From Cöthen to California

Classical Music in the Western Tradition from Bach to Adams

Robert J. Geise

Copyright © 2015 Robert J. Geise

All rights reserved.

ISBN: 978-0-692-66767-5

Table of Contents

Preface   i

Acknowledgements   x

1	Introduction to Classical Music	1
2	Listening to Classical Music	21

PART 1 - Music for Solo Instrument

3	The Baroque	39
4	The Classical Style – Haydn, Mozart, and Beethoven	57
5	The Classical Period	73
6	The Modern Piano - The Romantic Period	95
7	French Impressionism and the Piano	135

PART 2 – Chamber Music

8	Introduction to Chamber Music	151
9	Chamber Sonatas and Trios	159
10	The String Quartet in the Classical Period	187
11	The String Quartet Beyond Beethoven	205
12	Piano Quartets and Quintets; String Quintets to Octet	221
13	Chamber Music for Winds	233

PART 3 – Introduction to Orchestral Music – The Baroque and Classical Periods

14	Introduction to Orchestral Music	245
15	The Classical Period and the Birth of the Symphony	271

PART 4 – Orchestral Music – The Nineteenth Century

16	The Early Romantics	307
17	Nineteenth-Century France	325
18	Romantic Classicism	337
19	The Late Romantics	363
20	The Rise of Nationalism	397

PART 5 – Post Romanticism and the 20th Century

21	Impressionism – Debussy and Ravel	429
22	The Second Viennese School	439
23	Igor Stravinsky and Neo-classicism	459
24	Two Russian Giants – Prokofiev and Shostakovich	483
25	Populism and Traditionalism	499
26	The Avant-Garde and Minimalism	509

BIBLIOGRAPHY	535
NOTES	543
INDEX OF COMPOSERS AND COMPOSITIONS	605
INDEX	609

Preface

"I have never acknowledged the difference between 'serious music' and 'light music'. There is only good music and bad music."

— Kurt Weill

This book is intended for all those interested in classical music, from the casual fan to those who have developed a deep attachment to classical music. It is not aimed at someone brand new to classical music but meant to complement and provide more detail than books aimed at the newcomer.

'Classical music' denotes the Western classical musical tradition, which by convention specifically refers to the roughly three-and-a-half centuries of so-called 'serious' or 'art' music of Western and Eastern Europe, Russia and the United States (after 1860 or so). The term 'classical' music is obviously far too broad as it excludes most of the great music from the world's cultures. However, much of this 'world music' influenced many of the composers discussed here. Also, from around 1850 forward several key composers incorporated influences of indigenous music in their compositions. In instances where these influences were large, a 'nationalist' music was often the result, a fusion of indigenous folk tunes, or at least the influence of folk music, with classical forms.

> *"There is nothing more difficult than talking about music."*
> *- Camille Saint-Saëns*

I have chosen to highlight the roughly two-hundred and fifty-year period from J.S. Bach's appointment as *Kapellmeister* to Prince Leopold at Cöthen in 1717 through Minimalism in the 1960s and 1970s, the stopping point being the 'post-Minimalism' of John Adams. Most of what is regarded as Western 'classical' music was written within this period. For Bach, this new post at Cöthen allowed him to compose 'secular' music; he had spent most of his previous efforts on sacred cantatas and works for religious services. Before 1717 was the music of the Renaissance, which still owed much to medieval music and does not today enjoy the widespread popularity of music from the Baroque forward. On the other end, the 'jury is still out' on any long-lasting impact or influence of the classical music of the past twenty years or so.

The periods of music across this time span are the Baroque, Classical, Romantic, and 20th century. There is some overlap and further subdivision, for example, the turn of the 19th into the early part of the 20th century is called 'Post-Romantic' and the rest of the 20th century is often referred to as 'Modern'. But these four are the most popular periods in classical music; although the Renaissance, which preceded the Baroque, has been undergoing a renaissance. The music from the Baroque, Classical, and Romantic periods, dominates the catalogue and concert halls and its popularity shows no signs of diminishing. American composer Aaron Copland referred to this as "the overworked period of the 'Three B's", Bach to Beethoven to Brahms" (*ca.* 1720 to 1900). The music composed within this time forms the foundation of what we call 'classical music'; however, great music came before and great music has followed.

♪♪♪♪

The material is divided into the three major types of classical instrumental music: music for solo instrument (Part 1), dominated by the piano sonata; chamber music (Part 2), which is intimate music for a small ensemble (e.g., piano trio, string quartet), and orchestral music (Parts 3-5), which includes the two huge categories of concertos and symphonies, as well as other orchestral forms. Because of the large amount and variety of orchestral music I have divided it into the Baroque and Classical periods (Part 3), the 19th century (Part 4) and the 20th century (Part 5). Most general surveys focus on orchestral works and give chamber and/or solo instrumental music short shrift. While orchestral music will inevitably get more attention than chamber or solo music in any survey, the intent is to give solo and chamber music their fair share. Surveys that strictly go from composer to composer invariably favor the symphonic and orchestral canon, so the voices of non-orchestral composers, such as Fauré, get drowned out (Chopin would be the notable exception).

Part 1 and Parts 3-5 are arranged chronologically; Part 2 is arranged by chamber music genre. The reader can begin at any of the first three Parts and will be at roughly the same starting point. The division of solo, chamber, and orchestral music allows the 'Early Romantics' (Schumann, Chopin, Liszt) to be highlighted for their solo piano music (Chapter 6); the 'Late Romantics' (Chapter 19) and 'Romantic Classicists' (Chapter 18) for their symphonic works; and Fauré for his grossly underrated chamber works.

Each of the chapters is fairly self-contained. Some composers appear in Parts 1, 2 and 3 or 4, and others only in one part (e.g., Mahler and Bruckner). For composers who appear in multiple parts I have tried to distribute any included background and historical information among the various discussions on a particular composer. Notable exceptions to the division of solo instrumental, chamber, and orchestral music for a specific composer are the final two chapters in which the musical output of 20th century composers is covered together.

For several composers I had a choice of chapters in which to place them in Parts 3, 4, and 5. Some readers may wonder why only Janacek and Smetana are included as Czech nationalist composers, while Dvořák and Martinů are found in the chapters on Romantic Classicism and Neo-Classicism, respectively. Related to this is the placement of Sibelius as the last 'late Romantic' composer in Chapter 19 and not as the symbol of Finnish nationalism. Others will find the inclusion of Erik Satie in the sub-chapter on Minimalism curious but I feel that is, in hindsight, the appropriate location for a composer who defied classification while alive.

♪♪♪♪

The focus is on the forms and genres of instrumental music by the major composers. I have made no attempt to provide biographical details of composers; with most of them the coverage begins with their first major compositions. However, my intention was to produce a 'survey', not a 'history' of the 250 years covered, recognizing Professor Richard Taruskin's distinction that the former "makes little effort to explain why and how things happened as they did."

This book is not a listener's guide to specific works; being neither a musician nor a musicologist I am far from qualified to write such a book. Unlike many good books it does not provide details on what to listen for in a particular movement or piece. Harold Schonberg calls this "program-note writing." This type of examination can be found in CD liner notes or in other books, such as Jonathan Kramer's Listen to the Music and comprehensively in The All Music Guide to Classical Music.

With the occasional exception, any detailed discussion of the various versions and editions of compositions, either by composer, publisher, or other, is beyond the scope of this book. Some composers (e.g., Bruckner) continually revised their works, or (worse) allowed friends and publishers to hack away at them. Trying to follow the revision history can be mind-numbing, and of little interest to most listeners if only one version or edition is performed and recorded (not the case with Bruckner).

♫♫♫♫

Biographical information is deliberately sketchy, often only given to provide context and background to the composer's works. There are many 'classical references' or survey works published (see Bibliography at end of book). Some are aimed at the newcomer or 'casual fan' of classical music while others are for the serious classical music aficionado. A person in the latter group is one whose interest has developed to the point of collecting multiple versions of the same work and telling them apart. There are also several fine books that provide biographies of many composers, as well as many excellent works that detail the life of a specific composer.

I quote voluminously throughout the book from the many fine works of others, particularly those that are critical and opinionated as I find these works most interesting and entertaining. The abundance of direct quotes used in the book is because I found that most any point I wanted to make on a specific topic had already been stated very well by an expert.

In order to minimize redundancies I only go into details on a particular composer's life if those details relate to the music being discussed. Because the book is separated into 'solo instrumental', 'chamber' and 'orchestral' music, many composers will be explored in detail in the first section, but Mahler, Bruckner, Wagner and R. Strauss will not be discussed until the third section, as they composed primarily orchestral music (excepting songs for

Mahler and R. Strauss, which are beyond the scope of this book). Of these four great Romantic composers only Strauss remains known for any chamber music or concertos, and even these are relatively minor works compared to his operas and great tone poems.

The book is not intended to be a complete survey of the period covered; there are complete genres left out and many composers omitted or given short consideration. I have omitted the genres of opera and vocal music (e.g., the German art song or *Lieder*), so some very prominent composers (Verdi, Puccini, Hugo Wolff,) are not considered at all. Wagner is covered because of the incredible popularity of his overtures and orchestral extracts from his operas as well as his tremendous influence on the symphonic writing of Romantic and post-Romantic composers. The exclusion of these 'vocal' genres also keeps the book manageable. There are plenty of excellent books on opera and song cycles, including the comprehensive 'guides to classical music' by Penguin and *Grammophone*, which can direct the reader to the better recordings.

While many composers have inevitably been omitted, some very influential, I do feel there is sufficient composer diversity so as to adequately cover the course of music throughout this period. Certainly Edgar Varèse was, and remains, a very influential composer of the 20th century. Most current composers would likely consider Varèse a more influential 20th century figure than Bohuslav Martinů. However, Varèse's relatively small, but groundbreaking output remains unknown to most listeners. The greatest Brazilian composer, Heitor Villa-Lobos, could be covered under either Nationalism or neo-Classicism, or both. His combination of Bachian influences and Brazilian folk tunes is certainly unique. He was amazingly prolific with estimates of his works ranging from 1000 up to 2000; but most are unknown and unpublished. The inclusion of Gershwin, Ellington, and Bernstein was considered, but it was decided they fall just outside the scope of this book.

Within each part is explored the evolution of the form(s) as well as the composers who developed and perfected them. In many cases a recommended performance of a work (or two or three) is given immediately following discussion of the work(s). I do not provide recommendations for all works covered; many volumes do a very thorough job of this (see Bibliography appendix for 'Compendia of Recommended Recordings').

> "Being the art of pure fantasy, instrumental music must act without the intermediary of other elements."
> - Paul Henry Lang

Many of the recommendations of particular works are based on the available consensus of the best performances available. I indicate in the recommendations, as much as possible, the performer/orchestra/conductor, label, and (sometimes approximate) year of the recording (trying to avoid the issue date of the CD, which is often more recent). I avoid the use of catalogue numbers because the same recording can be re-released and re-coupled, so that there are often multiple releases with the same performance. As a rule-of-thumb, buy the newest release, it will have the best sound.

This is especially common with the large offering of 'recital' albums, which feature several works by several composers performed by one artist. The most common of these are the piano recital albums (e.g., Richter playing an assortment of works by Schumann, Liszt, Chopin, et al.) These collections are fleeting as the material is reshuffled and re-released. Therefore it is easier to simply recommend the performance of a particular work as opposed to the recital album on which it appears, as that can change quickly. The exception would be if the entire recital is being recommended as a single 'performance'. Richter's *Sofia Recital* would fall into this category whereby the recital is worth acquiring as a whole.

Many recordings are out-of-print but can be found on-line through re-sellers (eBay, Amazon.com), purchased and downloaded on-line, or have been re-issued under license by operations such as Arkivmusic.com. Therefore, although the catalogue number may no longer be valid and would not show up in searches limited to active releases, it does not mean these recordings cannot be acquired. For many recommendations I rely on professional reviewers as well as posted on-line reviews. For the most part the recommendations given are for 'modern' recordings (i.e., from the so-called 'stereo' era of the mid-1950s onward). These constitute the bulk of available performances either on CD or online. However, this does leave out many vintage recordings that are interpretively outstanding, even if they are sonically limited. For an excellent source on available historical recordings refer to Classical Music, ed. A. Morin (Backbeat Books, 2002). Mr. Morin and the fifty or so contributors "seem to have a working knowledge of every classical recording ever made…"

I do not attempt to rank or generate lists of greatest composers or works. While it is a necessary part of this book to recommend recordings, I have mostly avoided rankings, ratings and lists of works and composers. These are certainly useful in accessing classical music and there are several good books that rate and rank composers, compositions and recordings.

DEDICATION

To my wife and boys, Carmen, Joseph, Andrew and Zachary, who after eight years no longer have to ask me, "Is your book done?"

ACKNOWLEDGMENTS

I am grateful to the authors and editors of the books and countless liner notes I have used as secondary sources. Without the availability of their primary research and detailed knowledge this book would not have been possible. There are several types of sources for information on classical music in general, the composers and performers, and on the recordings available. I have used several of each type for my information and discuss in detail in the bibliography.

PHOTO CREDITS

Front Cover – Top photos of Germany by Robert Geise
  Bottom photos of San Francisco by Nicolette Lehman.
Back Cover – "Saalbau am Abend", Neustadt an der Weinstrasse (R. Geise)
All other photos within book by Robert Geise

- 1 -

Introduction to Classical Music

Like all art, music cannot be "pinned down as to what it says, yet it speaks"
— T.W. Adorno

"So long as the human spirit thrives on this planet, music in some living form will accompany and sustain it and give it expressive meaning"
— Aaron Copland

♪ What is Classical Music?

Roy Hemming has gone through the common definitions for 'classical' music and found them insufficient. He settled on defining it as "the vast area of Western music from the 15th century to the present, written primarily for performance by classically trained musicians." With a capital 'C', 'Classical' music has another meaning and refers to music of the Classical period, roughly 1750 to the first couple of decades of the 1800s. This period represents the masterpieces of Haydn, Mozart, and Beethoven (usually Franz Schubert is included, and will be here as well).

There was a time when Classical music was called 'serious' music, but even that is misleading because not all Classical music was composed with serious intentions. A possible distinction is that 'classical' music is a type of Western music that puts "art first, entertainment second," although this also presents problems because plenty of classical music was composed not to be profound but indeed to entertain. "It connotes something of lasting value, something conceived with certain standards in mind, yet far from elitist or restrictive." Conductor Michael Tilson Thomas calls classical music "Western civilization's most abstract and emotionally affecting art."

> *"Classical music is drama without stage or actors."*
> - Lawrence Kramer

♪ Evolution of 'Western' Music

> *"What makes the history of music...particularly troublesome is that what is most exceptional...has often the greatest claim on our interest."*
> - Charles Rosen

What happened in the years between the Renaissance and 20th-century music is the main focus of this book. Of course music has been around before recorded history. In the Western World the oldest well-known form is the monophonic (one voice, one melody) Gregorian chant from the Middle Ages. Monophony would be expanded to two voices ('diaphony') and these dominated all musical composition till the 13th century. In diaphony two voices would sing the same melody, separated by a set interval, the octave. This was a type of plainchant called *organum*. According to noted musicologist Alfred Einstein, as Europe was approaching the Renaissance "one could represent the whole history of medieval music as the history of the weakening, reduction and repression of the polyphonic principle in favor of the harmonic…"

♪ Music Before 1717 – The Renaissance

The Renaissance was "the period when the values of this world replaced those of the hereafter." The early 15th century saw the beginning of the Renaissance style in music. Up to this time musicians only achieved fame if one "was a man of genuinely creative gifts." Additionally, up to the middle of the 1500s, musical notation did no more than provide an outline for decoration and embellishment. The actual notes and melodies to be played were not written out in detail; musicians improvised. As musicologist Ruth Katz points out, once music began being written down, the methods of notation influenced music by imposing an ideal of clarity on composition. The 16th century saw the maturity of instrumental music and the birth of opera. The former was helped greatly by the availability of published scores.

All composers of the Renaissance looked to a church or to the court for employment. When Bach assumed his new post in Cöthen it did not require him to play the organ or compose organ or religious music; he was allowed to compose secular music. From his time at Cöthen come many of his concertos and orchestral works. This was a big change from his previous musical focus, which had still been very much like the Renaissance period which preceded the Baroque.

The "prevailing texture of Renaissance music is a polyphony of independent voices." Polyphony added a third or more voices that could be singing different melodies. The Renaissance saw the development of polyphony and simultaneous melodic lines of roughly equal importance, often without being able to detect a dominant melody, as opposed to single-line melody in the Classical and Romantic periods. Polyphony, still confined to vocal music, was fully developed in the 1400s.

The 15th and 16th centuries were the period of the 'Netherlands' schools, with the term being purely geographic as the region was dominated by French culture and civilization. The significant contribution of the Netherlands schools was their tremendous contrapuntal mastery, a type of polyphony that reached its height with Palestrina, Lassus, and Byrd in the 1500s. Burgundy, the first political state of the Low Countries, "assumed unquestioned leadership in the center of the musical world." Also in the 15th century royal courts became more influential than the Church regarding music, which led to a focus on secular music as well.

A prominent composer of the early Renaissance was **Josquin Desprez** (1450-1521), known simply as Josquin. He revealed a new world of sound, with music guided by imitation and a "succession of motifs, each leading a passage in which the voices wind round one another." Thus the groundwork was laid for future music in the Baroque as this "new world of sound" opened a straight path "to the triumph of criss-crossing in the fugues of Bach and Handel."

The other major change was from the four-part layout of alto, two tenors and baritone to the still-standard format of soprano, alto, tenor and bass. As a result music became more comprehensible and brighter in sound as each of the four voices now had its own center. Additionally, composers such as Josquin wrote for more than four parts, with five or six being common, adding further richness and brilliance; "a preponderance of polyphonic figuration carefully carried out to the smallest detail." His music marks the turning point from medieval to Renaissance and "his work is infused with warmth and poignant sorrow." Unlike all of his contemporaries Josquin's reputation remains intact and a large amount of his music survives. Just about all other composers of his time were soon forgotten after their deaths.

"Josquin is the master of the notes, which must do as he wishes, while other composers must follow what the notes dictate"
- Martin Luther

Instrumental music took a back seat to vocal music in the Renaissance. In the 16th century, at the height of the Renaissance, the musical scene was dominated by religious vocal music, especially for use at Mass or religious services. The church organ and lute became dominant while winds were reduced in importance with the rise of string ensembles. The lute was the favorite instrument of Renaissance madrigalists and the organ was the ideal Baroque instrument for the "rippling passage work, bold modulations…and fascinating ornamental superstructure" of keyboard toccatas and fantasies." The modern principle of thematic treatment was present in the Renaissance forms, in the madrigal and the canzone and in the more polyphonic *motet* and *ricercar*. Fantasies and toccata (*toccata* = 'touch piece') forms were also established, the fantasia being a piece of music unrestricted by any prearranged formal condition.

The instrumental fantasies and fugues furnished the backbone for the Baroque style of the early 1700s. The fantasies for various instrumental ensembles were the precursors of chamber music. In fact, the origin of variation form was Italian lute composers of the 1500s and their "desire to avoid mere repetition of the short (e.g., eight measures) periods." This carried over to Bach, who wrote many cantatas, the *Passions* and the great *Mass in B minor*. This also influenced Handel, who in the final phase of his musical production became a great composer of oratorios, the greatest of which is his *Messiah*.

"Being the art of pure fantasy, instrumental music must act without the intermediary of other elements."
– Paul Henry Lang

"The spirit of the Renaissance eschewed medieval longing for the beyond and reinstated love of life as cherished by the ancients." The Renaissance was "a time of high musical adventurous-ness," and it took music to new heights well beyond what preceded it in medieval times. Medieval music was in religious context simple and 'monophonic' with one single line, without chords or harmony. A greater distinction was made and there was more equality of function among vocal parts. Counterpoint ('pervasive imitation') was becoming more and more common.

> *"We get a picture almost as timeless as it is spaceless; a spiritual revelation throughout..."*
> - Wagner on listening to Palestrina

The polyphonic textures of the Flemish masters Josquin, Palestrina and Orlando di Lasso resulted in "the many-colored richness of a tapestry." Giovanni Pierguigi, nicknamed 'Palestrina' after his birthplace (c.1525-1594) was the greatest representative of this 16th century counterpoint and he was the greatest church musician of the latter 16th century. Except for a few madrigals, his entire output was sacred music. Palestrina was the "first Catholic church musician" and "became the creator of a church style par excellence." His masses "are among music's purest, most angelic manifestations," displaying a "tender and seraphic beauty." "His (religious) motets became a transfiguration of the (secular) madrigal." His tonal language was devout, with an "incense-diffusing softness."

> *"There are 'three colossi' in music...Palestrina, Bach, Beethoven."*
> - Giuseppe Verdi

Orlando di Lasso (1532-94) was a Netherlander who contributed much to the style of the High Renaissance. Lassus represented "the culmination of inter-nationalized Flemish art...the most versatile and universal composer of the 16th century." His style was a "combination of Germanic earnestness, profundity and artistic traditions with the secular world of the Italian Renaissance and a goodly share of Gallic wit." Lassus composed both erotic secular songs as well as spiritual madrigals. Some 2000 compositions embrace every form of his period and show Lassus comfortable with all of them. "He cherished the great traditions of his Flemish ancestors and liked to exhibit his great prowess in counterpoint...his oeuvre is a synthesis of what 200 years of musical culture had produced."

As we move to the High Renaissance and transition to the Baroque, we see an increased emphasis on homophony, i.e., melody, with prominent bass lines and harmony. The late Renaissance/early Baroque turned away from polyphony (less so in Germany and Northern Europe) as composers paid more attention to chords (i.e., harmony) than to counterpoint. This change was also driven by the rise of opera, which is not compatible with polyphonic writing. Besides its incompatibility with the rising genre of opera, polyphony declined ca.1600 because the Church, through the Council of Trent, decreed that church composers should reduce their dependence on "abstruse polyphonic designs."

This movement of the final decades of the 16th century, which led to the birth of opera, originated with the Florentine *Camerata*, led by Galileo's father Vincenzo Galilei. They were trying to re-create ancient Greek dramas and they wound up creating modern opera, as well as the dominant Baroque religious vocal forms of cantata and oratorio. The *Camerata* was opposed to polyphony; "they wanted a simple line, a simple accompaniment, natural characterization, and natural word-setting."

Indeed, the music the Florentines inspired was simple and 'pure'; the *Camerata* was secular, not religious and its focus was the dramatic and passionate, as opposed to the ceremonial. The melody (or melodies) would be written out by composer, as would be the bass line. Chords and harmony were filled in by the performer. There was plenty of freedom for improvisation and embellishment. Member of the *Camerata* Guilio Caccini pre-saged *tempo rubato*, thought to be a creation of the Romantic period, by speaking about not tying up singers in the ordinary measure of time but, "often making the value of the notes less by half, and sometimes more..."

Homophony ('being in unison'), consisting of different voice parts moving together in the same rhythm although on different notes (i.e., chords), dominated this period. Music was monodic rather than polyphonic and consisted of a single "melody going in company with a calm, even rhythm of chord change", referred to as 'triadic harmony'. There appeared the convention of the top line being the melody with the bottom line as bass to the harmony. Melody leads a "congruent line through an array of triads" (chords) and rhythm supports the melody "by providing a sense of regular steps." Later in the Renaissance, "Secular strains infiltrated sacred music" bringing back polyphony, "the knotty interweaving of multiple musical strands."

Many Renaissance instruments were ancestors of orchestral instruments we are familiar with. These include the lute, an ancient guitar and various 'viols' which were the forerunners of the violin, viola and cello. The recorder was a wooden flute which was used regularly in Baroque music and probably evolved into the clarinet and/or oboe, the latter found regularly in Baroque concerti. There were horns and trumpets, organs and harpsichords.

Unlike the Baroque with its terse, pulsating rhythms, the Renaissance of the Florentine *Camerata* was somewhat similar to the later Classical period in that both shared "clarity and balance with pleasant sweet sounds." The High Renaissance saw the emergence of carefully-controlled dissonances within a context dominated by consonance. In this time dissonances "were 'prepared' and 'resolved' according to well-defined principles, so as not to disturb the flow of counterpoint." Also, music publishing and printing, first started in the Renaissance, allowed a composer's works to be performed by any ensemble that could acquire a printed copy. Music no longer had to be hand copied, as had usually been done by clergy. Printing of secular music helped bring it to many different venues (royal halls, homes, learning institutions).

Claudio Monteverdi (1567-1643) was "the first artist to revive the spirit of antique tragedy and create a musical drama which was classical and modern at the same time." Monteverdi was not thrilled with the "strict rules and ever-murmuring polyphony of the Netherlanders." He was more interested in secular forms than in religious masses and motets (although he could compose anything well), so he became a great composer of madrigals, a musical setting of a short poem for two to six voices.

Madrigals are a "highly sophisticated part-song that sought to mirror and intensify the imagery and emotional content of a poem." There is usually musical accompaniment of some sort and they are "overrun with the most ingenious of polyrhythyms" derived from the "natural prosody of the words." Madrigals used music to describe the words of a poem and many were highly emotional in their word painting.

Monteverdi's madrigals, "with their variety of mood and technique, are a complete musical world in themselves," and introduced "dissonances which undermine the harmonic texture defined by Renaissance style." The textures of Monteverdi's madrigals could be extremely chromatic and, with his pungent harmonies, downright dissonant. In them there is "a repertoire of textures and techniques almost without parallel among his predecessors and his contemporaries."

> *"The artistic manifestations of a bygone age should not and cannot be judged by the standards of present-day musical life."*
> - Paul Henry Lang

Monteverdi presided over the transition from the decaying modal polyphony of the Renaissance to the 'modern era', starting with the Baroque, with its language of homophony and tonality, although polyphony would come roaring back in the high Baroque. He wrote mostly all his works for voice, but Monteverdi's huge contribution to the evolution of music was turning five-voice chamber mini works into concerted writing for voices and instruments. This 'concerted' form would lead directly to the pre-concerto forms of the Baroque and on to the Classical concertos of Haydn and Mozart.

Monteverdi's famous opera *Orfeo*, in 1607, made opera a vital, living form. He brought to opera elements of the madrigal as well as the pomp of the Renaissance. While Monteverdi set the stage for opera as we know it and gave significance to secular compositions, he still composed in the archaic twelve modes of the Renaissance. Harmony, which left only major and minor modes for the Baroque, had not yet taken over. Nevertheless, the music and innovations of Monteverdi served to link the music of the Renaissance to that of the Baroque.

♪ The Baroque

Instrumental music only emerged as a separate art form at the end of the 14th century, matured in the 16th, but did not truly flourish until the Baroque (1650-1750), especially the 'high' Baroque of Bach, Vivaldi and Handel. The birth year of Bach and Handel, 1685, had long been taken as a line of demarcation between unfamiliar "early" music and the classical repertoire we know. Music prior to this arbitrary dividing line was lumped together into a semi prehistoric repertoire called 'early music'. In reality, Bach and Handel were not at the beginning of anything, but rather, they were "outstanding late practitioners of styles and genres that were rapidly growing moribund in their time."

The term 'baroque' is believed to be derived from the Portuguese for 'misshapen pearl'. While the precise connection is not clear, it most likely derives from the distinctive architecture of the period. The Baroque began in the early 1600s in Florence, Italy. While instrumental music in the Renaissance had taken a back seat to vocal music, the Baroque saw a move away from vocal polyphony in favor of a single vocal line accompanied by a single instrumental line (*continuo*). Composers started to write specific parts for specific instruments and their individual qualities and distinctive characteristics (e.g., pipe organ, harpsichord, and violin). In addition, the dominant vocal forms of cantata, oratorio and opera emerged.

The Baroque spirit is restless, passionate, innovative and spacious. In Baroque music soloists are expected to 'ornament' or 'embellish' the melodic line, particularly upon successive repetitions of a particular theme or section. In other words, soloists did not play from music that was written out for them note-by-note. This did not happen until the Classical period.

The fully composed accompaniment of the Renaissance, which was a web of polyphonic lines, gave way in the Baroque to a sequence of chords, the *basso continuo* or *continuo*.

A critical development that began in the early Baroque period was the slow continuing move from the old modes to a harmony based on scale and key. This major-minor key system marked a new kind of tonality that carried music through the next three centuries. Baroque composers founded what we know as the system of keys (major-minor), which comprises modern tonality, to replace the ancient modes still in use up through the Renaissance. "The system of major-minor harmony, enmeshed with regular rhythm and phrase structure in smooth, clear forms" was first signaled in the music of Corelli, Couperin, and A. Scarlatti.

As we move into the High Baroque in the early decades of the 18th century, homophony yielded to much thicker contrapuntal textures, reaching its high point with the fugal forms of J.S. Bach. The high Baroque saw the full development of polyphony ('many voices at the same time') or counterpoint.

In counterpoint there is often no clear and dominant melody. Besides being the major form of the Baroque, polyphony characterizes much music of the 20th century. Bach's textures were very dense, spinning out melodies of extraordinary length, yielding music that was both weighty and profound. "At a time when many composers...were pruning and simplifying their styles in the interest of directness of expression, Bach remained faithful to an older esthetic tradition, seeking instead a maximum of...textural complexity."

The brilliant new generation of composers included Bach, Handel, Domenico Scarlatti (Alessandro's son), together with Rameau and Vivaldi. Together they provided the full richness of the high Baroque. For "it seems likely that composers before Handel's time did not have a strong feeling for instrumental color."

In the 1730s Handel switched from opera to oratorio and produced the most famous work of its kind, *Messiah* in 1741. Bach in his final years produced such monuments as the *Goldberg* Variations, written by Bach, according to legend, to be played by Johann Gottlieb Goldberg, harpsichordist to Count Keyserlingk (Russian ambassador to Saxony) to counter the Count's insomnia. Other works of Bach from his final creative period are the great *Mass in B minor*, *The Musical Offering*, and *The Art of the Fugue*.

While there was a form called *Sinfonia*, a mini-symphony that was the Baroque precursor to the symphony, the two major forms of Baroque composition involve a relatively large number of players were the suite and the *concerto grosso*. Bach's *Brandenburg* Concertos are the most famous example of the Baroque *Concerto Grosso*, and composers such as Handel and Corelli applied the term directly to sets of their works. The *concerto grosso* is one of the richest genres of the Baroque period and evolved into the *sinfonia concertante* of the Classical period, a concerto with more than one soloist.

The *Concerto Grosso* was made up of two sets of players, a string group (the *ripieno*) and a soloist group (the *concertino*). It contrasts two to four solo instruments against the main ensemble. Unlike the later soloist concerto form developed in the Classical period, the soloists were an integrated part of the whole and played along with the *ripieno*.

The Baroque Suite, on the other hand, could be for solo instrument, such as Bach's *English* Suites for solo keyboard, or for ensembles as with Bach's Orchestral Suites. The suite was an extension of the Renaissance dance suite. It almost always had at least five movements with several short (or longer) dance movements, which followed a longer opening movement (often titled 'overture'). The orchestral suite evolved into the Classical symphony through the efforts of Bach's son Johann Christian as well as Joseph Haydn. In the Classical period the symphony settled into a four movement work which retained one of the Suite's dance movements as the third movement minuet. However, the developments of sonata form for the first movement and rondo form, usually for the finale, were creations of the Classical period.

By around 1700 viols were completely replaced by the violin and its relatives, the viola and cello. The variety of winds was reduced and standardized. The Baroque concerto for soloist, as opposed to the *concerto grosso* for multiple soloists, juxtaposed a solo instrumentalist with a larger ensemble, which included the *continuo*. The *continuo* was usually a harpsichord and bass or cello that provided backup music designed to give the composition continuity in harmony and rhythm.

In 1730 Bach commented on music from the previous Renaissance period that, "taste has changed astonishingly, so that the former style of music no longer seems to please our ears." However, less than ten years later, Bach's music was being labeled 'bombastic and confused' as its heavy reliance on counterpoint was no longer in style. In the last decade of his life (1740s) there was "a swing away from 'reason' and back to 'the ear'." That is, a trend was towards simpler melodies and away from too much technical complexity. Ironically and in hindsight, Bach "was notoriously criticized…for the very attributes we prize most in his music today."

♫ Classical Period

> *"The melody is the charm of music and the most difficult to produce."*
> - Joseph Haydn

At the beginning of the Classical period in the mid-1700s there was a significant shift from the 'open' Baroque melody to a rounded, symmetrical melody that would characterize composers such as Haydn and Mozart, "like the same number of windows on the left and right sides of a house." Any emotion in works of the Classical period was "well contained within the form." Both of these great composers built their ideas on a classical elegant symmetry. The circular, rigid repetition forms of the Baroque gave way to linear, large-scale structures "proceeding from assertive thematic ideas through episodes of strenuous development to climaxes of overwhelming magnitude."

In Baroque music contrasts occur between, not within, movements and a piece of music limits itself "to the working out of a single texture" to yield a "unified representation of a single sentiment, or *Affekt*." In the Classical period because of sonata form (first and sometimes final movements), and the minuet and trio typically comprising the third (dance) movement, dramatically contrasting themes often occur within a movement, effectively creating a sense of drama in the work.

The embellishment that so characterized Baroque works was practically eliminated; Classical composers did not care for fugue or the immense, complicated forms of the Baroque. Even the cadenzas of concertos, an opportunity specifically intended to display virtuosity, were usually written out note-by-note by the composer, or in some cases by the soloist for whom the work was written.

The Classical period saw a debate over the role of music in society. On one hand music was first and foremost to be pleasing to the ear, full of enjoyable melodies. Others argued for music to express "otherwise intangible emotions and visions, however disturbing." The former view was able to hold on and characterize the Classical era, but the latter would take hold in the 1820s and 1830s and launch the Romantic period.

Baroque composers generally wrote music that functioned in blocks. The Classical style set contrasting themes of light and dark, tragedy to triumphant, in close juxtaposition. A new style of music developed in the middle of the 18th century between the High Baroque and Classical periods; it was termed the style *galant*. It favored lightness, simplicity, immediate pleasure and the pursuit of delight. The style *galant* was in opposition to the perceived overly complicated music of the late Baroque, with its thick contrapuntal textures and weaving polyphony. The great philosopher of the Enlightenment, Jean-Jacques Rousseau (1712-1778) referred to these complex forms of the Baroque as "remnants of barbarism and bad taste."

Galant represents a return to the simple over the complex, to melody over harmony. It was the rising preference for this style that was seized by C.P.E Bach, then Haydn and Mozart to establish the Classical Period, making their music "essentially accessible to anyone with open ears." From the Baroque through the Rococo to the Classical period, a major development was the rise of the middle class with its serious work ethic in contrast to the elaborate social life of the aristocracy. There now existed a mass market for printed music as a result of the steep rise in literacy, 'urbanism', and consumerism, which created a new kind of cultural space. The dominance of mainstream society by the emerging middle class resulted in the transition "from the scintillating gracefulness of the Rococo to the earnestness of classicism."

However, the scholar Maynard Solomon poses a less than glowing picture of the Classical style, 'perfected' by Haydn and Mozart. Solomon feels the period could be viewed as "a great repression in musical history" because it rejected the "advanced harmonic language, rich polyphonic procedures, and highly organized and complex forms" in the interest of the rationality and simplicity of the 18th century Enlightenment. This age of Enlightenment aimed for the "deification of man's mental life and the urge for the secularization of every other aspect…(to) render every authority answerable to reason."

Charles Rosen sees the Rococo period as possessing a lack of direction, without any integrated style and with elegance to the music only surface deep. An integrated style, as would characterize the Classical period, could not take hold until composers had reabsorbed and partly transformed the music of J.S. Bach and Handel. "The gradual reconquest of contrapuntal mastery was necessary" for the Classical style to take root. The greatest contribution of early Viennese symphonists was their recognition of the need for continuity. But it took Haydn and Mozart to resurrect elements of Baroque complexity and recapture some of the richness lost during the Rococo, style *galant* period. At its worst, the 'style *galant*' "combined the basic elements of old German and relatively new Italian musical trends" to yield "the most hackneyed and predictable harmonic progressions with melodic lines and rhythmic patterns that were simple to the point of dullness." Haydn and Mozart, separately and together, "created a style in which a dramatic effect seemed at once surprising and logically motivated."

The transition period between the Baroque and Classical periods was led by the all-but-forgotten composers Johann Adolf Hasse (1699-1783) and Carl Heinrich Graun (1703-1759), together with one composer who remains well-known (helped in part by his being J.S. Bach's son), Carl Phillip Emmanuel (C.P.E.) Bach (1714-1788). These composers set music on a path that would reach its heights with the music of Haydn and Mozart in the last third of the 18th century. Beethoven would take their forms and move them into the Romantic period.

Classical composers, as was the case in the Baroque, functioned under aristocratic patronage (or some still under sponsorship of a church, as with Mozart and the archbishop of Salzburg) and they were treated as skilled craftsmen. However, at the start of the Classical period music also began to move from churches and courts to more modest settings and was performed and enjoyed in middle-class homes. Songs (*Lieder*), chamber music and sonatas (solo instrument or duo) became extremely popular as they require limited performers and lend themselves well to intimate settings. However, at the same time the Classical symphony and concerto, seeded by C.P.E. Bach and brought to maturity by Haydn, required more elaborate orchestral forces. Concertos additionally required an increasingly capable soloist. This soloist would evolve into the virtuoso of the Romantic period.

♫ Romantic Period

The French Revolution glorified the individual as never before and gave rise to the Romantic movement in Europe. "Its chief characteristics were emotionalism, introspection, self-expression, originality, the cult of genius and sacralization." "The sacralization of music reached its climax in the person of Wagner and at the place Bayreuth" as did the concept of the musician as an independent artist. To the Classical period composer, "the artist's highest aspiration was to please," to the Romantic period composer "his art meant everything to him;" he was an idealistic individual, indifferent to public acclaim.

In post-revolution, post-Napoleonic Europe, artists and intellectuals detested the repressive, reactionary political situation but "could express their aversion in only the most oblique ways," leading them to transform "intensely personal thoughts, feelings…into artistic expression." Thus was Romanticism born.

Orchestras got bigger and bigger, adding more strings, horns, woodwinds, etc., and also giving percussion a larger role than it had in the music of Mozart, Haydn, and even Beethoven. The 'essence of Romanticism' is: "content more important than classical form." Alfred Einstein defines the "essence of romanticism" as, "the incessant absorption of fresh material from musical or outside sources and the moulding of all this into new unities." The Romantic spirit determined the art of the entire 19th century, and maintained its influence into the early 20th century. Composers were drawn to "experimentation with new forms, new colors, new textures" with an emphasis on sound, a "rich, sensuous, colorful sound."

Composers of the Classical period sought "to safeguard the purity of form" while the Romantic movement "concerns itself primarily with the expression of emotion" and rebels against tradition. The Renaissance and Classical period stood for order and clarity; the Baroque and Romantic periods stood for movement, disturbance, and doubt. However, this is not to say there was no romanticism in the music of Bach or Haydn.

With the dawn of the 19th century and Romanticism "the broad middle-class public now replaced the traditional elite" as the target audience of Romantic-era composers. Napoleon faced his downfall in the second decade of the century and simultaneously the aristocracy across Europe was losing its wealth and power. Additionally, there was a nationalist strain to Romanticism in the "reactions against French culture's century-long reign in Western Europe."

In the first half of the 19th century great composers were great pianists and/or great conductors. The four greatest pianists in Europe were Carl Maria von Weber, Felix Mendelssohn, Frederic Chopin, and of course Franz Liszt. The four greatest conductors were Hector Berlioz, Richard Wagner, Weber, and Mendelssohn. The first individualistic conductor appeared around 1820, one of them being the composer and leading influence on early Romanticism, Carl Maria von Weber (1786-1826), considered "the first of the true Romantics." The layout of his piano music is beyond anything that Beethoven and Schubert conceived but much of it has more glitter than substance. The huge influence he had on early Romantics is betrayed by the negligence of his works, excepting the opera *Der Freischütz*, in the past one hundred years or so, but they were extremely popular throughout the 19th-century. Johann Nepomuk Hummel (1778-1837) was a pupil of Mozart's who was considered almost on Beethoven's level in his day, and whose music "introduced a harmonic vocabulary much more 'modern' and sophisticated than Schubert's," that influenced Chopin, notably his Piano Concerto in E minor.

Early Romantics such as Schumann and Berlioz (but not Mendelssohn), displayed a youthful energy of revolt in their opposition to rule or authority in the 1830s. Within a decade (roughly 1830 to 1840) "the entire harmonic vocabulary of music changed." This brief period saw a significant move away from the diatonic harmonies of the Classical period to chromaticism, i.e., to "unusual tonal combinations, sophisticated chords, and dissonances." Mendelssohn, on the other hand, showed clear attachment to Classical styles and even 'rediscovered' J.S. Bach by performing his *St. Matthew Passion* for the first time in 1829. This 'rediscovery' marked the first time a major work had been revived and subsequently considered a masterpiece.

The 19th century was a secular and materialistic age in which musical Romanticism flourished, especially in Germany. Romantic composers "were more interested in what they put into their music than in how they put it together." The common bond of all these composers, starting with Schubert and distinguishing him from his Classical predecessors, was the world of pure sound in which they lived. While Mendelssohn and Brahms were content with Classical forms, Liszt, Wagner and Berlioz needed something looser, something which could follow the changing moods of a poem, story, or drama and still remain one piece of music.

It is no surprise that piano music and piano players dominated music of the Romantic period for "the keyboard was the perfect medium for conveying the intimacy and passion…of the romantic spirit." And the flamboyant keyboard virtuosos of the period "were celebrities idolized in the way of today's rock stars."

About halfway through the 19th century the "laws" of music, many of which had never been questioned and had been set in stone for 250 years, began to come under even more scrutiny than in the early Romantic. "The language of Bach, Mozart, and Beethoven…could no longer speak directly to the concerns of late-nineteenth-century mankind." The symphonies of Mahler, the music dramas of Wagner and the early ballets of Stravinsky represent some of the better-known works that bridged late Romanticism to the new paradigm that would unfold in the first half of the 20th century.

The transition from the music of the Romantic period to the 20th century would be one of turmoil and tragedy in society, along with experimentation by artists sometimes looking to the past while also rejecting it. The reactionary movements against the outsized orchestrations of Mahler, Wagner, and Strauss would radically alter the path of music after World War I. As man's understanding of the world increased exponentially, composers looked for objectivity and exactness in music. Even if the scope of one's listening ends before World War I, it cannot be said that the one hundred years or so since have not been interesting, producing the most musically varied period in history.

But just as 19th century Romantic composers reacted against the rigid forms of the Classical period, so 20th century composers would react against

Romanticism, its subjectivity and emotion, but most significantly, against tonality.

♫ 20ᵗʰ Century

> *"In the twentieth century musical life disintegrated into a teeming mass of cultures and subcultures...none has true mass appeal."*
> - Alex Ross

The 1900s saw a downscaling of the orchestra, aiming more for efficiency than for effect by numbers. Percussion became emphasized in this music, which made sense because it was intended and composed as "anti-Romantic" music. A tremendous taking off of atonal, polytonal, and dissonant music also marks the last century. There is an emphasis on rhythm over melody and harmony, which has not been seen since the Baroque Period. Clear lines of melody become hard to find as rhythm, harmony and tone color are more heavily emphasized. Harsh, percussive tonal effects of 20th-century piano music are produced from little or no use of the pedal. Whereas Bach and Mozart used dissonance only occasionally as an expressive device, 20th century music is rarely without it.

The early Modernist period of 1890-1914 witnessed enormously accelerated stylistic innovation, with innovation celebrated as a mark of vitality. A side effect was the production of works apparently simply for the sake of 'innovation'. A similar claim would be made fifty years later against some post-World War II *avant-garde* composers of complexity for complexity's sake. But despite many 20th century composers rendering melody suspect and looking to produce music absent of it, melody nevertheless "remains the heart of what matters in classical music."

'Modernism' actually began in France with Liszt, who at the time of his death in 1886 "was the most radical composer in the world," and anticipated "that the major and minor key system would eventually collapse." In fact, Liszt's music at the end of his long life was so radical it was widely rejected, with the public thinking he had gone mad.

The revolutionary Impressionist sounds of Debussy at the turn of the century made a strong statement that the old rules no longer applied, tonality was broken up, dissonance was not properly resolved. These all foretold of upcoming forms and techniques in the 20th century. Debussy started the breakdown of the old system, and "dared to make his ear the sole judge of what was good harmonically," without regard to whether it followed established 'rules' or violated them. With his 'radical' approach to music Debussy swept aside long-held and entrenched theories of harmony.

The Impressionist composers favored elusive melodies and harmonies. In their works, "orchestration shimmers with an impalpably pictorial quality...that veiled the beat...in an uninterrupted flow of dreamlike sound." Paul Henry Lang, who called Impressionism "the last stylistic synthesis of the century," summarizes the musical technique of Impressionism as "the clear articulation of a musical phrase turns into a swinging, undulating repetition, into a sounding mosaic comparable to the lapping of waves or rustling of leaves."

The world changed significantly with the First World War in the second decade of the century. The unprecedented loss of life in ended whatever remained of the Romantic Period, replaced by colder, 'objective' music (Schoenberg and disciples), works that looked to older forms for structure (neo-Classicism) or were now restricted by the iron fist of totalitarianism (Shostakovich). "The seemingly apocalyptic bloodshed of World War I only increased the desire for the reestablishment of security and norms."

After World War I some composers stopped composing, greatly decreased their output, or took a break from producing works of significance. Examples of this abound. Elgar produced only minor works after his Cello Concerto in 1918-19. Rachmaninoff took a break from 1917-26 and took until the 1930s to really get going again. Richard Strauss and Ralph Vaughn Williams composed during the 1920s, but their best works came either before or after this time.

Most notably, Jean Sibelius completely gave up, composing nothing for the last thirty years of his life. After his compact and muscular single-movement Symphony No.7 in 1924, only the symphonic poem *Tapiola* (1927) followed. Did Sibelius give up on symphonic form or did he somehow know that it had abandoned him?

Indeed, the writing of Schoenberg and his students (Berg and Webern) is closer to the contrapuntal, 'horizontal' compositions of Bach than to the harmonic, 'vertical' works of the Romantic composers. And this distance increased as these composers matured, moving from post-Romanticism to 'modern' compositions. Musicologist Lawrence Kramer defines 'modernism' as "a principled hostility to all traditions."

So in the 20th century we have, in a way, come 'full circle' from the strict counterpoint and polyphony of the Baroque being replaced in the Classical period by the melodic and homophonic sounds of Haydn and Mozart; however, still crafted within forms that evolved out of the previous period. The Romantics looked to abandon forms such as the symphony and fugal forms, which did not permit enough freedom to express their emotional music. Finally, the 20th century saw a reaction to the Romantic period and its subjectivity. Composers looked again for forms, either to the past in neo-Classicism and the neo-Baroque, or to create new methods based on 'new rules' (serialism).

The 20th century saw a great revival of counterpoint, which because of "its abstraction and refinement of thought" provided a perfect antidote to bloated post-Romanticism. It allowed a return to pre-Romantic era emphasis on "compositional problems rather than...personal feelings." This showed a "desire...for condensation of style and purity of expression" and away from "the thick chordal fabric" and "opulent tone mass" of late Romanticism to "pure line...sinewy melody...and transparency of texture." Twentieth-century 'modernism' rejected Romanticism and Impressionism; "composers turned away from the subjective...from heaven-storming passion; from landscape painting...from Wagnerian histrionics."

The 1920s produced many shocking works and saw atonality formalized by Schoenberg. Most all artistic efforts rejected and moved away from 'Romanticism', viewing it as a dinosaur of the pre-war world. However, as the 1930s progressed and totalitarianism started dominating so much of Europe, composers were rethinking the cold 'objectivism' of the disillusioned 1920s. Through music they searched "for the human resources that have been the fundamental answer to inhumanity throughout history."

The 'Second Viennese School', consisting of Schoenberg, Berg, and Webern, eroded major-minor tonality. In these works it is difficult to determine key, if one even exists. This transition was a period of free atonality during which increasing dissonance and chromaticism, along with "greater contrapuntal complexity...blurred the focus of tonality." They set the groundwork for the breakup of music in the 20th century, rejecting previous rules of tonality, away from composition as a "great structure assembled like a cathedral."

This free atonality evolved and was formalized in Schoenberg's twelve-tone method, which gives equal importance to all twelve notes of the chromatic scale, and does away with the traditional concept of 'key'. In strict twelve-tone compositions no note can reappear before its eleven companions have all been stated, resulting in 'equal importance' of all notes. The dissonances that appeared in works up until the turn of the century had always been resolved (e.g., return to 'home' key) but now were rarely resolved. It was this total chromaticism, formalized by Schoenberg's twelve-tone method that made the 'new' music of the Second Viennese School seem like "a revolutionary break with the past."

The twelve-tone method was "a direct outgrowth of the vast expansion of chromaticism in German and Austrian tonal music...prior to 1914." Anton Webern and his followers were committed to writing music that was "more rigorously athematic and atonal than that of (Schoenberg) himself." Although the 1920s saw a bitter, unrelenting struggle between serialism (Second Viennese School) and neo-Classicism (Stravinsky); in reality, both schools sought "the reestablishment of traditionalism and compositional control ." Although Schoenberg would make a very aggressive departure from tonality, he did revive the most traditional forms and genres of tonal music: sonata, suite, string quartet, and large-scale orchestral works.

Jazz, a form of music original to North America, increased greatly in popularity in America and Europe in the 1920s. Not surprisingly, its influence was felt by classical music and its rhythms absorbed into works by many composers between the wars. The influence also went in the other direction. A composer of popular songs, George Gershwin, first composed *Rhapsody in Blue* for piano and jazz band, but it has often been performed and recorded by piano with orchestra..

It is not possible to draw a clear line in time between the end of the Romantic period and the start of what we will call '20th century' music, with the "mind-bending harmonies and earthshaking rhythms" of Schoenberg and Stravinsky. Rachmaninoff produced purely Romantic orchestral music decades after Schoenberg composed his *Five Pieces for Orchestra*. Rachmaninoff was a contemporary of Stravinsky, both Russians who immigrated to the U.S. Their music could not be more different.

Unfortunately, classical music is stereotyped as "an art of the dead (that begins) with Bach and terminates with Mahler." In the first couple of decades of the 20th century there was, for the first time in musical history, a shift in public taste away from living composers to music by dead composers. Did turn-of-the-century artists and composers encourage this with their experimental (some would say 'radical') works? Or did artists simply react to the public's waning appetite for 'new' music, which allowed them to be more daring and less concerned with popular success? Adam Ross sums up Arnold Schoenberg's position as a result of this phenomenon as, "…the serious artist should stop flailing his arms in a bid for attention and instead withdraw into a principled solitude." This taste for long-dead composers only increased throughout the past century and into the 21st.

Artists spent the first quarter of the 20th century running away from Romanticism as far and as fast as they could. In fact, "the modernist strain in 20th century music, as it branched out from Schoenberg, would complicate itself exponentially." 'Modern' music was the product of a "desire to do away with all the poetical interpretations of music…characteristic of the whole 19th century…" and to replace it with the position that "music is to be music and nothing else." Sentiment is "the essential enemy," to be done away with along with the "enormous piling up of instrumental resources…and, above all, the voluptuous effect of romantic music." Sir Roger Norrington points out that "in the earlier part of (the 20th) century, music went through an abstract patch…it was thought that all music…mustn't tell a story." The 'modern' composer of the 20th century shuns repetition (until Minimalist composers); he states something once, thus also removing symmetry.

However, there were stops and starts, including the stock market crash of 1929 and the following world-wide depression, which led to the "Beethovenian urge to speak to all…being felt again." The symphony began to reappear with works by Honegger, Stravinsky, and others; "music was becoming simpler and modernism was in retreat." The atonal, modernist movement beginning with the Second Viennese School came under criticism that some modern composers were writing music seemingly "to fit intellectual concepts."

However, upon the end of World War II, some young composers, led by then-student in Paris Pierre Boulez, protested neo-Classicism. Boulez felt that musical progress had not only been stalled by Nazi Germany (the repression of 'modern' music in the Soviet Union could also be included) but that "neoclassicism had been a distraction…an unworthy capitulation to public laziness" the result of "a general lack of stamina among those who had carried forward…progress… before (World War II)." Indeed, the post-World War II *avant-garde* was swept along by the torrent of Webern's "incredibly tight organization" and "his kind of logic and musical purity." World War I brought the loss of "confidence in subjectivity" and a rejection of Romanticism and Post-Romanticism. As 'modern' composers regrouped to go forward after World War II, "something in the *Zeitgeist* latched on to the ideal of order and clarity in music…as if the musicians…(now) yearned for strict control backed by scientific principles."

> *"I can't be responsible for the audience: I'm not running a restaurant."*
> - composer Harrison Birtwistle

Indeed "in the 1930s/40s, the entire Romantic tradition was effectively annexed by the totalitarian state," most notably the Soviet Union and its satellites. Boulez and others felt that serialism, in addition to representing music at its most advanced, needed to play the role of disrupting "music's inclination to settle into familiar patterns," i.e., Neoclassicism. "By the middle of the 20th century, acoustic dissonance in music had reached its furthest possible extreme with the incorporation of 'white noise', which is all frequencies sounding at once." Thus, "dissonance, density, difficulty, complexity" would dominate Western music at the start of the Cold War.

- 2 -

Listening to Classical Music

"Nothing is, in a way, more exciting than a first discovery in music through listening"
　　　　　　　　　　　　- Alexis Weissenberg

"Listening to music (should be for all) a perfectly natural and simple process"
　　　　　　　　　　　　- Aaron Copland

"Listening to music is a skill that is acquired through experience and learning...the more you know about the subject of music, the greater will be your joy in listening to it."
　　　　　　　　　　　　- William Schuman

"If it sounds good, it IS good."
　　　　　　　　　　　　- Duke Ellington

It is said that a quick way to determine if one will enjoy a particular book is to read the first page. That may be an effective rule-of-thumb for readers but a similar approach, such as listening to the first minute, will not work when it comes to classical works. There are several reasons why this does not apply to music and could even be misleading and counterproductive. Excluding very short pieces (e.g., Beethoven's *Für Elise*) and 'bon-bons', many pieces of music barely get going in the first minute (think of the slow introductions in the first movements of Haydn symphonies), so it is often not representative of the piece as a whole. By comparison, an author's style is often apparent from the opening page.

Second, and just as significant, is the fact that a good book is thoroughly enjoyed and comprehended after only one reading. Many pieces of music require repeated listening just to begin to appreciate them. The vast majority of music from periods other than the Classical period requires repeated listening. Indeed, knowing something about a piece and/or the composer often enhances the listening experience by, for example, putting the work in historical context (e.g., works written during wartime). On the other hand, the music of Haydn and Mozart is immediately accessible despite its considerable musical depth.

> *"The end of all music is to affect the soul."*
> \- Claudio Monteverdi

Why do concerts featuring music of long-dead Germans still sell out? Why do recordings of their music still dominate the catalogue? Roy Hemming proposes that "these composers have something to say that still communicates with those who will listen." "Classical music asks its listeners to imagine a work with more fullness and complexity than most other music does." As noted by conductor/pianist Daniel Barenboim, "In music, two voices are in conversation simultaneously, each one expressing itself to the fullest, while at the same time listening to the other." Listeners should ask themselves two questions when approaching a work: "How much does the (composer) impose or suggest? How much may the (performer) assume and take upon himself?"

"The gulf which we have in our day between dance music, popular music, and so-called serious music, concert music, didn't exist" in past times. People danced to the symphonic minuets and orchestral *Ländler* and waltzes. Alternatives were very limited; basically, religious and secular music written for solo instrument or ensembles with or without voice. There was no Jazz, no Rock 'n' Roll, no Country and Western music. Sometimes Classical music is viewed as 'ancient' music composed by people who lived two hundred years ago. It was a different time; what is now termed 'Classical' music was actually popular music back then (excepting the music written for religious purposes).

This argument may have validity if one's tastes are limited to Bach, Mozart, and Beethoven. But Dmitri Shostakovich died in 1975, the same year he produced his final work, the Viola Sonata; Igor Stravinsky in 1971. Prokofiev and Sibelius were alive in the 1950s, although Sibelius had not composed anything of substance in decades. And the 'dean' of American Classical music, Aaron Copland, died less than twenty years ago in 1990.

> "...music...must never offend the ear...must never cease to be music."
> - Mozart

People listen to classical music for a variety of reasons. It is ideally suited as background music for study or work because many find it soothing and non-distracting; one can maintain the music in the background while thinking, writing, reading, whatever. Julian Johnson proposes that classical music "distances us from the distracting immediacy of everyday life." Listening to classical music can also have a calming influence on listeners, although not all musicologists agree that classical does relax us.

> "Music is never simply heard; it comes to us through practices of listening that help form our sense of the world."
> - Lawrence Kramer

Lawrence Kramer makes a distinction between music and classical music, pointing out that "All music trains the ear to hear it properly, but classical music...wants to be explored, not just heard." The listener wants to be actively engaged "with the music's capacity to absorb us." Every time we listen to music we purify it "by subtracting what is irrelevant from the undigested mass of sound that reaches our ears." Listening to music is not a passive act but requires a creative imagination and a separation of the music from any extraneous background sounds and other distractions.

> "The ear should be the final arbiter in all musical compositions."
> - Michael Derry

Kramer continues with the following, "...classical music demands a bit more effort from the listener than many (other forms of music)"...but "the music is worth the bother." And according to musicologist Paul Griffiths, recorded music presents us with a piece of music at three different points in time: "The now in which we hear it, the then in which it was made, and the further then of when the piece was composed."

> *"You must be able to relate what you hear at any given moment to what just happened before and what is about to come afterward"*
> — Aaron Copland

The American composer Aaron Copland proposes that we listen to music on three separate 'planes'. We can listen to a particular piece of music on one, two, or all three of the planes, and simultaneously. The first 'plane' is listening for pure enjoyment; Copland calls this the 'sensuous' plane. Humming along with Mozart's *Eine Kleine Nachtmusik* is an example. On this first plane the listener is simply a passive participant in the process, not seeking to explore anything more than the simple enjoyment of the notes.

"A composition is…an organism…a living thing…capable of being seen in a different light by various interpreters." Every composition has its own style, which the interpreter must not betray, but we also hear each piece "as refracted by the personality of the interpreter."

The second plane (the 'expressive' plane) involves listening for the meaning of the music. "Classical performances…retell the music's story without rewriting it." What is the composer trying to convey? Is there an emotion (sadness or joy?), a program or story attached to the music? The listener should not just be listening, but listen for something. With the piano there are endless shadings of color and volume. "With orchestral or chamber music, the tendency is to feel enveloped or suffused by the sound."

> *"Composition consists…of injecting a system of links into naïve musical ideas."*
> — Joshua Bell

For strictly 'absolute' music one might argue that this second plane does not exist, that there is no meaning to discover within the music. This may be true in the sense that 'absolute' music lacks a program, but it does not mean that it lacks meaning. "Something distinctive and particular…must happen in…a piece of music to make it live." Aaron Copland makes the important point that "in order to hear interpretation intelligently, you must be able to recognize what exactly the interpreter is doing to the composition at the moment that (s)he recreates it."

> *"Unlike a novel or a painting…a work of music gives up its full meaning only when it is performed in front of an audience."*
> — Adam Ross

Take Brahms' First Symphony. What meaning can a listener take from this? There is clearly no program; Brahms strongly disliked 'descriptive' music, so popular in the Romantic period. We know that Brahms waited years to premiere his *First*; he was over forty, and he had already established himself as a composer with several great works under his belt (German *Requiem*, the First Piano Concerto). He felt the pressure of Beethoven's legacy so he wanted to be completely confident in his symphonic abilities. Is this what we hear when we listen to Brahms' *First*? Does it come across as the work of a mature, confident composer who realizes the work will be compared alongside Beethoven's symphonies?

The third 'plane' Copland calls 'the sheerly musical plane,' consisting of notes constructed in unique manners to make music. These notes are combined to form the melodies, harmonies, rhythms and tone colors, usually according to the principles of a specific musical form, e.g., 'sonata' form.

> *"Likes and dislikes add to the music lover's zeal and interest."*
> — Eric Blom

Not all composers and their works are equally received by popular audiences, musicians and musicologists. Sometimes a very popular work is viewed by 'experts' as fluff or 'salon' music (i.e., music composed expressly to please an audience and lacking depth and complexity). The converse is also true in that there are critically-acclaimed works that simply never catch on with general audiences. A lot of 20th century music starting with Schoenberg's twelve-tone method, which led to serialism, falls in this category. With music composed by serial techniques the "listener hears only unrepeated and unpredictable musical events." Of course, the great masters (Bach, Beethoven, Mozart) are secure in their enormous popularity with all.

However, it is entirely probable that a listener will enjoy some or many works by a certain composer and not like, or be indifferent to, other works by the same composer. For example, one may enjoy Ravel's solo piano works but not particularly appreciate *Bolero*. Different listeners will draw a line in time at different points in the development of classical music. The most common stopping point is the turn of the 19th to 20th centuries to include Tchaikovsky, Rachmaninoff, Mahler, Richard Strauss, probably Sibelius, and possibly the early ballet suites of Stravinsky. It is apparent from the steep drop in their popularity and performance that music of the Second Viennese School ('founded' by Arnold Schoenberg), Paul Hindemith and early *avant-garde* clearly falls on the other side of that line. There are, as always, exceptions such as Copland's populist, Americana ballet suites as well as the more popular orchestral works of Prokofiev and Shostakovich. Based on this, we see there is a traumatic, world-changing (and certainly 'music-changing') event that coincides with this 'line' in time: the First World War. As a result, many listeners end their scope of favorite works somewhere in the first two decades of the 20th century.

♪ The Accessibility of Music

> *"Melody is not just a string of notes...(it is) the chief expressive resource of Western music."*
> \- Lawrence Kramer

'Motives' can be defined figuratively and descriptively as "molecules of melody" and more technically as "a few notes and a rhythm". They are the primary attention-grabber for most listeners, at least initially. Motives are indeed the glue that holds whole movements, even entire works, together. The most famous motif is probably the first four notes of Beethoven's *Fifth*. This motif not only dominates the opening movement; "...as a rhythm it figures largely in all the other movements as well."

The accessibility of music can vary greatly among the different periods. Music from the Classical period, a very melodic piece such as Mozart's *Eine Kleine Nachtmusik*, is not only immediately recognizable to many people, it is immediately enjoyable. There is a single melody, repeated several times throughout the serenade's first movement, which people naturally begin to hum. There is no heavy lifting here on the part of the listener to get 'beneath the surface' of the music, to determine what Mozart was trying to convey or describe through the music. It is not needed to put the work in the context of events in Mozart's life at the time of its writing. With the exception of his Requiem mass, Mozart's music gives almost no indication of how his life was going. It was simply intended to be exactly what it appears to be, music to be enjoyed.

> *"...everything is worth hearing, at least once...however much one may wince at the bare idea of repeating the experience."*
> \- Eric Blom

One can enjoy all forms of classical music from all periods. One's tastes may favor more melodic works such as the orchestral works of Haydn and Mozart, or you may prefer more esoteric works, such as 20th century chamber works. But music of the Classical period is probably the most immediately accessible and the reason the music of Haydn and Mozart remains extremely popular. The fact that the music of these two great composers is of exceptionally high quality ensures that the public will never tire of it, compared with the remaining ninety-five percent of their contemporaries, though popular in their day, are long-forgotten-to-obscurity.

Alan Rich points out in his foreword to Aaron Copland's <u>What to Listen for in Music</u> that in previous times (before the long-playing record and long before the CD) listening to classical works (any recorded music to some extent) took effort and money. Beethoven's *Fifth* in 1936 would have cost $160 at today's prices on four 78-rpm records. And the listener had to flip sides or change records every four to five minutes, much more of an issue in classical music than with popular music where most songs are less than five minutes. Since the explosion of the CD over the past twenty years there is now "music without effort", with the appearance that "every piece of music ever composed…is now available on discs."

The second half of the 18th through the 19th century ('Classical' and 'Romantic' periods) was dominated by homophonic music, which depends on harmony. Rhythm, melody, harmony and tone color combine to form an inextricable web of sound. "Harmony is…brought to life in the interplay of melody, texture and rhythm…it is the stage for the drama of melodic events." Melody is the horizontal combination of notes; it moves across the page in the notes of a musical score. Harmony consists of vertical columns of chords perpendicular to the single line of melody. This type of 'texture', dominant in the Classical period, in which the harmony supports and enriches the melody, is termed 'homophonic'. On the other hand, 'polyphonic' music combines several melodic lines in a unified musical fabric known as counterpoint.

The music of Haydn and Mozart through Tchaikovsky and Dvořák "generally has more immediate appeal for the listener than polyphonic (music)" due to the regular occurrence of 'hum-along' melodies and much greater lyricism. One is able to whistle many more tunes of Mozart than of Bach. However, "the contrasts in Beethoven's music demand more elasticity…than when listening to Bach or Mozart."

Although a listener need not know the details of programmatic music or be familiar with the circumstances surrounding it in order to enjoy it, that knowledge can enhance the listening experience. A recent example is Olivier Messiaen's *Quartet for the End of Time* written while he was held in a World War II prison camp and performed for the first time by the composer and three fellow musician inmates.

Music of the Baroque and the 20th century requires more effort on the part of the listener than the Romantic period and certainly more than the Classical period. This increased effort involves listening to works from these periods several, if not many times, before fully appreciating them. It also can involve being informed about the work and the composer. According to composer Aaron Copland the counterpoint and fugal forms so intricately developed in the music of the Baroque requires the most effort on the part of the listener. It requires multiple, if not many, repeated hearings to fully appreciate music composed in this complex form. Most would agree that the first movement of Bach's Second *Brandenburg* Concerto is very 'catchy' and recognizable but try humming anything beyond the initial melody and it quickly becomes difficult. However, the work stands on its own and there are no external circumstances or information available to enhance enjoyment of it. However, without having some understanding of what Anton Webern (1883-1945) was aiming for in his music (the effect, not the program), and what his influences were, it is hard to fully appreciate his compact, intense orchestral compositions.

> *"Only the very greatest musical works stand...detached from time. Everything else has period-value that requires appraisement by the listener."*
> — Eric Blom

The most difficult or challenging music to actively listen to is polyphonic or counterpoint. This is because counterpoint "moves by reason of separate and independent" melodies interwoven to form harmonies. All music before 1600 and much after (e.g., Baroque, 20th century) is polyphonic. Aaron Copland suggests that to truly and actively 'listen' to polyphonic music one must be able to hear each voice separately as well as hear them together. Of course this is easier said than done, but Copland does suggest a 'lab experiment' using Bach's chorale prelude *Ich ruf zu Dir, Herr Jesu Crist* as your beaker and Bunson burner.

The 20th century return to polyphony was part of the general reaction against 19th century music and Romanticism in general. It was a movement to replace subjectivity and emotion with objectivity. According to Copland, "the pull-away from Romanticism was the most important interest of the early 20th century." This movement is often labeled 'neoclassicism', and is applied specifically to such music as Stravinsky's from the 1920s.

> *"I could compare my music to white light which contains all colors. Only a prism can divide the colors and make them appear; this prism could be the spirit of the listener."*
> — Arvo Pärt

Migration of public away from living composers and 'modern' music as the 20th century progressed was, at least in part, caused by the increasing feeling among composers that "to pander to audiences who liked melody, harmony and rhythm" was to sacrifice "integrity on the altar of commercial success." Music of the past one hundred years has developed at an unprecedented pace so that 'modern' composers have left 'the public' stranded. 'Modern' music struggles to gain popularity because of the expectation of the listener, who does not approach 20th century music unbiased and with an open mind. Instead, one often expects to hear the melodic beauty of a Mozart concerto or the power and strength of a Beethoven symphony; that is, something familiar and non-threatening. If the listener expected something much different she would not be surprised at the apparent lack of a clear melody, the atonality, or the strangeness of unresolved dissonance. However, with each subsequent listening "you pick up new clues about how the composer has set up a theme..."

> "Listening to it once will only scratch the surface, akin to cuddling with your new pet, a porcupine."
> - J.H. Jacobson on serial music

A listener seriously approaching atonal 20th century works would make a mistake to expect the music to sound like Brahms or Beethoven. One needs to listen to the works for themselves, not against a reference point of a Classical or Romantic period symphony. Keep in mind that mostly all of serial music deliberately distances itself from the past. Although both Mozart and Schoenberg honed their crafts in musical Vienna, separated by more than a century, one can enjoy both a Mozart piano concerto and Schoenberg's *Variations for Orchestra* if one does not expect anything of Mozart's *cantabile* melodic homophony in the serial works.

♪ *'Absolute', 'Impressionist', and 'Programmatic' Music*

Any work with a sung text or story can be considered programmatic, that is, there is something behind the music. This includes opera, *Lieder*, masses, cantatas, among others. There are also orchestral works for which the composer has provided a detailed and descriptive program of what the music represents (e.g., the tone poems of Richard Strauss). But there are also many works that are programmatic but in a more subtle way, which leaves something or much to the imagination of the listener (e.g., Impressionist music, Debussy's *La Mer*).

'Absolute' music can be defined a few ways, including music written for no expressed purpose, music written for the sake of music, or in the case of Chopin's *Études*, music written to help others develop and perfect techniques. 'Absolute' music "speaks solely a tongue of its own, voicing nothing but abstract thoughts..." Each listener can have his own interpretation of the music. Some composers made efforts to write only 'absolute' music, and some (e.g., Brahms) went so far as to openly oppose programmatic music. Others, such as the Czech nationalist composer Bedřich Smetana, felt all music is or should be intended to convey something.

So much of 19th century Romantic works with literary programs "depend not one whit on its literary associations...but can be heard and enjoyed purely for itself" without even knowing the "extra-musical implications." However, programmatic music can be more effective when the listener knows the story behind it and what the composer is attempting to portray. Even in the case of the most programmatic music (e.g., a Strauss tone-poem) one cannot guess the program as "no music can specifically describe anything." Without knowing the descriptive titles and 'programs' makes it very difficult to visualize or grasp what the composer is attempting to depict through the music. At best, it can "express only mood and emotion;" music "succeeds or fails on purely musical terms." Particular instruments and combinations of instruments can be used to evoke imagery. A good example of this is Prokofiev's *Peter and the Wolf*, in which the narrator actually informs us at the beginning as to which instrument represents which character.

> *"Music that does not accompany words presents no image whatsoever to me...to me music resists description."*
> \- Harvey Sachs

Opinions vary greatly among experts on the significance of narrative in programmatic music. Great music can be enjoyed on its own and a "a good story cannot make up for poor music"; however, knowing as much as possible about the music only enhances the experience. Donald Grout sees two types of program for a symphonic poem (or any programmatic music). The first is the 'philosophical' because it lies in the realm of general ideas and emotions, unattached to particular incidents. The second is 'descriptive' in which a composer attempts to use music to illustrate nonmusical events. Examples of the two types are *Les Preludes* by Liszt and the thunderstorm 'scene' in Beethoven's *Pastoral* Symphony, respectively.

In the mid-1800s the 'common man' was being discovered, socialism as a form of government was being espoused, and Marx's Communist Manifesto was being read. Romantic ideals were detached from everyday life and artists and writers gravitated to 'realism' as a means of expression. After 1850 there emerged a preoccupation with storytelling and extra musical devices, with programmatic music the ultimate consequence.

An enthusiasm for literature grew among Western composers in the second half of the 19th century and many followed Liszt away from the traditional multi-movement, structured symphony. Adherence to form was de-emphasized as artists focused on what their creations 'said', on the feelings conveyed. Many embraced the one-movement, more loosely-structured symphonic poem based on pictures, myths, legend, nature, or abstract ideas. But musicologist Alfred Einstein points out in one of his *Essays on Music* that "music…does not always directly express the spirit of the time" (*Zeitgeist*). Artists instead may choose to represent a contradiction of the *Zeitgeist*, "the image of a desired ideal." This position opposes the commonly-held view "that art must always be a direct reflection of life."

It was common for Impressionist composers, especially Ravel, to compose a piece for solo piano and then later orchestrate it. This allowed the composer to create impressions and images using the entire color palette of an orchestra after creating a work whose powers of suggestion were limited by the piano. As a result, many orchestrated versions of piano pieces 'sound' different, as the melodies and themes previously monopolized by a single instrument can now be distributed across the entire orchestra. In many cases, the orchestrated version must be approached and considered differently by the listener. Let's look at Mussorgsky's *Pictures at an Exhibition*; both the original for piano and Ravel's brilliant orchestration. Ravel's orchestral showpiece is a significantly different work from Mussorgsky's suite for solo piano.

♪ Availability of recordings

The internet makes available many recordings that are out-of-print and otherwise difficult or impossible to acquire. It also allows the purchase of 'used' and new (legally) downloaded recordings at discount, thus lowering the cost of building a classical library and enabling more people to enjoy a wider variety of music. In many cases one may purchase a single multi-movement work without having to buy the entire 'album'. Technology also opens things up for a whole new range of abuses that are well chronicled.

> *"These talking machines are going to ruin the artistic development of music in this country."*
> *- John Philip Souza in 1906 to Congress*

Norman Lebrecht postulates that the Classical Music industry basically destroyed itself by responding poorly to two major technological advances: the rise of the digital compact disc (CD) and the online music downloading and file sharing mania. The former certainly preceded the latter, with music file downloading eventually doing major damage to CD sales. The fact that the two phenomena followed one another in time was a double whammy for the entire music industry.

The CD presented some major problems, including its virtual indestructibility. Record companies for years had relied on customers periodically replacing their favorite vinyl records, or later, their tapes and cassettes that got worn out or 'eaten'. With the CD only a one-time purchase was necessary; because of the digital encoding of the information the CD does not wear.

Initially, record companies skimped on the music offered on a single CD. Essentially, they offered LPs transferred to CD, often not even digitally remastered (indicated 'AAD'). The skimping was a result of a typical classical LP containing around forty-five minutes of music, while a CD can hold up to eighty. Most classical CDs released in the late 1980s into the 1990s were only 'half-filled'. This is why I have Carlos Kleiber's readings of Beethoven's *Fifth* and *Seventh* on two separate CDs. Deutsche Gramophone has long since coupled these two great recordings, making the combination on one CD one of the gems of the catalogue, and a real bargain at mid-price. Story has it that the eighty-minute capacity of the CD was to fit Beethoven's *Ninth* on a single disc. Indeed there were many versions of the *Ninth* released on a single CD in early days of digital releases.

But classical music fans did not fare as well with most other CDs, particularly multiple-CD sets. The most common ploy was to stretch over three CDs what could fit on two, and price this upwards of $40. Full-price two-CD sets were typically ~$30. Unfortunately, some very good recordings that have not been re-released and re-priced remain at this price. A recent release is András Schiff's *The Well-Tempered Clavier*, previously offered on two separate two-CD sets. Now one can obtain the complete Books I and II by Schiff in a 4-CD set for the price of a 2-CD set.

Eventually music aficionados had rebuilt their classical libraries digitally, and companies had to offer more music for less money to entice additional purchases or attract casual fans. This is the typical life cycle of a technology-based product whereby the early adopters overpay for the status of "first on the block" and to fund future R&D. However, once these people have their new toys, prices drop precipitously. Increased competition from "follower" companies also contributes significantly to this.

At first, record companies simply added a short overture to the typical symphony or concerto to extend the musical offering. A widespread example was the coupling of each of Brahms' four symphonies with one of his overtures or *Haydn Variations*, even though the Third and Fourth Symphonies fit together on one CD. However, in the early years of this century more and more CDs were being released that were mostly filled (offering seventy to seventy-five minutes of music). The Second and Third Symphonies of Brahms could now also be coupled onto a single CD.

By now the online downloading craze was in full swing and pressured the industry to enhance offerings. The most common offering remains the two-for-the-price-of-one CD couplings that allow a consumer to obtain the four Brahms symphonies for ~$15. In addition, record companies dug deeply into their recording archives to release decades-old performances. Recently, bargain-priced 'boxed-sets' of four or more CD's are being increasingly released, many re-packaging of previous sets that cost twice as much.

For at least fifteen years most CDs not only offer plenty of music, there are also several price points to choose from. A quality digital set of Brahms symphonies can be had for $15. Also with downloading we lose the insights, background information, etc., of liner notes, many of which are excellent sources of background and often detailed information. However, many recent releases have begun including digital liner notes included with the downloaded 'album'.

♪ Nicknames and Cataloguing of Classical Works

Many of the nicknames by which some of the more popular classical works are known were completely unknown to the composer. More often than not these nicknames were added by publishers (or sometimes the conductors of early performances) as a marketing device or to point out a unique feature of the work (e.g., the *Surprise* and *Drum Roll* in Haydn's Symphonies Nos.94 and 103). In most cases the subtitles assigned bear some resemblance to the work, but not in all cases. With Haydn's Symphony Nos.6-8 the subtitles *Morning, Noon* and *Night* were assigned by his patron Prince Esterhazy. While No.6 opens with music that could depict a sunrise, No.7 seemingly has nothing to do with midday and No.8 does not depict the nocturnal.

The logic was that if a catchy name were attached to a work it would be easier to remember and become more popular. This obviously worked as so many of the classical works that have retained or gained popularity over time have nicknames associated with them. Fortunately for us most of these works do actually deserve their fame, and many are masterpieces.

'Opus 120', 'K.497', 'D.850', 'Hob.XIX', what do these all mean? The easiest one to address is the 'Opus' (meaning 'work') designation. This is intended to be a chronological ordering of a composer's works; therefore, the lower the number, the earlier the composition. However, the opus was often not assigned when the composition was started or completed but when it was published. It was common for composers to allow works to go unpublished for years, so the opus numbering system is only an approximation of the order of composition. It more accurately reflects the order in which works were published and first performed in public. The result is that some symphonies are out of order (Schumann's) and occasionally a relatively early work will have a late opus number.

Opus numbers are used for many famous composers, including Beethoven, Brahms, and Dvořák. However, there are several key exceptions for which scholars later devised a cataloguing system. The best-known are the BMV, K., and D. (*Deutsche*) used for J.S. Bach, Mozart and Schubert, respectively. Keep in mind that the BMV (*Bach Werke Verzeichnis*) system used for Bach's works is not chronological; rather, it attempts to group his works together by genre. More information on cataloguing systems for specific composers is sprinkled throughout the book.

Part 1

Music for Solo Instrument

♪ Introduction

The repertoire for solo instrument is dominated by works for piano, and these are dominated by the piano sonata, one of the workhorses of classical music. Therefore, the masters have left us a huge amount of great music for solo piano. The piano is "the instrument par excellence for the expression of feeling, sensibility, mood, the inner life…" While there are plenty of compositions for violin alone, there are far more 'violin sonatas', which is a piano sonata with violin (or vice versa). During the 18th and 19th centuries there were far more people who played piano 'well' than violin. In most homes, several household members played the piano at a level to perform works being offered by Mozart and Haydn. In fact, it is believed that most of Mozart's piano sonatas were expressly written for 'students' or 'amateur' piano players of his day. This is because they lack the expected depth and complexity (excepting those in minor key) and are inconsistent with Mozart as a virtuoso pianist.

The major contributors to the solo keyboard repertoire include J.S. Bach with his masterpiece *The Well-Tempered Clavier*, Books I and II. This has been referred to as the 'Old Testament' of piano music. Bach also left us several sets of 'suites' and 'partitas' for solo keyboard. There must be a *New Testament*. That would be the thirty-two piano sonatas of Beethoven, the most impressive achievement of its kind. Chopin, given that mostly everything he composed is for solo piano, and is so unique in its melodic appeal and its requirements of virtuosity. Schubert and Schumann both wrote extensively for piano, the former extensively using the relatively structured form of the piano sonata, while Schumann practically invented the genre of 'piano miniature' or *Klavierstück*, gathering many short movements around a central theme (e.g., 'Scenes from Childhood'). All of these composers, excepting Schubert, were great pianists, as were Liszt (the greatest of his day in Europe) and Rachmaninoff later on.

♪ The Soloists

While some soloists are clearly stronger in certain parts of the repertoire, taste is subjective and the listener must decide for themselves which pianist they favor or whose violin playing is most likeable. Some listeners will be swayed by virtuosity but "virtuosity in itself is one of music's curses." For others, expression of feeling will be the determining factor in 'adopting' a particular soloist.

Instrumental soloists can be divided into three groups: pianists, violinists, and everyone else. The 'everyone else' category is probably significantly smaller than either of the other two, such is the dominance of the piano and violin as solo instruments; the instruments of choice for over two hundred years to demonstrate virtuosity. Virtually every composer of the past three centuries has written something featuring a piano or violin soloist.

In the area of solo instrumental music, the amount of music for solo piano dwarfs the music for all other solo instruments combined. In fact, most composers who wrote great piano sonatas composed nothing for another unaccompanied instrument. When it comes to violin and cello (excepting the great works of Bach), they almost always have to share the spotlight with the piano, or other strings in a chamber ensemble ('violin' and 'cello' sonatas, piano trios, etc.).

What differentiates the soloists whose recordings are available to us? More specifically, what contributes to a specific "interpretation"? All recorded artists are of the highest order, virtuosic and of high technical skill. Some pianists of older generations may not have been 'note-perfect', but made up for slight technical imperfections through the unique style and passion of their interpretations. Some unique features of an interpretation include differences in the timbre or tone of the piano being played. The artist has control over the piano s/he chooses to play. There are recording effects such as the acoustics of the recording location, the location of the microphones, as well any processing of the recording that results in differences. Some of these recording effects, particularly the acoustic of the venue, also apply to live performances.

In concert, the tempo of the work, as well as the extremes of tempo employed, will differentiate performances. Some artists are famous (or notorious) for wide tempo swings often seen as exaggerated or self-indulgent. A related issue is how much liberty the performer takes with the score or with the composer's (perceived) intentions. These are often indicated by tempi markings on the score, as well as scholarship and direct evidence from the composer himself or a contemporaneous performer. Some artists have no problem deviating from what is the consensus intention of the composer (e.g., the pianist Ivo Pogorelich). We cannot know which composers were sticklers and intended to set very narrow parameters for the performance of their works and who saw their score markings as strong suggestions but would expect their works to evolve over time and for interpretations to drift further with time from the original.

In most classical music the performers have to play the notes in the score; the performers cannot change melody, harmony, or instrumentation. After the Baroque period, composers did not permit free embellishment; even the cadenzas, designed to display virtuosity, were mostly written out and provided by the composer or an original performer of the work. However, there was plenty of *tempo rubato* and variation in dynamics.

But in performances from the post-Romantic, post-World War I era onward, all music has been intended to be played as written, with no unnotated variations in tempo (i.e., *tempo rubato*) or in dynamics. If one does not only follow what was notated by the composer, "you are playing romantically," a big no-no of the past one hundred years.

3

Music for Solo Instrument

The Baroque

The term 'baroque' is a French word derived from the Portuguese *barroco*, literally meaning 'misshapen pearl'. However, the French *baroque* was first used in the mid-1700s as a derogatory term meaning 'abnormal', 'bizarre' or 'in bad taste' resulting in the abandonment of thick counterpoint for the melodious music of the Classical period. Starting in the Romantic period of the 19th century, the term 'baroque' has a positive connotation.

The Renaissance and the Classical Periods form bookends around the Baroque. The Baroque fills the gap between Michelangelo (1475-1564) and the Pre-Classical Rococo period (1720-1760). When we think of Baroque we think of Bach (and the Bach family), Handel, and Vivaldi as the giants of the era, and they were, even though they came relatively late in the Baroque period, during the so-called 'late Baroque' (1700-1750). Bach produced an amazing number of works in an unprecedented variety of genres. Handel produced over 150 operas; Vivaldi around 600 concertos. Fortunately for them they were paid to produce these works and they often turned them out as commodities without thought for posterity. Handel was even a major celebrity in England (but not in his native Germany).

The High Renaissance "embodied calm, assured, and mature human clarity," while the Early Baroque "discovered the great possibilities inherent in the colorful tone of musical instruments" as instrumental music became the primary means to display virtuosity and ornamentation. The pictorial character of Baroque art is notably present in music. In the Baroque the 'old church modes' were replaced with our current major/minor system of keys and rhythmic ideas were developed that broke music into accented bar lines.

Baroque form is characterized by adherence to one mood and melodic idea per movement. In Baroque music it is rare that one moment is notably more dramatic than another. "A Baroque composition reveals its dramatic character in its first measure by the nature and shape of its melody." The instrumental fantasies and fugues of the late Renaissance furnished the backbone of the Baroque style of the early 1700s. The fantasies for various instrumental ensembles were the precursors of chamber music.

♪ Polyphony, Counterpoint and Fugue

Homophony and polyphony are far from mutually exclusive and the two have peacefully and very effectively coexisted now for hundreds of years. "The best homophony still contains a lot of the old contrapuntal virtue of smooth melodic progress in each part."

> *"Making counterpoint sound harmonious...is*
> *one of the hardest disciplines in music."*
> *- Jan Swafford*

Polyphony or Counterpoint is the interweaving of melodies and rhythms in a work or within a movement of a work. The technique gives the feeling that the multiple melodies are in dialogue with each other. 'Polyphony' is literally many simultaneous different sounds. Most melodies when played will eventually meet up with a counter melody, a rival that appears to either question or answer its companion melody. This second tune is usually more 'unstable' than its partner. "The purpose of Baroque counterpoint is not the opposition of different voices but the creation of harmonic unity out of independent parts."

Counterpoint "exalts the structural and formal values of music." The composition of counterpoint "requires consummate mastery of technique" but also "challenges the creative imagination." Counterpoint is often used in the development section of sonata form but not in the exposition. This makes sense if one thinks about the roles of these two sections. The exposition states the main themes while these themes are subsequently led through the development section via variation, modulation, and polyphony.

J.S. Bach was the master of the counterpoint; he took it to heights unmatched then or since. Bach's harmonic sense (was) frightening in its power, expression and ingenuity, with only a handful of notes making up a single melodic line. "Bach's fugue is the consummation of the species." "Every instrument that was capable of polyphonic expression received his outpourings." Bach mastered the fugue form and it achieved its height in his *The Well-Tempered Clavier*. His *Art of the Fugue*, one of his last works, "is a brilliant summation of virtually all the techniques of imitative counterpoint." But, unfortunately the form all but died with him in 1750.

The term fugue comes from the Latin *fugare*, to fly, indicating how each voice flies off from the next. Fugues, like other forms, have a structure to them, including a predominant main theme or subject, which gets imitated by subsequent parts ('countersubjects'). However, "fugues differ from other musical styles in that there is no separation into melody and accompaniment; all voices are engaged in simultaneous melodic utterance." On paper a fugue is a set of independent voices but is experienced as "one voice and now another coming to the fore, not all of them with the main theme." Fugue subjects are generally rather short and are of a well-defined character. There is an exposition, as in sonata form, and the parts of the fugue that do not contain the subject or countersubjects are called 'episodes' and are used as transitional devices that link sections of the fugue.

All fugues begin with a statement of the 'unadorned' fugal subject. This is the start of the exposition section, the only part of fugal form that is definitely set. The subject is then precisely imitated, usually by an additional three voices. After that, "a series of episodes alternate with statements of the fugue subject, seen each time in new aspects." As in Rondo form, the episodes do not contain the subject. As the piece proceeds the subject gets inverted and augmented. In the hands of a lesser composer, this type of polyphony can be repetitive and monotonous, but with well-thought out counterpoint a little music goes a long way by combining the same few melodies in different and creative ways.

The fugue is the highest expression or most complex form of counterpoint, the 'perfection' of polyphony and counterpoint. It consists of multiple voices or instrumental lines, usually three or four, following one another and imitating each other; not playing the exact melody of the previous line but one close enough to easily recognize that they are similar. This leads to the term imitative counterpoint. It is important to note that no voice or line is more important than the other; all voices, instruments, or parts (for fugues written for a single instrument such as keyboard) are given the same emphasis.

The "crystallization of imitative polyphony into its tightest, most succinct form," a fugue uses similar, but not exact, melodies that are slightly offset from each other. Unity is ensured by giving the melodies common features. The "themes" or melodies start up one by one and the same two or more melodies are combined in different ways. Fugues tend to start quietly and end loudly and are often preceded by a 'Prelude' (i.e., Prelude and Fugue).

"Fugue is...geometrical in the unfolding of its material, sonata form presents its subjects or themes in a more narrative manner." Fugal forms, such as the fugue and the concerto grosso, demand repeated hearings to be fully heard. An extension of the 'trio sonata', the concerto grosso is a fugal form that continued into the Classical period, although with less emphasis. By the time of Haydn and Mozart the *concerti grossi* had evolved into the *Divertimento*, Serenade and *Sinfonia Concertante*. Even these would eventually be completely replaced in the Romantic period by the concerto as we know it, written for a virtuoso soloist accompanied by an orchestra.

The fugue and counterpoint in general were greatly de-emphasized in the Romantic period during which composers moved away from, or even rejected, formal structures. If a Romantic composer such as Liszt found the symphony too restrictive with its four movements and first movement sonata form, it is not surprising that fugal forms would also be avoided. Interestingly, the concertante form would re-appear among neo-Classical composers such as Stravinsky, Hindemith, and Martinů, who were in the practice of putting a 20th century spin on Baroque and Classical forms.

> *"Hearing a fugue develop is like watching a densely formed cloud unfold and expand...as each voice is added, a great cathedral of sound builds in the ear and fills the body."*
> *- Maureen McCarthy Draper*

"In fugal writing...(Bach's) works summarize and bring to glorious completion a long line of development extending back for more than two centuries." However, fugal styles were used after Bach within movements of larger works (e.g., the finale of Mozart's *Jupiter* symphony) and counterpoint would make a huge comeback in 20th century music.

♪ Johann Sebastian Bach (1685-1750)

> *"What strikes me most markedly about Bach's work is the marvelous rightness of it...never since that time has music so successfully fused contrapuntal skill with harmonic logic"*
> *- Aaron Copland*

Perhaps the greatest composer, Johann Sebastian Bach is a giant figure in musical history, one who still heavily influences composers today. The music of Bach "not only attained an unsurpassed level of formal integrity but also transcends...traditional modes of musical expression, revealing the metaphysical essence of music itself: pure movement." Bach's genius was the ability to create "a brilliant work containing lots of intricate development within a coherent structure."

> *"He is the father and we the children."*
> *— Mozart on Bach*

His work is often set as the start of Western 'Classical' music, although nowadays most scholars mark this beginning during the Renaissance period, if not earlier. Several of his sons became composers, a couple of them very well known, Carl Phillip Emmanuel (C.P.E. Bach) and Johann Christian (J.C. Bach or the 'English' Bach because he spent much of his life as a composer in Britain). C.P.E. and his brothers "spoke frankly of having to distinguish themselves from such an outsize character as their father."

> *"A musician cannot move others unless he too is moved."*
> *- C.P.E. Bach*

During his lifetime Bach was always in the employ of church or court, with the job of turning out large quantities of religious and secular works. He was one of many such composers in Europe at the time who moved from church to church and court to court. This was when religion still dominated and Germany was divided into many states.

In 1717 Bach took an appointment in Cöthen with Prince Leopold. For the first time in his life he was expected to devote most of his time to the composition of secular music (chamber, keyboard and orchestral works), as opposed to the masses and cantatas that had consumed him in posts up to this point. This was happenstance for Bach as Leopold was a Reformed Calvinist and there was little need for 'religious' music.

Bach's employment and work ethic made him superhumanly prolific. Richard Wagner declared Bach's productivity as "The most stupendous miracle in all music." Consider also that he sired twenty children by his two wives. After his death in 1750, the gathering and publication of all of Bach's scores by the Bach *Gesellschaft* took forty-six years and occupies sixty huge volumes.

> *"Bach was a great river into which all things flowed; and all that his own age and the ages before him had done and dreamed of were his tributaries."*
> - Alfred Einstein

A natural question is how did J.S. Bach emerge from the glut of prolific Baroque court composers to be one of the great artistic geniuses of all time? There is no simple answer, but just as in his glorious Suites for Unaccompanied Cello, "Bach perceived possibilities in the instrument that were unnoticed by others," it can be generalized that he perceived possibilities in the musical forms available to him. It should be noted that he did not invent new forms but, as with Mozart a half-century later, perfected traditional ones. The roots of his legacy are the "unparalleled mastery of craft and an unwavering faith." As the eminent musicologist Alfred Einstein points out, "it is as though the 17th century Italians had only striven to develop all instrumental forms while leaving perfection for (J.S. Bach)." However, during his lifetime he was admired more as an organist than as a composer and he "thought of himself as a hard-working craftsman rather than as some sort of creative genius."

> *"Bach is Bach as God is God."*
> – Berlioz

Although not normally considered as such, Bach's music can be highly dissonant, with masterful use of counterpoint to resolve the dissonances. J.S. Bach "mastered with mathematical precision the formal problems of counterpoint." Nowhere is this more pronounced than in his works for solo keyboard. The major works for solo keyboard were written for the harpsichord but are now commonly performed on the piano. As has been pointed out, performances of Bach on the piano pose challenges because of differences with the harpsichord. Some musicologists swear by the harpsichord as proper for Bach's keyboard music. However, noted Bach pianist András Schiff claims Bach actually intended works such as the *Two and Three-Part Inventions* and *Sinfonias* for the clavichord, a precursor to the pianoforte and modern piano. In fact, Bach did try out some of his solo keyboard works on a 'new pianoforte' to compare to the usual harpsichord.

Schiff points out that "the most expressive pieces" of *The Well-Tempered Clavier* "require the singing and sensitive tone of the clavichord, not the percussive harpsichord."

All of Bach's keyboard works are masterpieces of technical composition and thoroughly enjoyable. The most famous and accessible are the *Goldberg Variations* and the two books of *The Well-Tempered Clavier*. Although these are all solo keyboard works, their appeal, as Murray Perahia points out, is in "Bach's genius to evoke timeless and true human emotions through the purity and spirituality of his writing-which, ultimately, stands apart from any specific instrumental environment."

According to Martin Meyer, Bach was the first to blend the bravura of the performer with the intelligence and emotion of his compositions. In fact, Hans von Bülow pointed out that *The Well-Tempered Clavier* had brilliant keyboard writing as well as spirituality.

> **A note on the cataloguing of Bach's works –**
> The BMV (Bach-*Werke-Verzeichnis*) designation is given to works by J.S. Bach after the cataloguing system devised by Wolfgang Schmeider. His system batched related works together but is not chronological.

The Goldberg Variations, BMV 988

Glenn Gould (1932-1982) made quite a reputation for himself with his Bach recordings on the piano, starting in the mid-1950's. He virtually 'discovered' the *Goldberg Variations* by recording them; before his release they had been primarily a curiosity among pianists and apparently not of interest to classical record companies.

These variations, which, if repeats are all observed, measure eighty minutes or more, were named for the harpsichordist Johann Gottlieb Goldberg, who played them to help Count Keyserlingk fall asleep each night. Keyserlingk, who was the Russian ambassador at Dresden, commissioned Bach to compose some solo piano music of a "soothing and cheerful character". The *Goldberg Variations* consist of an opening Aria stating the theme, followed by thirty variations with varying bass line as in a *passacaglia* (a work based on a repeated melodic bass line in ¾ time that is slow and dignified and begins unaccompanied).

Bach transcends the canonic and fugal forms and also overcomes the restrictions of staying within one key center "to attain the zenith of his art." The *Goldbergs* are "a journey of extraordinary transformations, in which the final return of the original theme is a deeply moving and satisfying experience." It is not known if these variations, played by Goldberg, were as effective as counting sheep.

> **Recommended – Goldberg Variations**
> The Canadian pianist Gould has seemingly recorded everything for the keyboard composed by Bach. Most have been released in multiple versions and couplings. Gould is rarely a 'safe' choice (for this go with Schiff); most listeners are either entranced by his interpretations or consider them over-the-top and are turned off by his humming accompaniment, audible on many of his recordings. But few question the mastery of his playing. Regardless, you want to have one of Gould's two recordings of the *Goldbergs* (from the 1950s or 1980s), but you will also probably want to have another interpretation as well (e.g., Schiff or Perahia).

"That genius who purifies and gives strength…and whose music seems written for eternity"
- R. Schumann on J.S. Bach

Dance Suites for the Keyboard – Suites and Partitas

The *English* and *French* Suites were unpublished in Bach's lifetime. Together with the six *Partitas* they form a triumvirate of Bach's solo keyboard suites. Each is an artistic monument of exquisite imagination and power. Bach gathered his harpsichord suites together into three collections while at Leipzig in the mid-1720s. They had most likely been written during his years at Cöthen (1717-1723). He viewed these solo suites as 'keyboard exercises', as indicated on the title page of the *Partitas*, the only set of the three published during his lifetime. Each suite is "a collection of stylized dances designed to display the grace and virtuosity of the performer…"

Although they seem to refer to some national flavor or spirit, neither the *English* nor *French* set "possesses characteristics consistent with their implied national identity". The *English* Suites (BMV 806-11) were composed before 1722 probably partly in Weimar first, then completed in Cöthen. A considerable Prelude opens all but the first of these suites, each of which has its own color and mood; "each (is) an extraordinary example of Bach's technique of spinning out material." The *French* Suites (BMV 812-17) were composed in Cöthen in 1722 so their composition probably began with the completion of the six *English* Suites. The *French* Suites are smaller in scale and more intimate than their direct predecessors.

The six keyboard *Partitas* (BMW 825-830) were written one a year between 1726 and 1731 in Leipzig. The title page indicates that Bach wrote these sets of dance suites "for music lovers, to delight their spirits." They represent "the supreme specimens of their kind…the summit of all Bach's dance suites." They are more expansive and artistic than, and even surpass the *English* and *French* Suites. In the *Partitas* (*Partita* being a dance suite) both French and Italian styles are integrated with German keyboard tradition to please both performer and listener. Not published until 1802, they led the publisher to exclaim that such splendid compositions for the clavier had not been seen or heard before.

The individual suites in all three sets (*English* and *French* Suites and the *Partitas*) have six or seven movements. In the *Partitas* the opening movements are not uniform: some are two minutes (Nos.1&3), while in Nos.4&6 the first movements are both at least six minutes. All have a distinctive style, some of a French overture, three contain fugues, one has improvisatory features of a *Toccata*, two are similar to preludes in other Bach works (here termed *Praeludium* and *Praeambulum*), and so on. All six *Partitas* follow the opening movement with multiple dance movements, concluding with a *Gigue* or 'jig', which is a fast dance with lively footwork. In Bach's keyboard suites, as well as in his Orchestral Suites and concertos, "one encounters a breadth of imagination, a logical power, and a degree of poignancy not found in any other composer."

> *Recommended – Bach Solo Keyboard Music*
> There are excellent performances of these works on either the harpsichord or piano. Excellent modern piano recordings of the *Partitas* and the two sets of *Suites* are available from András Schiff with his characteristic pristine objective approach (Decca). Murray Perahia has recorded a recent acclaimed set of the *English* Suites and the *Partitas* (Sony). On harpsichord one cannot go wrong with the six-CD set by Kenneth Gilbert for the *English* and *French Suites*, and *Partitas* (on Harmonia Mundi).

Other solo keyboard music

A set of early keyboard works are the *Toccatas*, which come from the period before his appointment at Cöthen. This set was probably composed 1705-14 and reference to them is included here because the *Toccatas* are a very early example of the free-style form of composition that would become popular for solo instrumental works starting in the Classical period through the 20th century (Prokofiev wrote toccata for solo piano). The *toccata* or *fantasia* had their origin in the Italian stylus fantasticus, a very unrestrained and free style form, which may possibly be traced to a form of composition inspired by the improvisational warm-ups of harpsichord players. Over time this form became more commonly referred to as *fantasia*, or simply fantasy.

> *"Very well...you play Bach your way, I play Bach his!"*
> - harpsichordist Wanda Landowska to a
> promising young musician

Pianist András Schiff responds to Mme. Landowska, "with due respect...that after two-and-a-half centuries it is virtually impossible to reconstruct (Bach's) way with complete accuracy."

The *Italian* Concerto (BMV 971) is a popular work and among Bach's most ebullient keyboard compositions. The slow movement contains a long-lined, florid melody which takes flight over a regularly recurring bass line. The sets of *Two- and Three-Part Inventions* (S 772-801) were written in Cöthen from 1720-23, and are forerunners to the great sets of *Partitas* and *English* and *French* Suites. The *Chromatic Fantasy and Fugue* (BMV 903) is a virtuoso work which "sounds much more effective on the instrument for which Bach intended it – the Baroque harpsichord."

The Well-Tempered Clavier, BMV 846-69; 870-93

> *"It was as though eternal harmony conversed with itself...shortly before the creation of the world."*
> - Goethe on *The Well-Tempered Clavier*

Now we come to Bach's supreme achievement for solo keyboard, the two books comprising *The Well-Tempered Clavier* (WTC). The conductor-pianist Hans von Bülow dubbed this monumental work as the "Old Testament of piano music." Each book contains twenty-four 'movements', twelve pairs of prelude and fugue. These can be considered as forty-eight two-part 'mini-sonatas' consisting of a prelude followed by a more substantial and complex fugue. These are similar to Domenico Scarlatti's binary 'sonatas', but Scarlatti did not have a masterful fugue as the second part of his sonatas. The binary form of Scarlatti's works and of the prelude/fugue of the *WTC* encourages the comparison, as well as the pieces being under five minutes.

Successive prelude/fugue pairs were composed in major/minor keys. The opening prelude (Book I, No.1 in C major) with its "wonderfully serene harmonic progressions," is followed by No.2 in C minor. The *WTC* was the first major work to "traverse the full complement of twenty-four keys" thanks to the advent of artificially adjusted "equal temperament" piano tuning in the 18th century. This eliminated the need to re-tune the clavichord in order to cover more than a limited number of keys. The preludes and fugues of The *WTC* can be performed convincingly on harpsichord or piano, "in different tempi and with different articulation, dynamics, touch, phrasing…" Baroque ornamentation is called for and the player decides "where and when some form of ornamentation is needed…" and when "a simple treatment of the material is more appropriate."

The prelude and fugue in each pair can vary drastically. Sometimes they are very similar in mood and thematic material; sometimes quite different. Many of the preludes were originally written to be free-standing pieces. Although manuscripts had been in existence for years, it took until 1801 to publish the complete and unified *WTC* books. We know that pianists knew and studied The *WTC* before this because Beethoven played the entire work by the age of eighteen. Later, Chopin used the works as a major influence on his *24 Preludes* and Schumann advised aspiring pianists to "Let *The Well-Tempered Clavier* be your daily bread".

The Well-Tempered Clavier is not only the sum of all works before it but it also points the way ahead. Of all Bach's works, the Preludes and Fugues in *The WTC* "contain the most lyrical effusion in the smallest space." Each fugue is a "study in musical conservation at the highest level" and there is an "underlying, almost all-pervasive spirit of the dance, which animates most of Bach's music and is a major source of its prevailing joy." Bach's fugues are "incredibly complicated networks of parts... developed ...from small thematic seeds of just a few notes."

Book I was completed in 1722 during his appointment at Cöthen and Book II over twenty years later in 1744 at Leipzig. Bach was developing material for Book I before 1722 and he actually started on some of the pieces that would comprise Book II shortly after completing Book I. The fugues of Book II are especially rich and expansive, with Bach ingeniously playing free counterpoint off against fugue with a distinct counter subject against the subject; that is, melody against melody. "Certainly the contrapuntal technique displayed in some of the fugues in Book II is nothing short of virtuosic."

It should be noted that some musicologists feel that of all Bach's solo keyboard music, the preludes and fugues of *The Well-Tempered Clavier* are the least suited to the piano and feel it and the *Goldberg Variations* are best performed on harpsichord. However, András Schiff, who has made acclaimed recordings of Bach's great solo keyboard works on a modern piano, believes that Bach intended the preludes and fugues of *The WTC* to be performed on clavichord and organ, as well as on the harpsichord.

> **Recommended – Well-Tempered Klavier Books I and II**
> András Schiff now has both books combined into one 4-CD set (Decca), the result more economical, making this a clear first choice. A good budget set is available on Naxos from Jenö Jandó. Recently, Angela Hewitt released her second complete set (2009, Hyperion).

Unaccompanied Cello Suites, BMV 1007-1012

The Cello Suites are very famous works, perhaps the most famous solo string works. With these unaccompanied suites Bach provides cellists "with their ultimate *raison d'etre*, their musical bible." In both the solo cello and violin works the solo instrument must not only provide the melody, but also "all the harmony its melody needs," as well as "also evoke a contrapuntal texture of up to four voices."

Pablo Casals, who discovered them over one hundred years ago, was the first to perform and record them. He reportedly played them before breakfast every day of his life. They have been championed by the great artists Mtislav Rostropovich, and Yo-Yo Ma, and recorded sets are available from many others. Casal's recording paved the way for future recordings by every prominent cellist, thus ensuring the ongoing popularity of these great works. Prominent works for solo cello are rare. Two hundred years after Bach's suites Zoltan Kodály, an amateur cellist, would compose his monumental sonata for solo cello, "trying to recreate the evocative melodies, sounds, colors and stories he had discovered on his ethnomusical travels; creating a world of zithers, cimbaloms, gypsy violins and voices on simply four strings of a lone cello."

Among the six Suites, which are written in the sonata da camera ('chamber' sonata) style, the Prelude of the Suite in G contains music of great lyrical energy and takes advantage of the strength of the cello's sonority. Bach creates a masterpiece that flows continuously through "spacious arpeggios (and) runs of increasing breadth (creating) a force of vital proliferation." The final suite, in D major, is for a five-stringed cello and has been described by Rostropovich as a 'symphony'.

Unaccompanied Violin Sonatas and Partitas, BMV 1001-1006

Bach's unaccompanied music for violin (three partitas and three sonatas) are supreme masterpieces and among the greatest music written for solo violin. These six works have been mainstays of the violin concert repertoire since the mid-seventeenth century and a regular part of the violin pedagogy since the eighteenth century." The set of six was completed no later than 1820, about midway through Bach's stay in Cöthen. "These are the most intricate works written for violin in the 18th century." Unlike almost all music composed in the early 18th century, these are truly 'solo' works and not composed over a supporting bass part (i.e., *continuo* or 'thorough bass'). Bach clearly emphasizes in his autograph score that these works are "without accompanying bass."

The *Chaconne*, which concludes the Partita No.2, is considered the Mount Everest of solo violin music and the "finest single movement written for an unaccompanied violin." It is "a quarter-hour-long soliloquy of lacerating beauty...(and) white-knuckle virtuosity;" essentially sixty-four variations on a four-bar theme. A *chaconne* is very similar to the *passacaglia* form but the melody of bass line is accompanied by harmonies from the very start. The movement, "a kind of death dance with a glimpse of heaven in the middle," represents the pinnacle of Bach's set for solo violin. Its "harmonic richness and contrapuntal intimacy...introduces the listener to an illuminating and inexhaustible meditation on the mysteries of life, death, and eternity."

The Sonatas are written in four-movement, *sonata da chiesa* ('church sonata') style with the arrangement of movements being slow-fast-slow-fast with the first two a prelude followed by a fugue. Each sonata opens with a rhapsodic slow movement. The third movements have typical sonata slow movement markings (e.g., *Largo, Andante*), while the finales of the three are marked *Presto, Allegro*, and *Allegro assai*, respectively. The Partitas, on the other hand, are in the *sonata da camera* ('chamber sonata') style and are suites of dances similar to the keyboard suites.

Several of our greatest virtuoso violinists have recorded these six works, but it is clearly not to every violinist's tastes to do so. It is a daunting task; these works are "outstanding for their complexity, making them arguably the supreme achievement of the violin repertoire." In fact, the number of quality recordings of these works is less than the number of available Cello Suites.

Recommended – Bach Violin Suites

Because the six works consume approximately 140 minutes of playing time, they lend themselves ideally to a 2-CD set. Those available include Itzhak Perlman on EMI's 'Great Recordings of the Century' series. Based on consensus of reviews, this is the set I chose and it is thoroughly enjoyable. However, you would not go wrong with Milstein's readings of these works, although you probably want to get the newer DG recordings and not the EMI recordings from the 1950's (for sound quality). And I cannot omit Heifetz's recordings, if it is pure fireworks you seek and do not care if you compromise on sound.

Bach's career was quintessentially 'provincial' – "humble, unglamorous, workaday. He remained for life in the musical environment to which he had been born." This is in stark contrast to his contemporary Handel. Bach spent all of his post-student years within a small area of Germany.

Bach did not achieve in Germany anywhere close to the fame achieved by Handel in England. However, Bach's music has steadily increased in popularity over the past two centuries and the 19th century celebrated him as the creator of pure music at its purest. Bach's current popularity is matched by very few other composers. In fact, after Mozart and Beethoven it is difficult to identify another composer as popular as Bach with the public.

♪ Domenico Scarlatti (1685-1757)

Although Scarlatti's compositions for keyboard (i.e., harpsichord) are called 'sonatas', they come nowhere close to what we now associate with the term 'piano sonata', such as those thirty-plus minute masterpieces by Beethoven and Schubert. But he is probably "the first composer with a fine ear for the more complex relationships" and his sonatas, approximately 555 of them, did show some hints of the Classical style before 1750, "an attempt to make a real dramatic clash in the changes of key, and a sense of periodic phrasing." Scarlatti, who composed only for the harpsichord, actually called them 'exercises' or 'studies', foretelling the future Étude form of Romantic piano composers. The characteristic traits of these 'sonatas', the short themes, tumultuous rhythms, octave leaps and rapid note-repetitions, are virtually his own invention.

While Vivaldi, with over 500 concertos is considered the 'concerto factory' of the Baroque, Scarlatti's 555 sonatas qualify him as the 'harpsichord sonata factory.' His sonatas are almost all single movement works in binary form (i.e., two sections within the one movement separated by the slightest pause) and were compared by poet Gabriele d'Annunzio to a necklace which breaks, producing a resounding hail of glistening pearls rolling around like precious bubbles. His keyboard writing was brilliant and showy one hundred years before Liszt dazzled Europe. Scarlatti was one of the first to "reveal a consistent step toward a solidification of the form from a melodic standpoint." However, he was unknown in mostly all of Europe's musical centers as he wrote his five hundred or so miniatures while in the employ of Spanish royalty.

> ***Recommended*** – Vladimir Horowitz is the master of Scarlatti on the piano; unfortunately, most of his recordings lack the quality of modern sound. However, because there are so many Scarlatti sonatas and you will most likely own multiple recordings, one of them should be a set by Horowitz. A Horowitz set can join a set by András Schiff (Decca), Ivo Pogolerich (DG), and/or Mikail Pletnev. The last is a particularly good bargain offering thirty-one sonatas on two filled-up discs at the price of a single bargain disc.

♪ George Friedrich Handel (1685-1759)

Handel's music is less complex and more accessible than Bach's. It is also more strongly melodic. "Much of the expressive force of High Baroque music depends on the improvised decoration." However, Bach's music, unlike most of Handel's, needs very little or no ornamentation. Contemporary performers actually complained that Bach's music left no space for ornamentation because he wrote everything out, fully notating the decoration of his vocal and keyboard works. In the words of Harold Schonberg, "He (Handel) did not have Bach's harmonic ingenuity or mastery of counterpoint, but who did?" Born in Saxony (Germany), Handel spent most of his life in England, composing for the populace of London. In 1706 he went to Rome for four years, learning and absorbing Italian opera. In Italy he was influenced by Corelli and the Scarlatti's. "The nobility of Corelli's ideals and the purity of his style struck answering chords in Handel's heart."

In 1711 he left Hannover for London, and there he made his career and became a national hero, not in his home country, but in his adopted England. Handel's fifty-year stay in London (1710-1759) showed how a musician could become rich and famous by appealing to public appetites.

Handel's stays in Hamburg, Italy and finally England were stations in the upward climb of a heroic life, which allowed him to grow continuously in breadth and freedom. He "was the quintessential musical polyglot." Handel's style was a hybrid of all his experiences and travels, German, Italian, English, as well as the French style that he assimilated into his work while in Hannover. The French style was popular with German nobles and so influenced court music.

Oddly, although Handel in his day was considered one of the greatest musicians ever (he achieved much more fame than Bach), mostly all of his music fell into neglect not long after his death in 1759 and remained overlooked for the next two hundred years. Only some of his choral works, but not his operas or instrumental music, retained a hold on the public. In fact, after Handel England had a long dry spell producing composers, only broken by Elgar in the late 19th century, almost a century and a half after Handel's death.

He was a prolific composer of operas, although few remain in the repertory. In the late 1730s the London thirst for Italian opera had waned and Handel adapted by beginning a journey that would mark him as the greatest composer of oratorios. Oratorios are dramatic works based on biblical subjects but they are not devotional religious works like masses and cantatas. His instinct was correct as the British music-loving public embraced the early oratorios *Saul* and *Israel in Egypt*. In 1741 Handel presented to the public the greatest oratorio, *Messiah*, which has remained the most popular by far of his works in this genre, as most of the others remain unknown.

Handel's music has made a comeback over the past couple of decades with the rise of the 'period' instrument movement, which heavily emphasizes Baroque music. As with his contemporary Bach he lost his eyesight late in life, but kept composing.

Opus 1 – Twelve 'Chamber Sonatas'
These works are variously for flute, recorder, oboe or violin and might serve as a 'school' of melody-writing. Handel spent five years in his early twenties in Florence and Rome, where he learned from A. Scarlatti and Corelli. These sonatas are in the Italian style and clearly show the influence of the Italian masters.

Harpsichord suites, 'The Harmonious Blacksmith'
Handel composed at least twenty suites for solo keyboard (i.e., harpsichord), analogous to Bach's sets of keyboard *Partitas* and *English* and *French* Suites. The most famous of Handel's by far is No.5 in E (HMV430), a four-movement work, including the typical opening Baroque 'Prelude', whose *Aria con Variazioni* Finale has become known as the 'Harmonious Blacksmith'. This finale contains a theme, aria, loosely-based on the English folk song 'Four Days Drunk', with five *variazioni*. Like much of Handel, the *Harmonious Blacksmith* is highly lyrical but virtuosic.

♫♫♫♫

In the last decade of Bach's life the musical style that he perfected came under criticism. The derogatory term 'baroque' was coined by critics who regarded the thick counterpoint of late Baroque composers to be dissonant and unmelodious. With Bach's death in 1750 and Handel and Scarlatti gone within the decade, the "learned contrapuntal style" also died as a result of the movement that evolved out of this criticism. In its place would come the 'lighter' and 'simpler' music of the Classical Period epitomized by Haydn and Mozart, which "demanded a singing style...fluffiness over deep content...a new style of melody...and gaiety over grace."

♪ François Couperin (1668-1733)
♪ Jean-Phillippe Rameau (1683-1764)

Couperin and Rameau were the key figures in French music of the late Baroque and both were virtuoso keyboard players. The art of French harpsichordists reached its summit with them. Like other late Baroque composers, Couperin wrote harpsichord music influenced by the works of the earlier Italian Baroque composer Archengelo Corelli. Couperin created a world of subtle feeling in his harpsichord music within the limits of binary form. His music, characteristic of the French Baroque, is not based on strong themes and does not contain coloristic or virtuosic effects; rather, he strives for a particular feeling or mood expressed in music, emphasizing melody with accompaniment.

> *"I would rather be touched by music than surprised."*
> - Francois Couperin

Couperin was chief harpsichordist to Louis XIV and was honored two centuries later with Ravel's neo-Baroque suite, *Le Tombeau de Couperin*, literally 'tomb' of Couperin, but actually signifying a memorial or tribute to the Baroque composer. Couperin composed over two hundred harpsichord pieces, bursting with ornamentation. Harpsichordist Wanda Landowska states that Couperin's (musical) language burrows into the depth of our inner life.

Both Couperin and Rameau wrote keyboard (harpsichord) suites that are lighter and less densely contrapuntal than those of Bach. They are considered prime examples of the rococo style, "in which the heroic dimensions of the

Baroque were cut down to a more human scale." Couperin, who admired the works of Corelli and Lully, produced the first French sonatas (in 1692; published 1726), fusing French with Italianate styles. They are 'sonata trios' scored for two violins and *basso continuo*.

A major literary contribution was Rameau's <u>Treatise on Harmony</u>, which he authored in 1722. This work offered the first complete theoretical formulation of the diatonic system (major and minor keys) that had replaced the old 'church modes' during the second half of the 17th century. Rameau was the supreme composer and musical theoretician of France's late Baroque and believed that there is a specified sequence of chords to express particular passions, revealing himself as a visionary, looking forward to Romanticism and Impressionism.

- 4 -

The Classical Style
Haydn, Mozart, and Beethoven

The Classical period (ca. 1760-1830) is when music for the keyboard as we know it today, really began in the form of sonatas and concertos. The piano sonatas of Haydn and Schubert, and the sonatas and concertos by Mozart and Beethoven paved the way for the future great piano music of the Romantic period and the 20th century. For all of Beethoven's declared independence from preceding influences, there was in reality "no radical movement away from the style of Mozart and Haydn comparable to the break…made by…Schumann and Chopin."

> *"I take Beethoven twice a week, Haydn four times, and Mozart every day."*
> - Rossini

♪ Mozart, Haydn, and Beethoven

> *"People make a mistake who think that my art has come easily to me. Nobody has devoted so much time and thought to composition as I. There is not a famous master whose music I have not studied over and over".*
> - Mozart

"By the late 1780s there was never any doubt about the supremacy of Haydn and Mozart," and by 1805 Beethoven had joined them to form the great Viennese triumvirate. Competing composers of instrumental music for public enjoyment were rarely taken very seriously. Haydn, Mozart, and Beethoven "were considered a coherent group at least as early as 1805…they…defined Viennese classical style…(that) influenced the subsequent history of music." All three used the coherent and systematic musical language provided by the High Baroque.

While there is no question that both Mozart and Beethoven receive the recognition they deserve, rarely is Haydn considered in their company. Haydn was a simple man, content with life and his music "is a reflection of a mind that was serene and strong in religious faith." He was Mozart's friend and Beethoven's composition teacher. However, if you consider their contribution to the evolution of classical music, it could be argued that Haydn made the greatest contribution of the three, greater than his contemporary Mozart, by whom he has always been overshadowed. When Beethoven left Bonn for Vienna in 1792, his patron told him, "…you will receive the spirit of Mozart from the hands of Haydn," alluding to the fact that although Mozart had died the year before, Beethoven would study in Vienna with Haydn, which he did, taking composition lessons with the great master who was past sixty.

> *"Haydn, Mozart, and Beethoven developed a new art."*
> — E.T.A. Hoffmann

At the time of his death Haydn was considered in Europe to be the greatest living composer. However, not long after he "was increasingly seen as the first and least in an evolutionary chain that culminated in Beethoven." Haydn scholar Richard Wigmore argues that 'Papa' Haydn has been scandalously underrated over the past two centuries and that Haydn's music has been a touchstone for all composers of instrumental music. Maybe part of the relative neglect until recent decades was that Haydn's music never said "look at me" the way Mozart did with his gift for the theatrical.

The contribution of these three giants can be summarized, however incompletely, as follows: Haydn invented forms (more accurately he took nascent forms to maturity); Mozart perfected existent forms but worked within the parameters established mostly by Haydn. He had little interest in establishing new musical forms, genres, schools, etc.; rather, "he brought to perfection those already in existence." Mozart "moved beyond Haydn...deep into the spirit realm."

However, it would be wrong to think that Haydn invented forms "out of thin air". The foundation was laid through the natural evolution of music from the Baroque to the Rococo and early Classical period. Haydn just put everything together and did it so effectively that past forms were virtually abandoned. Haydn's genius is validated by the fact that Mozart worked completely within Haydn's forms. If Mozart had found them inadequate or too restrictive he would have done something about it. Indeed, it took Haydn's other star pupil Beethoven to significantly move Haydn's forms forward, preparing the bridge between the Classical and the Romantic periods.

Haydn's music manipulates and thwarts the listener's expectations and keeps one "guessing as to the exact moment of a theme's return." He had a great fondness for practical jokes and was a "master of subtlety, surprise and subterfuge." Unfortunately, Haydn's "comic subversiveness...can still blind listeners to the full expressive range of his music."

While the music of both Haydn and Mozart share many more characteristics than differences, there are ways to distinguish the music of the two. Haydn allows his music to "grow dynamically from a small kernel;" an expansion based on Haydn's treatment of tiny motifs, as opposed to "the long, regular and complete melodies of Mozart." "The insistent repetition of smaller units is unusual for Mozart (although typical of Haydn)." "Haydn is interested in the directional power of his material, its dramatic possibilities." The lyricism of Mozart's works lies in the details, and the larger structure is an organizing force. "The opening of a work by Mozart is always solidly based, while with Haydn, e.g., the typical opening measures of a string quartet, it is "far more unstable, more immediately charged with a dynamic movement away from the tonic."

Haydn displayed a "mastery of subtle and complex compositional games." "Haydn was the most playful of composers," a "master of the surprise modulation, the dramatic silence, the asymmetrical phrase; and he added to this an aptitude for the facetious that no other composer enjoyed." Compared with Mozart, Haydn infused his music with un-Mozartian disruptions, giving it distinctive asymmetries that jump out at the listener and contrast with the usually highly symmetric and ordered Classical period forms. Haydn developed steadily over a long life and was not a Wunderkind like Mozart. Neither did he turn out music at the rapid rate of a Mozart, preferring to compose "with care and diligence."

Haydn's output has been compared to an iceberg, most of his music remains submerged while only a small amount is visible. For example, he composed 160-180 trios for the now-extinct baryton over a twenty year period before 1776. But for all of the intellectual and expressive virtuosity of Haydn's finest instrumental works, they "have relatively little of Mozart's sensuous allure," the bel canto that infuses Mozart, whose suave vocally-inspired melodies rarely have Haydn's sense of fun and mischief. Indeed, Mozart's "art...leads through opera" and opera "became the preferred medium of musical expression for Mozart."

> *"In every form he touched he produced an astonishing number of imperishable masterpieces."*
> — Jeremy Nicholas

Mozart is said to have composed his music in his head in its complete and mostly final form. He is quoted that "the committing to paper is done quickly enough", as well as, "I take out of the bag of my memory what has previously been collected into it." Thus, Mozart put music to paper quickly as what he committed to paper rarely differed from the music that was in his head. Few, if any, revisions or changes were needed.

Beethoven redefined forms and parameters and took them to unprecedented heights. "No composer has been more innovative than Beethoven...to alter the fundamental principles of the (classical) style he inherited," while rejecting no part of it. With him "each major work ventures into a different corner of his mind and heart...once he had solved a particular compositional problem, he would challenge himself with another." Haydn and Mozart stood for pure Classicism – rigidity of form, balance, order, unity and homogenized forms. These two great masters created or perfected many of the major genres that became the workhorses of Classical composition (the symphony, piano trio, string quartet, concerto with soloist).

Beethoven extended and expanded compositional practices inherited from Haydn and Mozart "by infusing them with new force and flexibility...more powerful emotional content, and an imposing monumentality." "Beethoven was in a position to select out of the work of Haydn and Mozart what was most forceful and effective… Haydn's forms permitted the release of Beethoven's energy." As with Haydn and Mozart, "Beethoven never relinquished his reliance upon the Classical structures;" but in addition, "he imbued them with greater freedom and fantasy, expanding their boundaries and maximizing their coherence." In place of Haydn's and Mozart's balance of harmonic and thematic development, Beethoven stresses thematic contrast and transformation, writing in a proto-Romantic style.

> *"What unites Haydn, Mozart and Beethoven is…their common understanding of the musical language which they did so much to formulate and to change."*
> — Charles Rosen

Haydn can count to his credit the 'invention' of (at a minimum) the modern symphony, earning the nickname 'father of the symphony' (with help from Johann Stamitz, Carl Friedrich Abel, and the sons of J.S. Bach), piano trio and string quartet. Mozart has one genre to his credit, the piano quartet. While Beethoven does not appear to have 'invented' any forms, he took virtually all existent forms to places they had never even approached before. For example, compare Mozart's last symphony, the Jupiter (composed in 1788), to Beethoven's Third, the Eroica (composed in 1803) in both conformance to structure and the diverse range of themes and emotions.

Beethoven bridged Classical and Romantic periods because he laid the groundwork for breaking the forms that had been established and adhered to so carefully during the Classical period. "The mature Beethoven underwent the influence of the liberating tendencies of the 19th century" and freed the symphony, string quartet, solo concerto, and sonata from the restraints and restrictions of the 18th century. "The whole immense wealth of (the 18th) century was concentrated in (Beethoven), and what he did was to make a new synthesis of classicism and then hand it down to the new century."

He "established the model of the composer as the angry, unhappy, original, uncompromising genius…" Beethoven spoke his mind openly in Vienna and did not care what people thought of him, regardless of their rank or position. Unlike Mozart, who always sought, or Haydn, who always enjoyed aristocratic patronage, Beethoven never allowed himself to be 'bought'. From a contemporary account we learn, "he has for years resided in Vienna in open hostility with many…the ill-judged candor with which he declares his opinion…an increase of difficulties and of invidious enemies."

It can also be stated that Beethoven said a lot more than both Haydn and Mozart with a lot less. Whereas Haydn composed around 100 symphonies (numbered up to 104), many of them masterpieces (particularly the last two dozen or so) and Mozart's last was numbered '41'; Beethoven needed only nine to completely evolve. Listen to Beethoven's First Symphony, then his final Choral symphony, keeping in mind he had only seven attempts in between, most of them (e.g., his Fifth Symphony) near perfect.

One can compare these three great composers in terms of the major genres of music in which they distinguished themselves. As symphonists all three can be considered on the same level, Haydn due to quantity and establishing the form, Mozart due to his perfection of the form, and Beethoven for moving the symphony far forward and producing at least three unrivaled works in the genre (Symphonies Nos. 3,5 and 9).

In terms of the string quartet, while Beethoven clearly sits on top by himself, Haydn is at least on the level of Mozart, although Mozart did add to the quartets a set of wonderful string quintets (adding an extra viola to give a timbre which he found well suited to the music he wished to make).

An easy call here is Beethoven's superiority with piano sonatas, regarding which he has no peer. But for piano concertos (Haydn is not really competitive) Mozart ranks ahead of Beethoven. While Beethoven's Fourth and Fifth concertos are musical masterpieces of originality, Mozart produced far more concertos of quality for keyboard and thus provides the most listening pleasure. Beethoven stopped composing piano concertos when he could no longer perform them as soloist because of his deafness.

It is also worthwhile to compare their social and professional situations. Haydn and Mozart spent much of their time and devoted much of their music-making efforts in service and as inherently inferior to nobility, although "Mozart lacked the temperament that allowed Haydn to remain a court servant over a long period." In fact, Haydn was the last prominent beneficiary of noble patronage that had supported European musicians and composers since the Renaissance. When Mozart moved to Vienna for the last ten years of his life after being released from the patronage of the prince-archbishop of Salzburg, he became possibly the first freelance composer in history.

Both Haydn and Mozart "still worked within the specific-piece-for-specific-occasion system" but it was Beethoven who was the first to hold "winning a place in posterity as the greatest goal of a musician." Beethoven was the first of the great composers to truly work as an independent artist, "and as such superior in his own mind to kings and nobles." "Beethoven was the first musician to become a legend in his own time." This combination of freedom from the bondage of patronage and an attention-grabbing persona not only established Beethoven as a legendary figure in Europe but set the stage for Paganini and Liszt as larger-than-life virtuosos.

Since Beethoven "we've come to expect (an) artist to take his fears, hangups, and conflicts and work them out through his art." His predecessors, including Haydn and Mozart, never saw themselves as artists creating works for posterity; rather, they supplied a commodity. Mozart did make attempts to break free of "the feudal order of things" but it usually landed him in financial straits. Mozart never experienced the stable and relatively generous patronage that Haydn did. Mozart considered the Archbishop of Salzburg his "unappreciative and miserly" patron.

> "Consider me a man whom God has
> granted a talent and a good heart."
> - Haydn

Haydn spent most of thirty years (1762-1790) employed in the service of Prince Esterhazy, a wealthy Hungarian nobleman and lived most of this period in either Eisenstadt or Eszterhaza. This is much different from the existence and lifestyle of Haydn's successors such as Mozart and Beethoven in Vienna; Chopin, Liszt and Berlioz in Paris; and Schumann and Mendelssohn in Leipzig. Haydn' life, apart from his marriage, was generally happy and well-adjusted, "certainly more stable than the mercurial, ultimately tragic Mozart and the scowling convention-defying Beethoven."

♪ The Classical Style and Sonata Form

The musical forms and genres of today were compiled over centuries and "evolved through the combined experience of generations of composers working in many different lands." As part of this evolution, some forms have passed completely out of use while others remain in use. In the previous chapter we saw how Bach perfected fugue and counterpoint as the dominant Baroque form. The Classical period moved away from polyphony towards homophony and new forms would be developed that, together with polyphony and counterpoint, have formed the foundation of 'classical' music for almost 300 years.

> *The goal is "to arrive where we started*
> *And know the place for the first time."*
> - T.S. Eliot in "Four Quartets"

♫ The Classical Style

The simplest way to summarize Classical style is "the symmetrical resolutions of opposing forces...in no other style do the parts and the whole mirror each other with such clarity." The Classical style is a reconciliation of conflicting ideals that "immeasurably increased the power of dissonance, raising it from an unresolved interval to an unresolved chord and then to an unresolved key." The Classical style created and integrated forms with a dramatic violence that the Baroque never attempted and the Romantic style preferred to leave unresolved.

The style *galant* of the mid-18th century "marked music's shift from church to salon, from fugue to sonata, demanding a singing style...fluffiness over deep content...(its audience) did not want to think." "The whole tendency of the classical style is against the heavy ornamentation of the Baroque... (It) purifies the lighter ornamentation of the Rococo." The style *galant,* with its sensibility and sentimental style, considerably tempered the technical requirements of composers of the mid-1700s such as C.P.E Bach.

Achievement of the 'classical style' required a new social situation to occur in the 18th century. Factors that established this new society in Europe were "the rising aspirations of the commercial class...and their growing interest in music as...proof of social distinction." Additionally, the population increase provided both a large pool of amateur musicians as well as a new and affluent public.

The style of the Classical period owed much to the Italian comic opera tradition. Its balance and stability provides the necessary framework and foundation for the drama, established through the development as well as the contrast of themes.

♪ Sonatas and Sonata Form

For details on Sonata Form, the leading books are by pianist and musicologist Charles Rosen. The details of sonata form, including modulation processes within parts of sonata; movement from the tonic to dominant, to subdominant, etc.; and how modulation was used to both create tension (e.g., by moving to relative minor); and how to resolve it (by return to tonic or modulation from minor to relative major) are well covered. Rosen uses many examples, including many scores to demonstrate his points through the actual music.

The term 'sonata' goes back at least as far as the 16th century, when it was "applied in a loose manner to individual pieces not patterned on specific dance types." The 'trio sonata', with its four-movement slow-fast-slow-fast format, traced its origin back to the contrasting slow and fast sections of the sonatas of the 1620s. The multi-movement, modern-day sonata emerged in Italy in the 17th century. By the late 1700s, "a sonata was any organized series of movements, and the proportions...changed according to whether it was the opening movement, a middle movement or a finale." By the Rococo period, 1735-50, the familiar three-movement fast-slow-fast format, derived from opera overtures of the pre-classical era, was predominant. Serenades and *Divertimenti* were created by adding marches and minuets.

'Sonata form' was not something already set down or established for composers to follow or adhere to and only occasionally do pieces fit such definitions as 'fugue' and 'sonata' form. Sonata form evolved out of binary form in the Classical era as a way of realizing the far-ranging musical goals of the period, including the sophisticated key changes that represented dramatic events effected by contrasts of themes, rhythms, and textures.

Specifically, what is termed 'rounded binary' form from this era and typically consists of A-A-B-A'-B-A', was essentially Sonata form in that 'A' represents the exposition; 'B' the development, and A' the recapitulation.

"'Sonata form' is not a definite form like a minuet...it is, like the fugue, a way of writing, a feeling for proportion, direction, and texture rather than a pattern." Neil Zaslaw sums up sonata form as the "ability to present and develop musical ideas and 'arguments' at unprecedented length while imparting a convincing aural unity to the whole."

The Classical period 'sonata' and 'sonata form' are inseparable from the 'Classical Style'. "The classical style appears inevitable only after the event...a step in the progressive realization of the musical language...since the 15th century." A major distinction of the classical style over the Baroque is the role of tension and contrast. In most Baroque music a low level of tension and drama remain relatively constant so that one section is not significantly more dramatic than another. "The most common Baroque form is one of simple and unified rhythmic texture," and the High Baroque looked for variety mainly through ornamentation.

> *"The dramatic character of the sonata calls for contrast."*
> *- Charles Rosen*

But in the Classical period, "the emotional force of the classical style is clearly bound up with the contrast between dramatic tension and stability." With modulations from major to minor keys and tonic to dominant, tensions are raised,. then relaxed. Second subjects in Classical sonata form are generally more intense than the first subject. "The dramatic character of the sonata calls for contrast." The opening and closing sections are more stable than the middle sections, resulting in a building up of tensions after the first subject and a return to stability and clarity to bring the movement to a close. The contrast between dramatic tension and stability gives the 'Classical Style' its emotional force. Its logic and stability "brought instrumental music to full maturity and independence in the Classical period."

Sonata form, also called 'first movement' or 'sonata allegro' form, usually applies to the first movement of a multi-movement work (sonata, symphony, quartet), but finales as well as single-movement works (e.g., overtures) can often be structured in sonata form. This is not to be confused with the instrumental works for solo or two instruments called 'sonatas'. Haydn more or less created the rules for classical sonata allegro form and then perfected it along with Mozart. Beethoven further elevated it and sonata form became the standard for compositional form for two hundred years.

The first movement consists of multiple contrasting themes that get resolved by the end of the movement and give sonata form its cyclic nature that "depends upon the unification of starkly opposite elements." The form consists of three parts: the exposition, the development, and the recapitulation. In many works there will be additional parts such as a slow introduction before the exposition (Haydn's late symphonies) and a coda can be added at the end to bring a feeling of finality to the movement. Sonata form is "a sophisticated large-scale structure built up of interlocking units" and parallels the literary model of an essay: presentation of ideas, development of those ideas, then a summary of the ideas and key points made in the essay. Because the recapitulation is essentially a re-statement of the first theme, sonata form can be shown as A-B-A. However, the distinction with three-part form is that the A and B sections represent larger (often much larger) divisions of music, sometimes greater than ten minutes each. Each unit in ternary sonata form is itself in a ternary form of stability-tension-stability. The alternation from stability to tension and from tension back to stability is often created with homophony and polyphony.

Exposition

The exposition presents the principal thematic material, usually with two major themes or sections. It presents the main themes that will be explored in different keys in the developmental section. In the Classical period, composers maintained overall unity of tonality primarily by staying 'close to home' and never wandering too far from the home key ('tonic') of the work. If there was a key change it was usually to the relative minor. Haydn and Mozart usually limited themselves to two themes, but later composers would present three or more themes in the exposition.

From the main theme grow other themes and variations "in such a way as to create an effect of organic unity." In the exposition these themes are exposed and contrasted, usually by presenting a serious, aggressive theme followed by lighter, song-like theme in a different key. The drama in a sonata-form movement is created by these contrasting characteristics or 'affects'. The "opposed affects" made possible in sonata form by contrasting themes and changing keys, among other devices, consist "of beauty and sadness, of consolation and tenor, of longing and anger, of pleasure and pain."

Often the themes are joined by a transition from one mood to another by use of a 'bridge' section. In many works the composer intends the exposition section to be repeated. Sometimes, repeating the exposition section of a first movement is critical to the success of the work; other times the practice is superfluous or redundant. "The use of repeats is transformed during the classical period." Up to the mature works of Haydn and Mozart the repeat was primarily the opportunity for expressive ornamentation, as used by composers of the Baroque. However, after 1775 structure replaced ornamentation as the principal vehicle of expression and the repeat provided a repeated hearing to the listeners in a live performance, an indication of the importance placed on the exposition by Classical composers.

One may read in a review of a particular performance of a symphony that the conductor does or does not 'observe the first movement exposition repeat.'

Past maestros regularly disregarded the repeat, resulting in shorter first movements. Recent conductors are more likely to follow the composer's wishes. Of course this lengthens the total time of the work(s) and sometimes has implications for CD layout and couplings.

Development
The Development section is the section that has held so much appeal for composers by virtue of its uniqueness. This section, which provides a vivid contrast between musical ideas, makes sonata form the only form in which there is "a special division reserved for the extension and development of musical material already introduced in a previous section." In the development material from the exposition is presented in contrasting ways to create drama and tension. The exposition is discussed and argued. The development heightens tension and delays return to the tonic through modulations and harmonic progressions. "The quality of the development is the test of the composer's resource, imagination, and technique."

Development utilizes devices such as 'repetition and contrast', statement of theme(s) in different keys (modulation), fragmentation of theme(s) into melodic-rhythmic units or motives. Repetition and contrast lead to unity as well as variety; the former establishing "a relationship between structural elements." The contrast "sets off and vitalizes this relationship," bringing with it a heightening of tension, which is resolved by repetition. The statement and development of themes in different keys builds tension and creates instability in anticipation of return to the home key.

The Development section was expanded by Haydn with the use of "the principle of thematic development in the 'working out' section (i.e., development) of sonata form. Haydn reserves all his harmonic surprises for the development." In addition to utilizing thematic development in his sonata-form movements, Beethoven also included thematic development in some of his scherzo dance movements, taking the third dance movement to levels beyond the traditional ternary A-B-A format.

Unfortunately, in English the word 'development' does not fully capture the intent; the German word *Durchführung*, meaning 'leading through', much better reflects the true intention of the development section. In the development there are plot twists and complications; themes interact freely and dramatically and these themes are "deconstructed and combined…often tonally unstable or ambiguous." The development tends to be unstable overall relative to the exposition and recapitulation; as such, it allows composers to show their gifts for imagination and variety. Development is not merely a development of themes, but takes into account and intensifies the order and the sense of what has gone before.

Recapitulation

The Recapitulation is a 'wrapping-up', a return of the first theme, and a restatement of previous themes and materials. It takes us back home to the tonic and opening themes. Recapitulation provides a symmetric resolution of the harmonic tension built up during the development. It serves to relieve the dramatic tension of the development section and re-establish the stability of the exposition. Thus, there are rarely any major modulations. To add a twist, "a recapitulation that begins in the wrong key is a familiar device...of Haydn and Beethoven." As opposed to the exposition, which looks ahead, the recapitulation looks back.

The second movement of a large, multi-movement work is usually slow and emotional, often song-like, and counterbalances the first movement. This form is often called 'song form'. It is also usually in a different key, such as the relative minor for a work in a major key. In a typical concerto, the soloist often dominates this movement with the orchestra providing a hushed accompaniment. It is often in an A-B-A form with 'B' contrasting with 'A' sections (e.g., happy to sad and back) or in theme-and-variations form. In the cases of extended second movements, sonata form may be employed by the composer. However, the typical 'slow' movement is not cast completely in sonata form because it has no development section, or only a short development. This form has been called 'abridged sonata form'. Of course, composers are not forced to place the movements in any particular order but before the 20th century convention usually dictated adherence to form. When movements are seemingly 'out-of-order', the effect can be very effective. One of the more famous examples is Tchaikovsky's Sixth, *Pathetique,* in which the slow movement is used to bring this symphony of despair to its conclusion.

Beginning in the Classical period, a dance-like movement was almost always the third movement in a four-movement work. "The tone is often courtly," although Haydn, with his ingenious sense of humor, often made his "jokey and/or folksy." These movements contain a minuet (A) played twice with a contrasting trio section (B) in the middle. The trio was made to contrast with the light and dance-like minuet. Both minuet and trio sections are often in ternary A-B-A forms themselves. This minuet-trio dance movement that symphonies originally took from Baroque orchestral suites evolved into the scherzo movement with Beethoven. In the Classical period it is this dance movement that is almost always omitted in a three-movement concerto. The minuet and minuet-trio are rigid forms, so any deviations from their standard pattern are very noticeable and are used to great effect.

Romantic composers replaced the minuet (and trio) almost entirely with a scherzo. The *scherzi* of Beethoven, while still dance-like in character with a middle trio section, contained heavier textures and more complex ideas and development. Beethoven did not simply replace the minuet with scherzo, but developed third-movement form much further to create elaborate sequences such as 'scherzo-trio A-scherzo-trio B-varied scherzo'.

The fourth movement, finale, is usually in *rondo* (A-B-A) form, and revisits earlier themes, particularly those in the opening movement. Rondo form consists of a recurring theme in the home key interrupted by contrasting episodes in related keys. Compared to sonata form, which can be considered circular as a whole, rondo form is continually circular with an A-B-A-C-A-D-A... pattern. In contrast to sonata form typical of opening movements, rondos in closing movements lack instability and tension, and are traditionally light and vivacious, with ironic or humorous effects. Even a finale in sonata form is more loosely organized, functioning to resolve the tensions of the entire work and to tie the previous movements together into a more or less cohesive whole. An exception is Chopin's Sonata No.2, in which he threw together four seemingly unrelated movements.

The finale is usually taken at a quicker pace and is significantly shorter than the opening movement, although of course there are many exceptions to this. Many composers effectively lend a feeling of 'racing to the finish line' to their closing movements, creating a buildup to the closing *tutti*. The final movement will usually operate with a recurring main theme (or refrain), with 'episodes' separating the reappearance of the refrain. With Beethoven and early Romantics the five-movement symphony appeared. The additional movement could be a march (Mahler), programmatic (Beethoven's *Pastoral* Symphony, Berlioz's *Symphonie Fantastique*), or a short 'bridge' passage to link two larger movements.

♪ Other Forms

Sonata form is the major accomplishment in the evolution of forms from the Classical period. The significant form representing the peak of contrapuntal writing is the fugue, covered in Chapter 3. Other forms are discussed below and in subsequent chapters.

Binary and Three-Part Forms

Binary Form, also known as two-part form (A-B), was a major form of the high Baroque period up to Haydn. There are two distinct sections, each of which is usually repeated, and represented as A-A-B-B. The first section (A) closes on a new key. 'B' opens on this new key but returns to and ends on the home key. Examples include the hundreds of sonatas by Domenico Scarlatti.

Three-Part Form (A-B-A) or 'ternary' form became very popular in the Classical period; the best examples are the minuets of Haydn and Mozart. Ternary form contains a melodic statement with a contrasting middle section sandwiched between. In A-B-A form (minuet-trio, scherzo) "the middle section represents a step outside the firm borders set by the primary section (A)"

Variation vs Development

Variation (or 'Theme and Variations', 'Variations on a Theme') form is "the most 'open' of musical procedures, one that gives the greatest freedom to a composer's fantasy...(it) is the form of shifting moods, alternations of feelings, shades of meaning." With Variation form "the game is to get maximum variety out of one piece of material." Variation form takes a tune or theme as a whole and subjects it to certain changes. The theme can be original, borrowed (Brahms' *Variations on a Theme of Haydn*), or even kept a mystery by the composer (Elgar's *Enigma* Variations).

The theme is most often first stated in its simplest form, then varied multiple times with each variation usually moving progressively further away from the theme. The last 'variation' or movement is often a coda-type affair with the original theme returning blended with some of the memorable variations melodies. Elgar wraps up the *Enigma* Variations with a return to the main theme blended with a recall of the famous and lovely *Nimrod* variation.

Variations on a theme can all stay within the same key; development is all about changing keys (modulation). In the development, a composer will take a motif and "play around with it", often employing polyphonic tools. It should be noted that traditionally in sonata form, polyphony is not utilized in the exposition section. The start of counterpoint can be used by a listener to signal the end of the exposition and the beginning of the development.

Alternatively, variation form is sometimes used in slow movements. "Anchored in...the theme, a set of variations allows the composer's imagination to cover a vast emotional territory." A statement of the theme in a minor key, as one of the variations, gives it a darker sound. The composer has a lot of options from which to choose: build new melodies around the theme while maintaining the harmony (i.e., the key); ornament the theme with changes in tempo or modulation from major to minor (or vice versa). Haydn, a master of the Theme and Variations form, often started with a very "plain and uncompromising theme then amazes us with the gold he extracts from it in the variations."

Rondo

Rondo form consists of symmetrical sections based on recurrence of the rondo theme. Its origin is the medieval song form forme fixe in which music was repeated but text would change. Rondo form sets up a refrain (A) that is returned to multiple times after intervals of new music (A-B-A-C-A-D-A...), "...like a series of short excursions, with a return home after each one." The refrain is always in the home key but the 'episodes' between its return contrast sharply in key and mood. Often, the principal theme, A, is varied slightly each time it returns. Rondo is the most common form for finales of multi-movement concertos and symphonies.

The merging of the rondo with sonata form is aptly called 'sonata-rondo' form, and is the common form used for final movements of concertos, as well as of many symphonies. It gives a joyful feeling to the concluding movement of the work and, when done effectively, creates a 'racing to the finish line' atmosphere in the music. The vast majority of popular songs are in rondo form, consisting of verses ('episodes') with repeated chorus/refrain, albeit with very little variation musically among the 'episodes'.

Minuet and Trio and *Scherzo*

The 'minuet-and-trio' and the *scherzo* are the most common formats of the dance-like movement of a work of four or more movements. The minuet-and-trio developed out of the Baroque dance suites and would dominate as the third movement form of Classical period symphonies and quartets. Beethoven would replace the stately minuet-and-trio with the scherzo. Both minuet and later scherzo forms are in a ternary A-B-A format ('B' = trio). Additionally, within the 'A' and 'B' sections there can be a further division into A-B-A format in longer movements (e.g., those in larger symphonies).

The tone of the minuet movement is often courtly, although Haydn with his ingenious sense of humor, often made his jokey and/or folksy.

Cyclic or Thematic Transformation

Cyclic form, in which a theme (or themes) recurs slightly altered throughout a work, became very popular with early Romantic composers, with Berlioz's idée fixe and Liszt's 'thematic transformation'. Cyclical form was very attractive to Romantic composers because it is a "dislocation of an accepted form" and enabled them to "use a traditional form but give it more personal urgency." Their facility with cyclical form allows the Romantic composer to seamlessly integrate the cyclical interruptions into the texture of the music without the momentary halt needed by the Classical period composers just before them.

72

- 5 -

Music for Solo Instrument – The Classical Period

In the 1770s Muzio Clementi and Mozart became the first true 'pianists'. The history of piano playing begins with Mozart and Clementi. In the last quarter of the 18th century extreme virtuosity almost disappears as keyboard music had become more sociable, with an emphasis on composition of works that amateurs could play, and pressure by publishers for scores that the public would purchase. Contemporary composers (i.e., Mozart and Beethoven) were usually glad to oblige their publishers in order to further establish their independence from the bondage of aristocratic and royal patronage. "Even more so than the string quartet, the (piano) sonata was…the province of the amateur musician."

Despite these factors, Mozart's music was never reduced to being 'easy', although he probably thought some of his music (e.g., several of his piano sonatas) was, by his definition. Beethoven's piano sonatas "showed still less consideration for the amateur than Mozart," providing the bridge from Classical sonatas routinely played by and written for amateurs, to the virtuosity of the early Romantic pieces of Schumann, Chopin, and Liszt.

In fact, the Beethoven piano sonatas were the first group of solo piano works substantial enough to comprise a program in a public concert hall. "Beethoven's music…demands more intense attention than other composers had dared to require." His piano sonatas are "the way for the professional concert pianist to demonstrate his pretensions to the highest musical culture." Their purpose is not to dazzle the listener with the player's virtuosity. However, within a decade of Beethoven's death Liszt, whose purpose was to dazzle the listener, had invented the 'piano recital', which remains today one of the more popular types of programs given in public. Liszt broke the mold of virtuoso pianist-composers playing only one's own music. His performances of Chopin's music greatly impressed even Chopin.

♪ Wolfgang Amadeus Mozart (1756-1791)

Unlike most all other composers, Mozart did not seem to make any mistakes or write any music one would consider to not meet his standards of excellence. "This most spontaneous of melodists…," Mozart's immediate accessibility and universal appeal are the result of the sophisticated simplicity of the music. To quote Romain Rolland, "Music is the harmonious expression of life" and Mozart's music is "addressed not to the intellect but to the heart" and always with feeling and passion but not with "offensive passion".

> *A note on the cataloguing of Mozart's works –*
> For works by Mozart, the 'Köchel' designation (indicated 'K.xxx'), named after Ludwig von Köchel who completely catalogued Mozart's works in chronological order (1862), is used. In the case of the Köchel designations, they do indicate the chronological order of Mozart's works, as best as Köchel could determine, so it is convenient that youthful works of Mozart are easily distinguished from mature ones. Mozart left few clues to the chronology of his works as he hardly concerned himself with posterity.

Mozart wrote eighteen sonatas for solo piano plus a couple of shorter pieces, most notably the Fantasia in C minor, K.475, often paired with the Sonata, K.457 in the same key. These C minor works are significant and "they strongly prefigure Beethoven's famous 'C minor mood'." Sonata K.457 together with Mozart's C minor Piano Sonata (K.491) exerted a potent influence on Beethoven. The sonatas as a whole are not particularly difficult or probing in nature (excepting the minor-key sonatas) and were probably regarded by Mozart more as pieces for students than as challenges or concert showpieces for virtuosi. The piano sonata was not one of Mozart's favorite genres; when it came to keyboard compositions he much preferred concertos, in which he expressed "strength and grace…in the most polished and ingenious manner…" Alternatively, Mozart preferred to áoin the piano to strings in a chamber ensemble in order to throw a keener light on the wonderful melodies of his piano trios and piano quartets.

The sonatas written for Paris in 1778, K.310, K.330-333 show a wide variety of style. K.310 in A minor is particularly impressive for showing Mozart expressing his own individuality more strongly and is one of his masterpieces in this form. On the other hand, K.333 in B-flat (often referred to as the *Linz* Sonata) is closer to the cantabile style of J.C. Bach although updated to Classical style. As a result, in K.333 past and present seem to meet. Only the last five sonatas were composed after Mozart settled in Vienna in 1781.

> *"The death of Mozart before he had passed his 35th year is perhaps the greatest loss the musical world has ever suffered."*
>
> - Edvard Grieg

> *Recommended – Mozart Solo Piano Music*
> Among the many complete sets of Mozart piano sonatas, the most highly-regarded is probably the set by Mitsuko Uchida (Philips), which also includes the shorter pieces. However, there are many excellent recordings by a variety of artists, including a re-release of a set by Richter, and a set by Gilels.

Mozart's works involving piano – eighteen sonatas, thirty-six violin sonatas, twelve piano trios and twenty-seven piano concertos – "propelled the pianist to the front rank of instrumentalists." By 1800 only the violinist was on equal footing with the pianist.

♪ Franz Josef Haydn (1732-1809)

Haydn, the "sanest and most spontaneous of all the great masters," began working for the wealthy Hungarian Esterhazy family in 1761 and would spend summers in isolation at one of their grand estates. During his first twenty years at Eszterháza, Haydn had limited live exposure to outside performances and "he was thrown upon his own resources (to) develop his own style in solitude, to experiment, to invent."

Most composers in Haydn's time were under the employ and control of church or courts. Haydn's contract with Prince Esterhazy contained such wording as "shall be under permanent obligation…," "…for the exclusive use of his Highness…" and language forbidding him from composing for others without "the knowledge and gracious permission of his Highness."

Haydn summed up the result of being cut off culturally from the rest of the world during these summers with, "I was cut off from the world…and so I had no choice but to become original." Things were not that bad as Haydn compensated for his "lonely" summers by spending winters in music-rich Vienna. Haydn's first solo keyboard works were composed in the mid-1760s and were written for harpsichord. Starting around 1771 with No.20, he wrote his piano sonatas for the *fortepiano*.

Haydn might have complained about his situation at Eszterháza ("It is a sad thing always to be a slave," "…poor wretch that I am") but he was generally one of the more content and well-adjusted of the great composers.

Although Haydn is labeled the "father of the symphony" and the "founder of the string quartet" neither label is accurate. There were many composers who were responsible for what would become the Classical symphony and string quartet. What Haydn added, in addition to his many simple country folk melodies, "was the synthesis of all this into a style of convincing logic and permanent validity…" What set Haydn apart from other long-forgotten court composers was his creativeness, his "strength and serious purpose (but with) wit and humor…the freshness and sincerity of his melodic style." Haydn was able to attain an unprecedented freedom of imagination by striking the "ideal balance of homophony and a specific modern instrumental polyphony (that was) thematic and melodic rather than rhythmic and motivic." He "seldom repeated himself…he was never at a loss for worthwhile, characteristic musical ideas."

As usual, Haydn wrote many more piano sonatas than Mozart but in this genre Haydn's were superior, as Mozart was composing his mostly as instructional pieces (excepting those in minor keys). Haydn's on the other hand are probing works, forward-looking to the great works of Beethoven and Schubert. Haydn's genius was balancing accessibility so that his music would be enjoyed by many, with the need to also please and challenge himself and more sophisticated listeners.

Haydn accompanied a "new world of art (music of the Classical period) from its inception to its supreme flowering." With this, Austrian peasant music became "a most personal expression…of love of life…moving about in a kaleidoscope of wit, humor, joy, and sorrow." Over a forty-year period Haydn wrote sixty piano sonatas. Of the sixty sonatas fifty-four survive. Of the sonatas at least two dozen are masterpieces. Haydn made it clear that he preferred the piano(forte) to the harpsichord. While his early keyboard sonatas were written for either instrument, the presence of dynamic markings on his sonatas from the mid-1780s onward make clear he was now composing specifically for the *fortepiano*, although he still indicated on sonatas from this period that they could be performed on harpsichord as well. Even today there remains a strong argument in favor of playing Haydn's piano sonatas on the harpsichord, clavichord or small *fortepiano* rather than on a modern grand piano.

Recommended – Haydn Piano Sonatas
Alfred Brendel is a great interpreter of Haydn's sonatas and has recorded the complete cycle twice. Other attractive offerings include two sets by Ax, a set by Andsnes, and the excellent sets by Schiff and Hamelin. The set by Schiff is "a miracle of wit, lyricism and beautiful playing."

Alternatively, Jenó Jandó's cycle for Naxos offers solid performance at a lower price, and allows one to slowly sample five sonatas at-a-time without a large investment. One should obtain sets from multiple artists to enjoy diverse interpretations. Because so many of Haydn's sonatas are represented among the above recordings, one can minimize duplication of sonatas.

A note on the cataloguing of Haydn's works –
The Dutch musicologist Anthony van Hoboken was responsible for the system used to catalogue Haydn's works. He accomplished this roughly fifty years ago. Hoboken assigned a roman numeral to each genre (e.g., III for string quartets; XVI for piano sonatas), then numbered the works chronologically so that *Hob. XVI:33* represents Haydn's thirty-third piano sonata and *Hob.III:77* is his seventy-seventh string quartet. Hoboken's designation sometimes appears in the abbreviated form, *H 3/77*, which indicates Haydn's seventy-seventh string quartet.

♪ Ludwig van Beethoven (1770-1827)

Beethoven's music remains the supreme form of his art because he believed in the limitless ability of man. He not only set no limits on himself (he clearly felt he had none) but pushed his fellow man (musicians, soloists, singers) beyond what was believed to be their capacity, believing men can always be better. He believed that creating music by the arbitrary limitations of musicians or by the limited expectations of audiences was the world of hack composers. How could music progress with that approach? Beethoven admitted some of his works, especially his works for solo piano, were (deliberately) extremely difficult (to draw attention to his virtuosity) and that most contemporary musicians (but, of course, not Beethoven himself) would struggle with them, some mightily. But he never thought his fellow musicians to be incapable of playing his challenging pieces. It makes no sense for a composer to write truly unplayable music because publishers will not publish it; however, it makes perfect sense that Beethoven required contemporary musicians to raise their performance skills to his lofty level. In fact, we are grateful for his approach because it is very likely that without the seemingly beyond-human demands Beethoven placed on his works, his compositions would not be the immortal masterpieces we know.

The Ninth Symphony was considered impossible to perform – the soloist parts alone stretch the boundaries of the capabilities of the human voice. But Beethoven was confident it could be performed, knew his fellow man had the ability to pull it off. Not only was the *Ninth* not beyond the capabilities of the available orchestra (a mix of professionals and amateur musicians), chorus and soloists, but the premiere was a smashing success! Beethoven did not produce his succession of masterpieces, each one greater than the preceding, by worrying about the perceived limitations of an orchestra and its players. He didn't formulate his works to meet musicians on their terms; he compelled musicians to meet him on his. And respond they did; repeatedly, and of a surprise to all but Beethoven himself, all involved rose to the occasion.

> *"Life can't be all bad when for $10 you can buy all the Beethoven Piano Sonatas and listen to them for forty years."*
> - William F. Buckley

Beethoven, unlike even Mozart, was the first musician to look "upon himself as an artist, and he stood up for his rights as an artist." All composers before Beethoven provided a commodity for the here and now; they did not think about writing for posterity or of their reputation among future generations. What also set Beethoven apart was his originality; "he was a creator, one of those natural talents, full of ideas and originality." Beethoven's "is the most powerful body of music ever brought together by one composer."

> "Each time Beethoven wrote a piano sonata he managed to rethink the form."
> - pianist Martin Roscoe

As with Mozart, Beethoven first came to fame as a pianist. However, the reasons for their fame as pianists were very different. While Mozart was smooth and fluent, Beethoven beat on the instrument mercilessly and became the "first of the modern piano virtuosos." As the capability of the piano expanded in the 19th century, he continuously pushed its limits. Richard Crocker points out that Beethoven's ear was "always turned toward the symphonic ideal rather than toward the capabilities of the (piano) itself." In Beethoven's hands "the piano went from gently tinkling 'harpsichord plus' to mighty powerhouse of the modern instrument." His imagination was sparked by the transformation of piano technology in the early 1800s. He "consciously made (his piano sonatas) so brilliant and so difficult that they are no longer accessible to the ordinary player…who felt that he had easily mastered Haydn and Mozart." Viennese society had been conditioned to be wooed by suave and elegant music-making, but "Beethoven planted bombs under their seats."

> "Never have I met an artist of such spiritual concentration and intensity."
> - Goethe on Beethoven

The 'giant' in this genre, as he is in several others, Beethoven composed thirty-two piano sonatas, giving us a treasure trove of keyboard masterpieces covering the gamut in emotion. His piano sonatas were deeply influenced over his career by those of Muzio Clementi (1752-1832) who composed sixty-four sonatas over almost fifty years, including all of Beethoven's creative years. As with his great string quartets, Beethoven's piano sonatas span his creative career, which is normally divided into three periods.

♪ Beethoven's Style Periods

There are not clean breaks between Beethoven's three periods when his entire output is considered. Charles Rosen considers this division "a fiction for the purposes of analysis;" only if one chooses certain sets of works (e.g., his string quartets) does the division into three periods seem natural. His 'early' period represents works up to 1802, including the Bonn years (1770-1792); the 'middle' being the years 1803-1813; the 'late' period being from 1813 until his death in 1827.

In his early period Beethoven struggled with the limitations of strict Classical period forms, which "limited themselves to…a purification of the feelings…(they) rarely plumbed either the heroic or the tragic levels of experience." Early in his career Beethoven had two somewhat opposed goals: the first was to prove himself as a composer of original music, the other was to demonstrate his mastery of traditional Viennese forms. We see a young composer who delights in his own strength. Some of his early works fall under the *Sturm und Drang* ('storm and stress') classification, including the Piano Trio Op.1, No.3; Piano Sonatas Op.2, No.1, Op.10, No.1, and Op.13 (Pathetique); and the fourth of the Op.18 String Quartets. With Beethoven's *Eroica* symphony, which marked "Beethoven's turn to compositions of unprecedented ambition," and other works of the mid- to late-1790s, music had begun "responding to the stormy currents of contemporary history."

As is the case with several other major genres, Beethoven used the model developed for the piano sonata by Mozart and Haydn, and while he knew and prized the models that these works represented, he had no intention of being limited by them but going far beyond them. As such, "they served him only as points of departure for a markedly more acute approach".

The forms of late Beethoven descend directly from Haydn's technique of growing music dynamically from a small kernel. In this technique, "the simplest, most condensed of musical thoughts (are) announced…at the very opening." Beethoven extended Haydn's technique to almost unimaginable limits, and with the *Hammerklavier*, "extended Haydn's technique to large-scale harmonic structure." He "extended classical harmonic language without violating its spirit." The fugues and variations employed by Haydn and Mozart still retained some Baroque nature. Beethoven, late in his life, had even managed to convert these into fully classical forms, with shapes and proportions analogous to the sonata. "The extent to which Beethoven manipulated conventions should not obscure how much he relied on them…to the end of his life he continued to employ and even revive many musical procedures" learned as a child in the 1770s.

Beethoven's middle period (1803-13) was the most exceptionally fertile and productive, giving us Symphony Nos.3-8; Piano Concertos No.4 and No.5; the Violin Concerto; the *Waldstein*, *Appassionata*, and *Les Adieux* piano sonatas; the Ninth and Tenth Violin Sonatas; the Op.59 *Razumovsky* String Quartets; and the *Archduke* and *Ghost* Piano Trios. "Probably only Mozart and Schubert…produced in a single decade (their final) as much music that is still performed frequently all over the world." Beethoven's middle period works led to the image of him as a tempestuous genius who shook his fist at fate and bridged the rationalistic 'Age of Enlightenment' to the stormy individualism of the Romantic era.

Beethoven did not sustain the outburst of creative energy seen in the middle-period decade of 1803-13. The fallow period that preceded his highly creative 'late period' were the years 1813-20 during which Beethoven wallowed in misery due to his total deafness. He was also occupied in a battle with his brother's widow for adoption of his nephew Karl, a fight he ultimately won. Once Beethoven came to grips with his deafness and associated depression he was able to develop in his music "the profundity and largeness of vision that are so uniquely his contributions to music."

In his late works, "struggle is sublimated into ecstasy...chaos strives for lucid formation...victorious conclusions are incessantly sought after and discovered;" Beethoven found in these forms "a new vehicle for his most imaginative musical thoughts." However, as Maynard Solomon observes, it is not easy to break down Beethoven's "late style into its sources...because many of its characteristics...its structures and "sound," are unprecedented in the history of music."

Late Period Beethoven was a "deeply unconventional composer" whose works were not well understood or accepted by his contemporaries. This is not surprising given his "deliberate flouting of the contemporary musical language." As opposed to the symmetrical and balanced melodies of most of the Classical period, in Beethoven's late works themes "were increasingly instilled with a new turbulence (using) contrasting motifs" and subjects that are "twisted and turned, fragmented and tossed about with infinite inventiveness." According to Paul Henry Lang there are numerous threads that lead from Beethoven to the Romantics, but he made "a new synthesis of Classicism and then (handed) it down to the new century."

♫ The Early and Middle Piano Sonatas

Beethoven's "earlier piano sonatas were intensely personal vehicles that united the imaginative flights of his keyboard improvisation with a mounting distinctiveness of expression and structural cogency."

Sonata No.8 in C minor, Op.13, *Pathétique*; No.14 in C-sharp minor, Op.27/2, *Moonlight*

The famous nicknamed sonatas are among the most well-known and best-loved piano works in the repertory. Beethoven gave us a treasure of beautiful melodies as he perfected the piano sonata. None of these melodies is more famous than the first movement of the *Moonlight* Sonata. The second movement of the *Moonlight* was described by Liszt as "a flower between two abysses."

Beethoven had nothing to do with the famous nickname, *Moonlight*, given to his Piano Sonata No.14 (1801); the work acquired that subtitle after his death. Beethoven's subtitle was *quasi una fantasia*, or 'fantasy-like'. Nevertheless, the *Moonlight* Sonata broke the mold of the three-movement Classical piano sonata – Beethoven unleashed a musical revolution, which starts with a brisk upbeat opening movement. The first movement does not sound like what we expect of a sonata. Instead, Beethoven opens with "this eerie, obsessive/compulsive, minor-toned introduction."

The *Pathétique* Sonata (1798-99) opens with a densely-packed low C-minor chord. "It does indeed capture all the pain and pathos that the subtitle implies." The sublime beauty and luminous melody of the famous second movement stands in stark contrast to the vehement outbreak of the first movement. The finale is optimistic but, in keeping with the subtitle, the pianist must avoid conveying cheerfulness. As with other C minor works of Beethoven, the passion and trouble that pervade this work are also positively resolved at the conclusion.

Sonata No.21 in C, Op.53 *Waldstein*; No.23 in F minor, Op.57 *Appassionata*

The model for Beethoven's middle period sonatas was drama, comedy, and tragedy. The years 1804-06 "represent a growth in artistic conscience for Beethoven," the height of his middle period powers manifested in the Op.59 string quartets, the Fourth Piano Concerto, and the *Waldstein* and *Appassionata* Sonatas. These sonatas, from 1804 and 1805, respectively, are the "twin peaks in the middle-period range of Beethoven's piano sonatas." They are both symphonic in character and dimension and stand in contrast as the *Waldstein* "exults in the major key" while the *Appassionata* "pursues its minor-key drama to the bitter end." The *Appassionata* along with the *Pathetique* and the *Moonlight* are works of melancholy with relief from the darkness provided only by the middle movements.

Beethoven's student Carl Czerny gives us his view of applying programmatic elements to his mentor's works, whether or not Beethoven intended such. On the finale of the *Appassionata* Sonata, Czerny states, "If Beethoven, who was so fond of portraying scenes from nature, was perhaps thinking of ocean waves on a stormy night when from the distance a cry for help is heard, then such a picture will give the pianist a guide to the correct playing of this great tonal painting." The designation of the *Appassionata* as a "great tonal painting" was surely all Czerny's idea while the nickname was attached by a publisher some fifty years later.

With the *Waldstein* and *Appassionata* Sonatas Beethoven begins paving the way for the Romantic period virtuoso by stretching the "potentialities of both instrument and performers to their outer limits." With Op.57 Beethoven "finally arrived at a conception of a sonata where all three movements have been formulated as one." In both works the "slow movements are organically connected with the finales." The *Appassionata* "begins in ominous mystery" and is thoroughly tragic to the extreme. The slow movement is like a calm between two storms. It was this stormy character and explosive dynamics that appealed to the Romantics. As Donald Tovey points out, "the tragic passion is rushing deathwards, " and the sonata ends "in a nihilistic frenzy."

The *Waldstein* possesses a sense of heroism and struggle that would be central to Beethoven's later sonatas. "The first movement of the *Waldstein* Sonata has a characteristic sound...unlike any other work of Beethoven."

Sonata No.26 in E-flat, Op.81a *Les Adieux*; No.27 in E minor, Op.90; No.28 in A, Op.101

Piano Sonatas Nos.24-27 mark a new direction taken by Beethoven in tone "often marked by a reflective lyricism, and a prevalent cantabile quality..." But it stops short of the clear Romanticism that begins with No.28. Nos.24-26 were composed in 1809-10 and No.27 in 1814. It is these 'transitional' (Classical to Romantic) piano sonatas that Schumann and Mendelssohn take as their starting point for their early works as teenagers.

Piano Sonata No.26, nicknamed *Les Adieux*, "bursts with youthful, clumsy ardor, intermingled with passages of desolate longing," for his patron and pupil Archduke Rudolph who had to flee Vienna because it was under heavy bombardment from Napoleon's troops. The key of E-flat is the same as the contemporary Fifth Piano Concerto.

Sonata No.27 is a two-movement sonata whose second movement possibly contains Beethoven's most beautiful melody. There is a "childlike purity of this melody, which seems to be sung by a country girl..." This second movement is the most cantabile ('song-like') of all Beethoven's sonata movements and possesses "an unreserved lyricism...the Rondo which lingers on the melodic beauty of the tender refrain...probes deep inside the world of Romantic feeling and thinking."

For some reason, most likely in addition to the more typical German character of Nos.27 and No.28, Beethoven decided to give the tempo descriptions of these two sonatas not in the customary Italian but in German (e.g., *Langsam* in place of *Adagio*).

Piano Sonata No.28 has a freedom of form and fantasy-like expressiveness such as the two earlier sonatas to which Beethoven attached the subtitle *quasi una fantasia* (Op.27, Nos.1&2). It is with No.28 that "the gates leading to the world of Romanticism are opened wide."

> *Recommended, Beethoven Middle Period Piano Sonatas –*
> Emil Gilels' set of the *Waldstein, Appassionata*, and *Les Adieux* sonatas (DG); Arthur Rubinstein's set of the *Moonlight, Pathétique, et al.* (RCA), and any set by Claudio Arrau.

"What is in my heart must come out and so I write it down."
- Beethoven

Many of Beethoven's great piano sonatas are cast in a minor key. "The basic chromaticism of the minor mode makes for a larger variety of procedures than the more diatonic major." Beethoven's struggle between "adherence to and a rebellious need to dissolve – or at least reshape – Classical style," definitely appeared to some extent in all middle period works but becomes clearest after 1815.

♪ The Late Piano Works

The Late Piano Sonatas

"Now I am writing a sonata which shall be my greatest."
- Beethoven on the *Hammerklavier* Sonata

With his late sonatas, composed 1816-22, Beethoven indicated that he was taking a new musical direction, and stated "it is somewhat better" than his approach to previous sonatas. In his late period Beethoven's works take on a 'neo-Baroque' characteristic with a "highly concentrated exploration of counterpoint and polyphonic textures." The years 1816-17 saw the completion of Op.101 and Op.106 and the last three, Opp.109-111, come from 1821-22. "Variation form joins fugue as one of the leading features." He also dispenses with the typical minuet or scherzo movement, excepting Op.106. Beethoven injects much variety into his slow movements, including the second movement of the two-movement Op.111 with four variations and an elaborate coda. The first movement of Op.111 "produced a synthesis of fugue and first-movement sonata form."

Sonata No.29 in B-flat, Op.106, *Hammerklavier*

The late piano sonatas, together with the *Diabelli* Variations, Op.120 and the Bagatelles, Op.126, "form one of the pillars of Beethoven's creative achievement in his last years." The final sonatas form a spiritual whole, with the *Hammerklavier* standing out as the giant among sonatas to this point. In terms of content and power, nothing for solo piano had approached it; it is a symphony for piano that took two years (1817-18) to compose. "The *Hammerklavier* is not typical of Beethoven…not even…of his last period." It was much longer than any piano sonata by anyone up to that time. With it, Beethoven attempted to produce "a new and original work of uncompromising greatness."

As does the contemporaneous Ninth Symphony, the *Hammerklavier* sonata restores the four-movement classic form but with "a magnification of scale and an intensification of contrast." Its technical and interpretive demands present a titanic challenge to performers and the "full-blooded, quasi-orchestral piano writing makes the utmost demands on even the finest modern instruments." It contains "passages of such contrapuntal density as to approach solid state…the most terrifying noises to come out of the piano until the late years of Liszt." The *Hammerklavier* is "a demonstration of power…monstrously long and scandalously difficult," it marked the "emancipation of piano music from the demands of the amateur musician…" In the finale Beethoven employs a fugue, taking as inspiration the deeply expressive B minor fugue that ends Book II of *The Well-Tempered Clavier*.

"The *Hammerklavier* is less the 'Mount Everest' of sonatas, more the Mount Etna, the concluding fugue an act of Titanic rage." The fugal finale of this sonata, uniquely labeled 'fugue in three voices with a few licenses' is a dramatic set of variations. It is one of the most pronounced examples of the new direction Beethoven took in his use of fugues and variations. Beethoven found in these forms "a new vehicle for his most imaginative musical thoughts." Although the stranglehold of sonata form on composition in the classical Viennese style had decreased by Beethoven's last years, he was still able to breathe new life into 'old' forms in a unique and inimitable way. This genius was most manifest in the *Hammerklavier*, "giving new vitality to old contrapuntal forms" with a gigantic fugue. In this grand sonata Beethoven initiated an extraordinary expansion of the style from his earliest years.

As with his other large-scale instrumental works, Beethoven achieves "the integration of unity and variety, large structure and small detail." This may be the first piano sonata written once Beethoven became completely deaf, although as early as mid-1801 Beethoven began referencing his loss of hearing in his correspondence. The huge third movement *Adagio* "is unequalled in the entire piano literature" and "anticipates all the elements of…Schumann, Chopin, Brahms." It leads into the finale, a "massive fugue created in wrath…" and which pianists continue to grapple with.

The *Hammerklavier* is an "arena for confrontation, for testing oneself to the utmost in open, unrelenting conflict." Beethoven is claimed to have said that this is a sonata that will make the pianist work; "I have written a sonata that will keep pianists busy for the next fifty years." The *Hammerklavier* Sonata made such an impression on his contemporaries that when some of them heard it for the first time they thought he was mad as well as deaf.

After the scale of the *Hammerklavier* sonata, which Charles Rosen claims is extreme even for his late period, in his last three sonatas Beethoven returned to the smaller dimensions of the Op.90 and Op.101 sonatas. He infused his final works in this genre "with a variety of rigorous polyphonic textures and an etherealized improvisatory tone." The final three sonatas (Nos.30-32, Opp.109-111) are all masterpieces culminating with the two-movement Op.111 in Beethoven's trademark key of C minor. They were all begun in 1820 and published between November 1821 and April 1823, a very creative period that also saw Beethoven begin his Ninth Symphony, the *Diabelli* Variations and the *Missa Solemnis*. Kurt Sanderling commented on Beethoven's final sonata, "Yes, Op.111 is about a glorious death, isn't it?"

Op.110 was completed on Christmas 1821. Beethoven had been ill most of the year and this sonata was the only substantial work he managed that year. This sonata has a sound unlike the other late sonatas, with "the recurrence of alternating and contrasting patterns (that) guarantees a richness of motivic forms." It is semi-programmatic; in it Beethoven uses techniques to imply sobs and grief.

In his final sonata, Op.11 from 1822, the "somber and dramatic" first movement is followed in the second movement by a set of otherworldly variations. "The vision is particularly elusive and its ultimate realization particularly sublime." It is in the key of C minor, a significant key for Beethoven shared with the Fifth Symphony. Beethoven's final piano sonata genre has led musicians and musicologist to give it all sorts of life-afterlife meaning. Besides being an "arena in which a life and struggle is to take place," the transition "from the gloom of C minor into the brightness of C major" signifies for pianist Wilhelm Kempff, "the final step from this world to the next."

> *Recommended, Beethoven Late Piano Sonatas –*
> Outstanding versions of the *Hammerklavier* sonata are available from Gilels and Pollini (both on DG). Pollini has a grasp of the elemental drama and thunderous spirit. Another excellent set of the final six sonatas is by Wilhelm Kempff. However, the weak link is the *Hammerklavier*, but it does include No.27.

To gather together these great works one would most likely not purchase a complete set of all thirty-two at once, so it is better to start by purchasing the more famous 'named' sonatas. The problem with complete sets is they are expensive. Additionally, you end up with all of the sonatas being interpreted by the same pianist. While this may eventually be something you seek, it is probably not for most listeners. Different pianists are better at interpreting different sonatas and, because Beethoven's sonatas cover such a broad range, one is better to sample from several or many artists.

The first set to acquire would contain the Moonlight sonata and probably the *Pathétique* sonata, along with one or two others. These two sonatas contain Beethoven's two most famous melodies from his piano sonatas, so they are instantly recognizable and accessible, even if not considered among his greatest for solo piano.

Bagatelles and Variations

Beethoven's last three piano sonatas (Opp.109-111) were completed by 1822 and it is as if he knew the "public taste was for shorter, less-demanding fare." After Beethoven, only Franz Schubert approached him in terms of piano sonata output, as future composers such as Schumann, Chopin, Brahms, and Liszt focused on less-structured forms for solo piano music, so-called piano 'miniatures'. Beethoven's late move to piano miniatures and variations after completion of his piano sonata canon was an example eagerly followed by the Romantics. Their short, often programmatic (excepting Chopin), pieces were foreshadowed by Beethoven's short piano pieces, which he called Bagatelles, Opp.33, 119, and 126. He also referred to these pieces by the German word *Kleinigkeifen* – 'trivia'.

The fragmentary quality of some of Beethoven's Bagatelles is a comic effect, excepting the Op.126 set, which is a true cycle. The famous piano piece *Für Elise* is actually a Beethoven bagatelle, WoO 59. The sets of bagatelles from the early 1820s are sometimes believed to be sketches for larger works that Beethoven never undertook. The pieces that comprise the bagatelles (the word literally means 'trifle') are "nothing more than ideas – motifs, combinations of sounds, lyrical moments."

Beethoven was the first composer to really plumb the depths of Classical variation form for solo piano; only Haydn's *Double* Variations in F minor comes close. Beethoven wrote around twenty sets of variations for the piano, including two early sets in 1802, the *Variations on an Original Theme*, Op.34 and the *Variations and Fugue*, Op.35 (*Eroica* Variations). He wrote more than a dozen sets of variations from 1793-1801 for either solo piano or piano with violin or cello. These early sets are "often deliberately superficial...sets of ornamental variations." As was often the case with Beethoven, he used his early period to master the particular forms that he would later take to new heights. The focus of his early stage (before 1802) was on "developing the implications of the various sonata forms in three- and four-movement cycles." There is also the set published posthumously as WoO 80, *Variations on an Original Theme*. For Beethoven, variation form was a school of energetic concentration.

Doubtless the piano sonata would never be the same but Beethoven did not crown his solo piano writing with a sonata but rather with a set of variations on a rather trivial waltz theme, the *Diabelli* Variations, composed a year after his final piano sonata. This fifty-plus minute masterpiece of thirty-three variations on Diabelli's waltz theme is the "real crown of his contribution" to solo piano, a "compendium of interwoven and juxtaposed voices, registers, and rhythms." It is "at once a stupendous practical joke and an intellectual tour de force," while "one of the most challenging works ever written, rivaling Bach's *Goldberg* Variations in depth of expression and mastery of form." The *Diabelli* Variations represent the peak of Beethoven's attachment to the harmonic variation style and away from the melodic variation style in which few risks are taken and which was perceived as superficial and ornamental. However, Charles Rosen sees them as "above all a discovery of the nature of the simplest musical elements."

Beethoven found Diabelli's waltz theme to have a fascinating harmonic structure. In addition to the almost one hour's worth of variations Beethoven supplied, Schubert and a young Liszt also provided variations of their own. As it was, the music publisher Antonio Diabelli had only requested one variation from fifty composers on a theme written by himself. Of course Beethoven's massive opus of thirty-three variations left all others forgotten; Diabelli published it separate from the others and called it "a great and important masterpiece.

> **Recommended - Beethoven Bagatelles and Variations**
> For the *Diabelli Variations*, Op.120 the recordings by Alfred Brendel (digital) and Stephen Kovacevich (analog from 1970s), both on Philips, are the top choices, as are Brendel's various sets of *Bagatelles*.

♪ Franz Schubert (1797-1828)

Schubert was the first major composer who was neither a conductor nor public solo performer, so he relied completely on others to promote and perform his music. This played a major role in so much of his music being neither performed nor published in his lifetime. Schubert's sonatas, symphonies, and chamber works were not widely disseminated before the 1840s. Before his death none of his symphonies, only one of fifteen string quartets, and an amazing three of twenty-one piano sonatas were actually published! Out of at least 600 *Lieder*, a form he practically invented, Schubert only saw 187 in print. While evidence suggests prospects were definitely looking up for him after 1825, nothing much materialized before his death in November of 1828.

Another factor was certainly his bohemian lifestyle; he led a middle-class life in a quiet, unpretentious circle of friends and fellow musicians. He and virtually all of his friends occupied the music-loving, art-loving, intellectual world. He just did not seem driven to see his music brought before the public, so had he lived longer it cannot be stated with any certainty that his increased prospects for publication would have materialized much. However, he was clear as to his purpose in life, "I have come into the world for no purpose but to compose."

The grand four-movement piano sonata began its decline in the 1820s. This decline contributes to the difficulty Schubert had in getting his large sonatas published while having an easier time with his songs or shorter piano works that could be performed as stand-alone one-movement pieces (e.g., the two sets of *Impromptus*, D.899 and D.935). Further evidence of the demise of the Classical sonata is the fact that Beethoven wrote his last sonatas five years before his death. During his last years he wrote sets of shorter movements and pieces, such as the *Six Bagatelles*, Op.126 and the *Diabelli Variations*, Op.120. It was after Beethoven had completed his final piano sonata in 1823 that Schubert started on his eight great sonatas.

> *"I finish one piece and start the next."*
> - Franz Schubert

Schubert is definitely an underrated composer, considering the volume of his output in his relatively short life. During a composing career lasting only seventeen years (1810-1827) Schubert amassed an incredible output of one thousand works. He also did not enjoy any financial success or social recognition of a Haydn or a Mozart as it was not until well after his death that his compositions were properly appreciated by the public. His orchestral works were largely unknown during his lifetime, being discovered later in the 19th century and he performed his chamber works with players within his social circle in Vienna. During his life and into the 1840s Schubert was known almost exclusively as a composer of 'art songs' or *Lieder*. Schumann, in his other role as leading music critic, "rested his case for Schubert's preeminence on (Schubert's) piano sonatas." As a result of his laid-back approach, self-employment and reliance on friends often for food and shelter, it took the world forty years after his death to wake up "to the fact that Schubert was one of the colossal creative figures of music…"

His music was highly original and his style broke significantly away from his immediate predecessors, Haydn, Mozart and Beethoven. Schubert is "in part the most significant originator of the new Romantic style and in part the greatest example of the post-classical composer." He "moves with great ease within the form which Beethoven created (but) considerably loosened what held it together." "Schubert is extremely direct…(he) may be the most accessible because after two bars you are completely in the landscape; it's very immediate." Schubert defies classification as Romantic, post-classical or Classical.

Of course, the influence on Schubert of these three great masters was still significant; no composer of Schubert's time could possibly escape it, especially in Vienna. But it "is amazing how consistently Schubert managed to avoid the influence of his titanic contemporary (Beethoven)." He actually had the most in common with Mozart. Besides living only into their thirties, during which they wrote an enormous amount of music, they both wrote music with alarming speed. Like Mozart, Schubert seemed to have the gift of putting complete works together in his head first, then quickly putting them to paper with few iterations or revisions.

His output is somewhat eclectic as it is distributed much differently among the various genres and forms than the works of other great composers. For example, he is recognized as the greatest *Lied* (song) composer, but wrote no concertos. His piano sonata output is perhaps second to only Beethoven's, plus he composed a large amount of music for two pianists. However, he never composed a piano concerto. Amazingly, Schubert composed his great set of piano sonatas without being a concert pianist and usually without easy access to a piano.

His works for solo piano are among the most impressive in the repertoire. Beethoven's true successor as a writer of piano sonatas is Schubert, and his way of writing for the piano is unlike any other. His "basic ideas are either extended melodies or melodic snatches...(but) rarely germinal motives." His sonatas possess "a marvelous flow of melody" plus his characteristic "handling of tonality, full of the most moving changes of key." "In most cases his works are held together by the unifying force of sustained lyricism." His late sonatas "stand on the same exalted plane as the great piano sonatas of Beethoven."

> There are several highly-regarded interpreters of Schubert's solo piano music, and they have recorded most, if not all, of his output in the form. Mitsuko Uchida, Alfred Brendel and Sviatoslav Richter are all known for their superb recordings of Schubert.

Fantasy in C, 'Wanderer'
This is often coupled with Schumann's Fantasy in the same key and is perhaps Schubert's most virtuosic piano work. It is actually a grand four-movement piano sonata, perhaps with a freer structure leading to its *Fantasy* designation. "Each movement is based somewhat ostentatiously on the same melody, like a gigantic set of variations."

Drei Klavierstücke (3 piano pieces)
These were published with Brahms' help in 1869, well after Schubert's death. It is not known whether Schubert intended for the three to be a set, he left no guidance, so Brahms bundled them together and gave them the very generic name for publication. These pieces were the last works for solo piano composed before the final three sonatas.

Six *Moments Musicaux*, D.780
These six pieces can be considered as a song cycle without words as it was composed between two of Schubert's great song cycles, *Die schoene Muellerin*, D.795 in 1823 and *Winterreise*, D.911 in 1827. The six pieces were not conceived as a unit. Four of the pieces were composed in 1827-28 with the third and sixth from 1823 and 1824, respectively. Some were first published individually. The title of 'musical moments' to these pieces is a misnomer as several are more than five or six minutes. The second piece in F minor is the most popular.

Impromptus, D.899 and D.935
The labeling of these two sets of four extended piano pieces was given not by the composer but the publisher. It was likely that, as with his Fantasy in C, if they had been published ten years sooner they would have been 'sonatas'; but given the trend towards freer sets of movements, exemplified by Beethoven's move to bagatelles and variations in his final years, the publisher preferred a loose connection among the four pieces in each set. However, just as with

D.780 these pieces are clearly misnamed as Impromptus because they are longer works without an extemporaneous or improvisatory nature. Instead, they are tightly knit, structurally cohesive works, often of great lyric intensity.

Robert Schumann felt that Schubert's D.935, because of the key sequence of the four pieces, had a greater degree of unity. The first and fourth piece also have unmistakable motivic associations, leading Schumann to propose that Schubert really intended the four pieces of D.935 to comprise a sonata. As with his *Wanderer* Fantasy, D.935 is, in reality, a sonata in all but name.

> *Recommended – Schubert solo piano pieces:*
> *Wanderer Fantasy* – Richter, coupled with Dvořák's piano concerto (EMI).
> *Impromptus* – one cannot go wrong with either of Brendel's sets, or with the recordings by Lupu and Perahia. *Moments Musicaux* – these six pieces are usually coupled with a sonata. Any of the above performers are recommended for this collection of pieces.

The Piano Sonatas

Schubert's set of piano sonatas is only second to Beethoven's and they are the best examples of the unforced melodic flow of Schubert's music. Despite this, as with the piano sonatas by Haydn, Schubert's set certainly seem underrated and under-appreciated, although his songs, symphonies and chamber music have all taken their proper places in music. Apparently the long shadow of Beethoven did not help, but only three of Schubert's sonatas were published while the two composers were alive anyway. The problem with publication of large-scale sonatas during Schubert's lifetime was that publishers wanted "less difficult but brilliant pieces in a lighter style." But Schubert dismissed this pressure for him to produce 'salon music', referring to this light fare as "wretched fashionable stuff."

Most of Schubert's sonatas were published posthumously. In fact, only three of the twenty-one were published during his lifetime, although many more were probably performed. The first to be published (in 1826) was D.845 in A minor (known now as No.16). The appearance of this sonata revealed Schubert to the public beyond a composer of *Lieder* (his songs had been his only compositions publishers were interested in, for the most part) and set him on the path as the natural successor to Beethoven in the piano sonata genre.

The tag line of *Reliquie* to D.840 in C was added by the publisher in 1861. This work was left incomplete by Schubert; the story goes he was having trouble working out the remaining movements. The two movements of this sonata are analogous to the *Unfinished* Symphony, a complete work in itself. Attempts to complete a minuet and finale for D.840 by scholars may shed light on why Schubert did not think the third and fourth movements added much, or perhaps detracted from the first two movements. The sonata works best if the two original two movements are accepted as a complete work.

D.784 in A minor (No.14) from February 1823 is a "bleak and austere work...an extraordinary feeling of world-weariness...conceived without regard for the limitations of the piano." The three movements of this sonata "show an almost total disregard for the conventions of Classical pianism. Harmonic figuration and melodic ornamentation...are absent."

Piano Sonata No.17 in D, D.850, was written during three weeks in the summer of 1825 (the same year as D.840 and D.845) while Schubert stopped off in the Austrian town of Gastein; hence, the nickname *Gasteiner* for this sonata. According to Misha Donat, D.850 "is the most brilliant and extrovert; Schubert intended the piece to be extremely energetic."

D.894 in G (No.18) is known as the Fantasy or Sonata-fantasy because publisher Tobias Haslinger did not want to publish the work, composed in 1826, as a four-movement sonata and so called it by its individual movements, *Fantasie*, *Andante*, *Menuetto*, *Allegretto*. That D.894 is over forty minutes, this was a contrived marketing ploy by Haslinger to take advantage of the rising popularity of collections of individual character pieces and the fading of symphonic-scale piano sonatas. Schumann considered D.894 'near-perfect' and was particularly fond of the sonata-allegro first movement.

Sonata No.19 in C minor, D.958; No.20 in A, D.959; No.21 in B-flat, D.960

The three final sonatas form a great triptych in which Schubert outdid his previous efforts in this form to create these masterpieces. As with most of his works, these final three sonatas were not published until well after his death, in 1839. With Beethoven's death in March of 1827 Schubert was at last free to challenge him on his own ground. However, the influence of Beethoven is still felt throughout these final sonatas, particularly D.958 in Beethoven's favorite key of C minor (Symphony No.5, *Pathétique* Sonata, Thirty-two Variations). Schubert lived only one and a half years after Beethoven's death, certainly not enough time to see what he truly could have accomplished, and in which direction his music would have gone. Would he have continued Beethoven's grand Classical form (keep in mind Beethoven had largely abandoned this with his final piano sonata in 1822) or fully embrace Romanticism within a decade or two?

Composed amazingly in only three weeks in September 1828, these are among the longest and most-involved piano sonatas, containing complex musical developments along with stirring melodies. With only two months to live, Schubert was struggling financially even more than usual but still managed these glorious sonatas. The large-scale finale of D.958 is a tarantella of almost manic energy, similar to the last movement of the *Death and the Maiden* String Quartet, and probably both inspired by the final *Rondo* of Beethoven's *Kreutzer* Violin Sonata. The main theme from the finale of D.959 was used, in a chamber arrangement, as the theme music for the TV show *Wings*.

D.959 in A has a slow movement that paints a picture of Schubert's "preoccupation with dark self-knowledge" using Romantic melancholy. The last movement of this sonata is based on the rondo finale of Beethoven's Op.31, No.1 in G, and is unquestionably greater than its model.

The long first movement of D.960 has a spiritual and meditative quality to it, an amazing effect from Schubert. The movement is, for the most part, played *pianissimo*, the effect being that the listener feels far away. This final effort of Schubert in this genre is also his most frequently performed and recorded piano sonata.

These last three sonatas along with D.784 were published by Anton Diabelli in 1839. Diabelli dedicated D.784 to Mendelssohn and the final three of Schubert's sonatas to Robert Schumann.

> *Recommended – Schubert Piano Sonatas*
> There are multiple excellent cycles, complete and incomplete, of Schubert's piano sonatas. The recommended versions would be by the leading Schubertians of recent times, Mitsuko Uchida, Alfred Brendel, Wilhelm Kempff, and Murray Perahia. Most offerings provide two sonatas per CD so one can sample many performers in building a collection. For historical recordings, Richter was very effective in Schubert's solo piano repertory. Also available is the rarely-recorded Grigory Sokolov's accounts of D.894 and D.960 (Opus 111, 2003).

Schubert's piano sonatas were long neglected by Romantic-period pianists as "difficult without any obvious virtuosity." But starting with Artur Schnabel in the 1930s, pianists took to the sonatas and they have been staples of the repertory now for decades.

Music for Four Hands or Two Pianos

"By 1800 music for piano was public, and anything interesting in the genuine private sector was confined largely to compositions for four hands." Schubert wrote only music for four hands (duets) but these works can and have been performed as piano duos, with two pianists playing separate pianos. The best-known of these works are the *Fantasie* in F minor, D.940, the *Allegro* in A minor, D.947 and *Grand Duo* Sonata in C, D.812.

> *Recommended –*
> An excellent two-CD live recording in Carnegie Hall by James Levine and Evgeny Kissin is available from RCA (2006), which contains the three works above.

- 6 -

The Modern Piano and The Romantic Period

♪ The Birth of Romanticism

Dictionary definitions of 'Romanticism' go something like this: an artistic movement or tendency, in reaction to Enlightenment ideals, which emphasized inspiration, subjectivity and the primacy of the individual with a strong emphasis on emotion and instinct. Author Harvey Sachs points out that Romanticism had to bring forward some great and heroic individuals. To deny this, would be to deny the Romantic era. By 1800 many composers had adopted a style that viewed art in relation to the artist, moving 'inward' from the traditional styles that viewed art in relation to nature.

Beethoven was one of the first great Romantic figures, "a symbol of greatness, heroism and genius for generations to come." Instead of viewing Beethoven as the bridge between Classicism and Romanticism, E.T.A. Hoffmann saw Beethoven as "a pure Romantic" whose music "sets in motion the lever of fear, of awe, of horror, of suffering, and awakens that infinite longing which is the essence of Romanticism."

According to eminent Beethoven scholar Maynard Solomon, the year 1816 or so was "one of the turning points in music history" as composers "were adjusting to the end of High Classicism," away from the intellectualism of the Enlightenment, to the anti-intellectual style of the nascent Romantic period. Music of the Classical period achieved unity in the identity of form and material. Its nature is a 'middle path'. 'Romanticism' was the reaction to what was perceived as extreme classicism and dissolves the Classical elements as it "overflows from the boiling cauldron of the overheated style of the period and forms its own world." "The Romanticists emphasized the individual components, the formal details, trying to achieve logic and unity by enhancing the importance of the elements of sentiment in the content."

The key word in Professor Lang's statement is 'sentiment' and the role that music would play for the Romantics because of their emphasis on sentiment. Whereas the Classical style insisted on initial clarity, Romantics preferred a "gradual unfolding and illumination of reality." Charles Rosen is careful to point out that music does not communicate or express emotions; it "represents sentiment only ambiguously, vaguely, and uncertainly." Music inspires and stimulates the expression of emotion.

> "No musician of the Romantic era could remain aloof from the necessity of coming to terms with the mighty phenomenon of Beethoven."
> - Alfred Einstein

Although there was a discontinuity of style between Beethoven and the generation that followed him, Berlioz, Mendelssohn, Chopin, Schumann, and Liszt all "looked to Beethoven as they formed their anti-intellectual styles."

The death of Beethoven in 1827 must have given a sense of freedom to these early Romantic composers. Beethoven was seen as a 'Romantic' by Romantics both because "he dared to breach the classical rules about structure and content" and because his social behavior was overtly non-conforming. Beethoven had brought into being the concept of 'absolute music', which the Romantics would construe "as the highest expression of subjective innerness." Additionally, the early Romantics would downgrade opera as an imperfect and impure hybrid form with inherent limitations due to spoken language. This would last until Wagner, and his *Gesamtkunstwerk* ('total art work'), in which he proposed the total fusion of 'symphonism' and opera.

The generation of composers that succeeded Beethoven often concentrated their energies on a particular alternative form to the symphony. Characteristic of many of these composers, "their first thoughts tended to be their best ones…the initial version tended to be the most forceful expression of their own individuality." Thus, there is an ongoing debate between Schumann's original versions of his piano miniatures (as well as his Fourth Symphony) and the changes he made later when he was a more mature composer. Many of the early Romantics produced brilliantly for a few years then lost inspiration or died young. Brahms would later break this pattern.

> *"The invention of the pianoforte was to music what the invention of the printing press was to poetry."*
> *- George Bernard Shaw*

Charles Rosen sums up the effect of Beethoven on the first generation of Romantic composers, "All that is most interesting in the next generation is a reaction against Beethoven…all that is weakest submits to his power." Beethoven was a "watershed between the century of musical craftsmanship (the Classical) and the beginnings of Romanticism; between illuminating rationalism and the philosophy of the subjective ego." However, Rosen goes on to conclude that the "Romantic style did not come from Beethoven…but from…Bach" and the influence of Bach on Beethoven was extremely limited. The music of Mendelssohn, Chopin, and Schumann made "continuous reference to Bach." Bach was revered during the 1800s for contrapuntal and harmonic density. The conception of polyphony and counterpoint for early Romantic composers came from their experience of how Bach sounded when played on a 'modern' piano.

Although both Schumann and Chopin miniaturized the piano sonata, unlike Chopin, Schumann had little appreciation or understanding of Mozart. In fact, Schumann felt that his music was closer to Bach than Mozart and while there is a return to the principles of the Baroque, the Romantic style is not a reactionary movement. For example, the piano music of Schumann and Chopin shows a lot of counterpoint, but not strict fugal counterpoint. This is because, for the Romantic composer, "the experience of counterpoint comes first;" the actual working out and structure of the counterpoint takes a back seat. Charles Rosen sums up this widespread technique as the effect of counterpoint without any 'real' counterpoint.

For example, in Mendelssohn's *Capriccio*, Op.1 for solo piano, the development section contains a fugue with almost no counterpoint, "the audible experience of fugue without actually constructing one."

"Perhaps nothing characterizes a style better than the way its composers try to sustain the interest in the return of a previously heard section." In late Baroque and rococo this was handled through ornamentation. In the last quarter of the 18th century Classical composers had adopted sonata recapitulation to recast an opening section harmonically. Neither of these approaches was attractive to or effective for Romantic composers, even beginning with Schubert. A common technique was to return the opening theme with more brilliant dynamics, as was a literal repetition at great length, sometimes in another key.

The above quote by Romantic poet Shelley was his reflection on the imminent birth of Romanticism; the same could be said for the opening of Beethoven's Ninth Symphony, a metaphor for the birth of this movement that dominated 19th century music.

During the high Classical period some composers began to take issue with what they saw as formal principles becoming rigid forms. Early Romantic composers went further by swinging the pendulum far in the other direction, looking back yearningly towards the Renaissance, focusing instead on lyricism, free melody, youthful enthusiasm and a general air of liberty. From the very beginning of the Romantic era, composers had a relaxed attitude towards symphonic and sonata forms. But Charles Rosen does not agree that the pendulum swung so far so quickly. He feels the Romantics balanced "the delight in structure" that had dominated the Classical Style, with "the delight in sound…they permanently enlarged the role of sound in the composition of music."

> *"The entire effect of music consists in accompanying and making perceptible the inner movements of the spirit analogously through outer ones…"*
> - Friedrich Schiller

The Romantic Period, essentially the 19th century, saw an increased focus on the individual and on individual's rights after the American and French revolutions. In Europe, the French Revolution and other subsequent ideological movements challenged the distinction between high and low culture (including music) on social and political grounds. The 19th century began with "boundless idealism and exaltation of the human imagination." Romantic composers wanted to break free of the rigidity of Classical forms and regarded themselves as more expressive and emotional than their predecessors. And while Haydn probably never imagined he was anywhere but Eszterháza, the Romantics, excepting Chopin, had a "taste for imagining oneself in strange lands or remote periods…the composer could disappear into the mountains or fields." Thus, literary works influenced and infused many of their works. Haydn was almost completely ignored by Romantic composers; they "surrendered him to the Philistines…he appeared much too clear…" The Romantic world of artists and writers stressed society as seen through the prism of the individual and did not emphasize society as an ordered structure.

Although at the beginning of the 1800s music was the most prestigious of the arts, the Romantics looked to other arts (painting, literature) for inspiration. For the Romantic artist sincerity became a key criterion of artistic value. Acceptance by the public became secondary, with some artists, anticipating the 20th century *avant-garde*, even believing that public rejection of a work provided it with moral credentials. The true Romantics of the 19th century "demanded something else of music; they demanded that they be 'transported'…music became for them a substitute for life." In literature "Byron's larger-than-life heroes and Walter Scott's "highly colored historical novels of romance and chivalry" were two of the leading sources.

Early Romantic composers such as Schumann could not completely break free from "the old aesthetic of the hierarchy of genres," although his works, along with those of Chopin and Liszt, "had already shaken it to its foundations." Schumann persisted in trying to adapt to the Classical models. It is perhaps why Schumann paradoxically influenced Brahms, the model of 'Classical Romanticism', but also had a profound influence on Debussy, who loved Schumann's music and "understood its capricious imagination (and) was able to adapt some of…the fleeting phrases (of) Schumann." The early Romantics lost faith and interest in the old structures, as well as in purely rational systems.

> *"Bach's characteristic feature was, even in its strictness, really Romantic."*
> \- Carl Maria von Weber

While they may have lost faith and interest in the strict forms of the Classical period, early Romantics possessed a new appreciation of J.S. Bach.

> *"As listeners to Bach's music, we may feel as if we were present when God created the world."*
> \- Goethe

The appearance of the modern piano, the most suggestive of all musical instruments, created the needed vehicle for Chopin, Schumann, and Liszt, and it would be the dominant instrument throughout the 19th century. In the

Classical era it was the pianists who had to bring their skills up to the level of the contemporary piano music. In the Romantic era players' skills would come to match the difficulty of piano music being generated. Romantic composers and pianists used the expressive capabilities of the piano to establish its role as the central instrument in the classical tradition. While Romanticism tended "towards extreme intimacy and absorption, it raised virtuosity to unprecedented heights," particularly with the piano and violin.

"The sonata was as archaic in 1840 as the Baroque fugue in Haydn's day." Romantic 'character pieces' for solo piano displaced the multi-movement sonata and "offered themselves as real, if fragmentary, expressions of sensibility." These character pieces were often collected together but rarely formed a coherent whole. Instead, grouping them together had an effect "to spread out the unlimited possibilities of feeling and reflection…available at the piano" and placed a high value on individuality. While some of the sets of piano pieces, particularly in the case of Schumann's, could be considered 'songs without words', one of the greatest achievements of the Romantic era was "the elevation of the song (*Lied*) from a minor genre to the vehicle of the sublime." Romantic composers of Lieder gave "the lyrical expression of Nature an epic status." In fact, Charles Rosen feels that the song cycle is the most original musical form created in the first half of the 19th century.

"The fundamental task and achievement of (the Romantic) was to attain the sublime through the trivial." Orchestral color only became a fundamental of form with the early Romantics; before this generation "tone color was (only) applied like a veneer to form." Carl Maria von Weber (1786-1826) was the first composer to break with standard forms of the day and "explore new types of color in the orchestra and piano." Weber was "the first composer with an eye for the intrinsic melodic value of folk materials." He mined local folk tunes and "breathed a mysterious, supernatural, Germanic spirit in this work." With Weber we have the first works to make a very noticeable move away from the balance and elegant proportions of the Classical masters.

Several early romantics, such as Johann Nepomuk Hummel (1778-1837) are "condemned to be a missing link between other great creators." He was a pupil of Mozart whose brilliant and improvisatory pianism, despite being "more impressive than profound…often foreshadowed that of Chopin."

♪ The Early Romantics

♪ Robert Schumann (1810-1856)

Like some other famous composers (Schubert and Mendelssohn), Robert Schumann was very creative and prolific in his short life. Only in opera was he unsuccessful. His legacy for solo piano is a large set of original thematic pieces drawn from his vivid imagination. He is considered the inventor of the tone poem for solo piano. Schumann gave us some of the most original solo piano music and it is a shame he battled demons for much of his life so that we are only left to imagine what his output could have been. The 19th century was a secular and materialistic age in which musical Romanticism flourished, especially in Germany. Robert Schumann can be considered to have brought this movement to its zenith.

> *"...through his music Schumann confesses to us his deepest secrets."*
> — cellist Steven Isserlis

His compositions are clearly divided into several periods, during which Schumann concentrated almost exclusively on one form. Prior to 1840 and between ages twenty and twenty-nine it was solo piano music. His first twenty-three works are for solo piano, mostly small pieces bundled together under a name. More often than not, there is little connection among the bundled pieces (e.g., the eight *Fantasiestücke*, Op.12). In 1840 Schumann turned to composing song cycles, picking up where Schubert had left off, broadening the concept of the art song. This total commitment to one form at the expense of all others (another example is 1842, Schumann's 'chamber music' year) is consistent with his manic personality, as Schumann also spent extended periods during which he composed nothing.

In 1833 Schumann started his own music magazine, *Neue Zeitschrift für Musik* (it is still published today) and as a critic he praised Chopin in one of his earlier opinions and introduced readers to Brahms in his final review, referring to him as a 'young eagle' and predicting great things. Chopin met Schumann in Dresden in 1835 and the next year in Leipzig. Schumann adored Chopin and introduced him to Germany by playing his music and giving him rave reviews in his magazine. He characterized Chopin and his music as a "cannon buried in flowers" and succinctly captured in four words the unique combination of power and beauty, the strength and sensitivity of Chopin's music. Schumann was also pivotal in bringing Schubert out of obscurity and wrote many articles to feed the Bach 'renaissance' (Mendelssohn also contributed much to this effort).

Schumann saw Bach, not Mozart, as "the origin of all that is poetic for his music." He studied Bach in depth leading to an unorthodox polyphony that surpassed even Wagner's. His compositions were characterized by an alternation of passion and satire allowing him "to yoke together musical ideas that seem incompatible at first sight." In 1850 Schumann went to Düsseldorf to take the post of Municipal Music Director, a post held by Mendelssohn twenty years earlier. Schumann, however, was nowhere near the conductor Mendelssohn was.

Around age twenty "Schumann became absorbed in the fashionable Romantic malaise of *Weltschmerz* (world-weariness). Starting around 1827

Schumann showed signs of mental instability and was haunted by the fear of going mad. "He constantly swayed between elation and despair with intermittent mental breakdowns and deep melancholy." Schumann's manic and neurotic personality would manifest itself in his music with the contrasting characters of *Florestan* and *Eusebius*. However, Schumann usually refrained from composing during his bouts of depression, waiting until he felt better.

He tried to broaden his reach for piano playing and ended up permanently injuring his hand, eliminating the possibility of a career as a concert pianist. Although his wife Clara would admirably fill this role well after Robert's death by concertizing throughout Europe over a career of sixty years, her ambitions as a composer were repressed by her husband. He also threw himself into the ice-cold Rhine River in February 1854 in an apparent suicide attempt, only to be rescued by passing fishermen. The last years of his life were spent in an asylum. He often wrote music first, then went back and gave it a title (e.g., *Carnaval*), and assigned tags to specific movements. Therefore, the names given by Schumann only "give a clue to the mood, and are not to be taken as a guide to the story."

Schumann "saw his piano music as a vehicle for some of his most intimate and directly personal messages." "Arguably, none investigated the Romantic's obsession with feeling and passion quite so thoroughly as him." Schumann "achieved the most powerful musical representations of pathological states of feeling before Wagner."

Schumann said, "I am affected by everything that goes on in the world...and...I long to express my feelings in music...anything that happens...compels me to express it in music." His three sonatas are all "striking, dramatic and powerful works, with moments of fantasy and intimacy" from which springs an "inspired flow of melody and idiomatic handling of the keyboard." Schumann's piano music is autobiographical but also original and poetic, reflecting his character and experiences, his hopes and dreams. His music hovers "between profound seriousness and pointed robust humor, between graceful charm and a 'smiling through tears'."

"The great art of the Romantic generation was to imply the existence of a program without realizing the details in any specifically extramusical sense." In many of Schumann's sets of short piano pieces there is no explicit program but only an implied narrative that helps to hold the work together. As with most music with extramusical references, Schumann's solo piano music can be enjoyed as abstract music without knowledge or attention to the underlying intentions of the composer. However, the listener will almost certainly appreciate the works more by placing them in their literary, psychological, and autobiographical contexts. "The moods and forms they encompass are myriad, filled with the most poetic flights of fancy and the wildest imagination."

Schumann's piano miniatures are "loosely knit structures...many small cameos...welding them all together onto one large canvas." In each set Schumann showed he had mastered "the technique of creating a cycle of 'fragments'." His greatest strength was "his ability to make a unity out of the most disparate material." These skills are epitomized in the sets *Carnaval* and the *Davidsbündlertänze*.

Schumann's piano works are challenging but not showy, with frequent and sudden changes in mood and key. Unlike Liszt, he was not a virtuoso and did not compose to dazzle the public. Schumann, like Chopin, dismissed virtuosity for its own sake, stating sarcastically, "As if there were nothing higher than the art of pleasing the public." But all three composers used "virtuosity in the service of poetical expression." Schumann's works for solo piano do present technical problems at least as difficult as those of Chopin and Liszt. What distinguishes Schumann is that "in his music technique is the servant of a richly fertile poetic imagination," and "his melodic genius lay in the picturesque transformation of a motif into different characters."

Pianist Garrick Ohlsson points out that much of Schumann's piano music "uses a lot of baroquish motor rhythms...has tremendous baroquish energy." Schumann's father was a writer, manuscript preparer, and bookseller so he grew up surrounded by literature, especially the romantic literature of his day. His style is actually more literary than musical and this carries over into his music in a unique way. If the public has difficulty with the music of Schumann, "it is more through the fear of being unable to follow the literary allusions and the constantly changing moods and incredible imagination."

Schumann's first published work was the *Abegg* Variations, Op.1 (1831), dedicated to Countess Pauline von Abegg. The complete title is *Variations on the Name 'Abegg'*. Schumann cleverly used A-B-E-G-G as the first notes of the work.

These were followed the next year with his Op.2, *Papillons*, a musical rendering of the ballroom scene, *Larventanz*, from Jean Paul's *Flegeljahre*. From 1829-39 Schumann composed almost exclusively for solo piano and all of his first twenty-three published works were for solo piano. It was during this time that Schumann virtually invented the genre of short, pictorial fantasy pieces for solo piano. He collected together these short pieces into the familiar sets, some unified, some not.

Fantasia in C, Op.17

This three-movement fantasia, originally titled *Dichtungen* ('Poems') is often coupled with Schubert's four-movement *Wanderer* Fantasy. The two are essentially substantial piano sonatas on the grand scale of Beethoven. "To wander is the Romantic tradition; one yields to it...or is driven and plagued by finding no escape." Schubert unifies the four movements into a "seamless and cohesive whole." The *Fantasia in C* of Schumann has some suggestive elements to it but is not as explicitly programmatic as many of his sets of short piano pieces. Schumann most likely refrained from titling his Fantasia a sonata because it "was freighted from the beginning with a heavy cargo of literary ideas." The composer toyed with the idea of Greek titles for the three movements, *Ruins*, *Trophies*, *Palms*, which Schumann subsequently changed to *Ruins*, *Triumphal Arch* and *Constellation*. However, neither trio of subtitles were included with the work upon publication in 1839.

The Schumann *Fantasy* was requested by and dedicated to Liszt to help fund a project to erect a statue of Beethoven in salute to the great composer. A melody from Beethoven's song cycle *An die ferne Geliebte* ('To the distant beloved') pervades this work. Although it is Schumann's homage to Beethoven, the *Fantasia* is totally un-classical as it "neither starts from a point of stability nor reaches one until the last possible moment." While proportioned as a Classical sonata the *Fantasia* does not 'work' like a Classical sonata in that it does not contrast themes of different character. Schumann succeeds in conveying an appearance of unity despite the fragmentary content. And instead of building tension as the exposition develops or in a development section, the first movement begins with great tension. In fact, most Romantic works of the 1830s imply a lowering of tension after the opening.

This is perhaps Schumann's greatest work for solo piano, one which Schumann said should be played "with passion throughout and fantastic energy." The first movement is certainly the most successful and most original essay in a large form among Schumann's long movements "with a sweep and energy that occurs nowhere else."

> ***Recommended – Schubert and Schumann Fantasies***
> The recordings by Maurizio Pollini find this great artist perfectly in his element. Pollini "strikes an ideal balance between visceral excitement and Classical restraint." This balance is a trademark of so many of Pollini's interpretations.

Sets of Miniatures for Solo Piano

The novelty of Schumann's ideas is best displayed in his piano miniatures, a form he created, as he had little use for existent forms. Schumann's best solo piano works "are often nothing more than a kaleidoscopic succession of miniatures…each born of a minute musical seed," but conceived and collected together as an entity. Each set, often connected only by an underlying uniformity of style, is a unique journey through Schumann's musical imagination including such varied images and topics as forests, childhood, dawn, night, butterflies, Carnival, and imaginary *Kapellmeister*.

His piano cycles repeat the same motifs throughout a particular cycle. These piano cycles were descended from the Baroque solo keyboard suites of Bach and Handel. Schumann's piano miniatures are "spiritual diaries as well as music." He was the first of the completely anti-Classic composers and, as with Chopin, form as it previously existed meant little to him. The deep influence of Bach is evidenced by Schumann's composition of piano parts to go with all of Bach's Unaccompanied Violin Partitas and Sonatas, including the monumental *Chaconne* as well as the Unaccompanied Cello Suites. Although Schumann seems to compose without rules, he was steeped in the great German classical tradition, particularly Handel, Beethoven, and Schubert, but especially Bach.

Schumann was the first composer to explicitly state, and to follow through with his music, "that content and idea dictate form, not the reverse", and he "established an entire aesthetic that verged on expressionism." Mood and color were much more important to Schumann than form; he preferred to create a kaleidoscope of texture and emotion. In his short piano pieces there is only the suggestion of a program, an implied narrative. The titles Schumann gave to his piano pieces served to bind the miniatures together in a 'unified' whole, but were also intended to ignite the imagination of the listener.

Schumann's 'radical' views, along with most of his music, were not accepted widely during his time, and he was not aggressive by nature to market himself (as were Berlioz and Liszt). Critics, academics, and others slandered his works as signaling the "end of music", or "a sign of the degeneracy of the times", and "decadence!", "the work of a madman." Although Schumann befriended and helped the careers of other young composers, most notably Chopin and Mendelssohn, they found it hard to return the favor. Composer-conductor Lukas Foss believes that Schumann's music reveals his generosity towards his colleagues. Although they liked Schumann personally they could find little to admire in his music. This is not shocking for the conservative, upper middle-class Mendelssohn who was far from adventurous in his music, but is somewhat surprising for Chopin, who had almost as little use for traditional forms as did Schumann.

> *"I am affected by everything that goes on in the world, politics, literature, and people. I think them over in my own way and then I express them in music."*
> - Robert Schumann

Papillons, Op.2
This set of miniatures brings us face-to-face with the young Schumann and was his "apprentice work, his graduation piece, and his masterpiece all rolled into one," the first work of genius. He had prepared for *Papillons* by composing a lot of music, without opus number, before.

The *Papillons* pieces have undeniable programmatic connotations to works of Jean Paul, specifically the Larventanz chapter of Jean Paul's novel *Flegeljahre*. Schumann provided in his letters the correlation of the individual pieces with passages of this chapter. It is the predecessor to Schumann's *Carnaval* set (see below), also a set of festive piano pieces representing characters in various dances.

"The succession of short pieces corresponds to the fleeting impressions and encounters at a masked ball." We have no clue as to why Schumann titled the set *Papillons* ('butterflies') and the significance of butterflies is not clear. However, "the suggestion of airiness and flight is clearly borne out by the music." Schumann portrays the dispersion of the ballroom crowd by having the music gradually vanish into nothingness to conclude the set.

Davidsbündlertänze, Op.6

The *Davidsbündlertänze* ('Band of David dances') set "is the subtlest, most mysterious, and most complex of all Schumann's large works." The set is not intended for public performance but is an example of the extreme intimacy between Schumann and the keyboard. The set of eighteen 'dances', few of which are actual dances, are essentially based on a tune from a mazurka by Clara Wieck, so the pieces comprise a set of variations onthis theme. Schumann grouped them together in two books of nine.

In typical Schumann and Romantic style, the opening dance has a restlessness and anxiety and is tonally unstable. Stability comes in the second piece, providing a stark contradiction to Classical forms that required unambiguous tonal stability upfront before progressing to instability and building tensions in the development section. Excepting the occasional 'event' such as the opening of Mozart's *Dissonance* String Quartet, the Classical Style dictated that instability had to come from a starting point of stability; instability could not simply appear at the outset of a work.

Schumann formed the *Davidsbund* ('band of David') to discuss and review music, and fight against what he, and presumably other members of the Bund, saw as 'safe' music produced by the "unimaginative bourgeois" and to expose "sham and pretentiousness in music." Schumann used pen names for its members and the pseudonyms 'Florestan' and 'Eusebius' to identify himself. His imaginary Davidites' mission was to slay the Philistines; for Schumann these were "the fashionable mass producers of trivial music and the thousands…who applauded their efforts."

When he associated a movement or piece with Florestan, the 'passionate extrovert', it usually showed his exuberant side, while music connected to Eusebius, the 'poetic introvert', was his more reflective and serious side, the repressed side of Schumann. Each of the movements of the *Davidsbündlertänze* set can be assigned to either of his alter egos based on these contrasting moods. His imaginary spiritual brotherhood counted among its members not only the alter egos of Schumann but many other composers and artists, including Mozart, Chopin, and Berlioz. Pianist Vladimir Feltsman feels the Florestan-Eusebius debate is "absolute nonsense. It's not interesting anymore (and) not needed to enjoy what is an excellent piece of music."

Clara focused on performing and left the composing to Robert, although she had made serious attempts at composition. Schumann attributed the inspiration for his impressive solo piano output from 1836-38 to Clara. Works from this period included the *Concert sans Orchestre* in F minor, Op.14, which is actually a piano sonata; and two famous sets of pieces, *Kreisleriana* and *Davidsbündlertänze*.

Clara Schumann gave us an idea of the barriers faced by women composers a century and a half ago, when she decided to give up composition for good she wrote, that "I once thought that I possessed creative talent…A woman must not desire to compose…not one has been able to do it…" To put Clara's situation in context, few women in the 1800s were admitted to the Paris Conservatory, and there was only one woman professor there during the entire 19th century (Louise Farrenc).

After Robert's death Clara Schumann tirelessly promoted her husband's music for another forty years by touring and giving concerts of his music as the greatest female pianist in Europe. Schumann shared the same romantic feeling toward music as the writer Johann Paul Friedrich Richter, a.k.a. Jean Paul (1763-1825), whom he admired:

> "…and of our sacred and vanished past, only one thing remains immortal – music."
> – Jean Paul

> *Recommended – Schumann piano miniatures*
> For the *Op.1 Abegg Variations* it is hard to beat Richter, although the teen-aged Evgeny Kissin might have with his Carnegie Hall Debut Recital (RCA, 1980). Perahia (Sony, 1988) shines in the *Papillons* coupled with the complete *Symphonic Études*. For the *Davidsbündlertänze* the nod for recent recordings goes to Pollini (DG, 2001).

Carnaval, Op.9

Carnaval is a set of variations published by Schumann in 1837 based on combinations of the notes E-flat, A, A-flat, C, and B, which by their German designations Es (S), A, As, C, and H, respectively, are the 'musical' letters of Schumann's name. Combining the German designations a couple of ways forms *Asch*, the birthplace of Ernestine von Fricken. He was under her spell before Clara Wieck. Schumann's cycles such as *Carnaval* and *Davidsbündlertänze* are based on the recurrence throughout of the same motifs. Schumann takes advantage of "juxtaposition of rhythms that are not quite together, creates the unsettledness that he is looking for."

As was *Papillons*, the pieces in *Carnaval* were inspired and influenced by the same characters from Jean Paul's *Flegeljahre*, the two brothers Vult and Walt who represent Schumann's opposing personalities. The personalities of the brothers correspond to the composer's outgoing and vivacious Florestan, who "was the extrovert, violent, and capricious side of Schumann's personality," and the sensitive and dreamy Eusebius. Schumann "steeped himself in the tales of E.T.A. Hoffmann, using them to fashion alternate artistic personalities."

Carnaval is a metaphor for masquerading, for becoming somebody else. The twenty-one miniatures, some deliberately designed to sound incomplete, fall into two categories: dance pieces and character sketches. Several of the pieces represent members of Schumann's imaginary *Davidsbund*, including Chopin and Paganini who, in their respective pieces, wage figurative war on the Philistines. Chopin and Paganini are the only characters who appear under their own names, without 'masks', with Paganini appearing as "a whiff of brimstone hovering over the dance floor." Other pieces represent other friends and of course, Florestan and Eusebius. Pieces with contrasting sections are considered to alternate between the two personalities of these imaginary figures.

The *Carnaval* set is related to the *Fashingsschwank aus Wien* set in that both were meant to capture the spirit of and were inspired by German carnival, or *Fasching*, season, which occurs just before Lent, much like *Mardi Gras*. *Carnaval* contains many of Schumann's most personal and eccentric inspirations.

Kinderszenen, Op.15

Translated as either "Scenes of Childhood" or "Scenes of Children" Schumann stressed that these thirteen pieces were meant to depict an adult's recollection of childhood and were intended to be played by adults. This is different from Schumann's *Album für die Jugend*, which were composed to be played by young people. They do not have the typical difficulty of Schumann and rightly so with titles for the pieces such as *Hobby Horseman*, and *Blind Man's Bluff*. In his pieces about childhood Schumann sometimes portrays, sometimes relives the experience of being a child.

Fantasiestücke, Op.12

These eight pieces are among Schumann's most popular and performed works. Titles of pieces in this set such as *Des Abends* ('In the Evening'), *In der Nacht* ('At Night'), and *Soaring* infuse the work with the extra musical feeling that made Schumann's piano music so influential to Debussy. Traditionally the Op.12 'Fantasy Pieces' set has been made up of eight pieces but a ninth has recently been discovered.

Symphonic Études, Op.13

This large set of variations was originally titled Variations pathétiques but Schumann settled on *Études in Orchestral Character for Pianoforte in the Form of Variations* in 1837 after going through several other titles. Begging to be shortened, history has settled on calling them the *Symphonic Études*. The theme for the *Symphonic Études* was provided by Baron von Fricken, whose daughter Ernestine was the object of Schumann's pursuits before giving up that chase and focusing his efforts on Clara Wieck; efforts that eventually proved successful and very fruitful, a marriage of two great musicians. In a novelty of sorts, Schumann returns to the theme rarely in the subsequent variations, a device used by Brahms and later composers in which the original theme is all but absent from the variations.

In addition to the thirteen *Symphonic Études* that Schumann published as the 'complete' set, Brahms discovered the five 'posthumous' *Études* that are often included in recordings and performances, although artists differ on where the additional five should be played. The theme is stated up front in the first piece and most of the subsequent variations are on Fricken's theme, excepting No. 3 and No.9. The finale is in rondo form and includes the main theme plus two additional themes taken from a German opera based on Walter Scott's Ivanhoe. In their scope the *Symphonic Études* go beyond all of Schumann's piano sets. They are immensely difficult to play.

Kreisleriana, Op.16

This collection of eight pieces is written around a set of related keys without any one feeling more important than the others. The odd-numbered pieces are passionate and even violent, while the slow pieces contain beauty and poetry. Both extremes are unsurpassed by Schumann in his other sets and *Kreisleriana* is generally regarded as Schumann's finest set of piano pieces. This set is named after the fictional character Kreisler, an eccentric, wild and gifted *Kapellmeister* created by writer E.T.A. Hoffmann in his book Fantasiestücke in Callot's Manier.

Pianist John Browning feels that the "Schumann repertoire is the most dangerous of all piano repertoire." He points to Vladimir Horowitz's observation that Schumann's piano music requires organized improvisation; it has to be tight but it also has to sound improvisatory. To Browning pieces such as the Fantasy, *Kreisleriana*, and the *Davidsbündlertänze* are "very dangerous to play in public; I think they fail more often than they succeed, even at the hands of some of the biggest artists."

Humoreske, Op.20; Novelletten, Op.21

The *Humoreske* set is the last of the great piano sets composed by Schumann between the age of twenty and twenty-nine. The six pieces are sophisticated but subtle and personal. Schumann composed this set, which he referred to as the *Grosse Humoreske*, within a week in 1839, described by him as "all week at the piano, composing, writing, laughing, and crying, all at once."

Novelleten is a set of eight pieces ('novellas') almost forty minutes in length. "As a whole, the *Novelletten* are extremely busy, very robust, masculine, generally good-humored." It is the longest but also the least-performed set of piano miniatures by Schumann. This is too bad because there is much variety among the individual pieces and in sympathetic hands the set is very enjoyable. However, many feel not all eight pieces measure up to the high standards of Schumann's more popular and more frequently-recorded sets of pieces. The pieces are all run relatively long and not all maintain Schumann's typical inventiveness.

Waldszenen, Op.82

The set of 'forest scenes' is an example of what Charles Rosen calls a 'landscape cycle' and was composed around Christmas of 1848. It is the only major set of piano miniatures composed by Schumann after age forty. Instead of the playful youthfulness of the piano sets of the 1830s, *Waldszenen* are filled with sentimental nostalgia with such titles for the nine pieces as *Lonely Flowers* and *House in the Woods*. They were inspired by forest romanticism, possibly specifically by a set of poems about hunting in the forest by Heinrich Laube titled *Jagdbrevier*. In the first of these 'scenes' the piano imitates a horn call at the opening, evoking the forest.

Pianist/conductor Christoph Eschenbach feels some pieces contain very deep, very poetic, even very sinister sections. "These are not woodland depictions without complications." Clara was so disturbed by some of the pieces that she would not play them. Eschenbach points to the fourth piece, *Haunted Spot*, inspired by a disturbing poem by Christian Friedrich Hebbel, although Rosen feels the inspiration for this piece is nothing more than "harmless urban fictions of country life." The well-known seventh piece (*Vogel als Prophet*) "is a very advanced, *avant-garde*, piece from that time," which could be mistaken for Debussy.

Gesänge der Frühe, Op.133

These 'Songs of Dawn' are five significant piano miniatures. They are such late compositions that Schumann actually wrote them after being committed to the asylum where he would die and represent the last solo piano pieces published in his lifetime. Pianist Peter Frankl, who has recorded the complete Schumann piano works, stated he "had the most trouble with this piece...sometimes it is accessible, but sometimes it really goes beyond our limits." And pianist Ronald Brautigam sees these pieces as "fragile music...best...to play it alone without an audience...one of the most moving of all his works, but...also one of the most difficult."

Many of Schumann's character pieces are connected to German literature. Such connections became fundamental to many works of his contemporaries as well as later Romantics. Schumann revised many of his solo piano sets trying "to endow the music with the healthy rational solidity" but at the cost of losing its fleeting visions and its sense of caprice.

> **Recommended – Schumann piano miniatures**
> If you enjoy Schumann's piano pieces you will have multiple recordings of some of the sets because of the couplings offered. Recommended CD's include Arrau (Philips), Lupu (Decca, 1996) and András Schiff (ECM, 2002), a live recital of *Humoreske*, *Novelletten* and *Piano Sonata No.3*. Also, any recording by Richter is recommended, with allowances for sound.

♪ Fryderyk Chopin (1810-1849)

> *"Such a poetic temperament as Chopin's never existed, nor have I heard such...refinement of playing...his execution was perfect in the extreme."*
> - Franz Liszt

Of the truly great composers Chopin is the only one known exclusively for his piano compositions. His fame is derived mostly from small-scale works for this one instrument. Chopin's music has always been very popular and remains at the heart of many piano recitals today. The uniqueness of Chopin's music is its "combination of melodic and harmonic resource of unprecedented charm and richness" as his works "link poetically expressive melody and restless harmony to high technical standards." He composed all his piano music over a period of only twenty years, so there is not a dramatic difference in style among his many works.

His music has always been 'in style' and the piano literature would be inconceivable without him. "Chopin's music is largely derived from his early experience of opera, the rhythms and harmonies of native Polish dances, and Bach," with the influence of Bach holding all his music together. But Chopin's piano music is more intimately expressive than Bach's keyboard works. Chopin wrote for an audience, a small audience but an audience nonetheless, and his counterpoint focuses on making an impact on listeners. Bach did not write for an audience; his keyboard works had two purposes – religious or instructive. His solo keyboard works all had pedagogic purposes.

Charles Rosen refers to Chopin's 'heterophonic' counterpoint – "two voices playing the same melody together in different rhythms." This heterophonic texture again points to the paradox of Chopin's forms by preserving "the supremacy of the Italian-style melody while allowing a richly interesting polyphonic development."

As with Mozart, the heavy influence of Italian opera on Chopin makes him "unique among instrumental composers to sustain melodies of great length." "Chopin has transferred Italian operatic melody to a keyboard texture and combined it with his study of Bach," from whom he "learned to make many voices out of one." He created a piano style that dominated the entire second half of the 19th century; his treatment of harmony influenced Wagner and anticipated Debussy in its near-Impressionism, only then yielding to the styles of Debussy and Prokofiev.

> *"...he may be called a perfect virtuoso...he produces new effects, like Paganini on the violin..."*
> *- Mendelssohn on Chopin*

Although Chopin is usually thought of as a swooning romantic he did not see himself this way. For one, he drew no inspiration from literary sources. As Arthur Rubinstein noted, Chopin's music "does not tell stories or paint pictures." He had no use for his fellow Romantic composers' music, although he was a friend to most of them, even though "Mendelssohn complained that you couldn't tell Chopin's wrong notes from his right ones." Some argue that Chopin's "music was more influenced by Classical and Baroque forms than anything else" and "Beethoven's thunder appealed to Chopin far less than Mozart's elegance and proportion and Bach's organizational powers and contrapuntal acumen."

Along with Schumann, Chopin fully exploited the possibilities of the miniature. His piano works are "the expression at once of the soul of the instrument and of his own." He found Beethoven too big and uncouth. The only two composers considered 'masters' by Chopin were Bach and Mozart. The paradox of Chopin's style is the unlikely combination of the strong influences of both J.S. Bach and, as with Mozart, Italian opera. From Bach comes a rich chromatic web of polyphony and from Italian opera a way of sustaining the melodic line. Both influences were discreetly absorbed into his own style. Chopin was "most original in his use of the most fundamental and traditional technique." He was both the "most conservative and the most radical composer of his generation." No other music of his time combined Chopin's "deeply moving simplicity with such complex art."

> *"Your objective with Chopin is to become one with the instrument."*
> *- pianist Ingrid Fliter*

Chopin excelled in every form for the piano and perfected many. Although his piano music is some of the most technically demanding, and challenged even the greatest piano of the time, Liszt, the music is not virtuosic for the sake of virtuosity. Instead, Chopin explores many musical depths and was a true romantic. Additionally, his is 'absolute' music, containing no program or theme, as Chopin wanted the music to stand on its own. He only applied abstract titles to some of his works. The famous nicknames given to many of his works (*Raindrop, Military, Winter Winds*) were marketing ploys assigned by publishers or became attached to his works later.

Despite his complete avoidance of program or deliberately descriptive music, Chopin did feel that music should have some meaning, just not explicit. Some argue that Chopin's *Ballades* are influenced or even based on poems by the Polish nationalist Adam Mickiewicz (1798-1855), specifically his collection *Ballady*. These poems were infused with folklore. However, the composer provided no explicit reference to the poems. If this is indeed the case, then this would certainly be the hidden meaning of the *Ballades*.

Chopin's handling of sonata form, particularly the development section, shows that while his music combined Mozart's elegance with the organization of Bach, his music is clearly 19th century Romantic. For Chopin the development section is not about working towards the resolution in the recapitulation. In fact, Chopin's recapitulations do not resolve previous tensions or reconcile harmonic and melodic oppositions. Instead, the 'resolution' brings further excitement by a return of original material; with greatly heightened brilliance Chopin brings back some of the main themes with a "magnified aura of brilliance, complexity, tension, violence and pathos." Chopin outdid his contemporaries in the variety and effectiveness of his treatment of the return.

Chopin, unlike Liszt, gave very few concerts to large audiences, preferring more intimate settings, partly because he played the piano 'gently' as opposed to being a 'banger' like Liszt. He performed in public only a dozen times and it is thought he may have acquired stage fright in his youth. His virtuosity "was devoted to the service of the most delicate and sensitive taste and poetic feeling." After settling in Paris in 1832 from his native Poland, Chopin composed extensively and was paid very handsomely to give piano lessons to well-heeled Parisians and their children.

It is good to mention Chopin's use of rubato, the practice of ornamentation in 18th and 19th century keyboard playing. In his music, as in the music of the Baroque, expression is largely conveyed through ornamentation. *Tempo rubato*, from the Italian meaning 'stolen time', involves differences in tempo, a speeding up or slowing down of the melodic line, while the left hand keeps the time. It is a delaying of the melody note until after the bass has been played. Any time 'robbed' by speeding up the melody must be 'given back' by slowing down somewhere else.

For example, "an eagerly awaited moment may be delayed a little by slowing the tempo." This is because the accompaniment (usually the left-hand baseline) remains steady ('steady-accompaniment). In fact, the most effective form of *rubato* is one in which the tempo of the melody ebbs and flows with 'steady-accompaniment'. If the time 'stolen' is not quickly 'repaid', then "tune and accompaniment will part company for good." "The true musician…takes something from time in order to give it to rhythm." Chopin used a very pronounced *rubato* and listeners unaccustomed to it were initially shocked by its effect.

As with all forms of decoration, *rubato* works best in slow movements. Rubato was used to a much greater extent in Romantic solo piano works than in the works of Mozart, which are played more strictly in time. However, tempo rubato, thought to be a creation of the Romantics, possibly traces its origins to the Florentine *Camerata* and Giulio Caccini in particular who spoke about not tying up singers in the ordinary measure of time but rather, "often making the value of the notes less by half, sometimes more…"

Excepting the two piano concertos and some early minor chamber works, Chopin composed only for solo piano. The piano in his time had a lighter action, making it easier to make it 'sing'. His piano music is 'sparkling', 'breathtaking', and the notes "scatter like pinpoints of flame." What makes Chopin's music unique is a combination of melody and harmony of unprecedented charm and richness. He combined "pure virtuosity with an aristocratic and poetic kind" of graceful, often melancholy, melody. Chopin's music was designed and performed for small, intimate audiences, he was not motivated to conquer a larger audience. This "made possible the kind of experimentation necessary to the development of Chopin's art."

While mostly everything Chopin composed is in the active repertory, it must be kept in mind that he stayed within a narrow comfort level throughout his career, music for piano (and predominantly for piano alone). However, "within his self-imposed limitation he was perfection itself," a genius as a pianist but also a creative genius of originality, a revolutionary who developed a new kind of piano playing and a sonority that released the instrument from the past, and fully exploited the coloristic resources of the piano. "An aura of mystery and magic surrounded…Chopin in his own day" and still does today; "…his music cast a spell on his listeners."

Ballades and Scherzos

Chopin's *Ballades* and *Scherzos* are often regarded as parallel cycles of four individual and self-contained works. Both sets were composed over a ten-year period begun in 1831, with the last work of each set completed in 1842. "The fusion of narrative and lyric in the Ballades is perhaps Chopin's greatest achievement." While Chopin wrote no programmatic music, the four *Ballades* are often seen as having a narrative motivation to them, possibly inspired by the poems of his countryman Mickiewicz, although Charles Rosen finds this highly doubtful. On the other hand, the Scherzos are claimed to have a dramatic motivation.

Ballade had been used to describe other non-musical works but Chopin was the first to label musical works as 'ballades'. As such, they can be considered 'songs without words'. He created this genre for solo piano, which is characterized by a narrative told through two major themes. However, as with all of Chopin's music, there is no program associated with these works and each one has a unique form. "Throughout his life Chopin's outmoded sense of musical decorum always resisted any attempt to impose an explicit nonmusical sense on any of his works." These four long, solo piano pieces combine drama and lyricism and in them Chopin "retains a feeling for a continuous, uninterrupted flow of repetitive melody..." and use contrasting, well-defined themes more often than other forms of Chopin's piano pieces. Components of Chopin's Ballades can be found in other forms he used (e.g., the Impromptus), but the length of the Ballades (ten minutes each) makes them longer duration than most of his piano works.

Ballade No.1 in G minor, Op.23 is very popular and recognizable. It is the most operatic and melodramatic of the four. The next *Ballade* in F major, Op.38 was dedicated to Schumann, who commented that Chopin's "music would inspire a poet to write words to it." The Ballade No.3 in A-flat, Op.47 is also very popular and presents "a kaleidoscope of images that reveal Chopin at his most elegant and poetic." The Third Ballade is lyrical with an underlying strength; it "gathers momentum slowly, like a story that takes its time to get under way."

The four *Scherzos* are similar to the Ballades in length and contain alternating passages of serious, gloomy and highly dramatic music compared to his works in other styles. This is the result of tension generated by the use of two sharply contrasted themes. Each of the four could be used as the scherzo movement of a typical 19th century large-scale piano sonata, and so could be considered fragments of sonatas. The Scherzos are full of pianistic fireworks with much lighter-spirited music. They are in ¾ time and not as lyrical as the Ballades. Chopin uses minor keys (in Nos.1-3) effectively to build tension but relies on the major for its relief. The Scherzos are combinations of ideas on a grand scale, each of which individually could be material for a miniature piece such as a prelude or nocturne.

Scherzo No.2 in B-flat minor, Op.31 is the most famous of the four and is powerful and expansive. The silences in this popular piece are "so urgent a part of its total effect," which is a very heated argument of dramatic and lyric elements. No.3 is "extraordinary...in the varied colors of its majestic chords and gentle showers of descending arpeggios. For style and substance, the Scherzo in C sharp minor is "where substance and high-octane virtuosity staggeringly mesh!"

Chopin is commonly criticized for "a clear incapacity for attaining the unity necessary in a large work," although Charles Rosen turns this around to state that Chopin was the only musician of his generation who felt invariably at ease with (large forms). Rosen cites each of the four Ballades and four Scherzi that are at least as long as the typical Beethoven movement.

> ***Recommended*** – Excellent single-discs of the *Ballades* and *Scherzi* are from Arthur Rubinstein (RCA) and Stephen Hough (Hyperion). Interestingly, Hough alternates *Ballade* with *Scherzo* as opposed to keeping the two sets of four together.

Études

Chopin took the *Étude* from the practice room to the concert stage. These works contain some of the most diverse challenges in piano writing. It is one thing to be able to play them; quite another to play them well. But they are more than just extremely challenging lessons, the mastery of which every serious pianist should seek. They are all that, but what makes them so great is that Chopin manages to infuse in these most technical pieces his usual beautiful lyricism. Charles Rosen sees the Romantic *étude* as "a form in which musical substance and technical difficulty coincide." It is a romantic idea that appeared in the Romantic era, "a short piece in which the musical interest is derived almost entirely from a single technical problem."

Chopin's *études* are quite different from Liszt's *Études d'execution transcendante* ("Transcendental Études"). Chopin invents pure piano sound, they are studies in coloristic counterpoint. Difficulties arise more from touch and balance than from speed or accuracy, although they are so difficult that Chopin is said to have preferred the performance of them by Liszt to his own. Liszt's are much broader in scope and each covers a wide range of pianistic problems. Naturally they are of enormous technical difficulty. Chopin's, while also being technically demanding, are arranged systematically so that each one concentrates on a particular technical point.

The first set, Op.10, was composed in 1829-32, mostly in Poland and dedicated to Liszt, who actually played the set for Chopin, generating a response from the Pole, "I should like to rob him (Liszt) of the way he plays them." The very first Prelude, No.1, is a direct reference to Bach with a modernized version of the very first Prelude of *The Well-Tempered Clavier*; both are basically a "string of arpeggios with an almost absolute rhythmic uniformity." "For Chopin and many others, *The Well-Tempered Clavier* was the foundation of all composition."

Book Two, Op.25, from 1832-37 came hard on the heels of the success with the first set and presents technical demands of a completely new nature. In the Op.25 set the chromaticism is more pronounced and the pieces flow from one into the next with a progression of virtuoso brilliance to make the set work as a whole, a unified work out of a series of different pieces.

Both sets had a profound effect upon Liszt, Brahms, Debussy, Scriabin, and Rachmaninoff, who achieved or surpassed them in complexity but did not reach the same artistic heights as Chopin.

> *Recommended – Chopin Études*
> In addition to Rubinstein's recordings, Mauricio Pollini's set from 1972 (DG) and Murray Perahia's disc, with the added bonus of Chopin's four *Impromptus* (Sony, 2004)

Nocturnes

These 'night pieces' contain some of the most beautiful piano music ever composed. They are "lyrical pieces with long dreamy melodies supported by lilting, broadly-spanned accompaniments." They span Chopin's entire career and show his development over time. Chopin modeled these pieces after John Field's (1782-1837) graceful series, which Field composed between 1813-35, totaling eighteen nocturnes. Field was the first Irish composer to make a contribution to European concert music and while he did not technically invent the nocturne he "cultivated it as both an idea and a genre." "At a time when most concert pianists were most interested in enlarging the power and range of the instrument, Field cultivated its possibilities for intimate expression," leading to his vast influence on Romantic piano music, particularly the miniatures of Chopin and Schumann.

One of Field's innovations was the "use of arpeggio figures wrapped in a cloud of sound from the sustaining pedal." His melodic idiom owes something to Irish and Scottish folksong and some of his nocturnes have a strong vocal character. Field was a pupil of Muzio Clementi. While his set may have served as a starting point for Chopin, Chopin had a better grasp of the form than Field, and by "enriching the harmonic content" Chopin made his nocturnes, which are "generally more somber and melancholy...more speculative and elaborate."

Chopin's slow music, such as the nocturnes, is often "progressively more and more encrusted with chromatic ornament." The Nocturnes are "wonderfully polished jewels of reflective lyricism and expressive nostalgia." They are "subtle mood studies intended (for) a small select audience..." As indicated by their name, all of these pieces contain melodies that are peaceful and tranquil, and are not typical of some of the virtuoso showpieces, or dance-like works for which Chopin is also famous. Although composed and published in a number of sets of two or three, it is most enjoyable to hear the nocturnes in toto. Although they are ordered, there is no reason not to listen to them in 'random' or 'shuffle' mode.

Chopin "was the first composer obsessed with the idea of reproducing the (operatic) bel canto ('beautiful singing') voice at the piano" and "...the idea of creating a continuously vocal style seems to be what he was about." "There's a sort of contrapuntal voice-led line in Chopin as a result of his devotion to and study of Bach." Nowhere is the *bel canto* style more apparent than in the nocturnes.

The first two nocturnes, Op.9, should be familiar, particularly No.2. It is often heard as 'background' music and used as such in some movies. The one I recall is Robert DeNiro listening to it in his apartment in the movie *City by the Sea*. It holds the same place in the piano pantheon as the first movement of the *Moonlight* Sonata, *Für Elise*, or Bach's *Jesu, Joy of Man's Desiring*.

> **Recommended – Chopin Nocturnes**
> Pollini's complete set (DG, 2005) is a beautiful culmination of this pianist's career-long devotion to Chopin's music.

Waltzes

The waltz probably traces its origin to German Bavaria in the late 1700s. However, it proved to be outrageously popular and spread throughout Europe by the time of the Napoleonic Wars. When Chopin arrived in Vienna from his native Poland in 1830 he "found the populace spinning furiously in three-quarter time". Chopin was surprised to find that waltzes were accepted and respected and their composers, such as Johann Strauss, were called *Kapellmeister*.

However, the waltzes that Chopin began to compose for the Viennese public, as well as those later in Paris, were far removed stylistically from those he encountered upon his arrival. They are more personal, more introspective. In many ways the waltz was a "rather limited genre" and Chopin's waltzes are a "testament to his genius and powers of invention."

> **Recommended – Chopin Waltzes**
> Two names: Rubinstein and Lipatti. Rubinstein's waltzes have many incarnations. For those by the great Dinu Lipatti, the 2-disc set of his complete Chopin recordings with 14 Waltzes, *Piano Sonata No.3, Piano Concerto No.1* and the *Barcarolle* (EMI).

Preludes

As with his Nocturnes, the set of *Twenty-four Preludes* (roughly forty minutes of music) contain exceptional melodies among the outstanding piano playing. They have an organic cohesion making them well-suited to performances as a whole. Most of these pieces are relatively short, many under one minute and are the "most impressive example of a set of tiny Fragments," which in this case form a cycle with one piece adding to another. However, Chopin most likely never performed the complete *Preludes* in a single performance. He believed that playing the pieces in small sets was the most effective presentation as it allows a full appreciation of the individuality of each miniature.

"In the Preludes there is a wonderfully nuanced play of contrast of character and sentiment" and may be the most concentrated expression of Chopin's style. One of the more famous preludes, No.15 in D-flat nicknamed *Raindrop*, with its poetic beauty is also one of the longer pieces and, unlike many of its companion pieces, can stand alone as it contains traditional development and a variety of ideas, whereas many of its shorter brethren are simply very challenging thirty second piano runs. The piece very effectively conveys rain falling relentlessly on a rooftop.

The Preludes are descended from Bach's *The Well-Tempered Clavier* but without the corresponding fugue partners. As with Bach's great preludes, most of Chopin's develop the initial motif without pause until the end. Although inspired by Bach's, Chopin's "are more concentrated...separate individual, and complete in itself." Whereas Bach's *The Well-Tempered Clavier* simply follows the chromatic scale, Chopin's take a more satisfactory tonal sequence: each prelude is harmonically related to its predecessor. This allows Chopin to often end one prelude and start the next on the same note. As he had done in both sets of his *Études* (Opp.10&25) "Chopin expended great subtlety to ensure a convincing movement from one prelude to the next."

Polonaises and Mazurkas

These two forms are taken directly from Chopin's homeland of Poland, and are popular Polish dance pieces in three-quarter time. The *Polonaise* was a ceremonial dance of Polish aristocracy, while mazurkas were peasant dances. Without attaching a program to the Polonaises, Chopin still manages to "evoke images of the high drama of Poland's history."

Chopin transformed the polonaise from lightweight fare, from "a stately processional dance...to a level of seriousness and emotional power never previously associated with it." For him the polonaise became "an image of heroism...emotionally charged, dynamically volatile keyboard epics." Polonaises Op.26, Nos.1&2 were published at age twenty-six in 1836. Polonaise Op.40, No.1 is the best-known, "a straightforward reflection of Polish national pride in the past as well as the future."

Chopin wrote a total of fifty-seven *Mazurkas* in his career, by far the most in any of his piano miniature forms, perhaps because he began writing them at age nine. The mazurka provided Chopin "with a repertoire of motifs, rhythms, and sonorities outside the main Italian, French, and German traditions of European music." "It was in Chopin's playing of the mazurkas that his liberty of rhythm seems to have been most remarkable."

One type of mazurka is a simple dance in triple time with off-beat accents that give "free rein to some of Chopin's quirkiest notions. However, a mazurka is not a specific type of dance like a waltz but a number of very different dances, not very strictly defined. This loose idea gave Chopin lots of freedom within the genre, and was probably why he wrote so many of them. "They constantly veer between simple, complex, charming and audacious." "From the mazurka...came much of Chopin's epoch-making harmony – affecting composers as distant as Wagner, Debussy, and Schoenberg." "They have an almost supernatural difficulty."

The Mazurkas of Chopin actually contain few Polish tunes but recall the rhythms, modes, and characteristics of Polish music with its unusual rhythmic patterns and irregular accents. His advanced treatment of the folk style uses only fragments of melody combined with great originality. The Mazurkas are Chopin's most personal invention and are more innovative than the corresponding Chopin Waltzes written at the same time. Of the short works the Mazurkas capture the full range of Chopin's genius and show a significant stylistic development unmatched by the other forms; "perhaps nowhere else do we feel so powerfully his combination of fastidious craftsmanship and passionate intensity." "The Romantic grotesque, central to Schumann and Berlioz, is found nowhere else in Chopin with such clarity as in the mazurkas."

In the Opp.17&24 works Chopin starts to "transform the mazurka from a miniature salon piece into something more ambitious." In his Op.41 set of 1840 "we find the first of Chopin's dramatic displays of imitative polyphony at the return of the opening theme," a technique used regularly in later mazurkas and "most spectacularly in the Fourth Ballade." As a traditionalist Chopin placed counterpoint above harmony. It is this presence of classical counterpoint and canonic imitation in some of the mazurkas after 1840 that make these the most learned of Chopin's works.

Sonatas

Schumann said that Chopin's Sonata No.2 in B-flat minor, Op.35 with its "feverish galloping of the opening movement" and the third movement funeral march was just a pretext for his gathering together "four of his wildest children." Schumann was making the point that the four movements do not seem to fit naturally together to produce a whole. In this sonata Chopin assembles four rather diverse pieces under one roof. Some critics point to the fact that the *Marche Funebre* third movement was composed two years before the rest of the work as support for Schumann's criticism.

In contrast, critic David Nice feels instead that "all the previous ingredients of Chopin's shorter pieces are knitted into a compelling whole." Chopin holds this sonata together not through the cyclical device of quoting from earlier movements, but by creating in the sonata a unity of tone and harmonic color. "Chopin's mastery of tone color is incontestable; his works reveal a range of sonorities unsurpassed before Debussy." Although the Second Sonata created a stir at the time and Schumann found "something repulsive about it," this radical experiment of Chopin's was sustained by "traditional elements and the conservative craftsmanship" that are the hallmarks of Chopin's works. His professional technique and craftsmanship were unequalled in his generation, and Chopin was the greatest master of counterpoint since Mozart. Anton Rubinstein observed that the second sonata was a "'poem of death' for far deeper reasons than the fact that it contains a funeral march."

The final movement is a dark minute-and-a-half of surly octaves moving at breakneck pace. According to Schumann the monophonic finale is a "musical line without melody and without joy." People have claimed an impressionistic 'wind over the graves' finale following the *Funeral March*. However, it seems dubious that Chopin thought or approved of this, given his strong disdain for programmatic music. The finale did directly inspire the "bizarre-sounding scherzo of Prokofiev's Third Symphony." In the finale Chopin seems to bring the music to the brink of atonality.

The Third Piano Sonata in B minor, Op.58 was clearly influenced by Hummel's Piano Sonata in F sharp minor, op.81. In his two piano sonatas Chopin "compromised neither his sense of style nor the energy of the form." Instead of using it for chromatic harmony Chopin uses the development sections for the "elaborately contrapuntal working out of the first theme" resulting in "a bewildering variety of surface change."

Great Chopin Pianists

Maurizio Pollini, Artur Rubinstein, and Dinu Lipatti are three great Chopin artists. Unfortunately, Lipatti died at age thirty-three in 1950 and his recordings are limited. Luckily, Lipatti's recording of the Waltzes is available in which "he communicated his feeling with almost hypnotic intensity." Rubinstein played for seven decades and recorded everything Chopin composed for piano in stereo. It is all now available on CD in several combinations. Rubinstein's "fresh and musically instinctive approach to Chopin has stood the test of time and remains the benchmark by which all subsequent performances must be judged." His playing of the waltzes "bristle with imagination, vitality and insight." Pollini also has released most of Chopin's solo piano masterpieces over his forty year career.

"Chopin carried you with him into a dreamland...Liszt was all sunshine and dazzling splendor..."
  - Sir Charles Hallé

♫ Franz Liszt (1811-1886)

Liszt is likely the greatest pianist in history, the Paganini of the piano. Others claimed to be the greatest pianist of their time in Europe (Mozart, Beethoven); but from all accounts, Liszt was on another level. Chopin may be better known for his piano pieces but he was not the performer Liszt was. Although Liszt composed concertos and symphonic music, he is known first and foremost for his piano music, which was reflective of his radical pianism. He was probably the first who composed "absolutely for public performance...he created material to fit and show them off." Liszt was a charlatan, according to pianist Stephen Hough, "a theatrical prophet who burned to communicate a poetic-romantic vision." While the public worshipped him, "right-thinking music lovers looked on with horror" and, as Charles Rosen states, "momentarily suspending their musical scruples."

Liszt had a "colossal technique, an unprecedented sonority," and he established "the genre of the bravura pianist, the pianist who would assault the instrument." Hans Christian Anderson is quoted after seeing Liszt command the keyboard that, "as he played…the instrument appeared to be changed into a whole orchestra." Before his virtuoso career was over Liszt completed "the transition of musician from servant to master."

Chopin and Liszt represent the two attitudes of the 19th century pianist and both made the piano the supreme means of Romantic self-expression. The first attitude, personified by Liszt, was of "heroic virtuosity…make the keys bleed." This approach emphasized technical prowess. Chopin represented "intimacy with the instrument" and emphasized "expressive richness." Both pianist-composers represented a "fresh infusion of Eastern European blood into musical art…(they) were among the earliest nationalists." Liszt was a great virtuoso performer; if Chopin is considered the 'pianist's pianist", then Liszt can be regarded as the "public's pianist." This is a suitable title for the man who invented the piano recital and who "represents the Romantic era at its most public."

These two great composers for the piano certainly influenced each other. Chopin made Liszt realize "that there was poetry as well as bravura to piano playing…that decoration could be functional," rather than simply flashy or taking a piece to vulgar excess. Liszt "tried to modify his bravura into a more poetic style," and refined his technique beyond merely that of a banger, learning from Chopin that "the piano could be much more than a virtuoso instrument" and that "virtuosity could have a musical meaning."

Liszt, the extrovert, showman and pianist to the public, used the piano "to create heroic self-portraits and vast panoramas." On the other hand, Chopin was introverted and a miniaturist (as was Schumann) who infused forms such as sonatas and preludes with intimacy and emotional intensity. This tempering of Liszt as pianist and performer was fortunate as many pianists of his day could very effectively "assault the instrument" as well as dazzle with their virtuosity. They were quickly forgotten. Despite his thundering virtuosity Liszt actually gave the piano a cantabile bel canto treatment (after the *bel canto* operatic singing style), making everyone else sound heavy beside him.

As is the case in most all endeavors, to attain holding power one needs a combination of style and substance, and both in large quantities. Needless to say both Chopin and Liszt had plenty of both as the sustained popularity of their solo piano pieces attests. While to play Chopin's music well requires a high level of technical mastery, Liszt wrote much music for super virtuosos only; works on "a heroic and even explosive scale;" the solo writing is "of almost fiendish difficulty."

Liszt is an 'early Romantic', along with Mendelssohn, Schumann, Wagner, and Berlioz. He far outlived all of them. At the age of nineteen he settled in Paris where he was exposed to the 'Berlioz approach' and discovered the meaning of color and a "visionary" Romanticism. Harold Schonberg characterizes Liszt's highly original and innovative piano writing as "tremendous operatic paraphrases for solo piano." He produced "a vast amount of great piano music accessible to an almost limitless public."

Liszt was somewhat late in his development as a composer. His works that remain popular and performed today were all composed after 1835 (after age twenty-five) but before 1850. Within a few years after 1835 Liszt had produced his *Transcendental* Études and *Paganini* Études. It is these vulgar yet great works of the 1830s and 1840s that have given Liszt his stature as a great composer, pianist, and public performer. Liszt repeatedly revised and recast so many of his works and routinely paraphrased earlier works, either his or someone else's. He was not very discriminating; "he had little feel for the quality of his musical material" but was concerned much more with what he could do with it.

> *"You either get Liszt or you don't. His music is to love or to loathe."*
> - Jeremy Nichols

His works for piano are fragmentary in nature, often not brought to the expected conclusion or resolution. Despite this apparent contradiction, by some incomprehensible process..."organic unity becomes established." Liszt's music underwent a revival in popularity in the late 20th century but his "greatest achievement was to complete the transition of musician from servant to master."

Liszt demanded more of a piano than those of his day could give. As a result, piano manufacturers were driven to create better pianos to suit the demands of the virtuoso. Technological improvements of the piano allowed the emergence of the keyboard virtuoso to stand aside the 'devil's fiddler', Paganini. Liszt was the ultimate keyboard virtuoso; he developed the piano to the same virtuoso status as Paganini did with the violin.

Piano Sonata in B minor

This is one of the great piano sonatas. It is incredibly original and its musical qualities are masterly. It is nothing less than one would expect from this fiery virtuoso. Liszt took only one shot at a full piano sonata and he hit a home run. It is a pivotal work between Liszt's early and late styles. Unlike Chopin's, it adheres much less to classical form in terms of development of themes, three or four distinct movements, etc. Instead, it is one massive movement presenting a sinister and mysterious atmosphere right at the opening with a satanic statement of the main theme; a theme that is made to do multiple duty. Liszt always invented his own forms, and would not use sonata form in his sonata or in his two piano concertos. His forms have a loose organization and his goal was "freedom of form, not formlessness."

This "thematic transformation", as it is called, is a metamorphosis that draws highly-diverse themes from a single melodic 'theme'. For example, taking one theme and altering it as a second subject, or making it the subject for the finale. The result is that the same theme shows up time and again differently, but very recognizable. It is an extension of the Romantic cyclic form in which each section is derived from the same motif. Liszt used this "thematic metamorphosis as a means of organic unification." By manipulating the main theme throughout the thirty-minute work, it served as the cement for the entire work. The concept of thematic transformation lies somewhere between traditional 'development' and the 'variations on a theme' form. It gave Liszt's music "its own kind of unity without falling back on old forms," which he was determined to avoid.

> ***Recommended - Piano sonata in B minor***
> The performances by Argerich (DG, 1960) and Richter (Philips, 1966) receive the greatest acclaim. More reserved, and more controversial, are versions by Maurizio Pollini and Stephen Hough. Hough's reading is in stark contrast to the virtuoso fireworks approach of Argerich and Richter.

"Often, it is only one step from the sublime to the ridiculous. The Liszt pianist should be careful not to take that step."
— Alfred Brendel

Prior to 1848 Liszt "crisscrossed Europe dozens of times as a traveling dazzling virtuoso of the piano." Starting in Bonn in 1838 and ending with a tour of Transylvania in 1847 he made over a thousand public concerts throughout Europe, causing Heinrich Heine to coin the term 'Lisztomania'. He "made a vast amount of great piano music accessible to an almost limitless public." Liszt invented the solo piano recital in 1839, probably to avoid sharing the bill with anyone else, as Liszt was a notorious egomaniac, although a mostly kind and generous one, making him somewhat of an enigma. He called these recitals 'soliloquies'. "Everywhere he went he was received with rapture," especially by females.

The decade 1848-1858 found Liszt in Weimar at his creative peak. He was done as touring virtuoso, no doubt the result of the toll of non-stop travel across Europe before the age of railroads. It was during this period that he meticulously revised many of his youthful works and produced the twelve symphonic poems, the *Faust* and *Dante* symphonies and *Totentanz*, a one-movement death dance for piano and orchestra. Liszt made Weimar the "headquarters of the progressive musical movement" in the middle of the 19th-century, and focused on conducting Wagner, Berlioz, and Schumann.

After Weimar, Liszt moved to Rome and was in Italy until 1870. Later in life his piano pieces were more experimental, often left incomplete and apparently unconcerned if they were ever performed in public. "Liszt's last piano works were composed very much for himself, without any compromise to public taste." He moved away from pure virtuosity towards more dissonance, even suggesting the Impressionist works soon to come from French composers. Liszt's final contributions were not as the fiery, virtuoso pianist but in bringing forward new concepts of form and harmony.

Liszt's great contribution to future composers and to the evolution of art music was in showing how "texture and intensity of sound, violence and delicacy of gesture could replace pitch and rhythm as organizing principles in the development of new forms." "In his concentration on tone color musician...the supremacy of pitch and rhythm over dynamics and color was turned upside down by Liszt." Liszt's genius shining through his vulgarity makes "us realize how misleading questions of taste can become when dealing with the 19th century."

Transcendental and *Paganini* Études

It was "with the étude and the characteristic piece that Liszt in the 1830s achieved one of the greatest revolutions of keyboard style." Out of this period came the *Transcendental* Études, the *Paganini* Études, and the Hungarian Rhapsodies. The first collection of études that most likely evolved into the Transcendental Études was composed when Liszt was only fifteen (1826). In 1838 he issued the reworked set as the Transcendental Études and yet again revised as the *Études d'execution transcendente* in 1852. Many of these revisions Liszt made in response to advances in piano making, to take full advantage of the current technology. In addition to the introductory first piece, *Preludio*, many of the pieces have descriptive subtitles such as *Landscape*, *Wild Hunt*, *Snowstorm*.

Both sets of Études "skirt the edge of the impossible in piano technique" and both would be later revised by Liszt and "pruned of their Romantic excesses." These Études are an example of how Liszt, rather than compose new ones instead "developed new effects of realization" to compensate for his weakness in inventing fresh material. "The étude is the most striking product of the 19th century Baroque revival." The Romantic étude of Chopin or Liszt is a genuine finger exercise and also an athletic exercise, as performance of these études is physically taxing.

> *Recommended – Transcendental Études*
> An excellent release is by the aforementioned Cziffra, in his other recent EMI Liszt re-release. Unlike the *Rhapsodies* (below), this recording is mono but Cziffra's magic with these pieces shines through.

Hungarian Rhapsodies

Pianist and musicologist Charles Rosen calls these flashy virtuoso pieces "the least respectable side of Liszt;" their charm lies in "the various noises that can be made with a piano." Liszt composed nineteen of these over a forty-year period. He published the first fifteen in 1851-53 and the final four in 1882-86. Written for solo piano, six were also orchestrated for orchestra. Whether orchestrated or played by piano alone, Liszt applies his idea of thematic transformation to these one-movement works by focusing his efforts much more on development than on exposition.

Both formats are a great collection of Hungarian Gypsy folk tunes mixed in with original melodies by Liszt. The orchestrated pieces sound much different from their solo piano versions. "In fact, nothing was ever too bad or too good to serve as material for Liszt's compositions." For example, contrary to the idea that the Gypsy melodies used by Liszt for these Rhapsodies are rustic folk songs, they are actually "cheap, urban popular music." and not folk music at all. As in many of Chopin's solo piano pieces (e.g., the Scherzos) all of the Rhapsodies alternate between fast and slow speeds for contrast.

> *Recommended – Hungarian Rhapsodies (solo piano)*
> The complete set is available by Roberto Szidon on two CDs from DG. The Brazilian Szidon's Liszt is not to everyone's taste. One can get ten of the more famous Rhapsodies (including *No.2* and *No.12*) on an EMI disc from the *Great Perfomances of the Century* series, with the great performance given by Georges Cziffra. A great version of *No.12* is included on Murray Perahia's *Aldeburgh Recital* release.

Other Piano Pieces

Liszt composed some works seemingly according to models established by Chopin. However, beyond their titles and use of rhythm they have little in common. The two ballades were composed 1845-48, shortly before Chopin's death. Ballade No.2 is much longer and is one of Liszt's finest works. As with many of his pieces, Liszt attached programmatic content to both ballades, evoking the Crusades with the subtitle of No.1 (*Le chant du croisé*) and casting the work "as a set of character variations on the crusader's 'song'." No.2 is thematically linked to the ballad *Lenore* and in the same key of B minor as his Piano Sonata, "similarly explores subtle methods of thematic transformation to achieve a range of evocative moods."

The two polonaises were composed shortly after Chopin's death, with No.2 more famous than No.1 and both "built on a technique of character variation…(each) adorned with more flamboyant pyrotechnics." Liszt's *Berceuse* is the most blatant homage to Chopin's work of the same title, bordering on plagiarism and also being in the key of D-flat.

The pieces grouped under *Consolations* are "often vaguely hymn like...with healing potential." Musicologist Lawrence Kramer even proposes some classical music, such as these pieces by Liszt, can actually provide a healing function for the listener. Based on the titles given them by the composer, it is likely he had something like this in mind.

Both Mephisto Waltz No.1 & 2 were originally intended for orchestra but ended up for solo piano. Twenty years separate them (around 1860 and 1880) and differences are obvious. No.1 is typical of the extroverted Liszt while No.2 contains sparer textures typical of his later works.

A major work, spanning several decades, is the trilogy *Années de peleringe* ('Years of Pilgrimage'). Books I and II were composed in the 1830s/40s at the height of Liszt's virtuosic powers, while the third book was written much later (1867-77) when Liszt had already been ordained a priest. The pieces comprising the books are programmatic pieces evoking places on Liszt's travels (pilgrimage) through Europe, they are "tone poems that sum up Liszt's emotions for the places he visited." The first year (Book I) is titled *Suisse* and portrays the Swiss mountain landscape. The nine pieces are youthful and energetic, virtuosic and showy, completely consistent with Liszt's rock star status at the time (1835) and include such portraits as 'Chapel of William Tell', 'Lake Wallenstadt', and 'Bells of Geneva'.

The seven pieces of Book II (the second year, *Italie*) were mostly inspired by Italian art viewed by Liszt through Italy (1837-49), including paintings by Raphael and sculptures by Michelangelo. The much later Book III does not have a specific place as a subtitle and is the product of a much different period in Liszt's life and career. As a result "the tempos are mostly slow and the moods meditative or mournful."

Recommended – Liszt Assorted piano pieces

Some pianists are very well-known as interpreters of Liszt; Stephen Hough is one of the best-known modern day specialists. He has at least two collections of Liszt piano music (one contains his controversial reading of the *Sonata*), both an assortment of better-known as well as more obscure works. Leif Ove Andsnes has a very appealing Liszt collection on EMI. If you enjoy Liszt, you will need several different CDs in order to get fully exposed to the breadth of his piano writing.

♪ The Late Romantics

♫ Johannes Brahms (1833-1897)

Brahms was born in Hamburg and there are apocryphal tales of how rough his childhood was and how his parents forced the teenager to play in waterfront dives and to be exposed to houses of ill-repute. This is revisionist history in an attempt to explain Brahms' gruff exterior and his social challenges. However, he was crude, "If I have failed to offend anyone here tonight I apologize." Usually cranky, he had strong opinions about most other composers, supporting some (e.g., Dvořák) while ignoring others. Brahms' lasting image is not the dashing blonde-haired man of his youth but of a shaggy beard and deliberately partly unkempt appearance, "like a grumpy Santa Claus…an overbearing professor." Discovered in 1853 by Schumann in Düsseldorf, Brahms became very close to Clara after Robert's death, a relationship that sparked much speculation among music historians. Contrary to popular belief Brahms possessed a caring side that his friends, particularly Clara Schumann, must have seen.

Brahms was the consummate 'Romantic classicist', the last of the "three B's" (with Bach and Beethoven) according to conductor Hans von Bülow. Devoted to traditional forms he abhorred programmatic music and wrote none. Brahms' style represented "the renovation of music as an abstract art and the resuscitation of its traditional forms" and he was "chiefly concerned with achieving structural integrity." But he did not merely preserve tradition. "Nowadays it seems obvious that Brahms…greatly renewed it," reviving the ancient art of polyphony combined with his expertise in variation form and organic development. Contrary to the theories of several prominent 20th century musicologists (Peter Latham, Donald Tovey) Brahms "had made a huge impact on the evolution of music in the 20th century." At its best his music "combines rigorous argument with expression that is rich, nuanced, and emotionally probing."

In Vienna Brahms was the leader of the 'absolute music' camp in opposition to the progressives such as Wagner and Liszt. The 'absolute' camp was supported by long-time and influential music critic Eduard Hanslick, who began his reign as the most powerful music critic in Vienna at the age of twenty-three in 1848. He would hold this title for half a century. From Hanslick the art of criticism was created. Unlike Bruckner, Brahms was not dissuaded by criticism. However, again unlike Bruckner, Brahms enjoyed the full support and endorsement of the powerful Hanslick.

The piano was central to Brahms' compositions and his musical thinking. His solo piano works divide neatly into three periods, all displaying different approaches to composition. His late solo piano music "hides within it, whole lexicons of the tenderest kind of private feelings." Despite the trend in his day to move away from classical forms and to fully embrace Romanticism, Brahms would not. He was the 'keeper of the flame' and preferred to follow the old masters and use counterpoint, variation and sonata form. "The sense of the irrecoverable past is omnipresent in the music of Brahms...(he) made music out of his openly expressed regret that he was born too late." Although Brahms could, as with Beethoven, be considered a consummate 'Romantic Classicist', as musicologist Jeremy Montagu observes, "Beethoven's piano was as different in tone from Brahms's as it was from Bach's harpsichord."

In his later years Brahms tended toward understatement but "even in his youth he was a master of the twilight tone." His works seem infused with a pervasive melancholy...a "pensive tone hangs over so much of the late Brahms." Alex Ross in his book Listen to This devotes a chapter to Brahms' late period and notes that he was the "first major composer who grew up within...our modern conception of 'classical' music." In hindsight many see Brahms as a 'pathbreaker', not as the conservative often portrayed. As did Bach, Brahms viewed "the entire range of music of the present and past as material to draw upon...a stance we see repeatedly in 20th-century composers." Brahms "infused new life into forms which the romantics had weakened" and he strived for "technical perfection in the classical sense...his ideals lay in the past." He was only interested in continuing "the spirit of Beethoven and Schumann" and "creating a series of abstract sounds" in the best forms to enhance and fully communicate those sounds.

Early Works

Brahms broke away from the Beethovian model he used for his three early piano sonatas and instead drew from Schumann's piano miniatures. But unlike Schumann, his friend and advocate, Brahms did not attach any programmatic or extra-musical meanings or titles to his piano pieces. Although Brahms did group miniatures together into sets, he did not combine them under a single descriptive title and avoided the forcing together of otherwise unrelated pieces sometimes practiced by Schumann. Brahms also adopted the 'variation principle' which he realized "offers large structures without the pitfalls of the sonata."

Although Chopin was the first to compose and title a musical work 'Ballade', Brahms use of the form was more serious than Chopin's much freer approach. In Brahms' four *Ballades*, Op.10, "the archaic effect of stanza and refrain is more literally indicated."

Handel Variations, Op.24; Paganini Variations, Op.35

These sets of variations come from the second period of Brahms solo piano evolution; a self-study of the variation form that would manifest itself in many future works. From 1853-63 Brahms was fixated on variation form, producing the *Handel* and the *Paganini* Variations as major works. "He was extraordinarily imaginative in developing simple ideas into innovative textures." In both collections Brahms "set out his variations as a string of short character pieces based on the formal and harmonic plan of the theme."

The orchestral work *Variations on a Theme of Haydn* began its life during this period as a work for two pianos. *Variations and Fugue on a Theme of Handel* (1861) show Brahms' expertise in Baroque counterpoint in the concluding fugue. The two books of *Paganini* Variations Op.35 (composed 1862-3) are his only sets that could be considered flashy.

Eight Pieces, Op. 76; Rhapsodies, Op.79; Opp. 116-119

These pieces, begun in the late 1870s, make up Brahms' third and final solo piano period, in which he composed eight short pieces (Op.76), two rhapsodies, then twenty short works in four sets, Opp.116-19. Many of these pieces are among the most introspective and probing of the entire repertory and contain "playing of such unmannered beauty that you seem to meet the elusive soul of Brahms face-to-face." "The sense of modernity at the fin de siècle was often deeply melancholy." Nowhere was this feeling more apparent than in the late works of Brahms, especially his chamber clarinet works and solo piano music.

Starting with the Op.76 pieces of 1878 there is "more security, confidence, and ebullience...the pieces are extremely sophisticated harmonically and rhythmically." In his last twenty years Brahms "tried to recapture variation and sonata form...to realize...the old ideal of musical construction...and to develop the thematic material organically..."

In his last years he "wrote a very tender, personal kind of music...(that had) a kind of serenity unique in the music of his time." The Opp.116-19 pieces are "vehicles for his most intimate thoughts", "a perfect expression of subtle feeling". Op.116 consists of seven fantasies, "a musical novella in seven chapters." Brahms' late piano music "hides within it, whole lexicons of the tenderest kind of private feelings."

Of the twenty pieces within the four sets, fourteen are labeled 'intermezzos' and "they tilt toward dark keys with many flats or sharps...(they are) too harmonically involuted and emotionally elusive to be considered occasional pieces." Brahms "combines technique with a mellow, golden glow." All of Brahms' piano pieces after the sets of variations were short and carried "Schumann's lovely sketches one step further."

> *Recommended – Brahms solo piano music*
> There are many good sets available: Lupu's recording of the two *Rhapsodies*, Op.79, and *Opp.117-119*; Angelich's recent release of the four *Ballades*, Op.10, the *Rhapsodies* and the *Paganini Variations*. A good bargain is the 2-CD set on Philips (1995) with Kovacevich performing *Opp.116-119* and the *Handel* Variations. Adam Harasiewicz offers the two books of *Paganini Variations* and Varsi the complete *Op.76* and *Op.78*.

♪ Gabriel Fauré (1845-1924)

"The master of charms."
- Claude Debussy on the music of Fauré

The above comment by Debussy was not intended as a compliment to Fauré; Debussy rarely dispensed with those for fellow composers. Most of Fauré's music is never encountered by casual fans of classical music, but what a hidden treasure are his chamber works and short piano pieces. His piano music "ranges from the gently reflective to the profoundly searching." Fauré's music makes few bright splashes but is difficult to play. He "is a lyricist…melodic evolution is continuous from first to last bar."

Fauré entered the Ecole Niedermeyer to study music at age nine and remained there for eleven years. As this institution turned out organists Fauré studied at first Renaissance and Baroque music. He was a pupil of Saint-Saëns and was exposed to the 'new' music of Liszt, Schumann and Wagner in a class given by Saint-Saëns. Throughout his life he was active in organizations and institutions, founding the progressive National Society of Music with d'Indy, Lalo, et al., and later led the Paris Conservatory where he was a mentor to Ravel. So he bridges the Romantic and Impressionist movements, or the Romantic to the 'modern'. He is "one of the most supple, elegant and refined of all composers" and considered the antithesis of Cesar Franck. 'Civilized sensibility' is a term often used and suitable to characterize Fauré's music.

Piano Pieces

Chopin was a major influence on Fauré and both applied a delicate sensibility to every note, producing music of lyricism and elegance, which is difficult to play but has little in the way of flashy virtuosity. It is definitely more subtle than Chopin's music, inhabiting "a world of ultra-sensitivity girded with searing passion." His Nocturnes (13) for piano are the best after Chopin's set and he also adopted some other Chopin labels for short piano pieces ('barcarolle', 'impromptu', 'prelude'), showing the influence of the Polish pianist on the forms used by Fauré, as well as on the music itself. Fauré's Nocturnes are the natural successors to John Field's and Chopin's and span a creative period of over forty-five years. They possess open airy textures and a profusion of melody. The *Nocturnes* and *Preludes* are Fauré at his most intimate and subtle and the *Barcarolles* "contain some of Fauré's most haunting inspiration."

As with Chopin's piano music any ornamentation is functional. Fauré characterized his reticent charm and unpretentious music as "the eminently French qualities of taste, clarity, and a sense of proportion."

Ballade in F-sharp, Op.19

This is Fauré's longest work for solo piano at over fifteen minutes. It was composed for solo piano in 1877-79 and orchestrated for piano and orchestra in 1881. There are very few differences between the two. The solo piano version clearly used Chopin's Ballades as its model. The orchestrated Ballade, along with the *Elegie* for cello and orchestra, are the closest Fauré came to writing a traditional concerto. The *Elegie* was originally composed for piano and cello in 1880; Fauré orchestrated it for solo cello in 1901. In the original solo piano form or orchestrated the *Ballade* is a good measure of Fauré's delicate poetry. In a famous story, the *Ballade* was presented to Liszt who turned it down, citing it as too difficult, a curious reaction from the greatest pianist of his day, who could play anything.

> *Recommended - Fauré Piano Music*
> Excellent collections are available by Kathryn Stott, who has recorded Fauré's 'complete piano music'. If this is an overdose, she also has a single CD recital, which includes some highlights of Fauré's short pieces. However, the single Stott CD does not contain the *Ballade*. One can get that from Paul Crossley's recital CD of Fauré, which also has the four *Valses caprices*.

♫ Edvard Grieg (1843-1907)

Grieg is the most prominent Norwegian composer, analogous to Sibelius of Finland, although Grieg wrote no symphonies and was much more of the Romantic than Sibelius. His career divides neatly into two distinct periods. First, as a Romantic composer in the early Romantic tradition of Schumann; compare their piano concertos, both in A minor. Grieg clearly took Schumann's as his model. In his second period, during the last decades of the 19th century, Grieg became a nationalist Norwegian composer, as did many other composers from smaller European countries. Compositions from this period include the ten books of miniatures called *Lyric Pieces*, a significant Nordic-flavored contribution to the solo piano repertoire.

However, Grieg was sensitive to accusations that he "merely churned out mechanical imitations of Norwegian folk music." German critics rudely called this 'Norsemanship'. Grieg felt that only in *Solveig's Song* from *Peer Gynt* could it be shown that he clearly imitated a folk melody.

> "The Chopin of the North."
> - conductor Hans von Bülow on Grieg

Lyric Pieces and Ballade

Grieg wrote these piano miniatures, collected as the *Lyric Pieces*, over the years. There are sixty-six pieces in total collected in ten volumes published 1867 to 1901. They have been characterized by the great Russian pianist Emil Gilels as "opening up a world of great intimacy of feeling."

Ballade, Op.24 is a set of variations on Norwegian folksong composed in 1875-76. It is Grieg's most important large work for solo piano.

> ***Recommended*** – For the *Lyric Pieces*, Gilels's set is a classic on DG "Originals". Andsnes' release (EMI, 2002) has the novelty of the Norwegian pianist using Grieg's Steinway at Troldhaugen. Most recently an excellent set by Stephen Hough has been released (Hyperion).

♪ Sergei Rachmaninoff (1873-1943)

"He (Rachmaninoff) was a six-and-a-half-foot-tall scowl"
- Igor Stravinsky

Rachmaninoff was a Russian who, like Tchaikovsky, wrote unabashedly Romantic music. Unlike any other composer he continued to write this music until almost midway through the 20th century. His famous *Paganini Rhapsody* (1934) and *Symphonic Dances* (1936) were composed long after the musical world had moved away from tonality and late Romanticism. Rachmaninoff was "the most effective anti-modernist standard bearer."

Rachmaninoff was a gaunt figure who displayed "powerful, sensitive, willful piano playing" which would make him famous as pianist as well as composer. He wrote "essentially the same kind of music throughout his life" in the melodic, melancholy style of Tchaikovsky. His solo piano music is highly virtuosic "without indulging in Lisztian pyrotechnics." He left Russia in 1917 never to return.

He wrote two piano sonatas and three sets of short piano pieces. The First Piano Sonata, in D minor, Op.28, was completed in 1907 around the time of his Second Symphony. It is a massive three-movement work of approximately thirty-five minutes in length. The *Second*, in E-flat minor, Op.36, in its usual 1939 version abridged by the composer, is more economical in form, better known and more often recorded.

Preludes

The largest set of pieces is the twenty-four Preludes, of which the very famous Prelude in C sharp minor is one. The C sharp minor was published on its own, followed by ten *Preludes*, Op.23 and thirteen *Preludes*, Op.32. These were composed between 1903 and 1910. The set taken together can be compared with Chopin's set. Much of Rachmaninoff's early popularity was due to the

C sharp minor *Prelude*, which "is couched in the melancholy nostalgic idiom that pervades much of his music."

Études-Tableux

The other sets of short pieces are two sets of *Études-Tableux*, or 'picture studies', designed, like the études of other composers, to be technical practice pieces. The performer "must surmount (technical and physical) challenges to create a vivid musical impression." These are more 'character-pieces, not pictures'. The first set, Op.33, was written in 1911 and the second, Op.39 in 1916/17. By using the label 'picture studies' Rachmaninoff is acknowledging the transformation of the piano *étude*, which began with those of Chopin and Liszt, into a programmatic miniature tone poem, but one which still requires and tests technical skills.

Both contain many instances of Rachmaninoff at his late Romantic best and "fuse technical and musical challenges with evocative poetic vision." The composer gives more emphasis in the Op.39 set to rhythmic sophistication and harmonic coloring than to melody. These pieces represent the final installment in this type of melodious Romantic music for solo piano; 20th-century composers could not run away fast enough from music like Rachmaninoff's. They saw it as outdated and lost in the 19th century.

Later on in 1931 Rachmaninoff would compose his *Variations on a Theme of Corelli*, Op.42, his last work for solo piano and the predecessor to his *Variations on a Theme of Paganini* for piano and orchestra.

Tonality, adhering to Classical forms, and evoking wide-ranging emotions, Rachmaninoff's music had no place with the *avant-garde*, who were moving music 'forward'. Having the benefit of hindsight we see that these composers simply took music in another direction, added more 'branches' to the classical music tree; time has certainly not forgotten the Romantic composers. In fact, "history may eventually come to regard (Rachmaninoff) as a precursor of the triumphant return to tonality." New readings of Rachmaninoff's piano concertos, Second Symphony, and his solo works for piano continue to be recorded and performed.

> *Recommended – Rachmaninoff piano works*
> *Piano Sonatas* – Nikolai Lugansky gives excellent performances of both sonatas (Naïve, 2012). *Preludes* (complete) – Vladimir Ashkenazy (Decca, 2 discs) – a great buy with *Sonata No. 2* filling out the set. *Études-Tableaux* – Recommended are any recitals by Richter, which will include excellent recordings of other works; Murray Perahia's Aldeburgh Recital (Sony). *Piano Concerto No.3* by the twenty-five year-old Leif Ove Andsnes with five *Études-Tableaux* (EMI); *Piano Concerto No.2* by Kissin/Pletnev (RCA/BMG, 1993) (with six *Études-Tableaux*).

7

Impressionism, Post-Romanticism, and the 20th Century

♪ French Impressionism

> *"There are details of music which cannot be heard but only imagined."*
> *- Charles Rosen*

Both Debussy and Ravel wrote heavily for piano and added substantially to the solo piano repertory. Although they are often associated and considered with each other, the two are not that similar. For example, Ravel was influenced by American jazz and blues and incorporated these elements into several of his later works, including the Piano Concerto in G and the Violin Sonata. Part of this association is due to critics' claims that Ravel copied Debussy. This annoyed Ravel who would quickly point out that he wrote his *Jeux d'eau* in 1901 before Debussy composed any piano music of importance, and that, if anything, Debussy had copied from him! Indeed, in Ravel's "piano music certain techniques actually anticipate Debussy."

These two colleagues and contemporaries are considered Impressionists (although Debussy much preferred the term 'symbolist') because they achieved by way of their music, particularly in pieces for solo piano, the same suggestive effects as Impressionist painters. However, Debussy's "principal extramusical influences came from literature, not the visual arts." Debussy also effectively achieved these effects in the orchestral pieces Images and La Mer. 'Impressionist' piano pieces are short, focused on a single idea without development. The Impressionist technique was the antithesis of the fugue, symphony, and sonata, which grouped "small musical units…into a great system of architecture."

With Impressionism, listeners feel different tone colors as different instruments and combinations of instruments produce different musical tones. Ravel attempted to de-emphasize any efforts to parallel his music with Debussy's, writing that, "I believe that I myself have always followed a direction opposite to that of Debussy's symbolism…" However, Ravel always admired Debussy and only spoke of him with respect. Debussy did not return the favor but "had some nasty things to say about Ravel."

The Spanish pianist Ricardo Viñes, who was Ravel's classmate at the Conservatoire, gave the premiere performances of nearly all of Ravel's and Debussy's piano music.

♪ Claude Debussy (1862-1918)

Claude Debussy is generally regarded as the greatest French composer, much more so for his innovations in taking music in new directions than for the volume of his output. Much of this reputation rests on the originality of his solo piano music. Some consider Debussy the first truly representative 20th century composer and his "music reflects...the complicated soul of the turn-of-the-century." In sound Debussy "imitated the dreamy qualities of light and air in Impressionist paintings." Through his music he was able to "connect sensory, emotional and imaginative experiences to one another."

> *"A benevolent god to whom musicians should offer a prayer before setting to work so that they may be preserved from mediocrity."*
> *- Debussy on Bach*

"Debussy's music does...strive to convey...the mists and the darkness...without the clear, well-marked structural organization that characterized the music of the past...the tonal world that Debussy created was not an outgrowth of the music that came before." Debussy "attempted to create the musical equivalent of a literature permeated with ambiguity."

> *"Music begins where words are powerless to express."*
> *- Debussy*

Debussy was opposed to his music being characterized as 'Impressionist'; he preferred 'Symbolist'. Many of his works were inspired by literature, especially poetry, as Debussy was an avid reader of the classics. Impressionist painters attempted to "depict personal responses to the fleeting, evanescent atmosphere of objects in the real world. They wanted to suggest rather than state..." 'Symbolist' authors sought "to evoke in a deliberate shadow the unmentioned object by allusive words." (Mallarmé) Thus, the development of Debussy's musical style was "...spiritually akin to Impressionism and Symbolism and drawn from...Borodin and Mussorgsky...of eastern music...of 18th century French composers (Rameau and Couperin)...and Oriental melody."

Debussy "used short melodic fragments that fit together like pieces of stained glass." He had an "infallible instinct for the one chord that would supply the right touch of color (and) make his piano music unique," using "fragmentary motives and little flashes of different tone colors side by side" to create "Impressionist effects such as shimmering light and shadow." Debussy "developed new theories of light and color in music" and "brought to music...a breathtaking landscape of unique surface beauties." Debussy shifted and juxtaposed chords for the sake of contrast rather than resolution. He tried to capture a fleeting impression or mood. Hearing exotic Spanish and Indonesian music in 1900 at the Paris Expo, Debussy went on to create a new palette of sound color.

> *"The century of aeroplanes deserves a music of its own."*
> *- Debussy*

Critics of his time claimed that "no one since Chopin so changed the character and technique of piano writing as did Debussy." He was "deeply mistrustful of tradition and 'theory' (and sought) to replace 'learning' with instinct as a guide to the creation of music." He baffled conservative musicians, his teachers at the Paris conservatory considered his music bizarre, incomprehensible and impossible to execute.

Upon touring the folk-music pavilions at the Centennial Exposition Universelle of 1899 in Paris, Debussy quipped, "I should prefer the creation of music that has neither motifs nor themes, a more universal music." The lasting influences he heard at this exposition included such diverse world music as the tunes of Africa, Arabia and Russia, and the gamelan orchestras of Southeast Asia.

> *"There is no theory. You merely have to listen...Music cannot be learned."*
> \- Debussy

Debussy "abhorred the egocentric hero worship of post-Romanticism, as well as the over dimensional proportions of (Wagner)." His impressionism was a conscious reaction against 'Wagnerism' and German music. Debussy felt that "the 'Wagnerian revolution', which had promised to open a door to the future, had in the end only closed the door on the past."

He claimed to detest the piano concertos of Mozart and Beethoven, and that the latter "definitely wrote badly for the piano." It did not seem to bother Debussy that this position put him in a very small minority; rather, he felt that a piano should sound as "an instrument without hammers."

Today Debussy is considered not only the greatest French composer but also the revolutionary who set 20th century music on its way and "destroyed 19th century rhetoric." His mature works for piano were the most significant contribution to the repertoire since Chopin, and represented a new invention in solo piano writing. His innovative treatment of sonority and imaginative approach to form, harmony and texture opened the door "to all the musical possibilities explored in the 20th century." The glowing transparency of Debussy's textures and harmonies are of the most original in music.

> *"I have no faith in the supremacy of the C major scale.*
> *The tonal scale must be enriched by other scales."*
> \- Debussy

His use of whole-tone scales created a mysterious quality to his music. This technique divides the octave into six whole tones, plus the 'home' note. The half-steps of the major scale are eliminated, as well as the character introduced by the use of major and minor keys. "Debussy's whole-tone scale undermined the dominant-tonic relationship." The whole-tone technique is very limited but, in the hands of a great composer, does produce the "elusive melodies and harmonies favored by Impressionism." In addition, Debussy "used chord changes to produce a fresh sound, not to heighten feeling" as Romantic composers did.

Preludes, Books 1 and 2

Debussy's revolutionary harmonic language and explorations of timbre would culminate in his second book of Preludes (1913) and the two books of Études (1915). Unlike the preludes of Chopin and *The Well-Tempered Clavier* of Bach, Debussy's Preludes do not follow any regular pattern of keys, so there is no need or logical reason to perform them in order.

Both books contain twelve preludes each and were composed very quickly for Debussy, in a matter of months. Book 1, published in April 1910, was composed between December 1910 and February 1911. They were not composed in the order in which they were published. Debussy started Book 2 directly on the heels of Book 1, by the end of 1911. It was published in April 1913. Some saw Book 2 as a letdown, Debussy's follow-up effort not containing as many striking pieces as his first.

These pieces represent the height of Debussy's use of solo piano to create impressions through music. The title and tempo marking of each prelude sets the mood for each piece, ranging from *La fille aux cheveux de lin* ("The Girl with the Flaxen Hair"), which is marked "very quiet and softly expressive," to the *Scherzando* ('playfully') marking assigned to *Ondine*. Other pieces tell us that certain pieces are intended to convey fallen leaves (*Feuilles mortes*), footsteps in the snow (*Des pas sur la neige*), fog or mist (*Brouillards*) and sails (*Voiles*).

It is not clear if Debussy intended each book of twelve preludes to be performed as a cycle because Debussy and Ricardo Viñes, who regularly premiered and performed Debussy's piano works, almost always only performed a selected three or four Preludes at a time.

Estampes

French for 'engravings' the *Estampes* are three musical depictions of particular moments at particular locales. *Pagodes* has characteristics of Asian music, *Soiree dans Grenade* takes listeners to Spain and is influenced by Ravel's *Habeñera*, while *Gardens in the Rain* contains suggestions of nursery songs.

Images

Debussy composed two books of Images for solo piano (published during his lifetime) as well as an orchestral set by the same name. The solo piano pieces were composed between 1901-07, with the first book published in 1905. Both books were the result of what Debussy termed "experiments with musical chemistry."

From the opening piece, *Reflections in the Water*, Debussy shows us his outstanding use of the piano as an impressionist device analogous to the paint and canvas of Impressionist painters. The second set from 1907 contains such evocative pieces as *Goldfish* and *Bells through the Leaves*. Debussy works his magic to effortlessly conjure up "reflections in water, church bells heard through rustling leaves and the quietude of moonlight."

Études

The two books of Études, each premiered in 1915, comprise Debussy's last solo piano work and come from his final creative burst that also produced three chamber works: the Cello and Violin Sonatas, and the Sonata for Flute, Viola and Harp.

The inspiration for his Études was a commission by his publisher to prepare an edition of Chopin's piano works. The pieces are very difficult, even for the composer, who commented, "You can be sure that (my fingers) come to a halt when faced with certain passages…this music hovers on the limits of performance."

The first book concentrates on harmonic intervals, thus the pieces are titled, *Study in thirds*, *Study in sixths*, etc. The second book addresses "principles of texture, sonority and tone color." The Études are "ultravirtuosic (and possess) "a certain icy fury."

Children's Corner

This piano suite was composed 1906-08 and "is a loving reflection of Debussy at his most human and humorous." The most popular of the pieces is *Golliwog's Cakewalk*, which brings rag rhythm together with motives from *Tristan*. Golliwog was a popular doll in the early 20th century.

♫ Maurice Ravel (1875-1937)

> *"The most perfect of Swiss watch-makers"*
> - Stravinsky on Ravel

> *"My only mistress is music."*
> - Ravel

Author and music critic David Hurwitz wrote that there used to be an entry in the Guinness Book of World Records that Ravel wrote the least amount of music of any great composer. Of Swiss and Basque parents, he is possibly the most successful 20th century composer if judged by the percentage of his works regularly performed and recorded. Ravel's breakthrough work was the six-minute piano piece *Pavane for a Dead Princess* in 1899. This is "a piece of melodic genius...(and) one of the great cut-off points between excessive Romanticism and 20th century modernism."

Although certainly influenced by Debussy, Ravel was no copycat but developed his own aesthetic, looking more to his predecessors (e.g., both *Jeux* and *Gaspard de Nuit* are both inspired by Liszt) and deriving forms from Classical and Baroque models. Ravel was far less progressive than Debussy and was only superficially influenced by his elder countryman. Whereas Debussy's forms followed no known rules and often evolved from colors and textures, Ravel worked from themes and was a more orthodox formalist with a stronger feeling of objectivity. Influenced by the structuring elements of the Baroque, Ravel's "innovative inelastic movement...greatly influenced Ligeti and...the whole Minimalist revolution of the 1960s."

Ravel wrote piano music throughout his career, from his *Serenade Grotesque* (1893) to his final major works, the two piano concertos composed in 1931. He "achieved a kind of clockwork precision in the musical processes...without sacrificing panache." "His love of all things mechanical is reflected in the clockwork precision and intricate logic of his writing." Ravel was such a perfectionist that by the time he committed 'a ripened conception' to paper it "needed not one jot of correction." He personified French *Joie de vivre* plus a "dash of Spanish influence and just a bit of American jazz." Ravel referred to his 'jazz stylizations' that later appeared in his piano concertos as "minute stylization in the manipulation (of) popular forms." He nonetheless maintained that the result was 'French' music.

His piano music borrows from the flowing figurations of Faure, the virtuoso piano Étude of Chopin and Liszt, as well as the heavy influence of his contemporary countryman Debussy. All of these combined to lead to the "nocturnal stillness and translucent brilliance of his...piano creations." Ravel's musical genius "expressed itself in the transformation and shaping of conventional ideas into the most viscerally exciting of musical gestures." His most markedly Impressionist works are the solo piano works *Jeux d'eau* (1901), *Miroirs* (1905), and *Gaspard de la Nuit* (1908), as well as the orchestral works *Rapsodie Espagnole* (1907) and the music for the ballet Daphnis et Chloe (1909-11). With the additions of *Valses nobles et sentimentales* (1911) for solo piano, *Ma Mere l'Oye* (1908) for piano duet, and Piano Trio of 1914, Ravel produced a run of great works leading up to World War I.

Many of Ravel's solo piano pieces were eventually orchestrated by the composer so that one can gather the same set of works performed on piano as well as by full orchestra. Ravel also orchestrated works of other composers, the most successful being his orchestration of Musorgsky's *Pictures at an Exhibition*. With this work the popularity of Ravel's orchestration far exceeds that of Mussorgsky's original work for piano.

Ravel was taken in early during World War I by the move toward 'objective' music through the use of 'old music' (i.e., neo-Classicism). For his piano work *Le Tombeau de Couperin* Ravel put it in the form of a Baroque suite. Ravel's first published work is a short piano piece titled *Menuet antique* that he composed around the age of twenty and premiered in 1895. It "already had the sophisticated precision of his mature style" and showed his characteristic innate elegance. Upon graduation from the Paris Conservatory he composed *Jeux d'eau* ('Water Games') and dedicated the work to his composition teacher Gabriel Fauré.

Miroirs

Together with *Gaspard de la Nuit*, this is Ravel's major work for solo piano that was not orchestrated. Composed 1903-05, its five movements convey five striking images; however, only one of the five pieces attained lasting popularity, the Spanish-flavored *Alborada del gracioso*, which would later also be orchestrated by Ravel.

With *Miroirs* Ravel "strikes out into uncharted territory…a significant change in his harmonic development."

Gaspard de la Nuit

"The world of piano music was turned upside-down by *Gaspard de la Nuit*," which climaxes with *Scarbo*, a musical portrait of a menacing goblin that takes keyboard virtuosity to its outer reaches. This famous three-part work from 1908, translated 'Devil of the Night', contains "formidable challenges" and much of *Gaspard* is violently passionate. It is an "alluring nightmare of a work" and is Ravel's masterpiece for solo piano.

The three scenes based on poems by Aloysius Bertrand are: *Ondine*, the water sprite; *Le Gibet* (the gallows) depicting someone's unfortunate trip to the gallows and includes a hypnotic tolling bell; and *Scarbo*, a malicious little goblin. Ironically, Ravel called them "three Romantic poems." *Gaspard* became a favorite of piano virtuosos after World War II, who consider it very difficult to play. It remains entrenched in the repertory of today's virtuoso pianists.

> *Recommended –*
> The version by Ivo Pogorelich is generally considered the best (1984 from DG). The performance by Martha Argerich is also highly recommended.

Le Tombeau de Couperin

This was Ravel's principal work of the war years (1914-17) and shows "his neo-Classical delight in rethinking popular idioms of the 17th century." It contains a brutally difficult fugue. It is a Baroque-like six-movement piano suite, even starting with a prelude, followed by fugue, toccata, menuet (not in that order) and other movements typical of the Baroque and paying homage to the harpsichord suites of Couperin and Rameau. In addition, each of the six movements pays tribute and is dedicated to a specific friend of Ravel's killed in battle in World War I. Ravel began the piano suite in 1914, was interrupted by the First World War, but completed the solo piano version in 1917 and orchestrated version in 1919 while convalescing in Normandy after being discharged from the army for poor health.

Ravel also composed a number of well-known pieces for piano duet (e.g., *Ma Mere l'Oye*, 'Mother Goose'). Again, some of these were orchestrated by him into famous orchestral suites.

♪ Alexander Scriabin (1872-1915)

> *"Chopin filtered through Grieg and Tchaikovsky"*
> \- Julian Haylock

Scriabin (or Skryabin) was a "divine tonal colorist," his music sensuous and "full of mysterious vibrations." Scriabin "represents the darker and more outlandish side of the Russian artistic psyche." He exploited "the voluptuous haziness of post-Wagnerian harmony." His piano works are "breathtaking in their melodic prodigality…infused with mercurial sensations, breathless palpitations…" Scriabin's earlier music was heavily influenced by Chopin, both in style and in titles for his piano pieces such as étude and prelude. These early works use conventional sonata form and cyclic procedures. But from around 1902-03 he became preoccupied with philosophy (e.g., Nietzsche) and he saw music as a bridge to mystical ecstasy. The resultant works "represent an intensive flowering of a more individual manner."

> *"I was once a Chopinist, then a Wagnerist. Now I am only a Scriabinist."*
> \- Alexander Scriabin on his evolving style

The influence of Rimsky-Korsakov gave Scriabin his interest in the synthesis of color and music but he developed a powerful personal style with unusual rapidity that was detached from other leading Russian composers. His music "speaks its own language entirely and has no Russian-ness' or nationalistic traces in it." He even experimented with twelve-note chords in his final two years and much of his music broke decisively with tonality. In his later sonatas (beginning with Op.62, No.6) Scriabin abandoned key signatures, leading to music "ever more incandescent, intoxicated, trancelike, and fevered." His "dissonances take on radiant auras of stability" in his later works for solo piano.

Scriabin almost simultaneously reached harmonic and timbral conclusions very similar to those of Schoenberg. Although neither composer influenced the other, there is a strong parallel with Schoenberg in Scriabin's late works, although Scriabin, while abandoning orthodox key relationships, never took the plunge into atonality. However, some call Scriabin's Piano Sonata No.7 "the world's first twelve-tone composition" because of how close it sounds to serial works and his new harmonic system proved "that tone alone no longer suffices."

Scriabin produced ten piano sonatas, composed from age twenty to forty-one, which are both Romantic and programmatic. They are the thread that joins together his entire output. He was the first Romantic pianist/composer to not be intimidated by the piano sonatas of Beethoven and Schubert. Most others (Schumann, Chopin, Liszt, and Brahms) wrote only three sonatas at most, if any at all (Mendelssohn). With his Fourth Sonata he broke free of all conventions and the last six sonatas were conceived as single-movement works and can be viewed as tone poems for solo piano. No.7 is titled *White Mass* while No.9, *Black Mass*. The late sonatas "rely less on thematic structure than on patterns of mood and harmonic and textural intensity." His last five sonatas certainly contain atonal moments.

His piano pieces evolved from Chopinesque early works to his final preludes that hinted at atonality and possibly at Webern in their fragmentary sparseness. Scriabin's output for solo piano was staggering, on a scale with Chopin and Schumann: in addition to the ten sonatas there are roughly eighty-three Preludes, twenty-three Pieces, and twenty-eight Études. His 24 Preludes, Op.11 reproduce the key sequence of Chopin's Op.28.

Luigi Rognoni characterizes Scriabin's piano music as "the Chopinesque model steeped in the sea of chromatic dissolution and tonal indetermination." Sonatas No.9 and No.10 are single-movement works in which Scriabin "achieved a maximum compression of form...astonishingly varied within their terse format."

> *"I can hurl myself against the whole world; I can subdue and dominate it."*
> - Alexander Scriabin

Involved with 'theosophy', an occult religion begun by Madame Blavatsky in which man is envisioned as ascending through a "series of incarnations to ever-higher spiritual spheres," Scriabin believed "in the coming regeneration of the world through a cataclysmic event." Pianist Yevgeny Sudbin characterizes Scriabin's mature style as "a mystical devil-worshipping avant-gardist."

Scriabin's Fourth Symphony from 1908, more a single-movement symphonic poem than symphony, was titled *Le poeme de l'extase*. Despite its title it is a pleasant essay in post-Wagnerism and was played during the first Soviet manned space mission. This is ironic not only because Scriabin never lived in the Soviet Union, but also because, had he lived longer, Stalin almost certainly would have crushed Scriabin's outrageous ideas, personality, and creativity. His Fifth Symphony from 1913, *Prometheus: the Poem of Fire*, contains an "elaborate program, ending with the world's beginning and a cosmic dance of the atoms." In *Prometheus*, Scriabin, "for the first time, propounds a space-time association between light-color and sound." It was the first actual attempt to synthesize music and colors using a 'color organ' that projected colors onto a screen. According to instructions from the composer the concert hall would be flooded "in synchronization with given harmonic-timbral effects in the orchestra." It was never put to use in concert.

> *"I am God. I raise you up and I am resurrected."*
> - Alexander Scriabin

There you have it, just in case you were still giving him any benefit of the doubt as a self-absorbed artist. Sting is self-absorbed; Scriabin was just plain nuts - delusional and narcissistic, with an ego that made Beethoven seem like Bruckner. His whole life was "a supernatural dream, and whose mind, possessed by demonic forces, penetrated deeper and deeper into the mire of mystical speculations, hallucinations, and dementia."

Despite producing some of the greatest post-Romantic piano music, Alexander Scriabin had an extremely radical view of religion that put him at its center as a god-like Wagnerian figure, a messiah. Scriabin's egocentrism increased exponentially in his orchestral works, which are the epitome of self-indulgence, and would have culminated in Scriabin's insane plan for the thankfully unattempted *Mysterium*. For some reason, Koussevitzky, who had a lot of money (through marriage) that allowed him to commission many 20th century works, bought the rights to whatever eventually would come out of the *Mysterium* concept. Unlike the *Gesamtkunstwerke* of Wagner, which were stage works with actors and props, Scriabin's vision for *Mysterium* literally would have occurred, at least in Scriabin's mind. This vision had as its climax the gathering of mankind to the Himalayas with the outcome the creation of a new race.

> *"Isn't he (Scriabin) losing his mind perhaps?"*
> - Rimsky-Korsakov

In a way Scriabin's early death in 1915 at the age of forty-three was symbolic. He symbolized "the last extravagant faith in the artist as spiritual force and in art as humanity's salvation." All would change with World War I and Scriabin, like Wagner, never had to come to grips with a world that turned against everything they personified.

♪ The 20th Century

♪ Béla Bartók (1881-1945)

Bartók had "a decisive, almost ideological belief in the example provided by the 'natural phenomenon' of folk music." Bartók's Hungarian nationalism and his quest for the indigenous folk music of Eastern Europe are discussed further in Chapter 20. Bartók "remained quite apart from the neo-Classical endeavors." He introduced decidedly progressive, even experimental, instrumental devices such as the piano as percussion instrument.

Bartók's late solo Violin Sonata (1944), commissioned by Yehudi Menuhin, is by far the best "20th century re-examination of Bach's approach to this genre." In its neo-Baroque character Bartók has "chosen to challenge Bach on his own ground" with a chaconne first movement and a fugue for the second.

Bartók's *Mikrokosmos* contains 153 miniature piano pieces arranged across six books. They are for students of the keyboard and range from simple to severely difficult in an orderly manner, much like Études of the 19th century. These pieces, composed over a long period from 1926-39, are the best-known teaching pieces by a 20th century composer. The brevity and sheer number of pieces compares with Grieg's *Lyric Pieces*. However, while the Norwegian's piano miniatures were Nationalistic Impressionism, the pieces in *Mikrokosmos* are pedagogic.

> *Recommended – Bartók's Mikrokosmos*
> Zoltán Kocsis (Philips, 2005) and György Sándor (Vox, 1960s) are both available as box sets with Sandor much less expensive on Vox but the trade-off is the better sound and track layout of the up-to-date Kocsis.

♪ Serge Prokofiev (1891-1953)
Piano Sonatas Nos. 6, 7, 8

This wartime triptych represents some of the most powerful solo piano writing of the 20th century. Composed during the war years these three great piano sonatas had been conceived as early as 1939. Prokofiev worked on the three simultaneously. No.6 "reflects the nervous anticipation of World War II;" No. 7, completed in 1942, "projects the anguish and the struggle of the war years as they were experienced in real time;" and No.8, completed in 1944, looks back to those terrible events retrospectively." By this time the outcome of the war seemed clear, as evidenced by Prokofiev's coda of the finale.

They constitute a trio of vehement, hard-driving sonatas, which were praised by the propagandist machine for their evocation of the Soviet war effort. Sonata No.8, composed during World War II, has a startling "contrast between simple lyricism and horrifying violence." Both Sonatas No.6 and No.7 have pounding first movements and No.7 has a diabolical finale. However, not all experts see these as masterpieces; the unhesitatingly controversial Richard Taruskin feels they are "ponderous."

Visions Fugitives, Op.22

Prokofiev's set of twenty *Fugitive Visions*, none exceeding two minutes, is a significant contribution to the 20th century piano miniature repertoire. Each piece has its own character and they "sound like moments of authentic inspiration, caught on the wing."

> **Recommended – Prokofiev solo piano music**
> The legendary recordings of all three sonatas by Richter are scattered among different releases and re-issues. A very persuasive account of *No.7* by Maurizio Pollini is also available (DG). For the *Visions Fugitives* individual pieces can be found by Richter or all twenty pieces together by Beroff (EMI, 1983, coupled with the five piano concertos).

♪♪ Dmitri Shostakovich (1907-1975)

Shostakovich composed two large sets of piano pieces, the *Twenty-Four Preludes*, Op.34 (1932-33) that owe much to Chopin's set of Preludes, and the neo-Baroque *Twenty-Four Preludes and Fugues*, Op.87 from 1951. The latter set is modeled on Bach's *The Well-Tempered Clavier*, although it displays influences ranging from another Baroque composer, Domenico Scarlatti, to the Russian choral tradition. In between, another work of note is his Piano Sonata No.2 in B minor, Op.61 from during the war in 1942. Unlike his countryman Prokofiev's "War Sonatas" (Nos. 6-8), Shostakovich's sonata shies away the drama and violence. In fact, Sonata No.2 expresses little of the agonies and tumult of war; Shostakovich preferred the symphony as the vehicle for such emotion.

PART 2

CHAMBER MUSIC

8

Introduction to Chamber Music

♪ What is Chamber Music?

> *"To know chamber music is to revere it...as one of the most satisfying manifestations of the human spirit."*
> - Homer Ulrich in <u>Chamber Music</u>

'Chamber music' (*Kammermusik*) implies ensemble music; therefore, two players are the minimum. Loosely defined, chamber music can be performed by as few as two, upwards to the point at which the orchestra begins. An ensemble becomes an 'orchestra' when individual musical parts are duplicated. The distinction gets blurred by the concept of a 'chamber orchestra'; however, these are more often too large to possess the required intimacy of true chamber music. Another definition defines chamber music according to its intended purpose and audience, as *Hausmusik*, or 'house music'. Chamber music is written and performed for the pleasure of the performers and a small audience in an intimate setting. The intimate nature of chamber music is what sets it apart from other forms of classical music in that it is not intended for performance in a large hall to a large audience.

> *"Some of history's greatest composers chose (chamber music) to express their most profound and intimate musical thoughts..."*
> - cmnw.org

Of the major categories, chamber music is the least accessible to those new to classical music and to the casual classical music listener. Chamber music does not rely on individual virtuosity or great splashes of sound; there are only the essentials. Unlike many orchestral or solo piano works there are few 'catchy' or instantly recognizable tunes that make immediate impressions on the listener.

Opera has the advantages of both visual performance as well as telling a story (the *Libretto*). Instead, chamber music is a medium for expressing subtle musical ideas. It is not a medium for storytelling and not usually suited to the virtuoso. As such, programmatic chamber music, telling a musical story through a small ensemble, is rare. Composers who were skilled in both chamber music and programmatic works (Dvořák, Mendelssohn, Schumann) did not mix the two genres. Schoenberg's *Verklärte Nacht*, composed for string sextet, is a notable exception, although the later version for string orchestra is more-often performed.

Chamber music requires repeated listening, a digestion of the material. Each repeated hearing can peel away another layer of the music allowing the listener to get closer to it and become more a part of it. As Eric Blom points out in his famous essay *An Essay on Listening and Performance*, "It is not enough to hear this or that Beethoven quartet once and then go on to something else. Such a work wants to be sought out, pursued and wooed again and again before it will allow us to boast of its conquest." There is a tendency for the listener to 'collaborate' with the performers.

Another key difference is the usual performance of chamber works in an intimate setting, as opposed to concert halls. The chamber musicians are a team, a unified group, and although one or more players may seem more important than their colleagues in a particular work (e.g., pianist in a piano quartet), there is no soloist, conductor, or star *mezzo*-soprano. One can almost always trace orchestral works back to a premiere performance about which details such as the conductor, orchestra and location are known. This is much more difficult with chamber music because it is inherently intimate and is not commonly performed in concert halls or to large public gatherings.

The succeeding chapters on chamber music are organized by genre instead of composer. The string quartet is generally regarded as the dominant, sometimes stated as 'the most perfect,' of chamber music forms. Because of the importance and number of works in this form, two chapters have been devoted to its coverage, with Beethoven as the turning point. After the string quartet the duo sonata is probably next in importance. These works are most often for violin and piano or cello and piano, but can also involve a wind instrument. Haydn established the genre of the piano trio (piano, violin, cello) and it has remained a popular form for 250 years, considerably more so than the string trio (violin, viola, cello). Chapters also cover the remaining popular forms of string quintet, sextet, septet, and octet with wind instruments often substituting for strings (e.g., "wind quintet").

♪ History of Chamber Music

Chamber music had its earliest origins in the late 16th century as music written for the pleasure of performers and of a few listeners rather than for practical purposes such as dance, liturgy or ceremony. From the end of the 1500s through the 1600s there was a rise in the popularity of ensemble music (three to six players) for viols or other instruments that signaled the birth of chamber music. The term 'consort' was used in some parts to designate an ensemble. 'Whole consort' indicated an ensemble comprised of instruments of the same family; 'broken consort' indicated mixed families of instruments. Some of the earliest works that can be classified as 'chamber' music were Telemann's *Tafelmusik* sets, among which were twelve quartets from 1737 for flute, violin, gamba, and cello (plus continuo).

The birthplace of chamber music, as we know it, can be taken as Mannheim, where Johann Stamitz founded his Mannheim school and began giving chamber concerts in the 1740s. The Mannheimers provided models for extreme contrasts between thematic groups, leading to 'sonata form'.

Johann Sebastian's most famous son, Johann Christian Bach followed the Mannheim model in seminal works such as his Op.11 for mixed wind and string quintet.

Around the same time some composers began producing quartets in Vienna and Munich. None of this music has endured and it was left to Joseph Haydn to endow the quartet with substance as none did before him. Chamber music began as amateur music performed in private homes by residents and their friends. Unlike orchestral music which was performed by professional musicians (with amateurs filling in the gaps as needed), chamber music in the Classical period was composed primarily for performance by amateurs in private. Schubert and his circle of fellow Viennese bohemian musicians were well-known for their intimate get-togethers to perform chamber music (much of it written by Schubert). As chamber works became more demanding (starting around the time of Beethoven), performance became the arena of professional musicians.

Chamber music as a substantial genre of music started in the Baroque. There was much music written for violin and harpsichord as well as in the trio sonata form, the dominant instrumental ensemble form of the Baroque, which was for two melodic instruments, usually strings, with *continuo* (keyboard and stringed bass instrument). The trio sonata was the central chamber music form of the mid- to late Baroque, from the late 1600s to mid-1700s, with prominent composers embracing the form: Corelli with his Opp.1-4; Purcell's *Sonatas of Three Parts* and *Sonatas of Four Parts* touch a "characteristically English vein of melancholy." In the last quarter of the 1600s chamber music, "disregarding the inroads of the concerted manner of composition," had finally made a clean break from orchestral music.

In Baroque trio sonatas the keyboard was relegated to the supporting role of continuo. However, at the beginning of the Classical era, as polyphonic writing faded out, the first violin took over undisputed leadership in the ensemble. The result was that the keyboard (first harpsichord, then piano) was relieved of its menial task and new chamber ensemble combinations with strings and keyboard (e.g., piano trio). The place of the keyboard was taken by another stringed instrument, forming the string trio, quartet, etc. In the second half of the 18th century the string quartet edged out the trio sonata as the principal instrumental ensemble in the home.

The 'sonata' is the earliest extended genre of 'absolute' instrumental music. But chamber music as we know it really began in the Classical period as composers wrote a separate part for each instrument. Up until that time, there were always ensemble members simply provided accompaniment (often not strictly written out by the composer), such as the *continuo*, and there was often duplication of parts among some instruments.

A major break came in the early Classical period and with Haydn. The 'chamber' music of the Baroque had left "the harmonic background...to the harpsichord player to extemporize from indications given by a figured bass (i.e., the *continuo*)." Haydn and Mozart, as well as Couperin and Rameau, did away with the *continuo*, and chamber players were left to provide their own harmonies. Chamber music from this point forward "consistently leaves nothing undetermined...or in permanent subordination." This led to the equality among the chamber players that endures today.

Haydn began composing in the rococo style with its superficial charm and elegance but soon he "began to weave the pretty rococo themes...into more serious, substantial musical fabrics" including peasant music from his childhood and a more polyphonic texture. Haydn bridged the rococo style to the Classical period just as the Rococo period (1720-1760) had bridged the Baroque to the Classical. During the Rococo period the harpsichord was discarded in trio sonatas, replaced by the viola, resulting in a string quartet ensemble of two violins, viola and bass. Eventually, a desire to make all four strings participate in the thematic work led to the bass being replaced by the cello.

> *"Four rational people conversing."*
> - Goethe on the string quartet

Advancements in winds and brass in the second half of the 1700s allowed chamber music to extend beyond strings and keyboard. Wind instruments could now hold their own with violin and keyboard. Classical composers developed the serenade and *divertimento* as an "idiom midway between orchestral music and true chamber music." The works in this idiom are excellent examples of the style *galant* of the mid-18th century. The first string quartets of Haydn were a natural product of the time, "stimulated by the extensive Austrian tradition of *divertimento* writing."

> *"The search for the origins of the string quartet is as vain as to search for the origins of man."*
> - Paul Griffiths

Mozart produced such masterpiece wind serenades as K.361 for thirteen winds. Works for wind ensembles were known in Germany as *Harmoniemusik*. In the Baroque this type of entertainment music had been referred to as *Tafelmusik* or 'table music'.

Divertimento is a general term for nocturnes, cassations, and serenades, which comprise a type of diverting entertainment music. They are light and cheerful, derived from the three-movement Baroque sinfonia. Viennese composers added movements; for example, the addition of a minuet dance movement yielded the template for the four-movement Classical symphony with its well-known fast-slow-dance-fast sequence of movements. *Divertimenti* bridged the orchestral suites of the Baroque to the more highly developed chamber music and symphonies of Haydn and Mozart at the end of the 18th century.

Examples of early chamber-type works in which winds join strings and/or piano are Haydn's *Divertimento* in E-flat for horn, violin and cello; Mozart's Clarinet Trio; and Mozart's Quintet for piano, oboe, clarinet, horn and bassoon. Beethoven would model his Quintet for the same combination of piano and winds as Mozart.

Even in the classical period, the cello in a typical piano trio of Haydn takes a back seat to the piano and violin. Only with Beethoven's piano trios does the cello approach equal footing with its companions. Haydn dominated chamber music in the decade after the death of Mozart. Beethoven produced masterpieces in 1806-12 but was then silent until 1824 when he began his late string quartets.

The great bulk of chamber music is written using the same template as symphonies, not surprising considering Haydn was responsible for stabilizing modern chamber forms and the symphony. This template is specifically a sonata-form opening movement, a slow second followed by a dance-like third movement, concluding with an upbeat finale often in rondo or sonata-rondo form. Many string quartets can be viewed as symphonies written for four string players.

In the 20th century Paul Hindemith (1895-1963) wrote a tremendous amount of chamber works. As a very accomplished violist (and member of the Amar Quartet) it is not surprising that he produced, in addition to viola concertos, four sonatas for solo viola and three for viola and piano. Amazingly, he composed at least one sonata for every standard orchestral instrument, including trombone, bass tuba, and bassoon, and for several different horns, some of which can be performed by saxophone. He also wrote chamber works for various combinations of instruments, including a quartet for clarinet, violin, cello and piano, a septet for winds, a sonata for horns, and a clarinet quintet.

"Even at the end of the turbulent 20th century, the usual definition of chamber music seems constant and secure: music performed by a small group of players…one on a part…emphasizing subtlety and intimacy…the traditional criteria still hold." However, although chamber music "had earlier been an overwhelmingly 'absolute' or 'pure music' genre," the 20th century saw a marked increase in 'programmatic' chamber music. Famous examples include the two string quartets of Janáček and Boulez's *Le marteau sans maitre*. Schoenberg's *Verklärte Nacht*, also programmatic and taken from a literary work, first appeared in 1899 as a string sextet.

For 150 years beginning with Haydn's Op.20 and Op.33 sets, the string quartet had dominated as the most highly-regarded chamber genre. However, 20th-century chamber music has refused to anoint any single ensemble as the leader, with composers writing for all combinations, adding percussion as a participant and even combining only percussionists.

♪ The Chamber Ensemble – The Players

There are many ensembles performing chamber music. Some have a permanent membership while others are comprised of artists coming together for the occasion. It is also very common for an individual performer, even a star such as Yo-Yo Ma, to join a chamber ensemble as a featured musician or soloist.

Popular ensembles often survive in name for decades but with changing rosters. The Juilliard Quartet, The Beaux Arts Trio, the Borodin Quartet, all existed for many years with varying rosters. However, although some of the players may change, these ensembles aim to retain their core sound and expertise. This is usually accomplished through continuity; in other words, one or two members stay with the group for a long period while other members come and go. Thus, a core group is always present.

For piano trio works the ageless Beaux Arts Trio, formed in 1955, is the standard. The three members also have recorded piano quartets and quintets by augmenting the trio with additional string players. Another excellent piano trio ensemble is the Florestan Trio led by pianist Susan Tomes, who is also a member of the quartet Domus.

In the case of works for two players (so-called 'sonatas'), the performers are presented as individuals and almost never considered an ensemble, even if the two otherwise form part of a trio, quartet, etc. One has to be careful about the chamber ensemble as the combination of the best musicians does not necessarily produce an effective group or even guarantee a good performance. It is analogous to a sports all-star team in which the total could actually be less than the sum of the parts, despite the individual talents. Such an ensemble could be ineffective if there is poor chemistry or if all members are not 'team players.'

Rarely are the best chamber ensembles composed of individual virtuoso performers, as virtuosity is not what chamber music is about. However, many virtuoso performers do partner with standing chamber groups, most often well-known pianists (e.g., Sviatoslav Richter with the Borodin Quartet for Dvorak's piano quintets) or join up with other solo artists to form a chamber 'dream team' (e.g., YoYo Ma, Isaac Stern, Jamie Laredo and Emmanuel Ax on Brahms' piano quartets, among others). Also, Menahem Pressler of the Beaux Arts Trio, probably the leading chamber pianist, is not found as a soloist on recordings of famous piano concertos. But Pressler has provided his considerable talents as a chamber musician to the Emerson String Quartet for recordings of Dvorak's Piano Quintet and Quartet in E-flat, as has pianist Leon Fleisher recently on Brahms' Piano Quintet.

- 9 -

Chamber Sonatas & Trios

Chamber music began with strings and remains dominated by strings (violin, viola, and cello). But chamber music allowed the keyboard to move beyond its previous ancillary *continuo* role into "a more honorable position" begun by Haydn with his many piano trios, and furthered by Mozart in his G minor Piano Quartet. The keyboard acquired a new function as partner to the strings, and before long, a dominant partner. By the late Romantic period, chamber works with a prominent piano role allowed the pianist "to regard himself as playing a concerto with stringed accompaniment."

The familiar chamber music forms were mostly developed and mastered during the Classical and Romantic periods. The most popular genres for duo and three players, respectively, are the violin sonata and the piano trio. The chamber sonata, a work usually for piano and a stringed instrument, but sometimes with a wind instrument in place of the piano or string, is second in prominence only to the string quartet among chamber forms.

While the 'piano sonata' denotes a work for solo piano, the 'violin sonata' indicates a work for violin with piano accompaniment. The violin sonata is one of the more popular forms of chamber music and by the far the most popular for two players. Unlike piano sonatas, solo works for violin or cello are usually indicated as 'solo' or 'unaccompanied' works. (e.g., Bach's 'Unaccompanied' Cello Suites). As discussed, piano players far outnumbered violin players, both amateur and professional; thus, music for solo piano, or that included piano, dominated the compositions of the day.

The cello sonata, coupling cello with piano, is common; many composers have composed at least one work in this form. The two instruments blend together very well; in fact, many find the combination preferable to violin with piano. The cello is second only to the violin as a stringed instrument in chamber music, as it is a participant in virtually all chamber works featuring stringed ensembles (piano and string trios, quartets, quintets, et al.).

Piano trios, with the trio being piano, violin and cello, are among the more popular chamber music arrangements. No less than six major composers (see below) composed significant works and/or prolifically in this form. The piano trio is a challenging medium; the composer must make sure the cello part is not overwhelmed by the pianist and violin, to avoid the reduction of the cello to a *continuo* role.

Violin sonatas, piano trios, piano quartets and quintets were considered piano music well into the 19th century, and as such "were expected to be simple enough in style and technical difficulty to appeal to amateurs." However, Mozart's publisher complained that his piano quartets were too difficult (for amateurs).

The piano trio of Haydn derives from the Baroque 'trio sonata' consisting of two string instruments accompanied by keyboard and a bass part (*continuo*). Prior to the trios of Haydn and Mozart the cello was simply a continuo instrument and composers did not write unique parts for it. Instead, the cello almost invariably reproduced the part of the keyboard (harpsichord) player's left hand. This is still the case in Mozart's First Piano Trio, in B-flat, K.254. This work from 1776 is actually more of a Divertimento, but with fewer movements. The rest of Mozart's piano trios are true piano trios.

Although the trios of Mozart and Haydn are true chamber works because the two strings have unique parts, the cello only reached parity with the other instruments in the piano trios and cello sonatas of Beethoven. Neither Haydn nor Mozart wrote cello sonatas, as this would have required a role for the cello that simply was not considered in their time.

♪ Wolfgang Amadeus Mozart

Violin Sonatas

Mozart liked to perform chamber music himself and preferred the part of the viola because he liked to be in the middle of the harmony. Mozart wrote many violin sonatas, including early works before the age of ten. But it is the more than twenty mature violin sonatas from the period 1778-88, including two sets of variations for violin and piano that cemented his contribution to this form.

In the sonatas up to this time the violin had generally been of secondary importance but in the early years of this ten-year period, beginning with K.304, the violin quickly increases in importance, mingles with the keyboard as equal partner, and achieves *concertante* status with the piano with the five sonatas K.376-80 from 1779-81. From these works onward Mozart establishes a duo sonata style clearly his own. His last four sonatas are masterpieces, concluding with K.547 in F from the summer of 1788.

> *Recommended – Mozart Violin Sonatas*
> For the last sixteen 'mature' sonatas (*Nos.20-35*) the choice is between Perlman/Barenboim (DG) and Goldberg/Lupu (Decca). Also good is the dynamic team of Dumay/Pires (DG) on a single disc containing *Nos.18, 21, 26, 27*.

Piano Trios

Mozart composed six piano trios, all in major keys. It was Mozart and Haydn who brought the piano trio to its maturity, further refined by Beethoven and Schubert. The major Romantic chamber composers (Mendelssohn, Schumann, Dvořák, and Brahms) all produced multiple piano trios that have long established themselves in the chamber repertoire.

The first of Mozart's piano trios is actually the *Divertimento* in B flat, K.254, from 1776, although Mozart had composed several pieces for keyboard trio that are actually harpsichord sonatas "adorned by an optional 'accompaniment' for violin (or flute) and cello." K.254 is still not genuine chamber music or piano trio because the cello simply doubles the piano left-hand; even the function of the violin is little more than ornamental.

However, the remaining piano trios of Mozart are true chamber music wherein the violin and cello are not simply accompaniment but participatory, although the cello part would have to wait until Beethoven to be fully emancipated and to stand on its own. These trios, starting with K.496, were written in a short span of less than two-and-a-half years in 1786 to 1788. The last two, K.542 and K.548, produced in 1788 at the time of Mozart's three great and final symphonies. K.548 shares the key of C major with the *Jupiter* Symphony.

The works are not particularly difficult, relatively speaking, the most challenging part logically being for the piano. Mozart intended these trios for consumption mostly by amateur musicians in Vienna. To make them marketable to that audience Mozart ensured his string writing did not require virtuoso performers. They are all spirited works in major keys and not intended to be as probing as his G minor Piano Quartet, K.478.

String Trios

Less popular than the piano trio, the string trio (violin, viola, and cello) comprises a minor portion of the popular chamber music repertoire, despite Haydn composing an astonishing sixty-seven of them. Because of the 'difficult' combination of violin, viola and cello the "genre almost invariably proves troublesome." The viola and cello are stretched to their limits to provide the harmonic texture provided by the second violin in a string quartet. In the Classical period the string quartet would establish itself as the dominant chamber combination for strings.

The most famous, and greatest, string trio is the *Divertimento* in E-flat, K.563, Mozart's last *divertimento*. It is "a distillation of Mozart's technique and experience...an essay in contrapuntal and harmonic richness." The mastery of Mozart's writing for four and five players in his mature string quartets and quintets is now concentrated within the limits of the string trio. It "stands alone, far above all other works in that form" and transfers the *divertimento* form into the realm of serious chamber music. K.563 is a perfect blend with two minuets but also with symphony-like movements "from the viewpoint of depth, expressivity, and seriousness of purpose."

Probably due to its six movements it was not classified as a string trio; divertimenti by Haydn and Mozart in Classical times usually had more than the three or four movements of 'trios' and quartets. Nonetheless, it is a massive work for its time, running some forty minutes with no movement shorter than five minutes. It is also one of Mozart's most mature masterpieces and its structure places it on the level of his mature string quartets and quintets.

The violin, viola and cello are given equal prominence in this work, significant because the violin was clearly dominant for Haydn and Mozart. However, this work looks forward to Beethoven, who more evenly distributes the musical work among the instruments in his piano trios, particularly with regard to the cello role. After a typical Mozart *allegro* first movement with "singing themes", we are given one of his greatest slow movements in the adagio second movement. Alfred Beaujean sees a look ahead to Schubert in the "broad melodic spans and long expressive breath" that characterize this movement. Paul Henry Lang feels that the trio "speaks of the poet's most subjective dreams and desires…"

Keep in mind that Mozart composed no 'bad' or even mediocre chamber music, all of it is of the highest artistic quality, with many masterpieces and several works that can only be described as 'miraculous'. Of the works that fall into the last category, this string trio/*divertimento* is not well-represented in recordings even though "rarely has a piece for such small forces achieved this sort of majesty and inventiveness." The popularity of a work does not always indicate quality, and vice-versa. Don't miss this gem.

> *Recommended – Mozart Divertimento in E-flat, K.563*
> Grumiaux Trio, a 1974 recording that joins Mozart's five string quintets on one of Universal's Trio series, making an incredible issue as the Grumiaux are joined for the quintets by Arpad Gerecz and Max Lesueur on additional violin and viola, respectively. Yo-Yo Ma, Isaac Stern and Jaime Laredo would be the alternate choice for *K.563*.

♪ Joseph Haydn

Piano Trios

Haydn's piano trios are "the greatest little-known treasure of the Classical era." Haydn runs away from his esteemed colleagues with a mind-numbing total of forty-five piano trios. Keep in mind that Haydn spent decades being paid by royalty to churn out music in volume (similar to J.S. Bach) and most other famous composers were not in as comfortable a situation for so long a period of time. However, keep in mind also that there were many other, long-forgotten 'hack' composers who were in a situation similar to Haydn. It is a tribute to this great composer that he created and/or perfected new forms and composed such high quality music when it was viewed by most (especially his patrons) as a simple commodity with no thought for posterity.

Haydn's earliest piano trios were composed for the harpsichord, but as the piano increased in popularity and became the favorite instrument of the amateur, the piano became a status symbol of the music-loving Viennese bourgeoisie. Because of the popularity of the piano among the public, piano trios tended to be lighter and less dense than string quartets as the former had to account for the many amateur piano players and their various limitations.

Also, the challenge of getting the piano to produce "agreeable sounds" with the strings prevented composers from enjoying the natural sound combination of string instruments that is so apparent in Classical string quartets and quintets.

Haydn was immensely popular in his time but within a couple of decades the view towards Haydn's music had changed drastically, summed up by Robert Schumann who referred to him as simply 'the old friend of the family'. Schumann saw in Haydn a composer who could offer him "nothing of greater import." Haydn's piano trios were assaulted from shortly after his death up until World War II under the guise of 'scholarship' and 'standard' editions of the trios. Included in the damage was "foreign material inserted by editors", and the putative 'complete set' of Haydn piano trios consisting of only thirty-one trios, with no attempt at chronological arrangement. Fortunately, the esteemed Haydn scholar, H.C. Robbins Landon has edited the definitive original texts, revealing the true output to be forty-five trios.

> *Recommended – Haydn Piano Trios*
> We are very lucky to have the complete forty-five piano trios, as edited and restored by Landon, available to us through the landmark 1970s recording by the Beaux Arts Trio (Phillips). This set, available on nine CDs, is a true treasure. However, if forty-five Haydn piano trios seems a bit much, other recordings exist *e.g.*, the dream team of Gilels, Rostropovich and Kogan (DG) or single discs by the Beaux Arts Trio (Phillips) that couple a few of the trios on a single disc. Alternately, one can selectively download some of the Beaux Arts versions.

♪ Ludwig van Beethoven

Different from mostly all of his contemporaries, Beethoven strived for equality of partnership in his chamber works. Beethoven's chamber works are not uniformly distributed across the three designated periods of his output ('early', 'middle', and 'late'). For example, he completed his violin sonatas by 1812 with Op.96. All of the preceding sonatas were composed before 1803. Similar is the case with the piano trios, the last of which, Op.97, Archduke, was composed late in the first decade of the 19th century while all the earlier trios were products of his early period.

Much different, however, is the case with his string quartets. His most important chamber music works are nicely distributed with the first six (Op.18) in the early Vienna period, started in 1798 and published in 1801. The three quartets of Op.59 are from the beginning of Beethoven's middle period (1805-06), followed by Op.74 and Op.95 from 1809 and 1810. The final five quartets, plus the single-movement *Grosse Fuge*, all were composed towards the end of his late period, over the years 1823-26.

Violin Sonatas

Beethoven's contribution to this form is very significant with his ten sonatas for violin and piano always cornerstones of the repertory. As was the case with other genres, Beethoven significantly advanced the violin sonata, making demands of the violinist not approached in Mozart's sonatas. "Beethoven faced the challenge of blending his expanded style of keyboard writing with a wider expressive range newly possible for stringed instruments." The most famous are No.5 in F, Op.24, known as the *Spring*, and No.9 in A, Op.47, nicknamed *Kreutzer*, after the violinist who would premiere the work.

His early sonatas, the three Op.12 and the Op.23, adhere to Classical convention. But the *Spring* Sonata (1800-1) begins the move away from established models so that the three Op.30 works that quickly follow in 1801-2 clearly show the disruptive and original features so apparent in his works starting just after 1800. The *Kreutzer* Sonata, its first movement characterized by its dramatic double stops, inspired a novella by Leo Tolstoy, which in turn inspired one of the rare programmatic chamber works – the *Kreutzer* String Quartet No.1 of Leoš Janáček.

Beethoven's tenth and final violin sonata, Op.96, was completed in 1812. He would compose no works in this form during his late period. The final sonata possesses a "heartfelt, exquisite communicativeness…providing a quietly imaginative coda to (Beethoven's) middle period."

> *Recommended – Beethoven Violin Sonatas*
> Many fine collections exist led by the Perlman and Ashkenazy partnership recorded in the mid-1970s in their youth. The recordings are fresh and the two famous named sonatas are available coupled (Decca) for those wanting to sample Beethoven's works for this combination without making a significant commitment. The partnership of Barenboim and Zuckerman would be a fine alternate.

Cello Sonatas

Beethoven's Op.5 cello sonatas had no precedent among the works of Haydn and Mozart, as they did not dare to put the cello one-on-one with the keyboard and thus did not produce any works for this pairing. At the end of the 18th century the cello had only recently asserted itself as a 'virtuoso vehicle', having been freed from its traditional role as a *continuo* instrument. Interestingly, the two Op.5 works, the first of their kind, were written in 1896 while Beethoven was in Berlin in the court of Prussian king Friedrich Wilhelm

II, an accomplished cellist. Without these circumstances it is possible Beethoven would not have had sufficient motivation to 'invent' the cello sonata. The Op.5 works, dedicated to the king, were both composed in two-movement format, an 'allegro' followed by a 'rondo', with the allegro first movement preceded in both sonatas by a tension-laden *Adagio sostenuto* introduction. The A major, Op.69 is probably the most famous of the set. As with many of Beethoven's late period works, critics had problems with the Op.102 pair, citing "melodies not infrequently rough, the harmony now and again hard."

The cello sonatas of Beethoven span the length of Beethoven's creative life; so taken as a whole, they give us an excellent insight into how the chamber music of this greatest composer evolved over time. He created a new genre in which almost equal consideration is given to both instruments. His contribution to this form includes not only the six ground-breaking sonatas (the two of Op.5, Op.17, Op.69, and the two of Op.102, but three sets of variations. These variations, all running around ten minutes in total, are the Twelve Variations in G on a theme from Handel's *Judas Maccabeus*, the Twelve Variations in F on one theme from Mozart's *The Magic Flute*, and the Seven Variations in E-flat on another theme (*Bei Männern, Welche Liebe Fühlen*) from Mozart's great opera. However, unlike the "atmosphere of experimentation and complex references" that pervades the six sonatas, these sets of variations "still belong to the category of domestic music-making and are innocent of intellectual ambitions."

> *Recommended – Beethoven Cello Sonatas*
> András Schiff and Miklós Perényi offer all of Beethoven's major piano and cello works on two CD. Also recommended are Ax and Ma, as well as the eminent Russian pair of Rostropovich and Richter.

Piano Trios

Beethoven's first numbered works, Op.1 were his first three piano trios, published in 1795. They set a new standard for Beethoven and for their genre and firmly distinguished themselves from Haydn's late piano trios. The three trios are fashioned on a grand scale; each with four movements they are musically and technically demanding. With their unprecedented tension Beethoven the "new" piano trio announces itself with its originality. And with this announcement sonata form would grow to titanic proportions.

Beethoven then took a break from composing any more works for this combination until his Op.70 in 1808. While Haydn and Mozart had taken the Baroque trio sonata for keyboard and/or string bass instrument (*continuo*) and transformed it into the Classical piano trio, Beethoven gave the form increased depth and breadth by expanding the contributions of the three players, especially the cello. Haydn and Mozart had established the piano trio with a subordinate cello part.

With Beethoven, the cello is given much more prominence as a solo instrument than with Haydn and Mozart, although the latter had started down this road with some of his trios. With his piano trios Haydn "never achieved a true trio style; the piano is always the dominant partner, the cello almost a sleeping one." Beethoven allowed the cello to do much more than follow the piano's bass line; he brought the cello onto equal footing with the piano and violin by giving it its own part. This resulted in Beethoven's piano trios being more fully trios, and expanding the capabilities given three full contributors as opposed to the cello being in more of a supporting role to the violin and piano. The rise to prominence of the cello allowed the birth of the 'cello sonata' with Beethoven. This form remained popular through the Romantic and neo-Classical periods, even finding favor with *avant-garde* composers such as Elliott Carter.

As often happens, the most popular Beethoven piano trios have long been labeled with nicknames. In this case, we have the *Archduke* and *Ghost* Piano Trios. The *Ghost* Trio (1808) derives its name from the eerie central Largo, whose spectral trills were associated in the composer's mind with an aborted project based on *MacBeth* and the witches in Shakespeare's play. The work is a marvelous example of Beethoven's concentration of thought: no scherzo is necessary because both the opening *Allegro vivace* and the *Presto* finale contain elements of such a movement.

The *Archduke* Trio (1810-11), on the other hand, is laid out on the grandest scale, with an Olympian opening *Allegro moderato*, a buoyant, characterful scherzo, a profound slow movement in variation form, and a skittish finale which, like the scherzo, calls for a touch of humor. "The opening movement has the noble sweep and grandeur of earlier heroic works, but the slow *Andante* movement (the emotional center of the trio) looks forward to the profound world of the later string quartets." In the *Archduke* Trio Beethoven creates not only a masterpiece for this genre but also one that, for the first time, presents the violin and cello as truly equal participants with the piano. It is "the most magnificent of all piano trios…the chamber equivalent of the *Emperor* Piano Concerto, full of golden melody."

Around the time of this trio Beethoven was finding it difficult to continue his 'heroic' style as "the age of heroes and nobles was drawing to an end…replaced by the middle class, the bourgeoisie." As a result "Beethoven…substituted…a warm, emotional style…for the grandiose gestures of the past." The *Archduke* was one of the first chamber works intended expressly for performance by professional players for a middle-class audience.

> **Recommended – Beethoven Piano Trios**
> To the recommended pairing for the violin sonatas, we add cellist Lynn Harrell to join Ashkenazy and Perlman for the top collection of Beethoven piano trios, available on two two-CD sets from the 1980s (EMI).

♪ Franz Schubert

Piano Trios

In his piano trios, as with his *Trout* Quintet, Schubert, "always…the inexhaustible melodist" embraces "the lighter tones of easy-going Viennese virtuosity." No.1 in B-flat, D.898 and No.2 in E-flat, D.929, were both composed in his final year, 1828, and both trios reveal the 'complete' Schubert: "noble melodies, piquant rhythms, persevering figurations, Romantic melancholy, harmonic variety – and great length."

Chamber music was a natural for Schubert, he grew up in an environment in which it was performed and was able to perform it himself with family members or with friends within the Viennese circle of Bohemian musicians. These performances often included his own works. Schubert offered this reflection on his B-flat Trio: "One glance at it and the troubles of our human existence disappear and the whole world is fresh and bright again…it is passive, feminine, and lyrical."

No.2 in E-flat is a massive trio, consuming over forty minutes with two large outer movement allegros. It is a darker, more serious work than its companion. Some critics view the E-flat as flawed and vastly inferior to the B-flat Trio. Complaints include that it is overly long and has less-than-inspired melodies. Others consider both of Schubert's piano trios to be chamber masterpieces.

Arpeggione Sonata, D.821

Rather than the feeling of profound tragedy found in so many of Schubert's works, the "gentle tempi" of this sonata "suggest mellow introspection and poignancy." The *Arpeggione* or *guitarre d'amour* was a six-string fretted cello/guitar hybrid invented in the 1820s that quickly faded into obscurity. This work was composed in 1824 and is one of the few Schubert works produced on commission, a major reason that Schubert lived hand-to-mouth, relying on friends to sustain his Bohemian existence. This sonata is nowadays performed as either a viola or cello sonata where it has taken its place in the respective repertoire of those instruments.

♪ Schumann and Mendelssohn

As founder and head of the Leipzig Conservatory and one of the leading contemporary composers, Mendelssohn was in the 1840s, the most influential musician in Germany. Although Mendelssohn's chamber works are considered by some to represent his greatest music, for some reason they have been relatively neglected while his symphonies, concertos, and overtures maintain popularity and widespread presence in concert halls and on recordings. Additionally, Mendelssohn's chamber music is made all the more enjoyable by its "elfin, scurrying scherzos." His best-known chamber works are his cello and piano sonatas and his six string quartets. But his first three numbered works were the three piano quartets, Opp.1-3, composed 1822-25, roughly when Mendelssohn was between thirteen and sixteen; "all three...have charm, vitality and musicianship." The Piano Sextet, Op.110, and his Second String Quintet in B flat, Op.87 are also fine works.

For Schumann 1842 is known as his 'chamber music' year as it was during this year that he absorbed himself in chamber music, producing both the Piano Quartet, Op.47 as well as the masterpiece Piano Quintet, op.44. Five years later Schumann would try his hand in the piano trio form.

Mendelssohn – Cello Sonatas No.1 in B flat, Op.45; No.2 in D, Op.58

Mendelssohn's two cello sonatas are mature works and among his finest chamber compositions. Mendelssohn treats both cello and piano as equal partners in these sonatas. The D major sonata, composed in four movements for Mendelssohn's brother Paul, is the stronger and the more frequently performed. It is "a brilliantly structured piece full of powerful contrasts."

The earlier B-flat Sonata is in three movements written in Leipzig in the fall of 1838. There is also the early *Variations Concertantes*, Op.17 for piano and cello and there are several recordings that feature some of Mendelssohn's *Lieder ohne Worte* ('Songs Without Words') piano pieces with the original vocal line taken up by the cello.

Schumann Violin Sonatas

Schumann composed three violin sonatas with the first two commonly coupled on recordings and the third rarely-heard (it was not published until 1956). No.1 and No.2 come from Schumann's first year in Düsseldorf as municipal music director. The second sonata is a more relaxed and far more expansive piece than the first.

Schumann – Fantasiestücke, op.73; Märchenbilder, op.113

The *Fantasiestücke* was written in 1849 as one of a series of miniatures for various solo instruments with piano. The three pieces "were conceived as a continuous suite" representing three changing moods, from "wistful nostalgia," to "sunnier blandishments," and finally to the "urgent resolve of the third."

The 'fairy-tale pictures' of the Op.113 are presented by viola and piano. It was composed in 1851 after the Schumann's moved from Dresden to Düsseldorf. The highlight of this four-movement work is the last movement, *Langsam, mit melancholischem Ausdruck*, a heart-easing lullaby sung eloquently by the viola.

> ***Recommended*** – Schumann *Fantasiestücke* (with cello) – Argerich/Gutman (EMI, 1995); *Märchenbilder* – Argerich/Imai (EMI, 1995).

Piano Trios

Mendelssohn composed two piano trios with No.1 in D minor, Op.49 remaining a popular staple of the chamber repertoire for listeners and performers. The work was completed a year after Mendelssohn's first cello sonata in the fall of 1839. With its lively and soaring melodies the four-movement trio achieves much of the greatness of Mendelssohn's *Octet*. Although cast in the primary key of D minor, the work appropriately concludes in the brightness of D major.

The second trio of the pair, Piano Trio No.2 in C minor, Op.66, is also in four movements but is markedly different from No.1 in its detail and complexity. Whereas the first trio rewards the listener immediately, one must listen to the second trio multiple times to maximize the sound rewards of the piece.

> ***Recommended*** - for *Piano Trio No.1* alone, the team of Argerich and the brothers Capuçon live at the 2002 Lugano Festival (EMI, 2003) injects urgency and passion into their sweeping account. For both Mendelssohn trios, the superstar team of Ma, Perlman, and Ax is recommended (Sony, 2010).

Schumann composed three piano trios. The first two, Op.63 in D minor and Op.80 in F are companion works, both composed in 1847. The contrasting keys set the works apart from each other. The First is a long and expansive work, running almost thirty minutes. It is "more personal (than Op.80), with long, warm melodies suffusing the first movement." Schumann's Second Piano Trio runs just shorter than the First; it is less diffuse with a more structured first movement. In 1851, nine years after his year of chamber music and four years after Op.80, Schumann composed his Third Piano Trio, Op.110 in G minor. This trio is energetic, full of both turbulence and warmth. In it Schumann uses looser structures than in the earlier works.

Fanny Mendelssohn (1805-1847) and Clara Schumann (1819-1896)

It is worth covering two female artists of exceptional talent but unfortunately little renown as composers in their own right. Fanny Mendelssohn Hensel was the older sister of Felix Mendelssohn and Clara Wieck Schumann was the husband of Robert Schumann. As composers, both women were held back by the widely-held view of their day that women did not work as professional musicians; nor did they have their attempts at composition published, regardless of quality. In fact, several of Fanny's works were published with her brother as composer; although once some of them became famous, Felix publicized the works' true composer. This was most likely the most expeditious path for the publication of Fanny's works.

Although most of their compositions remain unknown, each of them composed a significant piano trio, both of which were published. Clara Schumann's Piano Trio in G minor, Op.17 was composed in the winter of 1847 while she was pregnant with her fourth child. This break from her touring schedule as a leading concert pianist provided her the opportunity for composition. Clara's trio, "a well-proportioned work, sympathetically scored for the instruments employed," can stand next to the piano trios of her brother. The work displays a skillful use of counterpoint in the development sections of both the opening *Allegro* and the finale.

Fanny Mendelssohn's Piano Trio in D, Op.11, was a late work that was published three years after her death. The work is clearly influenced by her brother's works in the genre as well as by Schubert's two great piano trios. Because she was a woman and a woman of privilege, Fanny was always discouraged from any public or concert performances. She only performed privately in the family's salon. Nor was she actively encouraged to compose; however, we do not know the extent of encouragement received through her very close relationship with her genius brother. As mentioned, Felix did find ways to bring at least a small portion of his sister's music to the public and to acknowledge her as the composer. Fanny's Piano Trio premiered in April 1847 in Berlin; sadly, she was dead before the summer.

> *Recommended – C. Schumann and F. Mendelssohn Piano Trios* - The recommendation here is clear as the Dartington Trio has smartly combined both of these trios onto a single disc (Hyperion).

♪ *Johannes Brahms*

Taken all together and including the duo pieces (three violin, two cello, and two clarinet sonatas), Brahms left the most significant contribution to the chamber music repertoire since Beethoven. Alex Ross feels that while

Beethoven was clearly the model for Brahms' symphonies, the dominant model for his chamber works was Schubert. He composed chamber music over a forty year period with a marked difference between early and late works. The dividing line is roughly 1865 or his Horn Trio, Op.40. The earlier works are characterized by sustained lyrical melodies, showing the influence of Schubert on early Brahms. But after 1865 Brahms concentrated on a more rhythmic development and manipulation of melodies and melodic fragments, as well as contrapuntal structure.

His twenty-four chamber works are all at least very good and solid staples of the chamber repertory; many are great works. In his chamber music Brahms "cultivated an esoteric style founded on Viennese domestic traditions." However, "the intense fascination Brahms' chamber music exercised on other composers would be a powerful stimulus to stylistic innovation in the 20th century."

Brahms truly follows the Viennese tradition of Haydn, Mozart, and Beethoven, and restored chamber music (as well as large-scale concerto form) to the prominence it enjoyed during the Classical Period. Early Romantic composers (excepting Mendelssohn) did not emphasize chamber music. Brahms' chamber output is a treasure, covering virtually all forms. Including the two-instrument sonatas he composed no more than three of any one type. The breakdown of Brahms' chamber output is as follows: three each of string quartet, piano quartet, piano trio, violin sonata; two each of string quintet, string sextet, clarinet sonata, cello sonata; one each of piano quintet, clarinet quintet, horn trio, clarinet trio.

Violin Sonatas

Brahms wrote three violin sonatas, the First (Op.78 in G) in 1878, the Second (Op.100 in A) and Third (Op.108 in D minor) in 1886. They are mature works, filled with lyricism. As with much of his chamber music the violin sonatas are 'true' chamber music, to be enjoyed by the performers and a handful of listeners in an intimate setting.

Violin Sonata No.1 was composed around the time of the Second Symphony, Op.73, and the Violin Concerto in D, Op.77 in 1878. These three major works were among those composed by Brahms in the Austrian town of Pörtschach on Wörther Lake, a summer retreat for Brahms. This idyllic environment can be heard in these works, the Second Symphony often compared to Beethoven's *Pastoral* Symphony.

Brahms composed Sonata No.2 eight years later at a different summer getaway spot, this one in Thun in the Swiss Alps. This stay also produced the Cello Sonata No.2 and Piano Trio No.3. The three-movement Violin Sonata in A is concise but sunny and lyrical. The Third is symphonic and expansive and so makes a contrasting partner to Op.100. Although both works were written in 1886, No.3 would have to wait until 1888 for its premiere. Perhaps the contemporaneous *Double* Concerto, Op.102, influenced Brahms' approach to Op.108. It is known that Brahms' work on Op.102 slowed down completion of the Third Violin Sonata.

Cello Sonatas

Brahms wrote two cello sonatas, one around age thirty and one around age fifty. Brahms was attracted to warmth of tone so he favored the cello among strings along with the clarinet and horn among winds. Sonata No.1, Op.38 in E minor was his first effort at a duo sonata, all previous sonatas were for solo piano. With an extended first movement and its fugal finale the work stresses the darker, introspective side of the cello. No.2, Op.99 is a lighter work than Op.38 and was written twenty years later by the mature Brahms during a summer retreat in Switzerland. Three of the four movements are Allegros (*vivace*, passionate, *molto*) and the work gushes romanticism.

Having twenty years between them, one would expect some noticeable differences and indeed the sonatas have more than contrasting keys and a twenty-year sea of experience to set them apart. No.1 is in three movements while No.2 is cast in the symphonic four movements. The finales of the two sonatas present two different sides of the composer. In the E minor Sonata Brahms employs a "formal display of erudition" with a fugal finale, while the finale of the F major "wears its learnings more lightly" while also exuding a "full-blooded romanticism."

Piano Trios

More than twenty years before Brahms' First Symphony was performed, and while his friend and supporter Robert Schumann was still alive, Brahms composed his First Piano Trio, Op.8 in 1854 at the age of twenty-one. For Brahms, Op.8 represented the first chamber work worthy of an opus number. He had composed many chamber works that predate Op.8 as practice pieces but never published them. Unfortunately, he also destroyed works he was not happy with.

It is a youthful work full of charm, showing "an authentic Romantic flamboyance and all-or-nothing daring." Decades later in 1890 Brahms took the advice of the Viennese critic Hanslick and completely revised the trio, incorporating his maturity and the thirty-five years of composing experience he had gained since and shortening the work by a third. The 1890 version is still of significant length and remains the version of choice today. Misleadingly, Brahms kept the original opus number. Given the unfailing support Brahms received during his career from Hanslick it is not shocking that he was agreeable with his advice to improve the work. This 'first' trio is the most expansive of the three; in the other two (Opp.87 and 101) Brahms packs more ideas into shorter works.

Brahms did not return to the piano trio form for another twenty-five years, with the Trio in C, Op.87. In the interim he had composed the vast majority of his chamber works for strings with and without piano. The first movement of Op.87 was composed in 1880 and the remaining three movements in 1882.

Piano Trio No.3, Op.101, the shortest of the three at ca. 20 minutes, comes from the summer of 1886, which Brahms spent at Lake Thun in peaceful Swiss tranquility, far from the hustle and bustle of Vienna. This retreat also produced his Second Cello Sonata, Op.99.

♪ Dvořák, Grieg, Tchaikovsky, and Rachmaninoff

Dvořák Piano Trios

As with Haydn, Dvořák's life was one of the more peaceful of the great composers, and he was basically content with his lot in life. Both composers were respected, successful, and their lives were relatively free of stress and anxiety. Dvořák's chamber output is prolific – fourteen string quartets form its backbone, in addition to two piano quintets, four piano trios, two piano quartets, and one each of string quintet, string sextet, and string trio.

The two main influences on Dvořák's chamber music were Wagner and the fact that Dvořák was an accomplished viola player. The early influence of Wagner came from playing viola in an all-Wagner program with Wagner himself as conductor early after Dvořák's arrival in Prague (1857).

Dvořák's early chamber music for piano with strings contained much more advanced writing for strings than for the piano, although this would improve as the composer matured, culminating in his masterpiece Piano Quintet, Op.81 composed in 1887, and the Piano Quartet, Op.87 from 1889.

Also in these later works, the influence of Wagner was much suppressed because as Dvořák developed his craft he "retreated from an uncompromising Wagnerian stance and…returned to a Classical style." Dvořák's four published piano trios are large-scale works and are all beautiful and varied, especially the *Dumky* (No.4), which has six movements. The other three, No.1 in B-flat, Op.21 (1875), No.2 in G minor, Op.26 (1876), and No.3 in F minor, Op.65 (1883), all have four full movements, and are at least thirty minutes long with No.3 approaching forty.

The *Dumky* trio, No.4 in E minor, Op.90 composed 1890-91, is most famous as a result of its folk-tune character and charming simplicity. A *dumka*, derived from the Slavic word 'to meditate' is a Ukrainian folk song that has alternating moods and contrasting sections of liveliness; a "slow, elegiac section alternating with refrains of vivacity. The form can be indicated as A-B-A-C-A-B-A, with "A" the refrain. Many of Dvořák's chamber music movements are based on this popular folk form. He also uses it in his Op.51 String Quartet and for the Piano Quintet, Op.81. Dvořák had a deep affection for his homeland Bohemia and, as he matured, discovered "how this nationalistic strain could become an integral part of his compositions." The trio's six movements, with the first three tied together and the final three corresponding to slow movement, scherzo and finale, make it unconventional and add to its unique charm.

> *Recommended – Dvorak Piano Trios*
> Beaux Arts Trio on a 2-for-1 set from Philips

Grieg Sonatas

It is generally held that Edvard Grieg had trouble with large-scale works that employ sonata form. He never completed a symphony and composed only one major concerto, the great A minor Piano Concerto. His other works utilizing sonata form are in the chamber realm, including three violin sonatas, a string quartet, and the Cello Sonata. Even in these works Grieg rarely applies sonata form rigorously.

Grieg's three violin sonatas (Op.8 in F, Op.13 in G, and Op.45 in C minor) come very close to Brahms' set of three in representing the peak of Romanticism in this genre. These works are certainly not neglected, as there are several fine performances available, but they do not receive the attention they deserve as quality contributions to the chamber repertory.

Grieg's Cello Sonata in G minor, Op.27 is a wonderfully lyrical and romantic work. It "has a characteristic freshness and spontaneity, particularly the finale." Grieg was neither impressed by this work nor understanding of its success, commenting, "I myself do not rank it so high, because it does not mark a forward step in my development." The three violin sonatas and cello sonata "represent his dedication to the nationalist impulse (with) Norwegian dances and dance rhythms and Norwegian melodic idioms."

> *Recommended – Grieg Violin Sonatas*
> Augustin Dumay and Maria João Pires on DG (1993); Grieg *Cello Sonata* – Truls Mørk and Havard Gimse (EMI, 2002)

Tchaikovsky Piano Trio

Tchaikovsky wrote a single piano trio, Op.50 in A minor, dedicated to Nicolai Rubinstein (brother of Anton). Composed in 1882, this is one of the largest works of the piano trio genre (roughly fifty-five minutes) and has been called a "concerto for three instruments." It basically contains just two movements, although recordings almost always break up the massive second variations movement into separate tracks.

The first movement, with impassioned and sentimental lyricism so typical of this composer, really shows off a brilliant virtuosic writing for the piano part rarely seen in chamber music. In the variations (originally eleven but nine are more often performed) and finale coda Tchaikovsky presents "the charming theme in a number of contrasting guises" using forms such as the mazurka, waltz, fugue, and scherzo. The finale serves to wrap up the work, recalling the main theme of the first movement, which "is reintroduced in the company of thunderous chords and flashing arpeggios."

Rachmaninoff Sonatas & Trios

Although Rachmaninoff composed in the 20th century his works are 19th century Romantic in style and much closer to Tchaikovsky than to Prokofiev and Shostakovich. Therefore, his music is considered with other Romantics. He has suffered at the hands of critics because of this over the years, although he is more appreciated now given that his music has clearly withstood the test of time. However, the fact that Rachmaninoff was stuck in a bygone era has never hurt him with the public; his music has always been immensely popular, as well as frequently performed and recorded.

He wrote few chamber works and the Cello Sonata in G minor, Op.19 is his best-known. It is typical Rachmaninoff with its potent nostalgia and melancholy. Not surprisingly, because Rachmaninoff was one of the world's greatest pianists, the piano part dominates the work, causing some to characterize the work as a piano sonata with cello accompaniment. It is a large work in four movements that the composer completed in November of 1901 and premiered as pianist the next month.

Rachmaninoff composed two youthful piano trios, not surprisingly for Rachmaninoff both are in minor keys. One is a single-movement work (No.1 in G minor, Op.8), and the other in three movements (No.2 in D minor, Op.9). He labeled both of them as *Trio Élégiaque* (Elegiac Trios). Op.8 "has the gloomy charm of youthful morbidity (but)…superficial compared to the profound emotions of the D minor…composed in three huge and hugely despairing movements." The Op.9 is a beautiful elegiac memorial to Tchaikovsky and in it Rachmaninoff reveals "the sincerity of his grief in the music's overwhelming aura of gloom." Both Op.8 and Op.9 "are imbued with lyrical fervor and draw from the rich vein of melancholy so characteristic of Rachmaninoff."

> *Recommended – Trio Élégiaque*
> For intensity and Russian authenticity the choice is The Borodin Trio; for a refined treatment, The Beaux Arts Trio on Philips.

♪ French Sonatas & Trios

Many prominent French composers of the latter 19th and early 20th centuries (Franck, Saint-Saëns, Fauré, Debussy, Ravel) wrote very fine violin sonatas that remain in the chamber repertory. As for the piano trio in France, the year 1840 saw César Franck begin composition of his four piano trios and Édouard Lalo wrote three, but these have all but disappeared from the chamber repertoire. However, Saint- Saëns chamber output was more copious and more important and produced two piano trios. The better-known Romantic French piano trios (one each) are the trios of Fauré, Debussy, and Ravel.

♪ Camille Saint-Saëns (1835-1921)

The chamber music of Camille Saint- Saëns is unfortunately underappreciated, as his lighter fare retains greater popularity. In his chamber works, such as the early Piano Trio in F from 1863, the Violin Sonata No.1 in D minor (1885), and the Piano Quartet in B-flat, the logic of Saint- Saëns' music, "its neatness, finish, clear outlines…and rooting in the Classical tradition come shining through." He was a superb craftsman and master of the classic style. Saint- Saëns wrote another violin sonata (Op.102 in E-flat) and two cellos sonatas, Op.32 in C minor and Op.123 in F.

Saint- Saëns music is not richly romantic and was little influenced by Brahms or Franck. His chamber works show a "late flowering of Classical elements…a restrained utterance…more typical of composers a century before his time." He produced eighteen chamber works of a huge variety over his sixty-six-year composing career. While his chamber music clearly shows a mastery of all elements of composition, and no one denies his cleverness and originality, over the past century his music remains haunted by critics, who point to the lack of emotional depth, "a paucity of profound feeling," and "a lack of real inspiration in melodic writing."

♪ César Franck (1822-1890)

César Franck composed all of his key chamber and orchestral works in the last ten years of his life. Almost forty years separate Franck's three early piano trios and his piano quintet, a period during which Franck produced no chamber works. Instead, he slowly developed "his unique harmonic style, characterized by rich modulations and chromatic wandering."

Franck wrote what is perhaps the most famous violin sonata, his Sonata in A for Violin and Piano, in 1886. It is the most important and enduring sonata of the Romantic period and has been arranged for flute, cello, viola, and even tuba. He wrote it as a wedding present for and dedicated it to his fellow Belgian and violin virtuoso Eugéne Ysaÿe. Ysaÿe would form a chamber ensemble that still bears his name today. It "speaks the loudest of all his compositions…it's open-hearted and free although there's turmoil and argumentative-type writing."

Franck (1822-1890) was a Belgian who moved to Paris as a teenager. He combined not only French and German influences, but also fused classicism with romanticism. Franck had several similarities with Anton Bruckner including both being late bloomers. Like Bruckner, Franck labored for years as an organist only displaying the self-confidence to become a well-known composer around age fifty. Before he turned to producing several very good works in multiple genres, he composed very good organ music, which is still in the organ repertory but otherwise not well known today. As with Bruckner, Franck was deeply religious and his humility before age fifty apparently kept him from rejecting misguided advice of others.

"His music is characterized by a measure of contrapuntal excellence, formal innovation, and religious idealism." Some detect an atmosphere of mysticism in Franck's work, a factor which may have resulted in the rejection of his works in the decades after his death at a time when musical development focused on objectivity, removing itself from Romanticism by a return to counterpoint.

He was a pioneer of 'cyclic form', introduced first in his piano trios in the early 1840s, which is basically "musical development in which initial material was subject to manipulation within an entire composition." Franck's cyclic form has many similarities with Liszt's concept of 'thematic transformation' in its attempt to bind different sections of a work by unifying the themes. This can be done a couple of ways, including repeating a 'motto theme throughout the work, especially when it is unexpected. Another way is to derive all themes from "only a few primal themes…metamorphosed as the work progresses." Franck "sought to blend rigorous formal training with soaring lyricism." However, his music (and that of his students Chausson and d'Indy) was, and still, criticized for being too luscious and opulently chromatic. Franck was not fully appreciated nor considered a composer of stature by the public until after his death.

To most major forms he contributed but a single work, but each of the six was a masterpiece, and was composed during the last fifteen years of Franck's life. Three of these were orchestral works and three were for chamber ensembles. His three great chamber works were the Piano Quintet, the String Quartet and the Violin Sonata. The Violin Sonata in A (1886) is the best and best-known of the three. It is a "superb synthesis of Franck's own uniquely rich harmonic language and thematic cyclicism and the Viennese Classical tradition." Martin Bookspan summarizes the greatness of the work, stating that the Sonata "reaches out and involves performers and listeners in the strength and beauty of its lyricism." As with his famous and only symphony, the Symphony in D minor, Franck uses one of his favorite devices in this sonata, 'cyclic form', by recalling in later movements themes and material from earlier in the work. This is one more thing Franck has in common with Bruckner, who used cyclic form in his massive symphonies as a device to unify the parts with the whole.

The four-movement sonata begins *Allegretto* with a sweeping expanse of violins and closes "on a note of calm repose." The *Allegro* second movement, which may lead you to think that Franck has flip-flopped the traditional tempi of the first two movements, is a "restless, churning section with vivid accents and strong syncopation." The third movement allows the violinist to demonstrate technique with extended cadenzas while the last, canonic movement is the best example of Franck's "preoccupation with German polyphony." This finale shows a dialogue between the violin and piano as phrases are "tossed from one instrument and echoed by the other." After this the cyclic form appears as previous material is interwoven with new themes with the sonata concluding as "a mighty affirmation of victory."

> **Recommended – Franck Violin Sonata**
> Guillaume Sutre and Pascal Rogé perform the sonata, together with Franck's *String Quartet* and *Piano Quintet* by the Ysaÿe quartet (2007). Also recommended is Lars Voigt and Sarah Chang (EMI, 2004).

♪ Gabriel Fauré

Fauré's chamber output was significant but, as with his countryman Saint-Saëns, underappreciated and somewhat neglected, although his First Violin Sonata is well-known. In addition to the two violin sonatas he composed two cello sonatas. All four are excellent and substantial works in these forms. He also wrote a piano trio, a string quartet, two outstanding piano quartets and two excellent piano quintets. Fauré was a pupil of Saint-Saëns and a teacher to Ravel.

Ironically, Fauré did not originally see himself as a composer of chamber music; he stated he "would not have dreamt of composing a sonata or quartet." His chamber works remain in the repertory, "their particular flavour being unlike that of any other chamber music." The restrained Fauré manner and the step-wise smooth flow of the tunes is distinctly Fauré. He was neither a youth (Debussy) nor middle-aged (Ravel), when he composed his trio at age seventy-seven as one of his last works.

Fauré's chamber works "achieve a graceful union of classical form and romantic content." Taken together these ten works exceed all other composers' chamber outputs in the second half of the nineteenth century (excepting Brahms and Dvořák). In fact, some have stated that Fauré "is to French chamber music what Schumann and Brahms are to German." However, it does not help that critics regularly characterize Fauré's chamber works as "subtly refined", "elusive", and "reticent."

Fauré's chamber works do not threaten Brahms', but rival Dvořák's output, and surpass the works of his contemporary countryman Saint-Saëns. However, other than these two masters, Fauré takes a back seat to no other composer of his time when it comes to chamber music. He wrote mostly pairs of works in each genre (cello and violin sonatas, piano quartets and quintets), usually an early, accessible (but not 'youthful' or immature) work; later, a more serious, often darker and more 'difficult' work.

His relative obscurity derives from the fact that he wrote no symphonies and no concertos. Unlike the more famous composers, Fauré does not have an immediately approachable popular work that can function as a 'gateway' to his lesser-known compositions. Think of Beethoven's *Fifth* or *Eine Kleine Nachtmusik* by Mozart leading listeners to pursue other symphonies of Beethoven, with some people eventually navigating to the piano concertos, the piano sonatas, et al. Without this type of entrance way the 'door' to Fauré's music remains much harder to find and one has to know to look for it. His music will not find you.

Violin and Cello Sonatas

Of his two violin sonatas, the Violin Sonata in A is the more famous. It is one of Fauré's most popular works, his most popular chamber work, and one of the loveliest late Romantic sonatas. It was his first published chamber work (1876), and "the soaring, songlike lines of the violin writing are very much Fauré's personal language."

Violin Sonata No.2 in E minor, Op.108 was the first work (1916) of Fauré's final old master phase, in which the lyrical charm of his earlier works (e.g., the First Violin Sonata) is replaced by dramatic and impassioned compositions of emotional intensity. It should be noted that this darkening of his works' mood coincided with the outbreak of the First World War and the subsequent realization that Europe would never be the same because of it; the Romanticism of the 19th century had come to a devastating and final end.

Fauré, in his chamber works with piano, does not treat the piano as the virtuoso member of the chamber ensemble compared to the strings. Instead, Fauré "succeeds in unifying string and keyboard texture" by crafting understated piano parts. He follows the 'Mozartian formula' of using no more notes than are necessary. His music is uniquely dense but economical.

In 1917 Faure's Cello Sonata No.1 in D minor, Op.109 followed close on the heels of his Second Violin Sonata. Typical of Fauré's tendency to compose two works in each chamber music genre (excepting piano trio and string quartet), a sonata in G minor, Op.117 followed and completed the cello sonata pair. Both cello sonatas are products of his later period when his writing was leaner and sparer, even sometimes conveying bleakness. By now Fauré had lost his hearing and much of his music from the later years is markedly different in mood. Of his four violin and cello sonatas, only the First Violin Sonata was written before Fauré was seventy.

Piano Trio

This is one of Fauré's last works, composed in 1923 when he was 77, half deaf and in his words, perpetually fatigued. Any fatigue experienced by the composer is not apparent in his Piano Trio, a traditionally constructed three-movement work with a sonata-form first movement and a third movement in rondo form. The slow movement "is mostly a meditation on two themes."

♫ Claude Debussy

Early 20th century French chamber music was a "continuation of recent French classicism in the mold of Gabriel Fauré…and avoidance of German Expressionism's hothouse of individualistic emotions."

The violin sonatas of both Debussy and Ravel are late works in which Debussy's sonata shares some of the austerity more often found in Ravel. They also share a touch of bitterness that sets them apart from other, more popular works by these two Impressionists, although their violin sonatas have remained fixed in the violin sonata repertoire.

> "French music is clearness, elegance, simple and natural declamation. It (music) aims first of all to give pleasure."
> - Claude Debussy

Debussy's final three works were chamber sonatas in the classical forms he long opposed. They represent "a synthesis between the new directions he had pioneered in his earlier music and the clarity and refinement of…Couperin and Rameau." Paul Griffiths seconds this take on the late sonatas, feeling that they "slyly sneak glances at Rameau and Couperin." These works, all written during World War I, include the Cello Sonata in D minor and the Sonata for Flute, Viola and Harp, both from 1915, as well as the Violin Sonata of 1916-17. They show Debussy's style moving away from Impressionism to a more abstract music and are "perfumed with the palmy air of the French Baroque."

The Violin and Cello Sonatas are "as free-flowing and harmonically venturesome as *Jeux*," with the Violin Sonata being "the most passionate and violent of the three." The work is bright and hard, less dreamy than previous works and in a new style – "harsh, discontinuous, largely without a sense of key." It was Debussy's last work before his death in 1918 and it "manages to fuse elements of mainstream concert tradition with a wholehearted affinity for gypsy violin playing."

His Piano Trio in G minor is a work from his youth (1880), probably written without Debussy realizing the inherent difficulties of writing for piano trio. The lightness and clarity sound nothing like Debussy's mature works. Instead, it shows the young composer in search of his technique, struggling to effectively integrate melodies with the surrounding material. Debussy felt that 'German music' was "too heavy and unclear" and this youthful trio shows his early preference for lighter music. Somehow this "tuneful gumdrop of a piece" was not published until 1985.

♪ Maurice Ravel

Maurice Ravel was a master of instrumentation and orchestration, as evidenced by his large quantity of orchestral works before World War I. In the 1920s, however, his principal compositions were in chamber music, inherently less emotional and more objective. Ravel took a while to recover physically and emotionally from the turbulence of the war, his bout of dysentery, and the death of his mother. There are virtually no programmatic or impressionistic chamber works, including those by so-called Impressionists Debussy and Ravel. However, we are fortunate as this period of Ravel's creative output produced the Sonata for Violin and Cello, dedicated to the memory of Debussy, as well as the Second Violin Sonata (1927) to join his great Piano Trio of 1914.

Unlike Debussy's youthful, almost salon-like piano trio, Ravel's Piano Trio in G (1914) is one of the outstanding modern piano trios. Ravel claimed the four-movement work, composed in 1914 when he was almost forty, was 'Basque in coloring'. The second movement, *Pantoum*, with its whirling motion is interesting in that it is based on a Malay verse form and strictly follows that form in an extraordinarily intricate structure. The third movement, a linear *passacaglia* with "eleven statements of an eight-bar phrase, rising to a climax and then receding again," is in stark contrast to Pantuom.

Ravel's Violin Sonata, composed 1923-27, is sometimes designated No.2 because he had also composed an early one-movement violin sonata that was not published until 1975. The mature violin sonata shows "his most potent jazz stylizations." The seedy nightclub atmosphere of the middle movement titled Blues was Ravel's earliest attempt to introduce jazz elements in his works. The movement incorporates the major elements of jazz and 'the blues', including its poetic and melodic improvisation.

> *Recommended – French violin sonatas*
> Chen & Ehnes offer the Ravel, Debussy and Saint-Saëns (CBC, 2008) while Chang & Vogt substitute Franck's for Saint-Saëns' (EMI, 2004). Tetzlaff and Andsnes offer Ravel and Debussy as well as several others (Virgin, 2005).
> The piano trios of Debussy, Faure and Ravel are joined together on a marvelous disc by the Florestan Trio, experts in this repertory (Hyperion, 1999).

♪ 20th Century

There are three types of 20th century (solo or duo) chamber sonatas: the modern Baroque sonatas such as Bartok's solo Violin Sonata; the modern Classical sonata as exemplified by Prokofiev's sonatas; the 'modern' sonata by 'modern' composers such as Elliott Carter.

The chamber works of the great Russian composers Prokofiev and Shostakovich comprise a small portion of their musical outputs, as they were both more prolific in orchestral forms, with Prokofiev also contributing much to the solo piano repertoire. The chamber works of both show their neo-Classical leanings and "disclose a Classical clarity of form." While Shostakovich is mildly dissonant and conventional in form, Prokofiev can display a freer and harsher dissonance than his countryman; a wider range of emotion and moods "from dry humor to fierce abandon, from suave lyricism to intense drama." As Prokofiev was a gifted melodist, lyric melodies abound in his chamber music as in his other music.

♪♪ Serge Prokofiev

Violin Sonatas No.1 in F minor, Op.80; No.2 in D, Op.94b

The First Violin Sonata, one of Prokofiev's finest works in any genre, is "a distillation of wartime feelings;" an "exceedingly profound work (that) will yield immeasurable rewards for patient listeners."

Sonata No.2 is more lyrical, being originally composed for flute and piano, but quickly becoming more popular as a violin sonata. Although completed at the climax of World War II (1944) after the Soviet Union had sustained years of pummeling, the work, also in four movements, contains Prokofiev's typical "lyrical warmth with his playful mischief."

Cello sonata in C, Op.119

As with Shostakovich's works for cello, Prokofiev's single Sonata for Cello and Piano was inspired by the playing of the young Rostropovich. The bright key of C major is odd for a piano and string sonata but it does give the work a grandeur and positive attitude that distinguishes it from its many minor-key counterparts. In the work "true Classical sonata-allegro form meets stunning, voluptuous melody in the opening movement...he matches deeply lyrical 'Russian' tunefulness...then adds the kind of impish rhythms and virtuosic fire that will always say 'Prokofiev' to us." It was premiered by the dynamic Russian duo of Richter and Rostropovich in 1950.

> *Recommended – Prokofiev Cello Sonata*
> Truls Mørk (cellist) and Lars Vogt (pianist) combine for an excellent rendition of the Prokofiev *Op.119* (EMI, 1997).

♪ Dmitri Shostakovich
Piano Trios
Technically, Shostakovich composed two piano trios, the first when he was seventeen. But it is the Op.67 trio in E minor, completed just after his Eighth Symphony in 1944 that is generally referred to as Shostakovich's Piano Trio (without a number designation). The earlier trio is the product of a seventeen year-old in 1923.

The finale of Shostakovich's Op.67 Piano Trio consists of alternating dance sections with slower sections. The scales and rhythms of the dance themes are mostly based on Jewish tunes, "hammered into a brutal march," with the trio ending "in the more comforting key of E major." The work was intended as a lamentation for the victims of the Holocaust, the horrors of which had just been revealed in the Soviet Union.

The work premiered with the composer as pianist and two members of the Beethoven String Quartet, the Russian ensemble with whom Shostakovich enjoyed a close relationship.

Cello Sonata in D minor, Op.40; Violin Sonata, Op.134; Viola Sonata in C, Op.147
The Cello Sonata is cast in symphonic style with four movements and a first movement in conventional sonata form. From 1934, at a point when his music was under attack by the Soviet bureaucrats, this sonata nevertheless possesses Shostakovich's usual sarcasm and is "rife with cynicism, despair, and mockery." These characteristics show through in the scherzo with the "coarse, repetitive sawing from the cello" together with a heavy-handed melody by the piano. In the "rude, comically sinister finale," the composer ends the work abruptly after building momentum to generate false hope for a showy, brilliant finish.

One of Shostakovich's finer late works, the Violin Sonata was composed in 1968 as a sixtieth birthday present for his friend, violinist David Oistrakh. Oistrakh premiered the work publicly with pianist Sviatoslav Richter in May 1969.

The Viola Sonata was Shostakovich's last and the fact that it was composed in 1975 makes it the last work by a major composer who worked only in traditional forms. As a point of reference, noted avant-garde composer Elliott Carter was over sixty-five when the Viola Sonata premiered in late September of 1975, less than two months after Shostakovich's death.

Although there is a feeling of resignation throughout the sonata, it did not possess to the same extent "the morbid and gloomy moods found in most of the late quartets." Although much of the work is subdued and uncomplicated, it remains challenging to performers.

> **Recommended – Shostakovich Trios and Sonatas**
> All five works are combined in a set by the Kalichstein-Laredo-Robinson Trio (Koch, released 2007); if you can find them, the Oistrakh-Richter performance of the *Violin Sonata* (Vox) and the Bashmet-Richter of the *Viola Sonata* (Kniga, 1991).

♫ Paul Hindemith

Hindemith composed prolifically for string instruments, both solo and in chamber arrangements. Because he was most proficient as a viola player, some of Hindemith's most haunting tunes went into his viola music. He composed sonatas for viola with piano, as well as several for solo viola. Among his violin sonatas the Violin Sonata in C (1939) is his finest and "a masterly exploration of baroque techniques in modern terms."

As part of his 'workaday' *Gebrauchsmusik* or literally 'music for consumption' output (as opposed to music for music's sake), Hindemith composed sonatas, many strictly of pedagogic purpose, for virtually every instrument of the orchestra and more, including the saxophone. Much more so than his fellow neo-Classicist Stravinsky, Hindemith placed art and craftsmanship on the same aesthetic plane.

♫ Leoš Janáček and Bohuslav Martinů

Even at age sixty, just before World War I, Leoš Janáček was virtually unknown outside of Brno (Moravia) and even in neighboring Bohemia "he was thought of as…a hick." But from World War I until his death in 1928 he composed several orchestral works and a dozen chamber works, "virtually a life's work crammed into a dozen years displaying an unprecedented rejuvenated creative vitality."

Janáček's music and style were unique, very distinctive. He remained as free from dominaant Germanic influences as possible for a composer in Central Europe. "…the natural rhythmic patterns of the Czech language…informs the music itself…his music favors repetitive patterns, often set in stark contrast to longer, more lyrical, lines, or large blocks of sound." Janáček elicits much drama from a minimum of thematic development or contrapuntal elaboration, heightened by his "ability to adopt his music to the tonal and rhythmic characteristics of the Czech language." Janáček wrote only one mature violin sonata (1914-15; revised 1922), a short and concentrated work in four movements.

Janáček's earliest known duo sonata, from 1910 (revised 1912) is the popular *Pohadka* (meaning 'fairy-tale') for cello and piano, the tale being 'The Story of Tsar Berendvei'. Janáček bases the music on a folk tune and creates a work of "brisk, effective story-telling."

Like Hindemith in Germany but unlike his fellow Czech Janáček, Bohuslav Martinů composed a wide assortment of chamber works. In addition to works in the common forms of sonatas for piano with violin, viola, or cello, two piano quintets, and seven string quartets, there are works for woodwinds including a sextet for winds. Martinů employed two styles in his chamber works: the rhythmic effects of Stravinsky (absorbed into his style during his time in Paris) in his String Quartet No.2 (1926), String Quintet (1929), and String Sextet (1932); and a solidly contrapuntal, quasi neo-Baroque, style in, for example, his Piano Quartet of 1942.

> *"I am always more myself in pure chamber music."*
> - Bohuslav Martinů

He composed scores of chamber works in a wide variety of combinations that "reveal a creative mind of fertility and invention." He referred to some of his trios as 'Promenades' and 'Madrigal Sonatas' and was partial to the flute in his chamber works for winds. Martinů was a professor at Princeton University with Albert Einstein during World War II and found that the great physicist was an accomplished enough violinist to play Mozart sonatas. As a result, Martinů composed the *Five Madrigal Stanzas* in 1943 for piano and violin duo and dedicated the short work to Einstein.

> *"Martinů does not sound like other music."*
> - Virgil Thomson

Among his finer works is his Piano Quartet, one of the finest works from his extended stay in America through the 1940s. As Martinů was about to embark on his symphonic period it is not surprising to find symphonic elements in this chamber work. The Third Piano Trio, also composed in the U.S., is one of Martinů's most profound works with a deeply memorable slow movement. He is one of the few 20th century composers to tackle the piano trio genre. No.3 is the best of his three and "a seriously rewarding work of great creativity and marvelous dramatic thrust."

His Violin Sonata No.2 and No.3 were composed in 1931 and 1944, respectively. No.2 was written during the middle of his exile in Paris and exhibits the "motoric rhythms (of Roussel that) would throb through Martinů's scores for the rest of (his) life." This relatively short work is marked by subtle wit. Sonata No.3 is twice as long as No.2 and of symphonic proportions, written just before Martinů would begin his 'symphony phase' in America. It is "one of his darkest and most dramatic duo works."

- 10 -

The String Quartet - The Classical Period

The string quartet is the most popular chamber music form and why so many chamber ensembles are comprised of four string players (two violins, viola, and cello). It is also the form to which the most composers have attempted to make their own statements, even those otherwise not associated with chamber music (e.g., Ravel). "The string quartet (is) four-voice polyphony in its clearest non-vocal state." As Maynard Solomon puts it, the string quartet is "the most elevated, expressive, and learned genre of the Classical style...the most perfect, concise, and self-contained combination in all music..." "Its very timbre creates a sense of intimacy and personal feeling..." But because it is so self-contained it "demands scrupulous musicianship", for anything less is "mercilessly exposed in a string quartet."

The string quartet evolved out of the Baroque trio sonata for two violins and continuo (either cello or harpsichord). The *continuo* role was one of impersonal background, providing loose accompaniment, deferring to the violins. This secondary role would fade out as the cello would get its own distinct part, along with an added viola, to form the string quartet, the most important chamber form, perfected by Haydn and Mozart. In both of their many string quartets there is a wholly German character in which Mozart's "abundance of melodic force...is displayed with endless resource."

Haydn established the format of the string quartet and composed sixty-eight. The structure of the quartet and the symphony are similar so that the former can be thought of as a symphony for four players. Most string quartets follow a four-movement format of large opening movement, usually in sonata form, followed by a slow second movement. The third movement is the usual minuet or scherzo, depending on the period of the quartet (scherzo replacing minuet in 19th century works), then the finale, again utilized in much the same way as the closing movement of symphonies.

♪ Haydn and the Birth of the String Quartet

With hundreds of sonatas, trios, string quartets and symphonies, "Haydn both broke new ground and provided durable models." "Haydn brought all the weight of his symphonic experience to bear on his chamber music." Haydn perfected the Classical string quartet from earlier models and with the imaginative vision of chamber music as dramatic action, "endowed it with the power to bear dramatic and expressive weight without flying apart." He "developed a style in which the most dramatic effects were essential to the form...Haydn's classicism tempered his ferocity, but in no way curbed or tamed his irregularities." Although Haydn did not technically invent either the symphony or the string quartet he did firmly establish the lasting template for both by synthesizing the best of what came before "into a style of convincing logic and permanent validity."

Haydn brought several musical genres to maturity, including the string quartet from lightweight *divertimento* "toward the point where it would ultimately be recognized as the most challenging...and most pure...of musical forms of composition." In fact, Haydn's first twelve string quartets, six each of Op.1 & Op.2, were actually called *Divertimenti a Quattro*. In the first half of the 18th century the use of continuo made the trio sonata form a more efficient combination. The prestige of the string quartet among chamber music genres comes "entirely from its pre-eminence in the Classical period, from 1770 to the death of Schubert." It was with the six quartets of Op.3 that Haydn firmly established "the form and instrumental treatment of the quartet style as we know it today."

Haydn's most original achievement in his quartets was the dynamically conceived opening movement. Haydn's quartets represented for the string quartet a perfection of form. Haydn's sixty-eight string quartets are the centerpieces of his massive chamber output, with the forty-five piano trios not far behind. These two genres dominated his chamber output. Not only did Haydn produce a superhuman volume of chamber music, but mostly all of it is of the highest quality. This is especially true of the mature works.

Haydn's quartets were a huge influence on Mozart and the younger composer dedicated his best set of six quartets to the older composer hoping that "you (Haydn) will not consider them wholly unworthy of your favor." This great set became known as the Haydn Quartets. When Mozart actually surpassed his older friend with his string quartets, the tables were turned and it was Haydn's time to learn from Mozart, and this influence is clear in Haydn's quartets from 1785 to Mozart's death. But not before Mozart acknowledged the influence of Haydn on his own string quartets: "It was from Haydn that I first learned the true way to compose quartets."

> *"Haydn and Mozart egged each other on to fashion from this salon genre the intimate equivalent of a small symphony."*
> - Jessica Duchen

The string quartets of Haydn and Mozart highlight the differences in their general compositional styles. Haydn was given to jokes and surprises, a master of the unexpected. "His themes often recur in an unorthodox fashion." Mozart did not look to shock or surprise; "the expected thing takes place, but in ever new and interesting ways." The popular folk-like melodies were wedded by Haydn into his musical language in three places within his symphonies and quartets: towards the close of first movement expositions, the opening of finales and the trios of the third 'dance' movements. "The trios became more boisterous as Haydn grew older."

String Quartets - Op.17, Nos.1-6; Op.20, Nos.1-6

Prior to his Op.17 set of quartets Haydn had maintained the style *galant* dominant until 1760. With these two sets from 1771-72 he broke away from the *Rococo* (i.e., early Classical) characteristic of a single melody always being carried by the upper-most instrument, with the three other members of the ensemble providing harmonic accompaniment. In the Op.17 quartets the first violin takes on a virtuosic brilliance; "now he begins to dazzle even his colleagues." In the next set, Op.20, "Haydn shows a new regard…for the melodic possibilities of the cello," and Haydn takes a large step toward the musical equality of ensemble members that Beethoven would achieve in his trios and string quartets. These two sets of quartets are on a level that no other contemporary composer could equal or even approach.

A natural outcome of this was the return of counterpoint to instrumental music with a prominence not seen since the Baroque. But Haydn did not adopt a 'neo-Baroque' style but rather combined the contrapuntal devices of the past, which he had now come to master, with the melodic and formal developments of what became the 'Classical Style'. He successfully combines homophonic melodies with polyphonic textures.

The Op.20 set was significant in the development of the string quartet form and Haydn's ongoing efforts to deepen their musical character. "The individual character of each movement was Haydn's principal concern at this time." These six quartets were the first quartets from Haydn's *Sturm und Drang* period, the "hyper-emotive aesthetic movement" that lasted less than twenty years from the mid-1760's to mid-1780s.

String Quartets - Op.33, Nos.1-6, *'Russian'*

In the development of the string quartet, a major breakthrough came on Christmas Day 1781 into 1782 with Haydn's first set of string quartets in a decade, the six Opus 33 quartets. They represented a major breakthrough for the string quartet genre and are the other major set from Haydn's *Sturm und Drang* period. Haydn realized his 'discovery' or 'invention' of 'thematic development' in sonata form upon composing these string quartets in "quite a new and special way." "Haydn's technique of thematic development was able to accept almost any material, and absorb it." The intense, seriousness of the Op.20 Quartets, from the height of Haydn's *Sturm und Drang* period, was replaced by a lighter tone, a more balanced refined style in the Op.33 set. Some of the quartets received their first performance on Christmas Day of that year. The nickname is because of the dedicatee of the set, the Grand Duke Paul of Russia.

Paul Henry Lang proposes that the decade-long break from quartet writing was deliberate and intended to allow Haydn's symphonic writing to catch up with his quartets, these chamber forms maturing sooner for the composer than his symphonies. The ten-year pause "ripened (Haydn's) ideas and the last remnants of the style *galant* disappeared." What Haydn had learned in the decade before Op.33 is, above all, dramatic clarity. Lang also feels that the young Mozart had a major influence on Haydn during the 1770s: "the powerful influence emanating from the works of his young spiritual disciple and friend, Mozart."

A major advance in this set is the substitution by Haydn of the long-standing minuet dance movement with a scherzo. As a result, these quartets sometimes carry the label *Scherzi* Quartets. Also, in the Op.33 set we have the first appearance of the textural '*obbligato* accompaniment' in which the accompanying voices derive from the motifs of the principal voice, usually carried by the first violin. This could be what Haydn meant when he stated that this set was written "in an entirely new manner… (with) a greater variety of distinctive intervals and a more elaborate rhythmic scheme." '*Obbligato* accompaniment' is "essential to the method of thematic development," not only in Haydn, Mozart, and Beethoven, but also in almost all later Western European music.

The 'new manner' in these quartets provided the bridge between galant melody and 'learned' counterpoint, and sonata-form was fully established. Op.33 is the first set in which Haydn conceived the accompaniment as both thematic and subordinate. As a result, Haydn's thematic elements tend to be very short because they have to double as accompanying figures. Haydn's method of 'thematic elaboration' is displayed as he "builds the melodies up out of individual phrases, (growing) an entire movement from several microcosmic musical gestures," expanding and developing the fragments and then reassembling them at the end. In the Op.33 quartets Haydn gave melodic identity to "standard accompanimental fragments – (or) rhythmic motives…and then carefully and consistently used them in both melody and accompaniment." Charles Rosen points out that this "single innovation (was) the touchstone of classical counterpoint."

With the Op.33 set Haydn realized "that he was well on his way to mastering that most intractable of all musical forms, the string quartet." The revival of complex contrapuntal detail under Haydn's leadership replaced the banal accompaniment figures that had dominated instrumental works in the reactionary style galant of the Rococo period. In the quartets of Op.33 and later, "the independent solo writing entails an emphatic and complex contrapuntal display." This set of quartets contains two nicknamed works, No.2 in E-flat is known as *The Joke* and No.3 in C has the label *The Birds*, due to the chirping theme of the first movement.

String Quartets - Op.50, Nos.1-6; Op.64, Nos.1-6

With Haydn's Op.50 set we find cello writing far richer than in any previous string quartets, and the writing for the other instruments is filled with sparkle. In the Op.50 string quartets Haydn would return to a more substantial tone, but instead of the 'violence' of the Op.20 quartets, Haydn is eloquent and profound in the Op.50 set. These six quartets possess greater contrapuntal richness and show a "partial return to the rich and more 'learned' technique of the High Baroque" than the Op.33 set, which is leaner. Quartet No.4 of the Op.50 set contains Haydn's greatest fugal finale. An example of a Haydn 'surprise' or unexpected device and displacement of function is Op.50, No.6 with its opening theme beginning with a final cadence.

The Op.64 quartets represent the last set Haydn would write during his thirty years of service to the Esterhazy family. Five of the six (Nos.2-6) are mainstays of the string quartet repertoire. "The mature power and variety of the six quartets of Op.64…were never surpassed by Haydn." *The Lark*, No.5 in D, is most original in its wide spacing of registers and new range and openness of sonority.

The string quartets of Op.50 through Op.64, including the Op.54 and Op.55 sets of 1789, have a more dramatic character than previously displayed by Haydn and show a marked use of the chromatic line, which is greatly diminished in the quartets after the Op.64 set. The interesting point of this rise and fall in chromaticism is that it corresponds directly to Mozart's influence on Haydn's writing for string quartet. The rise corresponds to Haydn's Op.50 set composed in 1785 as the initial set after Haydn first met Mozart in 1781. The fall in chromaticism is first seen in the Op.71 quartets written by Haydn in 1791, the year of Mozart's death. Haydn reverted to diatonic scale formula upon his friend's death, no longer needing to compete or match Mozart's chromatic style.

String Quartets - Op.71, Nos.1-3; Op.74, Nos.1-3, *Apponyi*

These quartets were commissioned by Haydn's old friend Count Anton Apponyi upon Haydn's return from his first London trip for Salomon. Scholars noted that these were the first quartets written to be heard in concert halls, for an audience of around 800, instead of intimate aristocratic salons. The forceful introductions to all six quartets served as "a cue for any chattering to cease." Indeed, both sets were intended for concerts during Haydn's second Salomon-sponsored London tour in 1794. They are "more experimental and innovative than earlier compositions" and are full of "…flamboyant contrasts of texture, register, and dynamics." and "are marked by a profusion of arresting textures." "The dawn of Romanticism is noticeable in the string quartets of Op.74."

String Quartets - Op.76, Nos.1-6, *Erdödy*

This set contains some of Haydn's more famous 'name' quartets, including Fifths (No.2), *Kaiser* or *Emperor* (No.3), and *Sunrise* (No.4). No.3 contains variations on Haydn's hymn (and German National Anthem since 1922) *Gott erhalte Franz den Kaiser*. A major advance of the Op.76 quartets is the more profound and emotional slow movements that, according to Haydn scholar H.C. Robbins Landon, "are also bathed in a curiously impersonal and remote melancholy."

String Quartets - Op.77, Nos.1&2, *Lobkovitz*, Op.103 in D minor
The two Op.77 quartets were Haydn's last complete contribution to the genre and appeared at the same time (around 1800-01) Beethoven composed his six Op.18 string quartets. The sets from both composers were commissioned by the same person, Prince Franz Joseph Lobkovitz, himself an amateur chamber musician. Haydn first composed these as flute sonatas in 1799 but recast them as string quartets for publication in 1802. For these late two string quartets Haydn actually took Beethoven's lead, established in his Op.1 Piano Trios, of substituting a dynamic scherzo for the traditional minuet. "The texture (of both Op.77 quartets) is a perfect blend of homophonic and contrapuntal writing" and "in these quartets the highest point of Haydn's creative activity is reached." Tovey feels that Op.77, no.2 is "perhaps Haydn's greatest instrumental composition." They show Haydn at his most masterful, with strong themes and a perfect blend of homophonic and contrapuntal writing.

Haydn's last string quartet, Op.103 in D minor, indicates that the opening movement and finale were the toughest movements for Haydn as "he only had the strength to finish the middle movements of his last quartet."

Recommended – Haydn String Quartets
The best approach is to acquire a broad sampling by several of the leading Haydn ensembles. Suggestions include *The Haydn Project* by the Emerson String Quartet, which contains one quartet each from *Opp.20, 33, 54, 64, 74, 76,& 77* (DG, 2001); *Op.3, No.5*; *Op.64, No.5*; *Op.76, No.2*, Quartetto Italiano (Philips, 1965); Lindsay String Quartet: *Op. 20, No.4*; *Op.33, Nos.2&3*; *Op.55, No.2*; *Op.64, No.5*; *Op.76, No.3* (ASV, 1999); *Op.77, Nos.1&2*; *Op.42* and *Op.103* (Sanctuary, 2006). *Op.33, Nos.1, 2, 4* (ASV, 1996); Kodály Quartet: *Op.76, Nos.1-6* (Naxos, 1990). *Op.71, Nos.1-3* (Naxos, 1990). *Op.50, nos.4-6* (Naxos, 1998). For the true die-hard the Buchberger Quartet of Frankfurt offers the complete quartets in a boxed-set of twenty-three discs or by opus numbers on two- and three-CD releases (Brilliant Classics, 2006-09).

♪ Wolfgang Amadeus Mozart (1756-1791)

As with Beethoven's string quartets the twenty-six string quartets of Mozart give us a complete survey of the evolution of his style over the twenty-year period of 1770-1790. "The development of his genius is laid down for all to see."

The Opus 33 string quartet set of Haydn had a major influence on the younger Mozart. According to Alfred Einstein the effect was "one of the profoundest Mozart experienced in his artistic life." Upon hearing them around 1782, and "doubtless fired by a mixture of admiration and competitiveness", Mozart embarked on composing his own new set of six string quartets, which he completed in 1782-85, and dedicated to Haydn.

The *Haydn* String Quartets, K.387, 421, 428, 458, 464, 465

These were written not on commission but for Mozart's own satisfaction and to pay homage to Haydn. Mozart sent the quartets to Haydn in September 1785 and the older composer was so impressed by a private performance of some of them that he declared to Mozart's father Leopold, "Before God and as an honest man I tell you that your son is the greatest composer... He has...the most profound knowledge of composition."

> *"It was from Haydn that I first learned to write a string quartet."*
> - Mozart

Mozart continued this newly-formed mutual admiration society by replying to Haydn that the quartets were the product of the "guidance of a much celebrated man" and "his dearest friend." The six 'Haydn' string quartets "are, to be truthful, the fruit of long and laborious efforts." They were composed in two groups: K.387, K.421, K.428 in December to January of 1782/83; K.458, K.464, K.465 in the winter of 1784-85. Both sets show a great absorption of Haydn's idiosyncrasies by Mozart, presenting many varied and contrasting ideas. The slow movements, however, in their graceful gravity, show a profundity not found in Haydn.

Although in tribute to Haydn, these quartets now contained a full mastery and a new originality. Mozart continued by beseeching Haydn to "look with indulgence upon their defects." Despite Mozart's claim to less than perfection in these works, Haydn was correct in his assessment of the quartets dedicated to him. "For variety of thematic matter, concentration of musical thought combined with ease of manner, emotional range and sensuous appeal, the six ('Haydn') quartets must be ranked among the most perfect chamber works ever composed."

These quartets are contemporaneous with Haydn's Op.33 and stand "as the finest example of Mozart's genius." They "exhibit a perfect amalgam of the Rococo and Classical spirits." One effect Mozart clearly took from Haydn was the treatment of all four instruments as equal participants. Typical of the response to Mozart's 'radical' music not written to be crowd-pleasing fare, the *Haydn* Quartets were not very well received, attracting no great attention from either the listening public, musicians, or potential patrons who could provide commissions for additional works.

K.387 in G is the first of Mozart's six 'Haydn' string quartets, and it "quickly gives notice that Mozart...is here entering a new phase of his musical development." It opens with a "buoyant, transparent melody;" the piece "brims with rhythmic and contrapuntal invention." A highlight of this mostly joyous and ebullient work is in the final movement where Mozart shows his mastery of counterpoint, rapidly jumping from fugue to simple melodic passages. K.421 is in D minor, a dark key of haunting anxiety for Mozart that sets this quartet in stark contrast to the first. The key of D minor was used to this effect in several major works of Mozart, including the K.466 Piano Concerto, *Don Giovanni*, and the *Requiem* Mass.

K.458 and K.465 are famous as a pair because they are nicknamed The *Hunt* and *Dissonant*, respectively. The former got its name from the horn call in the opening theme, while K.465 opens with "what was then an almost alarming display of dissonant chromaticism." and its nickname refers to this "chromatic meanderings" of the slow opening of the first movement, with its "unresolved harmonies over a throbbing cello line" introducing the work, followed by a sunny allegro. The *Hunt* Quartet contains the "most profound of the slow movements" among the six quartets, the most poignant slow movement is found in the andante cantabile of the *Dissonant*.

Mozart wrote many other string quartets. The accomplished cellist, Emperor Friedrich Wilhelm commissioned three (K.575, 589, 590), nicknamed Prussian. These were begun in 1789 and were Mozart's last string quartets. He imbued all three with prominent cello writing. Mozart then began work on his last two string quintets, K.593 in D and K.614 in E-flat.

♪ Ludwig van Beethoven (1770-1827)

Now we come to the Mt. Everest of the string quartet form, Beethoven's set of string quartets in which he bares his soul as in no other form. Only in Beethoven's string quartets can a listener find every shade of emotion, every technical refinement, every significant musical purpose, spanning from his early maturity (Op.18) to the last months of his life. Beethoven has a universality, an "ability to embrace the whole range of human emotion, from dread of death to love of life…"

The string quartet as a genre had flourished in Vienna since the 1770s, but Beethoven's quartets are so far beyond what had come before and so significant that no set of quartets has approached them since. Beethoven "chose to stretch the string quartet toward symphonic dimensions." "The risk-taking and compositional challenges that Beethoven sets himself throughout the quartets are staggering and inspirational."

> *"Art demands of us that we do not stand still."*
> *- Beethoven*

Similar to his unrivaled output of piano sonatas, Beethoven set the bar for the string quartet as well. And as with the piano sonatas the quartets were written over most of Beethoven's compositional career from 1798 to 1826, thus providing a roadmap for the development and maturation of the composer. Beethoven's "direct and passionate expression of emotion...that (is) extroverted in his symphonies (is) deeply introverted in his late piano sonatas and string quartets." As Beethoven did with other genres that were developed by Haydn and brought to a certain point of maturity by Mozart, he again moves the genre of the quartet substantially ahead into uncharted territory. No other composer comes close in so consistently leaping far ahead of the crowd in such a variety of musical forms.

Beethoven waited until he was almost thirty and had achieved a level of maturity as a composer to take on the daunting string quartet form. He made sure he was prepared for this most demanding of genres and, with the legacy of the quartets of Haydn and Mozart looming, most certainly wanted to avoid turning out mediocre works. He mastered the string trio medium with Opp.3, 8, and 9 before adding a second violin for his Op.18 set of quartets.

Just as significant is the bridge Beethoven formed between the relatively rigid forms of the Classical period and the much freer works of the Romantic period. Beethoven blazed the path for the great quartets of Schubert, those of Mendelssohn, and the works of Brahms decades later. He did this with more than just his musical ideas. He was the first to react against the patronage model used by Bach, Haydn, and Mozart (and virtually all composers up to 1800) and asserted "the artist as a unique, dignified prophet of society." Beethoven paved the way for the 'independent' composer who composed a work on commission and was not shackled to any church or royal court. The downside was the likely lack of a steady paycheck and a roof over one's head, which in those days were luxuries for most people.

Beethoven's miraculous output of string quartets is, by convention and convenience, divided into an early, middle and late period. His three periods each produced a major set of quartets which shows his evolution out of the shadows of Haydn and Mozart to take the quartet to realms never before imagined. This neatly provides three sets of quartets that are often recorded as complete sets on two or three CDs for each set.

♪ The Early Period

The early string quartets (Op.18, 1-6) were the "most ambitious single project of his early Vienna years", composed in 1798-1800 and published in 1801. They are contemporaneous with Haydn's last two quartets, Op.77. Labeling them 'early' is misleading as these quartets were composed around age thirty and Beethoven had already written five string trios as a means of "dipping a toe into string quartet waters." The early quartets represent the natural progression of the rich string quartet legacy left by Haydn and Mozart, and they owe much of their influence to both of those composers, who perfected the form. Beethoven retains use of the minuet as the usual third dance movement in the Op.18 quartets but they are angry and nervous.

But there is plenty of new ground broken in them as Beethoven begins to distance himself from both Haydn and Mozart. The Op.18 quartets, while modeled on the two Classical masters' works, at the same time clearly suggest that the young Beethoven was "increasingly uncomfortable with the elegant confines...of the so-called Classical era..." by displaying "hard-edged accents and intensified dramatic contrasts." Beethoven took over where the two great Classical composers left off. This comparison is similar to Beethoven's first two symphonies compared to Mozart's last six and Haydn's *London* sets.

The Op.18 quartets served two purposes. Beethoven needed to demonstrate that he could produce string quartets in the Classical tradition of Haydn and Mozart, but he also wanted to produce quartets radically different from any previous. He succeeded on both accounts. Nos.4-6 experiment with different types and arrangements of movements but "essentially remain traditional and even conservative, reflecting Beethoven's main ambition: to master the most prestigious genre of the Classical style." They are "an interesting beginning to an extraordinary journey" that would culminate in his great late quartets.

Several of the Op.18 quartets underwent thorough revisions before publication, particularly Nos.1&2, and, as is often the case with bundled sets of works, the numbering does not represent the order of composition. No.1 in F was probably the second composed, although it is the most 'Haydnesque'. It has a "fine slow movement – one of the great tragic utterances among his earlier music." No.2 in G is in the key Beethoven chose for some of his wittiest works. The 'wit' in this specific work is the use of a scherzo as the central theme of the ternary slow movement, followed by a full scherzo third movement. It is fitting that Beethoven cast this quartet in his wittiest key as this is the most 'Haydnesque' of the set.

Op.18, No.3 has neither a scherzo or minuet slow movement but a brief allegro between the slow movement, which is a study in contrasting sonorities and textures and the dazzling finale written against the background of tarantella, a frenzied Italian dance that jumps from major to minor keys, sometimes at a breathless pace. Op.18, No.4 in C minor has never been as "widely admired as its companions (with an) awkwardness...not to be found elsewhere in Beethoven's string quartets." Nonetheless, "the music crackles with vitality, wit, and daring ingenuity," while the finale "often speaks with a gruff Beethovian accent," despite being filled with Haydn's disconcerting wit.

The fifth work of this early set shows more of an influence of Mozart than of Haydn. It is modeled on Mozart's K.464 Quartet in the same key of A major and in the reversal of the slow movement and minuet. Op.18, No.6 is characterized by its startling shifts of mood and juxtaposing of "material of diametrically opposed character." The last of the 'early' quartets looks forward to the late string quartets (e.g., Op.135) "with its seemingly mystical dilemma (and its) dynamic, thrusting scherzo." The *scherzi* of the previous five Op.18 quartets were "a good deal better-behaved."

♪ The Middle Period

Beethoven's middle period saw the expansion of formal proportions and expressive power. Only six years separate the Op.18 quartets (1800) from the first three string quartets of Beethoven's 'middle' period in 1806. However, from 1800 to 1806 "his style had changed almost beyond recognition" as Beethoven gained inspiration from Mozart's most imaginative and most radical conceptions.

The *Razumovsky* Quartets, Op.59, Nos.1-3

The Op.59 string quartets, "uncompromising in their severity and intellectual rigor," represented "a continental divide in the history of the quartet." These quartets prove that "by 1806 Beethoven was the equal of Haydn and Mozart – if not Bach – in any species of polyphony." The three Op.59 Quartets possess "concentrated power and energy that tap into the same breadth of vision that Beethoven was striving for in his greatest orchestral works."

The extreme technical demands and unprecedented 'broad canvas' of these three quartets "challenged the traditional notion of chamber music as a vehicle for domestic music making." No.1 and No.2 have substantial Adagios that are highlights of both quartets. In the first of the Op.59 Quartets (in F major) the slow *Adagio molto e mesto* provides a "pervasive atmosphere of grief." Beethoven indicated with an inscription that this movement represented "a weeping willow or acacia tree on my brother's (Kaspar's) grave." It was Kaspar's son Karl whom Beethoven tried to adopt after the death of Kaspar from consumption. These episodes provided a subplot for the movie *Immortal Beloved*.

The quartet ensemble that premiered Op.59, No.1 in early 1807 thought Beethoven was playing a practical joke with this music of unprecedented difficulty. He had recently come to grips with his deafness, realizing it could be overcome and Beethoven's creative genius flourished. He stated that he did not write Op.59, No.1 for present musicians "but for a later age."

The *Adagio* of the No.2 Quartet (in E minor) is a serene movement characterized by Carl Czerny as composed by his teacher while "contemplating the starry heavens and thinking of the music of the spheres." This quartet is distinguished by the fact that it is the first significant string quartet cast in the key of E minor (Haydn and Mozart avoided this key for their quartets).

The third of the Op.59 Quartets (in C major) is unlike its two fellow quartets of the triptych. It is Classically-proportioned such that Beethoven even used a minuet in place of a scherzo, in seeming violation of what had become standard practice in his four-movement works. The influence of

Mozart is pronounced in No.3 with references to the concluding *Allegro* of K.387, the first of the 'Haydn' Quartets, and to K.465, 'Dissonance', as the opening movement of No.3 mimics K.465 in that it "only gradually gropes its way towards the home key."

These quartets represented a continuation of the heroic impulse of the *Eroica* Symphony applied to the string quartet; an expansion of the traditional 18th century quartet boundaries to a point where "one may legitimately speak of these quartets as 'symphonic quartets'." These works are contemporaneous with some other major compositions: the Fourth Piano Concerto, Op.58, the Fourth Symphony, Op.60, and the Violin Concerto, Op.61. Unlike the six quartets of Op.18, and even the late string quartets, the three *Razumovsky* Quartets are not very similar but rather are "a trio of sharply characterized, consciously differentiated individuals." A notable exception would be the use of some Russian elements in all three as a nod to their dedicatee, Count Andreas Razumovsky who commissioned the works.

Quartet in E-flat, Op.74 *Harp*

Compared with Op.59, Nos.1&2 this quartet is "altogether well-behaved," although the "bold individuality of its slow opening page" caused one reviewer to point out the "unnecessary jumble of harsh dissonances," and revealing just how radical any of Beethoven's string quartets were for their day. It is generally considered of a lesser stature than the other middle-period quartets as its strongest parts are its two middle movements, the romantic and intensely beautiful *Adagio* and the "diabolical scherzo, full of hammering figures."

Quartet in F minor, Op.95 *Quartett serioso*

This string quartet stands alone between the 'middle' and 'late' string quartet periods. It was composed more than a decade before he started on his final masterpieces that "formed his main creative preoccupation during the final three years of his life." "Its abrupt transitions, changes of mood, and flighty coda in the finale look forward to Beethoven's late masterpieces in the form." It is one of the great works of Beethoven's middle period and "stands at the gateway to the third."

Op.95 is the tersest and most austere of all Beethoven's string quartets and one of the most intensely dramatic of all Beethoven's middle period works with extremes of contrast and the compression of its drama. The *Serioso* tag was applied by Beethoven himself, who curiously claimed it "was never to be performed in public." The label is very fitting as Beethoven never wrote a more terribly serious composition.

♫ The Late Period

> Music heard so deeply
> That it is not heard at all
> But you are the music
> While the music lasts
>   - T.S. Eliot, inspired by the late String Quartets

It is with these quartets that Beethoven fully acts as Beethoven. As he did with the symphony and piano sonata, Beethoven provides for the string quartet genre a huge leap forward in terms of structure and complexity. The late piano sonatas and string quartets are difficult experimental works. After the Napoleonic wars aristocratic patronage and enlightened attitudes began to crumble. Responding to these trends, Beethoven's late works "crystallized avant-garde currents among Viennese intellectuals." "As his hearing faded, he seemed to have developed a deep inner hearing…he longed to touch the infinite…to embrace all humanity." Unlike his middle period quartets, the late string quartets possess an "exceptionally strong unity that binds (them) together." Several movements within different quartets are linked by related moods and structures.

Beethoven claimed he gave himself more freedom and fantasy than usual in the late string quartets. With them the traditional development of themes is abandoned to be replaced by fragments of ideas, sometimes repeated, interrupted or varied. In all of them Beethoven uses a "serene set of variations" as the "expressive heart of the work as a whole," and "variation form joins fugue as one of the leading features." Examples include the *Adagio* of Op.127; in Op.131 it is the large central movement alternating among *Adagio-Andante-Allegretto*; and in Op.132 it is the 'holy song'. For this reason Beethoven's late quartets are 'harder' to listen to than most of his earlier quartets. The melodic lyricism of the early period quartets is much more accessible. Additionally, listeners can benefit from knowing that enjoyment of the late quartets is different from enjoyment of the early ones. The intricate texture of these quartets is the major obstacle they present to listeners, along with the unorthodox layout of their movements.

These last five string quartets and the *Große Fuge*, characterized by sharp contrasts of mood and an extraordinary range of emotion, are the "sublime soliloquies of a lonely soul" and "represent…the supremist height to which music has attained." Although most apparent in this 'great fugue', all of the late quartets "show a new-found interest in the discipline of the fugue." As with many sets of works, the opus numbers are not strictly chronological.

With Opp.130-132 Beethoven plays "with our sense of the passage of time" taking the listener on a long, multi-movement spiritual journey in each of these three quartets. The reaction to the late quartets was exemplified in a Leipzig review that characterized the *Große Fuge* as "incomprehensible, like Chinese…" and a review by Ludwig Rellstab stating that Op.127 "contains only the ruins of the youthful beauty and manly nobility of his genius, often buried deep under arid rubble." Audiences could not comprehend Op.130 or "withstand the shock of the new." Possibly on account of this the last two quartets, Op.131 and Op.135 were not performed in public during Beethoven's lifetime.

Beethoven's five late string quartets and the *Große Fuge* "are generally agreed to represent the summit of instrumental music in the West." Alfred Einstein asks, "Does there still remain alive in (the late quartets) a last trace of that 'sociability' that Haydn's and Mozart's, and even Beethoven's own Op.18 had exemplified?" In these quartets "there is no poignancy or sentiment. Rather, there is the spiritualized equivalent of those moods,…(the quartets) reveal themselves as the most divinely inspired music in the literature." Each is considered here individually as each is of such significance to the genre. These mystical, demanding string quartets would have to wait until the 20th century and the sets of Bartók and Shostakovich to be joined by similar works in this demanding genre.

Quartet in E flat, Op.127

This quartet is the first of a trio (along with Op.130 and Op.132) commissioned by the Russian Prince Nikolas Galitzin. The prince had to be patient while Beethoven completed the *Missa Solemnis*, the *Diabelli* Variations, and the Ninth Symphony. Once Beethoven could turn his attention to the string quartets he turned out Opp.127, 132 and 130 in six months (Feb 1825, July 1825 and Aug 1825, respectively). Op.127 is "a natural outgrowth of the last piano sonatas," in the traditional four movements, "perhaps to reestablish Beethoven's control of the medium." To give an idea of public and critical response to much of Beethoven's late period music, the contemporary critic Ludwig Rellstab stated that Op.127 "contains only the ruins of the youthful beauty and manly nobility of his genius, often buried under arid rubble."

Quartet in A minor, Op.132

While Op.127 stands alone, Opp.130-132 are thematically linked, despite the commission by Prince Galatzin for three string quartets being fulfilled by Beethoven by Opp.127, 132, and 130. After the 'traditional' Op.127 the next three quartets are "experimental works that create a variety of new formal structures." Harold Schonberg refers to Opp.130-132 as "the great trinity;" these quartets "carry music to a height that actually seems to transcend music." It is this 'musical transcendentalism' that inspired and was carried forward by Romantic composers.

The A minor String Quartet contains one of Beethoven's most famous and greatest chamber movements, the third movement of the five. This movement, which exudes an unearthly calm, is Beethoven's "song of gratitude to God after recovering from a serious (abdominal) illness." The "music here appears to become an implicit agency of healing, a talisman against death." This long slow movement, which alternates between *Andante* and *Adagio*, ends with a heavenly calm that is "rudely interrupted by a parody of a march" to start the two-minute fourth movement. The long German title attached to this 'song' is translated, 'holy song of thanksgiving from a convalescent to the Deity, in the Lydian mode.' To give an idea of the breadth that could be absorbed by Classical style, Beethoven uses Gregorian chant in this string quartet.

Quartet in B flat, Op.130 and *Große Fuge*, Op.133

The *Große Fuge*, Op.133 was the original finale for Op.130, which Beethoven eventually removed from this quartet and published as a separate work. It was met with such stiff resistance that he had to acquiesce and provide a new delicate and transparent finale, an *Allegro*, roughly half the length of the *Große Fuge*. It "is as different as could be imagined...though Beethoven (still) managed to incorporate...fugal writing." The *Große Fuge* was published as a separate, one-movement work and is an example of thematic conflict unsurpassed in music.

On recordings the *Große Fuge* is available as a stand-alone work and also incorporated into Op.130 as an alternate finale (as the Takacs Quartet does). "Like the fugal finale of the *Hammerklavier* Sonata, the *Große Fuge* shows Beethoven's writing at its most intractable," and "can alienate with its sheer furosity and scale." At the time it was called by some "the work of a lunatic." "Its subject is marked by immense leaps, the contours of its lines are jagged, its harmonic trajectory veers toward brash dissonance."

Completed in January 1826 Op.130 was the last composed of the trio of quartets commissioned by Prince Galitzin. With the 'lighter' finale in place of the *Große Fuge*, this quartet almost takes on the feel of a *divertimento* or even a Baroque suite, but not so fast. The third movement of Op.130 "may appear to be a nostalgic reminiscence of Mozart and Haydn," but it is actually much more 'modern'. The replacement *Allegro* finale for the *Große Fuge* was the last piece to be completed by Beethoven before his death.

Quartet in C sharp minor, Op.131

This quartet, considered by Beethoven to be his most perfect single work, consists of seven movements, amazingly played without a break, giving the work a great sense of structural integration. However, typical of Beethoven, he also commented that the seven movements were "stuck together out of various odds and ends." It is the only late quartet with such instructions from the composer. It really is five movements as two movements are nothing more than very brief introductions, or bridges, to following movements. It opens with an intimate, other-worldly fugue.

> *Beethoven had "climbed so high that one begins to lose one's breath.*
> - Berlioz after hearing a performance of *Op.131 and Op.135*

Quartet in F, Op.135

With a short repeated opening phrase Beethoven presents a metaphysical dilemma in this quartet using the minor key to ask, "Must it be?" This fateful question is answered in the major, "It must be!" Beethoven alludes to the struggle to resolve this dilemma by including the transcription "the decision grasped with difficulty" on the score of the work.

But the music in Op.135 is, by comparison to its four predecessors, much more fresh, light and playful. It is also cast in the traditional four movements. With his last quartet "Beethoven came home at last…(and) turns sharply back, not forward…(with its) withdrawal from the…fierce drive and passionate expressiveness of the earlier (four late) quartets."

Recommended – Beethoven string quartets

The better string quartet ensembles in these works are usually consistently strong across the periods. Complete sets are usually divided into three sub-sets corresponding to the three periods. Highly recommended are the sets from the Takacs Quartet and The Lindseys. The Emerson String Quartet is celebrated for its precision and execution, but some say they sacrifice passion and warmth in some of their recordings. The best approach is to acquire the quartets by a variety of ensembles so as to appreciate the different approaches to these masterpieces.

- 11 -

The String Quartet Beyond Beethoven

♪ Franz Schubert

> *"...but who can do anything after Beethoven?"*
> \- Franz Schubert

> *"Schubert's goal had never been precise four-part writing, nor did he often achieve it."*
> \- Homer Ulrich

Instead, Schubert searched for textures in the warmth of instrumental color. His chamber music dwells "on lyric moments and rich harmonies at the expense of figuration and tonal plans." Indeed, 19th century composers could not approach Beethoven's late string quartets; their inner logic lay beyond them.

Schubert left us fifteen string quartets that are at least partially complete, with the greatest being the four late works. In most of his chamber and symphonic works "Schubert works within the late and loosely organized post-classical style." "The 'great' Schubert shows himself first in the C minor String Quartet of 1820." His last seven chamber works from 1824 onward were written on a larger scale and contained many orchestral effects compare with previous chamber compositions. However, these large-scale works "are still based on intimate, economical chamber music techniques."

The first of these seven works was the A minor String Quartet, nicknamed *Rosamunde* because Schubert borrowed the *Andante* theme from his incidental music for the play of the same name. The overture from this play is also a popular Schubert work. The A minor is his first mature string quartet intended for the public. His previous twelve quartets had been composed for in-home performance by his family quartet, which consisted of Schubert, his father, and his two brothers. Amazingly, this quartet is the only chamber work by Schubert to be published while he was alive.

With the one-movement *Quartettsatz* ('Quartet movement') in C minor we find that "the inner joy and vivacity that filled the earlier works is gone," replaced by a restless, more serious expression.

The string quartet, *Death and the Maiden* in D minor from 1824 (designated No.14), uses Schubert's song of the same title as the theme for the somber second movement variations. It was composed within one month of the completion of his melodious *Octet* and around the time of Beethoven's Ninth Symphony, also in D minor. Interestingly, the record shows that Schubert attended the premiere of Beethoven's final symphony and "Beethoven's titanic figure loomed large over Schubert's life." It is not a happy work but dark and brooding, written at a time when Schubert said "I feel as though I am the unhappiest, most miserable man on earth." As with Beethoven's *Ninth* the first movement of *Death and the Maiden* also has turbulent main themes offset by lyrical secondary themes. "What Schubert could only suggest in his *Lieder* here finds exhaustive expression."

In many ways the most orchestral of Schubert's chamber music is his fifteenth, the G major String Quartet. It is also ahead of its time, with its harmonic freedom and unrest taking the place of Schubert's usual songfulness. This quartet "offers perhaps the most striking example of Schubert's departure from the lines of true Classicism." With the late String Quartet in G major "Schubert returns to classical principles in a manner almost as striking, if not as complete, as Beethoven."

> *Recommended – Schubert string quartets*
> Emerson String Quartet (DG, 1987), part of a 3CD 'Trio' offering with other chamber works of Schubert. The Philips release by the Quartetto Italiano remains a classic. For a recent release of *Death and the Maiden quartet*, the Takacs Quartet are on target.

♪ Romantic Period Quartets

♫ Felix Mendelssohn

Some view Mendelssohn (1809-1847) as a composer who peaked very young with his *Octet* and *A Midsummer Night's Dream* Overture, written as a teenager, and argue that his style never really developed any further.

After Beethoven and Schubert, Mendelssohn contributed the next best set of string quartets from the first half of the 1800s. He wrote a total of six and succeeded brilliantly in all. "Mendelssohn had a genuine understanding of what Beethoven was up to in his last years." The late period Beethoven of eccentric and imaginative sonatas and string quartets served as a major model for the young Mendelssohn, who was able to discover his own originality and eventually turn Beethoven's model into his own individual, personal and uniquely Mendelssohnian works. But his first two quartets draw blatantly and explicitly from several of Beethoven's late string quartets; the dependence of the first movement of No.2 on Beethoven's Op.132 is "so flagrant as to constitute a public homage to Beethoven."

The Quartet in F minor, Op.80 was written just after the death of his sister Fanny, with whom he was extremely close, in May 1847. He tells us that he "could not think of work, or even music, without feeling the most intense emptiness and barrenness in the mind and heart." His sense of anguish upon this loss resulted in the Op.80, "perhaps the most intensely tragic work" he ever composed, "characterized by extreme, often unresolved tension." This work drew again from Beethoven's Late Quartets and the influence of Schubert's D.703, *Quartettsatz* in C minor, is felt in the opening movement.

Unfortunately, while Mendelssohn clearly mourned for Fanny through this quartet, the composition did not provide relief from the grief as he wrote later in the same year, "Now I must gradually begin to put my life and my work together again, with the awareness that Fanny is no longer there: and it leaves such a bitter taste that I still cannot see my way clearly or find any peace." So he kept himself in a constant state of overwork, during which he would cancel engagements (or resign as director of the *Gewandhaus* concerts) to relieve matters only to book additional concerts in England. Mendelssohn was dead at age thirty-eight not long after his sister's death and shortly after finishing his final string quartet.

> *"This constant hurry in which he lives year after year makes me breathless just thinking about it."*
> *- Fanny Mendelssohn*

The other string quartets, for the most part, show the more genial side of Mendelssohn's nature, the one with which we are familiar. Two of these quartets comprise his Op.44, composed during a time that, according to Mendelssohn, "work is now quite wonderful and merry."

Mendelssohn's opus numbers are confusing, and rarely reflect the chronology of composition. For example, among the *Four Pieces*, Op.81, the last of the four was composed in 1827 while the third in 1843. For Op.12 & Op.13 the opus numbering represents order of publication as Op.13 was composed two years before Op.12.

After Schubert and Mendelssohn the string quartet became an archaic and academic form as "music generally seeks to avoid the kind of linear definition implied by the string quartet." For most Romantic composers, but not the Classical Romantics Dvořák and Brahms, the quartet became a "proof of mastery, and a nostalgic recall of the great classicists," but not a work central to their output. Even disregarding the Romantic composers who composed no chamber music to speak of (Liszt, Wagner), this explains why several composers of the 19th and early 20th centuries made a very limited number of attempts at the form (Smetana), some once and only once (Franck, Fauré, Debussy, Ravel), and some avoided the form altogether (Chopin, Rachmaninoff, R. Strauss).

♪ Robert Schumann

Schumann's set of three string quartets (Op.41, Nos.1-3), written in Schumann's "chamber music year" of 1842, are among the least known and performed of any set of string quartets by a major composer. Perhaps a contributing factor is the criticism they have received from some for being little more than piano works arranged for string quartet. These quartets represent an "extreme simplification of the string quartet form. The three quartets were curiously composed with bridges (later deleted by Schumann) from one quartet to the next. The composer either intended the three to be played together or at least intended to provide the option. For the most part, Schumann's most enjoyable music almost always include the piano; his concerto, miniatures, quintet, and quartet that include piano are all among his most enduring and popular works. However, his string quartets remain in the repertory and recorded, but are "very difficult, thorny, with lots of problems." Compared to Brahms' dense string quartets the Schumann quartets are leaner and more airy.

♪ Smetana and Dvořák

Bedřich Smetana composed two string quartets, the first in E minor (1876), subtitled *From My Life*, and the second in D minor composed between June of 1882 and March of the following year. Their autobiographical and programmatic nature would inspire other Czech string quartets, most notably, the two by Janáček and Martinů's *Fifth*. Smetana revealed his intentions in his detailed program notes for the work. "My intention was to paint a tone picture of my life…four instruments conversing among themselves about the things that have so momentously affected me."

The heart of the First Quartet is "in the glorious slow movement in which the composer recalls the happiness of his first love." In the polka movement Smetana reminisces about his youth. The composer's deteriorating hearing is captured in the finale. Smetana claimed Quartet No.2 picked up where the first ended but now Smetana has lost his hearing and presents the "swirling sound" of music he now hears. According to him the first movement of No.2 "is quite unusual in style."

Dvořák wrote no chamber sonatas for string and piano and only his Piano Trio No.4, the excellent *Dumky* trio, is well known. However, Dvořák makes his mark in chamber music in works for ensembles of four or more players. Dvořák's fourteen string quartets, plus two one movement works for string quartet (*Quartettsatz* form the bulk of his chamber output and contain not only "his most experimental work" but "many of his most beautiful inspirations."

Dvořák's stay in America (1892-95) resulted in a major stylistic change in his music, with his two "American" works, the Op.96 Quartet and the Op.97 String Quintet, showing the impact of the composer's hearing of spirituals and Native American music. The Op.96 String Quartet even earned the label *American*. It is easily Dvořák's most popular chamber work because it is "folksy, concise, and easy to follow."

Dvořák's two late string quartets, Op.105 in A-flat and Op.106 in G, were both completed shortly after his three-year stay in America (1892-95). Op.105, started before but completed after Op.106, was Dvořák's last chamber work and also his last work of 'absolute' music; only tone poems and operas remained. Dvořák began Op.105 just before leaving America for

Prague. Neither quartet shows the New World influences or his so-called 'American style.' Both are more Classical in outlook and seem to celebrate Dvořák's return home "and his confident mastery of the quartet medium."

♪ Johannes Brahms

After a period of forty years or so during which chamber music was not emphasized by early Romantic composers, the genre was revitalized by Johannes Brahms. Brahms' chamber music output is certainly one of quality over quantity, as he limited himself to usually no more than three works in any of the chamber forms. However, his total chamber output exceeded his symphonic output. One of these forms was the string quartet, of which Brahms produced three. The genre of string quartet gave Brahms as much pause as the symphony. In fact, there were as many as twenty attempts (all destroyed by the composer) before Brahms was satisfied to apply the label "No.1" to a string quartet.

While for some other major composers the string quartet represents the peak maturity of their chamber output (Haydn, Mozart, Beethoven, Schubert), Brahms' string quartets simply join his other various and high caliber chamber works. Much of this is because, as was the case with his First Symphony, Brahms waited until maturity to tackle this most difficult musical form. The wait was worth it as his string quartets are among the most poignant of his works.

Some musicologists have noted that these quartets "suffer from their complexity;" Brahms worked on the two quartets that comprise Op.51 (No.1 in C minor: No.2 in A minor) on and off for eight years, giving the pair a "worked over nature." Brahms did have a tendency in some works to try to fit a 'quart in a pint jar'; packing so many ideas into a work and pushing the limit of what the form could hold. Throughout the C minor Quartet we hear Brahms' "immediately identifiable language, rich in poignant harmonic suspensions, rhythmic displacements, nervous passion, and melting lyricism." The A minor is more expansive than its partner quartet, making "more room for more expansive lyricism." Both quartets are "deeply serious and uncompromising pieces" and as a result the public has "been known to find both pieces somewhat forbidding."

By the time Brahms set to work on the Third String Quartet in B-flat, Op.67, he had lightened up a bit. The work stands in contrast to the Op.51 pair in its cheerfulness, "too delightful for words, with its delightful, mocking conclusion." Although he still had not reached his mature 'autumnal' phase, he did use some folk-like themes in the Third Quartet.

♪ French Romantic String Quartets

Because the string quartet is viewed as the most challenging chamber form to compose, more composers have accepted the challenge and produced a single work in this form than in any other. Some of the better known quartets are highlighted in these sections. The following French composers wrote one string quartet each.

The Debussy and Ravel quartets are usually coupled together on CD, and although they debuted ten years apart, they are not that similar. The Debussy String Quartet in G minor, Op.10, premiered in Paris in 1893 and was performed by the Quattor Ysaÿe, led by the famous Belgian violinist Eugene Ysaÿe. Debussy chose as his first major work a string quartet, which could "be taken as a symbolic renunciation of Wagner." Written when the composer was thirty it remains his most popular chamber work, which according to a critic of the day, is "so vigorous, so thoughtful in its passion." The string quartet "fuses Debussy's harmonic and colouristic traits with Classical forms and cyclic treatment of themes." "Its varied tonal effects, soulful beauty, and freedom of form and structure provide an excellent musical counterpart" to Impressionism and Symbolism.

The Ravel String Quartet in F has a transparent, silken texture. Although "written at a time when poetry and painting were overt influences upon his music" Ravel's string quartet contains "no poetic or visual allusion." It premiered in 1904 by the Heymann Quartet in Paris. In it Ravel sticks mostly to old German forms handed down from Haydn, Mozart and Beethoven: perfect sonata form in the first movement and a three-part scherzo. Debussy saw the work and told Ravel, "In the name of the gods of music…do not touch a single note." The *pizzicato* violin playing throughout the entire second movement (designated "quite lively" by Ravel) "makes the violin sound like an entirely different instrument."

Fauré's String Quartet, Op.121 in E minor from 1924 represents his final chamber work and his only chamber work without piano. It is "enigmatic and other-worldly, (it is) Fauré's last (musical) utterance." In the work Fauré produces "a rarefied distillation of the whole miniature musical culture" he had created in his piano pieces. It is a "remarkable example of contrapuntal mastery" with a profound central Andante movement.

Recommended – French String Quartets
Faure and Franck – Dante String Quartet; Debussy and Ravel – Emerson String Quartet (DG); Alban Berg Quartet (EMI)

♪ Borodin, Grieg and Tchaikovsky

The Second String Quartet of Alexander Borodin (1833-1887) in D is "by far the single most popular piece of chamber music" produced by a Russian..."it is beautifully composed...sweet, gentle..." Borodin was a noted research chemist who found time to compose some excellent music, including three symphonies, the third of which was left unfinished. His String Quartet No.2, famous for its slow movement *Nocturne* (sometimes performed in an arrangement for string orchestra), like Tchaikovsky's quartets, taps a vein of Russian melody. While he took several years to complete many of his major orchestral works, the String Quartet No.2 occupied Borodin for only two months in the summer of 1881.

Borodin had a great gift for "pouring out long, exquisitely singable melodies...and glorious themes." The Second Quartet was written as a twentieth anniversary gift and "as an expression of love for his wife." It is meant to evoke the couple's happiest days in Heidelberg, where they met. The effect of Russian folk music is far less pronounced on Borodin's chamber works than on his orchestral music, but "one can (still) detect the same folk elements and reaction against musical conservatism."

Borodin took heat from other Mighty Five composers when he turned to chamber music, especially his string quartets. His friends saw the string quartet as "teutonically academic 'pure' music" that was incompatible with the Russian nationalist school they were looking to propagate. However, the skill of Borodin allowed him in his quartets to fuse the Beethoven and Mendelssohn style with a completely individual and Russian quality.

Edvard Grieg produced some quality chamber works, which are sadly overlooked, including a cello sonata, three violin sonatas, and the G minor String Quartet. The quartet, composed in 1877 and premiered the following year, was influential and used by Debussy as a model for his string quartet in the same key. According to Grieg, his quartet "aims at breadth, vigor, flight of imagination and above all, fullness of tone for the instruments." The melodies of the third movement "all have the rhythmic verve and earthy energy of folk dances."

Tchaikovsky composed three string quartets with No.1 from 1871 being well-known (in D, Op.11). The D major Quartet was the first composition to carry Tchaikovsky's reputation outside Russia. Overall, it is probably the most effective of Tchaikovsky's few chamber works. This quartet contains the very famous second movement *Andante cantabile*, a very effective contrast between the first and third movements. The second movement "has been arranged for every conceivable instrumental combination." Filled with Russian folk song melodies and peasant dance character, it shows the tunesmith Tchaikovsky at his Russian nationalist best.

> **Recommended –**
> The fittingly-named Borodin Quartet has recorded the work more than once but their 1962 version, with their original lineup, remains definitive (BBC Legends). The Emersons offer the above two quartets plus Dvořák's *American* quartet. (DG)

♪ 20ᵗʰ Century

The 20th century made considerable contributions to chamber music from many diverse composers. The genre continues to provide the best vehicle for music on an intimate scale, with each instrument receiving considerable, if not equal, treatment.

One cannot speak of the history of the string quartet and omit those of Bartók and Shostakovich. The sets of string quartets by these two composers are by far the most significant set of quartets in the 20th century, and probably the most important chamber works of the past century. Although Bartók's quartets are clearly intended for the virtuoso string player and "tax the players to the utmost,…they continue to fascinate, rather than scare off, prospective performers." While Bartók's quartets are 'absolute' music, some of Shostakovich's are programmatic in ways similar to some of his symphonies. Shostakovich's quartets give listeners "deep insights into the character of a complicated, and immensely resourceful, composer."

♪ Béla Bartók (1881-1945)

Bartók wrote his six quartets over a thirty year period from 1909-1939 and was working on a seventh at the time of his death. They link to Beethoven's late string quartets from one hundred years earlier. Bartók's string quartets trace "not only his personal creative evolution but the deeply tragic *Zeitgeist* of half a century as well." These quartets are all "very elaborate works and all very different from one another." Bartók "found in the string quartet an ideal medium for the intensely serious music he wanted to write – cogently expressive yet fully discursive." "The grave opening fugue" of Bartók's Quartet No.1 "owes much to the example of Beethoven's Op.131" string quartet. It is apparent that Bartók was aware that any set of string quartets composed would be assessed relative to Beethoven's gold standard, and the connection he makes leaves no doubt that Bartók was indeed aware of this.

> *"I consider a genuine peasant melody as much a masterpiece, for instance, as a Bach fugue or a Mozart sonata."*
> - Béla Bartók

Bartók was the last great nationalistic composer. His very early works were of a late Romantic style with influences from Richard Strauss. But at the turn of the century he began incorporating authentic Hungarian folk music, as well as ideas from indigenous music of other parts of Eastern Europe and beyond. This was a product of Bartók's decision to explore and discover the music indigenous to his homeland and elsewhere. He displayed **variety and** skill in integrating "the essence of his national folk music heritage with the highest forms of Western art music."

Bartók's music "has a great deal of the strange, unpredictable violence of barbaric impulses in its harmonies as well as in its rhythms." In his string quartets he "created a series of works that are unsurpassed in the variety of their sonorous effects...(and) each succeeding one disclosed new musical possibilities." With savage and barbaric rhythms, "exotic turns of phrase" derived from indigenous folk music and the variety of texture Bartók's string quartets seem cold and impersonal compared to late Romantic works.

Together with fellow Hungarian Zoltán Kodály, Bartók invented "a new brand of folk-based musical realism" in which these two nationalistic composers would get as close as possible to the 'folk' and sought to find, record and absorb what peasants were actually singing and playing, as opposed to doing what most other nationalistic composers did, namely subject indigenous music to a "destructive urban influence," and "the contaminating influence of cosmopolitan culture." Paying "heed mainly to people on the social margins" he travelled through Hungary, Transylvania, Slovakia, Romania, Croatia, but also Turkey and North Africa to find these people and their music. His scholarly work includes systematizing 13,000 Hungarian folksongs; arranging 2,500 Romanian folksongs, in addition to collecting many indigenous Bulgarian, Serbian, and Slovak songs and preparing them for publication.

> *"The melodic world of my string quartets does not essentially differ from that of folk song, only the framework is stricter."*
> *- Bela Bartók*

Bartók's music rarely actually quotes folk themes but rather "he has completely absorbed and assimilated the folk tradition into his own musical thinking." Combining the folk tunes of his native land with Debussy's approach to harmony and color, along with a mastery of counterpoint, make Bartók not only one of the key composers of the 20th century but a unique one. Much of Bartók's work borders on atonality, even in the first decade of the 20th century, "but Bartók's ardor for folk melodies prevented him from going over the brink" and completely abandoning tonality. In fact, Bartók moved to liveliness and clarity in his *Music for Strings, Percussion and Celesta* of 1936. Although highly chromatic, much of his music "has a sense of a note that functions as a tonal center. This is sometimes called 'chromatic tonality'." His use of folk music resulted in "finding his basic material in music that came from societies rather than individuals...and a more generalized expression."

Bartók's string quartets traces his "personal creative evolution" over thirty years, starting with the "hothouse romanticism" of the first quartet, but also "the deeply tragic zeitgeist of half a century as well." The first two, from 1908 and 1917, respectively, are relatively conventional but in three movements. Both quartets retain elements of the late romantic sound world but also show hints of the Bartokian dissonance that would burst forth in the 1920s. String Quartet No.1 shows "almost every melodic fragment appearing in various guises," and was one of his first works "to synthesize the influences of peasant song and art music." It is not yet in focus but shines a bright light for us to see what Bartók was aiming for. He would achieve much greater stylistic definition and show many features of his mature style in his Second Quartet. The Second String Quartet was completed just before the end of World War I and is the most popular of the six. It "begins with music of exacerbated personal feeling" but ends "in an exuberant medley of village dances."

Quartet Nos.3-6 "are in a new, wild, cataclysmic world...that frightened listeners and players of the day...and include the famous Bartók *pizzicato*" – the effect produced by "the rebound of the string against the fret board." The Third is in one continuous variation movement divided into four distinct parts and contains the harshest dissonance of the set. Here "Bartók came closest to the extreme radical tendencies around him...(as) traditional forms are clouded over or completely eliminated." The five-movement Fourth String Quartet is "audacious in concept and brilliant in execution" and is an example of a work in symmetrical arch form. Nevertheless, the first movement is in sonata form, tone clusters and all. In the work Bartók has paired up the two outer movements, as well as the second and fourth movements, with the middle movement serving as a 'bridge' or 'keystone' to the entire structure.

In both the Fourth and Fifth Quartets "a unique central movement is flanked...by neighbors of similar character..." The result in both quartets is a symmetric A-B-C-B'-A' form in which 'C' is the bridge movement. Each individual movement is also symmetrically shaped. In Quartet No.4 the middle movement "is an almost motionless 'night music'," the outer movements possess a high degree of thematic development while "advanced shapes and textures are now concentrated in the inner movements." The *Fourth* is a cyclic quartet, themes from the first movement return to conclude the final movement. In Quartet No.5 the middle of the five movements is a wild scherzo flanked by slow movements. In both quartets there is a "sonata-like balance between movements of scherzo and nocturne type."

The Sixth and final quartet, the only one in a traditional four-movement format, was the last composition Bartók would write in Europe before immigrating to America. He wrote it while deeply disturbed over rising

Nazism and the outbreak of war, and "it is not difficult to hear (in it) some of the anguish Bartók (felt) as the civilized world tottered on the brink of destruction." The premiere was given in New York in January of 1941; at the end of the same year Bartók's adopted country would enter the war.

As with Beethoven's late quartets, Bartók's six push the technical capabilities of string players and require an "ensemble of virtuosi, as they tax the players to the utmost." "In their breadth of vision and profound humanity (they) are the legitimate progeny of Beethoven's." Some experts feel that Bartók's six quartets are the only set that can hold a candle to Beethoven's great late string quartets.

> ***Recommended – Bartók String Quartets***
> The Emerson String Quartet delivers technically flawless results of the six quartets (DG, 1988). They made their reputation largely due to this release. However, there are the usual reservations when it comes to this ensemble. Some find their performances too polished and not 'rough' enough to capture the full color and nationalistic flavor of Bartók. An excellent alternative (1998, Decca) is the Takacs Quartet, who master the polarizing components of these works. This set comes with extensive liner notes on how each quartet was written. Highly commendable performances are also by the Tokyo, Hungarian, and Juilliard String Quartets.

♪ Leoš Janáček (1854-1928)

Janáček's two string quartets are rare examples of programmatic chamber music, particularly the *First* (from 1923) in which the composer aims to portray an actual story ('The *Kreutzer* Sonata') by author Leo Tolstoy, with each instrument assuming the part of a particular character of the novella. The title of Tolstoy's story is taken from Beethoven's famous violin sonata. Janacek used his First String Quartet to show his passion for the rights of women and to protest the tyranny of men over women, with Tolstoy's story of an unhappy wife lured by a seducer and killed by her jealous husband as the backdrop.

Besides their programmatic nature these two chamber works are unique because they sound like no other works, probably because of Janáček's attempt to connect literature to the most purely musical of classical genres. String Quartet No.2, nicknamed *Intimate Letters*, was inspired by the composer's obsession with Kamila Stösslova, thirty-eight years younger than he. There is no evidence that Kamila had interest in Janáček, other than as a source of flattery and attention. The four movements of the work, completed in 1928, "are a drama of volatile, fluctuating emotion…"

♪ Serge Prokofiev (1891-1953)

Prokofiev produced two string quartets at different periods in his creative life, both in three movements. The *First* (in B minor, Op.50) was composed in the United States in 1930 towards the end of his fifteen-year exile from Russia. It is a "predominately serious, deeply felt work" that is strenuously wrought and is more daring harmonically than the second. String Quartet No.1 has propulsive energy; "Prokofiev only allows the occasional withdrawal into private lyricism in the first two movements." The "long emotional *Andante* (is) the quartet's crowning achievement (communicating) deep feelings and powerful passions through a direct and muscular approach, avoiding all sentimentality, (and ending) with a sense of inner strength and fortitude." It is worth noting that in 1930 Prokofiev had not yet lived in the Soviet Union; he had left Russia before the revolution.

The F major quartet, Op.92 subtitled 'On Karbadinian Themes', contains ('Soviet-approved') Ukrainian folk themes. The imposed parameters aside, this quartet is "one of the most immediately attractive quartets in the repertoire." It was completed at the end of 1941 while he was in the Caucasus Mountains, where he had moved with other leading composers for protection from the advancing German army. He became familiar with Kabardian folk music and incorporated, in an uncompromising way, the "music's primitive power and combination of childlike naïveté with menacing belligerence" making it an immediate success when performed in Moscow the following year.

♪ Dmitri Shostakovich (1906-1975)

The fifteen string quartets of Shostakovich comprise "a series unparalleled in the 20th century for its all-inclusive breadth." They show the composer's characteristic "long, flowing contrapuntal movements, wandering and almost improvisatory in nature." As with Bartók's, Shostakovich's quartets possess barbaric scherzos. He began the quartets at age forty in 1948 and they "became his favorite medium (giving) him the freedom to write labyrinthine narratives full of blankly winding fugues."

As with his symphonies and concertos, the string quartets of Shostakovich gained popularity in the 1980s with complete cycles appearing on CD and recognition as ranking alongside Bartók's at the pinnacle of 20th century chamber music. If Shostakovich's symphonies present a history of events he lived through, his string quartets represent a private, autobiographical portrait of the composer.

According to conductor Mariss Jansons Shostakovich's "...symphonies and quartets give an unmistakable depiction of the struggle of the individual against authority." Over thirty-five years Shostakovich's string quartets "increasingly served to make an indictment against the isolation and desperation of the individual in the inhuman system." The fifteenth and final quartet from 1974, the year before his death, consists of "six movements of unrelenting gloom."

> *"We still have a lot to learn from the composers of the Classical era..."*
> — Shostakovich

> *"One should not look for any particular depth in my First String Quartet"*
> — Shostakovich

Consistent with other composers looking over their shoulders at Beethoven, Shostakovich did not complete his First String Quartet until 1938, after he had already completed five symphonies. This is a brief quartet, only around fifteen minutes. In contrast to the Fifth Symphony, the First String Quartet displays none of the "rigorous struggles of the Fifth;" instead, Shostakovich challenged "the hallowed genre with deliberately shallow material." It is neo-Classical and "so full of spring-like innocence."

> *"Nobody is likely to write a work in memory of me, so I had better write one myself."*
> — Shostakovich on his *Eighth String Quartet*

Shostakovich's string quartets contain between one and seven movements with some structured closer to Classical *Divertimenti* or Baroque suites than traditional chamber quartets. No.2, from the summer of 1944, opens with an 'Overture' and concludes with a 'Theme and Variations'; String Quartet No.3 (1946) and No.8 share a five-movement format with two scherzo-like movements following the first movement.

String Quartet No.4 was composed in 1948 but not premiered until after Stalin's death. The composer feared his Fourth Quartet would be labeled with the latest denunciations from the dictator's culture police. These denunciations included pointing out the "anti-democratic tendencies" of certain works considered "being foreign to the people." Stalin's cultural 'soldiers' were on the march to push back what Soviet leadership saw as an "enthusiasm for difficult forms of instrumental music without text."

The most popular and most heard by far is String Quartet No.8, composed in 1960 in just a few days during a visit to Dresden. Shostakovich dedicated it "to victims of fascism and war." No.8 is "one of the most extraordinary autobiographical pieces in musical history." The musical material is largely heterogeneous consisting largely of quotations from his previous works. To his friend Isaak Glikman, Shostakovich admitted the quartet was "pseudo-tragic." This quartet, dominated by slow tempi, is "intensely poignant and personal in the slow movements, bitter and driven in the faster sections...beautifully integrated and balanced in its use of homophonic and polyphonic textures." The Eighth Quartet was scored for strings by Rudolf Barschay, producing what is known as Shostakovich's 'Chamber Symphony'.

> *"At his best...he mourns...for all victims of all tyrannies."*
> - Jan Swafford

Works quoted in this string quartet include some by the composer (the First and Seventh Symphonies, Cello Concerto, and the Op.67 Piano Trio), Tchaikovsky's *Pathetique*, as well as some quotes from Wagner's Ring cycle. The composer sprinkles in quotes from many of his works, in addition to using his trademark four-note D-Eb-C-B signature. "The fury of some sections could outpunch heavy rock music." The work is filled with "sounds that are as bleak, shrill and harsh as the events to which they respond...without the tortured circumstances of Shostakovich's life...his music would not have aspired to such tragic heights." Although he would live another fifteen years after completion of the Eighth Quartet and Shostakovich was only halfway through his total output in the form, the work serves as both a requiem and a memorial.

In opposition to the highly charged and autobiographical No.8, Shostakovich's Tenth String Quartet from 1964 is "entirely abstract, gentle and optimistic in tone." It is "one of Shostakovich's most serene and untroubled compositions," interrupted by "the sustained violence" of the furious *Allegretto* second movement.

Another of Shostakovich's popular string quartets is No.15, composed while he was very ill and within a year of his death. "Few works...confront the end of life in a more personal, poignant, and anguished way..." It is an elegiac work of six adagios played without pause, "conveying a mood of brooding grief." In between the opening Elegy and the concluding Epilogue are a Serenade, *Intermezzo*, Nocturne, as well as a funeral march. The final movement provides a summary of the themes from the five earlier movements. The unchanging rhythmic patterns "hold the listener's attention, providing an extremely moving musical experience." The *Fifteenth* was the first Shostakovich string quartet in decades not to be premiered by fellow Russians, the famed Beethoven String Quartet. "Increasingly bleak and despondent, his fifteen quartets represent a diary of his ever more desperate, tormented existence."

> **Recommended – Shostakovich String Quartets**
> The complete fifteen is probably beyond the interest and ambitions of most classical music fans. The *Eighth* can be had either coupled, or on its own on a budget CD by the Emerson String Quartet (DG). For complete sets, the box by the Fitzwilliam Quartet (Decca) was produced with input and approval by the composer. A good alternative would be the Borodin Quartet, which some feel has a much more 'Russian feel' than the performances by the Fitzwilliams. Recent efforts include the excellent cycle by the Mandelring Quartet (Audite, 2005-09) available on five separate discs (in SACD format) of three quartets each or as a boxed set.

The string quartet as a genre is still going strong in the first decade of the 21st century. The form should remain a major source of new chamber compositions; current-day composers remain attracted to the string quartet both for the challenge presented by the difficult form but also for the synergistic music produced by the seemingly perfect combination of string players.

- 12 -

Piano Quartets & Quintets
String Quintets to Octets

String quintets, sextets, septets and octets are much rarer than string quartets, but there is still much great music in these forms. The piano quintet is one of the rarer chamber genres because of the challenge of combining a string quartet, the most perfect of chamber combinations, with a dominant soloist. The combination of string trio and piano to form the piano quartet is a more common genre, but still much less so than the violin sonata, string quartet or even the piano trio.

To what extent the piano dominates, as opposed to being an equal partner with, the strings depends on the piece of music, the composer, and the pianist. Many famous virtuoso pianists (e.g., Argerich and Richter) were able to be partners and 'share the stage' with chamber ensembles and produce extraordinary results.

The three great piano quintets of Schumann, Brahms, Dvořák (Op.81) have long been taken together as a chamber music triptych. But before these were conceived, Franz Schubert composed the first chamber work for piano and four strings, his *Trout* Quintet. However, this was not technically a string quintet because it was composed for violin, viola, cello and double bass with piano.

♪ Germany and Austria

♫ Wolfgang Amadeus Mozart

Mozart 'invented' (actually perfected) the piano quartet by adding a viola to the piano trio, which brings the viola's distinctive sonority. Mozart's two piano quartets, K.478 in G minor (1785) and K.493 in E-flat (1786), were novel in their treatment of strings as partners with piano, in the true spirit of chamber music, instead of simply providing accompaniment to piano. These works moved piano music beyond the keyboard-dominated *galant* pieces of the Mannheim composers and J.C. Bach. Mozart's piano quartets laid the foundation for similar works of the Romantic period in which the strings are given full responsibility with piano in establishing ensemble texture.

With his six string quartets dedicated to Haydn, Mozart refined and improved the string quartet style begun by the elder master, but Mozart found his greatest inspiration in writing for the string quintet ensemble, which can produce even richer textures with an additional viola. Both composers sometimes flip-flopped the second (slow) and the third (dance-like) movements in their quartets, as Mozart also did in his string quintets. "Placing the minuet second…throws the expressive weight…towards the latter half" of the work. It often results in a more equal balance between the halves. The shift in a work's center of gravity is even more pronounced if the finale starts with an *adagio* introduction. Haydn used this order often in his string quartets until 1785.

The String Quintets

The string quintets are Mozart's greatest achievement in chamber music. The additional viola highlighted his love for rich 'inner-part' writing (second violin, second viola, cello) as opposed to quintets of contemporaneous or preceding composers which were in the concertante style with first violin and first viola as soloists and the remainder of the ensemble serving as accompaniment. The *concertante* style lacks the complex intimacy of chamber music which Mozart sought and mastered in his string quintets.

In addition to the six works that form Mozart's 'string quintets' is his most famous string quintet, what we all know as *Eine Kleine Nachtmusik*. This work is cast with a different ensemble than his string quintets, a string quartet plus double bass (a combination Schubert would employ) as opposed to a string quintet plus second viola. It is also frequently performed by a larger ensemble, e.g., a chamber or string orchestra.

Mozart took the form of the string quintet popular in his day (two violins, viola, and two cellos as utilized by Boccherini, a cellist) and adapted it for two violas instead of two cellos. In the Italian's string quintets the first violin and first cello dominate everything. By contrast, Mozart composed for five equal instruments "with occasional prominent solos and dialogues for two of them." "Mozart's first viola in no way steals the limelight like Luigi's (first cello)."

The additional viola gives a different timbre to the ensemble than a string quartet, one which Mozart obviously found appealing as he wrote six works for this combination. Mozart was known to prefer playing the viola over the violin and was proficient on both. This preference helps explain the dominant role he gives to the 'first' viola in these works. The result of the two violas is a feathery and velvety tone, which gives them a unique sound.

The six string quintets were written at various times in Mozart's life and are not a unified group as is his set dedicated to Haydn. With the exception of No.1, K.174, the other string quintets are considered among Mozart's mature chamber output. K.174 is an "immature if delightful divertimento-type composition written during his Salzburg days at the age of seventeen." Although mostly resembling an immature divertimento work by his standards, the finale of K.174 "is the most complex contrapuntal work that Mozart was to write for many years to come."

Mozart must have realized the shortcomings of this piece because when he needed a third string quintet to publish along with K.515 and K.516 (the standard number for a set of chamber works back then was three or six) he added a transcription of K.388, a wind octet, rather than use his First String Quintet. This transcription, which was wholly successful, has been catalogued as K.406 or K.516b and is the String Quintet No.4 in C minor. It is said that Tchaikovsky was particularly fond of the *adagio* from K.516, which he claimed brought tears to his eyes.

Quintets Nos.3-6 were composed in pairs between 1787-91, with No.3 in G minor and No.4 in C minor, K.515/516 produced in 1787-88, and No.5 in

D and No.6 in E-flat, K.593/614 in the last two years of his life. Mozart most likely composed the first pair to impress the new Prussian emperor Friedrich Wilhelm II, an accomplished cellist and chamber music enthusiast who had recently appointed Luigi Boccherini, composer of so many string quintets, court composer. Both K.515 and K.516 begin with the cello part highlighted and were, at the time, "grander in scope than anything that Haydn had ever conceived even for the orchestra."

As heard in both K.593 and K.614 "the brilliance of the individual instruments is more remarkable…each (instrument) is often pitted against the other four, with passages of exceptional virtuosity." In Quintet No.6, K.614 we have Mozart's last major chamber work. It is interesting that in the minuet and finale of this quintet Mozart clearly recalls the style of Haydn. Despite having outgrown the elder's influence, this quintet is clearly a tribute to his friend. The finale is derived from Haydn's Op.6, No.6 and, although contrapuntally complex, is Haydnesque throughout. With it Mozart makes a lasting tribute to the man he clearly saw as mentor, friend, as well as great composer.

> *Recommended – Mozart String Quintets*
> There really is no competition for the complete set of string quintets by the Grumiaux Trio with the addition of Gérecz and Lesueur (Philips). "Playing on this level is rarely encountered…belongs in the pantheon of great Mozart recordings." If the 3CD 'Trio' set is purchased, the addition of the great string trio *Divertimento in E-flat* (K.563) makes an exceptional bonus. There are many great renditions of *Eine Kleine Nachtmusik*; my favorite is by Karl Böhm and the Berlin Philharmonic (DG).

♪ Franz Schubert

Trout Quintet

The *Trout* Quintet is a piano quintet "suffused with the warmth and intimacy of *Hausmusik*." It was commissioned by the cellist Sylvester Paungartner, who happened to like Schubert's song *Die Forelle* ('The Trout'). Schubert borrowed a theme from that song to use in the quintet for Paungartner, hence the nickname.

As with the use of two cellos later in his Quintet in C, Schubert was also unconventional in his combination of strings in the 'Trout', using a double bass as the fourth stringed instrument instead of a second violin. The bass "is largely an independent voice that provides a foundation for the piano (and) strings." The work contains five movements with variations on *Die Forelle* inserted after the scherzo and before the finale.

Quintet in C
For his great String Quintet in C (D.956) Schubert added a second cello, following Boccherini, instead of a second viola as done by Mozart in his set of quintets. This made sense for the Italian as he was an established cellist and used the first cello part as a featured part and the second cello as accompaniment. The additional cello very effectively amplifies the texture, giving the work a "vastly expanded range of sonorities" and a depth achieved by very few string quartets.

Written two months before his death the Quintet in C is Schubert's greatest chamber work and one of the finest chamber compositions of any period; some believe the finest.

♫ Robert Schumann

Piano Quartet, Op.47; Piano Quintet, Op.44
The Piano Quartet in E-flat was composed in just a month back-to-back with his Piano Quintet of the same key during Schumann's chamber music year of 1842. The Piano Quintet was the first composed of the great triumvirate (joining Dvořák's and Brahms' piano quintets), also within a month in September - October 1842. Schumann's Piano Quintet was the first work expressly composed to combine piano with the forces of the string quartet. Schubert had composed quintets for piano with other combinations of strings (e.g., the aforementioned *Trout*). Many of Mozart's middle period piano concertos, particularly the eight from 1783-84, were written for small orchestras so that the winds could be omitted and the works performed as piano quintets. This was in response to the difficulty in securing large ensembles but also to make the piano concertos more attractive to amateurs and chamber ensembles for performance in private or small gatherings. Clara Schumann called her husband's work "Magnificent – a work filled with energy and freshness…"

The *Andante cantabile* third movement "manages a careful balance between 'light' salon music and true romantic poetry." The finale of Op.44 is "based on catchy opening tune that returns several times in several different settings." In fact, for the second part of the finale, this tune becomes the subject of an almost baroque-sounding fugue preceding the thrilling and exciting finish. In this finale Schumann shows a mastery of counterpoint (from his study of Bach), pitting an augmented first movement main theme against the leading theme of the finale.

The Piano Quintet and Quartet were expressly written for Clara as pianist. The Quintet became her signature work, appearing on many of her programs after her husband's death. Clara would often perform Schumann's piano chamber works with Brahms and violinist Joseph Joachim.

Both the Quartet and Quintet "treat the piano as a soloist constantly in the spotlight." As with the Piano Quintet, Schumann's wife Clara gushed over his Piano Quartet, "a beautiful work, so youthful and fresh, as if it were his first." Completed in October of 1842, it was rehearsed for the first time in December of that year with Mendelssohn filling in at piano for the pregnant Clara. The Piano Quartet is "so buoyant and so full of life. It's really infectious music" with a slow movement that is "one of the most inspired things ever written by anybody." The work highlights Schumann's practice of the "continuous use of short…sequential patterns within larger sequential structures…(to) impel the music forward without varying the pattern."

> ***Recommended*** – The Mandelring Quartet with pianist Claire-Marie Le Guay bring fresh expression to these two great works (Audite, 2010). The Beaux Arts Trio augmented by violist Samuel Rhodes (of Juilliard Quartet fame) and violinist Dolf Bettelheim perform these two piano chamber works, along with Schumann's *String Trios* (Philips).

♫ Felix Mendelssohn

Octet in E-flat, Op.20

Mendelssohn was called "the Mozart of the 18th century" by Robert Schumann. The comparison is not as exaggerated as it may seem; for one thing, Mendelssohn actually outdid Mozart as a composer at a younger age. His two masterpieces before the age of twenty, the *Octet*, Op.20 at age sixteen and *A Midsummer Night's Dream* Overture of 1826 (Op.21) at age seventeen were well ahead of what Mozart had composed at a similar age.

With his *Octet* Mendelssohn established a new genre of a chamber work for eight string players, which are actually two string quartet ensembles. But, as Louis Spohr commented, "all eight instruments work together." And Mendelssohn was indeed seeking true ensemble playing for this mature masterpiece from his youth. Spohr's comment is consistent with the instructions provided to the players by the composer: "This octet must be played in the style of a symphony in all parts…" It is constructed as a symphony with an *Allegro* first movement that is twice as long as any of the three that follows. There is an *andante* slow movement, a scherzo and the finale marked *presto*, as with a typical four-movement symphony.

The *Octet* indeed looks ahead to the classically configured works of Mendelssohn's future and already possesses their refinement and elegance. The work sticks to sonata form and never attempts to break new ground. This is not surprising for Mendelssohn as he was a composer who stuck to convention, not a risk taker or trail blazer. Donald Tovey commented on the *Octet* that, "Eight string players might easily practice it for a lifetime without coming to an end of their delight in producing its marvels of tone color." The work, scored for two opposing string quartets, is a shining jewel of chamber music.

The *Octet* is a supreme model of cyclical form early in the Romantic period in which the opening theme of the scherzo shows up again in the finale. This masterpiece would be a model for later attempts in cyclical form.

> ***Recommended – Mendelssohn Octet***
> The recommendation is the offering from the same ensemble, Hausmusik on EMI (1990 & 1991 for Mendelssohn and Schubert, respectively). The Mendelssohn CD also comes with a performance of his *A major String Quintet*, Op.18.

♪ Johannes Brahms (1833-1897)

After the genius of Haydn and Mozart and the elevation of the form to the sublime by Beethoven and Schubert, chamber music lay dormant for almost forty years. It took Brahms, who "had learned to venerate" the past masters, in the 1860's to revitalize the genre. Brahms does not break any molds, he was not an inventor and "he did not expand the means of his art." Instead, he engages the "daunting legacy bequeathed" by the giants before him. While Brahms may not sound like Mozart or Haydn, "there is a deeper generic structure…that signifies its ancestry." In other words, the roots of Brahms' chamber works are undeniable.

The popularity of chamber music in the 20th century is largely due to Brahms' masterpieces composed at the end of the nineteenth. Of his seventeen works for three or more instruments, "among them there is not one in which it could be said that 'Homer nodded'."

Piano Quartets

Brahms' three piano quartets are great listening music and represent the pinnacle of the form. The third and fourth movements of Op.25 are among my favorites and contain some of the finest, and most varied, chamber music with piano. As with all of Brahms' chamber music, these works are chocked full of beautiful melodies. Brahms' characteristic achievement of "that personal compromise between classical and romantic" shines through in these large-scale chamber works.

With the G minor (Op.25) and C minor (Op.60) quartets the first movements are characterized by the "makings of tragedy" and "profound disturbances", whereas the A major (Op.26) "is all grace and romance." The C minor Quartet came together over twenty years - the first and third movements of the C minor Quartet were originally composed in 1850. Both movements were revised in the 1870s when Brahms added the slow movement, with its beautiful cello solo, and final movement. The A major Quartet, Op.26, is a massive work over fifty minutes in length, roughly ten and fifteen minutes longer than Op.25 and Op.60, respectively; the first movement *Allegro non troppo* taking well over fifteen minutes. In Op.26 Brahms extracts from the main theme a seemingly endless array of "variations and permutations". And in the G minor Quartet the *Rondo alla Zingarese* ('Gypsy Rondo') finale "precisely evokes the exuberance of a Gypsy wedding band."

> *Recommended – Brahms Piano Quartets*
> Fine performances of the three quartets in one set are available from the teams of Ax, Ma, Stern, and Laredo, the chamber equivalent of an 'all-star' team (on Sony, 1990), as well as from the Beaux Arts Trio (Philips).

Piano Quintet

Brahms wrote this famous chamber work around age thirty and it is definitely one of his finer early works. It exists in other forms: it was originally intended as a string quintet, then a sonata for two pianos before reaching its final form as a piano quintet. It is still performed in the two-piano version (as Op.34b), but not as a string quintet. Brahms' transformations of this work clearly paid off as it has enjoyed lasting fame in this form, with its "potent combination of driving passion (and) lyrical grace…"

Brahms' Piano Quintet provides an example method of what Schoenberg, who later orchestrated Brahms' G minor Piano Quartet, called "developing variation," whereby the composer "continuously building on germinal ideas; the first movement theme is "series of variants of its opening measure."

> *Recommended – Brahms Piano Quintet*
> For the version for two pianos, a live performance by Martha Argerich and Lilya Zilberstein (EMI, 2003) from her perennial series of recordings from the Lugano Festival is recommended and also one of the few available.

String Quintets and Sextets

Brahms wrote two string quintets (Op.88 in F and Op.111 in G) and two works for string sextet (Op.18 in B-flat from 1860 and Op.36 in G from 1865). The sextets, which are early sunny works, are better-known than the quintets, but both pairs contain plenty of the typical Classical-Romantic melodies associated with Brahms. The First Sextet was written when Brahms was in his twenties, a time when he destroyed many more of his compositions than he sent for publication. It shows the influence in his youth of the chamber music of the great Classical composers.

The First String Quintet is from 1882; the Second was composed in the summer of 1890. Brahms had expressed thoughts to his publisher Simrock that Op.111 could be his final composition, but thankfully changed his mind, producing his four late chamber works with clarinet, as well as his great sets of late solo piano pieces (Opp.116-119). The string quintets are more congenial than the sextets and, being later works, they reflect the more mellow and mature Brahms. The Op.18 String Sextet in B-flat is "sunny and pleasant in outlook…it hearkens back to the music of Mozart and Beethoven." Op.36 is "quieter and more reflective than the first sextet," and did not achieve the quick success of Op.18.

♪ 19th Century France

♫ Cesar Franck (1822-1890)

Franck's Piano Quintet was premiered in 1880 with Saint-Saëns the pianist. To get an idea of the response to Franck's music, even from his contemporaries, Saint-Saëns is said to have hated the work and walked off the stage when finished, not staying or acknowledging the audience's applause. Despite Saint-Saëns' unprofessional behavior at its premiere, after his Violin Sonata this is Franck's most successful chamber work.

♫ Gabriel Fauré

Piano Quartets

Fauré composed two masterpieces for piano quartet, Op.15 in C minor and Op. 45 in G minor. The First Piano Quartet, composed in 1877, followed his other chamber masterpiece of his early period, the First Violin Sonata, Op.13, and is his most popular chamber work after the Op.13 sonata.

The Second Piano Quartet was probably composed in 1885 or 1886. While it is not as popular as the First it is superbly crafted and melodically generous. In this work, as in some of his other chamber works (e.g., the Op.108 Violin Sonata), first movement themes are hinted at in later movements, but in a much more subtle way than Liszt's 'thematic transformations' or Franck's 'cyclic' form.

As in the First Quartet the two middle movements are contrasted, a violent scherzo and a serene *Adagio*. Of the *Adagio* Aaron Copland wrote, "its beauty is truly classic if we define classicism as intensity on a background of calm." The finale of this quartet is relentlessly driven, even compared to the furious energy of the Op.15 finale, which manages an occasional pause for reflection.

Piano Quintets

Fauré's two piano quintets are much less popular than his two quartets. They "inhabit a more private world," and "contain some of the darkest and most violent moments in (his) chamber music." Both show his characteristic "intellectual, contrapuntal writing" and Fauré's "ever-gutsy sensuality." However, these two chamber works have a hypnotic effect upon repeated listenings that "puts you completely under its spell." Fauré's textures unfold smoothly and organically; they "evolve into one another." His is the "language of seamless flow, almost never of dramatic interruption." In the quintets the piano fits "as unobtrusive equal in the dialogue" with the strings, together creating a "pervasive web of harmonic richness."

Even though Fauré's deafness was getting worse, leading to the loss of his post at the Paris Conservatory in 1920, which put him in financial straits, these last seven years of his life produced "an outpouring of powerful and vigorous chamber music." The works from this final period include the Second Piano Quintet and Violin Sonata, two cello sonatas, the Piano Trio and the String Quartet, his final work (Op.121).

> *Recommended – Fauré piano quartets and quintets*
> The Domus ensemble is recommended for the both piano quartets (Hyperion, 1985). For the piano quintets Anthony Marwood joins Domus (Hyperion, 1995).

♪ Eastern Europe

♫ Antonín Dvořák

Through his association with Brahms and pressure to move to Vienna, Dvořák considered a move away from the incorporation of Bohemian elements in his music towards a more Germanic music in the line of Beethoven, Schubert, and his friend Brahms. He chose not to follow this path but to renew his devotion to Bohemian folk music with his mature Piano Quintet, Op.81, the Piano Quartet No.2, and the 'Dumky' Piano Trio, all composed from late 1887 to early 1891.

Dvořák's piano quartets and quintet are fine examples of his nationalistic, Bohemian style. Although he rarely quoted folk songs, "Dvořák wrote melodies that grew naturally from Bohemian soil...(and) are subjected to a Classical Germanic craftsmanship learned from Brahms and Beethoven."

Piano Quartets

Dvořák contributed two very fine piano quartets, one early and one more mature (No.1 in D, Op. 23 and No.2 in E-flat, Op 87). Both are in typical Dvořák style, deeply rooted and indebted to Slavonic folk tunes with strong nationalistic undercurrents and hints of gypsy spirit. The Op.23 was composed in 1875, the same year that saw Dvořák produce his *Serenade for Strings* (Op.22), Symphony No.5 (Op.76), and the B-flat Piano Trio (Op.21). It did not premiere until five years later in Prague.

Early after his arrival in Prague (1857) Dvořák played viola in an all-Wagner program with Wagner himself conducting! This resulted in a strong Wagnerian influence on the early Czech composer, which Dvořák held to in his early years of composing, probably delaying establishment of his unique style we know today. Fortunately he soon retreated from an uncompromising Wagnerian stance and returned to a Classical style beginning with his early chamber works.

The mature Dvořák showed his development with more original and inventive scoring for Op. 87, as well as "far more assured" piano writing, exploring its "capacity for rich, massive sonorities". This work is "built on the grand scale of Brahms' Piano Quartets."

> *Recommended – Dvořák piano quartets*
> For both quartets together Domus is the choice (Hyperion, 1988). For *Op.87* and the *Piano Quintet* on the same disk, the choice is also clear: Menahem Pressler (of Beaux Arts Trio fame) joins the Emerson String Quartet to produce "a beautifully played Dvořák program with charm and warmth."

Piano Quintets

Dvořák's Piano Quintet, Op.81, is the result of his attempt at revising his first quintet. Instead of doing that, he decided to simply compose a brand new one. Fortunately for us this decision resulted in a masterpiece of the chamber repertoire and one of the most popular chamber works.

By the time Dvořák took to composing Op.81 in 1887 he was a much more accomplished composer. As with the second piano quartet, Dvořák's piano writing was mature by this time, after being rather routine in his earlier chamber works in which Dvořák focused on "masterly string writing" as a violinist and violist. He took much longer to move beyond "stock figurations" and to compose marvelously for the piano as well as the strings.

The first movement is a signature of Dvořák's mature chamber works, "understated, lyrical opening prepares the way for the main business of the first movement." The second movement is a *dumka*, alternating slow and fast themes.

> *Recommended – Dvořák Piano Quintet*
> I recommend the recent and polished offering from an ensemble of artists, including Sarah Chang on violin and Leif Ove Andsnes on piano. The recording is coupled with Dvořák's *Violin Concerto*. An historic recording, if a performance from

> 1985 can be considered 'historic', is Sviatoslav Richter joining fellow Russians, the Borodin Quartet. This is a live performance without the polish of most studio recordings, but with the spontaneity of a live performance. It is coupled with the much lesser-known early *Piano Quintet, Op. 5* of Dvořák.

♪ 20th Century

♪♪ Arnold Schoenberg

Verklärte Nacht was originally composed in 1899 by Schoenberg for string sextet, although the later version he orchestrated for string orchestra is the better known. It is purely post-Romantic, with a program taken from a poem by Richard Dehmel, and does not yet show Schoenberg as the atonal maverick he would shortly become. As Schoenberg made his sharp break from post-Romanticism he distanced himself from the relationship between Dehmel's literary poem and his own tone poem.

♪♪ Dmitri Shostakovich (1907-1975)

> *"He is talented, but...has no gift for melody."*
> *- Prokofiev on Shostakovich*

Shostakovich's Piano Quintet in G minor, Op.57 (1940), was the result of a request by the Beethoven Quartet of Moscow for a new string quartet. In reply, Shostakovich wrote a piano quintet he could play together with the renowned quartet. The popularity of this work is undoubtedly largely due to its positive emotion as opposed to the "intense soul searching" that results in the dark and brooding nature of so much of his music. The Piano Quintet draws inspiration from Bach; so much so that Prokofiev declared the first two movements, a prelude and a fugue played without a break, to be too 'Bachian' for his liking. It was otherwise well-received, even winning the Stalin Prize but Prokofiev thought it revealed his countryman's reluctance to take risks, even claiming Shostakovich to be "bereft of melodic invention." Shostakovich's Piano Quintet, "a work of a neo-Classical stance, where the keyboard and the string quartet are juxtaposed in an effective manner," was his most significant contribution in the neo-Baroque vein.

13

Chamber Music for Winds

Many of the septets and octets in the chamber repertory were composed for a blend of winds and strings. These are discussed below, along with works for wind-only ensembles, including wind octets, which were called *Harmoniemusik* in 19th century Germany. The nucleus of the *Harmoniemusik* ensemble was two bassoons to provide the bass part plus two horns and a combination of oboes and clarinet.

The first true chamber works for winds were probably the wind quintets composed by Franz Danzi (1763-1826) around 1780 while he was a cellist in Karl Theodor's orchestra at Mannheim. His compositions are dominated by works for winds, including several quintets for piano and winds. Although a wide variety of Danzi's chamber music for winds is still performed, available recordings are dominated by the three sets of wind quintets (Opps.56, 67, 68). The wind quintets are light works, lacking the development and depth of chamber works by Mozart and Haydn for similar forces.

Germany and Austria

Mozart

Flute Quartets

Mozart had met the amateur flutist and surgeon Ferdinand De Jean, who commissioned from the young Mozart three flute concertos and three flute quartets for his own use. The actual number of works commissioned varies by account. Mozart had trouble getting interested in this commission; at the time "he (had written) only one flute concerto (and he arranged an earlier oboe concerto for flute) and at least one flute quartet." Mozart disliked the flute but ultimately composed four quartets, four concerto works and a *sinfonia concertante* that highlight the instrument.

K.285 in D, an early chamber work, was completed on Christmas Day in 1777. It follows the expected sonata-form first movement, slow movement, and rondo finale. "Brief and straightforward, it keeps the spotlight firmly on the flute, offering beautifully idiomatic writing for that instrument in the process."

K.298 in A is the major work of Mozart's four flute quartets.

Serenades for Winds

Serenades and divertimenti were genres that bridged the orchestral suites of the Baroque with the orchestral and chamber music forms that firmly established themselves in the Classical period. They are lighter works, intended for outdoor public performances. Nevertheless, Mozart left several masterpieces of this type and he was one of the few composers before the 20th century "to write all-wind music at the top of his form."

The three wind serenades qualify as 'Harmoniemusik', *Harmonie* being the German term for wind band in the mid-1700s. This music was very popular in Mozart's day, consisting of music scored for groups of winds, ensuring flexibility of tonal color. Also, winds were better suited for open-air performances, allowing varied instrumental combinations.

Serenade No.10, 'Gran Partita' in B-flat, K.361
The most common combination for *Harmonie* was the wind octet made up pairs of oboes, clarinets, horns and bassoons. To these eight parts Mozart, for K.361, added an additional pair of horns, two basset horns, and a double bass as the only string of the ensemble. Serenades were the most popular type of *divertimento* in the Classical period. They are occasional 'informal' pieces and it is in the ad hoc nature of these works "that the idealism of Mozartean music manifests itself most palpably."

Together with the Clarinet Quintet, K.581, the *Gran Partita* Serenade 'for 13 Wind Instruments' is one of Mozart's two greatest works for chamber wind ensemble.

Serenade No.11 in E-flat, K.375; No.12 in C minor, K.388
Serenade No.11 was originally composed for sextet, two each of clarinet, horn and bassoon, but Mozart later expanded it to the usual *Harmonie* octet ensemble with the addition of two oboes.

Being in a minor key tells one that the K.388 Serenade will not be as light and playful as those in major keys. It is a "powerful, penetrating piece that encompasses many of the emotional realms Mozart explored in his great operas." This is especially true of the "spectacular, hauntingly beautiful set of variations" of the finale. This serenade would subsequently be re-cast by Mozart as the String Quintet, K.406.

Clarinet Trio, K.498
Mozart first heard clarinets on a visit to Mannheim in 1777-78, fell in love with the sound, and began writing works for clarinet as soloist and incorporating the instrument into other orchestral works. He would quickly come to prefer clarinets to oboes. Once Mozart showed how well the clarinet worked as a key performer in a chamber ensemble, this repertory firmly established itself. The flexibility of the clarinet is shown by its use in quartets and quintets with strings alone or with piano and strings. Mozart's Clarinet Trio was composed in 1786.

Clarinet Quintet in A, K.581
Along with Brahms' Clarinet Quintet this late (1789) chamber work for clarinet and string quartet is among the two greatest of its kind. It was written in 1789 and, as with K.498 above, for the renowned clarinetist Anton Stadler, for whom the famous Clarinet Concerto, K.622, was also written. This work

is considered by many to be Mozart's greatest chamber work for winds.

The balance among the five instruments is unified as in his great string quintets, with the clarinet assuming the role of the first violin. Mozart "allows the clarinetist to display great virtuosity." The work has one of Mozart's most beautiful slow movements, the second movement *Larghetto*.

Wind Quintet in E flat, K.452

> „For my own part, I think it's the best work I've ever composed."
> - Mozart in letter to his father (1784)

The combination of instruments for this delightful work from 1784 is piano with oboe, horn, clarinet, and bassoon. This ensemble was unknown up to this time for use in such "an elaborate, refined piece of chamber music that is every bit as demanding as a string quartet."

Most classical pieces for wind ensembles were light-spirited serenades and divertimenti intended to entertain the public, and did not include a demanding piano part. The piano writing is of the same style and difficulty as Mozart's contemporaneous piano concertos and there is a 'concerto' element to this quintet with dialogue taking place between the piano and different winds.

Horn Quintet in E flat, K.407

The Horn Quintet was written in Vienna probably in the end of 1782 for Ignaz Joseph Leutgeb. This work, for the unusual scoring of horn, violin, two violas, and cello, is "full of gentle, amiable music" is more of a miniature horn concerto than a true chamber work because the horn dominates and the strings provide accompaniment. "The viola has a range similar to that of the horn, and this work's sonority emphasizes the mellow middle range of the horn and violas rather than the bright upper register of the violin."

As with his string quintets Mozart, who always favored the viola as a player, again shows his mastery in extracting from this instrument far more than any previous composer. As usual the limitations of the natural horn are not obstacles to Mozart; instead they are "exploited wittily and skillfully."

Oboe Quartet in F, K.370

Written in 1781 for the oboist Friedrich Ramm toward the end of Mozart's stay in Berlin, this is "one of the jewels of the repertory…with…infectious high spirits." Mozart was focusing on chamber music during his time in Berlin, producing this great work for oboe and string trio in which the composer grants the oboe a very prominent role.

> **Recommended – Mozart Chamber music for Winds**
> *Clarinet Trio* – Kovacevich, Brymer, and Ireland (Philips, 1969);
> *Clarinet Quintet, Horn Quintet, Oboe Quartet* – Academy of St. Martin-in-the-Fields Chamber Ensemble (Philips, 1980)

♪ Ludwig van Beethoven

Wind Quintet in E-flat
The influence of Mozart is especially pronounced in Beethoven's chamber music for strings and winds together. Beethoven paid tribute to Mozart's Wind Quintet (K.452) with this *Harmoniemusik*, his Wind Quintet of 1797, by casting it in the same key and using the same combination of instruments. One marked difference is the piano here is much more dominant and virtuosic than in Mozart's Quintet.

Septet, Op.20
This work is scored for violin, viola, cello, and double bass string section plus a wind trio of clarinet, horn and bassoon. It consists of six movements in light, entertaining divertimento for and the mid-18th century *Rococo* style *galant*. This became one of Beethoven's most popular early works during his lifetime, which upset him. Beethoven "denounced it for lacking seriousness" and even attributed his *Septet* to Mozart later in life.

♪ Franz Schubert

Franz Schubert was the bridge that moved the music of Haydn, Mozart, and even Beethoven, into the 19th century.

Octet in F, Op.166 (D803)
Schubert's *Octet* was first performed in the spring of 1824 in Vienna at the house of the clarinetist who commissioned the work. It is scored for the same winds as Beethoven's *Septet*, but Schubert added an additional violin to combine the forces of string quintet (the fifth string being the double bass) and wind trio. It is believed that Schubert was asked to model it after the *Septet* so that the ensemble would have that work, plus Schubert's new *Octet* to perform at the same gathering. One month after the completion of his *Octet* Schubert would complete his Fourteenth String Quartet in D minor, titled 'Death and the Maiden'. The melodious *Octet* stands in stark contrast to the surrounding string quartets with their poignant, soul-searching qualities.

The *Octet* is a substantial work, taking approximately an hour to perform. After the two significant symphonic-like opening movements of twenty-five minutes, followed by a light-hearted and brief *Allegro vivace*, Schubert gives us an unusual theme and variations. This form was popular in Schubert's time for allowing each of the players "a few moments in the spotlight." The closing ten-minute finale returns us to the symphonic textures of the opening movement.

♪ Johannes Brahms

Late Chamber Works with Clarinet; Horn Trio

Brahms' last four chamber works were all written for the clarinet as the featured instrument. Brahms' fell for the clarinet toward the end of his career, inspired by his friend, clarinetist Richard Mühlfeld. In his late clarinet works Brahms seems to have found the perfect instrument to capture his mood at the end of his career. Chances are if Brahms and Mühlfeld had not crossed paths we would have none of Brahms' four great late clarinet works. Once Brahms discovered the marvelous tone colors of the clarinet, he concentrated on writing his final chamber works for the wind instrument.

The final four clarinet chamber works consist of the famous Clarinet Quintet in B minor, Op.115, the Clarinet Trio in A minor, Op.114 and the last two works, the Clarinet Sonata No.1 in F minor and No.2 in E-flat, Op.120/1&2. The Op.120 sonatas are sometimes performed as viola sonatas (with piano). In his late clarinet chamber works Brahms "found at last a perfect medium for the expression of his own humanity." In his last decade Brahms reacted to the post-Romantic movement "by endeavoring to restore the balance and clarity of the past."

The Clarinet Quintet was composed in 1891 and it is "the paradigm of his autumnal style." The whole mood of the work is subdued. By effective use of harmony it is without extreme tension. The clarinet at the opening of this work "gleams forth over murmuring strings in a single harmonious tone. It melts into a lustrous shimmer…the mood is perfectly blissful."

However, this mood gradually darkens as the first movement progresses, which, according to Lawrence Kramer, hints at Brahms feeling "old and creatively exhausted." In the first movement we hear "the sound of a romantic longing very familiar to members of Brahms' generation."

In addition to the late four works for clarinet there is also the much earlier *Trio for Horn, Violin and Piano* in E-flat, Op.40. This trio can be considered to conclude Brahms' early chamber period and "in many ways looks back nostalgically to his youth."

♪ French Chamber Music for Winds

♪ Camille Saint-Saëns (1835-1921)

Sonata for Oboe Op.168; Bassoon, Op.169; Clarinet Op.170

These three sonatas for piano and wind instrument were all written in Saint-Saëns' final year. The composer claimed to have admirable intentions with these late works, admitting, "I am using my last energies to add to the repertoire for these otherwise neglected instruments." These works are cherished by wind players, who welcomed them enthusiastically into the limited repertoires for their respective instruments. He intended to write a sonata for as many as six different winds, but only completed half. The three sonatas are Romantic in sentiment but their basic structure and simple musical lines look back to the Classical era. They have simpler melodies and textures than his other chamber works and set the tone for 20th century chamber wind composition.

Composers such as fellow Frenchman **Darius Milhaud** (1892-1974) composed chamber works to include clarinet and he rearranged his *Scaramouche* for Two Pianos for many different instrument combinations and ensembles, including versions with clarinet, with saxophone, and for wind sextet. The English composer and Milhaud's contemporary **Arnold Bax** (1883-1953) had composed a *Trio for Flute, Viola and Harp* a few years before Saint-Saëns' wind sonatas (1916) and Bax later produced a *Fantasy Sonata for Viola & Harp* (1927) and a Clarinet Sonata (1934).

♪ Claude Debussy

Sonata for Flute, Viola and Harp

This trio, referred to as a 'sonata' in English, is part of Debussy's final three works (1915-17), all for chamber combinations. The other works are the Violin Sonata and the Cello Sonata. In all three Debussy had made it clear that his music was becoming more abstract and he was moving away from pictorial music-making (i.e., Impressionism). However, in contrast to Debussy's Violin Sonata and Cello Sonata, the *Sonata for Flute, Viola and Harp* is "a great deal less harmonically adventuresome."

> "Where are the old harpsichordists who had so much true music?"
> - Debussy

Debussy also composed two eclectic works, the *Rapsodie for Sax*, and the *Rapsodie for Cor Anglais*.

♪ 20ᵗʰ Century

♫ Igor Stravinsky

Stravinsky knew his neo-Classic works would never approach the popularity of his early ballets. In a way, he peaked very early as a composer and rode the wave of that early success through a dynamic career during which, for the most part, the musical world considered him the 'greatest living composer'. Stravinsky was partial toward winds as shown in two of his better-known chamber works.

Octet

A work that exemplifies Stravinsky's neo-Classicism, the *Octet* was composed in 1923 and scored for flute, clarinet, and two each of trumpet, trombone and bassoon. This work is an example of *Harmoniemusik*, which at the time was the term used in Germany for music performed by a wind ensemble, often an octet. The *Octet* caused surprise for the young Aaron Copland and many others because of its "mess of 18ᵗʰ century mannerisms." It did, however, according to Copland, bring "the latent objectivity of modern music to full consciousness." In Stravinsky's *Octet* the subjective element was expunged completely.

Symphonies of Wind Instruments

This work, which actually appeared nine months before the *Octet*, is a neo-Classical divertimento, updated for the 20ᵗʰ century and Stravinsky's first completed work after his move to Switzerland. Of his *Symphonies of Wind Instruments* Stravinsky said, "it lacks all those elements that appeal to the ordinary listener…the music is not meant to 'please' an audience…" Stravinsky was not off-target here with his assessment; with its "lamenting cries (and) meandering chants", Alex Ross characterizes this work for twenty-four wind and brass players (or twenty-three as Stravinsky would remove the French horn in the 1947 revision), as "the consummation of Stravinsky's hard-edged, steel-tipped style." It is "only a system of sounds, which…group themselves according to purely musical affinities."

The *Symphonies* forms a connection among several of Stravinsky's influences and compositional styles. It looks back to his great ballet scores of his 'Russian' period, but also ahead to Stravinsky's embrace of neo-Classicism in the 1920s. It mixes Russian folk tunes but also chorales that look forward to his later sacred works. It uses the term 'symphonies' literally as 'sounding together' as the winds produce a "kind of disjointed, collage-like form." However, the work fits almost no definition of 'symphony' up to that point or since.

It premiered in 1921 in London under Koussevitzky and is dedicated to Debussy (who had died two years earlier). Ironically, the great French composer was not flattering to Stravinsky privately and in correspondence, but to the young Russian composer on the rise, Debussy appeared supportive. The ten-minute piece in four episodes was summed up by Stravinsky as, "An austere ritual which is unfolded in terms of short litanies between different groups of homogeneous instruments."

♪ Paul Hindemith

Hindemith and Martinů, two neo-Classicist contemporaries, revived the spirit of Classical chamber music in the first half of the 20th century with their prolific output of chamber works, for all sorts of combinations of strings, piano, and, as with Mozart's chamber works, for wind instruments.

Hindemith (1895-1963) was a prolific composer and wrote chamber works for many instruments of the orchestra. His chamber output is by far the most varied by any 20th century composer, writing at least one sonata for piano with virtually every instrument of the orchestra. Many of these works were intended as instructional tools for players and thus are not virtuosic. However, because Hindemith could play every instrument at least adequately (he was a virtuoso violist) they are all of high quality and remain widely-used for their value in the training of instrumentalists.

The *Quartet for Clarinet, Violin, Cello, and Piano* is one of his more popular chamber works. All four instruments are full partners. This work is underperformed due to its odd instrument ensemble.

Kleine Kammermusik, Op.24:2 is a wind quintet scored for flute, oboe, clarinet, horn, and bassoon. Hindemith made it clear that it was written (1922) for the Wind Chamber Music Society of Frankfurt. "While invoking the outdoor wind *divertimenti* of the 18th century, (it) sneers at the late 19th century's sonorous and emotional indulgences." This work and the seven works that comprise Hindemith's *Kammermusik*, "contain almost none of the post-Romantic tendencies found in contemporaries…but reflect Hindemith's…headlong plunge into the world of German modernist music in the 1920s." It consists of five movements with lively outer movements as bookends to a waltz, a calm and simple slow movement and a movement of cadenzas. However, it does contain "an undercurrent of bitterness and irony, perhaps a reflection of the social and political unrest in Germany at the time." It is an excellent example of unpretentious 'workaday' music (*Gebrauchsmusik*).

♫ Martinů, Janáček, and Bartók

Bohuslav Martinů (1890-1959) was a contemporary of Hindemith's and similarly looked back to the Baroque and Classical periods for the settings of his 20th-century neo-Classical works. As Hindemith did, Martinů turned out a large volume of chamber works for many combinations of instruments. One wind instrument he favored was the flute, usually joining it with piano and/or violin. These chamber flute works include the *Sonata for Flute, Violin and Piano* (H254, 1937) as well as the *Sonata for Flute and Piano* (1945), the *Trio for Flute, Cello and Piano* (1944) and the flute trios titled *Promenades* for flute, violin and harpsichord and *Madrigal-Sonata for Flute, Violin and Piano* (H291, 1942) For larger chamber forces Martinů contributed for strings alone a sextet and a quintet, and for winds and strings the *Quartet for Oboe, Violin, Cello and Piano*, and the *Nonet* for winds and strings.

Among **Leoš Janáček's** (1854-1928) many chamber works, his most famous is for wind sextet titled *Mladi* or 'Youth'. The work premiered in 1924 at the composer's seventieth birthday party. *Mladi* "bubbles forth with great enthusiasm and fresh ideas" as the composer recalls childhood memories through music. Janáček uses the repetition of tiny thematic figures to build the work up into a convincing whole. *Mladi* is scored for wind quintet (flute, oboe, clarinet, horn and bassoon) plus bass clarinet.

Another work is the *Concertino* for piano, two violins, clarinet, French horn and bassoon. It was written the year after *Mladi* and, according to Janáček, "comes from the youthful mood of *Mladi*," although it is more 'modernistic' in style and feel. As with most of his great instrumental works, it was written during Janáček's last years; he was over seventy when he wrote the *Concertino*.

The *Concertino* is a programmatic work, depicting nature scenes recalled from Janáček's youth, with a hedgehog, a squirrel and birds being depicted in the first three movements. In the fourth movement the animals all come together. In the *Capriccio* of 1926, composed between the *Concertino* and the *Sinfonietta*, Janáček creates a very unique and flexible sonority with the unusual and highly original instrument ensemble of left-hand piano, flute (or piccolo) and six horns.

In addition to **Belá Bartók's** (1881-1945) six great string quartets, he also composed a three-movement clarinet sonata called *Contrasts* for clarinetist Benny Goodman, the "King of Swing" and violinist Joseph Szigeti, with the composer in a supporting role on the piano. The title indicates that Bartók is exploring timbral differences among the instruments. The fast dances of the outer movements bracket the relaxation (*pihenö*) of the middle movement with its "whispered nocturnal flutterings and trills heard in country fields, forests, and along mountain streams."

Part 3

Introduction to Orchestral Music: The Baroque and Classical Periods

- 14 -

Introduction to Orchestral Music

♪ Types of Orchestral Music

It is convenient to divide orchestral music into works with and without soloist(s). Among the former the dominant form is clearly the symphony, with other forms including overtures, 'tone' or 'symphonic' poems, suites, serenades, and sets of variations on a theme. The term 'symphonic music' includes here all orchestral music that does not involve a dominant soloist. The distinction between some of these is not always clear-cut; for example, some 'overtures' of the early Romantic period could be classified as tone poems. Also, works such as Tchaikovsky's orchestral suites are not much different from his symphonies. Works with soloist(s) had been called concertos since before the Classical Period, but can also be designated as a concertante (with more than one soloist) and even *concerto grosso* (a Baroque form that has been used in 'modern' music).

The form of both concertos and symphonies is often very similar, with concertos usually adopting a fast-slow-fast format for its typical three movements and the symphony inserting a minuet or scherzo as the third movement in a four-movement work. In some symphonies the slow movement and the scherzo may exchange places. Although most symphonies have the standard four movements, three and five movements are not uncommon, and there are well-known two-movement symphonies (Schubert's *Unfinished*).

The opening movement of traditional symphonies and concertos is usually in sonata form, described in detail in Chapter 4. The purpose of the second movement of both concertos and symphonies is to contrast the opening movement; therefore, it has traditionally been a slow movement (marked *Adagio*, *Andante*, etc.).

The form of the third movement (for symphonies) is most likely 'dance-like' and depends mostly on the period in which the piece was composed. This movement is usually excluded from concertos, although there are exceptions such as Brahms's four-movement Second Piano Concerto, in which a massive scherzo movement is added after the opening movement.

The finale of a symphony or concerto is often structured similarly to the first movement, in sonata-like form (e.g., rondo or 'sonata-allegro' form), but usually does not have an extensive development section. So the last movement is often significantly shorter than the first, although this generality does not apply for certain composers. The finale is traditionally a 'happy ending' with tunes that are more dance-like, having evolved from the gigue ('jig') finales of pre-Classical suites and symphonies.

♫ Overtures and Tone Poems

The term 'overture' in classical music can mean several things, but is most often introductory music for some larger work (e.g. an opera). In the case of an overture in a work by Bach, it is simply an opening movement, usually the longest, followed by several shorter movements, often dance suites (e.g., the *English* and *French* Suites for solo piano and the Orchestral Suites).

Many overtures that have become famous and are performed as stand-alone works were originally instrumental preludes to operas. Many of these operas themselves are long-forgotten, but their overtures live on. Other overtures were written as stand-alone pieces and are known as 'concert overtures'. These are often designed to conjure up images to go with the music, and sometimes include literary themes. The concert overture corresponds to a single symphonic movement in length as well as in shape and structure.

For example, Beethoven wrote several non-operatic 'concert' overtures but composed only one opera, *Fidelio*. These overtures are five to ten minutes in length and are ideally-suited as the opening piece in a concert program, which is often comprised of overture, concerto (with soloist), and symphony. Many overtures are composed in binary sonata form without development section, not too different from rondo sonata form commonly used in the finales of symphonies and concertos.

Not only are Wagner's opera overtures very popular, but just as much so are instrumental excerpts from within the operas. Many orchestras perform and record parts of Wagner's operas without the corresponding vocal parts. This is particularly true of the four operas that make up his monumental 'Ring' cycle, based on Teutonic legends, containing the famous *Ride of the Valkyries*. Other composers who composed overtures that are equally, or even more popular, than their operas are Rossini, Mozart, Berlioz, Dvořák, and Franz von Suppé.

The other single-movement form of orchestral music, popularized later than the operatic overture, is the 'tone poem', or as Liszt referred to his, 'symphonic poem'. Their forerunners were the 'concert overtures' of the first half of the 19th century. These are usually longer in length than the overtures. They are also sometimes composed as a set related to each other by some common theme (*Legends* by Sibelius, *La Mer* by Debussy). Many tone poems are of patriotic and nationalistic sentiment (*Finlandia* by Sibelius), based on legend or folklore (*Don Juan* by Richard Strauss) or inspired by scenes from nature (Dvořák).

An early example of an 'overture' that is actually a tone poem is Mendelssohn's fine *The Hebrides* (or *Fingal's Cave*) overture, inspired by the composer's trip to the isles of Scotland. Interestingly his Third Symphony is nicknamed 'Scottish' and his *Fourth* is nicknamed 'Italian', so Mendelssohn (or his publishers) clearly associated his symphonies with particular countries.

Perhaps his greatest overture is the Overture for his incidental music to Shakespeare's *A Midsummer Night's Dream*. According to Harold Schonberg, Mendelssohn "never wrote a more perfect work" and this overture "has remained eternally fresh." Mendelssohn wrote other programmatic overtures that are popular on their own, including, *Calm Sea and Prosperous Voyage*.

The Romantic period 'tone' or 'symphonic' poem is a single movement orchestral work having narrative or illustrative meaning. The genre was at the height of its popularity from 1850 with its 'invention' by Liszt to the 1920's and the final tone poems of Sibelius. Unlike a lot of 'overtures', which are often in sonata form or sonata-like form, tone poems do not adhere to any defined structure; by their nature they are loosely structured.

Tone poems were made popular in the Romantic period by Liszt, R. Strauss, Dvořák and Sibelius. The loose structure of tone poems can be directly attributed to Liszt and the "seemingly fragmentary nature" of his piano works. Liszt took the thematic concert overtures of Mendelssohn and Berlioz, some of which told stories and described scenes, and expanded the dimensions and liberated "the descriptive impulse from the formal and functional expectations of the overture as a genre." Neither Liszt nor Strauss composed traditional symphonic works (nor did Wagner) but instead favored the symphonic 'poem' to point out the "prevalent unhappiness with symphonic form among the avant-garde." The *avant-garde* apparently was Liszt and Strauss, along with Wagner, as opposed to 'traditionalists' such as Brahms and Bruckner. This former group, led by Liszt, Strauss and Wagner, felt that "Beethoven had done all there was to do with the symphony."

Sibelius wrote several great tone poems which, together with his seven symphonies, represent a considerable portion of his orchestral output. As for Dvořák, his four tone poems were composed late in life after he had already left a lasting symphonic legacy.

♪♩ Suites, Divertimenti and Variations

Suites

The term suite was adopted in France just before 1700. After 1650 new dances, often based on regional dance tunes, and non-dance movements were added to what would soon be termed suites. For example, intermezzi were now usually placed between *sarabande* and gigue, and the prelude was placed at the beginning as the first movement, so that the 'dance' suite actually began with an extended non-dance movement. Novel dance movements include minuet, *gavotte*, *bourrée*, as well as airs, rondo, *chaconne*, *passacaglia*, and variations of previous movements.

Works were classified as suites since the Baroque and the term has been used into modern times, although the music sounds much different. More modern suites of the Romantic period were brilliantly orchestrated with sharp contrasts between movements. The movements in suites are generally shorter than in symphonies and do not explore the depths of typical symphonic movements in full sonata form.

Examples of well-known Romantic suites are by Tchaikovsky, Bizet, Grieg (*Peer Gynt*), and Sibelius (*Karelia*). The line between suite and symphony is not always clear, so a hybrid form called the 'symphonic suite' exists. This classification has been applied to such works as Debussy's *La Mer* and Rimsky-Korsakov's *Schererazade*, which can also be viewed as sets of thematically connected tone poems.

Divertimenti

Divertimenti evolved from Baroque suites and concerti grossi to appear in the Classical period with Mozart composing dozens that survive. They are called 'Serenades' 'Cassations' and *Divertimenti* and are lighter than symphonies and concertos, without the development and the antagonism between orchestra and soloist. *Divertimenti* possess the elements of the Baroque suite with light mood and several short, loosely related, dance-like movements, but they also have a symphonic element with some serious movements and a first movement in sonata form. They also serve as a bridge from chamber to orchestral music as most can be performed by smaller ensembles or full orchestras. The crossover from chamber to orchestral music is usually taken as the point at which there is duplication of musical parts, so that in chamber music each member of the ensemble has a unique part to play.

Divertimenti often are comprised of more than four movements. Unlike later concertos and symphonies, with the standard three and four movements, respectively, the serenades and *divertimenti* could have many movements. The standard form being five or six movements, including the four standard movements of the Classical period sonata or symphony plus a theme and variations and/or a scherzo-type movement.

Because most *divertimenti* were performed by small orchestra, sometimes even quartets and quintets, this form also bridges the trio sonata to the Classical string quartets of Haydn and Mozart. Haydn's early string divertimenti eventually led to a split by Haydn into two stylistically opposed forms: his initial string quartets and later *divertimenti*. While the lighter form of the *divertimenti* was in decline the string quartet was beginning its ascension to the summit of chamber music forms. Paul Henry Lang had another take on the role of the *divertimento* form, feeling that it was "not a stepping-stone to quartet or symphony" but rather, "an independent type of music sharing the…spiritual and technical maturity with" these other more 'serious' forms.

By the late Classical period the sinfonia concertante, divertimento, and serenades had run their course as a leading genre of music. Beethoven wrote only two serenades, the *Sextet*, Op.81b and the well-known *Septet*, Op.20 (ca.

1800). The virtuoso soloist, usually pianist and, less often, violinist, began to dominate the scene and composers adjusted concerto writing to suit this new breed of musician. However, some examples of works in these forms continued to appear, most notably the *Triple* Concerto of Beethoven and the serenades and *Double* Concerto of Brahms. The form fell into disfavor with the early Romantics but returned later in the 19th century, revived by Dvořák, Brahms, Tchaikovsky, and Elgar.

Variations

This form has been embraced by many composers across periods "because of the opportunities it affords for real inventiveness, skill in counterpoint and pictorial orchestration."

Beethoven composed several well-known sets of variations for solo piano and the variation form is very popular for the solo instrument. The most famous of his sets of variations are the *Diabelli* Variations for solo piano. Along with J.S. Bach's *Goldberg* Variations the *Diabelli* Variations are two towering masterpieces of variation form. There are also well-known orchestral pieces consisting of a theme, followed by multiple variations. Sometimes the theme is the composer's original but often the theme is 'borrowed' from another composer, and only the variations are original. In this case the title of the work will usually indicate 'Variations on a Theme of (composer)…'

♪ Evolution to the Symphony and Concerto

The Florentine *Camerata* of the late Renaissance took an "extreme and hostile stand against the principles of High Renaissance polyphony." It was led by Count Giovanni de Bardi (1534-1612) and counted Galileo's father Vincenzo Galilei (1533-91) among its members. The *Camerata* believed they were reproducing the dramas of ancient Greek and wanted a simple line, a simple accompaniment. Indeed the music is simple and pure. However, especially in Northern Germany (i.e., Bach) polyphony would continue to dominate straight through the Baroque.

In Italy would emerge Claudio Monteverdi and the first steps "in the direction of the 'musical speech' known as recitative over a *basso continuo*," or "solo singing to a simple accompaniment." The earliest 'orchestral' music accompanied 17th century French opera theater and provided ballroom music for the French court. From this the Baroque style would appear in the 17th century.

"The first man to think instinctively like an orchestral composer…Claudio Monteverdi" – employed the first 'modern' orchestra of thirty-six to forty players for *Orfeo* in 1607…drawing "a spectacular variety of ear-tweaking combinations." The orchestra was an innovation of the early 1600s, growing out of the larger instrument ensembles utilized in 'new' opera. This point in history marks the beginning of modern orchestral music, with strings and winds dominating. There was a vast improvement of instruments along with the appearance of the harpsichord to join the organ as the primary keyboard instrument. The violin took over as the lead string instrument from the viols and became the favorite orchestral and solo instrument.

Melody now became conditioned by harmony and, in contrast to the movement of the Florentine *Camerata*, linear counterpoint gave way to complex polyphony and contrapuntal textures. But until the concerto became popular towards the end of the 17th century, the orchestra would be limited to accompaniment of voices (opera, court, or church music). Eventually instrumentalists sought the attention that vocalists had been receiving and the instrumental soloist would be born. This instrumental soloist would lead to the composer-performers of the Classical period (Mozart and Beethoven) and eventually to the virtuosi of the Romantic period (e.g., Liszt and Paganini).

In 1700 public concerts were still unknown. With the rise in public concerts at the end of the 1700s dramatic techniques from programmatic music forms (i.e., opera) had to be applied to 'absolute' music such as symphonies and concertos. Thus, sonata form and three- and four-movement orchestral works took on a plot, complete with action, characters (expressed musically), a climax and *dénouement*. Beginning in the middle of the 18th century publication of musical scores became commonplace; composers wrote not just for his orchestra but for others as well. It was therefore in everyone's best interests to standardize the leading orchestras and ensembles across the courts and churches of Europe.

"Between the instructional works of the late Baroque (*Goldberg Variations, The Well-Tempered Klavier*, Bach's keyboard Partitas) and the Romantic *étude* lies the development and spread of the public concert." In fact, by 1800, according to influential Viennese music critic Eduard Hanslick, the concert had become "the main medium for music *per se*;" however, in 1800 subscriptions for concerts were nonetheless expensive and thus reserved for the privileged. Concerts would become reasonably priced in the mid-1800s. In the last quarter of the 18th century composers realized the possibilities of large ensembles and wrote music to reflect the new fact of concert life. From 1780 on composers wrote symphonic works with large heavy-sounding ensembles in mind. However, because these were often unavailable Haydn and Mozart had no choice but to use smaller, thinner ensembles. According to Charles Rosen, this adaptation by Classical composers to the reality of the age has been misunderstood by musicologists over the recent decades. What has resulted are an entire movement and recordings of 'authentic' and 'period' performances of Classical orchestral works, despite these not representing the authentic wishes of the composers.

After 1750 orchestras "abandoned the sharp terrace dynamics of the baroque" and began the transition to the orchestra of the Classical Period with its "new stylistic principle of graduated transition dynamics." In the early 1700s some sonata movements were cast in a different key for the first time. For example, Corelli would often cast a succeeding slow movement in the relative minor of the preceding movement. From 1730-50 composers were on the edge of violating the Baroque form in their trio sonatas with the practice of contrasting moods within a movement and the transformation to the Classical Viennese style of Haydn and Mozart. This journey would first pass through the Rococo period, characterized by the style *galant*, which ran roughly from 1725 to 1760.

Up until the mid-1770s composers only wrote down the 'outline' of the music, leaving the performers to orchestrate, harmonize, improvise, and embellish as they saw fit. The *continuo* accompaniment at this point was referred to as 'unfigured bass', which was employed by composers because of commonly understood progressions. Composition "was the creation of abstract patterns of pitch and rhythm, which were subsequently realized – by composer or performer...in instrumental tone color, texture, and ornament. Slight chromatic alterations of the composer's text were generally expected from performers."

This gave way in the mid-1700s to the 'figured bass' because of more varied harmonic progressions. Eventually, any discretion remaining to the continuo player would be removed as composers (e.g., early Haydn) were "now wishing to exercise even more refinement in the spacing of chords and the handling of inner parts" (i.e., harmony). By the late 1700s ornamentation by the performers became rarer, the obbligato accompaniment replaced the improvised accompaniment and continuo playing quickly lost its role of filling out the harmony. It is gone altogether by the early 1800s.

"The orchestral music of (most) of the 18th century was still a 'chamber art'." Typical orchestras were composed of around two dozen instrumentalists, roughly equally divided between strings and winds plus percussion, if called for. "It wasn't until as recently as 1800 that the orchestra emerged in something like its modern form..." "The institution of public concerts had been the greatest stimulus of all to the development of complex, large-scale instrumental forms, most notably the Classical symphony." "It was the gradual spread of the public concert that emancipated music from its dependence on court and church." Along with the decline of aristocratic patronage and court music came the "rise of trivial 'salon music' that attended the rise of the bourgeoisie."

Professional orchestras did not exist in Beethoven's time; orchestras were a mix of amateur, professional and semi-professional players. Trumpeters and drummers were borrowed from military bands and horn players from among hunters. The modern art of conducting was in its infancy and not yet a dedicated profession. The 'modern' orchestra as we know it today (as opposed to the 'modern' orchestra of Monteverdi's time) was formed in 1830s and 1840s Europe. At this time the Paris Conservatory Orchestra was probably the leading orchestra, it was certainly the largest. It was a permanent orchestra with professional players and existed chiefly to perform symphonic music. German orchestras, e.g., the Leipzig *Gewandhaus*, were beginning to develop into virtuoso concert orchestras, but most were still basically opera ensembles. The symphony concert was only an occasional event, whereas opera was performed regularly, even every night during 'opera season'.

The orchestra expanded significantly by adding winds to sustain harmonies. This freed the violas and cellos to provide a livelier accompaniment to the violins. The Mannheim Court Orchestra, assembled by Palatinate elector Karl Theodor, was the pre-eminent orchestra in Europe from 1720s to 1770s. Described by Christian Daniel Schubart at the time as "the musical Athens of the German-speaking world," the orchestra was comprised of fifty players, led by Stamitz and Cannabich, who displayed unparalleled precision, power and virtuosity for their time. Mozart's take on Mannheim was direct: "The orchestra is excellent and very strong."

Its breathtaking *crescendos* led to the phrase 'Mannheim Steamroller' (and to the modern-day instrumental recording ensemble). The skill of this ensemble and greater flexibility of their orchestral fabric set the stage for the perfection of the symphony in Vienna by Haydn and Mozart. By end of 1700s the orchestra had settled into its well-known four-section pattern of strings, woodwind, brass, and percussion. From his *Sturm und Drang* period to the Salomon *London* symphonies, Haydn's symphonies track the growth and development of the orchestra. A typical Haydn symphony of the 1770s utilized ten strings, pairs of oboes and horns, and a bassoon and/or harpsichord as the continuo for a total of less than twenty Ezsterháza players. For Haydn's *London* symphonies, Salomon provided him with an orchestra three-fold in manpower. Parallel to this increase in orchestra size (and volume) was the need for ensembles to acoustically fill larger public concert halls as opposed to the more intimate royal and aristocratic settings.

Around 1820 conductors appeared who no longer doubled as musicians. Freed from the keyboard, they introduced the use of the baton and read from the full score. Early great conductors included Mendelssohn and Berlioz, the latter stressing the importance of the conductor in interpretation over mere time-keeping. Rimsky-Korsakov, Debussy, and Ravel "applied timbres to an orchestral canvas with the individuality of a master painter's brushstrokes."

♫ Evolution of the Symphony

The symphony as established and perfected by Haydn and Mozart at the height of the Classical period, evolved out of the sinfonia, an Italian opera overture, and the French orchestral suite, frequently called 'overture'; "...indeed, the whole German symphony was a result of a concert development of the old opera sinfonia." The sinfonia was, in Baroque times, an orchestral piece in three very short movements (quick-slow-quick) played as the overture (i.e., opening orchestral piece) to an Italian opera. Over time the movements grew longer and were eventually performed separate from the opera. Emerging from the opera overture, the symphony became a hotbed for instrumental intrigue and virtuosity.

The 18th century saw a shift from Italian opera to German symphony, with accelerated development as German composers (sons of J.S. Bach, in addition to Stamitz, early Haydn, and many lesser composers) sought "the creation of an original expressive language." Opera was already too developed and not flexible enough for their needs; the symphony could more easily be adapted to new purposes. By the middle of the 18th century composers were beginning to experiment with a new textural clarity and a way of organizing contrasting musical themes primarily by their gravitating towards specific key centers. A novel symphonic tonal drama was developed – sonata form. Johann Stamitz (1717-57) with his Mannheimers, "livened up the sweet Italian sinfonia" and introduced the "frequent, unpredictable placement of…abrupt changes," revealing early signs of Classical symphonies "in a rapid alternation of light and dark."

One can look to Bach's Orchestral Suites as a perfect example. In these an introductory movement, which probably evolved into the opening orchestral exposition of symphonies and concertos, is followed by "some quick music", then some slow music. After this, a series of "dances would follow, among which would probably be a minuet". These Baroque suites became the *Divertimenti* and serenades in the early Classical period as sonata and symphonic forms (as we know them) began to take shape. In the evolution of the Baroque suite into the sonata and symphony of the Classical period, only the minuet was retained by Haydn as the one dance movement. This dance movement is usually the third movement and contrasted with the typically slow second movement.

> "Virtually all musical roads lead back to one
> of two composers: Haydn or Bach."
> - critic David Hurwitz

The *concerti grossi* and orchestral suites of the Baroque and the serenades and divertimenti of the Classical period were both the forerunners of the symphony and a bridge between chamber music and symphonic music. Generally speaking Classical serenades and divertimenti were composed for public performance, sometimes festive occasions, so they often did not possess the intimacy inherent in chamber works.

Somewhere in the early Classical (Haydn or CPE Bach) decided to conclude the four-movement format with a fast, lively finale possibly in sonata form, but whose tunes will fall into more clear-cut sections and be more dance-like than the tunes of the first movement. Obviously, many of the tunes encountered in the last movement will be similar to the themes of the first movement. Often the first movement seems to describe the beginning of the journey and the final movement a feeling of approaching our destination. We are now at the point of the first great symphonic output, the symphonies and concertos of Haydn and Mozart.

In a period of less than 100 years (1720-1810) composers wrote more than 16,000 symphonies; we have rejected ninety-nine percent of them.

A couple of decades later Beethoven brought the symphony to its peak as "the form in which the composer tries to come to grips with big emotions." Beethoven's First Symphony in 1800 was instrumentally and musically a summation of the first half-century of symphonic composition. He then redefined the symphony developed by Haydn and Mozart (as well as Beethoven's First and Second Symphonies) with his Third Symphony, the *Eroica*. With this great symphony he expanded the form to allow for philosophical and even metaphysical statements.

The symphony in the Romantic period was de-emphasized. A new kind of virtuoso instrumental composer emerged in the Romantic era, while Berlioz expanded orchestral forces to unprecedented levels. His *Requiem*, composed only ten years after Beethoven's death, was scored for an orchestra of 182! Although Liszt and Berlioz wrote symphonies, they were programmatic works, and Liszt quickly found the one-movement symphonic poem to be more to his liking and less restrictive. Wagner made no secret that he felt the symphony as a form had run its course. Although Schumann and Mendelssohn wrote successfully in the form, their symphonies do not approach the level of Beethoven's output. It would not be until Brahms in the 1870s, along with Bruckner, Tchaikovsky, and Mahler, that the symphony would regain most of its previous stature.

By 1880 late Romantic period orchestra sizes of 100 were not unusual. Mahler's Eighth employs an enormous force: a chorus of 500, a children's choir of 350, seven soloists, and, of course, the huge orchestra typical of Mahler. Wagner's most celebrated descendents were Richard Strauss and Gustav Mahler. The former "drove orchestral virtuosity to previously undreamt-of heights…that demanded every player be a consummate master of his instrument." Mahler was an introspective counter-weight to Strauss's extroversion. After World War I the cost of massive orchestras became prohibitive and composers began to write for smaller forces. This partly led to the rise of neo-Classicism between the wars.

Symphony Orchestras
Roughly a dozen orchestras have dominated the major classical record labels over the past fifty years of recordings, half of them in the U.S. and the others in Europe. They are considered the 'top tier' orchestras. Mostly all great conductors have been associated with at least one of these orchestras and many with several of them. In the U.S. it is not surprising that the top

orchestras are in the largest cities: New York Philharmonic, Chicago Symphony Orchestra, Cleveland Orchestra, Boston Symphony Orchestra, and Los Angeles Philharmonic. In Europe, several countries in Western Europe are represented with the London Philharmonic and London Symphony Orchestra in London, the Berlin Philharmonic in Germany, the Vienna Philharmonic in Austria, and the Concertgebouw Orchestra in Amsterdam. In addition, the St. Petersburg (formerly Leningrad) Philharmonic and Moscow Philharmonic in Russia rank with these top orchestras.

> *"I'm not interested in having an orchestra sound like itself. I want it to sound like the composer."*
> *- Leonard Bernstein*

Some orchestras are famous for their own unique sound. Often this is more appropriate for certain types of music than others. The 'Philadelphia Sound', produced by the Philadelphia Orchestra under Eugene Ormandy for almost fifty years, favored the strings and produced a very supple sound that leant itself well to heavily romantic works such as a Rachmaninoff piano concerto. Unfortunately, the two principal conductors who followed Ormandy, Riccardo Muti and Wolfgang Sawallisch, have tried to roughen the Philadelphia Sound, possibly in an effort to make their mark on the orchestra. On the other hand, the Chicago Symphony Orchestra is famous for its 'rough' sound and for its brass section. One can see how particular works were better suited for a particular orchestra, depending on its "sound".

For decades the Cleveland Orchestra was probably the best all-around American orchestra, thanks to the leadership of George Szell in the 1950s and 1960s. Chicago had its brass and characteristic muscularity and Philadelphia had its 'sound', but the orchestra in Cleveland probably excelled in the widest repertory. In the 1950s three of the five leading American orchestras were led and gained even more prominence under the leadership of Hungarians who had come to the U.S.: Ormandy in Philadelphia, Reiner in Chicago, and Szell in Cleveland. A fourth great Hungarian-U.S. conductor was Antal Dorati, who led the Minneapolis (now Minnesota) Symphony Orchestra. In the late 1950s Leonard Bernstein became the first American-born conductor of a leading U.S. orchestra, the New York Philharmonic.

The Berlin Philharmonic under Herbert von Karajan for decades produced a sound that was characterized as 'highly polished'. This sound was not for everyone; critics pointed out that it resulted in Karajan and the orchestra approaching every work in the same manner, without taking into account the period of the work. Whether the work was a Bruckner symphony or Vivaldi's *Four Seasons*, the Berliners performed both with the same, highly-polished and refined sound of a modern orchestra.

This has led to Karajan's recordings with the Berlin Philharmonic literally filling up the bins of music stores as he recorded and released almost every major work, some symphony cycles several times (e.g., Brahms four symphonies, Tchaikovsky's six symphonies). Toward the end of his life when he had worn out his welcome with the Berliners, Karajan moved to Vienna to record the staples of his repertoire with the rival Philharmonic in the Austrian capital. This was in the mid- to late-1980s when 'digital' recordings or 'DDD' were the rage in classical music and the maestro wanted a legacy of digital recordings. While many of these recordings were judged inferior to early recordings with the Berliners (Tchaikovsky symphonies), his final take on some of Bruckner's symphonies, particularly the *Seventh* (his final recording) and *Eighth* are considered among the greatest interpretations of those works. Ironically, one of the reasons for this widely-held view of these final recordings is that Karajan may have finally moved away from his applying his usual overdose of polish and allowed the Viennese players more freedom in the performance (rise and fall of classical music).

♪ Development of the Concerto

> *"The most important fact about concerto form is that the audience waits for the soloist to enter, and when he stops playing they wait for him to begin again."*
> - Charles Rosen

Only with the Renaissance did the accomplishments of instrumental virtuosos begin to be valued as truly artistic. Some Renaissance instrument virtuosos were "flashy and full of 'inspired' effects like sudden changes of tempo and contrasts of register...that will hardly be matched until...Liszt and Paganini."

It is very interesting to trace the development of the genre termed 'concerto', which consists of a soloist or set of soloists with orchestral accompaniment. The concerto form first appeared around the end of the 17th century, with the rise of the concerto principle of ensemble playing, that of pitting two dissimilar groups of players against each other. The difference could be the size of the groups or the different instrumental makeup of each group.

The *canzon* or chanson and the *ricercar* were representative forms of early Baroque ensemble music, which spawned additional varieties such as the *fantasia* (fantasy) and the *capriccio*. The *canzon*, which displayed some regular periodic formal structure, was a distant ancestor of the classical symphony. A hybrid form of the fantasia and the *ricercar* appeared that was termed 'sonata'. Eventually, the term 'sonata' was adopted for works with soloist and *continuo*. A popular form was the 'trio sonata', which employed two 'melody' instruments (e.g., two violins), a stringed bass instrument such as the cello, and *continuo* (most often a harpsichord). 'Trio' refers to the three-voice texture of these sonatas as a result of the two melodies with the bass line. This early Baroque sonata had very little to do with the sonata as we know it today (from the Classical period onward).

The *sonata da camera* ('chamber' sonata) in early Baroque referred to any music (e.g., trio sonata) that was not church or opera. *Sonata da chiesa* ('church' sonata) were four-movement sonatas cast in serious contrapuntal form. One product from the evolution of this loose 'form' was the 'trio sonata', a cyclic form in four movements that "became the essence and symbol of baroque chamber music."

The Baroque chamber sonata employed stylized homophonic dance movements that were similar to the orchestral dance suites. The *concerto grosso* evolved into the solo concerto, in recognition of the rise of virtuosic players. The trio sonata evolved into the solo sonata, duo sonatas and string and piano trios. A tendency towards individuality was in place among the dominant instrumental forms of solo sonata, trio sonata, and *concerto grosso*.

Within a couple of decades the concerto became the high Baroque era's most important orchestral form. In the last quarter of the 1600s the *concerto grosso* emerged as the dominant concerto form of the Baroque, along with the 'solo' concerto, which was close in prominence to the *concerto grosso* during the Baroque. The *concerto grosso*, which pitted the ripieno against the concertino, evolved into the sinfonia concertante in the Classical period. The *sinfonia concertante* was a popular form in the early Classical period along with the serenade and *divertimento*. Both Haydn and Mozart set the standard in these forms. The solo concerto was destined to have a long and important history and would virtually replace the concerto grosso in the Classical era.

With the high Classical period the performer's adherence to the written score was complete. Gone was the embellishment of the Baroque and Rococo. So-called interpretation was limited to dynamics and tempo; melody and harmony had to be left exactly as the composer intended. In the late 1700s concerto composers were usually virtuosos who composed pieces specifically for their own public appearances, as a vehicle of self-promotion. The fact that Haydn was not a virtuoso instrumentalist explains his relatively small concerto output and the lack of profundity in his keyboard concertos.

The most important element of the 'modern' or 'solo' concerto "is the dialogue between the main protagonists – soloist(s) and orchestra." This interplay traces back to the *concerto grossi* of Corelli, Handel, and Bach in the Baroque with the concertino, a small group of soloists, facing off against a larger ensemble or orchestra, the *ripieno*. "The Baroque concerto is a loose alternation of *ripieno* and solo sections." Starting with Haydn, the concerto form that is familiar to us was firmly established: that of a single soloist pitted against the orchestra. Three of the typical four movements of the symphony are present with the usual dance-like third movement omitted. The first movement is modified from its usual full sonata form to "give the soloist-protagonist a dramatic life against the orchestra's…besides the drama…of the subjects, we get that of these two protagonists."

In the three movement Baroque concerto the first and third movements normally followed a rondo-like structure, in which large *tutti* passages alternate with solo interludes. The middle movement was the forerunner of orchestral slow movements, but much less sophisticated with a simple melodic pattern repeated again and again. This fast-slow-fast structure became the signature of the Classical concertos of Haydn, Mozart, then of Beethoven and throughout the concertos of the 19th century Romantic era.

In concertos of the Baroque period, such as Vivaldi's *Four Seasons*, the soloist plays along with the orchestra. He is viewed as part of the orchestra as a whole but is featured and highlighted as an individual player from time to time during the concerto; for example, in the famous cadenza at the end of the first movement of *Brandenburg* Concerto No.5. The years 1735-50 saw the appearance of the three-movement fast-slow-fast concerto format, derived from opera overtures of the pre-Classical era. Classical composers added marches and minuets to this format to yield *divertimenti*.

In the Classical period there is separation of the soloist from the orchestra. The soloist does not play along with the orchestra during the opening orchestral section. This opening ritornello is purely orchestral in the concertos of Haydn and Mozart, essentially the opening statement of the exposition section of the first movement. This orchestral opening also serves to build up listener anticipation for the dramatic entrance of the soloist. This entrance occurs at a definite point in the opening movement, marks the end of the opening *ritornello*, and clearly separates the soloist from the orchestra.

Classical concertos generally follow a pattern of orchestral playing of theme(s), often called *tutti*, alternating with soloist sections. The opening *tutti* often "offers a parade of the main ideas of the movement." The early, middle, and late sections often correspond, respectively, to the exposition, development and recapitulation of sonata form. The middle or slow movement really developed under Beethoven to bind compositions together. Most follow a song-like sonata form without the development. Finales in Classical concertos are often cast in rondo or sonata-rondo form.

The Romantic concerto "seeks to deepen and enrich the possibilities of feeling…with all its expressive warmth and its wealth of pianistic textures." Romanticism places a premium on both feeling and individuality. Romantic piano music parallels "with the development of the grand virtuoso concerto…a rise in the number of shorter pieces for piano and orchestra."

In Romantic piano concertos of the 19th century, as well as Rachmaninoff's of the 20th, "the piano encounters an 'objective' expression of feeling in the orchestra and proceeds to make it 'subjective'." This creates a dialogue between two perspectives: the objective represented by the orchestra and the subjective perspective of the piano and soloist. In the Romantic period works labeled 'serenades' were usually for string symphonies, wind ensembles or chamber orchestra. Serenades for full orchestra (e.g., Brahms) were intended to be 'lighter' and without the full development of themes and adherence to forms so as to distinguish them from symphonies. As European music moved into the 19th century Romantic period the serenade, *divertimento* and cassation were fading fast as forms, and would not be appealing to early Romantic composers. However, Brahms and Dvořák, as 'classical romantics', would each produce two orchestral serenades.

Many great piano concertos were written for the composers themselves to perform; most great violin concertos were written for someone else, often the leading virtuoso violinist of the region. This is another reason why there are fewer violin concertos than piano concertos. The cadenza became the vehicle to show off the virtuosity of the soloist. The virtuosic improvised cadenza at the end of a movement became in the Classical period, a dramatic necessity in a concerto. The rock guitar solo that has survived in music for five decades now is a direct descendent of the classical cadenza, designed to highlight the virtuosity of the soloist.

The concerto went on hiatus toward the end of the 19th century. While downgraded in prominence by early Romantics such as Liszt, Wagner, Berlioz, and Chopin, at least Chopin and Liszt wrote piano concertos, as did Mendelssohn, Schumann and Grieg. Brahms gave new life to the concerto with his four 'Classical Romantic' works and Saint-Saëns provided some concertos of modest success, but Bruckner and Mahler disregarded the form altogether. The neglect or outright rejection of the concerto as popular form seemed to be an integral part of the late Romantic.

Debussy had no use for the concerto (or for symphonies either), and the Second Viennese School may have used concerto in the titles of some early works, but these were hardly intended for a soloist to display virtuosity (e.g., Berg's *Chamber* Concerto for violin, piano, and thirteen winds). Schoenberg and his leading disciples did eventually compose difficult and very technical concertos, but only after they had established themselves and gotten past their reactionary days. The Berg Violin Concerto dates from 1935 and the Schoenberg, Op.36, followed it in 1936. Both were premiered by Louis Krasner, who also commissioned Berg's Violin Concerto.

In England, Elgar enjoyed some success with his concertos for violin and for cello, but his music fell out of favor between the wars and was generally seen as a relic from the Romantic period, taking decades to return to popularity. Only Rachmaninoff remained committed to continuing the tradition of concerto for virtuoso through the first half of the 20th century.

♪ Orchestral Music of the Baroque

The virtuoso concerto soloist did not really exist yet during the Baroque. While there were some great concertos written featuring soloists (e.g., Bach's violin concertos), most works were of the *concerto grosso* style in which a set of soloists and instruments were featured against a larger orchestra (e.g., Bach's *Brandenburg* Concertos).

♪ Jean-Baptiste Lully (1639-1687)

"The guiding theme of music in (the 1600s) was marked by a constant decline in polyphony," led by the Florentine *Camerata*. The transplanted Italian Giovanni Battista Lulli became Louis XIV's composer of chamber music and music master of the royal family. Lully rejected the musical style of his homeland Italy and established French classical drama, with its 'overture' opening new paths for instrumental music. He invented this 'French overture' or opening orchestral movement to an opera. 'Overture' is actually from the French word 'to open'. The overture was adopted in France starting in 1640 for the opening movements of ballets and operas.

Lully invented and popularized a new genre for the late 17th century – French lyric tragedy with dramatic dialogue its primary concern. He created a structure in which the overture would be followed by selected dance movements from the particular ballet or opera, forming a 'suite'. Eventually, suites were composed by this formula independent of any ballet or opera, and called 'orchestral suites'.

The term 'French' or 'Dance' suite was adopted in France just before 1700. After 1650 new dances had often been based on regional dance tunes. This overture model was used heavily by Purcell, Bach, and Handel as the opening movement to the suite form. In these 'suites' an opening movement, often called 'overture', would be followed by several dance movements, usually alternating between fast and slow. Bach uses an extensive overture, which is the most important part of the suite, followed by four to six dance movements intended for listening entertainment. He combines fugal construction with concertante writing (i.e., for several soloists) based on that of Vivaldi.

♪ Arcangelo Corelli (1653-1713)

The Italian 'violin school' of the 1600s, which included the craftsmanship of Stradivari, was led by Corelli, who "united all the threads developed by his eminent colleagues...keeping a just balance between instrumental sonority and polyphonic construction." Corelli was the first important composer to focus primarily on instrumental music. Corelli's monumental works crowned the 17th century efforts to create instrumental ensemble music. Throughout the 1600s the craftsmanship, as well as playing technique, of the violin underwent steady improvement.

Corelli was a Baroque violinist ("father of violin playing") and composer of many trio sonatas and concerto grosso. He was the first composer in history to establish himself exclusively as a writer of instrumental music and was a pioneer of chamber music. Corelli's 'chamber sonata' form, consisting of alternating dance movements, proceeded by an overture (as invented by Lully), became the 'orchestral suites' of the Baroque. He altered the fast-slow-fast three-movement format by adding a first slow movement, establishing the slow-fast-slow-fast format. The initial slow-fast movements would carry into the Classical period, combined as a longer first movement. Famous examples are Haydn's London symphonies with a slow introduction to the first movement allegro. Corelli's most significant contribution is the perfection of the *concerto grosso*.

Corelli spent thirty years composing six sets of sonatas and concertos, with twelve works in each set. Over this period, beginning in the 1680s, Corelli "was preoccupied with new expressive devices, new ways of making the violin to sound, and new concepts of melodic beauty." He is best-known for the *Twelve Concerti Grossi*, Op.6 from 1682, of which the most famous is No.8 in G minor nicknamed *Christmas*. In these works there is an amazing richness of sonority with "delicately stylized dances, wildly rushing allegros, pleasant drone basses, and broadly flowing largos." The concertos of Op.6 are neatly split into eight da chiesa ('church sonata' form) and four da camera ('chamber sonata' form) and "clearly manifest the sense of key emerging during the 1600s." Also with Corelli "the church sonata became eloquent with a lyricism found before only in vocal music."

He also composed the two sets of twelve trio sonatas each, Op.2 and Op.4. These works would serve as a foundation for the concertos by the eminent composers of the late Baroque. In the sonatas of Corelli, as with French 'suites' of the period, the first movements (usually titled overture or sinfonia) are always the most important and are cast "in a mixed homophonic and imitative style…a few have lyric melodies, but almost all have…expressively melodious bass lines."

♪ Henry Purcell (1659-1695)

England's one bright musical moment of the late 17th century, Purcell, who studied in Paris with Lully, brought together ideas from French, English and Italian influences, often resulting in a clash of styles and usually "bringing about corresponding harmonic mismatches." His *Twelve Sonatas of Three Parts* (1683) were composed two years after Corelli's Op.1 set.

Purcell looked forward as well as back (e.g., he used Renaissance-period viols in some pieces) and "had the old modes in his blood as he embraced the new tonality." Looking forward, his "harmonic boldness (was) unknown again until the later Wagner or even Stravinsky," and his innovative infusion of folksong in his music foretold such nationalist composers as Dvořák. After Purcell England would suffer two hundred years before producing another world-class composer in Edward Elgar.

♪ Antonio Vivaldi (1678-1741)

Vivaldi was a concert-composing machine, a master of the Baroque concerto who composed at least 450 concertos and as many as 650 total works. He established the 'fast-slow-fast' three-movement layout of typical concertos that has been the template for almost 300 years. Vivaldi "enlarged the solo passages in the concerto grosso until the solo violin became the dominant instrument of the whole ensemble...Under his hands the concerto became a passionate fresco of dramatic contrasts."

Vivaldi "advanced the concerto more than any other composer...he invested his concertos with descriptive or 'programmatic' writing." The best example, of course, is *The Four Seasons*. These four violin concertos are the pinnacle of descriptive art in the Baroque, with each of the four concertos brilliantly evoking "the particular atmosphere, flavor, and spirit of each season." In these four concertos "Vivaldi experimented with a range of textures intended to suggest everything from frozen wastes and driving rain to bird song." These descriptive concertos are the first four in a twelve-concerto cycle called by Vivaldi "The Contest between Harmony and Invention." This Baroque programmatic music also has descriptive sonnets attached to provide a vivid narrative to the music. It is by far Vivaldi's most famous work, and in addition to the most famous first movement of the *Spring* concerto, contains several other memorable melodies.

Many listeners will comment that a lot of his concertos sound the same, they are dominated by the violin, as are Bach's. Igor Stravinsky commented that Vivaldi wrote the same concerto one hundred times. Bach modeled his concertos on Vivaldi's but took the Italian concerto to unprecedented heights, capped off with the six *Brandenburg* Concertos, widely hailed as the peak of the Baroque concerto. On the other hand, some feel Vivaldi actually led "a flight from counterpoint in the early 18th century, accelerating progress towards the Classical style" that dominated the last quarter of that century. Like Bach and Haydn, Vivaldi was employed to produce music in volume as a commodity; however, many of his works display virtuosic brilliance. "Vivaldi developed tremendous rhythmic drive in the fast movements and pathos or poignancy in the slow."

Recommended – The Four Seasons

The *Four Seasons* is one of the most popular of all classical works and one of the most recorded. There are many performances featuring high-profile violinists as part of the marketing of this popular work, which always ranks near the top of classical music listeners poll. The differences are mainly in orchestra size and whether the performance is 'modern' or 'period'. Three excellent versions are those by Nigel Kennedy, Janine Jansen and The English Concert.

♪ Georg Friedric Handel (1685-1759)

Handel's twelve *Concerti Grossi*, Op.6 ("written in the grand style" according to the composer) are considered the peak of the form and were heavily influenced by Corelli's *Concerti Grossi*, Op.6 as was his earlier Op.3 set. The Op.3 works "join winds to the strings for rousing and delectable music." The Op.6 concerti, composed in one month in the autumn of 1739, were subtitled Twelve grand concertos in seven parts and together with Bach's *Brandenburg* Concertos are considered "one of the twin peaks of the Baroque concerto" according to The New Grove Dictionary. Compared to Bach, Handel often abandoned contrapuntal writing in favor of melodies and homophony, especially in slow movements.

All twelve Opus 6 concertos were composed in a one-month flurry of activity in the fall of 1739. In designating these twelve concertos as his Op.6, and emphasizing this point, Handel was paying tribute to Corelli's Op. 6, the set of twelve *concerto grossi* that perfected the form twenty-five years earlier. In fact, Handel had worked alongside Corelli in Rome when young. In addition to the Op.3 and Op.6 *concerti* Handel composed fifteen solo sonatas in 1724 as his Op.1; nine trio sonatas as Op.2 and seven trio sonatas in his Op.5.

> **Recommended –** For *Op.6* the "clear winner in the period instrument category" is by the Academy of Ancient Music and Andrew Manze. These are "performances of eloquence and infectious vitality...that add a feeling of zestful chance-taking." These are not "the old plush Handel, but dramatic and swaggering."

Handel also wrote music for outdoor gatherings and celebrations in England. The two most famous sets are the *Water Music* and the *Royal Fireworks Music*. Both are upbeat, celebratory groupings of pieces containing some famous themes. The *Royal Fireworks* premiered in July 1717 upon commission by King George I and was performed for the king on a barge on the River Thames. Besides the choice of performance on either 'modern' or 'period' instruments, the *Royal Fireworks Music* can be performed either in the original version (wind and percussion instruments) or the version orchestrated for inclusion of strings. Handel preferred the orchestral version for public performances.

> ***Recommended*** — The differences among recordings are the same as those above for Vivaldi's concertos, that is, size of orchestra, 'original' versus 'modern' instruments.
> *Water Music, Music for Royal Fireworks* — The Academy of Ancient Music gets the nod, led by Christopher Hogwood. For the complete Water Music, no one has surpassed Charles Mackerras and The Orchestra of St. Luke's.

Bach and Handel, the two giants of the waning Baroque, represent an ideal contrast, a national personality with roots deeply embedded in Germany versus "a citizen of the world who finally settled down in Britain." Bach "seemed unaware of the existence of a public" while Handel "enjoyed life fully and…showed an unlimited creative capacity."

♫ Johann Sebastian Bach (1685-1750)

Bach's "work exhibits a remarkable unity of creative genius — a stylistic uniformity that transcends the differences between all the genres in which he composed." Richard Crocker points out that "Bach was less attracted to trio sonatas, more to virtuoso solos."

Brandenburg Concertos

Bach, being influenced by the works of Vivaldi, brought the concerto to the level of universal genius with his six *Brandenburg* Concertos, "Perhaps the most brilliantly diverse instrumental anthology ever assembled." The Brandenburgs are a "microcosm of Baroque music, they contain an astonishingly vast sample of the era's emotional universe." The individual concertos are all composed within the format of the concerto grosso, but all are not true concerti grossi. Indeed, they blur the line between orchestral and chamber styles as at least two of the *Brandenburg* Concertos (e.g., No.6 is a sextet) are intended for one instrument to a part. Concertos Nos. 2, 4, and 5 employ a virtuoso soloist of trumpet, violin, and harpsichord, respectively. Bach fittingly called them *Six Concertos for Diverse Instruments* and this is the title he indicated at the head of his manuscript.

No two concertos are scored for the same combination of instruments. Each concerto has a different solo instrument or group of instruments and can be thought of as a "Baroque jam session, the way different instruments take the spotlight." For example, in the famous first movement of the Fifth concerto, the soloist plays the harpsichord and even a cadenza before the movement wraps up. The *Fifth* is more a harpsichord concerto than a true *concerto grosso*. Also, Bach varies the size of the ensemble used as well as the number of soloists in a given concerto.

The *Brandenburgs* were written over a period of several years in Cöthen, collected in 1722 and presented and named for Christian Ludwig, Margrave of Brandenburg. However, Prince Ludwig must have had poor taste in music as he had no use for the concertos and did not even bother to put Bach's manuscripts in his considerable library.

The *First* is the most elaborate and the only one not in three movements (it has four). The solo group (the *ripieno*) includes a violin, three oboes and two hunting horns. The accompaniment (the *concertino*) is provided by the usual strings and continuo. The *continuo* role in the Baroque *concerto grosso* can be filled by bassoon and/or low strings and/or harpsichord.

Concerto No.2 has a wide variety of soloists (trumpet, flute, oboe and violin) and is well-known for its piercing trumpet solos. The first movement is probably the most familiar movement of any of these concertos. The trumpet used to play this music in Bach's time had no valves so these virtuoso trumpet parts were very challenging to perform, with the trumpeter relying only on varying lip pressure, such as with a modern-day bugle.

The *Third* is one of two concertos (the *Sixth* being the other) written for strings alone. Thus, strings comprise the soloists as well as the *concertino*.

Concerto No.4 is a true *concerto grosso* with a *concertino* consisting of the solo violin and two 'echo flutes'. What exactly the echo flutes were is not known for certain; they may have been related to the recorder.

The *Fifth* is also a true concerto grosso with flute, violin and harpsichord comprising the *concertino* of which the harpsichord is given virtuosic treatment. This contrasts the usual role of harpsichord as accompanying continuo. Therefore, the *Fifth* is considered a harpsichord concerto. *Brandenburg* Concerto No.5 contains perhaps the best example of a Baroque precursor to the cadenza that would become a standard feature of the Classical concerto. But instead of an unaccompanied solo part for piano or violin Bach provides an extended solo for the harpsichord.

The *Sixth*, like the *Third*, employs strings only but this is a true concerto grosso. The soloists are two violas and a cello with the *ripieno* (also omitting violins) comprised of violas, violas de gamba, cello, as well as harpsichord and/or bass as continuo. The *Sixth* is a serious exercise in counterpoint, employing imitative techniques of round, canon and fugue. This "kaleidoscope of counterpoint is endlessly varied and fascinating."

Recommended - Complete Brandenburgs –

The English Concert led by Pinnock, Tafelmusik, and Musicus Concentius Wien led by Harnoncourt are recordings that provide excellent and different takes on these prototypical Baroque *concerti grossi*. These ensembles give "authentic" performances, as opposed to larger-scale orchestral versions.

Harpsichord Concertos

Bach's harpsichord concertos are his contribution to the keyboard concerto repertoire. Some of these concertos are also performed on the piano. As with Bach's solo keyboard works it is largely up to individual tastes whether one prefers the more 'authentic' harpsichord, or the modern piano.

None of Bach's surviving concertos for solo harpsichord or multiple harpsichords were originally composed for the instrument. They are adaptations of previous Bach concertos or the music of other composers, something that was common in his day. For example, No.1 in D minor, BMV 1052 and No.5 in F minor are believed to be based on lost concertos of the composer; No.3 in D major, BMV 1054 is an adaptation of his famous Violin Concerto in E, BMV 1042; and the Concerto for Four Harpsichords in A minor, BMV 1065 was based on Vivaldi's Concerto for Four Violins in B minor, op.3, no.10.

It is not known why Bach chose not to compose a concerto 'from scratch' for the harpsichord. It is possible that Bach felt that the harpsichord, relegated to the role of *continuo* in the Baroque, did not merit his original efforts so he simply made necessary changes (i.e., in key) to existent works.

> *Recommended - Harpsichord Concertos*
> Trevor Pinnock and his English Concert. On piano, the offerings by Murray Perahia are very good.

The Orchestral Suites

These are evolved from a form developed by Lully in France during the 1600s. Bach's suites represent the high point of the Baroque suite and he composed dozens, mostly for solo keyboard (the *English* and *French* Suites, *Partitas*), but also the famous sets for solo violin (almost always joined to the three solo violin sonatas) and solo cello. Only four of his orchestral suites survive; he certainly wrote more.

The orchestral suites were intended to be more for entertainment than the more challenging suites for solo instrument, so they are less complex than the solo works. These works also look forward to the symphonic form that would develop later in the century.

The Third Suite contains the famous *Air*, which is frequently found on its own in 'best of Baroque' collections.

The Art of the Fugue, BMV 1080

This is one of the great master's last works; left incomplete, it is a collection of contrapuntal movements for which Bach provided no defined sequence or instrumentation. It demonstrates practically every composing technique available to Bach. Although left unfinished at his death Bach started the work in the early 1740s. Despite its complex contrapuntal nature "there is nothing about its character to deter the casual listener."

Bach seems to have written it for the sheer intellectual exercise. In the work Bach took "a mathematical delight in the interweaving of contrapuntal variations on the same theme." Some scholars believe Bach intentionally left its completion to "those select few who truly understood his art."

Paul Henry Lang speaks of the "same unfathomable and mysterious musical world...conjured up in Bach's *The Art of the Fugue* and in the last string quartets of Beethoven." As with *The Well-Tempered Clavier* Bach only intended this work to be performed in private.

Because no specific instruments or ensemble are indicated by Bach, *The Art of the Fugue* has been arranged and recorded by anything from full orchestra to solo keyboard, and much in between. Because these are all arrangements, they all have their weaknesses, but scholars seem to favor either a small string or chamber ensemble with some leaning to the solo harpsichord or organ. It is up to the listener to decide and if one really likes this work, recordings of different ensemble versions are worth obtaining.

A Musical Offering (BMV 1079)

This work is more a set of exercises than a composition and can be considered chamber music. It was composed by Bach as an 'offering' to Frederick the Great at Potsdam in 1747, who supplied Bach with the 'royal theme'. It consists of twelve canons and fugues split in half by a trio sonata, resulting in a total of sixteen movements of around fifty minutes. In the 20th century Anton Webern would transcribe the six-voice *ricercar*, emphasizing through instrumentation "the independence and opposition of voices through tone color and phrasing."

A Musical Offering is unique in its symmetry, beginning and ending with a *ricercar*. Five canons succeed the opening and precede the closing *ricercar*. As does *The Art of the Fugue*, this work "demonstrates the full arsenal of the Baroque composer of fugues..." "More than almost any other work in the Baroque period, must be heard, lived with and experienced fully in order that its scope may be understood and its purpose revered."

The Violin Concertos

In the late 17th to early 18th centuries the Renaissance viols gradually gave way to the Baroque violin family. Bach's Violin Concerto in A minor, BMV1041 and Violin Concerto in E, BMV1042, as well as the Double Concerto in D minor, BMV1043 for two violins, were composed at Cöthen (1717-1723). Earlier at Weimar (1708-1717) Bach had studied the Italian Concerto form of three movements (fast-slow-fast) perfected by Vivaldi in his concertos. Bach, not being satisfied to simply imitate his Italian contemporary, also combines the concerto grosso style of Corelli with the elements of the Italian concerto to advance the concerto for soloist and orchestra to new levels.

As many musicians did Bach used some of Vivaldi's concertos as 'jumping off points' for his own works; he 'Germanized' some of Vivaldi's concertos. But what set Bach's 'plagiarism' apart and made it special was that "with his own more vigorous breath (he would) inspire them with new life…he could touch nothing that did not grow…to the utmost completeness and grandeur."

The *Double* Concerto is one of his greatest works with a most beautiful slow movement. In fact, it can be said that performers of the concerto for two violins "stand or fall by the treatment of the…*Largo*." By adding a second violin soloist this concerto is considerably more contrapuntal than Bach's solo violin concertos.

♪ 'Original' and 'Modern' recordings

> "Who says that Bach wouldn't have used modern instruments if he'd had them?"
> - conductor Karl Richter

'Original' or 'authentic' performances on period instruments produce clearer, thinner sounds, allowing listeners to hear the individual voices of the players. Modern instruments give a plush, homogeneous blended combination of sounds. The 'modern instrument' sound, both on solo instruments and in ensembles, originated in the Romantic period with vast improvements in instrument technology, including the cast-iron frame piano.

There are several very well-known ensembles that perform 'authentic' interpretations of music on 'period instruments' and so-called chamber orchestras and ensembles. Some of the better-known of the latter group are the Academy of St. Martin-in-the-Fields (ASMF) and the English Chamber Orchestra (ECO), both of which have been widely recorded, especially the ASMF under Marriner. The ECO is well known for its cycles of Mozart piano concertos with the soloist (Murray Perahia or Daniel Barenboim) conducting from the keyboard.

There are many examples of 'period' or 'original instruments' ensembles. Roger Norrington and his London Classical Players achieved fame with a series of recordings in the 1990's including Beethoven's symphonies. There are many others with The English Concert led by Trevor Pinnock and The Academy of Ancient Music led by Andrew Manze (founded by Christopher Hogwood) being the most well-known and long-running ensembles.

> "Could we not…let 'authentic' and 'non-authentic' performers live side by side in peaceful co-existence?"
> - Andras Schiff

As with many issues of performance and authenticity, there are two camps, one being the period instrument supporters, many of whom are also scholars on the subject. The other camp, while not in stark opposition to the authentic crowd, finds period performances interesting but hard to believe that composers of yesteryear would not use all available resources of today (e.g., modern piano). After all, that is exactly what many of them did in their time. Pianist Hélène Grimaud notes the 'original' instruments of the Renaissance and Baroque were not used by choice but of necessity.

Many later composers tried to introduce Bach into their own periods, e.g., trying to update Baroque music into the Romantic period. Bach's *The Well-Tempered Klavier* inspired the Twenty-four Preludes of Chopin, who could play both books of *The Well-Tempered Klavier* by memory. There were efforts by Mendelssohn and Schumann, Liszt with his transcriptions, and Busoni with his piano arrangements of select Bach works such as the the *Chaconne* from Violin Partita No.2 in D minor. This continued into the 20th century with conductor Leopold Stokowski's well-known transcriptions, including his very famous orchestration of Bach's *Toccata and Fugue* in D Minor. These are all the "result of 'progressive' efforts to bring Bach closer to the particular period" of a given composer. The preludes and fugues of *The Well-Tempered Klavier* clearly influenced Shostakovich's *Twenty-Four Preludes and Fugues*, Op.87 as they were composed after Shostakovich attended a two-hundredth anniversary celebration of Bach's death.

The rise in period instrument performances could be seen as a backlash against this and an effort to return music "to its roots", ostensibly to composers' original intentions. The drawback to this line of thinking and to period performances is we do not know how the composer would want his music performed today. Even if scholars have a fairly good idea of how it was originally performed, that is not the same as Haydn wanting performances of his symphonies today limited to what was available in Vienna two hundred years ago.

- 15 -

The Classical Period and the Birth of the Symphony

> "Beethoven crashes the gates of heaven
> while Mozart comes down from heaven."
> - Otto Klemperer

"Haydn and Mozart…created a style in which…the expressive and the elegant could join hands." This fusion of dramatic surprise and formal perfection came to be termed the 'classical style'. Out of the Classical period came the forms and structures that dominated classical music until the early 20th century. These include 'sonata' form, which is the most dominant and the most significant form developed in the Classical period.

The *sinfonia*, orchestral suite, and *concerto grosso* of the Baroque evolved into the sinfonia concertante and the modern concerto and symphony. The key difference between the *sinfonia concertante* and a Classical concerto is that the latter attempts to 'pit' the soloist against the orchestra; in the *sinfonia concertante* the soloist(s) are integrated with the orchestra in an extension of the Baroque *concerto grosso*. As a result, a *sinfonia concertante* falls somewhere between a concerto and a symphony. Also evolving out of the Classical period are 'variation' and 'rondo' form, as well as the 'scherzo' movement, which replaced the 'minuet and trio' starting with the more mature symphonies of Beethoven.

A classical work or movement can be cyclical (e.g., A-B-A, Rondo) or progressive. Progressive form uses various transformational devices to either resolve a conflict (the 'Classical' model) or leave the tension unresolved (opening or final movements of Shostakovich symphonies), using motives and thematic ideas to make a 'whole', almost make a 'whole', or deliberately avoid making a wholly self-contained melody.

In most works of the Classical period a melody ('primary') quickly encounters "a partner or a rival…a counterpart or contrary," that allows the primary melody to address the "impulse to significant change." The successful composer of symphonies, as started by Haydn and Mozart, is able to give their works "that mysterious unity" to make the movements of a work "seem…like different aspects" of a single whole. Such a composer also "convinces us that each finale is the inevitable outcome" of all that came before it in the earlier movements.

♪ Joseph Haydn (1732-1809)

"The consistency of Haydn's output is almost greater than any other composer." According to pianist Howard Shelley the five qualities Haydn combines in his works are wit, drama, beauty, energy, and contrast. And Rimsky-Korsakov declared Haydn to be the greatest of all masters of orchestration.

> *"Since God has given me a cheerful heart, he will forgive me for serving him cheerfully."*
> *- Joseph Haydn*

The 'father of the modern symphony', Haydn left us 104 symphonies, which firmly established the four-movement format with the progression of opening movement usually at a brisk pace, followed by a slow second movement (*Adagio, Andante*). Haydn's third movements were "lusty, peasant-like minuets," which later evolved into a scherzo. The symphony concluded with a final movement similar to the first movement in tempo and breadth, but serving to 'wrap things up' as opposed to introducing themes and developing variations on them. "Haydn's impressive series of 100-odd symphonies gives the most comprehensive, continuous picture of stylistic development from 1760 to 1780, and after." "For Haydn, the overall form of sonata or symphony was basically a series of contrasting movements, whose character was sufficiently varied yet sufficiently related to form a complete musical experience." According to Paul Henry Lang the symphonic principle, carried to such a high degree by Haydn in his mature symphonies and string quartets, consists of "developing a pregnant idea through all imaginable metamorphoses."

> *"There is no one who can do it all – to joke, to terrify, to evoke laughter and profound sentiment, and all equally well – except Joseph Haydn."*
> - Mozart

Haydn's early *Divertimenti* established a broad writing style that diverged into his early symphonies (with the addition of larger forces) and his early string quartets. The quartets characteristically were more serious than the early *Divertimenti* he composed specifically for string quartet combination, "music to be listened to for its own expressive value." The stand-outs among Haydn's very early symphonies are Nos.6-8, nicknamed *Le Matin, Le Midi, Le Soir* ('Morning', 'Noon', and 'Evening'), his first public appearance of his symphonies. In these, he reverted to older practice and drew almost entirely on established traditions. All three employ *concertante* parts against a *concerto grosso* background.

Haydn's symphonies speak primarily to the listener; his mature symphonies in particular were intended for public consumption. His string quartets, on the other hand, speak to the players with many passages written expressly for the enjoyment of the performers.

Sturm und Drang
Haydn was "always trying to push boundaries" of convention as far as he could, "as if to say to people 'Yes, it might be a rule that you're not supposed to do this, but look how effective it can be'." Haydn's first symphonic masterpiece was his *Farewell* symphony, No.45 in F-sharp minor. Haydn shows himself as the musical jokester at the symphony's concluding sections by having each of the musicians exit the performance as their part concludes.

The *Farewell* is one of the famous symphonies of Haydn's short-lived *Sturm und Drang* period. It was revived in 1838 by Mendelssohn who conducted it with his *Gewandhaus* Orchestra. In keeping with Haydn's intentions Mendelssohn had the players leave the stage with their scores once each part ended. Mendelssohn described Symphony No.45 as "a curiously melancholy little piece."

The *Sturm und Drang* ('Storm and Stress') movement started in the 1760s by a group of students in Strasburg and led to a "new expressive freedom, a freedom from convention." The name of the movement came from a play by Maximillian Klinger. From 1766-1773 Haydn had his *Sturm und Drang* period, composing symphonies (Nos.26, 35, 38-9, 41-52, 58-9, and 65) with strong emotions, and a "dramatic, passionate, and at times demonic tone" that "appears here to give battle to the style *galant*." Haydn's music "took on a new emotional intensity (and) dramatic sense of urgency and energy." Symphony No.46 in B is one of the first examples (if not the first) of 'cyclical form' – a few phrases of the minuet that closely resemble the main theme of the finale, reappear in the last movement.

The most effective (No.39, No.44 'Trauer', No.45 'Farewell', No.49 'Passione', No.52) are in dark minor keys, and are more personal than his later cheery works. They possess a stark emotional vitality with "tempestuous fast movements and dramatic changes of tempo and dynamic." The dark minor keys of Haydn's *Sturm und Drang* symphonies Nos.26, 49, 39, 44, 45, 52 (all composed 1765-75) give them a "curiously relentless character which eventually distorts the traditional style." The style is "harshly dramatic and fiercely emotional without a trace of sentimentality." Some feel these, and not his later symphonies, are the pinnacle of his symphonic output. However, this dramatic, highly personal and mannered style was almost at once abandoned by Haydn.

Haydn does show his ability to cover a wide range of emotions, from the later *London* Symphonies for public performance to using minor keys for introspective works. With the *Sturm und Drang* symphonies Haydn tuned to the dramatic literary spirit of the age, or *Zeitgeist*. This pitted the ideals of subjectivity, originality and passion against what this "angry-young-man movement…perceived as the stultifying rationalism and classicism of the older generation." In the literary sphere this movement had Johann Goethe as its hero. It did briefly restore and encourage "subjectivism, emotional excess, spontaneity, violence, even a kind of anarchism."

The Paris Symphonies

In 1779 Haydn's long time patrons the Esterhazy house allowed him to take paid commissions from the 'outside world' for the first time. Among many commissions that would come his way from all over the continent and England were several sets of famous symphonies, sets known to us as the *Paris* and *London* symphonies.

Symphonies Nos. 82-87 are termed the 'Paris' symphonies, composed 1785-86 for a Parisian audience at a Masonic concert. These six symphonies are joined together and can be had on two CDs. In addition, the set of three symphonies, Nos.90-92 represents a second set of *Paris* Symphonies also written for the Comte d'Ogny. With his exposure to Mozart's music starting in 1781, Haydn's music "became broader than it had ever been, deeper, more expressive." These symphonies show no striking novelties, but a "deep inner balance" and "a perfect matching of dimension with energy," allowing the works to "attain striking character with a minimum of means." The *Paris* Symphonies blend "an approachable, popular style with a broad emotional range and inventive mastery of form." Additionally, the use of folk-like material becomes increasingly important in Haydn's works from 1785 on. Although composers long had an interest in folk music, "it is only in the 1780s that the classical style (with Haydn) was able thoroughly to assimilate and to create elements of folk style at will."

Of the symphonies composed just before the first *London* set No. 88 and No.92 *Oxford* are the best known. No.88 is one of the most beloved of all Haydn symphonies. To the glorious *Largo* of Haydn's Symphony No.88, "which has the most holy religious character," Brahms allegedly claimed, "I want my Ninth Symphony to sound like this."

H.C. Robbins Landon summed up the joyful and vibrant *Oxford*, which "combines the greatest contrapuntal mind since J.S. Bach with a rich symphonic style." "Not a measure (of the *Paris* symphonies)…is not marked by Haydn's wit." No.92 has a lot of jokes and happiness but also sorrow and tragedy. The first movement is "Haydn's most massive expansion of sonata form until then." This symphony was the last and greatest of the symphonies written for Paris. The nickname comes from the fact that Haydn re-used it at Oxford when he received an honorary degree. With the composition of the *Oxford* Symphony in 1788 Haydn entered his final period of creative activity. His symphonies reached their highest order in which simple rondos replaced by "finely developed sonata-rondos worthy of the artistic quality of the initial movements."

> *"There's something extraordinarily heart-warming about Haydn's wish to entertain."*
> - Roger Norrington

The commissions for the *Paris* and *London* symphonies in the 1780s and 1790s, respectively, allowed Haydn to take advantage of the much larger forces at his disposal. In both of Europe's leading cities, Haydn could compose for an orchestra of fifty to sixty players as opposed to the twenty or so permanently employed at Eszterháza. This allowed Haydn to take important steps in the development of the symphony. Included in this evolution is the use by Haydn of a slow introduction at the opening of several of these symphonies. "The slow movements of many of the later Haydn symphonies have the improvised intimacy of much of his chamber music." In fact, the slow introduction to Classical works had been an exterior device until Mozart's String Quintet in D and Haydn's late symphonies. These works "reveal new relationships between the introductions and the following allegros."

The London Symphonies

By the 1780s Haydn was composing music for patrons all over Europe: symphonies, masses, quartets for French, Spanish, Austrian, and of course, Hungarian patrons. In addition, there are also the many, mostly-forgotten, operas. This resulted in an international fame, which preceded Haydn to England at the call of another patron, Johann Salomon, whose two sponsorships resulted in the final twelve *London* Symphonies. Haydn's freedom from the Esterhazys and his move to Vienna in 1790 was another signal, together with Mozart's career and that of the soon-to-be-in-Vienna Beethoven that the era of the composer as servant was ending.

There were two trips to London, each representing six symphonies, Nos.93-98 in 1791-92 and Nos.99-104 in 1794-95. Both trips were smashing successes. The symphonies, filled with abundant musical invention and expressed with a noble simplicity were completely appropriate to a London bourgeois audience. While the twelve are often considered together, they are actually two sets of six symphonies, each set a distinct commission. The two groups are drastically different but all twelve symphonies are intended as crowd pleasers, although they are certainly great works. The public welcomed them with much fanfare. "For beauty, power and range, there is no comparable symphonic body created in so short a time." Haydn had at his disposal from Salomon a large orchestra and in these symphonies "the different orchestral colors are less contrasted and opposed than blended to form a new kind of mass sonority."

On his first trip Haydn arrived in London on New Year's Day 1791 and stayed until mid-1792. He provided two sets of three symphonies for both concert seasons, Nos.95-97 for the first season (spring 1791) and Nos. 93, 94, 98 for the second (spring 1792). Symphony No.96, 'Miracle', was the first of the new symphonies to be premiered in London. He would return to Vienna but be back again in London under arrangements with Salomon in February 1794. He would again provide three new symphonies (Nos.99-104) for each of the two concert seasons (February to March 1794 and February to May 1795), and left for Vienna in August 1795.

Haydn conducted all twelve premieres in London. The *Military* Symphony (No.100) quickly became his most popular work. The symphonies when performed in Vienna were well-received but never with the ecstatic reviews Haydn received in England. Haydn lived fourteen more years after completing his final symphony, aptly nicknamed *London*.

Haydn's later music, from the 1780s onward, "rarely displays the extraordinary passion of the finest works of the 1770s." What was lost from the extreme effects of his earlier *Sturm und Drang* symphonies was compensated in the *London* sets by a harmonious combination of elements and a bringing together of the ingredients into the most efficient relationship. The *London* Symphonies may not be "more powerful than (his) finest works of the 1770s, but they are certainly more efficient." In his maturity Haydn uses a "sophisticated control to relate phrase rhythm to large harmonic movement (endowing) the music with great energy." A trademark of the *London* Symphonies is the slow introduction to the first movement, a device used in eleven of the twelve symphonies. The elaborate slow introductions of the *London* Symphonies became a dramatic gesture. The key to the success of these slow introductions is their "lack of a precise definition…(a) nebulous quality" that keeps it from sounding like an actual opening.

Another trademark Haydn device that distinguishes much of his music from Mozart's is the 'surprise return'. This is one of Haydn's best-loved and most dramatic effects. The most famous example is the 'surprise' in the slow movement of Symphony No.94, leading to the work's nickname, *Surprise*. There are more surprises to this symphony than just the famous 'wake-up' surprise of the slow movement. Haydn was very proficient at suggesting the arrival of the surprise but delaying it "until the listener no longer knows when to expect it." Not surprisingly, the other London Symphonies acquired nicknames, some that make sense and some that do not. The label of *Miracle* for No.96 is a misnomer, but *Drum Roll* for No.103 was gotten from the opening timpani roll, while No.101, *The Clock*, has a tick-tock accompaniment to the main theme of the slow movement. Mozart's influence is seen in Symphony No.99, the first Haydn symphony to use clarinets, Mozart's preferred wind instrument.

The introduction to Symphony No.104, 'London', is a good example of Tovey's portrayal of Haydn as "heedless of rules, who traded in the inspired-unexpected" so that Haydn "could strike one of those tragic notes of which (Haydn) knows the depth as well or better than the gloomiest artists." Something often overlooked, especially in 'modern' performances of Haydn's symphonies by leading orchestras and conductors, is that even as late as his *London* Symphonies Haydn conducted while also accompanying at the keyboard, although the role of this keyboard part was more so that the conductor could follow the score with the players than to give the keyboard any true musical role. The virtuoso conductor, first seen with Beethoven but viewed as eccentricity by players, would only establish himself in the Romantic era with great conductors such as Mendelssohn and Berlioz.

> **Recommended – Haydn Symphonies**
> *Sturm und Drang* – Pinnock or Ivan Fischer; *Paris* Symphonies – Antal Dorati and the Philharmonia Hungarica (Decca, 1972). *London* Symphonies – Colin Davis and the Concertgebouw (Philips) on two double CD sets with "classical lightness and sympathetic shaping." Sir Thomas Beecham's interpretations with the Royal Philharmonic are timeless on two 2-CD sets (EMI, released 1992). Charles Mackerras' offerings of four of the nicknamed symphonies (*Clock, London, Military*, and *Miracle*), with the Orchestra of St. Luke's, remain satisfyingly fresh. The four have now been repackaged in a 2-CD set.

Haydn was the patriarch of European musicians for the last twenty years of his life (after the passing of Mozart in 1791). He was "adored from St. Petersburg to Seville…proving that a man of genius could rise to high levels of social esteem while remaining…a servant."

The Haydn renaissance after World War I was due largely to the "passionate advocacy" of Sir Donald Tovey and the restoration of so many of his neglected works (the vast majority of his total output), led by H.C. Robbins Landon, who, according to Haydn historian Richard Wigmore, was "that prodigious one-man Haydn industry." Haydn spent over forty years in the east Austrian city of Eisenstadt in the employ of the Hungarian Esterhazy family. The city today still holds an annual Haydn festival.

Haydn did not enjoy modern copyright protection; as soon as his publisher released a new work, knock-off copies appeared. These copies would often revise parts to suit specific orchestral ensembles, or to make the works more 'marketable'. In worst cases, Haydn's original intentions were eviscerated and what remained was a total mutilation. Unfortunately, many of these bastardizations established themselves in the standard repertory version and would be performed for 150 years. Luckily, someone decided to undertake the monumental but necessary task of correcting this mess. H.C. Robbins Landon, the eminent Haydn scholar, took on the task and it is mostly his meticulous editorial work that allows Haydn's original intentions to be heard today in his symphonies.

Regarding the concerto output of Mozart and Haydn, Mozart made much more of a contribution with his twenty-seven piano concertos, five violin concertos, four horn concertos, and various concertos for wind instruments. The most famous of the latter group is the Clarinet Concerto. Haydn, not being a virtuoso performer on keyboard (or any other instrument) wrote less than a dozen piano concertos, several of which were most likely not composed by Haydn, and only a couple of violin concertos. However, his two most well-known concertos are for trumpet and cello soloists. The Trumpet Concerto in particular is popular for its upbeat rhythms, its virtuosic solo trumpet playing, and especially for its final movement, which makes an appearance periodically in commercials. The Trumpet Concerto is often coupled with Hummel's Concerto for Trumpet, a contemporary of Haydn's. Both concertos were written for the newly-invented 'keyed' trumpet.

> **Recommended – Haydn concertos**
> Here I must recommend the collection of Haydn's three most popular concertos, two of them played by household names, coupled together on one CD with Wynton Marsalis (trumpet) and Yo-Yo Ma (cello), plus one of the violin concertos.

♪ Wolfgang Amadeus Mozart (1756-1791)

Mozart "perfected as he created the form of the classical concerto." While Mozart did not contribute to the concerto repertoire for cello or trumpet, he wrote several excellent wind concertos and took the piano concerto to new heights in terms of form and substance. Harold Schonberg summed up Mozart's music very succinctly, "Mozart's music is at once easy and hard to listen to: easy because of its grace, its never-ending melody, its clear and perfect organization; hard, because of its depth, its subtlety, its passion." And Alfred Einstein pointed out that "to a certain part of the 19th century his work seemed to possess so pure, so formally rounded, so 'godlike' a perfection..." Although he began composing at age six, it was only after Mozart made his final break from Salzburg in 1781 at age twenty-five that we hear the personality, concentration, and richness that characterize his masterpieces.

♫ Piano Concertos

Haydn failed in two major forms in which Mozart had great success: the dramatic concerto and opera. These two forms are much more related than it may seem. Mozart derived his classical concerto form directly from the operatic aria, with the concerto soloist like a character from an opera. Mozart intended a dramatic contrast between soloist and orchestra modeled on the operatic aria. As the audience waits for the entrance of the soprano in opera, so they wait for the pianist to enter or re-enter a concerto. In Mozart's piano concertos "the piano's exposition is...a free adaptation of the orchestral ritornello."

Mozart fully exploited the dramatic possibilities of concerto form, reshaping the contrast between soloist and orchestra. He "bound himself only by the rules he reset and reformulated anew for each work." With Mozart's mature concertos (after 1775) "the entrance of the soloist is an event, like the arrival of a new character on the stage of a drama." "In terms of Mozart's style, dramatization means development...and modulation."

It was within the decade from 1777 to 1786 that the piano concerto as we know it was established by Mozart. Beginning in Salzburg and continuing in Vienna Mozart established the piano concerto as a serious composition with complex interaction and dialogue between soloist and orchestra. It became much more symphonic with an enriched orchestra and enlarged dimensions compared with the concerto model established by C.P.E Bach. Slow movements are usually andante instead of the adagio movement typically found in symphonies, and finales are fast and brilliant rondos.

The style *galant* of the mid 1700s helped the pianoforte supplant the harpsichord as the keyboard instrument of choice as *galant* music sounded sweeter on the piano. Mozart was the driving force and with his final eight concertos he certainly elevated the form to near-perfection. He learned to "integrate elements…of both generations of Bachs, folding Johann Christian's *galant* manner into Johann Sebastian's…rich…polyphonic textures." Beginning with No.20 (K.466) he produced eight masterpieces, concluding with No.27 (K.595). His mature piano concertos are not only considered among his greatest works but are unsurpassed in the genre.

Mozart's concertos are "independent creations based on traditional expectations of the contrast between solo and orchestra…" Mozart essentially invented the piano concerto as we know it by greatly augmenting the basic concerto structure laid down by C.P.E. Bach, elaborating on sonata form and adding immense richness. This was apparent mostly in his first movements where he allowed a dramatic element into the music.

While Mozart composed in each musical genre of his time and "none is without a matchless contribution from his pen," in no genre did he reach greater heights than in his piano concertos. "The miracle of Mozart's style was to make a clearly marked event…like the entrance of…the soloist in a concerto, seem to rise organically from the music…This conception of articulated continuity was a radical departure in the history of music." Mozart took the piano concerto to "an exalted level" infusing them "with an otherworldly purity and spirituality." In his twenty-one original and full-scale concertos for piano and orchestra he paved the way for the genre "to be expanded and intensified by Beethoven, Brahms, and the great Romantics who followed."

It should be noted that Mozart did not publish his mature piano concertos during his lifetime as "the keyboard concerto was a personal vehicle for his appearances as soloist…the principal way of presenting himself to the public."

Piano Concerto No.9 in E-flat, K.271; No.19 in F, K.459

Mozart did not accomplish this right away; in fact, the first concerto that can be considered as markedly different from predecessors is his *Ninth* (K.271), composed in 1777 at age of twenty-one in Salzburg. This concerto was the first classical-style masterpiece to be completely purified of the Rococo mannerisms. The concertos before K.271 reflect the less serious approach to the form of J.C. Bach and "had not broken, except in small details, with the common sociable style of his contemporaries." It was also the first of Mozart's piano concertos to appear in print, published in Paris around 1780. We know little of the French pianist 'Mademoiselle Jeunehomme' for whom Mozart composed this concerto.

The next eight concertos, through No.19, show Mozart's progression and gradual maturity with the form. After coming to Vienna from Salzburg in 1781 Mozart got ready for the 1782-83 concert season with his three Piano Concertos Nos.11-13. Mozart characterized these works as "a happy medium between too hard and too easy...pleasing to the ear." Not certain of the makeup of his audiences Mozart stressed that the concertos contained passages to please both connoisseurs and non-connoisseurs alike.

With the *Ninth*, Mozart composed a concerto that some feel is on par with his final masterpieces. Alfred Einstein called it "Mozart's *Eroica*", because in its power Mozart seeks to be "entirely himself", and like it was for Beethoven, Mozart's Ninth Piano Concerto provides a clear statement that what will follow will be nothing like what has come before it.

The originality of this concerto is also worth noting. The piano enters in just the second measure, something that was very strange for its time. "Where listeners would have expected a lengthy orchestral introduction of the movement's themes, Mozart instead prefaces this with a little orchestral flourish answered by an amiable rejoinder from the soloist." Aside from its structural innovations, the *Ninth* "has a depth of feeling and an elegance of manner...that have made the concerto endure." As for the slow movement, Charles Rosen points out that "as an expression of grief and despair, this movement stands...almost alone among Mozart's concerto movements; not until (the slow movement of Beethoven's Fourth Piano Concerto) is the same tragic power recaptured."

The principal lines of the classical piano concerto were laid down with Mozart's Piano Concerto No.9, K.271 but the technical range of the concerto form would not be fully explored until eight years later with the six great concertos of 1784 (Nos.14-19).

Piano Concerto No.19 was written at the same time (1784) as his *Haydn* String Quartets and it shows influences from the older master. "This concerto is the last of the miraculous harvest of 1784," the year that produced concertos Nos.14-19. It is likely that Mozart wrote this concerto purely for the pleasure of the Viennese listening audience. "The first two movements of (K.459) are heavy with Baroque sequences and contrapuntal imitation." Mozart avoids outright virtuosity in the elegantly polished first movement. He delays soloist-orchestra confrontation and any feeling of tonal tension until the final movement, "the greatest of all Mozart's concerto finales...a complex synthesis of fugue, sonata-rondo-finale and *opera buffa* style." Even though some tension is introduced in the finale, Mozart offsets that by ending with a fine example of the Classical period 'happy ending' after the cadenza.

Piano Concertos No.21 in C, K.467; No.22 in E-flat, K.482; No.23 in A, K.488

Piano Concerto No.21 in C, K.467 is the pendant work to K.466 but is a work of symphonic majesty. Charles Rosen compares the following of K.466 with K.467 to the *Jupiter* Symphony following the G minor (Symphony No.40). "This concerto is Mozart's first true essay in orchestral grandeur." It is the tranquil breadth of K.467 that leads directly to the compositional style seen in the *Prague* and the *Jupiter* Symphonies. The second movement of K.467 is one of the more well-known, "over a troubled accompaniment we hear one of the world's astounding melodies…"

No.22 is the third of the piano concertos Mozart composed in 1785, "both grand and gentle, it offers remarkable contrast to its two immediate predecessors…both of them hyper-inventive and audaciously personal." K.482 and K.488 that followed are soft interludes in the series of Mozart's late piano concertos. Clarinets, Mozart's favorite woodwind, dominate this concerto and woodwinds play a larger role than in any of his other piano concertos, including a considerable amount of solo work for bassoon. The orchestration is brilliant and charming.

No.23 is one of Mozart's most popular piano concertos. It is chamber music-like showing "little ambition by way of pianistic brilliance… (it is) lyric and softly moonlit." The opening movement is very comforting, "no worries in it...the worries come in the second movement." Especially notable is the finale "in which the piano and orchestra cavort…in an exhilarating and satisfying manner…to create one of Mozart's seemingly most perfect masterpieces."

Piano Concertos No.20 in D minor, K.466; No.24 in C minor, K.491

Concerto No.20 and No.24 are the only two minor key piano concertos of Mozart. There was "no hint of the turbulence that was to emerge" with the D minor Concerto in 1785 just two months after the light-hearted F Major, the cheerful No.19. K.466 has always been held in high regard even when Mozart's reputation was low, especially by Romantic composers of the 19th century who, as a result of this concerto, viewed Mozart as the greatest of 'romantic' composers.

"The soft but tumultuous strains that begin" the D minor "project unease, portending tragedy." This "gloomy texture" was unusual for Classical concertos as most "began with a melody that listeners could seize upon for guidance while entertaining pleasant anticipation of its return." It possesses "brooding chromaticism and stormy outbursts" although the final section in D major represents "a clear instance of an 18th century happy ending."

As was the case with No.20, Concerto No.24 in C minor (1786), with its "darkened mood, chromatic instabilities, and stormy patches" was not well-accepted or understood by audiences in Mozart's day. They both anticipate

Beethoven's stormy emotional intensity. Mozart biographer Hugh Ottaway has an explanation for the reaction by Viennese audiences. K.466 marks Mozart's move away from 'social' music toward more profound, but less accessible, music. This brooding minor-key concerto and subsequent reflective and complex works were difficult to assimilate on first hearing, causing listeners to be puzzled; ultimately they rejected them.

Interestingly, the first movement of K.491 is closely related to Haydn's Symphony No.78 in the same key. "With all its dramatic power, K.491 comes closer to the late chamber music style of Mozart…we reach the inward-looking detail of the string quartet." Although K.491 has a tragic feel like its companion in D minor, it is "more intimate (and) it evades the theatricality of (K.466)." Because of their overt emotionalism these two concertos would become very popular with Romantic-era pianists and audiences, two of the few of Mozart's work to hold a firm place in the repertoire during the 19th century.

Piano Concertos No.25 in C, K.503; No.26 in D, K.537; No.27 in B-flat, K.595

Concerto No.25 has never been one of the public's favorites among Mozart's mature piano concertos. Although a magnificent work in the grand Classical style, the "almost neutral character of the material" makes it a cold work to many listeners.

Not only did the Viennese public have trouble with Mozart's minor key piano concertos (Nos.20 & 24), but the residents (and rulers) of the Hapsburg capital found his later concertos too complicated. Emperor Joseph II complained famously, "Too many notes, dear Mozart, too many notes." Michael Steinberg feels that Piano Concerto No.26, 'Coronation', was composed in direct response to this public reaction and is less complex "meant more to please and charm than to stimulate the mind and stir the emotions." The work brings back the charm and light-spiritedness of the Rococo and the style *galant*. Mozart possessed an "ability to draw the utmost poignance of expression from the simplest means." But Charles Rosen feels the *Coronation* Concerto is "the most 'progressive' of all Mozart's works…it was extremely popular throughout the 19th and most of the 20th centuries…with its loose melodic structure it can be seen as the greatest of early Romantic concertos."

Mozart's final developmental style was characterized by an economy of means, exhibited, for example, in the most chamber-like of his piano concertos, his final one. Piano Concerto No.27 is one of two concertos from the final year of Mozart's life, the other being the Clarinet Concerto. With their tone of intimacy, they "depend more upon the delicate interplay of chamber music than upon the dramatic interplay of concerto style." However, his last piano concerto, as well as Symphony No.40, both in Mozart's final style, show modulations as brutal as any of his other works.

> **Recommended - Mozart Piano Concertos**
> There are two approaches. One can purchase a complete set of the concertos from Barenboim or Perahia (both functioning as soloist and conductor). Perahia's set, recorded with the English Chamber Orchestra from the mid-1970s to mid-1980s, "provides the ideal mix of purity and profundity." However, one only gets one soloist's take on all works. It is preferable to select and purchase individual CD's (with two concertos each) to provide a variety of soloists, conductors and orchestras. The best purchase to experience Mozart's piano concertos, is the two-CD set played by Clifford Curzon of concertos 20, 23, 24, 26 and 27 with Kertész or Britten conducting.

Concertos for Strings

Mozart composed five violin concertos, a couple of one-movement works (a Rondo, an *Adagio*) and the *Sinfonia Concertante*, K.364, which is a concerto for violin and viola. K.364 is a 'double' concerto analogous to Brahms *Double* Concerto for violin and cello, except Mozart's was a neo-Baroque Classical concerto and Brahms' a Romantic Classical work.

The violin concertos were all written together from September to December of 1775 in Salzburg and are not the sophisticated works that his piano concertos are; they are fairly conservative in structure in style. These violin works also do not require virtuoso violin playing. No cadenzas exist for these concertos so it is believed Mozart saw himself as soloist and would improvise the cadenza himself. This is reputed, however, as Mozart rarely performed as a concert violinist, but often as pianist. He also preferred the viola over violin parts in chamber works.

On the other hand, the *Sinfonia Concertante* is one of Mozart's greatest concerto masterpieces in which both violin and viola soloists are treated as equal partners. In K.364 the "sonority inspired by the solo viola part which Mozart probably wrote for himself to play, is unique."

The *Third*, *Fourth* and *Fifth* ('Turkish') violin concertos are the more popular but not on the level of his late piano concertos. The *Fifth*, which "sparkles with the wit that is typical of Mozart at his happiest," is nicknamed *Turkish* because of the march that follows the rondo section of the finale.

> **Recommended – Mozart Violin Concertos**
> Perlman, VPO, Levine give classical performances that highlight the *cantabile* nature of these works. Violinist Gidon Kremer, with Harnoncourt directing the Vienna Philharmonic, takes a different, less lyrical approach that de-emphasizes the 'cantabile', or song-like feel, of Mozart's music. This set, which also includes the *Sinfonia Concertante*, makes a good complement to the lush and traditional Perlman/Levine.

Wind Concertos

In addition to his piano and violin concertos, Mozart wrote a number of wind concertos, including four concertos for horn. His Clarinet Concerto, K622, is a large-scale concerto with a well-known melody in its first movement. It is his greatest wind concerto and one of his greatest orchestral works overall, as well as Mozart's last completed major work. This work joins Mozart's Clarinet Quintet in A (K.581) and Clarinet Trio in E-flat (K.487) to form a set of three works giving a dominant role to the clarinet. With its wealth of melodies, contrapuntal rigor and the magnificent treatment of the clarinet, K.622 is "hardly the trifling showpiece that some of his earlier wind concertos are (and) far removed from the empty virtuosity of other clarinet concertos."

The Oboe Concerto in C (K.314) represents Mozart at his most charming, filled with soaring melodies. There is also the Bassoon Concerto in B-flat, K.191, a relatively early work from 1774 and the only surviving work of a possible five concertos Mozart composed for bassoon. Although this wind instrument has limitations in both range and power, Mozart shows his skilled use of orchestration to overcome this. Mozart possessed unparalleled understanding of winds as well as wide experience with them.

Mozart, under commission for a number of flute works, relieved himself of some of the drudgery of the commission by recycling his Oboe Concerto into his Flute Concerto in D, K.314. However, there are sufficient changes (including the key signature) to allow us to regard it not so much as a knockoff but as a valuable addition to a too-slender repertoire. The concerto is lighthearted, exemplary in its balance between soloist and small orchestra, and sufficiently virtuosic to satisfy a demanding soloist.

Mozart's four concertos (K.412, K.413, K.447, K.495) for natural (that is, valve less) horn remain popular. Nos. 2-4 are all in E-flat major with the first in the key of D. Because of the limitations of the natural horn, Mozart was limited to the natural pitch (and overtones of that pitch) of the horns available and in how he could use the soloist regarding the normal pattern of key and theme relations. Any tune composed for the horn soloist would have to be cast in the appropriate key.

The numbering does not correspond to the order of composition. As was the case with his other wind concertos, the horn concertos were written for a friend who was an outstanding player, in this case Ignaz Leutgeb. K.447 stands out above the others for its subtlety and depth.

> *Recommended - Mozart Wind Concertos*
> Vienna Philharmonic, various soloists led by Karl Böhm
> Mozart Horn Concertos – Dennis Brain, generally considered the greatest horn player, in vintage recordings from 1953 with the Philharmonia led by Herbert von Karajan.
> Flute Concerto – Emmanual Pihad, principal flutist of the Berlin Philharmonic, with his bandmates and Abbado (EMI, 2001).

♪ Symphonies

Mozart's symphonies, like much of his music, were heavily influenced by his older contemporary Haydn, whose complete set of 104 symphonies is considered by many, as a whole, to be superior to Mozart's. Mozart's final six symphonies taken as a group can be considered with Haydn's final twelve symphonies (the *London* symphonies). However, while Haydn's *London* symphonies were crowd pleasers and were received as such, Mozart had become less popular as his compositions moved into uncharted territory in which the conservative music-going crowd in Vienna was not comfortable.

During his ten-year Vienna period, which was the last ten years of his life (1781-1791), Mozart's musical production was amazing although, as mentioned, his popularity dropped as the Viennese public did not take to his more mature works, masterpieces though they were. The late works were viewed as too different by the conventional minds of Vienna, as even his patrons, as well as other musicians, reacted with statements such as, "he leaves the hearer out of breath" and "far too many notes". But these works were "of much greater depth, confidence, brilliance, and power," definitely looking forward to the great works of Beethoven. Vienna delighted in light music to lift their spirits, take their minds off life's troubles. They wanted *Eine Kleine Nachtmusik*, not a somber, lengthy piano concerto in a minor key (No.20 in D minor or No.24 in C minor).

The Middle Symphonies

Symphony No.25, the 'Little G minor', marks the beginning of his great run of symphonies (Nos.25, 29, 35, 36, 38, 39, 40, and 41) that culminates with the 'big G minor', No.40 and the *Jupiter*, No.41. As does Haydn, Mozart effectively uses the minor key to convey Sturm und Drang in his symphonies.

Symphony No.29 in A, K.201, is the last of Mozart's Salzburg symphonies, with the andante being the highlight of the work. Together with No.25 and No.28 it forms a trio of symphonies widely considered Mozart's first mature efforts in the genre. Earlier Mozart symphonic efforts had been little more than three-part Italian opera overtures. With the trio of Nos.25, 28, 29 Mozart shows an extent of contrast, a deepening of expressivity, and an imitative treatment of themes that highlight his later great symphonies. It is in these three symphonies that Mozart not only masters the form but finds his own voice as a symphonist.

Symphony No.31 in D, K.300a, nicknamed *Paris* for whose orchestra and citizens it was commissioned, has only three movements with the minuet omitted, and was the first of Mozart's symphonies to feature his favorite woodwind, the clarinet.

The Final Symphonies

Symphony No.35, *Haffner*, was created in 1782 by dropping the introductory march and one of the minuets from a recently-completed serenade, resulting in a four-movement symphony. The serenade, requested by his father for another Haffner celebration, does not survive. Mozart had previously provided the K.250 serenade for a Haffner wedding affair. It is confusing, but the *Haffner* Symphony is indeed derived from a serenade, but not from the *Haffner* Serenade. He also beefed up the instrumentation by adding pairs of flutes and clarinets to the outer movements.

His next symphony, No.36, *Linz*, was composed in 1783 to honor Count Thun-Hohenstein of Linz. Although this is the first Mozart symphony to begin with a slow introduction in the manner of Haydn (he would do the same in his next symphony, No.38), it is all brightness after that, "bathing in a refined, agreeable light that projects gentleness and high hopes." In this regard, the *Linz* is the last Mozart symphony to retain the light and elegant atmosphere of his early serenades, and to be composed for a specific occasion. His last four symphonies would be much different.

There is no symphony numbered 37 so Symphony No.38, 'Prague', is the next in line. Mozart loved Prague and enjoyed much success there, but Mozart's affinity for the Czech city could not prevent even him from portraying a dark and complex environment that reinforces Prague's reputation as one of the darkest cities in Europe. The *Prague* Symphony contains "perhaps the richest and most complex introduction before Beethoven's Seventh Symphony." It was composed in Vienna at the end of 1786 in anticipation of Mozart's trip to Prague in early 1787. His stay in Prague "provided Mozart with the greatest popular successes he was ever to know," including the commission for his greatest opera *Don Giovanni*.

The last of Mozart's symphonies, the three masterpieces Nos.39-41, were all composed in a creative spurt of activity during the summer of 1788. This was the first time Mozart had shown a sustained interest in symphony writing since the early 1770s. The preceding six symphonies were composed for isolated occasions, as indicated by their nicknames (*Prague, Linz, Paris, Haffner*). Symphony Nos.39-41 were inspired by Haydn's 'Paris' Symphonies, with which they share the same large dimensions, the same breadth and assurance. While Haydn established an ever-evolving model for the symphony, Mozart relied on and followed Haydn's examples. "This gave Mozart the opportunity – and the obligation – to make the detail of the symphonic plan more exciting and expressive."

Symphony Nos. 39-41 do not appear to have been commissioned by anyone or for any specific occasion, and were most likely simply the product of an inner compulsion to compose new works. His final three symphonies express "the healthiest reactions on each other", according to Donald Tovey, and "excite wonder even for a composer whose entire musical output is a creative miracle." Musicologist Alfred Einstein gushed that these symphonies are Mozart's "last and most perfect gifts to orchestral music," and that all three hover "between grace and melancholy…clarity and joyousness…on a dark background."

The lengths of these symphonies depend heavily on whether or not the conductor observes the repeats in the movements. Depending on that, the first two movements of these symphonies can be up to twice the length together as are the combined time of the third and fourth movements. The four-movement structure of each of the three symphonies is similar; a long opening sonata movement with much development, followed by an equally long slow movement. These first two movements are then followed by a quick minuet/trio as the third movement, and a compact finale to wrap up.

Symphony No. 39 in E-flat, K.543
The first of the three final symphonies (from 1788) is a "lighthearted score, full of abundant joy and ebullience." Unfortunately, K.543 was not performed until after Mozart's death. This symphony also highlights Mozart's recently found interest in the clarinet as an orchestral instrument. The clarinet as we know it today was a new instrument for that era. He substitutes clarinets for the two usual oboes of his scoring, and the effect is pronounced in the minuet third movement, in which "the characteristically liquid sound of the clarinet is heard throughout the work…" In Symphony No.39 Mozart's clarinet writing imbues the work with its own special atmosphere. Charles Mackerras adores its "wonderful clarinet writing and Haydnesque ingenuity."

Symphony No.40 in G-minor, K.543
According to Sir Donald Tovey the G-minor Symphony "accurately defines the range of passion comprehended in terms of Mozart's art." This symphony is one of only two Mozart symphonies in a minor key, which creates in the work a special timbre and unique coloring.

Wagner characterized this symphony as a work of "indestructible beauty." It opens with pulsating violas producing poignant passion, throbbing "behind the gentle yet intense song of the violins." The finale of the G minor Symphony is despairing and impassioned in its dramatic complexity. Conductor Sir Charles Mackerras feels that this symphony is "so full of anxiety, it's almost hysterical." Sir Charles also points out that Schumann felt it was a pleasant, almost jolly symphony.

Symphony No.41 in C, K.551, *Jupiter*
The nickname Jupiter was not given by the composer but by Johann Peter Salomon of the Haydn *London* Symphonies, who cited the work's loftiness of ideals and nobility of treatment. Assertive and forthright, it is music of majesty and sweep. The final movement of this great work is generally regarded as Mozart's supreme achievement in counterpoint, concluding his symphonic contributions with a heroic double fugue.

Mozart learned from Haydn and mastered symphonic counterpoint in his last three symphonies. Particularly in the *Jupiter*, the finale of which is one massive display of the mastery of polyphony, ending with a "magnificent coda where all five principal themes are interwoven in one of music's greatest triumphs." This is the culmination of the inspiration of Bach on Mozart to "introduce all kinds of contrapuntal devices" with "contrasting themes are lined up, harnessed, and sent galloping down the final stretch in one of the most...overwhelming passages..."

At the beginning of the last decade of his life Mozart became very familiar with the music of Bach and Handel. Mozart considered fugue the "most artistic and beautiful of all musical forms." (Mozart) Eric Blom in The Musical Companion suggests that the "immense technical skill with which its elaborate fabric is woven" can only "be apprehended by the imagination."

Recommended – Mozart Symphonies 38-41
The late Charles Mackerras studied, conducted and recorded these symphonies for decades and gave his final word as an octogenarian on Mozart's final four masterpieces with the Scottish Chamber Orchestra (2008). Also recommended are Sir Charles' Teldec recordings from the 1980s with the Prague Chamber Orchestra. For more traditional Mozart, the set of these six symphonies by Böhm and the Berlin Philharmonic has set the standard for decades.

Serenades and *Divertimenti*

These forms are primarily of the Classical period, developed by Haydn and brought to their zenith by Mozart. The serenades and *divertimenti* of Mozart and Haydn were composed for instrumental forces ranging from octets (many various combinations of strings and winds) up to the typical orchestra size of their day. These generally upbeat and lively works were written for festive occasions, such as weddings and other celebrations, and often performed outdoors. Mozart was not very concerned with the formal unity of these works (as with a symphony) and thus his works in this genre are generally collections of loosely-connected movements.

Mozart's *Eine Kleine Nachtmusik* is by far the most well-known serenade. It was finished in August of 1787 for string quintet with double bass, but became famous with string orchestra. The instantly-recognizable opening melody "makes a direct appeal even on the casual listener."

Mozart's K.361, the Serenade for 13 Wind Instruments, *Gran Partita* is a good example of the crossover from chamber to orchestral music with six pairs of winds (plus double bass as *continuo*) duplicating parts.

Mozart composed three other Serenades that are well-known, two of which are substantial works and Mozart's most symphonic in this genre. These are the *Haffner* and *Posthorn* Serenades (K.250 and K.320, both in D major). The third is the shorter *Serenata notturna* (K.239). The *Posthorn* is so nicknamed for the solo section for the posthorn in the second minuet (sixth of the seven movements). Mozart used this primitive horn in no other composition. The third and fourth movements, both in G major, contain elaborate concertante writing for flutes, oboes, and bassoons. The *Haffner* is even meatier than the *Posthorn* with eight movements, including three minuets. The *cantabile* solo violin writing highlights much of this serenade.

K.239 was composed while Mozart was still in Salzburg. It has a *concerto grosso* character with a string quartet group set off against a group of strings without double basses. This work's three movements show how far this work from the mid-1770s was from the great Haydn and Mozart symphonies of the next two decades. It begins with a slightly pompous March followed by a minuet and concludes with a movement in rondo form.

> *Recommended – Mozart Serenades*
> An excellent set is by Böhm and the Berlin and Vienna Philharmonics containing four serenades on two CDs.

♪ Ludwig van Beethoven (1770-1827)

According to Beethoven scholar Barry Cooper, Beethoven's goal was "not just to create music but to create music of the highest artistic worth." Harvey Sachs, author of The Ninth, calls Beethoven's music "big-caliber artillery pointed at the future." Beethoven's first concert for the Viennese public was in April of 1800. The program premiered his Septet, Op.20 his First Symphony, and a performance of a piano concerto, probably the Op.15.

♪ The Concertos

Piano Concerto No.1 in C, Op.15; No.2 in B-flat, Op.19; No.3 in C minor, Op.37

> *"I turn my ideas into tones that resound, roar and rage until at last they stand before me in the form of notes"*
> - Beethoven

When Beethoven premiered or performed his first four piano concertos (he did not perform the *Fifth* in concert) "Beethoven the virtuoso felt free to improvise on the text set down by Beethoven the composer." The concerto was for him mainly a "youthful preoccupation intimately bound up with his prowess and ambition as a public pianist…the concerto was mainly a personal vehicle for the composer-virtuoso's performances"

Piano Concerto No.2 in B-flat was actually completed first in 1795 and at least the first movement may have been drafted as early as 1785 in Bonn (at age fifteen). But it was not performed until Beethoven revised it in Vienna in 1798 and only published in 1801. During that period he composed his C major Concerto, probably written in 1795-98, which came to be No.1. There is disagreement as to which concerto was played by Beethoven at his public debut. Piano Concerto No.1 was probably begun in 1793 and was virtually in its final form some time in 1795. No.2 has by far the most complex history of any of Beethoven's concertos, a checkered history from the late 1780s to 1801. It underwent multiple revisions resulting in no fewer than four distinct versions and "shows Beethoven struggling toward mastery of a high galant style long since achieved by Haydn and Mozart."

As with his symphonies, Beethoven owes a lot to Haydn and Mozart for his first two piano concertos. Both "are fairly unadventurous…in the nature of the piano writing," although there is plenty of new ground broken in these to give a hint of things to come. For example, the opening of the first movement of No.1 "has a Promethean strength of purpose…the sheer muscular strength of the music expands the Haydn-Mozart tradition into something altogether more epic."

However, with his Third Piano Concerto, in C minor Op.37, as with his *Eroica* Symphony, he has clearly entered uncharted territory and this concerto represents a clear advance over its predecessors. With it Beethoven established the "model of Classic-Romantic concerto form for the 19th century." Finished in 1800 "a new note of passion enters the music" with "the dramatic opening theme obviously influenced by Mozart's C minor concerto (No.24) and is "full of Mozartean reminiscences." The modulations and key changes in this concerto were surprising to Beethoven's contemporaries. For example, Beethoven drifted into a remote key (E major) for the slow movement, whereas Mozart stayed much closer to home in the slow movements of his concertos by only side-stepping to the relative minor or major. Piano Concerto No.3 premiered in April 1803 on a program that also included Symphony Nos.1&2.

Piano Concerto No.4 in G, Op.58; No.5 in E-flat, Op.73, *Emperor*

Piano Concerto No.4 in G (1805) is the most eloquently lyrical of all Beethoven's piano concertos. It is unique in that it opens with the soloist, instead of the usual statement of themes (i.e., exposition) by the orchestra. As with Beethoven's C minor Concerto, the G major relies heavily on Mozart's masterpieces in form and the "entrance of the piano in the first measure…immediately brings to mind the opening" of Mozart's Piano Concerto No.9. The middle movement, while less than five minutes, is most arresting, "a vividly etched dialogue between piano and strings."

Beethoven knew about the onset of his deafness by 1801 at the latest. He wrote only one more concerto for himself after 1808 and made no appearances to a large audience after 1814. The *Emperor* Concerto of 1809 was a product of one of the most difficult periods of his life. His hearing had deteriorated badly and Napoleon was laying siege to Vienna.

"And yet out of this chaotic existence came the bold and life-affirming Fifth Piano Concerto." It provides a startling contrast to No.4 with its magnificent opening and with its "storming solo cadenzas, has a royal majesty;" thus, the nickname *Emperor*. At the time it was the longest and most difficult showpiece yet attempted in the concerto literature.

It was composed as Napoleon was about to launch another attack on Vienna. The key of E-flat major was used by Beethoven in his *Eroica* Symphony and in this piano concerto to convey a nobility of spirit and grandeur. Premiered in Vienna in 1812 after the dust had settled. Beethoven's pupil Carl Czerny was the soloist because the composer was too deaf to perform its public premiere. Beethoven had premiered his previous four concertos. Unfortunately, this initial performance was a failure; fortunately, it soon became a success.

In the Emperor Concerto Beethoven takes advantage of recent advances in piano instrument evolution to create this most expansive music, which was "so far ahead of its time that (even today) the (piano) has continued to grow into the music." Bold new touches include Beethoven beginning with three very powerful and brilliant cadences, followed quickly with an opening solo cadenza, followed by a usual exposition. The cadenza normally comes at the end of a first movement in sonata form, just before the concluding coda. Only a piano composer of Beethoven's skill could prevent the first movement piano writing from being reduced to "bombast of scales, *arpeggios*, trills, thunderous chords, and the like." The slow second movement, co-opted by Leonard Bernstein for a love song in *West Side Story*, is a brief dialogue between soloist and orchestra before the transition to the glorious finale. The "serene bliss" of the second movement "follows the galvanizing drama between piano and orchestra in the first movement…" After the "heroic struggle of the first movement…Beethoven achieves a sublime rest in the second movement." The finale is an "irrepressible joyride" and one of Beethoven's "most delightful and positive conclusions."

Recommended – Beethoven Piano Concertos

A most enjoyable live set of all five concertos is by Brendel with Levine conducting the Chicago Symphony Orchestra. Not everyone likes this set but there is just something very spontaneous and fresh about the performances. As for single discs, the coupling of No.4 and No.5 on DG by Kempff with Leitner and the Berliners has stood the test of time. Also, Fleisher with Szell and Cleveland are good.

Except for some sketches Beethoven left for a sixth piano concerto (in D) that he never completed, after the Fifth Piano Concerto he did not return to the concerto form for the remaining eighteen years of his life. A full set of first-movement sketches survives for this unfinished and obscure concerto.

Violin Concerto in D, Op.61

The year 1806 was quite a year; Beethoven produced his Fourth Piano Concerto, Op.58, his only Violin Concerto, Symphony No.4, the *Appassionata* Piano Sonata, and the three Op.59 string quartets, showing a "stylistic range that can only be called Protean." If a mortal composer had completed just one of these great works within a twelve-month period it would have been considered an outstanding year.

As with the Fourth Piano Concerto, the Violin Concerto is an intensely lyrical and intimate work. "The opening theme quietly announces its expressive world in concerted woodwinds." As innocent as the opening seems today, the four timpani beats to start an orchestral work were quite a novelty in 1806 and probably surprising to many listeners. It was disturbing to critics, who had difficulties with new developments after the decades of well-structured, 'conservative' works by Classical-period composers.

Leon Plantinga points to the pastoral nature of the concerto's beginning, similar to Beethoven's *Pastoral* Piano Sonata and his soon-to-be-composed *Pastoral* Symphony No.6. The opening of this concerto "summons up the imagined simplicity and contentment of bucolic life in the countryside."

The premiere was on December 23, 1806 with Franz Clement as soloist. Clement must have been an outstanding musician because Carl Czerny, who has provided a first-hand account, said Beethoven completed the concerto only two days before the concert and that Clement sight-read the solo part at the premiere without rehearsal. However, the solo part played by Clement "seems to have differed appreciably from the version we know."

♪ The Symphonies

Beethoven had a tendency to follow up "one major work with another that was its mirror opposite." The *Pastoral* Symphony "provides an antidote to the *Fifth*, which is "all geothermal heat;" the *Eroica* "begat the decidedly unheroic *Fourth*;" and the "transluscent delicacy" of Piano Concerto No.4 yielded to "an exuberant display of power" in the Emperor Concerto. Beethoven's *Third*, *Fifth* and *Ninth* Symphonies all offered themes of fate dramatized with truly marvelous economy.

Beethoven's first two symphonies owe a lot to the influence of Mozart and Haydn, and Beethoven struggled "to get beyond this influence and to establish his own style and career." However, there is plenty in these two early symphonies to hint at what was to come from the greatest symphonist.

Symphony No.1 in C, Op.21; No.2 in D, Op.36

Clearly set apart from the works of Haydn and Mozart, it begins with dissonance instead of in C major, virtually unprecedented in 1800. Vienna was not sure what to make of Beethoven's First Symphony, with one critic characterizing it as "a caricature of Haydn pushed to absurdity." Already in the *First*, although marked as a typical 'minuet' Beethoven is moving away from the menuet third movement, beginning the evolution of the movement to the more dramatic scherzo form. Menuet form, the one carryover from the stylized dance suites of the Baroque to the Haydn-model symphony of the Classical period, was simply not going to cut it with Beethoven.

The works of Beethoven that we view today as 'radical' for their time were viewed with fear and suspicion by critics and public alike. Even a work that might have been viewed as curious but not outlandish, the Second Symphony, evoked hostility. The work caused a Viennese critic to characterize it as "a gross monster, a hideously writhing wounded dragon."

Symphony No.3 in E-flat, Op.55, *Eroica*

But neither the First nor Second Symphony could have prepared Vienna or the world for the immensity of Beethoven's next symphonic effort. With the Third Symphony we do not have a gradual, 'next step' in the evolution of the symphony but a complete revolution of the form, "the first of Beethoven's immense expansions of classical form." The *Eroica*, with its opening E-flat chord played twice, began Beethoven's significant move away from the symphonies of Haydn and Mozart, who had "limited themselves…to the attainment of noble mirth, to a purification of feelings." The first movement "is fundamentally a show of strength…Beethoven, in his early thirties, flexes his muscles." The *Eroica* shows clearly for the first time Beethoven's appeal "to the heroic, to the religious, to the moral."

> *"Everything is different from today."*
> - Haydn after the premiere of Beethoven's *Eroica*

At fifty-five minutes the *Eroica* symphony is roughly twice the length of the typical classical symphony (almost as long as Beethoven's *First* and *Second* combined). It is significantly longer than Mozart's final two symphonies. The initial public reaction and critical review were negative; one reviewer finding "too much that is glaring and bizarre." Another warned of the length as well as the "strange modulations and violent transitions…if Beethoven continues on his present path both he and the public will be the sufferers. His music could soon reach the point where one would derive no pleasure from it…"

However, the figure of Beethoven was so large that most criticism against his music was tempered with a tone of respectful self-doubt and it did not take long for the public to embrace the *Eroica*. Despite the initial resistance at the premiere of many of his works, "the musical public of Beethoven's time was much more receptive to new ideas than later generations...to accept the *Erocia* Symphony within a few years of its composition...was indeed a remarkable proof of musical intelligence."

Beethoven originally titled this symphony "Bonaparte", but changed it to 'heroic', "in memory of a great man" instead of explicitly in honor of Napoleon, who had disappointed Beethoven by declaring himself 'emperor'. Berlioz, born in the year in which the *Eroica* appeared, could not help but assign programs and find extra musical references in the *Eroica* as well as the *Ninth*. Berlioz considered the *Eroica* to be "inspired by a modern hero, reminiscences of the ancient Iliad play...no less evident a role." Berlioz referred to the *Ninth* as Beethoven's "vast musical poem."

> *"Some say this is Napoleon...Bah! For me it is simply 'allegro con brio'"*
> — Toscanini on Beethoven's *Eroica*

The opening chords, struck twice, indicate the freshness and the boldness of this work, a "willful break with tradition." The chords are "rapped out with neither ceremony nor apology." The "purity of form and depth of poetic intention are perfectly matched...the very ethos of heroism." The *Eroica* Symphony "miraculously balances the tension of extremely opposing musical ideas...exquisite tenderness, terrible power and humor can exist side-by-side." The first, second, and fourth movements are roughly of equal weight with the third movement "to give a bit of emotional respite."

Up until the *Eroica* Symphony of 1805, Beethoven had his roots planted in the 1700s. However, many of his sets of works in various genres (e.g., his Op.18 string quartets), with their massive sonority, Romantic expression, and unconventional form were more rugged than any of Mozart's or Haydn's works. His early 'named' piano sonatas, such as the *Pathétique* and *Moonlight*, probed deeper than those of Haydn and certainly those of Mozart. Beethoven drew upon the work of contemporary masters Mozart and Haydn and challenged himself to push their models beyond limits. "From the *Eroica* Symphony onward, (Beethoven's) music is that of a genius in full control."

Symphony No.5 in C minor, Op.67

In 1808 Beethoven produced only four major works with two being the Op.70 Piano Trios. The other two are his Fifth and Sixth symphonies. After the relatively mild Fourth Symphony, Beethoven returns to the 'heroic' nature of his Third Symphony with his *Fifth*. Both symphonies have attention-grabbing openings. Harvey Sachs contrasts the openings of the *Third* and *Fifth* as intense-positive (cast in a major key) and intense-negative (in C minor), respectively.

The most famous symphony opens with the most famous four notes of any musical composition, what Beethoven supposedly referred to as "Fate knocking at the door." In fact, the opening four notes are an "exceptional example of how much mileage a composer can get out of a few notes…" This "four-note rhythmic figure…recurs in all movements in various guises" and foreshadows the idea of 'thematic transformation' that would be used regularly by Liszt and be so popular among Romantic composers.

From the beginning Beethoven makes it clear that this symphony is "one of the most violent, conflict-ridden pieces ever composed." The whole work is "an effort to get from turmoil in C minor to triumph in C major…while the orchestral sonority evolves from dark to bright." Beethoven fuses together the last two movements by ending the scherzo with a "coda that serves also as a suspenseful introduction to the finale…(that) ends with a striking turn toward bright C major." E.T.A. Hoffmann described the link between the symphony's third and final movements as "a fear which tightly constricts the breast" giving way to "radiant blinding sunlight," as the tension built up in C minor is resolved in the blazing triumph of C major. "The triumphant effect of the eruption of the last movement," is a result of the resolution to the key of C major, "after a long stretch of harmonic ambiguity."

The premiere of the *Fifth* took place in December 1808 in a concert that also included the premiere of Beethoven's *Pastoral* Symphony as well as his Fourth Piano Concerto.

Symphony No.6 in F, Op.68, Pastoral

Beethoven based this symphony, which "represents a retreat from the militancy of the *Fifth*," on a descriptive pastoral symphony by Heinrich Knecht when he was a young teenager. Knecht's symphony, from the early 1780s, was titled *A Musical Portrait of Nature* and shares with Beethoven's *Pastoral* descriptions of thunderstorms and giving thanks after the storms. Beethoven struggled with the idea of program music, knowing that "all painting in instrumental music, if pushed too far, is a failure…listeners should be allowed to discover the situations themselves." That is most likely why Beethoven claimed the *Pastoral* to be an "expression of feeling rather than painting." It is not programmatic in the same sense as Romantic works evoking landscapes and nature; its images, even the explicit thunderstorm scene, are generalized and the sentiments portrayed are done so within the Classical tradition.

The *Sixth* was completed in 1808 with sketches that began in 1806. Beethoven conducted the premiere, which also included the premiere of his Fifth Symphony and a performance of Piano Concerto No.4, three days before Christmas of 1808 (the two great symphonies have consecutive opus numbers). The two works brought trombones into the concert hall for the first time. It must have been quite a concert! The name *Pastoral* and headings of the five movements were all Beethoven's doing, although he was careful to warn listeners not to expect pictures in the *Pastoral* Symphony.

Berlioz in 1834 commented on the storm (fourth) movement of this symphony, "It is no longer an orchestra that one hears, it is no longer music, but rather the tumultuous voice of the heavenly torrents blended with the uproar of the earthly ones, with the furious claps of thunder, with the crashing of uprooted trees, with the gusts of an exterminating wind, with the frightening cries of men and the lowing of the herds. This is terrifying, it makes one shudder, the illusion is complete." Not surprisingly from Berlioz, this description is more than a little 'over the top', or as Paul Griffiths points out, "is evidently done for effect – if splendidly." The thunderstorm of the fourth movement "is the fulcrum of the *Pastoral* Symphony. Its intrusion is what gives meaning and narrative direction to the whole."

Because of the poetic 19th century imagination the *Pastoral* Symphony remained Beethoven's most popular through much of that century. While that might seem initially surprising, in hindsight it makes sense as the *Sixth* is indeed the most romantic of Beethoven's orchestral works and exerted a great influence on the Romantic generation of composers who followed him. Excepting the thunderstorm scene, the *Sixth* is "bathed in a benign luminous energy," in the traditional pastoral key of F.

Symphony No.7 in A, Op.92; No.8 in F, Op.93

The Seventh and Eighth Symphonies are often viewed as a contrasting pair, deliberately composed this way by Beethoven. The symphonies preoccupied him for over a year beginning with sketches for both in the summer of 1811. As with the *Fifth* and *Sixth*, the *Seventh* and *Eighth* have consecutive opus numbers, although the former two are rarely considered together. As with the *Fifth* and *Sixth* these two symphonies certainly stand in contrast to each other, one energetic followed by a serene work.

The *Seventh* is "massive, muscular, louder than any of his other works...it is one long explosion of superhuman energy." It is "short on themes but long on rhythmic drive," which gives a galloping, dance-like character to the work, while the *Eighth* is "short and deliciously witty" and "full of sly humor." Composer George Benjamin gushes about this symphony, claiming "it seems to be the most infectiously joyous thing man has ever made." And he points out that at the symphony's conclusion, "the music seems to descend into a black hole and then surface again more ecstatically than before."

Premiered in 1814 to a relatively cool reception, the *Eighth* did not create a furor. This angered Beethoven who, for some reason, considered the *Eighth* to be "much better" than his *Seventh*, which had been received with the expected enthusiasm reserved for the work of a great master. The *Eighth* is sometimes labeled 'neo-Classical' because it calls "to mind the lightness and clarity of the 18th century Viennese style." Indeed, the "civilized gaiety" that marked the classical style "makes its last appearances in the allegretto of Beethoven's *Eighth* and in some of the movements of the last string quartets." Once Romanticism took hold, wit was "swamped by sentiment."

> **Recommended – Beethoven Symphonies**
> Symphony No.3 *Eroica* – Barbirolli/BBC SO (1967); Symphony No.5 & 7 – Carlos Kleiber/VPO, mid-1970s. Symphony No.6 *Pastoral* – Bruno Walter, Columbia SO (Sony/CBS, 1959); Paavo Järvi, German Chamber Philharmonic, Bremen.

Symphony No.9 in D minor, Op.125, Choral

Contrasted with even Haydn's late symphonies, the listening public did not yet have the deep appreciation required for Beethoven's *Ninth*. The scope, with its four soloists, chorus, and enlarged orchestra was unprecedented. Not only did movements become longer but individual sections within movements became much longer. It is Beethoven's most compelling and memorable vision of a free, democratic society and "the most profound message of brotherhood and hope." The choral finale is a declaration in favor of universal brotherhood. It was used at the opening of the United Nations and to celebrate the fall of the Berlin Wall.

The Viennese public wanted 'easy-listening' and catchy tunes, not the heavy-lifting required for Beethoven's final symphony, roughly twice as long as any symphony of Mozart and Haydn. In addition, the *Ninth* requires much larger forces including a full chorus and vocal soloists. Not happy with his recent treatment by the Viennese, Beethoven considered holding the premiere in Berlin, until persuaded by some prominent citizens of Vienna.

The *Hammerklavier* piano sonata and the Ninth Symphony were conceived almost simultaneously and both far outdid any of Beethoven's preceding sonatas and symphonies. In the Ninth Symphony, Beethoven returns to his heroic style of his middle period, "turning once again to the *Eroica* Symphony…with its grand-manner Empire style." "The Ninth consolidated and elaborated on elements of his earlier creations, and transcended them." Beethoven used the same solution to the finale of the *Ninth* that he used for the *Fifth*, his other minor key symphony – a powerfully triumphant movement in the relative major. However, Beethoven's plans for the *Ninth* initially were as two separate works, a purely orchestral symphony and what became the finale, a setting of Friedrich Schiller's poem 'Ode to Joy'.

Author Harvey Sachs feels Beethoven's *Ninth* symbolizes in music, as Byron did in poetry, man's quest for freedom of mind and spirit from the repression that had taken hold in Europe in 1824 in the aftermath of revolution and Napoleon. The first movement is dark and cloudy, it "begins quietly but not calmly, in an atmosphere of uncertainty…something vaguely menacing seems to be moving towards us." On the opening of the symphony Nietzsche stated "the thinker feels himself floating above the earth in an astral dome."

Richard Wagner, who chose to conduct the *Ninth* at the Bayreuth cornerstone-laying festival in 1872, had lots of thoughts on this movement, including the comment that "to the shrewd professional musicians of its own time it must have looked like the work of a bungler." But he also remarked about the first movement, "What this movement is cannot be expressed in words," although author David Benjamin Levy tries by pointing out that in the first movement, "Beethoven compresses human life into a quarter of an hour." Wagner also offered that in the *Ninth* Beethoven "forced his way through the most unheard of possibilities of absolute tonal language." Even Hector Berlioz, one of the greatest musical analysts, through up his hands and conceded that, "to analyze such a composition is a difficult and dangerous task that we have long hesitated to undertake." Instead, he simply characterized the *Ninth* as the "starting point for the music of the present."

Beethoven's plans to set Schiller's *An die Freude* ('Ode to Joy') poem to music had begun taking place while he was still in Bonn. The *Ninth* had the longest gestation period of any of Beethoven's works. The final text for the fourth movement uses only half of Schiller's poem and Beethoven "freely rearranged (the eighteen sections of the poem) in accordance with his own poetic vision." In anticipation of the premiere of his *Choral* Symphony Beethoven described it as "a new grand symphony, which ends with a finale…with solos, and chorus of singing voices, the words from Schiller's immortal well-known *Lied*: To Joy."

The symphony consists of a contemplative third-movement *Adagio*, in which "the simplest harmonies are presented so solemnly that they seem imbued with unutterable significance," and a movement on which conductor Arturo Toscanini commented, "one ought to conduct it on one's knees." The contemplative movement is combined with three movements full of violence, exuberance, and rapture. Its harmonies move "in simpler progressions but in curious rhythms;" it "swirls continuously upwards from despair to struggle to acceptance to joy…it is in a dynamic A-B-C-D form." However, Beethoven was able to control the violence in his compositions by stripping away any constraints of decorum and cutting away anything superfluous.

A contemporary review in *The Harmonicon* read as follows: "The opening is…full of rich invention and of athletic power, from the first chord till the gradual unfolding of the colossal theme." As in his *Hammerklavier* Piano Sonata of the same period Beethoven places the demonic scherzo before the *Adagio*. The *Ninth* is the only symphony in which Beethoven does this and Charles Rosen feels this is because the *Scherzi* of this symphony and sonata were "conceived partly as a parody of the first movement."

> *"Art and science can raise men to the level of gods."*
> - Beethoven

After the dissonance at the start of the final movement, the *Ode to Joy* choral finale "emerges from the orchestral narrative of the first three movements…with audacious brilliance." "The contrast between the marvelously peaceful conclusion of the third movement and the jagged, dissonant, blaring opening blast of the fourth never fails to jar." Beethoven pushes the four soloists to the brink of human capacity, then even beyond. But how could he not expect to bring out the 'super' human given the universality and spirit of this symphony? To not demand performance at human limits would mitigate the enormity of the work. After all, does not the solo bass sing in the first verse *Alle Menschen werden Brüder*, "All people become brothers"?

In this revolutionary finale to a symphony "the variation set is completely transformed into the most massive of finales, one that is itself a four-movement work in miniature." As was the theme-and-variations finale of the *Eroica* Symphony, "the variation finale of Beethoven's Ninth was a model for both Schumann and Liszt." One of the variations is even in Turkish march format. The symphony was an extraordinary success as "Beethoven managed without intellectual condescension to strike the populist note…in the compulsively singable, anthem-like tune of the finale."

The 'Ninth', as no symphony had before, "represents struggle…so monumentally anguished a cry." Conductor Jos van Immerseel believes that when performed according to 'historical specifications', as he does with his *Anima Eterna* players, the *Ninth* reveals Beethoven "not as a master of the universe but as a human composer expressing thoughts and emotions."

> *Recommended – Symphony No.9*
> Karl Böhm/Vienna Philharmonic (DG) – one of his last recordings; Furtwängler (EMI) – a historic performance in 1951 at the re-opening of Bayreuth after World War II. Karajan/BPO, 1977 (DG) – the best *Ninth* of multiple cycles..
> Complete Symphonies, 1-9 – Karajan/BPO, 1963 (DG). Although he made two more complete efforts, this second one remains the consensus favorite. It also was the first Beethoven symphony cycle to be recorded in stereo. Karajan had not yet applied the ultra-gloss polish to the BPO, so this set remains fresh and spontaneous, appealing to those who avoid the ultra-refinement of later Karajan.
>
> *Conductor Spotlight - Herbert von Karajan*
> Conductor of the Berlin Philharmonic for thirty years, he was renowned for the refinement and polish of his orchestra, a style that his record company (DG) fully leveraged by releasing virtually the entire repertoire, first on LP then digitally on CD, by Karajan and the Berliners. His marketability was his stature and in the belief that one could purchase any Classical work led by him and be assured of a good, if not always outstanding performance.
>
> However, not all saw things this way. Critics point to the over-refinement of his music- making, leading to recordings that were too polished and 'overrefined', a swirling homogenization of the sound. This led to the view that he and the BPO provided "safe

recordings" of much of the repertoire. Indeed, Karajan and the BPO did record an unprecedented survey of Classical music and sold more than 200 million records, far outpacing any other Classical artist. Martin Bookspan in his classic book <u>101 Masterpieces of Music and Their Composers</u> never misses an opportunity to dismiss many of Karajan's ultra-refined and polished-until-glistening interpretations. It is clear Bookspan feels that Karajan's treatment of most music drains the life out of it. This is not shocking; the polish that Karajan applies is characteristic of most of his readings.

Late in his career in the 1980s and with digital recording, his releases (sometimes with Vienna Philharmonic) became even more polished and refined (*e.g.*, his final Tchaikovsky symphonies with the VPO). Many of his better recordings are from the 1950s with the Philharmonia and from the 1960s/70s with the BPO. His recorded output approached the absurd, sometimes releasing four recordings of a given work over a couple of decades, and maintaining all four available in the active catalogue. Extreme examples include the seven (!) releases of Tchaikovsky's *Pathetique* Symphony Karajan has recorded back to 1939. He released three complete Beethoven symphony cycles, he re-recorded much digitally in the 1980s. Karajan is by far the most recorded artist as he recorded virtually the entire Austro- German repertory two or three times over thirty-five years as the most prominent conductor in Europe.

Sorting through all of this there are many gems in his discography. Composers who brought out the best in the BPO under Karajan include, of course, Beethoven, but he is equally admired for his unrivaled Richard Strauss and Bruckner, as well as his Brahms and Sibelius. Sibelius was still alive when Karajan recorded some of his symphonies with the Philharmonia in the 1950s. As Richard Freed stated in the March 1990 issue of *Stereo Review*, "all of Karajan's most characteristic performances were...free of anything smacking of gratuitous interpretive overlay."

Overtures

Beethoven composed a significant set of overtures, eleven in all, composed over a twenty year period 1801-22. He naturally shaped his overtures as he would a single movement of a symphony. The earliest, from 1801, is *The Creatures of Prometheus* and the last, The *Consecration of the House*, op.124, was performed as a companion piece at the premiere of the Ninth Symphony. Four overtures (the *Fidelio* and the three *Leonore* overtures) are related to his only opera *Fidelio*. The story around the four overtures is confusing but concerns Beethoven's ongoing revisions of the overture for *Fidelio*, and the fact that the opera had three incarnations (1805, 1806, and 1814). *Leonore III* in particular is a splendid concert piece.

In addition to the overtures associated with *Fidelio*, the most popular and most recorded are *Egmont*, Op.84 (1810) and *Coriolan*, Op.62 (1807), the former inspired by Goethe's play (from 1775-87) and lead character, the Count Lamoral van Egmont, Dutch hero executed in 1568 by the Spanish governor of the Netherlands for being a rebel against the "holy Roman church." *Coriolan* was based on a long-forgotten play, not by Shakespeare, about the outcast Roman general Coriolanus.

In the CD era these overtures did yeoman duty as fill-up on releases of single Beethoven symphonies. As the industry moved toward filling up CDs by coupling two Beethoven symphonies, these overtures became less common coupled with symphonies on new releases.

♪ Franz Schubert (1797-1828)

Schubert was the first among several great composers to be bitten by the 'Beethoven curse'. This 'curse' refers to the composers who never got to attempt a tenth symphony because if Beethoven had been limited to only nine, who could possibly be allowed to exceed the master in output?

Schubert was not heavily influenced by Mozart, Haydn, or even Beethoven, whom he visited on his deathbed. Although, as with Mozart, "there are poignant passages in…Schubert's music where beauty and pain seem inseparable," of the three Haydn had the greatest influence. In his early music, such as his early symphonies, Schubert does experiment with the "forms and textures of Mozart and Haydn" but then he proceeds "to go along a road of his own without ever turning back." Schubert's sonata form was not as organized as Haydn, Mozart, and Beethoven. His movements in sonata form tended "to wander and become diffuse," as form had to be compromised to accommodate Schubert's lyric instinct.

While Schubert did complete his Ninth Symphony ('The Great' to distinguish it from an earlier symphony in the same key of C), he left the Eighth 'Unfinished' leaving us with two of the most beautiful movements in music. It is still debated whether Schubert deliberately left the *Eighth* unfinished, feeling he had nothing more to add to it, or if he went on to the *Ninth* and simply never got around to finishing it.

Aside from the *Eighth* and *Ninth*, his earlier symphonies are much more traditionally classical in form and duration. Critics have often looked unfavorably upon Schubert's first six symphonies with the benefit of hindsight and unfairly using his Eighth and Ninth Symphonies for comparison. In the early symphonies Schubert, in his late teens to early twenties, focused on "a consolidation of techniques" and not on the new departures found in his final two symphonic masterpieces.

The Fifth Symphony, "elegant and lightly scored," can be performed by a chamber ensemble and is a throwback to the Haydn style. The slow movement of the *Fifth* has "a glorious outpouring of melody."

Symphony No.8 in B minor, *Unfinished*

The *Unfinished* Symphony is markedly different from the earlier symphonies of Schubert. His 'early' symphonies, of which Nos.3, 5, and 6 are well-known, were light-spirited in the manner of Haydn or Mozart. The *Unfinished* Symphony, as with Tchaikovsky's *Pathétique*, is in the key of B minor, "the darkest, grimmest, most 'pathetic' mood." Schubert's Eighth Symphony "is valued for the lyricism of its themes, not for its overall form."

Why unfinished? Did Schubert finish it and the last movements got lost? Only two pages of the third movement scherzo remain. Did he intend to leave it a two-movement work after perhaps realizing that any additional movements would detract from the impact of the first two? Did Schubert intend to finish the work later, having put the two movements aside to move on to another work? It is believed that Schubert intended this symphony to be a monumental work but only completed the first two movements, which were not discovered until 1860 and premiered in 1865. Scholars are divided among these theories because Schubert left few records of his activities. However, not knowing only adds to the allure of this great symphony.

Scholar Alfred Einstein felt that we are wrong in calling Schubert's "incomparable song of sorrow" his 'Unfinished' Symphony. Its two movements represent as complete a work as any. It contrasts sharply with Schubert's six earlier lightweight symphonies.

Symphony No.9 in C, *Great*

Schubert attended the premiere of Beethoven's *Ninth* in 1824 and shortly after began work on his own Ninth, also of a grand scale. It is full of glorious melodies but, great as it is, he never heard it performed. Robert Schumann found it in 1839 and it was given its premiere in the same year under Mendelssohn. The efforts of these two early Romantic composers contributed significantly to the 'discovery' of Schubert's vast output.

Robert Schumann gushed about the *Ninth*, "All the instruments are human voices...like a novel in four volumes..." Schumann used his *Neue Zeitschrift für Musik* to recognize the great masters of the past. He repeatedly drew parallels between Schubert's and Beethoven's ninth symphonies, showing Schumann's tendency to get emotionally carried away, as he continued, "It bears within it the core of everlasting youth." However, Alfred Einstein sided with Schumann by claiming that *The Great* "declares Schubert to be Beethoven's peer."

> ***Recommended – Schubert symphonies***
> *Unfinished Symphony* – Sinopoli with the Philharmonia, Abbado with the London Symphony Orchestra or Carlos Kleiber's coupling of the *Unfinished* with *No.3* (all on DG). *Ninth Symphony*, 'The Great' – Szell with Cleveland or Böhm conducting the Staatskapelle Dresden (DG, 1990). The early symphonies – Sir Thomas Beecham with Royal Philharmonic, an excellent triptych; not surprising given Beecham's famous recordings of Haydn's *London* symphonies.

As previously mentioned, Schubert's works were largely unknown until after his death. For example, his ninth and final symphony was unearthed by Schumann, who got the manuscript from Schubert's brother Ferdinand in 1839. It was quickly given its premiere in Leipzig under the baton of Mendelssohn. The last two Schubert symphonies "had an enormous influence on composers...from Bruckner to Dvořák," helping to revive the symphony as a leading genre. Also interesting to note is that Schubert did not compose in the concerto form, unless such works have not been unearthed yet or are gone forever.

There is confusion as to the numbering of Schubert's symphonies, not surprising because most of them were composed long before they were published. If he had not died so prematurely it is likely Schubert would have achieved the deserved fame in his lifetime.

PART 4

Orchestral Music

The Nineteenth Century

- 16 -

The Early Romantics

"Berlioz, Schumann, Liszt and Wagner stand out as energetic, crusading writers, bent on elevating the public's taste and reforming the musical life of Europe." The lasting presence in Vienna of the symphonies of Mozart, Haydn, and Beethoven "discouraged the composition of new symphonies by Viennese musicians during the next half century." For the Romantic composer, Haydn was mostly viewed as a primitive forerunner of 'modern' music; a revival of genuine sympathy for his work had to wait for Brahms.

♪ Robert Schumann (1810-1856)

Although many speak of Schumann as being conflicted, tormented, and even 'schizophrenic', others believe Schumann was simply taking various aspects of his personality "and then reconciling them into some synthetic whole." In late 1840, after a decade of composing exclusively for solo piano, Schumann turned to writing *Lieder* for a year, then dedicated himself to orchestral and chamber music. His new bride Clara encouraged Robert to make this move and attempt to master larger forms. The switch paid off quickly with 1841 producing the First Symphony, the *Overture, Scherzo, and Finale*, the first version of what became Symphony No.4, and the one-movement fantasy for piano that evolved into the first movement of his Piano Concerto.

Piano concerto in A minor, Op.54

Schumann's famous piano concerto began as a one-piece 'fantasy' for piano and orchestra. The fact that he did not set out to compose a traditional concerto is not surprising given Schumann's avoidance of traditional forms. The creative process that resulted in the piano concerto was a long one. He began sketching the *Fantasy* in 1833 and finally completed it in 1841. In 1845 he added two more movements, first the rondo third movement, then an *intermezzo* to link the self-contained Fantasy with the rondo, resulting in the concerto as we know it. In spite of its piecemeal genesis, this concerto remains Schumann's most successful large piece.

The premiere was given by Clara, who "always wanted a large bravura piece by him." But her husband had not composed a technical showpiece but rather, as explained by Schumann, "a compromise between a symphony, a concerto, and a huge sonata...I cannot write a concerto for the virtuosi."

> *Recommended – Schumann Piano Concerto*
> This is one of the most-often recorded concerto, usually coupled with Grieg's *Piano Concerto*, also in A minor. There are several excellent performances, among them Richter with the Warsaw National Philharmonic led by Rowicki, and Perahia with the Bavarian Radio SO under Davis (Sony, 1989).

Robert Schumann composed four symphonies, but they are not numbered in in the order composed. Critics through the years have claimed 'weak orchestration', that the works are symphonic lightweights. However, it appears that Schumann, as well as Mendelssohn (who suffers the same criticism), have become appreciated as more than tunesmiths, and that their symphonic works actually possess depth. Yet many conductors over the years have made slight to major reworkings of parts of Schumann's symphonic scores, ostensibly to 'correct' for the perceived shortcomings of the orchestratration. One theory holds that some of the 'problems' with Schumann's orchestration (e.g., doubling of instrument parts) were due to the inferior (i.e., many amateur players) orchestras Schumann had at his disposal. This explanation makes even more sense for the *Rhenish* Symphony if Schumann orchestrated that work keeping in mind the resources available to him in Düsseldorf. Mahler re-orchestrated parts of Schumann's symphonies, as did George Szell, while Leonard Bernstein, a great interpreter of these symphonies, preferred to conduct them untouched.

While none of Schumann's symphonies is considered a masterpiece, they do contain much music to enjoy. The Third Symphony (1850), *Rhenish*, is particularly tuneful in its unconventional five movements, with the three central movements functioning as romantic mood pictures. These movements find "symphonic space for evocative sound-pictures, notably of a ceremony in Cologne Cathedral" in the fourth movement. In a way this movement is a tone poem within the five-movement symphony and also owes much to Schumann's study of Bach.

Interestingly, composer Lukas Foss places Schumann's four symphonies on par with Schubert's and Mendelssohn's. I find this interesting because Schumann's symphonies are a fairly consistent set, but none stands far above another. To critics all four suffer from the same 'shortcomings'. Schubert's split clearlz into two sets, the early Haydnesque and the last two great symphonies, and Mendelssohn's five are significantly inconsistent. His *Scottish* and *Italian* Symphonies stand far above his other three.

Conductor Wolfgang Sawallisch (Staatskapelle Dresden, Philadelphia Orchestra) states that he has found musicians "object" to performing Schumann's symphonies. He points out the difficulty of the symphonies because the melody continually gets interrupted and "you never have big melodies, like a Tchaikovsky symphony." In his symphonies Schumann tries to fuse fantasy-oriented forms with which he is very comfortable (i.e., his piano miniatures) with larger-scale forms with which he clearly is not.

Symphony No.1 in B-flat, Op.38, *Spring*
The period of the First and Fourth Symphonies produced some of Schumann's best chamber works, including the Piano Quartet (Op.47), Piano Quintet (Op.44), and the three string quartets (Op.41). Schumann originally attached descriptive titles for each movement but discarded them because he wanted

his First Symphony to be "absolute music in the Beethovenian mould." In the First Symphony Schumann borrows Berlioz's idée fixe using a brass fanfare motto theme to unify the whole work.

Symphony No.4 in D minor, Op.120

Symphony No.4 contains the novelty of four movements played without a break and also uses 'thematic transformation', both foreshadowing works of Liszt. Schumann uses a single cell, this time the first five notes of the brooding slow introduction, out of which much of the material develops. The symphony "represents Schumann's most radical and ingenious attempt to bind together all four movements." The main theme, dubbed 'Clara' theme by Schumann, is contained in the first five notes of the brooding slow introduction, which subsequently returns in many guises throughout.

Schumann may have gotten the idea for a symphony without breaks from Mendelssohn, who used the device in his violin and piano concertos. It was originally finished in 1841, designated as 'No. 2' and premiered the next year in a concert that also included his *Overture, Scherzo and Finale*. Schumann was not satisfied with it so it underwent major revision in Düsseldorf in late 1851 and premiered a year later. The result is thicker orchestration. Both versions survive today but the revised edition is more often performed. Interestingly, Brahms preferred the original version, blemishes and all, as does conductor Wolfgang Sawallisch who recorded one of the outstanding Schumann Symphony cycles with the Staatskapelle Dresden Orchestra in 1973. However, Lukas Foss recommends that if a great composer was dissatisfied with a previous version and replaces it with a 'new and improved' one, we should trust him. It was the only one of his four symphonies that Schumann subjected to revisions.

Symphony No.2 in C, Op.61

This work, composed through most of 1846, has dark, disquieting undercurrents (despite being cast in C major), full of struggle, with a dark and haunting *Adagio*, as Schumann wrote this symphony while not completely recovered from a nervous breakdown. Peter Ostwald believes that the "very lugubrious kind of chromatic events in the opening of the Second Symphony" are due to Schumann being severely ill when he worked on the symphony. It uses a motto theme from the horns, similar to the First Symphony. It is the least-performed of Schumann's four symphonies.

Symphony No.3 in E-flat, Op.97 'Rhenish'

As with his First Symphony Schumann drew from extra musical influences for his final symphony in 1850, originally to be called "a piece of life by the Rhine." The Third Symphony marks the start of Schumann's late period, which includes works such as the Violin Concerto, Cello Concerto, *Manfred* Overture, Piano Trio No.3, and the collection of piano miniatures,

Waldszenen. The two concertos and the piano trio from this period are very difficult works.

Schumann's Third Symphony in E-flat shares the same key with Beethoven's Third, *Eroica*, the latter an undeniable influence. Schumann was criticized for this symphony's five movements (the only precedent was Beethoven's *Pastoral*), in particular the chorale-like, baroque-polyphonic fourth movement, with "all those short entrances, one group after another…like an echo coming back." This movement is widely believed to be inspired by the Great Dome in Köln (Cologne), which Schumann probably saw often after he settled in nearby Düsseldorf.

> ***Recommended*** – Sawallisch and the Staatskapelle Dresden (EMI) and Bernstein and the Vienna Philharmonic (DG).

"Schumann did not completely succeed in his symphonies, partly because he never learned to think in terms of orchestral sound." His style of dense, intricate and intense figuration was highly effective for his short pieces but not for the wide-open spaces of the symphony.

Overture, Scherzo, and Finale

Schumann dubbed this work his 'Symphonette' and it "has a Mendelssohnian grace and lightness of touch" as well as a driving energy in its final movement. It is essentially a symphony without a slow movement and was completed in Schumann's 'year of the symphony', 1841, which also saw the completion of the B-flat and (the initial version of the) D minor Symphonies (No.1 and No.4, respectively). Conductor Marin Alsop finds this work to be "charming and so Mendelssohnian and so whimsical…and has some fantastic counterpoint in the last movement."

Cello Concerto

Schumann felt his Cello Concerto was one of his most joyful pieces, and he may have been the first to use the cello in a truly 'romantic' way. At the time it was the most technically challenging cello concerto and established a new model for the genre; the first important work of its kind since Boccherini's seventy years before. It has "a continuously developing lyricism, largely meditative in the first two movements."

According to New Jersey Symphony Orchestra principal cellist Jonathan Spitz, the Cello Concerto "was among Schumann's last great works before his final breakdown." In it Schumann "lays bare his emotions…with a hopeful yearning for a world that doesn't have" his pain and vulnerability. Clara Schumann raved about the work "written in true violoncello style…the romantic quality…wholly ravishing." As with his Piano Concerto, the Cello Concerto has no opening orchestral *tutti*, just a brief orchestral gesture before the soloist enters.

Violin Concerto

The least-known of Schumann's concertos was his last major orchestral work. Composed ostensibly for the famous violinist Joseph Joachim, it remained unpublished upon Schumann's death in 1856. His Violin Concerto has never taken hold in the repertoire; it remains similar to Dvořák's Piano Concerto: the least successful work of its kind by a major composer. However, Schumann's Concerto generally receives rave reviews from string players. Violinist Yehudi Menuhin found it to be the 'missing link' between Beethoven's and Brahms' concertos. Cellist Steven Isserlis gushed recently that it is indeed a "magnificent work with both Handelian grandeur and some of the most gentle, inward-looking music to be found in any concerto."

Schumann, an accomplished pianist, was at his weakest in concertos for string soloists (the Violin and Cello Concertos), although his Cello Concerto enjoys a stronger place in a smaller repertory. Dvořák, an accomplished strings player, produced a masterpiece of a cello concerto, a very good concerto for violin, but a relatively mediocre piano concerto.

Schumann's Violin Concerto simply has too much competition from the violin concerto repertoire. It faces the 'top tier' of works by Beethoven, Mendelssohn, Bruch, Sibelius, Brahms, and Tchaikovsky, which dominate the concert halls, followed by the 'second tier' by Wieniawski, Paganini, Lalo, Glazunov, Dvořák, Elgar, et al. It also has to battle for concert programs with 20th century violin concertos such as those by Stravinsky, Shostakovich, Prokofiev, Berg, and Adams. So credit must be given when it does get programmed, as the New Jersey Symphony Orchestra did in 2009, with concertmaster Eric Wyrick as soloist under James Gaffigan. Wyrick says he plays "lesser-known works, which still deserve to be heard."

♪ Felix Mendelssohn (1809-1847)

Mendelssohn was "by far the most restrained of any of the great Romantic composers in the 1830s and 1840s." Schumann called Mendelssohn the Mozart of the 19th century; "his devotion to clarity and balance look back to the Classical era." Mendelssohn had a gift "for lyrical melodic lines and delicate, transparent textures" but also was best, among his contemporaries, at controlling large-scale structures. Mendelssohn was an upholder of tradition, of classicism, a "versatile, craftsmanlike composer whose work effortlessly mediated between the poles of classicism and romanticism."

His music "has clear lines and beautiful organization" and "avoids the sweeping Romantic gesture." His works are "masterpieces of refinement, lightness, clarity, and control," his musical ideas were "tender, wistful, whimsical, or spritely." He was a "sweet, pure, perfectly proportioned master." The graceful and light qualities of Mendelssohn's works have led some to note that "there is indeed something elfin about it." Conductor Erich

Leinsdorf contrasts Schumann and Mendelssohn as follows: Mendelssohn "was absolutely perfect and was always on the surface of things. Schumann was never perfect and always delving deeper into things."

There has always been a debate as to whether his music "ever developed beyond the supreme fluency and grace of his early masterpieces." Mendelssohn was at his most daring up to the age of twenty-one and it has been proposed that "he never lived up to his initial creative promise." Perhaps because he approached perfection in compositions as a teenager (*Octet*, *A Midsummer Night's Dream Overture*), he was somehow expected to subsequently improve on these. But that would have been against his fabric; he did not look to break new ground. He had trouble coming to grips with Chopin's piano music because of its novel approaches to harmony.

Mendelssohn in his music always looked to avoid offense and he was suspicious of anything "that threatened the established order of things." Instead, he aimed to be a flawless technician, and his music almost completely lacks the element of surprise common in the music of other composers. There is an essential weakness in his style in that he "rounds off his phrases, his paragraphs, and eventually his sections with a certain comfortable sweetness.

He was mistrusting of the crop of early Romantics (Liszt, Berlioz, and even Chopin), again because he saw their music as a threat to the "established order of things." Mendelssohn's music was purely diatonic, without the harmonic bite in the music of the early Romantics. This feature made his music immediately accessible and especially appealing to the aristocracy, who for the most part wanted to enjoy music; not to think about it or be surprised by it. Berlioz was heard to say that "he (Mendelssohn) loves the dead too much," and Mendelssohn saw Berlioz's greatly expanded use of the orchestra as "a frightful muddle, an incongruous mess…" Simply put by Harold Schonberg, although classified a Romantic composer, Mendelssohn and "the Romantics did not speak the same language."

In 1835 he took over the *Gewandhaus* Orchestra of Leipzig and turned the city into the musical capital of Germany. His upbringing in a conservative Jewish bourgeois home led him to be risk averse. However, this aversion to the "radical harmonies" of some of his contemporaries did not stop him from conducting their works at Leipzig. Alfred Einstein points out that "real conflict was lacking in his life as in his art." With Berlioz, Mendelssohn represented the first of the 'modern' conductors and he established Mozart, Haydn, Beethoven, Bach, and Handel as the backbone of the repertory, replacing obscure and long-forgotten composers who were undeservedly dominating concert programs in Mendelssohn's day. Mozart, Haydn, et al. have remained the backbone of the repertory ever since.

♪ The Concertos

Mendelssohn composed two piano concertos as well as three single-movement works for piano and orchestra. The concertos are staples of the repertory. Of the single-movement works the *Capriccio Brilliante* in B minor, Op.22 from 1832 bounds "along with inexorable vivacity." Two additional single-movement works for piano and orchestra are the *Rondo Brilliante* in E-flat, Op.29 and *Serenade and Allegro Giocoso*, Op.43.

His First Piano Concerto was begun in Rome in 1830, finished the next year and performed by the composer for the King of Bavaria in Munich. Although it lacks cadenzas, it is still a virtuosic showpiece, so that Liszt immediately added it to his repertory. As he would also do later with his Violin Concerto the three movements are blended into each other, this time with a transitional brass fanfare. This piano concerto was the first three-movement concerto to be performed without breaks between movements. Liszt would also adopt this approach for his works for piano and orchestra.

> **Recommended – Mendelssohn works for piano and orchestra**
> Stephen Hough with Lawrence Foster and the CBSO have recorded both concertos as well as *Opp.22, 29 & 43*. This is a clear first choice, with Serkin and Ormandy a good alternative.

Mendelssohn's is the most popular of all violin concertos (in E minor, Op.64). The first major work of its kind since Beethoven's thirty-eight years earlier, was composed from 1838-44 with revisions along the way. It is the "most successful synthesis of the Classical concerto tradition with the Romantic virtuoso form," and included the unprecedented placement of the cadenza between the development and recapitulation in the first movement instead of at the end of the movement.

Mendelssohn's friend Ferdinand David was the soloist for the premiere in Leipzig with Mendelssohn's *Gewandhaus* Orchestra. However, Mendelssohn did not mimic Beethoven's severely elegant classicism but instead "produced the quintessential Romantic concerto," one of his "most sublime and original…compositions." It was first performed in 1845 in Leipzig to instant acclaim and "revealed a forcefulness hitherto largely concealed behind amiable whimsy or tenderness."

The work possesses a "masterful integration of virtuosity and musicality. It is full of melodic lines that spin seemingly effortlessly from the violin…" In traditionally-structured violin concertos of the Classical and Early Romantic periods the soloist enters after a long orchestral introduction. In contrast, the soloist enters quickly, after just a few measures, in Mendelssohn's Concerto. Another key difference is Mendelssohn's use of musical ties or bridges to smoothly link the three movements together so there is no break between movements. Within the movements there is fire and drama, grace and beauty to go with a devil-may-care flair in the finale.

🎵 Symphonies and Overtures

Mendelssohn produced a significant set of overtures; the best was the first, *A Midsummer Night's Dream*, which he composed when he was seventeen. This overture, as perfect as the *Octet* of the previous year, has remained eternally fresh. Later, he would add 'incidental music' to this overture. His other famous overture, *The Hebrides*, is one of the greatest of all concert overtures; in it Mendelssohn sought to capture the wild seascape of these islands."

The youthful string symphonies are smaller, lighter and less ambitious than his five numbered works. Among Mendelssohn's five major symphonies, the Third, *Scottish,* and Fourth, *Italian,* both have country-based nicknames and enormous popularity in common. In these two symphonies Mendelssohn "transformed his personal travelling experiences into poetic sound images." But beyond this the two works are starkly different.

A Midsummer Night's Dream Overture, Op.21

Written in 1826 at age seventeen this work cemented Mendelssohn's status as a genius while he was still a youth. In the music an "elfin spirit leaps out…with an ethereal shimmer of strings we enter fairyland and a new conception of orchestral writing." Mendelssohn would return to Shakespeare's play years later in 1842 to compose incidental music to supplement this overture.

Symphony No.4 in A, Op.90, *Italian*

> *"The liveliest thing I have yet done…"*
> - Mendelssohn

Although it follows No.3 in number order, this symphony was begun in Rome during Mendelssohn's tour of Italy in 1831 and completed in two years. It was premiered in London with the composer conducting. However, Mendelssohn withheld the work from publication during his lifetime because he could never quite reconcile the finale with the rest of the work; thus, the Op.90 designation.

In the symphony Mendelssohn stated that he was trying "to convey his impressions of the art, nature and people of Italy." From the opening, with its instantly recognizable horn-call theme, the symphony sweeps us willingly along in its joyous burble. In the slow movement there are "garlands of flute tone woven around the strings."

Hebrides Overture in B minor, Op.26 'Fingal's Cave'
In 1829 Mendelssohn visited Scotland and began this extremely popular overture. It was completed the next year during his time in Rome. Mendelssohn gave it a major revision and it premiered in 1832. It is "especially engaging...one of Mendelssohn's inspired ideas – simple and beautiful." Although Mendelssohn deplored program music, his trip to Scotland had an extraordinary effect on him and inspired the theme of the overture. *Fingal's Cave* has remained one of the most popular of all concert overtures, partly because listeners believe the composer was extremely effective in describing the wind and waves that one experiences in the Hebrides. His other descriptive maritime overture, *Calm Sea and Prosperous Voyage*, Op.27, written around the same time also remains popular.

Symphony No.3 in A minor, Op.56, *Scottish*
The *Italian* opens immediately with a bright, melodic theme that is instantly recognizable. The *Scottish* opens with a brooding mood and develops slowly, with many different somber colors, starkly contrasting the keys of A major and A minor. It is a melancholy and serene reflection of the landscape of a responsive soul. Mendelssohn would probably say he was contrasting his experiences in both places.

Sketches of the Third Symphony date from his stay in Scotland but the symphony was not completed until more than ten years later in 1842. It was premiered by the Leipzig *Gewandhaus* under Mendelssohn. Each movement runs right into the next without pause, unique among his symphonies and a device he would repeat in his famous E minor Violin Concerto. The setup of the first movement with its slow introduction leading into the *Allegro* main theme is taken from Haydn's symphonies. This lends credence to the belief that Mendelssohn had begun at least sketching parts of this symphony a decade or more before its premiere in 1842.

Although he was inspired by Italy and enchanted with Scotland so as to produce his two most famous symphonies, he had no interest in incorporating the music of those lands into his works, just as he "deplored music with explicit extra musical references." "No national music for me!" Mendelssohn was known to have exclaimed. This clear rejection however did not prevent some from claiming that "in the whole first movement (of the *Scottish*) we breathe the heavy thick air of a Scottish highland mist." The Third proves Mendelssohn's ability to very effectively combine absolute and programmatic music.

> *Recommended – Mendelssohn symphonic music*
> The recording of the *Scottish* and the *Hebrides* Overture by Maag and the LSO has long been critically acclaimed. For the *Italian* Abbado/LSO or Sinopoli/Philharmonia (both DG) or the more recent Andrew Litton/Bergen Philharmonic (BIS, 2010).

> For a complete set of the overtures, it is hard to beat Klaus Peter Flor and the Bamburg Symphony Orchestra (RCA).

Mendelssohn's influence in Britain was great, dominating aspiring British composers throughout the 1800s, which only served to extend the composer drought in England, finally quenched by Elgar and Vaughn Williams at the end of the century. Also, the influence of England showed in his *Scottish* Symphony and in *The Hebrides* Overture.

♪ Frederic Chopin (1810-1849)

"Chopin solved many of the problems confronting Schumann by avoiding them," writing no symphonies and engaging a full orchestra only in a supporting role for his piano concertos. In Chopin's two piano concertos, both written before the age of twenty, the soloist is the dominant protagonist supported by the orchestra as opposed to the equal treatment of soloist and orchestra by Mozart and Beethoven. In fact, it has been said that Chopin's concertos should be called 'for piano with orchestra', not 'for piano and orchestra', to indicate the secondary role of the orchestra as opposed to the back-and-forth between soloist and orchestra in most other concertos.

Both of Chopin's concertos contain beautiful slow movements. Liszt commented on the slow movements of both of Chopin's concertos. He found the *Larghetto* of the First to be "of an almost ideal perfection…" and for the second movement of the Second, "passages of surprising grandeur may be found in the *Adagio*…"

Chopin premiered both works in Poland before he left for Paris at age twenty. The concertos are numbered in reverse order of composition; No.2 in F minor, Op.21 was actually begun in 1929 while No.1 in E minor, Op.11 was begun the following year but premiered before the *Second*.

> **Recommended – Chopin Piano Concertos**
> Chopin *Piano Concerto No. 1 & 2* – Zimmerman either leading the Polish Festival Orchestra or with Giulini and the LAPO.

♪ Franz Liszt (1811-1886)

Liszt, more than anyone else, invented the symphonic poem. He and Berlioz (both were in Paris) created the program music craze, which would culminate with the tone poems of Strauss and Sibelius, but also serve as a major influence on the operatic works of Richard Wagner. As with his solo piano works, Liszt applies his concept of thematic transformation in his orchestral works, the repeated reworking of a melodic idea which serves to maintain unity of material.

♪ Piano and Orchestra

Both piano concertos are cast in a single continuous movement with multiple "sections merging freely and lacking the customary development." Although both of Liszt's piano concertos are virtuoso showpieces they "show a profound understanding of the integration between soloist and orchestra." Liszt essentially avoids the use of first movement sonata form. Their layout is closer to the symphonic poem than to the standard concerto. Liszt effectively links the sections of the concertos using his 'transformation of themes' technique.

Piano Concerto No.1 in E-flat opens with the orchestra's "forceful opening gesture" followed by a "cadenza of thundering octaves and clangorous chords," much as with Beethoven's Fifth Piano Concerto. By contrast, in the opening of the Piano Concerto No.2 in A, instead of a display of power by the soloist, the piano provides "a sweetly harmonious, sensitive, responsive accompaniment to the woodwinds and muted strings."

Liszt worked on his first piano concerto in the 1840s, revised it ca. 1851, and it was not published until 1857, although the first performance was given in 1855 in Weimar with Liszt as soloist and Berlioz on the podium. The concerto is "extroverted to the point of exhibitionism…a perfect mirror of the flame-throwing pianist…" Béla Bartók found the E-flat Concerto to be "the first perfect realization of cyclic sonata form, with common themes treated on variation principles…" Bartók is referring to Liszt's technique of thematic transformation in which a basic theme "undergoes constant transformations and disguises,…" it always serves the "structural purpose of unity within variety." In his piano concertos Liszt wanted to roll together several movements into one, and this technique helped him do that.

The Second Concerto, as with the E-flat concerto, was sketched out, finalized and orchestrated by Liszt over a period of years, possibly starting in the early 1830s, completed in 1848, and premiering two years after No.1. The Second Concerto is one long movement subdivided into a number of contrasting sections indicated by tempo changes with several brief cadenzas sprinkled in. "The seven-note recurring, swooning theme announced at the outset by the clarinets" provides continuity and unity. Three themes recur several times "in the work in different guises…binding (Liszt's) concerto together with thematic logic." Rather than using the full orchestra Liszt prefers "to focus on the individual timbres of instruments." Liszt did a final revision of this concerto in 1861.

Liszt's other major work for piano and orchestra, *Totentanz*, ('death dance') is a vivid dance of death using the very fitting and effective plainchant melody *Dies Irae* (Day of Wrath) as the theme for its set of six variations.

This is not the first, nor last, time this famous plainchant melody plays a prominent role in a work by an early Romantic composer; Berlioz had used the *Dies Irae* theme in the 'Dreams of Witches' Sabbath' fifth movement of his *Symphonie Fantastique* and Rachmaninoff used it in more than one work. All three of these works "reveal an experimental approach to the matching of soloist and orchestra."

> *Recommended – Liszt Piano Concertos and Totentanz*
> Richter with Kondrashin and LSO or Krystian Zimerman with Ozawa leading the Boston Symphony (DG, 1988)

♫ Symphonic Works
Tone Poems
While Liszt is known foremost for his highly influential piano pieces, his invention of the symphonic or tone poem heavily influenced symphonic writing in the Romantic era and beyond. He helped to revive symphonic composition by miniaturizing the symphonic legacy of Beethoven and emphasizing those aspects that were most exciting. He also composed two large-scale programmatic symphonies, the *Faust* and *Dante* Symphonies. The symphonic poems starting with Liszt's in the 1840s were the hottest flashpoint in the altercation between 'program' music and 'absolute' music.

Liszt took the ideas Berlioz established in his programmatic orchestral works and created the symphonic poem in an effort to use symphonic material in a novel format. As with Berlioz, Liszt too allowed Shakespearean influences on his music, resulting in the tone poem *Hamlet*. The relationship between title, program, and music varies considerably from one work to another. Even if some of his tone poems did not possess an actual program, they all were suggested by a 'poetic' idea.

The main contribution of Liszt to the advancement of program music was his transformations of *Leitmotive*, whereas Berlioz simply transferred themes into a succession of different scenes. The use of 'thematic transformation' in the symphonic poems provides unity, variety and narrative-like logic "by transforming the thematic material to reflect the diverse moods needed to portray a programmatic subject."

Although he wrote twelve tone poems in total, only about half of them are commonly collected together in recordings. If they are bombastic and even vulgar, they are also tremendously exciting and extremely well-orchestrated. *Les Preludes* is Liszt's most popular tone poem by far, based on a four-part French poem by Lamartine, it also is in four parts, with similarities to a first movement of a symphony. The four parts of the poem deal with love, destiny, war and the countryside, so these four different themes require four distinct moods.

Hungarian Rhapsodies
The *Hungarian* Rhapsodies are similar to the symphonic poems but are orchestrations of six of the solo piano rhapsodies. They are "the very essence of gypsy soul and wild abandon." Because the numbering system of the six orchestrated rhapsodies does not match up with the numbering of their solo keyboard counterparts, there can be some confusion.

♪ Richard Wagner (1813-1883)

Like Berlioz, Wagner was a self-taught composer who was unable to play any instrument on a professional level. He developed the latest of all great composers while also receiving the least formal training. But Wagner "made up for his deficiencies by instinct and a profound musicality." He seemed to fully absorb whatever he could learn with amazing rapidity, including "hours…poring over scores of Beethoven symphonies." Wagner produced thirteen major operas and 'music dramas', the final ten are cemented in the operatic repertory.

Wagner's music is characterized by "a high degree of…restless, searching tonal instability," "his melodies and harmonies often move chromatically…Wagner often used dissonant chords." He "took chromaticism as far as it could go within the key system" and expanded "the tonal harmonic system to near bursting point." "His aesthetic was perhaps the most grandiose that Western music has ever known" and he was "the most subjective of all artists."

"Wagner's achievements…were the culmination of Romanticism…(he) is the incarnation of his age." His one lasting achievement "was his positioning of music at the very center of public life, from which it has never been dislodged." Wagner's "rapturous musical creativeness" produced previously unknown orchestral brilliance and richness, a result of a novel means of dividing and blending strings and winds. In his operas "the text merely floated on top of the rich orchestral sonorities." Wagner saw the typical opera in his day as "a chaos of unconnected sensual elements," and he himself would create "the perfect blend of poetry and music."

"Practically every 19th century composer…saw Beethoven as his spiritual as well as musical preceptor." Beethoven's *Ninth* was Wagner's musical ideal throughout his life. He claimed his operas were a continuation of that great symphony. After being bowled over by a performance of the *Ninth*, Wagner characterized it as "so perfect and so moving…a stream of inexhaustible melody, gripping the heart with ineluctable force." Cosima (Liszt) Wagner related how her husband believed that Beethoven's intent with his Ninth Symphony was to "write a great symphony of joy in the spirit of the Freemasons and to precede it with struggle and mourning…"

Wagner's love of Beethoven's *Ninth* came from his view of its finale as 'music drama', an art form Wagner picked up and took to its highest level. For Wagner Beethoven's *Ninth* "caused the orchestra to burst into speech with a message for all mankind," "sounded the death knell of 'pure music', and finished off the symphony as a viable independent genre." Liszt and Wagner felt "that the mantle of Beethoven had fallen on their shoulders" and "that music was to be valued for its emotional or symbolic content."

> *"For upon it (the Ninth) the perfect art work of the future alone can follow."*
> - Richard Wagner

Presumably, Wagner fancied himself the creator of "the perfect art work of the future." Wagner's literary work <u>Art Work of the Future</u> (*Das Kunstwerk der Zukunft*) from 1849 outlined how he saw music as no longer having "an independent existence and (would) merge, instead, with drama and the other arts." The German word coined for this 'total art work' was *Gesamtkunstwerk*; "only the total work of art, incorporating dance, music, drama, and poetry, could redeem humankind from the abyss."

He not only wanted to be the greatest composer ever but also the greatest master of stagecraft. This put him and his followers at odds with the camp occupied by Brahms and the 'romantic classicists'. The Brahms camp was not interested in being the greatest anything, or "capable of one-upping Mozart or Beethoven;" instead, they sought for their works to be appreciated on their own merits.

His sense of entitlement was surpassed only by his arrogance and ego. He brought out from his devoted followers something Messianic, displaying "a degree of megalomania that approached actual lunacy,...he stands for all that is unpleasant in human character." As despicable a person as Wagner was, whose racist theories on Teutonic supremacy would tragically carry into the 20th century and be associated with Nazism, his significance "must endure. His work...cannot be ignored." "Through much of the latter half of his century, Wagner...personified the European artistic avant-garde."

But Wagner had genius to go with his gargantuan ego and because of him music would be drastically changed forever. "An imagination so powerful...a technique so novel and so impressive, that neither music of his own day nor that of succeeding generations...is conceivable without him." The writings of Friedrich Nietzsche and his concept of "rule by the best," and of "man rising to superior fulfillment...seduced the imagination of Europe" Nietzsche's idea of selective evolution to *Übermensch* or Superman, the 'artist-genius', was certainly attractive to Wagner (and also to Richard Strauss). Proponents of German (or 'Aryan') supremacy responded eagerly to Nietzsche's theory of the rights of the strong over the weak." For a long time Wagner received the support of Nietzsche.

Early in his career (1834-37) Wagner jumped around from Magdeburg to Königsberg, and finally an opera position in Riga (modern-day capital of Latvia), making and leaving behind large debts and many enemies. This pattern of quickly wearing out his welcome and staying one step ahead of those he owed would characterize the rest of Wagner's career due to his arrogance, recklessness, selfishness, and dishonesty.

> *"One cannot judge Wagner's opera after only one hearing, and I certainly don't intend going a second time."*
> - Rossini

His first opera, *Rienzi*, premiered in 1842 in Dresden, was a great success and Wagner was an instant hit. *The Flying Dutchman* was staged the following year. In 1845 *Tannhaüser* premiered in Dresden, followed five years later by *Lohengrin*. These were all still operas, more or less modeled on the existent grand-opera formula, with inspiration from Wagner's genius. The elaborate outsized music dramas would come later, although the three early operas after *Rienzi* did show Wagner's taste for German mythology as the source for his material. Wagner did later come to the conclusion that "all great art must be based on mythology."

He believed all great art is based on legends and myths. Of course the source of Wagner's genius was his extreme personality, his egotism, even his alleged messianic complex. If he had been more 'normal' or 'well-adjusted' it is doubtful he would have produced the masterpieces he did. Their conception and creation required the combination of traits, however offensive, that make Wagner a unique figure in musical history.

Wagner produced one mature large-scale orchestral work, *Siegfried Idyll* in 1870 as a Christmas present to his wife Cosima (Liszt's daughter). He originally intended it to be a string quartet but wound up expanding it, possibly finding the quartet genre to be too limiting, as he was accustomed to pushing the bounds of an orchestra. It uses themes from the third act of Siegfried, the third of four music dramas in *The Ring* cycle.

Wagner's musical dramas filled the ever-widening gap between symphony and opera during the second half of the 19th century. He preferred the term 'music drama' to 'opera' for his later operas. He believed he was taking this form to new heights and that 'opera' was too limiting and could not contain his idea of an all-embracing work of art.

Wagner used the *Leitmotiv*, which is a short descriptive motto, a brief musical idea that describes a particular character, event or certain state of mind. The *Leitmotive* were metamorphosed "through a process of constant manipulation" to achieve in Wagner's words an "endless melody." These thematic *Leitmotive* were a means of weaving long spans of music into a continuous fabric. His goal was "unbroken drama expressed in unbroken music." This means of linking different parts of a long work with recurring themes goes back at least to Berlioz's *idée fixe*.

> *"I need a theatre such as I alone can build."*
> - Wagner

Der Ring des Nibelungen

Wagner's masterpiece musical drama cycle *The Ring* consists of four full-length music dramas based on Teutonic legends. The project consumed Wagner for twenty-six years from the start of *Das Rheingold* to the completion of the fourth and final work in the cycle *Götterdämmerung* ('Twilight of the Gods') and "illustrates Wagner's unrelenting effort to make music overwhelmingly convincing." Unusual for opera composers, Wagner wrote all his own librettos. Work began in 1850 with the start of the libretto and finished with the first performance of *The Ring* cycle at the first Bayreuth Festival in August 1876.

Harold Schonberg sums up the theme of these four operas as "gods, goddesses, earth-mothers, and Aryan heroes, all manipulated so that the theme of redemption through love wins out." In less than twenty years the regular Wagner festivals produced at the Bayreuth *Festspielhaus* "had acquired an oppressive atmosphere of obligatory reverence." When Sibelius went to Bayreuth in 1894 he observed that "the faithful absorbed the master's works 'as if they were receiving Holy Communion'."

There are two types of recordings of Wagner orchestral music (aside from complete operas). Both types are great showpieces and allow orchestras to really flex their sonic muscles. The first consists of both overtures and preludes from particular music dramas, which are very popular as stand-alone works, and there are many fine sets. The overtures from his first four successful operas have become very popular.

The other type is excerpts of parts of the music dramas themselves, but without singing. The most famous example is *The Ride of the Valkyries* from *Die Walküre*. Wagner's "music without words" is just as popular as his operas and more accessible. The music of Wagner's operas and music dramas was extremely influential on late-romantic orchestral music and composers, most notably Strauss, Bruckner, and Mahler.

> *"An old, primitive love poem, imperishably reborn in ever-new forms and repeated in the poetry of all the languages of medieval Europe, tells us of Tristan and Isolde."*
> - Richard Wagner

One of the most famous and influential of orchestral excerpts is the *Prelude and Liebestod* from his music drama *Tristan und Isolde*, completed in 1859. "The opening chords of *Tristan* were to the last half of the nineteenth century what the *Eroica* and the Ninth Symphonies had been to the first half – a breakaway, a new concept." *Tristan* was composed while Wagner worked on *The Ring* (1856-59). The harmony in it is sometimes called atonal..."for Wagner a stable key is an uninteresting one...keys are not established by direct routes but by indirect ones, by remote modulations."

The harmonic relationships in *Tristan* are pushed to their breaking points; the chromaticism of this work would influence virtually all post-Romantic composers. However, Richard Taruskin does not see Wagner's *Tristan* as "pointing toward the coming collapse of tonality" but rather, he debunks this "routine citation" as "the historicist tendency to write history backward with an eye toward giving the present a justification." 'Historicism' being the myth of purposeful, goal-oriented evolution through history.

Not surprisingly the opera initially was criticized as too 'dissonant' and too 'modern'. These two adjectives have been frequently used against contemporary music up to the current time. One major difference between criticism in Wagner's day (or Beethoven's) is that the opinions given by professional music critics were usually in line with the public. For decades now there has been a large disconnect between the public's perception of 'modern' music and other arts and the judgments given by 'experts'.

Wagner's last opera, *Parsifal*, with its theme of Christian mysticism, purity, and redemption utilizing the Arthurian legend of the knight Parsifal's quest for the Holy Grail, was finished in 1882 with the premiere in July at Bayreuth. The composer, exhausted from decades of non-stop activity, died in Vienna the following February at age sixty-nine. *The Ring* and Bayreuth had established themselves as huge successes, his operas were in demand all over, Wagner spent much time in his later life writing wildly on a wide variety of subjects in which he was not expert. But given his narcissism and egotism this was irrelevant, for he considered himself expert in all matters confronting Man. His rants about topics, such as racial purity, his anti-Semitism and claim that Christ was not a Jew, while also dismissing Christianity as stemming from Judaism, were especially disturbing and would influence future movements and madmen.

Wagner, reputed to be the most radically innovative composer of the 19th century, was actually, according to Richard Taruskin, not a futuristic utopian but the very opposite, "a reactionary with a social vision of restored pre-modern harmony in direct reaction to the social discombobulations caused by modernization." However, his influence on composers for at least fifty years after 1870 was undeniable. Strauss, Bruckner, and Mahler are the most obvious, but also Dvořák, Debussy, and even the Second Viennese School of Schoenberg (the clear influence of *Tristan* on *Verklärte Nacht*). Only with the neo-Classical school of the 1920s would composers such as Stravinsky successfully break from the entire Wagnerian apparatus.

17

Nineteenth-Century France

♪ Hector Berlioz

Extremely rare, if not unique among important composers, Berlioz was not a prodigy or an immensely gifted child and "never even learned to play a useful instrument correctly." Harold Schonberg captured the contradiction that is Berlioz: "Only a genius could have overcome his lack of basic knowledge. He could not play piano, found Bach to be a bore, and played guitar and kettledrums. But only his lack of knowledge...led him (down) the paths he took." 'Genius' hardly overstates things as the largely self-taught Berlioz became a master of academic counterpoint and understood the harmonic implications of melody as well as anyone. One path he took that is surprising, given his lack of basic musical knowledge, is that of greatest music critic of his time.

This allowed him later on, in his own words, to compose freely and in silence. H did he grow up in a musical household with musical parents, nor was he encouraged in his early musical pursuits. His father was a physician and Hector was to be one also, and his mother "sincerely believed that anybody becoming a professional musician was automatically on the road to hell." As a result, "the forms he used were different and self-evolved...sometimes...brilliantly successful" but often he struggled "as he tried to shape his materials." He gave his works such labels as, 'concert opera' and 'dramatic symphony.' Unlike virtually every other contemporary composer, Berlioz did not learn the piano or get early exposure to counterpoint by learning Bach's *The Well-Tempered Clavier*. For many of the early Romantics, Bach's work "was the foundation of all composition."

> *"He (Berlioz) believes neither in God nor Bach."*
> - composer-pianist-conductor Ferdinand Hiller

Because of his "super-heated imagination" and his genius, Berlioz thought about and approached music differently from all other composers. Berlioz was "the first composer consistently to derive his inspiration from the nature of the instruments." "With Berlioz you have a wide range of different possibilities for each instrument. No instrument has just one given character." Aaron Copland elaborated on Berlioz's genius, pointing out that the Frenchman mixed instrumental colors "so as to produce a new result" as opposed to all previous composers who "used instruments in order to make them sound like themselves."

Berlioz wrote almost no intimate works, such as string quartets or solo piano works, and if he did they are obscure. Instead, "the more colossal the means that he set in motion, the better he felt." He did not see solo instruments or small groups of complementary players; he saw a hundred instruments (as a whole) - the symphony orchestra. Berlioz only employed huge musical forces, "preoccupied...with extreme and gigantic aims." "To his inflamed imagination the classical symphony seemed too generalized and ambiguous in meaning." He saw programmatic and descriptive music as a solution to this. This perspective, along with his vision and genius, led to Berlioz's creation of the modern orchestra, which has been the dominant "instrument" of classical music for almost two centuries.

The innovations and influences of Berlioz on contemporaries and on Romanticism of the 19th century were enormous. Unlike his contemporary early Romantics with whom he is inevitably grouped (Mendelssohn, Schumann, Chopin), Berlioz fully embraced his role as pioneer and innovator; in this way he was much closer to Wagner. In fact, Mendelssohn and Berlioz were opposites among the early Romantics: "Mendelssohn was sanitized to perfection" while Berlioz represented "excessive enthusiasm or exaggeration."

> *"Berlioz's instrumentation is so disgustingly filthy...one needs a wash after merely handling one of his scores."*
> *- Mendelssohn*

Berlioz fought passionately for the cause of Romanticism, "the projection of the ego in the work of art, as well as the artist as inspired lunatic." Berlioz and Liszt both "exploited a satanic public image, and enjoyed a Gothic taste for the macabre."

Berlioz was the father of modern orchestration and used the orchestra to create "a new kind of tonal power, resource and color." Berlioz wrote extensively on music and the contemporary art scene with "sharp satire and wit, mingled with considerable bitterness." His textbook <u>Treatise on Modern Instrumentation and Orchestration</u> of 1844 was the first scoring manual offered by a major composer and was very influential on several generations of musicians. By reaching for the extraordinary, Berlioz "produced an unceasing inventiveness in...orchestral color." Berlioz subordinated "all other musical means to the effect of orchestral color." He was the first composer to differentiate between 'instrumentation' (what instruments can and cannot do well) and 'orchestration' (the creative combination of instrumental colors). His for-the-time monstrous opera *Les Troyens* (1858) can stand aside the musical dramas of Wagner with extravagant sets and costumes, and running four-and-a-half hours.

Berlioz was the ultimate French Romantic composer but he had roots in the Classical era. As proof, he was critical of Chopin not only for what Berlioz saw as weak orchestration in his piano concertos (a common criticism even today), but also for Chopin's departure from traditional forms. He was the "first to express himself autobiographically in music." And his idea of attaching a detailed program to his *Symphonie Fantastique* led directly to the symphonic poem form invented by Liszt. Berlioz called his symphonies 'instrumental dramas'; "the universal romantic urge...induced him to convert the symphony into a 'drama with voices'."

> *"Next to God, it is Shakespeare who has created most."*
> *- Hector Berlioz*

In his music Berlioz attempted to fuse the literary, or *fantanstique*, with symphonic form. The influence of the classics in literature on his programs and compositions is in evidence all over his works, from *Romeo and Juliet*, to the opera *Les Troyens*, to *Harold In Italy*. The influence of Shakespeare led to the concert overture *King Lear*. However, while not admitting influence from, and certainly paying no homage to, great past musical masters, "there nevertheless was a great deal of tradition in his music," which increased in his mature works. Even in the frequently wild music of his youth, this tradition served to temper the "uncontrollable instincts of youth (with) restraint, clarity, and proportion."

> *"One must try to do coolly the things that are most fiery."*
> *- Hector Berlioz*

As Harold Schonberg pointed out, unlike his love of past literature, especially Shakespeare, when it came to music Berlioz only had interest in what lay ahead. He did not look back to the tradition of Bach and Haydn and he "ignored most of Mozart." His inspiration from the past was only Beethoven, and even Paganini claimed "Berlioz was the only man capable of making Beethoven come alive again." "Of all who dared rival Beethoven in the symphony, none did so with greater courage and enthusiasm than young Hector Berlioz." "Beethoven (to Berlioz) stood for all that mattered and…against all that was trivial in music."

Berlioz sincerely believed that his music derived from Beethoven's symphonies. He felt he was "continuing the symphonic ideal…through program music…a poetic idea in music." Paul Henry Lang finds fault with Berlioz's thinking, holding that "the symphony responds to the abstract-musical only." The formal sonata form cannot hold up when submitted to an extra musical program which determines the course of procedure.

If he did not entirely invent the idea of programmatic music he certainly led to its popularity. Berlioz was so firm in his position of music as story-telling that he wrote no abstract or 'absolute' music. His works are only orchestral as he wrote no chamber music or music for solo instrument that remains. He composed a number of orchestral, and for their day radical, works that were very influential to later Romantic composers (Liszt and Wagner in particular) and some operas (with mixed results). Berlioz was so ahead of his time that he was little influenced by fellow early Romantic composers, commenting after hearing the *Prelude* to *Tristan and Isolde* that it was "a sort of chromatic moan, full of dissonant chords…"

Symphonie Fantastique

For his *Symphonie Fantastique* (1830), his first major work and a work of immediately striking originality, Berlioz provided a fantastic program. The full title is "Episode in the Life of an Artist: Symphonie Fantastique in Five Parts." For example, "A young musician…poisons himself with opium in a fit of amorous despair." The 'young musician' in this fantasy is supposed to be Berlioz, in despair over his unreciprocated fascination with Harriet Smithson. The dose, being too low to result in death, the "musician is plunged into a deep sleep accompanied by the strangest visions," which Berlioz puts into "musical thoughts and images." The movements of the symphony describe what "Our Hero experiences in the course of his drugged dreaming," "a kind of five-act drama of nightmares and hallucinations."

> *"A feverish masterpiece of romantic ardor…moving as a battle of the elements."*
> - Debussy on *Symphonie Fantastique*

This work is the first great 'Romantic' symphony, complete with a love- and drug-induced orchestral nightmare and with detailed program notes provided by the composer so we can go along for the ride. It is amazing to think that this symphonic masterpiece with all its orchestral imagery was completed only three years after Beethoven's death and while Berlioz was still a Conservatory student. Even Beethoven never imagined taking the symphony where Berlioz took it. Berlioz felt Beethoven's *Ninth* was "a starting point for the music of the present," and he produced the 'Fantastic Symphony', as new and astonishing a work as the *Ninth*, a little more than a year after he encountered Beethoven's last symphony. Berlioz was the "first major figure in European music who grasped and publicly defended the difficult, groundbreaking works of Beethoven's last creative phase." No other composer produced so graphic a picture of a young artist as Berlioz did in his first major work, with "concepts of color and sonority that forced all future composers to revise their estimates of orchestral sound."

The flute melody provides "the unity of his symphonic whole" and the reappearance of the idée fixe (a recurring theme or motif that represents a character or idea) in all of the movements represents his obsession with Harriet Smithson. Berlioz gave this *idée fixe* "both character and importance right from the beginning…the theme recurs in each movement, binding them…more tightly together." In the *March to the Scaffold* movement he murders the object of his obsession in a nightmare and is sentenced to the gallows. The *Witches Sabbath* in the last movement is presented with a strict fugue. This finale shares some features with the finale of Beethoven's *Ninth*, including a violent introduction.

Harold in Italy

This is actually Berlioz's attempt at a programmatic concerto for viola written for the virtuoso Paganini to play. However, because it turned out to really be a symphony with a viola solo, Paganini was disappointed because the viola does not have the prominence that the soloist has in other concertos, such as the violin concertos to which Paganini was accustomed. In *Harold* the viola assumes a narrative rather than a concerto role.

Harold is in four-movements but with the usual adagio omitted. Instead, the two middle movements are picturesque scenes. As with the flute melody of the *Symphonie Fantastique*, in *Harold* the unity of the symphonic whole is provided by the main theme (the *idée fixe*) spoken by the viola.

Overtures

The overtures of Berlioz, some written as openings for his operas, others composed as Romantic concert overtures (a nascent genre at the time) all have themes and phrasing that hint at themes developed more fully in *Harold In Italy* and in the *Symphonie Fantastique*. For example, the ending of *Waverly* Overture is a similar, 'lighter' versions of the ending to *Harold*.

Around Christmas of 1830 Berlioz set off for Italy but he was viewed as a 'dangerous character' in Genoa and Nice. According to Berlioz the Italians at the time "saw in every Frenchman an agent of the revolution." While in Nice Berlioz composed the *King Lear* Overture and began *Le Corsaire* Overture, before he was banished from Nice and continued on to Rome. The connection between Shakespeare's play and the passages in Berlioz's Overture are unclear. Berlioz did not leave any specific programmatic guidance so commentators are left to their own imaginations. *Le Corsaire* Overture had to wait thirteen years until Berlioz managed to return to Nice and the inspiration to complete the work was rekindled. The product is a carefree, witty, and thoroughly delightful overture. Berlioz would revise *Le Corsaire* ten years later and give its premiere in April 1855, a quarter-century after its initial sketches.

The *Roman Carnival* Overture was extracted from the composer's opera Benvenuto Cellini, and the two main melodies of the overture come from this opera. The bulk of the music is taken from the carnival dance scenes in the opera. It is an orchestral showpiece that shows off Berlioz's brilliant skills as an orchestrator. The overture "is wonderfully alive, marvelously sonorous – because of its orchestration." As with most of Berlioz's orchestral creations the *Roman Carnival* is not typical of its time; "rather, it is a work of a true original, whose orchestral craft and melodic imagination were unlike those of any other composer."

> **Recommended – Berlioz Symphonic Works**
> *Symphonie Fantastique* – The recordings by Charles Munch with the Boston Symphony (RCA) and by Colin Davis with the Concertgebouw (Philips) continue to lead the field.
> *Harold In Italy* – again Colin Davis, a great Berlioz conductor, with the London Symphony Orchestra and Nobuko Imai as viola soloist (Philips, 1975). Overtures - Colin Davis's recent release on RCA with the Staatskapelle Dresden.

Berlioz is one of the few major composers only covered in one section of this book. The other notables are Wagner, Bruckner, Richard Strauss, and Mahler; all late Romantics who employed massive orchestras and huge forces, as did Berlioz earlier. It is therefore not surprising that they all (excepting R. Strauss to some extent) eschewed chamber and solo instrumental music, forms apparently unable to provide sufficient scale to capture their musical visions. Other than Bruckner, the aforementioned composers were also recognized as great conductors in their day, as was Berlioz. Even Wagner, not one to part easily with compliments, was moved after seeing Berlioz conduct, "I was simply all ears for things of which I had not dreamed until then…"

As Wagner grew in popularity, then established dominance as leading musicians such as Liszt became his disciples, the music of Berlioz fell into neglect for almost one hundred years. He became increasingly bitter as he "was left on the periphery of the musical establishment" in Paris but did have a successful conducting career outside of France. He remained a marginal figure until a revival of his works after World War II. Modern criticisms of Berlioz came from Stravinsky, who found his reputation as an orchestrator 'suspect', and from Pierre Boulez, who has claimed Berlioz's "awkward harmonies" make him want to scream. Much more of his music has been heard in the past fifty years than ever before.

♪ Cesar Franck (1822-1890)

French composers mostly avoided writing symphonies, until Saint-Saens, with the success of his Third Symphony, 'Organ' Symphony and Franck's *Symphony in D minor* inspired other French composers (d'Indy, Chausson) to quickly follow with their own symphonies. Franck's fame is mostly due to six great works very late in his career, three orchestral and three chamber works. The great orchestral works were the tone poem Psyche (1887-88), the Symphony in D minor, and the *Variations Symphoniques* (1885) for piano and orchestra, essentially a piano concerto. Franck was unique among French composers in that he gained his fame primarily as a composer of 'absolute' music and not with vocal music, opera or symphonic poems (although he produced works in these genres).

In these works Franck was willing "to go to the edge of tonality to convey restlessness, yearning, and a feeling of transcendence," providing a bridge between late Romanticism and the 20th century movement in France. He is called "the father of modern French music." Franck's harmonic language was influenced significantly by the chromaticism he heard in Wagner. Because this influence was felt later in his life he appears to be a late bloomer with these six great works all being composed by Franck after the age of fifty.

Symphony in D minor

The Symphony in D minor has an "odd combination of Wagnerian mysticism (and chromaticism) and Bachian rigor." Although its harmonic language is clearly Wagnerian, Franck went out of his way to stress that its form was like the symphonies of Beethoven, with a "recapitulation…but here it is in an alien key…the finale, just as in Beethoven's *Ninth*, recalls all the themes…" Many were unconvinced and its detractors dismissed it, even fellow French composers. Gounod dismissed it as "the expression of impotence pushed to dogmatic lengths." The rejection of this symphony in Franck's time was actually a rejection of the infusion of Wagner into the symphonic tradition symbolized by Beethoven.

The symphony shares the key of D minor with Beethoven's *Ninth* and Beethoven's final symphony "haunts the work no less pervasively than it had haunted Bruckner's Third Symphony." The central motif, taken from the last movement of Beethoven's Op.135 String Quartet ("*Muss es sein?*" "*Es muss sein!*"), developed in the first movement, was also incorporated into the second movement and "returned in its original form in the coda to the finale."

Just as described in the chamber sections on his works, Franck applies what his pupil Vincent d'Indy coined 'cyclic' form to his Symphony in D minor as well, attempting to bind different sections of the symphony by unification of the themes. It is similar to Liszt's thematic transformation technique. Aaron Copland, in his classic What to Listen for In Music, says that this is done in a couple of ways. One is to repeat a motto theme throughout the work, especially at unexpected moments. Another is to derive all themes from "only a few primal themes…metamorphosed as the work progresses."

Symphonic Variations

Franck makes it clear by not calling his *Variations Symphoniques* ('Symphonic Variations') a concerto that the virtuoso piano playing so typical of Romantic piano concertos would not be emphasized in this work. Instead, the composer employs a concertante style and a "deft dovetailing of piano and orchestra." Franck started the work in the summer of 1885 and he completed it before Christmas. The work was dedicated to and premiered by French pianist Louis Diémer, "one of the glitterati of the French musical scene."

Franck uses cyclic form and thematic transformation. The work is interesting and unique in its design with "a set of six free-flowing variations enclosed by an introduction and finale." What makes it unique is that the themes of the outer sections, in which the finale "is built mainly on the piano's very first theme," are "different from the variation melody."

> **Recommended – Franck orchestral works**
> *Symphony in D minor*: Pierre Monteux leading the Chicago Symphony Orchestra (RCA, 1961); *Symphonic Variations* – Clifford Curzon with the London Philharmonic under Boult is the clear forerunner here, and it is joined on disc by the Schumann and Grieg piano concertos (Decca, 1955).

♪ Camille Saint-Saëns (1835-1921)

Camille Saint-Saëns was "probably the most awesome child prodigy in the history of music." He had total recall, meaning that if he heard a piece of music just once, it would forever be branded in his memory. He was a leading pianist and organist (Liszt called him the greatest organist in the world), a good conductor, a critic, and as a composer he "worked prolifically in all forms." As a pianist he avoided the public demand for the flamboyant virtuoso (although he allied himself with Liszt). Instead, he "was an exponent of purity, clarity, refinement, and Classicism." Saint-Saëns began his career as a progressive, a champion of Berlioz, Wagner, and Liszt. But as the 19th century gave way to the 20th, Saint-Saëns, who turned sixty-five in 1900, became a reactionary to the current music, be it Mahler, Stravinsky, or Schoenberg. And he despised Debussy's music.

His music has never been held in high regard by critics, and in his day he "did not make much headway." Over the years his works have been characterized as not probing very deeply, being lightweight, "all technique and no ideas", "elegant but superficial…the French Mendelssohn" (as if it is a slight to be compared to Mendelssohn!). French critics characterized it as "bad music that was well written." What prevented Saint-Saëns from being a really great composer was "being unwilling to sully his facility with depth or originality." Sibelius said that in the history of music there were only three child prodigies – Mozart, Mendelssohn, and Saint-Saëns. Sibelius felt that Saint-Saëns certainly never reached the heights of Mozart and not even Mendelssohn.

One reason for this general feeling towards his music is that his most popular works are more superficial while his deeper, more probing chamber works are, unfortunately, not among his most performed. Saint-Saëns is in good company, with Mendelssohn and Tchaikovsky, when it comes to popular composers who do not enjoy the same level of acclaim among 'critics' and 'experts' as they do with the public. The reasons given by the experts include one or both of the following: 1) they were 'tunesmiths' but lacked depth; 2) they stayed strictly within traditional forms so their works did not contribute to the progress of music. In Saint-Saëns' defense (or maybe not) it should be pointed out that he was the first composer to write film music, composing background scores for many 'silent' movies.

The comparison with Mendelssohn is interesting. Both had unlimited potential which critics have always felt was not fully reached. The depth of their music is questioned by 'experts' but in reality has been underrated as evidenced by both composers having many varied works as mainstays of the repertory. For Saint-Saëns, three of his piano concertos remain popular (with No.2 & No.4 more so), as does his *Organ* Symphony (No.3), the Third Violin Concerto and the Cello Concerto. His *Carnival of the Animals* continues its popularity as a logical CD coupling with Prokofiev's *Peter and the Wolf*. Saint-Saëns may be regarded as the "heaviest of lightweights" but his orchestral works are "full of wit, color, melody and imagination."

Symphony No.3 in C minor, 'Organ'

Given Saint-Saëns skill as an organist and extensive knowledge of the instrument, it is not surprising that he would include a prominent role for organ in one of his symphonies. The work is dedicated to and, in its application of thematic transformation, influenced by Liszt. It premiered in 1886 in London with the composer at the podium. Not given virtuoso treatment, the organ complements the orchestra, serving to support the strings in the lyricism of the *Adagio* and provide "a luscious depth." Saint-Saëns pulls out all the stops in the finale as the organ sounds "triumphant chords" with its "majestic full voice" in the final section of the symphony. This symphony led Charles Gounod to make the exaggerated claim of his countryman Saint-Saëns as 'the French Beethoven.'

'French Beethoven' or not, Saint-Saëns' *Third*, as with Beethoven's *Fifth*, is in C minor and ends in a triumphant C major. In tribute to Liszt, Saint-Saëns included a part for piano. The first and second as well as the third and fourth movements are linked by means of smooth transitions. In the finale the organ plays a key role in the transformation of the main theme into a hymn.

> *Recommended – Saint-Saëns' Organ Symphony*
> There are three recommendations, the first the classic by Charles Munch and the Boston Symphony from 1959 (RCA). In addition, the versions by Daniel Barenboim with the Chicago Symphony (DG, 1976) and James Levine with the Berlin Philharmonic (DG, 1990), now with added fill-up on CD, lead a crowded pack.

Concertos

Camille Saint-Saëns wrote five piano concertos which are light and spirited and do not refute his reputation as a composer who lacked emotional depth. On the other hand, the concertos are thoroughly enjoyable. Concertos No.2, No.4, and No.5 remain popular and are established in the piano concerto repertory. All five concertos are examples of Saint-Saëns' ability to blend Gallic charm with sparkling technique to create a very enjoyable listening experience. No.5, nicknamed *Egyptian*, is amusing; it is Cairo observed from a café table in Paris.

France's main composers have not produced many concertos, but Saint-Saëns is an exception. His Cello Concerto stands as a masterpiece with its "blazing heart-on-sleeve melodies and melancholy strains…(it) shows off cello's capacity to sing and growl."

> *Recommended – Saint-Saens Concertos*
> Piano Concertos – for a complete set of *all* of Saint-Saëns' works for piano and orchestra, first choice is Stephen Hough with Sakari Oramo and the City of Birmingham SO (Hyperion, 2001).
> There are two approaches to the *Cello Concerto*: Ma's version (with the Orchestre National de France and Maazel on CBS/Sony,1983) "shows off the cello's capacity to sing" in a lyrical account that approaches it as a Romantic concerto. DuPre and Barenboim (Teldec), on the other hand, show "off the cello's capacity to…growl" in a raw, driven account, typical of this great cellist whose intensity made one wonder if her instrument actually survived the performance.

- 18 -

Romantic Classicism
Brahms, Dvořák, Tchaikovsky, and Rachmaninoff

There was no symphonic activity in Western Europe between the works of Liszt and Brahms, although in Russia, Tchaikovsky, Borodin and Rimsky-Korsakov all composed symphonies in the 1860s/70s. Wagner considered the symphony "redundant" by the 1840s. But the symphony made a comeback in the 1880s with Brahms, Bruckner, and the later symphonies of Tchaikovsky. In America, the Boston Symphony Orchestra was founded in 1881, the Chicago ten years later; in Europe the Berlin Philharmonic was formed in 1882.

Brahms settled in Vienna in 1862 and Bruckner arrived six years later. Like Brahms, Bruckner was in his forties before he composed a work he felt worthy of being called his Symphony No.1. To Brahms the symphony was a noble genre and his four symphonies are all works of the highest rank. However, the second half of the 19th century saw a battle take hold over sonata form with combatants entrenched on both sides. The 'Brahms camp', "upholding the primacy of sonata form" faced off against the looser harmonic and tonal ideas of the more innovative literary concepts of the Wagnerian progressives.

In the marketing terminology of today Brahms would be considered a customer-oriented composer, creating music for 'consumers'. His music was accepted immediately and quickly became popular. The same could be said of the melodious works of Tchaikovsky. Brahms' works did not cause a stir; the biggest stir he ever created was including a Latin text drinking song (*Gaudeamus igitur*) in his *Academic Festival* Overture, most likely to shock the academics at the University of Breslau, who were honoring him with an honorary doctorate.

This chapter titled 'Romantic Classicism' covers Brahms, Dvořák, Tchaikovsky, and Rachmaninoff. It could have also been titled 'Classical Romantics'. Of the four composers, Brahms and Dvořák leaned more towards classicism whereas the music of the two Russians is among the most Romantic at the turn-of-the-century. Both Tchaikovsky and Rachmaninoff "represented Russian melancholy expressed in German forms."

♪ Johannes Brahms (1833-1897)

Brahms' symphonies are powerful and mature works that did not begin to appear until he was forty-three years old and had composed many other orchestral works, including failed attempts at a 'first' symphony. Brahms was well along in establishing himself as heir-apparent to Beethoven; his orchestral works could stand next to Beethoven's. This feeling existed, almost a desire for someone to take up again the symphonic torch, because the early Romantic composers such as Mendelssohn and Schumann were relatively weak in symphonic works, while Chopin and Liszt mostly avoided them.

Responsible for "the renovation of music as an abstract art and the resuscitation of its traditional forms," Brahms was chiefly concerned with achieving structural integrity. At its best his music "combines rigorous argument with expression that is rich, nuanced, and emotionally probing." Brahms and his music were embraced by the musical camp in Europe longing for a return to strong symphonic works. They felt that the strong tradition established in the classical period had sputtered since the death of Beethoven (up to the 1860s-70s). Brahms is also credited with reviving the strong chamber music tradition that had similarly been dormant because the same early Romantic composers did not emphasize chamber forms either.

The influences on Brahms' compositional approach reach back as far as the vocal polyphony of Palestrina and Lasso. The contribution of Brahms to classical music and the value of his works is often generalized as the preservation of the Classical tradition. However, some view Brahms' works as ground-breaking and modern; "without which serial music of the 20th century would be unthinkable." Arnold Schoenberg attributed much of his musical debt to him and referred to Brahms' method of composition as 'evolving' or 'developing variation' (*entwickelnde* Variation), consisting of a constantly changing thematic core from which he built up his large instrumental forms.

♪ The Symphonic Works

What Brahms started, a return to strong symphonies, was continued by Bruckner with his large, brooding symphonies and their religious or spiritual movings; and by Dvořák with his excellent symphonies and the Czech's chamber contributions as well. Brahms rejected programmatic works and "stooped to no trickery of orchestral effects;" instead, he chose "to create absolute music beautiful for its own sake." His symphonies contain uplifting themes, music of "immense power...full of inspired individual touches." By studying Schumann's huge library of music from the past, Brahms was to "metamorphose from the comparatively unbridled Romantic into the great musical classicist of the second half of the 19th century."

There were two camps in the late Romantic period that could be termed 'conservative' and 'progressive'. With Schumann as his greatest influence and mentor, Brahms was in the former; the progressives counted Wagner, Bruckner and Liszt as their main members. There was juicy battling back and forth among composers in Vienna in those days. Brahms had little use for Wagner and Liszt, and pretty much ignored Bruckner and Mahler. Brahms and Wagner loathed each other both personally and professionally. Mahler, who respected Bruckner (Bruckner worshipped Wagner), characterized Brahms as "a mannequin with a somewhat narrow heart."

The Viennese music critic Eduard Hanslick, who apparently had the influence, and the personality, of the food critic in the movie Ratatouille, either contributed significantly to creating this divide, or gained notoriety from it. He was firmly in the camp of Brahms and Schumann, praising their works, while strongly opposed to Wagner and Bruckner. Hanslick published his critiques in Vienna's *Neue Freie Presse* (New Free Press). He lumped together Liszt, Berlioz, and Wagner as the "three most offensive and lunatic composers" of all time. Hanslick regularly trashed the symphonies of Bruckner and was vehemently opposed to music that claimed to paint pictures such as programmatic tone poems. He believed strongly that music is a completely abstract art. The praise by Hanslick of Brahms' First Symphony certainly helped it gain traction. "Seldom, if ever, has the entire musical world awaited a composer's first symphony with such tense anticipation," Hanslick gushed; and further, "The new symphony…is a possession…the nation may be proud, an inexhaustible fountain of sincere pleasure and fruitful study."

Symphony No.1 in C minor, Op.68

Brahms delayed his first symphony as long as he could as "he had before him the fearsome specter of the Beethoven Ninth" and that "the creation of true music depended on craftsmanship acquired by years of study." He was being hailed as the next Beethoven and was not going to enter that competition until he was sure of his command over the medium. In a letter he wrote to conductor Hermann Levi, Brahms supplied this as a possible explanation for stalling composition of his first symphony, "I shall never compose a symphony! You have no idea what it feels like to hear a giant like that (Beethoven) marching along behind you all the time."

Efforts toward producing the actual first symphony occupied Brahms for at least fourteen years. Because he destroyed most of his manuscripts we have no idea how many times he came close to finishing it or how many times he considered it done, only to go back and rework significant portions. By the time he finished the First in 1876 Brahms had been famous since the German Requiem of eight years earlier.

In the *First* several features point to Beethoven: the key of C minor (shared with Beethoven's *Fifth*) and echoes of the Ninth's 'Ode to Joy' in the main theme of the finale. There is a "Beethovenian spiritual journey of (its) outer movements" and "like Beethoven's *Ninth* (Brahms' *First*) goes through stages of struggle and reflection to attain a final victory." Also, the intensely dramatic introductions to both the opening and closing movements recalls Schumann's Fourth Symphony. But Brahms' *First* is a triumph of symphonic form in its own right as he "succeeded in establishing a motivic continuity, first heard in its embryonic state in the slow introduction to the opening movement, which is continued throughout the four movements."

Serenades No.1 in D, Op.11; No.2 in A, Op.16

While delaying his First Symphony, Brahms practiced in the symphonic form without committing to a full symphony by writing his two serenades for orchestra in 1857-59. They are both in the serenade tradition of Mozart with five to six movements. Brahms was satisfied with Serenade No.1, saying, "I am very pleased with my first attempts at writing for orchestra...". He also wrote to Clara Schumann, "The concert (at which Serenade No.1 premiered) appears to have gone fairly well." The two serenades were viewed by Brahms as a hybrid of serenade and symphony; well-crafted pieces but lacking the "emotional density" of the symphonies.

> *Recommended – Brahms Serenades*
> István Kertész leading the Vienna Philharmonic (Decca), offered together with the complete Brahms symphonies.

Symphony No.2 in D, Op.73

Although Brahms seemingly took forever to bring his First Symphony to the public, he only needed five months to complete No.2. It is 'pastoral' in nature and stands in contrast to No.1 in which Brahms appears to have seen himself in a head-to-head competition with Beethoven in the monumental outer movements of the *First*. However, Brahms seemed to approach the Second without the looming shadow of Beethoven hovering over it. If his First Symphony succeeds in making the symphonic connection to Beethoven's powerful canon, Brahms' *Second* stands in contrast, for it is, according to the composer, "cheerful and sweet" with "nothing clever about it...with melodies flying about so fast..."

The cheerful and sunny *Second*, with its idyllic fundamental nature, grows from the seed of the first three notes played by the cellos and double basses. It was premiered in December 1877, the year following his *First*. The lushly scored first movement "begins with a dipping-and-rising three-note figure, the thematic kernel of the entire piece." The *Second* was a smashing success and 'got the monkey off Brahms' back and solidified his place as a great symphonic composer.

Symphony No.3 in F, Op.90

Brahms cast his middle symphonies in the sunny keys of D and F major, respectively, with No.2 sometimes referred to as his 'Pastoral' symphony. The *Third*, never quite achieving the great popularity of its companions, is "an odd mix of overt heroism and dense formal logic" and is sometimes viewed as the 'poor sister' to Brahms' other three symphonies. It is the shortest and least performed of the four symphonies. It was completed in the summer of 1883 and the premiere given a few months later in December by the Vienna Philharmonic and Hans Richter.

Michael Steinberg labels Brahms' *First* as 'heroic', his *Second* as 'pastoral' and cheerful, and the *Fourth* as 'tragic'. But "the *Third* leads neither to victory nor to tragedy, but ends in resignation and hard-won calm." The opening of the symphony is assertive and fiery but ambiguity and surprises soon appear. Brahms alternates between major and minor keys to create contrasting moods; tension and suspense are built up but answered with ambiguity and not resolved in the first movement.

Symphony No.4 in E minor, Op.98

The *Fourth* was begun within six months of the premiere of the *Third*. Brahms took a year to complete it and he conducted the premiere in Meiningen in October 1885. Due to the timing of his symphonies, many consider the four in pairs. No.1 and No.2 premiered in 1876 and 1877, respectively; No.3 and No.4 in 1883 and 1885.

Symphony No.4 was the result of Brahms' lifelong struggle to infuse "the strict musical architecture of the Baroque...with the passion of the Romantic era." Brahms succeeds splendidly, and in the *passacaglia* finale "epic tragedy and melodic lyricism find their most powerful expression." The "combination of tragic feelings and heart-rending melancholy" runs throughout the symphony.

Some have approached this work as "a vision 'seen through a glass darkly,' sustaining the soul with the grandeur of its conception." "The finale of Brahms' *Fourth* is...a *tour de force* of styles past and present...an apocalypse in strict time, musical history stripped to the bone." Brahms expert Walter Frisch called the fourth movement "perhaps the most extraordinary movement written in the post-Beethoven and pre-Mahler era."

Academic Festival Overture, Op.80; Tragic Overture, Op.81

Brahms composed only three short works for orchestra, these two overtures and the *Haydn Variations*. The *Academic Festival* is a medley of four university songs, including the Latin drinking song *Gaudeamus Igitur*, reserved for the grand conclusion. It is Brahms' most accessible orchestral work. It has a playful energy combined with warm romantic lyricism, a result of its mixture of sonata form technique and traditional student songs. Written for very large orchestral forces, the *Academic Festival* Overture is Brahms' most recognizable and accessible orchestral work.

The *Tragic* is the serious partner to the light-heartedness of the *Academic Festival* and is characteristic of the mature Brahms. Brahms had plans to compose incidental music to Goethe's *Faust*, but only completed an overture, which he allowed to stand on its own as the *Tragic* Overture.

Variations on a Theme of Haydn, Op.56a

This is one of the greatest orchestral works of the 'variation on a theme' form, in the company of Elgar's *Enigma Variations* and Strauss' *Don Quixote*. Originally conceived as a work for two pianos, it was composed and premiered in 1873. It was Brahms' last orchestral warm up before he completed his First Symphony in 1876. "On a melody (*St. Anthony Chorale*) of great dignity and beauty..." Brahms added variations that are the "acme of perfection" both in terms of design and content.

Brahms mistakenly thought the 'St. Anthony Chorale' theme was by Haydn, but it is probably by Haydn's student Ignaz Pleyel. No one is certain, except that Brahms got the most out of the theme in producing this magnificent orchestral work. With these variations Brahms dissects "a single tune, examines it from every…angle, and puts it back together."

Although Brahms' music has aged very well over the past century or so, and he is admired by modern listeners for his "richness of expression and unerring taste," in his time he was found by many to be "dry, artificial, and (even) grotesque." Author Alex Ross feels that Brahms' lasting popularity is partly due to what sets him apart from most other musical giants – he addresses us on "roughly equal footing, as one troubled mind commiserating with another." His music has a 'sunset' quality about it and "the tone of late-night consolation" that he so often uses to relieve tension in his music "may be Brahms's chief gift to the human race."

> *Recommended – Brahms Symphonies*
> As the 'Classical Romantic' there are two approaches to Brahms' symphonies and most conductors fall somewhere in the middle. Toscanini and Szell stressed lean textures and quick tempos. Romantic maestros (Furtwängler) extract more passion with weightier textures and generally slower pacing. *Symphony No.1* – Karajan at his peak with the BPO (DG, 1960s). *Symphony No.2* – Light treatments of Brahms' *Pastoral* Symphony are from Monteux and Beecham, conductors not often linked to heavy Germanic works. *Symphony No.3* – the 1970s version by Karajan/BPO (coupled with *No.2*) is preferable to his later digital accounts. *Symphony No.4* – unquestioned favorite among critics and music lovers is Carlos Kleiber and the Vienna Philharmonic (DG). This focused and passionate interpretation remains the benchmark. Complete sets – Furtwängler (EMI) and Kertész (Decca). The two overtures and the *Haydn Variations* can be found as fill-up on many CDs. Kertész's set has the added bonus of excellent versions of Brahms' two orchestral serenades.

♪ The Concertos

Brahms worked in Classical forms but with Romantic overtones. He was the 'Classical Romantic', and he completely shunned the programmatic music popular during the Romantic period. It is not surprising at all that he made no attempts at opera. He may not have "touched the profoundest depths of inspiration as did Beethoven" but he combined "his powers of invention" and the uplifting quality of his themes in perfect companionship with his orchestration, which never stooped to any "orchestral trickery." Brahms resisted the trend in his day to use the concerto as a "vehicle for virtuoso display with orchestral accompaniment." Instead, he was more inclined to lean on classical models of Mozart and Beethoven, "creating a more equal partnership between soloist and orchestra."

Harold Schonberg characterized Brahms as the "keeper of the flame"; his "music combined a sensitivity and rich romantic sentiment with a formal intellectual control unmatched by other romantics." Brahms occupied in the second half of the 19th century the position held by Mendelssohn in the first half, an ingenious composer who was content with old forms and, as a result, did little to advance the forms.

Brahms began work on the First Concerto intending it to be his first symphony so many hear the piano concertos more as symphonies with piano accompaniment. As with several other works, the First Piano Concerto took a tortuous path to its final format, starting as a sonata for two pianos, before he redirected things toward a first symphony, and finally settled as Piano Concerto No.1. It shows signs of being a youthful work, which it is, and its large opening movement conveys conflict, maybe even anger, certainly setting it apart in mood from his later, more mature works.

Piano Concerto No.1 in D minor, Op.15; No.2 in B-flat, Op.83

Brahms' First Piano Concerto, begun in 1854, was premiered by Brahms in 1859 in Leipzig. Within the work there is great tension between orchestra and soloist, a *"Sturm und Drang* turbulence," but the "concerto is not a war; it is a creative debate rooted in conflict." According to a critic present "the public was wearied and the musicians puzzled." It was seen as too big and too demanding and was shunned by soloists for almost a century because it supposedly did not highlight the piano enough. The composer Edouard Lalo summed up this sentiment by complaining that a soloist needs to be "given the main role and not be treated as a soloist within the orchestra." Feelings such as these prevented the concerto from being a popular choice for performers and it was not until the 1950s that the D minor Concerto became the popular work it remains today.

Given Brahms' complete disdain for program music and for his music portraying anything extra-musical, it is curious that his friend the violinist Joseph Joachim thought the concerto's brutal opening produced a jarring and disorienting effect meant to represent Brahms' friend Robert Schumann tumbling head over heels in his failed suicide plunge into the Rhine.

There was considerable time between the composition of the two concertos and they are significantly different, in addition to the Second having a fourth movement. Piano Concerto No.2 is more mature and balanced compared to the First, with Brahms now in his late forties. Instead of the traditional three movements Brahms inserts a big scherzo after the opening movement. The scherzo is "classically-grounded…very much from Beethoven tradition…

heavy in orchestration."

Brahms strategically placed the scherzo between the "epic first movement and luscious *Andante*," the latter opening with a beautiful solo cello melody, which "functions as a palate cleanser in between substantial courses." The dance-like final movement is curiously lighter than the second movement scherzo.

> *Recommended - Brahms Piano Concertos*
> Gilels with the Berlin Philharmonic under Eugen Jochum is widely hailed as the gold standard for their probing qualities in these concertos. The catalogue is dominated by Szell and the Cleveland Orchestra who have backed up recordings of these concertos by Serkin, Fleisher and Curzon.

Violin Concerto in D, Op.77

This concerto shares its key with Brahms' Second Symphony, Op.73, composed at around the same time, in the summer of 1878. Both are considered "sunny, idyllic works abounding in melodic simplicity and charm." Its "expansively woven melodies, its rhythmic robustness and warm flow of harmony" are all typical Brahms.

The Violin Concerto was written to challenge the new breed of performer who was just beginning to emerge in Brahms' time. This performer was the musically intelligent virtuoso. For Brahms this performer was the violinist and friend Joseph Joachim. In fact, the concerto is a product of Brahms' extensive consultations with Joachim, as the composer was not familiar with the details of the violin. However, the music is pure Brahms, despite the contributions of his friend. Joachim was naturally the soloist at the premiere in 1879 conducted by the composer.

In response to the difficulties of the concerto and the demands placed on the soloist, conductor Hans von Bülow remarked that other violin concertos in the repertory were written for the violin, but "Brahms had written one against the violin."

> *Recommended – Brahms Violin Concerto*
> There have always been two types of performance and we do not know Brahms' preference, nor Joachim's style. The first is personified by the fireworks of Heifetz with Reiner and Chicago Symphony (RCA). The other is the lush romanticism captured best by David Oistrakh, whose best of several recordings is with Klemperer. This work is as popular as any other in the repertory and recordings are many. Digitally-recorded readings include those by Kennedy, who brings something new and different to performances, and Hillary Hahn, one of the brightest young violinists on the scene.

'Double Concerto' in A minor for Violin and Cello, Op.102

There are not many double concertos in the repertory written beyond the Classical period. Beethoven composed his *Triple* Concerto for piano, violin and cello, which is widely regarded as one of his weaker orchestral works; "one of his least memorable creations, suffering from unimaginative piano writing." Balancing one instrument against the orchestra is a challenge; making three all 'cooperate' while also making significant contributions to a great work is very difficult, apparently even for Beethoven.

However, Brahms used his *Double* Concerto as a vehicle for the cello as solo instrument. Supposedly he could not find a satisfactory way to balance a solo cello with the orchestra, although he was more successful than Beethoven in balancing violin and cello. As it turned out, Dvořák was able to do the former two decades later with his great Cello Concerto, to which Brahms contrasted his own lack of success with the great Czech composer's success, "had I known that it was possible to write such a concerto for cello soloist, I would have done it." "Throughout the concerto both soloists pit themselves against the orchestra in a bid for supremacy."

The *Double* Concerto was composed in 1887; a "magnificent piece...it has a powerful sense of suppressed energy." In this, his last orchestral work, Brahms at fifty-four, "sums up the emotional experience of a lifetime and proclaims its Romantic feeling in every bar." As with many of his later works it has been labeled as 'autumnal' in mood because it is relatively subdued (compared with his younger works) and avoids extreme harmonies.

♪ Antonín Dvořák (1841-1904)

"Dvořák was singularly endowed with the ability to synthesize the two German traditions – the 'classical' and the 'futurist'." Part of the appeal of his music is the blending of "tight control of formal structure," while making the listener feel as if "the music can go anywhere at any time."

♫ The Symphonies

Dvořák completed nine symphonies, which together form a substantial contribution to the symphonic form. His most famous are the Seventh, Eighth, and especially the *Ninth* ("From the New World"), but the emphasis on his final three unfortunately has led to the undeserved neglect of the previous symphonies. This is especially true of the *Fifth* and *Sixth*, which are not performed frequently enough given their stature. The numbering of Dvořák's symphonies is very confusing as they were originally numbered in the order in which they were published, which was very different from the sequence in which Dvořák composed them.

And it is even worse than indicated by simple differences in composition and publication dates. Some symphonies were performed years before publication. For example, what is now known as Symphony No.2 in E flat, Op.10, was begun around 1872, orchestrated the next year and given its premiere by Smetana in 1874. After this initial performance, Dvořák spent years revising the work, gave it to his publisher Simrock sometime around 1890, but Simrock did not publish it until 1912. Today the numbering has been resolved, although one can still find vintage LP recordings of the *New World* Symphony as 'Symphony No.5'. It took István Kertész and his complete cycle of Dvořák symphonies in the 1960s to bring the early works out of obscurity. Prior to Kertész's trail blazing complete cycle in the 1960s, Dvořák's first four symphonies were virtually unknown.

Symphony No.4 in D minor, Op.13
This symphony was begun in late 1873 and completed within a few months. However, it would not be performed for another twenty years. The neglect of Dvořák's early symphonies, particularly Nos.1-4, remains a mystery. For example, his first two symphonies were not published until 1960! They have unfortunately been relegated "to an obscurity which is out of proportion to their significance and…true worth." By comparison, Tchaikovsky's early symphonies (Nos. 1-3) have been considerably more popular. The key difference is that, unlike Dvořák's, Tchaikovsky published his early symphonies shortly after he completed them.

Symphony No.5 in F, Op.76
This symphony, the first of Dvořák's symphonies that did not spend decades in obscurity, was completed in the summer of 1875 and premiered four years later. It "marks the beginning of his true maturity as a symphonic composer." Dvořák got the attention of Brahms and the critic Hanslick, who were both judges for the Austrian State Prize Dvořák applied for. Brahms brought Dvořák's music to the attention of Simrock, the Berlin publisher.

While composing the *Fifth* Dvořák was still unknown and struggling financially. However, the symphony shows a "cheerful assurance" and "gives no hint…of the frustration he felt at his lack of recognition." Although it enjoys nowhere near the status of his final three, the Fifth Symphony "can easily stand beside his better known, later symphonies."

Symphony No.6 in D, Op.60
This was the first of Dvořák's symphonies to be published and was mistakenly known as his *First* until the 1950s. It was composed in late 1880 and premiered in early 1881 in Prague. Brahms' influence on this work is ubiquitous, particularly from the recently-premiered Second Symphony. However, Dvořák's D major symphony stands on its own despite being quickly superseded in popularity by his final three symphonies.

The strong Bohemian nationalistic flavor of the work was a deliberate effort on the part of the composer. After the success of such works as the first set of *Slavonic* Dances and *Moravian* Duets, Dvořák saw himself as the musical spokesman for Bohemia. He was determined to compose a 'Czech' symphony. Melodies influenced by Czech folk music are heard from the opening of the work but are at their most pronounced in the third movement marked 'furious' ('furiant'), a scherzo containing a vigorous folk dance.

Symphony No.7 in D minor, Op.70

This work, the first of his great triptych, was begun in December 1884 and finished by Dvořák in March 1885. The premiere in London, which was led by him, must have been well-received as Dvořák commented that it was "immensely successful and at the next performance will be a still greater success." In fact, the Seventh was the first of Dvořák's symphonies to achieve and hold popularity. The symphony was commissioned by the Philharmonic Society of London after the success in London the previous year of Symphony No.6 (at that time known as No.1). This made expectations extremely high and Dvořák put the work through a thorough revision before bringing it before the public.

Dvořák had recently heard Brahms' Third Symphony and it had a great influence on him, who set about composing his *Seventh* after hearing it. Brahms was a champion of Dvořák, and a well-meaning critic.

Symphony No.8 in G, Op.88

Dvořák's *Seventh* was composed in a little more than two months from late August to early November 1889. The work was first performed in Prague in February 1890 under the baton of the composer. Since the premiere of his Seventh Symphony Dvořák had written a second set of *Slavonic* Dances as well as two of his greatest chamber works, the Piano Quintet, Op.81 and the Piano Quartet in E-flat. It was Dvořák's preference to complete a work quickly but to also avoid revisions, if possible. For a composer such as Dvořák it contains drastic experimentation with "ideas linked by rhythmic rather than melodic features." He had indicated that he tried in his *Eighth* to work out individual ideas in a new way. In this he succeeds but without failing to give the work an impression of formal unity.

The five years that separated Dvořák's Seventh and Eighth Symphonies "witnessed a sea change in his approach to composition." While the *Seventh* was "consciously molded in the traditions of Viennese Classicism" the *Eighth* is unorthodox in the classical sense. Both the first and second movements are of unusual structure. The very opening of the work is unusual, a cross between a typical introduction for a symphony and an exposition, moving towards the central key (typical introduction) but at the fast tempo of the rest of the movement.

Symphony No.9 in E minor, Op.95, "From the New World"

> *"Whatever I have written in America, England or elsewhere is and always remains Czech music."*
> - Antonin Dvořák

Dvořák was invited to America by philanthropist Jeannette Thurber to be director of the National Conservatory of Music. Dvořák and his family spent the better part of two-and-a-half years (Sept. 1892 – April 1895) in the 'New World', with one return trip home during that time. He worked on this symphony from December 1892 to May 1893. The *New World* Symphony "is the majestic culmination of Dvořák's evolving symphonic style." The plaintive melody of the slow movement, with its 'hymn like chords' and 'quasi-spiritual' style, was adapted by Harry Burleigh, a student of Dvořák's, into the spiritual hymn *Goin' Home*. Richard Taruskin points to this symphony's "hidden program adapted from Longfellow's *Song of Hiawatha*." In fact, Dvořák stated that the scherzo of the *Ninth* was suggested by the feast scene in *Song of Hiawatha* where the Indians dance.

Symphony No.9 continues to spark debate as to Dvořák's meaning of *New World* Symphony. Did he simply mean he wrote it while in the new world or "did it imply that the thematic content...was in some sense inherently American?" Either way, Dvořák's final symphony was acknowledged as a masterpiece from its very first performance, a great public triumph for him by the New York Philharmonic under Anton Seidl in December 1893. In addition to his most successful symphony, Dvořák composed two chamber masterpieces while in the U.S., the Op.96 String Quartet in F, appropriately nicknamed *American*, and the String Quintet, Op.97 in E-flat. Both were written while the Dvořák's vacationed in the Bohemian village of Spillville, Iowa.

Recommended – Dvořák Symphonies
Complete symphonies – István Kertész and the LSO (Decca, 1963-66). The outstanding survey by the conductor who brought the early symphonies out of obscurity, this cycle remains fresh and spontaneous. This boxed set also includes *Scherzo Capriccioso* and the overtures *In Nature's Realm*, *Carnival*, and *My Home*.
Symphony Nos.7,8,& 9 – George Szell and the Cleveland Orchestra (Sony/CBS, 1959) usually packaged together with the *Carnival Overture* and works by Smetana.
Symphony Nos.8&9 – For this coupling the consensus remains Rafael Kubelik leading the Berlin Philharmonic (DG, 1995). Kubelik also offers the complete symphonies with the BPO.

Dvořák also composed several other notable symphonic works, including the two sets of *Slavonic* Dances, *Legends*, and a number of great overtures and tone poems. He joins Strauss and Sibelius as the three great composers of tone poems from the late Romantic Period.

♪ Overtures and Tone Poems

In Nature's Realm, Op.91; Carnival, Op.92; Othello, Op.93

Composed in 1891-92 these form a tone-poem triptych, which had the ambitious original title of "Nature, Life, and Love". Perhaps Dvořák had second thoughts about covering so much territory in less than forty minutes, but these three overtures, taken together, "marked the birth of modern Czech music," initiated by Dvořák with these related overtures and developed further by Martinů and Janáček. Although rarely are the three overtures performed together as Dvořák intended, a 'nature motive' (i.e., a *Leitmotiv*) runs through all three works and is supposed to represent a "symbol of nature as the basis of all life."

Carnival has remained the most popular of the three, probably because of the exuberant energy of quicksilver shifts from cymbal crashes to vibrant Bohemian dance rhythms, reflective of Dvořák's childhood memories of village celebrations.

The Noonday Witch, The Water Goblin, The Golden Spinning Wheel, The Wood Dove, Opp.107-110

Composed in 1896 after Dvořák returned from America, these four works form a cycle of symphonic ballads based on Czech tales and legends. They are Dvořák's way of re-engaging with the Bohemian heartland after his three-year stay in America. Derived from Czech folk music, they are probably the most advanced if Dvořák's works, they point forward to Janáček and to the tonal language of the 20th century. These are good examples of how "central European folk tales are decidedly darker than those of Western Europe and do not always have a happy ending."

Based on the folk-inspired ballads of Karel Jaromir Erben, the four poems represent some of his most pungent orchestration and unfailingly expressive melody. Short descriptions of the stories associated with them are follow. In *The Water Goblin* the goblin takes revenge after believing to have been betrayed by a human. *The Noonday Witch* tells of a hobbling old witch who tries to catch naughty children at midday. Parents used this tale to keep their kids in-line by threatening them of falling into her clutches. It is a variation on the boogey-man legend.

The *Golden Spinning Wheel* is a tale of chivalry involving a complex murder plot in which a woman murders her stepdaughter so that her own daughter can marry the king. That is a fairly stock story until the golden spinning wheel appears, made from the bones of the dead stepdaughter, a

Stephen King-like development in this macabre tale. Of course, good triumphs over evil, the dead girl is brought back to life just in time to be taken by the king as his true bride.

Another tale of a murder plot is *The Wood Dove*. This time a wife poisons her husband and, through the wood dove he drives her to suicide from his grave. The main theme is fittingly a funeral march from which all subsequent variations derive. The premiere was led by Janáček in Brno (1898) and Mahler conducted the first Vienna performance the next year.

> *Recommended - Dvořák Tone Poems and Overtures*
> The set to get is by Rafael Kubelik and the Bavarian Radio SO (DG, 1992). A recent recommendation is the set by Charles Mackerras with the Czech Philharmonic (Supraphon, 2010).

♪ Miscellaneous Orchestral Music
Slavonic Dances, Op. 46 and Op.72
The Op.46 (1878) set of orchestral dances finally launched Dvořák's fame beyond the borders of his native Bohemia. The publisher Simrock (who was also Brahms' publisher) wanted Dvořák to produce a set in the Bohemian tradition, as Brahms had done with his *Hungarian* Dances. Brahms originally composed his *Dances* for piano four hands and Dvořák composed his eight Op.46 dances in both orchestral and piano duet versions.

Op.46 was such a success that Simrock requested a second set. Dvořák complied, but not until 1886. The earlier set is youthful and perky while the latter group is powerful and nostalgic. The Op.46 dances are "orchestrated in bright primary colors...propelled by the rhythmic patterns and characters of traditional Czech folk dances." The Op.72 pieces are "more sophisticated concert dances, several steps removed from their folk origins."

> *Recommended* – Szell and Cleveland, at the height of their success, provide the classic complete set (Sony, 1960s).

Symphonic Variations, Op.78
This work was completed in 1877 and, like many of Dvořák's works, was not published until 1888 and after revision by the composer. The main theme is an original of Dvořák's, taken from one of his songs. After the theme is presented he then manages to squeeze twenty-eight variations into less than twenty minutes of music. For the concluding variation Dvořák decided to use a polka for an immensely vigorous dance.

Serenades, Op.22 in E; Op.44 in D minor

Dvořák's serenades look back to the serenades of Mozart, who was still very popular in Dvořák's Prague, with the minuet second movement of Op.44 and the five movement layout of Op.22. The Op.22 for String Orchestra was composed and premiered in 1875, around the time of his Fifth Symphony. It is a relatively early work that shows residues of the short-lived influence of Wagner on the Czech composer with some "poignant Siegfried Idyll-style harmonies." Because of Dvořák's "astonishingly inventive use of texture," it shares a popularity as great as Tchaikovsky's Serenade for Strings.

The Op.44 for wind instruments was composed in January of 1878 and premiered that November. Its scoring is very similar to Mozart's *Gran Partita* Serenade, to which it makes a graceful allusion. Its "melodic invention is of the highest quality."

♪ The Concertos

Although Dvořák composed three large-scale concertos, only the Cello Concerto is a 'great' work, probably the greatest concerto for cello and orchestra. Of the other two, the Piano Concerto does not stand up against other Romantic piano concertos, such as those by Brahms, Tchaikovsky, Schumann and Grieg. "It is not often played, even in Czech Republic...it may be rare because it's so difficult and not 'pianistic' at all." Dvořák was much better at writing for strings or for piano as a chamber participant. He had trouble providing the confrontation between keyboard and orchestra needed for an effective concerto.

Violin Concerto in A minor, Op.53

His Violin Concerto fares much better in comparison to other great works by Brahms, Tchaikovsky, Mendelssohn, and Bruch. While not as frequently performed as these other works, it remains in the repertory. This concerto was written for the famous violinist Joseph Joachim right after completion of the *Slavonic* Dances, possibly influencing the dance-infused finale.

Cello Concerto in B minor, Op.104

The greatest of all cello concertos is also the longest in the repertory. Brahms commented that had he known that it was possible to write such a concerto for cello, he would have done it. Thinking it not possible to compose a Romantic concerto on a grand scale for cello and orchestra, he instead wrote his Double Concerto with the cello joined by violin as soloists.

> *Recommended – Dvořák Cello Concerto*
> My personal favorite for intensity of the outer movements is Pierre Fournier with Szell conducting the Berlin Philharmonic. The consensus favorite is Rostropovich with the Berlin

> Philharmonic under Karajan, usually coupled with Tchaikovsky's *Rococco* Variations. Another excellent version is by Jacqueline du Pré with Celibidache and the Swedish Radio SO. Married to Daniel Barenboim, du Pré left a great catalogue of the repertory for cello. She died far too young.

♪ Piotr Tchaikovsky (1840-1893)

"Beethoven speaks to humanity... Tchaikovsky wanted to talk to everyone individually"
- conductor Yuri Temirkanov

Tchaikovsky is one of the greatest composers of orchestral music and his symphonies do not disappoint. His Fourth, Fifth and Sixth Symphonies are workhorses of the repertoire and the others hold their places in concert halls. Each symphony "affords multiple insights into the musical personality of an emotional, sensitive man and artist", who tragically was prone to bouts of intense depression. Tchaikovsky was an emotional and sensitive man and used the symphony more as a "means to express his most inward thoughts and feelings" than as "a form for developing reasoned musical discussion."

Unlike his fellow Russian composers of the 19th century who sought to establish Russian music distinct from the West, Tchaikovsky did not resent the influence of the West and the resultant Westernization of his homeland. He "had much more sympathy with the life and art of the West. This may be the reason why today he is the most popular of all the Russian composers." In fact, Tchaikovsky's sustained popularity is a good example of the "gulf between people's taste and the expert's opinion."

The symphony for Tchaikovsky was really "a means to express his most inward thoughts and feelings." Out of his inner turmoil he produced musical ideas "that often haunt the mind as well as delight the ear" and "no 19th-century composer was more convinced…of the necessity of intimate personal disclosure through music." His music is the most accessible of the late Romantic composers. Because of his extraordinary talent for lyricism and 'catchy' melodies, one can fully appreciate his works on first listening. Beethoven, on the other hand, takes multiple hearings to get the full measure of his music. There is something to be said for the skill and talent needed to write music that people can immediately take to, without it being 'hack' or 'salon' music. The ability to do this was the genius of Tchaikovsky.

♪ The Symphonies

Most of Tchaikovsky's symphonies, including the final great three, are cast in minor keys to produce a melancholic atmosphere. The symphony for Tchaikovsky was "less a form for developing reasoned musical discussion than a means to express his most inward thoughts and feelings."

Symphony No.1 in G minor, Op.13, *Winter Daydreams*; No.2 in C minor, Op.17, *Little Russian*; No.3 in E, Op.29, *Polish*

Composed 1866-7 Tchaikovsky's First Symphony premiered early in 1868 but did not achieve its final form until 1874. Today's version was not heard until 1886. The nickname 'Winter Daydreams' was actually given by Tchaikovsky, showing the influence of Schumann and Mendelssohn, who each had nicknamed symphonies. The influence of Mendelssohn is felt specifically in the Scherzo, with references to *A Midsummer Night's Dream* and the symphonic dance movements of Mendelssohn.

In the case of the *Little Russian*, No.2, as is usually the case with nicknames, this one was not made by the composer himself. It was very well received in its premiere in February 1873 because of "melodic themes borrowed from Ukrainian folksong" and because, unlike his First Symphony, the music "reflects a wholly unmorbid side of the composer's personality." At around thirty-four minutes the Second is the shortest of Tchaikovsky's symphonies by ten minutes.

The nickname for the Third Symphony, which took Tchaikovsky only a few weeks to compose in 1875, was given by the conductor of the premiere performance. However, there is nothing Polish about it, but the nickname stuck anyway. Like all of Tchaikovsky's symphonies from No.2 onward, the Third opens with a slow introduction to the first movement before the main themes and exposition.

Symphony No.4 in F minor, Op.36

The Fourth, Fifth and Sixth Symphonies of Tchaikovsky are justifiably very popular works within the symphonic repertory "offering tremendous drama and outpouring of indelible melody." The *Fourth* in particular, is a perfect example of Tchaikovsky's genius to capture his "oscillation between extremes of melancholy and frenzied activity, between resignation and optimism." Today this would be diagnosed as manic depression and indeed Tchaikovsky was a manic depressive who was tormented throughout his life, particularly by his sexuality. As sad as this was for the health of this great composer, we can look back and realize that Tchaikovsky's ongoing and painful struggle resulted in his use of music and composition to release the inner tension via outpourings of creative work – "great eruptions of fiery passion as well as the expression of profound defeatism."

The *Fourth* was composed mostly in 1877 and premiered the following year. The composer thought it was "the best thing I have done" up to that time. A greater technical mastery suddenly showed itself in this work and others composed around the same time (e.g., the Violin Concerto).

Tchaikovsky often came very close to assigning meaning to the movements of his symphonies, making them 'program' music. We have his letters to get an idea of what he had in mind. The first movement contains the germ of the entire symphony, with the main idea representing *Fate*, which according to the composer, is "that force that prevents the impulse to happiness from attaining its goal." Conjuring up *Fate* as a theme in each of the four movements creates a parallel of Tchaikovsky's *Fourth* with Beethoven's *Fifth*, in which the latter claimed to take Fate "by the throat." Tchaikovsky was less triumphant in his encounter through composition with *Fate* as the *Fourth* is "deeply pessimistic." Tchaikovsky characterized Fate as "that ominous power that hinders our striving after happiness."

The *motto* theme that opens the *Fourth* and reappears at critical times during the work encapsulates *Fate*, which Tchaikovsky felt controlled his destiny. He provided the following thoughts on the first movement, with typical melancholy, "All life is an unbroken alternation of hard reality with swiftly passing daydreams and visions of happiness." The scherzo, labeled 'stubbornly *pizzacato*' allows the string players to put their bows down throughout the entire movement; strings are only plucked leading up to the explosion that is the Finale.

Suite No.3 in G, Op.55

The four suites of Tchaikovsky are analogous to the two early serenades of Brahms. Both are lighter symphonic works composed of shorter movements without a fully-developed sonata-form first movement. As with Brahms' serenades, these shorter multi-movement works of Tchaikovsky still allow his flair for colorful orchestration to shine through. Whereas Brahms used the serenades as warm-ups for his first symphony, Tchaikovsky already had composed his first four symphonies and indicated his feelings on the suites as, "I want to compose a suite so that I may have a good rest from symphonic music." He stuck to his plan and composed three of the four suites after his Fourth Symphony and before the *Manfred* Symphony.

Suite No.3 from 1884 is the best and most popular of the four suites, and with its twenty minute final movement (in the form of a theme and variations) is as long as some Tchaikovsky symphonies. The composer was clearly satisfied and proud of his work, as he wrote to his publisher that, "There never yet was a work of greater genius than my new Suite!!!"

Manfred Symphony, Op.58

The *Manfred* Symphony, based on the long dramatic poem of Lord Byron, was composed between May and September in 1885, eight years after the

Fourth and three years before the *Fifth*. It is Tchaikovsky's longest symphony by almost ten minutes and is the only explicitly programmatic of his symphonies. Of course, implicit programs have been assigned to some of the other symphonies, in particular the *Pathétique*, either by the composer himself, or by an assortment of critics, musicologists, and publishers.

To connect the music to Byron's poem Tchaikovsky attached short descriptions to each movement. The inspiration for a programmatic symphony based on this subject came while reading Byron's poem while in Switzerland. After he finished he thought about using only the first movement as a tone poem and discarding the rest. Fortunately, he decided to retain the four movements intact as a symphony.

Tchaikovsky establishes the central theme (*idée fixe*) at the outset in low register woodwinds. This is the *Manfred* theme. The first movement is about Manfred wandering in the Alps and establishes the his state of mind.

Symphony No.5 in E minor, Op.64

Tchaikovsky's *Fifth* was composed in the middle of 1888, eleven years after the *Fourth*. However, in those years Tchaikovsky did compose the Manfred Symphony and four orchestral suites, some of which approach a symphony in size and scope, in addition to his Second Piano Concerto, the Serenade for Strings, and *Capriccio Italien*. Just before he began work on No.5 he had travelled, as an ambassador for Russian music, to Berlin, Prague, Paris, London, and other major European music centers.

Tchaikovsky's *Fourth*, *Fifth*, and *Sixth* symphonies are all concerned with fate, either through the use of a 'fate motif' or through program notes left by the composer himself. The *Fifth*, with its beautiful, romantic, lush melodies, shows off Tchaikovsky's gift for melody as few of his other works do. In fact, the slow movement alone contains at least three different romantic melodies. In the final movement Tchaikovsky uses a false ending before a triumphant coda in the major, drawing some parallel to Beethoven's fate-themed *Fifth*. A writer once made the comparison between these two symphonies as, "If Beethoven's *Fifth* is Fate knocking at the door, Tchaikovsky's *Fifth* is Fate trying to get out."

Symphony No.6 in B minor, Op.74, "Pathétique"

Premiered in 1893, the famous subtitle *Pathétique* refers to passion, not pathos, "though by its close the symphony has done away with the difference." The nickname was provided by brother Modest after the composer rejected his brother's first suggestion of 'Tragic'. The very start with bassoon, then the strings repeating the opening theme, makes clear the symphony is not going to be bright and cheery.

After the brass-dominant opening, the development section "is a large self-contained whole in which one closed logical theme encloses another." The second part of the section of the development "shatters the stillness; sheer turmoil follows", preparing for the lyrical recapitulation.

An immediately apparent feature of this symphony is the unconventional ordering of the movements, especially by ending with the slow movement. Most symphonies end with a rondo-form *allegro* movement triumphantly returning previous spirited themes. Instead, Tchaikovsky chose to end his life's work with a lamenting *Adagio* conveying grief and anguished intensity.

The dramatic contrast between movements is also striking with the third movement being a march with a famous melody followed by the slow fourth movement, which allows the symphony to move to a deliberately gloomy end. The music symbolically dies out with "the long dying-away of a lamenting theme to a low groan on bassoons and lower strings that is the sole substance of the finale," "ending what Tchaikovsky had virtually composed as his own epitaph." There is a "peculiar alternation of melancholy mood and almost hysterical gaiety, of grief and joy." As with his other symphonies (excluding the Third) Tchaikovsky uses mostly minor keys to create the melancholy feelings in these symphonies and in his famous First Piano Concerto.

Tchaikovsky died nine days after conducting the premiere either from drinking tainted water (the official version) or by taking his own life, or both. It was said right after his death that the *Sixth* "reflected a conscious premonition of death on (his) part."

> *Recommended – Tchaikovsky Symphonies*
> We are lucky to still have Mravinsky and Leningrad Philharmonic available for *Nos. 4-6* (DG, 1960). This great conductor and his orchestra give us idiomatic and thoroughly Russian performances of unmatched intensity. For a complete set (with *Manfred*), Jansons and the Oslo Philharmonic on Chandos is recommended. Recommended performances of individual symphonies include Muti's *Manfred* with the Philharmonia (EMI), Szell's *Fourth* with the LSO (DG), Gergiev's *Fifth* with the VPO (Philips) and any of Karajan's from the 1960s with the Berlin PO (DG). Dorati's version of *Suites No.3&4* with the Concertgebouw from the mid-1960s is recommended as is Karajan's great performance of the *Third Suite*.

♪ The Concertos

Piano Concerto No.1 in B-flat minor, Op.23

The year 1876 saw the premiere of one of the greatest piano concertos, Tchaikovsky's First, which contains the most famous opening of any piano concerto. Thus, the concerto "begins at a peak of magnificence that it never regains" as the "opening melody crumbles away and the piano goes off in search of a new theme."

Interestingly, the concerto premiered in Boston, not in Europe or Russia itself. Its dedicatee, Nicolai Rubinstein, gave the concerto a cold reception and a critical mauling, citing "its grandiose, Listzian pages, black with notes" that were "diametrically opposed to Rubinstein's refined and intimate style." This led the confidence-challenged Tchaikovsky to quickly dismiss his concerto with, "It turned out that my concerto was worthless and unplayable; passages were so fragmented, so clumsy, so badly written that they were beyond rescue…" However, as soon as Tchaikovsky could join Rubinstein in his dismissal of the great work, the latter quickly changed his verdict and became the concerto's biggest advocate. When Tchaikovsky dedicated his Second Piano Concerto to him, Rubinstein insisted this time, "there was absolutely nothing to be changed." Rubinstein died before he could play or hear the premiere of the concerto, which was not received with anywhere close to the enthusiasm of the first, despite being a fine work. Tchaikovsky's Second and Third Concertos suffer unfair neglect because they could never live up to the success of the *First*.

Violin Concerto in D, Op.35

Just as with the lone violin concertos of Beethoven and Brahms, Tchaikovsky cast his only violin concerto in the key of D, which includes the notes of the four 'open' strings of a violin. Tchaikovsky's Violin Concerto was written in 1878 and premiered in December 1881. Hans von Bülow was on the podium again, as he was for the premiere of Piano Concerto No.1. However, instead of in Boston, the premiere of this concerto was given in Vienna, with Adolf Brodsky as soloist in place of the work's dedicatee, Leopold Auer. Auer, who originally declared the concerto unplayable, would later recant and become one of the work's biggest champions. The infamous Viennese critic Eduard Hanslick claimed that in Tchaikovsky's concerto "the violin was beaten black and blue."

Tchaikovsky completed this famous concerto in less than a month. The work is so chock full of beautiful melodies that the gorgeous opening tune never has to be repeated, just as Tchaikovsky had done in the first piano concerto with its timeless opening theme. And no Romantic concerto ends "with greater finesse or panache, not even Rachmaninov."

Variations on a *Rococo* Theme, Op.33

This brilliant virtuoso display piece is a cello concerto cast in variation form instead of the more traditional fast-slow-fast format. This work shows off Tchaikovsky as a great melodist, this time using a light-hearted theme as the starting point. Tchaikovsky is tipping his hat to the style *galant* of the mid-1700s but in an utterly Romantic fashion. The work shows little of the "tormented and overwrought soul who could sometimes pound the listener into submission with emotional extremes."

The work is seldom performed as first composed by Tchaikovsky; several of the variations were rearranged before its premiere in 1877 by cellist Wilhelm Fitzhagen, for whom the work was composed. Fitzhagen also deleted one of the original variations (the eighth) and shortened the coda. Tchaikovsky completely approved of these revisions and cuts, although not all versions of events recount it that way.

> *Recommended – Tchaikovsky concertos*
> *Piano Concerto No.1* – Argerich with Dutoit and the Royal Philharmonic or the famous Van Cliburn recording with Kondrashin conducting. *Violin Concerto* – Heifetz pulls out all the stops with Reiner and the Chicago SO. Kennedy with Kamu and the LPO (EMI) is also good. *Rococo Variations* – Rostropovich (BPO, Karajan) or Ma (Pittsburgh SO, Maazel, 1992).

♪ Sergei Rachmaninoff (1873-1943)

"I feel like a ghost wandering in a world grown alien. I cannot cast out the old way of writing, and cannot acquire the new."
- Sergei Rachmaninov in 1939

Sergei Rachmaninoff (1873-1943) was the last of the 'Romantic' composers. One could view Rachmaninoff as being born too late or being stubborn in holding onto the past. He was passionate about music, which flew in the face of the obsession with artistic objectivism that dominated the 'ice-cold intellectual climate' in between the two World Wars. Rachmaninoff was not an orchestral innovator; instead, he looked back to the romanticism of Tchaikovsky. Although only one year older than Schoenberg and Ives, his music seems generations removed from theirs.

Rachmaninoff was last in the line of composer-virtuosos that began with Mozart and ran through Chopin and Liszt. While his most famous works are for piano (solo or with orchestra) he also composed some significant symphonic music. He was also an outstanding conductor, at least of his own compositions, as he limited himself to interpreting his works, and was considered one of the greatest pianists of his time. Fortunately, he did make recordings of himself as soloist, and some survive and are serviceable sonically thanks to modern engineering.

Rachmaninoff believed that, "a composer's music should express the country of his birth, his love affairs, his religion, the books that have influenced him, the pictures he loves. It should be the sum total of a composer's experience." With this view guiding his music Rachmaninoff made himself an object of ridicule who "could…do nothing right by most contemporary critics and composers." Even today he remains to some critics nothing more than "an inspired tunesmith and purveyor of sumptuously-orchestrated...Slavic melancholy...big tunes that aspire and then decline in nostalgia." Even prominent composers such as Copland and countryman Stravinsky took potshots at his distinctly old-fashioned music.

However, "his music's surface brilliance masks an innate sentimentality;...his output is far more varied than is encompassed in the image of the romantic melodist." Rachmaninoff's music remains highly popular, especially his four piano concertos, the second and third of which have become two of the more popular works in the repertoire.

Piano Concertos

When Rachmaninoff was seventeen he set about composing his First Piano Concerto, Op.1 in F sharp minor. The premiere was given in 1892 (opening movement only) and twenty-five years later he thoroughly reworked the second and third movements. This revised version of his received its initial performance in New York in 1919. The concerto therefore contains elements of both the young and the more mature composer.

The Second Piano Concerto in C minor, Op.18, published in 1901, is full of luscious melodies, like much of the music of Tchaikovsky. The very recognizable second theme in the third movement was used for the popular Sinatra song *Full Moon and Empty Arms* in 1945. This concerto was Rachmaninoff's greatest public success and premiered in November 1901. It was contemporary with the Cello Sonata, which Rachmaninoff completed in December of that year. Both reflect positive personality changes.

The Third Piano Concerto premiered in New York in 1909 on Rachmaninoff's first American tour. It is the grandest of the four and longer and deeper than No.2, even with the cuts forced on the composer. It "has none of No.2's more indulgent or excessive qualities." but at the same time makes extreme demands of agility and power on the pianist. Despite its great length "almost everything grows from the first movement's initial bars." Much of Rachmaninoff's popularity was "at a time when audiences...were often actively resistant to modern music...Rachmaninoff was the only (composer) who seemed capable of successfully maintaining the...style of the 19th century 'classics' into the 20th century." His Second and Third Piano Concertos were popular repertory works at a time when modernist works (e.g., those of Stravinsky, Schoenberg, and Bartók) were specialty items at best.

Piano Concerto No.4 (1926-27) was written in the U.S. and revised later in 1940 although ideas for it began to take shape as early as 1914. With Europe changed forever by World War I, Rachmaninoff realized there was little appetite for his gushing romanticism. He found it difficult ("I cannot cast out the old way of writing.") to bring his style in line with the times because, as with Elgar and Sibelius, he had been very successful. The premiere with the Philadelphia Orchestra under Ormandy was seen a dismal failure that led to Rachmaninoff composing nothing for five years. This reaction is reminiscent of the effect of his First Symphony.

Rhapsody on a Theme of Paganini - Rachmaninoff only composed five major works after he left Russia in 1917. One of these was his last work for piano and orchestra, the *Paganini* Rhapsody, composed in the summer of 1934 at Lake Lucerne. The theme is from the last of Paganini's *Twenty-four Caprices* for solo violin, a simple and catchy tune previously employed by Liszt and Brahms. In a twist, the composer does not state the theme until after the first variation. There are a total of twenty-four variations. Although called a rhapsody, the work is tautly constructed. Many feel this is Rachmaninoff's finest work for piano and orchestra, including those who find his works hyper romantic and sappy.

As with Tchaikovsky's *Rococo* Variations for cello and orchestra, this work is a piano concerto in 'variation on a theme' form as opposed to the sonata form usually followed by Romantic concertos. In contrast to his popular piano concertos, the *Paganini* Rhapsody is "stripped-down, sinewy, athletic, save for the gorgeous 18th variation," which is the "most unabashedly…romantic of the (variations) in its expressive gestures." The work "embodies his late style at its brilliant and witty best, it has one of the world's irresistible melodies," and even pays tribute to "the demonic Paganini in its use of the Gregorian *Dies Irae* chant."

Rachmaninoff's four piano concertos, the *Rhapsody on a Theme of Paganini*, the Second Symphony, and solo piano works "are more firmly entrenched in the concert repertoire than those of any other 20th century figure," including Stravinsky. This serves to highlight the listening public's continued ongoing affinity for Romantic music over true '20th century' or 'modern' music. However, critics and scholars have never given his music its due, despite one hundred years of sustained popularity. "Rachmaninoff may have contributed nothing to 20th century form or harmony, but he did suffuse the old forms with something highly personal, as Tchaikovsky did."

Recommended – Rachmaninoff Piano Concertos
For the complete set the live, fresh and spontaneous collaboration between Hough with Andrew Litton and the Dallas Symphony (Hyperion) is highly recommended. Janis with Dorati leading the Minneapolis and London Symphony Orchestras in the *Second* and *Third* from 1960/61 is memorable. The 1957 performance of the *Fourth* by Arturo Benedetti Michelangeli (DG 'Originals') has been highly regarded for decades, as has Richter's 1959 performance of the *Second* (DG). Andsnes performs *Piano Concertos 1&2* live with Pappano and the Berlin Philharmonic, part of a cycle completed in 2010. Horowitz in his 'golden jubilee concert' in 1978 performed the *Third* at Carnegie Hall with the NYPO under Ormandy is historic.

Symphonies

On the heels of the great success of his First Piano Concerto Rachmaninoff set out to compose his First Symphony. However, this was a disaster on several levels, including an inebriated Glazunov conducting the work. The composer characterized it as "weak, childish, strained and bombastic." Cesar Cui compared the work to "a program symphony on the Seven Plagues of Egypt." The work disappeared quickly after its failed premiere and was not rediscovered until after World War II. Rachmaninoff sunk into a state of distress that paralyzed him artistically for three years. Upon recovery he took the music world by storm with his glorious Second Piano Concerto, Op.18 in C minor. It was an instant success and has remained so.

He had more success with his Second Symphony in E minor, Op.27, although Rachmaninoff waited more than ten years after the failure of the First. The E minor Symphony was finished in 1907 and conducted in St. Petersburg by Rachmaninoff early in 1908. After the disaster surrounding the First Symphony Rachmaninoff was prepared to swear off the form, "Curse them! I don't know how to write them...I don't want to" he wrote to a friend. Fortunately, he did know how to write symphonies and the *Second* was a success and has remained popular. There is an "overwhelming nostalgia" to the introduction of this symphony. Both the Second Symphony and Third Piano Concerto "display...a greater confidence in the handling of large-scale structures."

Symphonic Dances, Op.45

Thirty years after his successful Second Symphony, Rachmaninoff completed his *Symphonic* Dances, Op.45, which are representative of his late style. It even includes the novelty of an alto saxophone. Although adventurous for the composer with its "mild metric shifts, jagged rhythms, and chromatic harmonies," it was still very conservative for 1940. The composer commented on the work that "it must have been my last spark."

Rachmaninoff originally planned to call his final work 'Fantastic Dances' and toyed with the idea of using *Midday, Twilight*, and *Midnight* as titles for the three pieces. The work was dedicated to and premiered by Eugene Ormandy in Philadelphia in 1941. The work got off to a rough start with audiences because the orchestra was ill-prepared at the premiere. Although rarely performed until recent years, some now considered it Rachmaninoff's greatest orchestral work. It is in three movements; the finale quotes the *Dies Irae* chant melody used previously in the *Paganini* Rhapsody and the Third Symphony, an interesting choice in a work of dances.

- 19 -

The Late Romantics

Bruckner, Mahler, Strauss, and Sibelius

If the music of Brahms and Tchaikovsky avoided public uproar, some of their contemporaries and immediate successors did create controversy (Strauss, Mahler) or encouraged ridicule (Bruckner).

The 1960s saw a renaissance of Bruckner and Mahler and the start of a popularity for their symphonies never previously realized. Mahler's rise was catalyzed by scholars deciding that he was the father of, or at least the inspiration for, serialism. This is certainly a tough association to accept as one would think that the 20th century *avant-garde* would want to run away as far as possible from the bombastic orchestral monstrosities of Mahler and his post-Romanticism.

Although the men and their symphonies were different, Mahler and Bruckner have been closely associated in discussions of classical music. Unlike Mahler who often attached programs and corresponding chorale sections to his symphonies, Bruckner's symphonies are pure absolute music. Mahler would also rise to this challenge, possibly influenced by hearing Bruckner's symphonies, but Mahler's symphonic works would be more programmatic than Bruckner's. While there may be an atmosphere of mysticism and/or spirituality surrounding Bruckner's massive works, this hardly approaches anything of a specific, programmatic nature.

Both Mahler and Bruckner adopted Austrian folk song themes in their symphonies for their *Ländler* (dance) movements. Bruckner "embraces the naïveté of the folk music of Upper Austria," his homeland while Mahler used the melodious folk tunes of his native Bohemia. "Basic to Mahler's melodic inspiration and harmonic world is the folk song in all its vital and most genuine essence." But beyond that, most of the comparisons and similarities have been exaggerated. One difference that sets their symphonies apart is that Mahler's symphonies get going a lot quicker than Bruckner's, which have "almost always an impetuous and fiery first movement of vast proportions." "The Mahler symphonies represent the last great expression of that dynasty which went back to Beethoven;" Mahler carried "the formal process and the spiritual dimensions of romanticism to the point of saturation." With Mahler each symphony "offered a different answer to the question of what the genre could be at the turn of the 20th century." In Bruckner's symphonies we rediscover "the symphonic tradition of Beethoven filtered through the Wagnerian experience." "The Bruckner symphony brims and blazes with an inner spiritual fire."

Although Sibelius might seem to belong in the chapter on nationalist composers, I have chosen to put him among the late Romantics, as he is the last of the great symphonic Romantic composers. While he personifies Finland and his music evokes the Nordic north, unlike Bartók, Smetana, and Vaughan Williams, he did not actually seek out native folk music as an influence on his music. Perhaps because he did not hide his ardent patriotism, Sibelius's music was simply heard as Finnish. The decision to include Sibelius with Bruckner, Mahler, and Strauss is in recognition of the bridge his music forms between late Romantic and early 20th century orchestral music. Particularly, works such as the fourth symphony pointed to the cold, austere style that would dominate 'modern' music.

♪ Anton Bruckner (1824-1896)

> *"I could write the way other people want, but I dare not."*
> - Anton Bruckner

According to Deryck Cooke, Bruckner was the first Romantic composer to take up the "metaphysical challenge" of Beethoven's Ninth Symphony. In fact, music historian Alfred Einstein takes the position that it was Bruckner, not Brahms, who "once more attained the monumental stature of true symphony." He points out that Brahms' symphonies are really rooted in chamber music. Nowhere is the distinction between Bruckner and Brahms more apparent than in the former's ability to restore the great *Adagio* form of Beethoven and the "somewhat incoherent outer movements."

Bruckner comes from the symphonic tradition of Beethoven, "but when it comes to musical expression…he's really the link between Wagner and Mahler in his musical grammar and in how he uses musical form." "There are aspects of Bruckner's writing that Mahler carried forward in a more modern way." According to Cooke, "To express his own personal vision he had to create a new type of symphony – vast, stark and rough-hewn."

Bruckner was a "direct descendent of the old Austrian instrumental church-music composers" and renewed the symphony as an "expression of transcendent emotion and a confession of personal faith." This is not surprising as Bruckner was a devout Catholic, a "humble church organist" whose belief in the mysteries of the Church permeated his music. While church organist in Linz, Bruckner studied harmony and counterpoint under the renowned music theory teacher Simon Sechter.

Using "dance forms and solemn chorales" Bruckner gives expression to "love of nature, piety…and mysticism." Unlike Mahler, Bruckner did not wrestle with questions on the meaning of life; his faith in God was unshakeable. He believed that the purpose of his work was to give glory to God and his music concentrates on man's awareness of God. Bruckner's symphonies employ "preclassical structural devices" and they bear "unmistakable traces of organ improvisation."

Falling under the influence of Wagner early on, Bruckner turned from early organ and choral religious works to the symphony. Bruckner was captivated by Wagner's music "with its luxuriant orchestra, its harmonic daring, and its complex motivic textures." He eventually established a unique symphonic style and, unlike Wagner and Liszt, he did not embrace programmatic music. Bruckner was a "romantic of the first order…as he made pure sound the basis of his symphonies." Bruckner's worship of Wagner bordered on the pathetic; he actually dropped to one knee and kissed Wagner's hand on one occasion, stating, "Oh Master, I worship you." This was too much even for the egomaniacal Wagner who promptly told the church organist to pull himself together.

However, his early alliance with Wagner put Bruckner in the cross hairs of the most notorious music critic in history, Eduard Hanslick of Vienna, perhaps because Hanslick recognized that Bruckner's music "is much more revolutionary than people usually perceive." Rumor had it that Hanslick lay awake nights plotting the destruction of Bruckner and the critic actually tried to prevent performances of his works.

Bruckner was an extreme late-bloomer, as all of his major works were composed after the age of forty. Even starting in middle age he lacked self-confidence and deferred to critics, friends and publishers, allowing them to eviscerate his works, apparently to make them more palatable. For example, he favored abrupt contrasts as opposed to smooth transitions, a feature his students and friends thought undesirable for the public. These well-intentioned 'editors' aimed to tailor Bruckner's works to what they thought the public, publishers, and critics wanted to hear instead of what Bruckner intended. Luckily much scholarship and effort has given us most of his symphonies as Bruckner intended them, although several have more than one 'definitive' edition. Not surprisingly Bruckner's original intentions are superior to any of the versions 'improved' by others.

This resulted in a confusing maze of versions for many of his symphonies, both authentic and eviscerated; Bruckner's students did not hesitate to take a knife to his symphonies. Three of these students were the brothers Schalk and Ferdinand Löwe. As a result of this, his symphonies did not premiere as Bruckner originally intended. An additional factor making him agreeable to continual revision could have been the fact that "his success as an improviser at the organ gave him an unconscious prejudice against setting his work in stone for all time."

The Bruckner Society of Vienna (founded in 1927 in Leipzig) has tried to restore the symphonies to Bruckner's original intentions, or as close as possible. The result is two 'definitive' editions, named for Robert Haas (published in the 1930s) and Leopold Nowak (post-World War II). Both were Austrian musicologists and the head of the Society at the time a 'definitive' edition was released. Nowak's later editions are purportedly "based on a more literal reading of (Bruckner's) hand-written scores." Therefore, conductors today can choose which edition they wish to perform and this decision will be noted on the recording (see below recommendations for recordings of the Fourth Symphony).

In addition to the issue of the 'Haas' and 'Nowak' editions for many of his symphonies, there were multiple versions of some symphonies published during Bruckner's lifetime; for example, the '1888-89' version of the Third Symphony. In fact, the Third Symphony exists or has existed, in at least six versions (worked on by the composer from 1873-89) and as many as nine. The Bruckner Society has sought to restore Bruckner's true intentions to his symphonies and remove damage done by the composer's well-intentioned but misguided students and publishers. The bottom line is confusion due to several of Bruckner's symphonies having two definitive editions ('Haas' and 'Nowak') of multiple versions by the composer or by the composer along with Löwe and the brothers Schalk.

What this boils down to for the listener are multiple performance versions of the same symphony, allowing one to listen to and enjoy the various editions of each version and choosing a favorite to own or owning multiple. Some of the differences are significant in terms of timing and scoring; in other cases, there is basically one version and very little to distinguish the Nowak and Haas editions (e.g., Symphony No.7).

> "A little, timid, silly-looking organist with gargantuan ideas."
> - Jan Swafford

The obstacles to Bruckner were many. He was humble to a fault and his lack of self-confidence and deference to almost anyone else led to constant revisions of and cuts to his symphonies. He was socially inept, from a poor rural background trying to make his way in Vienna. He actually tipped a conductor who led a performance of one of his symphonies and pathetically worshipped at the feet of Wagner. He was under constant attack by the notorious Viennese music critic Eduard Hanslick. Wagner was the critic's actual target but the egomaniacal composer was too popular and established and probably didn't care what Hanslick said anyway. Bruckner, by openly aligning himself with the Wagner camp, made himself an easy target for the critic's venom and could offer no resistance. Hanslick simply could not envision a world of music in which Brahms and Strauss, or Schumann and Bruckner shared the same concert stage.

One has to believe that Bruckner's deep, unwavering faith allowed him to persist with his music, despite obstacles and rejection. Although he allowed others to eviscerate his symphonies, hoping to make them more likely to be performed, he continued to write in the same symphonic style over and over. His opening movements take forever to develop, his adagios, while some of the most beautiful, are also some of the most gargantuan symphonic movements. Bruckner's strong religious instinct remains central to his creativity, and the "awe-inspiring grandeur, innocence, and sense of space" expanded the boundaries of the symphony in his day as Berlioz had in his.

Bruckner's symphonies have been likened to Gothic cathedrals. His mastery of counterpoint "makes his nine symphonies into densely woven polyphonic designs." Just as some people may feel all such cathedrals look alike, so to some, all of Bruckner's symphonies may sound the same. But as with cathedrals, each symphony has its own individual character and presence. He shied away from complex textures, preferring instead to build emphatic statements in blocks of sound. Bruckner detractors are also bothered by the repetition of material that is just not very stimulating. What is true is that Bruckner's symphonies begin alike, and in the same way as Beethoven's *Ninth*, with "a vague agitation in the strings out of which a theme gradually condenses and then builds up in a crescendo."

Bruckner was not respected at all in his lifetime, his music described with words such as 'dull' and 'pompous'; "…the highly charged intensity of his style was attributed to neuroticism." Brahms referred to Bruckner as "that country bumpkin who wrote symphonic boa constrictors." In fact, only since around 1960 has Bruckner been recognized as one of the outstanding Romantic composers. As with Gustav Mahler, his popularity has taken off in recent decades as his symphonies have been championed and recorded by leading conductors. Bruckner's standing as a great Romantic symphonist is solidified, but during his lifetime his symphonies never caught on and his music had no following. When they were performed the public reaction was one of confusion at the scale of the works, and that was when they were well-received. Additionally, Bruckner paid to have his works performed. He even withstood the humiliation of almost the entire audience walking out during a performance of his Third Symphony (dedicated to Wagner) with Bruckner himself conducting. Interestingly, the story goes that one of the few people remaining to the conclusion was a young student sitting up in the balcony, none other than Gustav Mahler, who remained to cheer the work.

Even today critics of Bruckner's symphonies complain not only about their length or that the first movements seem to take forever to get going. Put bluntly, many feel he wrote the same symphony nine times, although this exaggeration is more to make a point than to be taken literally. A similar accusation was tossed at Vivaldi for writing the same concerto six hundred times; but at least the Baroque Italian 'concerto machine' was paid well to churn out scores of very similar *concerti*. On the contrary, Robert Dearling feels that "in beating his own symphonic path Bruckner rarely retraced his steps. Each symphony is unique in form and distinct in style, even though his musical language is immediately recognizable."

The works of Anton Bruckner are massive, "but underneath…were clearly organized blocks of melodies and the mortar to hold them together." The symphonies contain a narrative continuity throughout the sixty, seventy, eighty minutes of music, with some single movements longer than the four combined movements of a Mozart or Haydn symphony. Bruckner wrote slow movements that went on for twenty minutes or more, often marked *feierlich* or 'solemn'. This was accomplished in part in the finale by revisiting themes that had been developed in the opening movement.

Alfred Einstein, who called Bruckner "a Romantic of the first order", said, "he made pure sound the basis of his symphonies." Einstein went further to characterize Bruckner's symphonies as breathing a cosmic spirit, as rich in invention and "primitive creative power". In his music we share Bruckner's experiences of "doubt and joy, despair and exultation."

Arnold Schoenberg stated that the scherzo movements of Bruckner's symphonies, "evoke some kind of religious ideal involving nature...a kind of message that is allied to the Infinite." His symphonies contributed significantly to the advancement of the genre as a massive "visionary expression with a broad yet cogent development of...material." Critic Harold Schonberg sees the essence of Bruckner's symphonies to be the "slow, inexorable, solemn procession of harmonies." And according to Max Graf, a student of Bruckner who later became the leading Viennese music critic, Bruckner's symphonies provide "a world of spirits in the bass, which accompanied the harmonies like shadows in the depths...the fundamental steps of the bass...had cosmic importance."

Today, of Bruckner's nine symphonies the most popular are the Fourth ('Romantic'), Seventh, Eighth and Ninth; the last of which he left unfinished in three movements. Symphony No.4 was the first to get a favorable reception from the music-going public in Vienna.

Symphony No.4 in E-flat, 'Romantic'

The *Romantic* Symphony has a pastoral feeling and atmosphere, with Bruckner's characteristic prominent use of horns. The horn call sounded at the opening is the first movement's central theme and concludes the final movement as well. For Bruckner, this symphony is relatively light fare and pastoral in mood from the opening horn call. Bruckner attached the label 'Romantic' to the symphony himself, although the work is not programmatic nor is it any more 'romantic' than his other symphonies.

The original version dates from 1874. Never performed or published, Bruckner revised it into an almost new work, replacing the finale and extensively reworking the first two movements for a 1881 performance in Vienna, then made additional minor changes for a performance in Karlsruhe in the same year. This symphony has a convoluted revision history, with Bruckner and friends continuing to make cuts and changes through 1886. The resultant version of 1886 and the version performed at Karlsruhe are the only two authentic versions, both published by the Bruckner Society as the Haas ('1878/80') and Nowak editions.

Symphony No.5

The *Fifth* is Bruckner's only symphony that begins with a slow introduction. It also contains a huge finale, "staggeringly complex yet always logical." The slow second movement has become famous on its own.

Conductor Franz Welser-Möst feels there is a deep link between Beethoven's *Ninth* and Bruckner's *Fifth*, beyond the similarity of reassembling previous motifs in the introductions to the last movements. Both symphonies "emerge from darkness into light." This conductor also sees Bruckner's fugal development in the finale as "incredibly modern and so totally weird" in that "it passes through several keys and throws everything upside down," yet Bruckner shows great mastery and keeps the fugal structure intact.

Symphony No. 7

Bruckner's early symphonies were dismissed as the unplayable music of a wild man. But the success of the *Seventh*, after the ridicule and failure of his previous symphonies, finally ensured Bruckner's reputation and stature.

The spacious and lyrical *Seventh* abounds in rich Wagnerian harmonies and is the "most generously melodic of the symphonies…and one of warm serenity." The quiet opening, followed by an ascending arpeggio that leads to the first theme has been compared to the opening of Beethoven's *Ninth*, as well as the A-B-A-B-A form of the *Adagio*. The slow second movement has become famous on its own. The symphony has the typical four Bruckner movements with a funeral-like *Adagio* (an elegy for Wagner that was actually played at the Bruckner's funeral), a scherzo like a thunderstorm dissected by a *Ländler* trio section, and an expansive, organ-like finale that builds in cumulative layers and volume to the finish.

Of added advantage to the *Seventh* is the fact there is no confusion as to Bruckner's true intentions as there are no major differences in the editions available for performance. The *Seventh* has always remained very much in Bruckner's original version, although there are Haas and Nowak editions.

Symphony No. 8

This massive work is often considered Bruckner's greatest achievement. The third movement, the beautiful *Adagio*, "unfolds in visions of religious ecstasy" and was considered by the composer (and probably correctly) to be his greatest single movement. In the finale Bruckner "unleashes the brass as if a dozen cavalries were coming."

Bruckner sent the original version to conductor Hermann Levi, who was hesitant to accept the gigantic symphony that dwarfed anything before it. Predictably, the crushed Bruckner set about drastically revising the score in 1887 "somewhat pruned and with many dramatic new features." Hans Richter gave the premiere of the revised *Eighth* in 1892. The version conducted by Richter is not definitive as it contains cuts to the '1890 version' later restored by both Haas and Nowak. Given its size it is not surprising that the *Eighth* presents the largest differences between the Haas and Nowak editions and conductors are fairly evenly split between them.

Symphony No.9

This symphony was begun by Bruckner nine years before his death but never completed. He worked on it for almost a decade, from September 1887 to October 1896, but could not bring himself to finish it. Although he had finished the first three movements by November 1894, he could not compose a concluding fourth movement before his death in October 1896.

Bruckner did get through most of the final movement but being part of a Bruckner symphony, not surprisingly it exists in at least six versions. Bruckner's 'unfinished' symphony looks ahead to both major schools of the first half of the 20th century, the neo-Classicism of Stravinsky and the Second Viennese School. It looks to the former with the pounding rhythms of the scherzo; to the latter with its "wide interval leaps and grinding dissonance."

"…the violence alternating with near-serenity shows Bruckner coming to terms with the warring elements of his tormented personality and giving them form." The *Ninth* was not performed until 1903, more than six years after the composer's death. The premiere was led ironically by Ferdinand Löwe, who along with other well-intentioned friends, had eviscerated many of Bruckner's previous symphonies.

Both Bruckner and Mahler left their final symphonies unfinished, a fact that draws comparison between the two great Austrian composers. In Mahler's case, his tenth numbered symphony was incomplete.

Recommended – Bruckner symphonies
Complete sets – Eugen Jochum recorded two complete cycles, one with the Berlin Philharmonic (DG) and a later set with the Dresden Staatskapelle (EMI). Jochum was a distinguished Brucknerian and these remain the standards among complete sets. George Tintner in his complete cycle (Naxos), recorded most of the symphonies (with the Royal Scottish National Orchestra) using the earliest published version. However, better versions of certain symphonies are available from notable Brucknerians; *Symphony No.4* – Klemperer and the Philharmonia (Novak edition, EMI); *Symphony No.5* – Karajan and the BPO (DG, 1975); *Symphony No.7* – Karajan leading the Vienna Philharmonic (DG) in the great maestro's last recording. An alternate choice is Riccardo Chailly's reading with the Concertgebouw (Philips); *Symphony No.8* – Herbert von Karajan leads the Vienna Philharmonic in a gorgeous reading; *Symphony No.9* – Bruno Walter and the Columbia Symphony is a great vintage recording of Bruckner's final *Unfinished* symphony (late 1950s) as is Giulini and the Vienna Philharmonic (DG, 1989).

♪ Gustav Mahler (1860-1911)

If Bruckner is about religion and his symphonies musical processions to the glory of God, then Mahler is about mysticism: searching for answers to universal questions and struggling with the inadequacy of the answers found. Conflict-ridden, Mahler saw himself in the role of an architect whose gigantic structures arose practically bar-by-bar and contrary to every rule of conventional formal language. Listening to his massive symphonies, one can share his "futile struggle to make sense out of life." Some critics, e.g., Harold Schonberg, contrast Beethoven's heroic triumph over his struggles with Mahler as a wimpering weakling, even suggesting that Mahler reveled in his misery.

Mahler makes his view of the symphony clear with the following statement, "A symphony is a world, it must embrace everything." He is the "quintessential representative" of *Weltanschauungsmusik*, 'music expressive of a world outlook', a term coined by German music historian Rudolf Stephan. Mahler intended his symphonies to be "so great that the whole world is actually reflected therein…" "In (Mahler's) music there is everything. It is universal. You find nature, sarcasm, love, hatred, the grotesque, tragedy and comedy…people find echoes of their own fears, doubts and suffering."

With this view we can see why his symphonies are as massive as they are. In fact, some of his symphonies require the most colossal performing apparatus, not just an enormous orchestra but several large choruses (in No.8) and a multitude of vocal soloists. Mahler broke up the opera-oratorio and sonata-symphony forms and "recast them into one immense musical edifice." He justified the scale of his symphonies by comparing them to operas, which take up an entire evening. Mahler tried to do in his symphonies what Wagner did in his music dramas: create his own world. "Just as Wagner had introduced the symphony into opera…Mahler restored opera to the symphony."

He used his symphonies to explore nature in its widest sense – life and death, earth and universe. As such, his music is pantheistic where Bruckner's was religious. Mahler summed this up, "My music is, everywhere and always, only a sound of Nature."

Mahler was the first composer to instruct conductors to perform the music according to their personal preferences. Different interpretations of most symphonic works will sound the same from night to night, orchestra to orchestra, even conductor to conductor. But two concerts of a Mahler symphony can differ by as much as ten minutes. The moods of many sections of his symphonies are also under the control of the conductor. Mahler gave so much latitude to the conductor perhaps because he saw himself, and was viewed by the public, as a conductor who composed music, not as a composer who conducted.

A non-religious Jew, forced (for practical reasons) to convert to Catholicism because of his prominent opera post in anti-Semitic turn-of-the-century Vienna, Mahler spent his life pursuing spirituality, "in search for his God." His symphonies capture his complex emotions and thoughts at different points on this journey. His early symphonies are "steeped in the mysticism of natural beauty," his symphonies gigantic musical discourses on "life, death and renewed life." The meaning of life obsessed Mahler to the point that Mahler acolyte (and later great conductor) Bruno Walter, who spent years with Mahler at Hamburg theatre and Vienna Opera, felt that "each of Mahler's symphonies was a new attempt to answer the questions eternally plaguing him."

"If we want thousands to hear us...we have to make a lot of noise."
- Gustav Mahler

Mahler's symphonies, despite being massive and illustrative of "the breakup of Classical models," were still direct descendants of the symphonies of Beethoven. "Mahler extended Beethoven's concept of the symphony as a bold personal statement." Harold Schonberg takes this further to propose that the slow movements of Mahler's symphonies (as well as those of Bruckner) were actually "unconscious attempts to rewrite the adagio of (Beethoven's) Ninth." Schonberg the critic was not sympathetic to Mahler and he could only manage back-handed compliments such as, "There are sections in most of his symphonies where the undoubted brilliance of Mahler the musician conquers Mahler the Deep Thinker."

Mahler's symphonies are all presented in distinct movements, "but they are strongly linked by connections not so much of material as of narrative." He was last in the line of the Viennese symphonists (the 'First Viennese School') from Haydn to Bruckner and was a prime influence on the Second Viennese School.

"Tradition is laziness! In every performance the work must be born anew."
- Gustav Mahler

Rare for most great composers, Mahler was recognized in his day as a great conductor (as were Mendelssohn and Richard Strauss); Schumann, Brahms, and Bruckner, on the other hand, were not very effective conductors, even of their own works. In fact, he was more prominent as a conductor while alive than as a composer, overlooking no detail, always striving for unattainable perfection from his orchestras. He revitalized the Vienna Opera in his ten years there before coming to New York. Mahler composed mostly in summers between busy conducting seasons.

Mahler had a reputation for being despotic, and held the head conducting post of the New York Philharmonic from 1909 to 1911, a brief tenure during which he is credited with improving the orchestra. Terminal illness forced his resignation in February 1911 and he returned to Europe where he died three months later.

However, it is held that he predicted as a composer "my time will come" although the actual quote from Mahler is, "My time will come when his (Strauss') is up", acknowledging that Strauss, not he, "already enjoys immortality here on earth." It did, but he would have had to live to be over one hundred years of age to enjoy it. Ever since his 100th birthday in 1960 his music has gained enormous popularity as prominent conductors such as Leonard Bernstein championed his symphonies. By the 1970s and 1980s Mahler was one of the more popular symphonists in concert halls and on recordings. The dominance of the CD format over the past two decades has helped even more as his massive symphonies, which used to occupy several records, fit either on a single disc (e.g., the very popular *First* and *Fifth*) or accommodated on two discs. Sometimes a double CD set of Mahler will offer two symphonies.

Mahler composed five orchestral song cycles (if *Das Lied von der Erde* is counted as a song cycle and not a vocal symphony), nine complete symphonies and left the *Tenth* unfinished. He used many of his song melodies in his symphonies as well as some texts of his songs for the vocal movements of symphonies. He revised most of his works repeatedly, sometimes after each performance he conducted.

Symphony No.1

It is ironic that Mahler's instrumental legacy (along with his *Lieder*) is limited to his massive symphonies because he initially struggled with symphonic form. In fact he hesitated to call his First Symphony, completed in 1888, 'symphony' at all but rather a 'symphonic poem'. It surely would have been the most massive work to be called a 'poem' but he did eventually settle on it being a symphony, after discarding a fifth movement, the so-called *Blumine*. This is included by some conductors in modern recordings, despite its omission by the composer, who felt the *Blumine* movement was not sufficiently symphonic. However, feelings are mixed on whether the *Blumine* movement adds anything to the overall symphony and whether including it actually defies the wishes of the composer. According to critic Martin Bookspan putting this 'extra' movement back within the rest of the First Symphony "convinces me that Mahler was right in ultimately dropping this movement."

The First Symphony, occasionally labeled *Titan*, is a powerful, all-instrumental work and, for a first published symphony, is as successful as Brahms' *First*. However, as Brahms did, Mahler did have several "failed" attempts at a first symphony, which were not up to his standards to present to the world as a symphony. In Mahler's case he composed at least four earlier works but no manuscripts survive. However, the fact that we know they did exist helps explain how Mahler had mastered so much by his 'First' symphony. The *First* starts "with an elemental hum – the note A whistling in all registers of the strings," over almost sixty bars. Mahler called the effect an 'unending spring', some think of it as 'dawn in the forest.'

For the first time a symphonic composer subjected 'low class' popular music (Austrian folk tunes) and natural sounds (e.g., the opening is supposed to evoke dawn) to symphonic treatment. The folk elements in Mahler's symphonies, most notably the *Ländler*, are "deliberately left unassimilated, unfused with the strikingly advanced orchestral style in which they are embedded." He also draws themes from his *Songs of a Wayfarer* cycle of *Lieder*. Another novelty is that although the extensive first movement follows sonata form, the music rarely leaves the home key, "and absolutely nothing dramatic happens until the very end (of the opening movement)."

Mahler faced some trouble arranging for a first performance of the symphony because most conductors considered it too modern. As a result, he took the work to Budapest and conducted the premiere himself to a cool reception. In particular, the "mock funeral march and the turbulent finale presented the conservative (Hungarian) audience with problems." Mahler himself conducted more performances of his First Symphony than any of his other symphonies. The finale is very exciting (a similar finale is found in Mahler's *Fifth*) opening with what David Hurwitz describes as "CRASH! SCREAM! THUD!"

Symphony No.2 in C minor 'Resurrection'

The *First*, while being rather large in scope and orchestral requirements, was chamber music compared to some of the symphonies Mahler had in his future, starting with the great Second Symphony (nicknamed *Resurrection*), among the largest compositions in the history of music. In this symphony Mahler reveals his ongoing struggle between religion and spirituality. Mahler claimed the connection between the First and Second Symphonies was the funeral march first movement of the Second Symphony symbolizing the burying of the 'hero' of his *First*. "It is the hero of my First Symphony whom I bear to his grave."

This symphony, in C minor, contains a massive instrumental opening movement. This represents a symbolic struggle with death, and concludes with an equally massive choral finale based on Klopstock's *Resurrection Ode*, which had a profound influence on Mahler when sung by a boys' choir. Thus the finale and its references to the afterlife serves as rebuttal to the death obsession of the opening movement. The first movement grew out of a symphonic poem called *Totenfeier* ('Funeral Rites') that Mahler had composed around the same time as the First Symphony.

For example, the implied questions of the first movement, "Why do you live? Why do you suffer?" are answered explicitly in the finale with the words, "O believe, you were not born in vain! Have not vainly lived and suffered!" So after all of these questions and seemingly some answers, the *Second* is "essentially optimistic", progressing "from a song of death to a song of hope."

In attempting to explain what conclusions, if any, he reached in this symphony for us to take, Mahler explains, "there is no judgment...there is no punishment and no reward...we know and are." It is hard to tell whether this was a conclusion Mahler felt was final and was satisfied with or, more likely, it represents the point he was at in his constant struggle with such universal questions. In all of Mahler's symphonies there is "always the hope of the new mingled with the death of the old."

Mahler left us detailed insights for each movement in program notes he provided. Of the first movement, which he called 'Funeral Pomp', he asks, "is life just an empty dream? Do our life and death have meaning?" Mahler believed we must answer these questions in order to go on living. The second through fourth movements were conceived by Mahler as an interlude (*intermezzi*), the *Andante* second movement "a blissful moment in the life of the dear departed and a sad recollection of his youth and lost innocence."

In his Second, Third, and Fourth symphonies Mahler included sung texts to help clarify the narrative and "to supply added variety and invoke the magisterial example...of Beethoven's *Ninth*." The similarity of Mahler's Second to Beethoven's Ninth includes the use of a choir and the dissonant crash at the start. The first appearance of a voice is a solo soprano soaring heavenward. The work "begins with a furious orchestral assault and progresses to a huge choral and orchestral climax."

Mahler was Director of the Vienna Opera for ten years (1897-1907), a period which also produced Symphonies Four through Eight.

Symphony No.4 in G

The Fourth Symphony was completed in 1901 although the song that forms the final movement, "The Heavenly Life", was completed in 1892 and had been performed alone. This song is Mahler's attempt, through symphonic song, to describe a child's vision of paradise.

In comparison to some of his monstrosities, the Fourth is an overture for chamber symphony. It is 'only' around forty-five minutes and actually employs an orchestra of 'normal' size. Conductor Iván Fischer characterizes it as "a chamber or neo-Classical symphony." These factors help to make it Mahler's most lyrical symphony and one of his most accessible. The twist in the *Fourth* is a finale featuring a soprano soloist singing text extracted from German folk poetry. In typical Mahler form the text is about yearning for heaven while tolerating a miserable existence on earth.

Symphony No.5 in C-sharp minor

The Fifth was composed in the summers of 1901 and 1902 and conducted by Mahler in Köln in October of 1904. It is the first of his final four purely orchestral symphonies, all in a minor key (the Fifth, Sixth, Seventh, and Ninth). Conductor Markus Stenz proposes that one "could probably get a perfect feeling for the universe of Gustav Mahler" by listening only to this one of his symphonies. Jonathan Kramer states that the Fifth was Mahler's first attempt at "purely musical expression." He goes on to draw the distinction between the *Second* and the *Fifth* to be that the former "proceeds from death to resurrection" while the latter "moves from death to life."

Although the *Fifth* is dominated by wind music, the famous *Adagietto*, "a compound of airy lightness and ornate melancholia," uses only strings and harp. "It's kind of timeless, almost defying gravity in the way it flows." Mahler kept revising the orchestration of his Fifth Symphony until his death. As with Symphony No.1 (if the *Blumine* movement is included) and No.2, the *Fifth* is cast in five movements that fall into three parts. The middle section serves to bridge the first and third parts.

Symphony No.6 in A minor

Although Mahler removed the subtitle *Tragic* just before publication, the question remains whether Mahler was expressing a death wish with his Sixth Symphony? At the time he was composing this symphony he was also setting Rückert's *Kindertotenlieder* ('songs on the death of children') to music. His wife Alma felt the *Sixth* was "the most completely personal of his works…" It is his most 'Classical' in form and layout and many consider this to be Mahler's most cohesive and tautly organized symphony. But Alma worried about her husband's apparent fascination with music of death. Even as Alma was giving birth to his children he would voice "his darkest emotions" through the music he was composing at those times.

"This strange, dark, massive work confused listeners." Maybe this was not unintentional as Mahler felt that the *Sixth* contained "riddles" that could only be solved by first digesting its five predecessors. The symphony uses a wide assortment of percussion instruments and devices, along with his standard gigantic orchestral forces.

The final movement is massive, by far the longest at over thirty minutes, and most complex of the four movements. The extended drama of the finale makes "the tragic aspects of the symphony become most clear," and "the ending…is the most pessimistic and shattering in the whole repertoire." The symphony ends "unremittingly in the minor" without Mahler's typical "transformation into a glorious ending or peaceful resignation."

Symphony No.7 in E minor
'Awkwardly structured', 'beguiling', Mahler's 'problem symphony'; these are some of the phrases used through the decades by critics of Mahler's Seventh. Even the noted Mahler champion Deryck Cooke found "something irreducibly problematic about this symphony."

The symphony has a five-movement symmetric structure, with a 'bridge' scherzo movement connecting two extended *Andante* movements which Mahler labeled *Nachtmusik* I & II ('Night music'). As usual Mahler devotes a movement expressly to the theme of death, not with a funeral march but with the scherzo, here "unmistakably a dance of death." Romantic composers found appealing the incorporation of people's nocturnal imaginations into their music. While Mozart's 'A Little Night Music' and the *Serenata Notturna* are delightfully upbeat, Romantic and post-Romantic composers such as Saint-Saëns in his *Danse Macabre*, Richard Strauss in the *Alpine* Symphony or Rachmaninoff in the *Symphonic Dances*, took advantage of popular beliefs in sinister happenings, perpetrated by ghosts and evil spirits, once the sun had set on the day.

As is the case with Mahler's symphonies it is not programmatic, and if Mahler has a story to tell with it the plot line is all over the map. Unlike Beethoven's *Ninth*, which is clearly positive, a celebration of the brother hood of man with Schindler's *Ode to Joy* as the 'plot', Mahler's *Seventh* see-saws back-and-forth between death and life; between the macabre and the joyous, reflecting the neurosis of its composer.

The work features instruments and combinations rarely heard in symphonic music, including mandolin and guitar.

Symphony No.9 in D minor
Bruckner and Mahler are often coupled and considered together. Although they do not have as much in common as the association might suggest, there are clear similarities. Both composed massive symphonies, on a scale previously unapproached. They both had spiritual themes and overtones to their music, although they approached spirituality in very different ways. Bruckner was a devout Catholic, church organist and, while very insecure about his talents as a composer, secure in his faith and beliefs. Mahler was a Jew who converted to Catholicism out of necessity (because of bigotry in Vienna and the musical post he held). He was neurotic and constantly struggled with his spirituality, searching for answers to universal questions through his music, specifically his massive symphonies, and to mysteries beyond our capabilities; mysteries which Bruckner accepted as part of his faith.

Although Mahler's conversion to Christianity does not appear to be a true conversion, the mysticism of Roman Catholicism probably attracted Mahler, along with the focus on the mystery of the afterlife. His Second Symphony, 'Resurrection', attests strongly to this. After the grandiose symphonies that became his trademark, culminating with the *Eighth*, 'Symphony of a Thousand', Mahler's last two completed symphonies, *Das Lied von der Erde* and the Ninth Symphony, "breathe an inner serenity and resignation."

What makes the *Ninth* unique is a "synthesis of the sharp-edged style of the *Sixth* and *Seventh* with the rarefied, contrapuntal technique" of his symphonic song cycle *Das Lied von der Erde* resulting in "music that is more closely allied with…Schoenberg than with Mahler's earlier romanticism." The *Ninth* was completed in 1908; the previous year Mahler's world had fallen apart both professionally and personally. First he was forced to resign as music director of the Vienna State Opera due to the rampant anti-Semitism in the Viennese press. Within a couple of months his daughter Marie died at age five and he learned that he had a serious heart condition. It is in this condition that Mahler set out to compose his Ninth Symphony.

This symphony contains a mad, macabre *Rondo-Burleske* third movement that releases "the inner tensions of the first two movements." In the "broadly sweeping *Adagio*...Mahler makes overt his farewell...into a purely spiritual realm." It is "a magnificent conclusion to his symphonic struggles."

Recommended – Mahler's Symphonies

It is not recommended to purchase a complete set from a single conductor. Even the best Mahler interpreters do not get all nine symphonies 'right.' I have combed the reviews of experts and the large volume of recommendations offered online and have put together the following recommendations for the individual symphonies:

Symphony No.1 - Solti/Chicago Symphony (Decca, 1990); Kubelik/Bavarian RSO (DG, 1967); Horenstein/London SO (Unicorn, 1970s). *Symphony No.2* - Rattle/CBSO (EMI) and Bernstein/NYPO (DG) are classic recordings from the 1980s, with Bernstein's interpretation worth the price just for the conclusion. A vintage disc is by Klemperer/Philharmonia (EMI). *Symphony No.3* – Rattle/CBSO (EMI, 1997); Horenstein/LSO (Archipel, 1961). *Symphony No.4* – Szell/Cleveland Orchestra (CBS/Sony, 1965); Maazel/Vienna PO (CBS/Sony, 1985). *Symphony No.5* – Tennstedt/London PO (EMI); Barbirolli/New Philharmonia (EMI or Warner Classics, 1969); Rattle/Berlin PO (EMI/2002). *Symphony No.6* – Bernstein and the Vienna PO (DG, 1990) or NYPO (CBS, 1960s); Barbirolli/New Philharmonia (EMI, 1960s). *Symphony No.7* – Either of the Bernstein/NYPO (Sony, 1965; DG, 1985).

Symphony No.9 – The modern recommendation is Karajan and his Berliners (DG, 1982) in a rare Mahler recommendation of Karajan. The vintage jewel is again from Barbirolli and the New Philharmonia (EMI, 1964).

The elemental power of Beethoven's music haunted composers throughout the 19th century. He was viewed as the Napoleon of composers who in the Romantic period became a "heaven-storming hero of mythical proportions." Many composers after Beethoven were superstitious about composing beyond a ninth symphony. They probably were on to something. Mahler was superstitious about beginning a ninth symphony, feeling completion of a ninth of his own would be an affront to Beethoven and because Beethoven, Schubert, and Bruckner had all died after completing, or in Bruckner's case, leaving incomplete, their designated 'Ninth'.

Mahler was obsessed that he would die after composing his *Ninth*, so he "attacks death head-on with music of profound violence and irony." He died before finishing his *Tenth*. Bruckner, a deeply religious Catholic, left his Ninth unfinished (his eleventh actual symphony because Bruckner did not count two early symphonic attempts). Schubert left his famous 'Unfinished' Eighth Symphony unfinished, but finished his 'Great' *Ninth*. He did not live to compose a tenth.

In the cases of Bruckner and Mahler, the numbering is chronological but does not represent their total symphonic output. Bruckner has two early symphonies that are designated '0' and '00' before he composed the one he called his *First*. Mahler's actual ninth symphony is *Das Lied von der Erde*, but the neurotic Mahler still wanted to write more symphonies beyond this one but felt that if he called it his *Ninth* fate would ensure it would be his last.

Despite the paranoia, Mahler did actually complete his *Ninth* and begin his *Tenth*, after his actual ninth, *Das Lied von der Erde*. Bruckner's *Ninth* was left in only three movements but, like Schubert's *Unfinished*, it is hard to imagine any improvement would be made by additional movements. Even other composers shared this superstition, feeling "that punishment awaited those who challenged certain forces." Even Arnold Schoenberg subscribed to this and wrote in 1913, "It seems that the Ninth (symphony) is the limit…those who had written a ninth symphony were too close to the Beyond." It is interesting that of major symphonists after Beethoven; only Shostakovich wrote multiple complete symphonies beyond number 9. The symphony retained a high-mindedness and social ambition for over one hundred years. "This all but fizzled out in Austria and Germany with the death of Mahler."

But Mahler was, on balance, a romantic; his music more backward than forward-looking. "Through a loosened key structure he created a mysterious language that is full of intense yearning." Despite his unconventional harmonies, he was no more ahead of his time than Richard Strauss, while Debussy and Schoenberg were composing works in the first decade of the 20th century that were far more advanced than even Mahler's last works (the Ninth and unfinished Tenth Symphonies).

He continued to the end to use Beethoven's symphonies as a template for his own. Even though Mahler's symphonies represent a breakup of Classical models, he tried in several of these works to re-write the *Adagio* of

Beethoven's *Ninth*. But swollen with emotion and bloated with endless struggles, this is very subjective music, taking the elements of Romanticism almost to the absurd. To portray Mahler as a forerunner of Neoclassicism or somehow the inspiration for the formalism of Schoenberg's twelve-tone method and subsequent serialism requires one to ignore the substantial evidence to the contrary. Critic Harold Schonberg believes some scholars are too anxious to make Mahler the link between Wagner and Schoenberg.

Mahler sought to answer in his symphonies the questions, "Why have you lived?" and "Why have you suffered?". He insisted that "we must resolve these…if we are to continue living." This thinking would seem to hardly have any impact on such 20th century 'objective' composers such as Stravinsky (once he began his neo-Classical period in the 1920s), who stated that it was not music's job to "express anything," and that his Symphonies of Wind Instruments was not meant to "arouse passions" in the audience. However, a century after Mahler's death "the most serious and accomplished musicians of our time continue to devote themselves to solving the existential and musical conundrums he created."

♪ Richard Strauss (1864-1949)

"The anguished idealism of Mahler contrasts utterly with the cool, practical, sardonic attitude of Strauss towards music and the world."

> *"New ideas must search for new forms"*
> *- Richard Strauss*

Richard Strauss in his youth composed 'absolute' music according to classical traditions. His father was a professional horn player and drilled into his son a commitment to tradition. His early quartets, symphonies (D minor and F minor) and his *Serenade for Thirteen Winds* show no sign of the music dramatist to come. His early chamber works include two piano trios, a string quartet, a very substantial cello sonata, and a piano quartet.

But in his very early twenties he was influenced to convert to programmatic music, to be guided by the works of Berlioz, Liszt, and Wagner. His association with the poet/musician (and first violinist of the Meiningen Orchestra) Alexander Ritter, while Strauss was principal conductor at Meiningen, exposed him to "the concept of music as expression" and took the young composer from absolute music to an interest "in composing music with a literary or philosophical outline." Ritter drew Strauss away from traditional Viennese sonata form "in favor of a freewheeling, moment-to-moment, poetically-inflamed narrative."

> *"We must study Brahms long enough to discover that there is nothing in him."*
> - Alexander Ritter

In 1889 tone poems were all the rage in Europe, "what the *concerto grosso* had been to the Baroque." Strauss's embrace and perfection of this form would label him as "Liszt's natural successor." Strauss "carried the symphonic poem to more daring feats of description" beyond Liszt by providing explicit and specific descriptions of the music, compared to Liszt, whose tone poems dealt with generalized programs. This detailed program results in the recorded versions of many of his tone poems having many short movements, each with descriptive information regarding the imagery or sound world intended by the composer. Most of Strauss' tone poems have fairly detailed plots to help the listener follow along.

Strauss before 1890 and the age of twenty-five wrote the dissonant symphonic fantasy *Aus Italien* (1886), his first move away from classical tradition, as well as the tone poems *MacBeth*, *Don Juan*, and *Death and Transfiguration*. Strauss, clearly lacking the modesty appropriate for his age, dubbed *Aus Italien* "the connecting link between the old and the new." After *Aus Italien* Strauss' tone poems did not evoke pictures or scenes but "man in struggle and search," embroiled in "the three great adventures: battle, love and death," shown through *Don Juan*, *Don Quixote*, *Till Eulenspiegel* and *Zarathustra*. With *Ein Heldenleben* Strauss continued this approach but now the focus was on Strauss himself as 'hero'.

From 1890-1911 Strauss was "The World's Greatest Composer". His detailed tone poems demanded larger and larger orchestras and "generated a constant atmosphere of excitement and electricity." The works were tied to specific programs, usually literary and required orchestras of unprecedented size and virtuosity. As with Berlioz and Liszt, Strauss used Shakespeare as inspiration for a tone poem, *MacBeth*. However, Strauss seemed to contradict himself when he made statements such as, "I don't like programs at all", but he felt "the poetic form is not…a musical description of certain events of life." He felt this would be "quite contrary to the spirit of music."

Over a ten year period (1894-1904) he produced five more symphonic poems that got progressively bigger and more sensational: Tod und Verklarung (1890), *Also Sprach Zarathustra* (1896), Till Eulenspiegel's Merry Pranks (1895), Don Quixote (1898), *Ein Heldenleben* (1899), and *Sinfonia Domestica* (1904). Strauss "retained for Germany the supremacy of music which had culminated in Wagner." This made Strauss one of the more important men in German society because only in music did the rest of the world still seem to acknowledge German superiority.

Strauss was a great orchestrator, able to manipulate the parts of the orchestra to fulfill the programmatic requirements of his works. A major orchestral development of his was giving equal treatment to all instruments, so that any instrument (even a saxophone) at any time could be "thrust into soloistic prominence," and pushed many beyond their capabilities. Strauss' orchestra is "aggrandized and enlarged choreographically" and he "elaborates it to the highest degree of acrobatic virtuosity."

> *"Strauss...could make music...perform dazzling miracles against nature."*
> - Barbara Tuchman

The orchestral complexity of Strauss's music pushed the virtuoso capabilities of any orchestra, as well as conductor. He wrote themes of immense vitality and sweep, dazzling and overwhelming listeners with his superabundance of energy. It was certainly a huge advantage that Strauss was an outstanding conductor, possibly one of the greatest ever, holding conducting posts at Meiningen (succeeding Bülow), then at Weimar starting in 1889, thirty years after Liszt held the same post. As such, he was able to very effectively coerce an ensemble to bring his works to life.

> *"So young, so modern, yet how well he conducts Tannhaüser."*
> - Cosima Wagner on R. Strauss

In the post-Romantic Germany of Mahler, Strauss, and Schoenberg, "dissonance speaks of personal feeling, in line with the Austro-German Romantic tradition." Because this tradition has the "most all-embracing harmonic logic, that dissonance was most powerfully felt" in their music. Despite the tone poems of Strauss seeming revolutionary at the turn of the century, they belong more to the post-Romantic world of Mahler than to the atonal experimental world of the first half of the 20th century. However, "the anguished idealism of Mahler contrasts utterly with the cool, practical, sardonic attitude of Strauss towards music and the world."

Strauss "exercised little or no influence on the new school of composers." To them his tone poems were "vulgar, over orchestrated." Music critic Harold Schonberg is not kind to Strauss's legacy, stating that today it is hard for a listener "to take the huffings and puffings" of his tone poems. Schonberg continues that Strauss's "pure sensationalism" is dated and, worst of all when characterizing an artist, claims Strauss was "flawed by the desire to put effect over substance."

> *"Schumann and Brahms are only imitators and will not survive. Apart from Wagner there is really only one great master...Liszt."*
> - Richard Strauss

The most influential music critic of Strauss's day, Eduard Hanslick of Vienna, simply did not feel that the music of Wagner/Strauss could co-exist with that of Brahms and the classical tradition. Critics and the public had to choose a side, one could not be loyal to both the Wagner camp and to Brahms. Strauss' first major tone poem was *Aus Italien*, inspired by a trip he took to Italy. The work picked up where Liszt and Berlioz left off. Those two masters of programmatic symphonic works usually stayed within traditional patterns of theme and development. Strauss did not.

Don Juan, Op.20, was his first tone poem to be published and his first masterpiece. Strauss took the tone poem to its highest level and perfected the symphonic poem invented by Liszt years earlier. Starting with *Don Juan* and continuing through his subsequent great tone poems Strauss sought to make "music perform a non-musical function" by having it play the role of literature, that is, to describe characters, emotions, and events.

Strauss's tone poems have detailed plots that the music is designed to depict. Many of his works have many short movements to allow for this greater detail. The titles of specific movements indicate what the composer is trying to depict through music (e.g., festivities, storm at sea, a death). The accompanying liner notes can help by telling what to listen for and by elaborating on the composer's intentions. However, Strauss believed that "the program was mainly a stimulus to his imagination, and that the music should and could stand on its own." Also, he felt that "those who really understand how to listen to music probably don't need it (a program) at all."

Most composers of suggestive/programmatic music were not as specific as Strauss but instead left a good amount of the details to listeners' imaginations. The 'Impressionists', such as Debussy, produced music more suggestive of "the mood of a scene, or a general feeling." Thus, Debussy in *La Mer* and Respighi with *The Pines of Rome* do not paint specific pictures with the orchestra but try to provide the impetus for listeners to paint their own, so as to elicit an individual reaction to the suggestions of the music.

Critics, other composers, and much of the public did not hold back their attacks on Strauss and his 'musical modernism'. Similar overreaction to 'new' music would be common over the next thirty years or so as composers from Stravinsky to Schoenberg attempted to move musical tradition to its next logical place, ironically trying to distance themselves from the 'excesses' of post-Romanticism. As for shots from other composers, one of Russia's 'mighty five' composers (unidentified) said some of Strauss's works are a "mockery of music". But Strauss had some very influential supporters as well. Conductor Hans von Bülow, whom Strauss succeeded at Meiningen, dubbed him 'Richard II', as heir to Wagner.

Don Juan, Op.20

Based originally on the hero, *Don Juan*, in a Spanish play from 1630 by Tirso de Molina, it spurred many additional works on the same character, the most famous being Mozart's *Don Giovanni*. The poet Byron also called on Don Juan and his dashing exploits; however, Strauss used the hero from a poem by Nikolaus Lenau, who is not simply an incorrigible woman chaser, but a more complicated figure.

From the opening, the intense lyricism of the music vividly portrays the "irrepressible adventurer." According to Tovey the work culminates "in a superb gesture of welcome to Love wheresoever it might be found." There are alternating thematic episodes including the famous *Don Juan* theme, which fittingly opens and sets the atmosphere for the work – "a heroic proclamation from the four horns in unison."

The work was completed in 1888 and the premiere was well received the following year with Strauss conducting. The music is extremely self-confident for a twenty-five year old. The critic Eduard Hanslick predictably denounced *Don Juan* as 'ugly' but then he "detested everything that was not Brahms or Schumann."

Tod und Verklärung, Op.24

Composed just after the completion of *Don Juan*, *Death and Transfiguration* was first performed in 1890. This tone poem can be a little rough because of its subject of death and dying. Strauss depicts a dying man's last hours spent dreaming of his youth. Alexander Ritter, Strauss' friend and mentor wrote some verses for this work, which Strauss appended to the score.

The composer avoided too explicit a program because he based it on an idea rather than on a literary text. The idea traces a dying man's memories from the innocence of childhood through his life and final agony when faced by death. Strauss effectively uses the orchestra to convey the pain the man is feeling. This may not be the subject everyone is looking for in music.

As in *Don Juan*, Strauss uses a recurrent theme to signal the key component of the work. In this work Strauss called it the 'Idealism motif', which appears in the middle and is pronounced during the final 'transfiguration'. Debussy claimed that the 'transfiguration' in this work "takes place before our very eyes." Strauss, in this tone poem, wanted to "represent the death of a person who had striven for the highest artistic goals" and the 'idealism motif' was used to portray the soul upon death finding "perfected in the most glorious form in the eternal cosmos that which he could not fulfill here on earth."

Till Eulenspiegel's Merry Pranks, Op.28

Strauss's fourth major tone poem was composed in 1895 and first performed that same year. Till was a German folk hero from the 1300s, a 'merry prankster', with some legends painting him as a Robin Hood type figure. The title subject, a happy knave, was originally going to be the subject of Strauss' second opera, but he settled on using the merry prankster as the star of a tone poem instead. As with Don Juan, Till gets his own theme, which appears multiple times with variation as part of the music narrative. Strauss uses variations on Till's theme cleverly and effectively to communicate the state or situation Till finds himself in at a particular point in the story.

Strauss elicits very effective sound images from violins, brass, and clarinets and uses "every kind of instrumental device (to portray Till's) adventures…" Debussy was awed by the "mad rhythm that sweeps us along…to share in the hero's pranks." Strauss returned the favor by declaring Debussy "a remarkable and altogether unique genius." Not surprisingly, the critic Hanslick pronounced *Till* "the product of decadence."

Also Sprach Zarathustra, Op.30

From its opening 'Sunrise', made famous in Stanley Kubrick's *2001: A Space Odyssey* in 1968, to the final *Nachtwanderlied* ('Night Wanderer's Song'), Strauss's intentions with *Zarathustra* were incredibly ambitious. This tone poem, completed in the summer of 1896 and consisting of nine sections, is freely based on the writings of philosopher Friedrich Nietzsche. Nietzsche's philosophy and optimistic views on our development through time, had seduced the imagination of Europe at the time of Strauss.

Each section that follows the famous opening, explores a section and theme from Nietzsche's text, including *Von der großen Sehnsucht* ('Of Intense Yearning') and *Das Grablied* ('Song of the Grave'). Again, the critic Hanslick found the opening of *Zarathustra* "tortured and repulsive."

Don Quixote, Op.35 (1898)

This is the "most programmatic piece by music's most programmatic composer." Strauss' full title was *Fantastical Variations on a Theme of Knightly Character for Large Orchestra*. He takes his musical depictions to another level, even using a wind machine to help depict an imaginary flight through the air. Strauss represents his hero in this tone poem using multiple themes presented in the introduction movement. Each theme is intended to represent a different aspect of Cervantes' character. The variations theme is then presented by solo cello, the featured instrument. This is followed by eleven variations which narrate Don's adventures and misadventures. Strauss referred to the variations as "ramblingly tragicomic." It was completed in the last days of 1897 and premiered three months later in Köln.

Ein Heldenleben, Op.40 (1898-99)

Nietzsche's notion of the Superman, the artist-genius, "who shook off the chains of tradition and history as the intolerable burden of the past," inspired Strauss to write *Ein Heldenleben* ('A Hero's Life'). The six-part tone poem is played without a break, "varying in tempo and tone but all (parts) drawing on the same supply of thematic material." Debussy felt that the six-part *Ein Heldenleben* was like a "book of images, even cinematography." It does contain in the 'Battle', according to Romain Rolland, "the most splendid battle that has ever been painted in music."

The work is autobiographic, depicting the hero (Strauss) taking on his enemies and conquering them. One such enemy is the music critic Eduard Hanslick, and the composer snipes at Hanslick in one section of this tone poem. Strauss described this work as a "largish tone poem...with lots of horns, always expressive of the heroic." This is Strauss' last symphonic poem in the true Lisztian tradition.

After 1911 his best tone poems were behind him and he could not top previous successes in sensationalism. With the *Sinfonia Domestica* of 1904 and *An Alpine Symphony* of 1915, it appeared that Strauss had gone to the tone poem well too many times. The public did not embrace these works as it had the earlier masterpieces and favor toward Strauss fell off. However, *An Alpine Symphony* is the last symphony from the Austro-German tradition to retain a place in the standard repertory. Music aficionados were instead embracing Prokofiev, Stravinsky, Bartók, and Schoenberg, much of whose music made Strauss's post-Romantic bombast sound old-fashioned.

In response, Strauss turned to opera and produced three masterpieces. Two were based on ancient stories and created quite a stir. Both *Salome* and *Elektra* were derided as too "sensual and decadent" for the first decade of the last century. However, his third operatic success was much different; *Der Rosenkavalier* ('The Knight of the Rose') is a light, comic opera that has always been received very favorably. Perhaps Strauss's claim that he was trying "to write an opera such as Mozart's" had something to do with his avoidance of any controversial themes or subjects and decision to demonstrate that he could indeed produce music of transparency and character, an opera filled with beautiful music.

Strauss's final works were composed during the Second World War and include a Concerto for Oboe, another for horn (his second), the *Metamorphosen for 23 Solo Strings*, and *Four Last Songs*. His legacy has been justly damaged by his perceived loyalty to the Nazis and the fact that "he never put up much of a fight against the horrors of the Nazi regime." Being opportunistic and apolitical, Strauss would go in and out of favor with the authorities. He "wanted to have the best of both worlds...to be left alone to write his music and make money." Strauss tried to remain in the Nazi's favor but also pushed the limits of what he could get away with because of his prominent standing. He said things that could have landed other people in a concentration camp. During his final years after the war his reputation took hits as many saw him, at best, as indifferent to the horrors of the Third Reich. At the extreme was Klaus Mann fuming over Strauss' denunciation of his father, author Thomas Mann. The younger Mann saw Strauss as a "rotten character...completely lacking in...impulses of shame and decency."

History and public opinion has been as conflicted about Strauss as he was in his relationship with the Nazis. It is frequently pointed out that he made no effort to leave Germany. Strauss offered as an explanation that someone had to stay behind to make sure that German culture was not completely destroyed by Hitler.

As tolerant as he may have seemed to the Nazis, he did not display anti-Semitism in his personal or professional life, as he guarded his Jewish daughter-in-law and some of her family members. He was an advocate of a young and unknown Arnold Schoenberg, arranging financial support for the struggling composer. Most of his operas prominently featured Jewish librettists, producers, etc. He also worked actively to protect Jewish musicians and conductors.

♪ Jean Sibelius (1865-1957)

Sibelius was a nationalist and nature poet in the post-Romantic tradition. He "found fresh new means of expression while working within accepted traditions." Although Sibelius' compositional output was diverse and included chamber music and solo piano music, he is known for his symphonies, his dark and brooding tone poems, and his Violin Concerto. Sibelius painted "with darker shades of the musical palette" to evoke "the atmosphere of his beloved native land." In fact, "whatever elements he borrowed from the Finnish folk tradition give his music a degree of character found nowhere else." His seven symphonies are all different, not an easy achievement.

Sibelius admired "severity of form, and profound logic that created an inner connection between all the motifs." He strove, especially in his symphonies, for compression and aimed to create unified organic structures, Romantic in tone, but Classical in concentration and economy. Sibelius' unique style "favored pithy, compact motifs, rather than extended melodies." Alex Ross points out that Sibelius, like so many Romantic composers (think Schumann and Tchaikovsky) took a perverse pleasure in surrendering to melancholy, finding joy in darkness. Sibelius "succeeded in stamping his own voice on seemingly worn-out, antiquated symphonic forms."

While Sibelius' tone poems were programmatic and often nationalistic and infused with much Finnish folklore, his seven symphonies are purely 'absolute' music. However, many listeners find in them a musical evocation of the composer's homeland.

♪ Symphonies

> *"A symphony is more a confession of faith at different stages of one's life."*
> — Jean Sibelius

Symphony No.1 in E minor, op.39

As David Hurwitz points out, Sibelius' stature rests primarily on his symphonies, his ability to conquer "the largest, most serious, and most complex of all musical genres." All of Sibelius' symphonies are chock full of short motifs and *ostinato* patterns (persistently repeated musical phrases and/or rhythms), with "haunting lyrical passages of yearning, melancholy, and nostalgia." The first two symphonies are "typical orchestral dramas of the heroic soul" that show Sibelius' knack for "breaking down themes into murmuring textures."

Sibelius finished the *First* at age thirty-four in the fall of 1898. Sibelius conducted the premiere the following April. The work signaled Sibelius' emergence as a master of the orchestra. If you think that Sibelius's First Symphony from 1899 is actually a long-lost Tchaikovsky symphony, it was heavily influenced by Tchaikovsky, whose Sixth Symphony premiered less than six years before Sibelius' *First*.

Symphony No.2 in D major, op.43

With his Second Symphony, which premiered in 1902 in Helsinki with the composer conducting, Sibelius establishes his signature that distinguishes his orchestral music – short, abrupt phrases, dark and brooding moods, and unified symphonic themes influenced by Bruckner. This last feature serves to tie the symphony together by, for example, returning to first movement themes in the Finale. "There is a subtle coherence to the work that counters its seemingly shapeless quality." This symphony served as a more clandestine way of demonstrating Finnish patriotism versus the blatantly (and therefore censored) patriotic *Finlandia*.

Many of the movements are based upon a collection of fragmentary ideas which fuse and coalesce as the music proceeds. The melodies of the finale are "decked out in all the lush raiment of late 19th century orchestration." Robert Layton attributes the wide and enduring popular appeal of the Second to "a combination of Italianate warmth and Nordic intensity." As Beethoven did in his Fifth Symphony, Sibelius links the third and fourth movements with a bridge passage from the minor to a flowing melody in the major.

Symphony No.3 in C, op.52

Sibelius' Third Symphony, begun in 1904, is a "terse, elusive work" that is actually "a sustained deconstruction of symphonic form." The work marked the end of Sibelius' Romantic period and the beginning of his pursuit of "new formal methods based on fragmentation and recombination." The lean textures, orchestration, and dimensions of the *Third* initially confused listeners expecting the thicker, more epic Second Symphony. It is neo-Classical in spirit and the typical Sibelius atmosphere is created by alternating dominance between the deep strings and the winds, creating a very effective contrast. Sibelius found himself drawn more to "the sensuous radicalism of Debussy," seeing "new possibilities in...orchestral color," and away from Austro-German influences of Strauss, Mahler, and Schoenberg.

Symphony No.4 in A minor, Op.63

> *"Give me the loneliness either of the Finnish forest or a big city."*
> - Jean Sibelius

As the 20th century got moving, Sibelius "moved away from the lush orchestral aspects of Romanticism" which especially characterized his first two symphonies. Indeed, the Fourth Symphony "exemplifies the 20th century urge to lighten the orchestral texture." as Sibelius adopted a more austere style. It also stands in contrast to the tuneful and relaxed *Third* and the heroic and extroverted *Fifth*. The *Fourth* "is the quintessence of Sibelius – a model of concision, intensity, and thematic unity;" the best example of how Sibelius had moved from the influences of Tchaikovsky, Grieg and Borodin to a style in which "emotion is tautly controlled within unified but unconventional formal structures in a spare, clean-lined, orchestral texture."

In 1911 Sibelius completed his Fourth Symphony (premiered April of 1911), a drastic change from the three before it, which used "elements of nationalistic rhetoric, melody, and color". The "material is handled with the utmost economy." Words used to describe the *Fourth* include 'austere', 'remote', and 'dissonant'. It represents Sibelius' rejection of the gigantism of post-Romanticism, specifically the tone poems of Strauss and the symphonies of Mahler.

This compact and austere symphony actually pre-dates the 20th century *avant-garde*. "Sibelius' 4th symphony experimented with passages of indeterminate tonality." In fact, stripping away the lush Romantic textures of his music and leaving the choppy, compact melodic statements (e.g., the short, repetitive main motive in the finale of the Third Symphony), one finds the foundations of 20th century modernism. The *Fourth* is full of abrupt changes of mood; the third movement is "haunted, with textures of an almost Webern-like spareness."

In the *Fourth* we have Sibelius' "bleakest expression" to-date, demonstrating a general "disenchantment with the world." It represented "music as forbidding as anything (in Europe) at the time." The music has a "claustrophobic grimness," seemingly slowed down by an external "gravitational force on the music...it keeps visiting the same unresolved conflicts." Sibelius described the *Fourth* as a "protest against the music of today." With the *Fourth* Sibelius began stressing "the organic evolution of material during the course of a work." The *Fourth* "ends not with a bang (as most Romantic symphonies) or a whimper (Wagner operas and Strauss tone poems) but with a leaden thud."

As early as 1911 the mood in Sibelius' music was changing, although he would still produce several great works over the next two decades. However, if the composer was disenchanted with the world in 1911, Sibelius was still to live through two world wars, the Great Depression, a flu pandemic, and the rise of Nazism and Fascism, as well as the Soviet Union.

Symphony No.5 in E-flat, Op.82

The Fifth Symphony shares similarities with the *Second*, more so than with the *Third* and definitely more than with the *Fourth*, which breaks away from the lush melodies of the first three symphonies. Sibelius composed the *Fifth* as a mighty symphony at a time when "many composers chose to concentrate on more economical forms," in 1915 during the First World War. In fact, Sibelius' *Fifth* is one of the few big orchestral pieces composed during World War I. It is "an unconventional and staggeringly original work." Instead of the thematic development expected from the apparent sonata form, Sibelius' material evolves incrementally through trancelike repetitions.

The Fifth Symphony is in the heroic key of E-flat (same as Beethoven's *Eroica* Symphony). Sibelius worked it through three versions from 1915-19 and the original version was four movements and much longer than the final product we know.

Symphony No.6 in D minor, Op.104

In the Sixth Symphony Sibelius returns to the neo-Classicism of his *Third*, "as if the composer were trying to flee into a mythic past." Roger Dettmer in the All Music Guide feels this symphony is "the purest, most inward...for some...the most hypnotic, to be heard countless times without ever revealing all of its secrets." The *Sixth* is in a straightforward four movements. Written on the heels of World War I and premiering in 1923, Sibelius was apparently oblivious to what was going on musically in Europe around him, or simply was determined to follow his own path, for the *Sixth* is contemporary with the initial twelve-tone works of Schoenberg, the "most outrageous expressionist experiments" of Hindemith and the "iconoclasm of *Les Six* in France."

Symphony No.7 in C, Op.105

The *Seventh* "has a seemingly inexhaustible capacity for evolving new material from the same basic germinal ideas." This symphony fuses the dark (Fourth Symphony) and the light (the *Fifth*) sides of Sibelius "into one continuous structure…anchored on a grand theme for solo trombone." The Seventh, in one continuous movement, is "the acme of formal unity" held together by long ostinato passages consisting of a "rustling of strings under fragments of solo woodwind melody." Sibelius used transformation of themes (see sections on Liszt) in his one-movement Seventh Symphony. He accomplished this transformation "by tugging at both ends of the one movement and dropping two others into the gaps that opened in the middle."

> *Recommended – Sibelius symphonies*
> Complete set, including several tone poems – Ashkenazy leading the Philharmonia (Decca) consistently conveys the unique atmosphere of Sibelius' music. Symphonies 2&5 – Karajan and the Philharmonia (EMI, 1960) or a recent recording by Vänskä and the Minnesota Orchestra (BIS, 2012).

♪ Tone Poems and Legends

Along with his symphonies, Sibelius composed one of the more significant sets of tone poems. Several were nationalistic in nature, based on Finnish legends and folklore. Sibelius utilized the symphonic poem to express "his visionary, myth-based musical style…" From his first in 1892, *En Saga*, which tells no story but is simply 'about Finland', to the dark orchestral coloring of *Tapiola*, his final masterpiece, his tone poems give "shape to what a wanderer feels as he walks alone." Sibelius' final tone poems also marked the seventy-year run of popularity of the Romantic tone poem.

Finlandia, Op.26, is a tone poem of nationalist pride that "compresses centuries of Finnish folklore and the country's fiercely independent spirit into eight minutes of music." It was composed in 1899 as one of six 'Historic Scenes'. Its "raw emotionalism dominates…Finlandia grabs both heart and gut."

Sibelius' last tone poem is *Tapiola*, Op.112 from 1926. In it he evokes the forests of his native Finland, as well as the forest god Tapio, in which "the connection to traditional tonality grows ever more tenuous." The work is one of "especially remarkable concentration that testifies to (Sibelius') dazzling sonic imagination."

Sibelius took no part in the experimentation and reactionism of the first quarter of the 20th century (atonality nor neo-Classicism) and composed nothing of significance after *Tapiola* and the Seventh Symphony. Instead, when he decided to stop composing, despite living another thirty-two years, he had "arrived at a final synthesis in a style of Classical tranquility."

Tapiola can, somewhat arbitrarily, mark the end of "Romantic Period" music as we know it. Not only did the sun set on Sibelius' career, but also on the subjective and suggestive emotionalism that marked music of the late Romantic period as the 19th century gave way to the 20th.

Four Legends from the *Kalevala*, 'Lemminkäinen Suite'

The *Kalevala* is an epic Finnish poem that contains the national legends of Sibelius' homeland. The epic was used as source material several times by Sibelius in his tone poems, as it is an ideal source for nationalistic programmatic music. The Four Legends are: *Lemminkäinen and the Maidens of the Island*; *The Swan of Tuonela* (the most famous, often performed, recorded without the other three parts); *Lemminkäinen in Tuonela*; and *Lemminkäinen 's Return*. In the final Legend Sibelius vividly describes Lemminkäinen galloping through the wild forest of his homeland. These tone poems were completed in December 1895 to January 1896.

> *Recommended – Sibelius Tone Poems*
> Any of several sets by Ormandy and the Philadelphia. The combination of Sibelius' music and the 'Philadelphia Sound' is always a winning combination. More recent and also good are the Finnish recordings by the Lahti Symphony Orchestra under Osmo Vänskä (BIS).

Violin Concerto in D minor, Op.47

Sibelius despised the piano and thus wrote no music for it. This is the most recorded of 20th century violin concertos, with Shostakovich's First Violin Concerto probably just behind it. It was composed in 1903, between the Third and Fourth symphonies, and premiered a year later. Its rejection caused Sibelius to revise it for a second 'premiere' under Richard Strauss in Berlin. "This time the reviews were merely indifferent." The work languished for three decades until it was rescued by Heifetz's performance of "unblinking conviction" under Beecham, the most ardent Sibelius advocate. This original Heifetz recording was made in late 1935.

The finale of Sibelius' Violin Concerto was characterized by Donald Tovey as "evidently a polonaise for polar bears." This work is more a soloistic concerto than a symphonic one. Sibelius opposes, rather than meshes, the soloist and orchestra.

> *Recommended* – Heifetz rescued this concerto from obscurity and his version with Hendl and the Chicago SO (RCA) has always set the standard. On CD this is usually coupled with Glazunov's *Violin Concerto* and Prokofiev's *Second*.

> *"All the doctors who wanted to forbid me to smoke and drink are dead."*
> — Sibelius, who lived to ninety-one

In the 1920s and 1930s Sibelius was "lionized as a new Beethoven in England and America" but "dismissed as a kitsch composer in" Austria-Germany. Simultaneously, he was essentially ignored in France or Italy. As his symphonies became very popular in America he attained celebrity. He was voted favorite living composer by NY Philharmonic audiences. For the 1932-33 season of the Boston Symphony, Koussevitzky programmed the complete cycle of Sibelius symphonies. Critics who railed against 'modern' music opposed composers such as Stravinsky and Schoenberg and what they stood for and promoted. They found in Sibelius "the last of the heroes...who would rescue music from cerebral modernism." Sibelius owed his fame in America partly to Olin Downes, music critic of *The New York Times* for thirty years.

As stated above, Sibelius did not achieve the same level of fame in continental Europe, which favored the 'more intellectual' modern music (e.g., Stravinsky). In Berlin and Paris "his expansive symphonies and evocative tone poems" did not have much "intellectual market value," some critics even going so far as to characterize his great Violin Concerto as "boring Nordic dreariness".

While Olin Downes gave Sibelius his constant support in *The Times*, critic-composer Virgil Thomson, of the *New York Herald Tribune*, who was squarely in the Stravinsky camp in America, skewered Sibelius in his reviews. Thomson's prominent reviews are thought to have brought about the decline of Sibelius's popularity in the mid-20th century. Thomson tore into the Second Symphony as vulgar, self-indulgent, and "provincial beyond all description." Author Theodor Adorno piled on with unequivocal dismissals such as "the work of Sibelius...fundamentally lacks any good qualities." And composer René Leibowitz did not help matters by titling a work <u>Sibelius: The Worst Composer In the World</u>.

Sibelius began his never-finished eighth symphony in 1924 and through most of the thirty remaining years of his life he would claim the work "was almost ready for performance." It is not clear how much effort he actually put into it or how close to completion he actually got. Renowned music critic Harold Schonberg, even in the third edition of his excellent book <u>The Lives of the Great Composers</u>, expresses an unfavorable view of Sibelius that seems somewhat dated. It may be that these views carried forward from previous editions but his statements are not consistent with Sibelius' current status. While most of his violin works may be "salon trifles" as Schonberg claims, certainly his Violin Concerto is a masterpiece of the repertory. And his seven symphonies, each being different and representing a clear evolution forward, together with his numerous tone poems, add up to more than "an honorable place among the minor composers."

Sibelius has enjoyed a comeback over the last few decades due to the rediscovery of the melodic early 20th century tonal composers "who found fresh new means of expression while working within accepted traditions." His symphonies, tone poems, and his Violin Concerto, are all well-represented in the catalog in new performances. Author Alex Ross points to the characterization of Sibelius' unique style by Milan Kundera (in *Die Weltliteratur*) as "antimodern modernism." One might reword this as 'traditional modernism.' Kundera points to Sibelius' "personal style that stands outside the *status quo* of perpetual progress."

The music of Sibelius certainly foreshadowed the style of music to come, more so than contemporaries such as Tchaikovsky and Rachmaninoff. Beyond the end of Sibelius' composing career, although he was to live another thirty years, the Classical music landscape would be dominated by 'modern', 'experimental' '20th century' composers.

The social, cultural, and political structures of the Western World had splintered. Add to this the rise of Nazism taking Europe into World War II and the spread of communism across half of Europe after the war. Sibelius would have seen communism take hold next door, producing the Soviet Union. Maybe he did not compose any major works after 1927 because the ideas he wanted to convey through his post-Romantic aesthetic no longer had a place in a world ravaged by war and at the mercy of ruthless dictators and oppressive new forms of government. As a Finn, Sibelius lived through Finland's struggle for independence and subsequent civil war. One theory on why he abandoned composition points to a "reaction to the post-Civil War repressive society," in which the working class lived under oppression by the Finnish middle class. Others claim "age, burn-out and painful self-criticism" as being closer to the truth. The actual reason remains a mystery.

- 20 -

The Rise of Nationalism

The nineteenth century saw the rise of nationalism in music, particularly in Russia, Hungary and the areas of the Austrian-Hungarian Empire that would become Czechoslovakia after World War I (Bohem ia and Moravia). In the second half of the 1800s fervent nationalism blended with Romanticism in the music of Smetana and Grieg. Music began to be used to express a country's longing for freedom or a country's pride in its traditions. Although certainly Haydn and even Mozart incorporated folk material into their music it was used "only when needed within an already formed style."

Nationalism became "one of the weapons by which composers in those countries sought to free themselves from the domination of foreign music." To add a native touch, composers mined the indigenous music of their homeland, not to lift tunes directly, but for inspiration to make their compositions identify with their respective countries, as Sibelius became synonymous with Finland.

> *"Music does not happen in a vacuum; it invariably contributes to and reflects the culture of which it is part."*
> - Ruth Katz

Musicologists have divided nationalist composers into two camps: the emotional, fervent patriotism of Grieg (Norway), Sibelius, and Smetana (Czech), versus the nationalism of Janáček (Czech), Bartók (Hungary) and Vaughan Williams (England), who "systematically incorporated the folk music and rhythms of their countries into their music." National music was spurred by the "impulse to get below surface politeness to the roots of things." Excepting the blatant use of folk tunes in compositions, "the characteristics and the emotions they evoke are often in the ear of the listener." More often, it is simply that listeners come to associate a certain composer's personal style, inspired by their country, with a particular nation.

These composers moved the use of folk material well beyond Haydn and Weber so that the incorporation or influence of indigenous tunes served a purpose beyond the music itself. These composers yearned for a vanished youth, mourned "for a pretechnological past" and lamented "for a lost world" with "elegies for the golden age." Sibelius' music "sounds Finnish" even though he never consciously made use of folk tunes. Grieg (hopefully) joked that "in fact, I am sure my music has a taste of codfish in it."

Dvořák was "the most inventive and spontaneously musical of all national composers." Bartók, like countryman Kodály, used genuine peasant folk tunes and "remained loyal to…that hidden empire of peasant music." As Bartók and Kodály did in Eastern Europe, Vaughan Williams went into villages to collect folk tunes and traditional melodies of the English countryside. But their works survived and are popular and relevant today, with some being "canonical masterpieces" (e.g., Vaughan Williams' *Fantasy on a Theme by Thomas Tallis*).

Historian Barbara Tuchman in The Proud Tower offers a reason for the rise in nationalism at the turn of the century and into the early 20th. She points to the retreat of religion before the advance of science, giving as one example Nietzsche's infamous statement, "God is Dead." As a result, "love of country began to fill the empty spaces in the heart." As formerly people would fight for religion, that fervor would now be redirected towards defense of their country. This fervor was also fed by the formation of unified 'countries' such as Germany, Italy, Czechoslovakia, which brought together people of the same nationality previously separated into many 'German' or 'Italian' states.

♪ Russia, Glinka and 'The Mighty Five'

♫ Mikail Glinka (1804-1857)

In the early 19th century educated Russians, and thus Russian art music, were split between the rural, Orthodox Church Slavs and the privileged French-speaking, cosmopolitan elite who were the result of Peter the Great's modernization (i.e., Westernization) project a hundred years before epitomized in the founding of St. Petersburg. The resentment towards this Westernization of their country and the dominance of German and French influences on Russian culture planted the seeds for Glinka and Russian nationalism in music. This resentment manifested itself in many ways, including a disruptive demonstration at a Liszt concert in St. Petersburg intended to protest Western influences.

Glinka is credited with creating the 19th century forms of Russian music and becoming the first Russian nationalist, using folk styles as his guide. Glinka began "the attempt to build a national Russian school on a foundation of folklore," which was continued by the 'Mighty Five'. The folksongs heard during his childhood "sank deep into Glinka's mind so that later he could effortlessly incorporate their shapes into his own melodic invention." He struggled, writing non-distinctive music of various forms, mostly based on Western models, before his two great nationalist operas *A Life for the Tsar* (1836) and *Russlan and Ludmilla* (1842). While in Italy attempting to compose in 'Italian manners', Glinka realized, "I could not sincerely be an Italian…a longing for my own country led me gradually to the idea of writing in a Russian manner."

Starting with the 'first Russian opera', *A Life for the Tsar*, Glinka did for Russia "what Weber had done for Germany…combined the naïveté of folk music with the sophistication of the classical traditional to create" truly national music, although Russian nationalism is more evident in the libretto than in the music. *Russlan and Ludmilla* is much more nationalist Russian than *A Life for the Tsar*. *Russlan*'s rhythm "has a recognizably Russian exuberance" with a pungent harmony and a "coloristic use of chromaticism quite distinct from conventional Western practices." With these two seminal Russian operas Glinka changed the course of Russian music, and established the dramatic style followed later in the Russian masterpieces *Boris Godunov* and *Prince Igor*, by Mussorgsky and Borodin, respectively. Glinka's orchestral fantasy *Kamarinskaya* (1848) paved the way for all the folk theme-based Russian orchestral works of the second half of the 1800s. It also brought Glinka's nationalist style to full maturity.

Up to this point all Russian orchestral music had been dominated by foreign influences. Glinka devised forms and procedures to be used as models for future Russian composers. These models, based "more readily in terms of full melodic statements and subsequent variation," would result in a school of Russian composition distinct from the German model "of a musical fabric woven from small melodic entities and spanned out upon an evolving tonal scheme."

> *"Rimsky-Korsakov...suggests fierce whiskers stained with vodka."*
> - Anonymous

The principal Russian nationalists of the second half of the 19th century were nicknamed 'The Mighty Five" although they preferred to call themselves 'The New Russian School'. It consisted of Cesar Cui, Mily Balakirev, Modest Mussorgsky, Alexander Borodin, and Nicolai Rimsky-Korsakov. Balakirev was "the overbearing leader of the (Mighty Five) who encouraged its Russian nationalism." He composed two 'Overtures on Russian Themes'. The last three in particular were the driving force behind Russian nationalistic music. They were amateurs who were not formally trained in harmony or counterpoint. As such, they had no foundation that would cause them to perpetuate the dominant Germanic musical style. Instead, they were forced "to discover their own ways of doing things, and…they used the materials nearest at hand, folk songs." They did struggle with the balance in their compositions between the influence of the West (mainly Germany) and their incorporation of native Russian folk idioms.

♪ Modest Mussorgsky

Mussorgsky was the most original composer of the Russian nationalists and was firmly convinced that art must mirror the conditions of real life. "His music seems to penetrate the Russian soul." Mussorgsky left many works unfinished, probably due to his alcoholism. The more famous completions and orchestrations were taken up by Rimsky-Korsakov, who sorted out much of the shambles left behind, and by Ravel. Biographer David Brown calls him "a unique figure who invents a world of stunning novelty."

> *"Mussorgsky's music is utterly and damnably awful...it is the most vulgar and squalid parody of music."*
> — Tchaikovsky

His solo piano masterpiece, *Pictures at an Exhibition*, famous in the version orchestrated by Ravel, which premiered in 1922 under Koussevitzky and the Boston Symphony Orchestra. The work is a set of character pieces that are dazzling, weird, funny, and touching. His well-known tone poem *Night on Bald Mountain* is his only orchestral work. Mussorgsky characterized this work as "witches' music, in the form of a tone poem." He thought of the work as "something new and is bound to produce a satisfactory impression on a thoughtful musician." Rimsky-Korsakov revised Mussorgsky's final version of *Night* after Mussorgsky's death, smoothing it out and improving the orchestration to the point that the Rimsky-Korsakov version is considerably different from what Mussorgsky left.

> *Recommended – Pictures at an Exhibition*
> For the original solo piano version it is tough to beat the legendary live performance by Richter, part of "The Sofia Recital." For both the piano version and Ravel's orchestration, Mercury offers Byron Janis (piano) and Dorati.

♪ Alexander Borodin (1833-1887)

Borodin was as good a research chemist as a composer, so he was only able to devote himself part-time to music. However, his works are of high quality and won him great respect in his time. His symphonies and string quartets show the "determination of the Russian nationalists to compete with foreign composers in absolute music." In his research efforts as a chemist (he obtained a Ph.D.) he worked on benzene derivatives with Erlenmeyer at Heidelberg, with organic halogens in Pisa and is the co-discoverer, with Wurtz, of the "Aldol" reaction. As a result, he produced a small number of musical works, most of which took considerable time to complete.

His famous Second Symphony was begun in 1869 but only completed seven years later. As if that was not enough, he was not happy after the first performance and Borodin revised the symphony and the revision given its premiere by Rimsky-Korsakov. It was worth the wait; Borodin's Second Symphony was an instant international hit with strong national colorings to illustrate "scenes of Russian heroic antiquity and oriental voluptuousness." Borodin saw his Second Symphony "as a picture of old Russia."

As with the other Mighty Five Russian composers Borodin "tried consciously to make (his) music sound Russian…the contours of the melodies and the rhythms have a decidedly Russian feeling." The fact that Borodin's symphonies remain successful today and his String Quartet No.2 is perhaps the best-known piece of Russian chamber music is evidence of Borodin's accomplishments.

♪ Nicolai Rimsky-Korsakov (1844-1908)

Rimsky-Korsakov's music is an "inspired mix of imagination and orchestral skill." As a master orchestrator, he "knew every instrument's capabilities and invented new tone colors for them." His influences ranged from Iberia for Capriccio Espagnol to seductive Eastern melodies for his most famous orchestral suite *Scheherazade*. Working on the completion of the orchestration for Borodin's opera *Prince Igor*, the influence of Borodin's *Polovtsian* Dances "helped turn Rimsky's mind towards exotic themes." Rimsky-Korsakov was more conservative than the other Mighty Five composers and he "eventually embraced the more disciplined approaches he had learned from his Western European contemporaries." However, he still found a way for his music to be a driving force for Russian nationalism with works such as *Russian Easter* Overture.

Composed in the summer of 1888, *Scheherazade*, Op.35, is a programmatic symphonic suite based on the thousand year-old tale of the *1001 Arabian Nights*. Rimsky-Korsakov stated that he intended to create in the work a "kaleidoscope of fairy-tale images and designs of Oriental character." "Never had (Rimsky-Korsakov's) virtuoso brush strokes painted a more luxuriant canvas," as the work "unfolds as a lush and exotic musical representation of the *1001 Nights*." The composer ultimately abandoned the subtitles of the movements because he did not want *Scheherazade* interpreted as clear-cut programme music.

Rimsky-Korsakov got the inspiration for the orchestral showpiece *Capriccio Espagnol* from his visit to Spain, claiming "the Spanish themes of dance character, furnished me with rich material for…orchestral effects." It is "one of the all-time tours de force of instrumental imagination," and is often coupled with *Scheherazade* and the *Russian Easter* Overture.

> **Recommended – Scheherazade and Russian orchestral showpieces**
> The recommendations here are the Amsterdam Concertgebouw, the world's best orchestra for these colorful works, in *Scheherazade* led by Kondrashin (Philips), Muti and Philadelphia (EMI, 1984) or a more recent exciting account by the Kirov Orchestra and Gergiev (Decca, 2001). An alternative would be any of the recordings by Stokowski. Good collections are available by Jansons and Järvi that contain several Russian showpieces by the above composers.

♪ Alexander Glazunov (1865-1936)

Glazunov was the last of the great Russian nationalists who "single-handedly kept the nationalist flag flying with a series of enchanting symphonies, concertos, ballets, and quartets." He followed the 'Mighty Five' but continued their cause for a characteristically Russian music, a style that had been forged by the time Glazunov rose to prominence. Glazunov would add the innovations of Liszt, Wagner, and Brahms to give Russian nationalism a more international style.

For example, his Violin Concerto (1904) shows the influence of Liszt with its one extended movement. It is one of the most popular of all violin concertos. By the time he achieved prominence as a composer, "the Romantic style that he clung to was already in terminal decline." However, "against the prevailing tide of modernism he kept Romanticism alive until the 1930s." He was a first-class orchestrator and a melodist of rare distinction. Borodin was Glazunov's inspiration and mentor and Shostakovich his most celebrated student.

♪ Great Britain

Edward Elgar, Ralph Vaughan Williams and Frederick Delius, all born within fifteen years of each other, were responsible for the Renaissance of English music; they "lifted British music from its post-Handel and post-Mendelssohn doldrums." Back in the 17th century Henry Purcell (1659-1695) had represented the culmination of the English musical tradition that had started with John Dunstable in the 1400s, followed by John Taverner and Thomas Tallis in the 1500s.

Despite the take-off of nationalism in music during the 19th century, nationalism was a potent force long before 1800. As the concept of 'nation', as opposed to 'state', "proved to be a concept brimful with motivating force" we see signs as early as the late 1600s, sparked by the seventy-plus year reign of Louis XIV, which led to the cultural and political dominance of France, and resentment from other European 'nations'.

In England, a nationalism could be clearly detected at this time (1691) in the music-drama *King Arthur* by Henry Purcell, with libretto by the poet John Dryden. Also of note is the fact that *King Arthur* was not commissioned by royalty or the upper crust but intended for performance in a commercial theatre.

Purcell, who was also the organist at Westminster Abbey, was prolific, producing church music, songs, chamber music and *Dido and Aeneas*, the first English opera in 1689. He "wove all the elements of the European Baroque into the fabric of English music." But despite his striking melodies and harmonies "that at times anticipated the chromaticism of the Romantics," his music was largely forgotten after his death.

After Purcell's death in 1695 England would go 200 years before producing another native-born prominent composer. Between 1759 (death of Handel, who was born in Germany) and the emergence of Elgar in the 1890s, England did not produce one major musical figure. English musical tradition, which had a strong line of succession from Dunstable to Purcell (over two hundred years) went dormant for almost 150 years, during which the high Baroque, Classical, and most of the Romantic period passed it by. Britain was known to Germans during this time as the "land without music." The appearance of Elgar's *Enigma* Variations in 1899 unleashed "a flood of pent-up musical energy" among potential English composers who would follow Elgar. It was as if the success of one of their own (Elgar) was needed to instill the necessary confidence to overcome the apparent inferiority complex of the "British composer." Vaughan Williams succeeded Elgar as the "representative of English music on the international scene."

Harold Schonberg attributes this lack of emerging talent in Britain to the effect of 'imports'. The dominance of Handel's influence and music after his death in the 18th century, and the strong force exerted by Mendelssohn in the 19th, excluded the development of any English composer in the more daring and creative Romantic mold of Chopin-Liszt-Wagner. Certainly Mendelssohn was a genius but a conservative, gentlemanly genius who "did not rock the boat." As a result, English composers followed Mendelssohn's lead by "writing very proper and not very original music." Of course what worked very well for Mendelssohn manifested itself in very mediocre music in the hands of much lesser talents. Fortunately for England and for music Elgar came along and broke his country out of this rut.

♫ *Edward Elgar (1857-1934)*

Elgar represented the first prominent British-born composer since Henry Purcell. Britain enjoyed several transplanted composers, most notably Handel, but also Mendelssohn and Haydn for extended stays. Elgar embraced 19th century German tradition. Of note, he was the first major composer to record a large number of his own works as conductor.

Enormously popular in his day, Elgar was recognized as England's greatest composer. He was "sometimes viewed as the artistic exponent of the virtues of the empire." Richard Strauss proclaimed Elgar as the "first English progressivist." Although Elgar's music feels 'very English', his biggest influences were Brahms and Strauss. Also heavily influenced by Wagner, Elgar characterized *Tristan* as "…the Best and the whole of the Best of this world and the Next." He was somehow able to convert "the Wagnerian apparatus of leitmotifs, chromatic harmony and velvety orchestration-into an iconic representation of the British Empire at its height." His music, excepting the Cello Concerto, can be summed up as an amalgam of Wagner, Tchaikovsky, and Franck. Elgar's is a "plush, expressive-but-not-excessively-so orchestral style." The "mixture of idealism and imperialism prevalent during" the late Victorian and then Edwardian eras "found perfect expression in his music," "an emotional kaleidoscope" that distilled the essence of Edwardian England.

His reputation tanked in the years between the wars during 'music modernism', neo-Classicism and strong anti-Romanticism, but rose up again in the 1960s and remains strong today. After World War I the music of Schoenberg, Bartók, and Stravinsky rendered Elgar's music, which nobly celebrated the British Empire, obsolete; indeed, "the guns of August blasted away the context of his music." His output was considerable and varied: two well-established symphonies, two great concertos (for violin and cello), several works for string orchestra, overtures, marches, and the *Enigma* Variations.

Elgar, unlike countryman Vaughan Williams, not only did not look to folk tunes of his country for material and inspiration, he openly opposed this. "He believed that it was a composer's business to invent tunes, not to…base them on the quaint sounds of the past." It is ironic that Elgar's music is considered very 'English' and 'sounds English' "but his music is not in the least touched by English folk song."

Enigma Variations, Op.36

One of the more famous examples of the theme and variation form, the Variations on an Original Theme, 'Enigma' portray friends of the composer with minimal attempt at hiding the identity corresponding to each variation (Elgar used initials or pseudonyms). The variations are "both virtuosically orchestrated and vividly contrasted, covering a…diverse range of moods."

Composed in 1898-99 the G minor melancholy theme, according to the composer, was meant to convey "my sense of the loneliness of the artist…" The theme is never actually stated. According to Elgar, it is very well known, leading to lots of speculation as to its identity, never revealed by Elgar. With each of the fourteen variations Elgar portrays one of his friends and the mood and emotions felt as a result of each of those friendships. Variation #9, *Nimrod,* is the most famous and beautiful variation representing Elgar's friend Augustus Jaeger. The final variation ties together the opening and *Nimrod* themes.

Violin Concerto in B minor, Op.61

Elgar's Violin Concerto is of the greatest violin concertos, probably the longest and "arguably the most difficult," and "with a deeply personal impulse underlying the music…as personal a concerto as has ever been written." Nowhere is this more in evidence than in the "infinitely subtle, reflective slow movement." The concerto pushes players to the limits of their endurance.

This work lacks much of the pomposity detractors cite in Elgar's music but is "resigned, melancholy, moody, introspective, even tormented." It is the last great concerto to open with a full-length orchestral exposition in the tradition of great Romantic violin concertos. The premieres of Elgar's Violin Concerto and First Symphony marked the zenith of his fame from 1908-10.

The Symphonies

Elgar's First Symphony, composed in 1907-08, was hailed as the first great British symphony. Elgar was still an optimist at this time as World War I had not yet taken that from him. He insisted that the symphony had "no program beyond a wide experience of human life…and a massive hope in the future." The "massive hope" that lies at the heart of this work would be shattered in a few years.

Symphony No.2 (1911) was not well received initially and the work was marginalized after Elgar's death. However, the symphony is popular now, championed by Sir Adrian Boult. The composer thought his second symphony was one of his finest and most personal works. Listening to it, "one can sink as into a comfy chair."

Cello Concerto in E minor, Op.85

Together with Dvořák's famous concerto, Elgar's Cello Concerto is at the top of any list of great concertos for this instrument and on equal footing with his Violin Concerto. Composed in 1919 just after the war, it is "filled with sadness and disillusionment" and is Elgar's requiem to the "end of a civilization." This great concerto doesn't sound like Elgar, his symphonies or his Violin Concerto. Instead of their "victorious swagger" and "rhapsodic virtuosity" the Cello Concerto is "a musical conversation of shyness and economy and a virtuosity of daring and attack." Sir Adrian Boult, an eminent interpreter of Elgar's music, felt that Elgar had "struck a new kind of music, with a more economical line, terser in every way" with lean textures. It was Elgar's last work to be received with widespread acclaim.

Serenade for Strings, Op.20

Elgar's Serenade for Strings is a "remarkably original masterpiece …characteristic of its composer, with its mood of wistful reflection…and its moments of sudden lyrical sweetness." It is an early work from 1892 cast in the key of E minor.

♪ Ralph Vaughan Williams (1872-1958)

> *"Every composer cannot expect to have a worldwide message, but he may reasonably expect to have a special message for his own people."*
> - Ralph Vaughan Williams

Vaughan Williams composed in many forms: symphonies, concertos, short orchestral works as well as many songs and much vocal music such as masses. He published his first work while a teenager and finished his Ninth Symphony shortly before his death, putting the crowning touch on a creative lifespan of almost seventy years.

In 1908 he went to France to study composition with Ravel. While he probably learned technical aspects from Ravel, Vaughan Williams' style and approach to orchestral works, with his use of folk tunes, are far removed from French Impressionist music. From Ravel he did claim to learn that the "heavy contrapuntal Teutonic manner was not necessary." Vaughan Williams rejected the 19th century German tradition in favor of British nationalism, turning to English folk song and choral tradition for inspiration and musical influences. He "saturated himself in folk song (and)…was able to free himself from foreign influences." He quotes some folk tunes (but not as much as is commonly thought) and their spirit certainly infuses his music to create a unique national music for England. He created this in a neo-Baroque manner that used old forms such as *passacaglia*, fugue, and *concerto grosso* exhibiting his fondness for counterpoint. His *Norfolk Rhapsodies* is a trio of works from 1906-7 that has been described as "an orchestral stew of several existing (English) folk airs."

Vaughan Williams had seen too many of his fellow English composers "dragged on a rope behind the chariot of German theoreticians." As a result, he is considered uniquely British, as opposed to Elgar who held on to 19th century German Romanticism. Harold Schonberg sums up Vaughan Williams' "love of all things British" musical philosophy this way: "Better a limited but honest music than imitation."

Fantasia on a Theme by Tallis

His first masterpiece was the *Fantasy on a Theme by Thomas Tallis*, originally completed in 1910 but revised in 1919. It is one of Vaughan Williams' most famous works and his first large-scale work after his studies in France with Ravel. It shows "a massive, broad, bare choral style" that pays homage to the madrigals and polyphony of the golden age of English music. Vaughan Williams' appreciation of Tallis (1505-1585) came from his two years of work editing the English Hymnal (1904-6), during which he came across and was impressed by the somber splendor of a Phrygian-mode tune contribution by Tallis to the 1567 *Psalter* for the first post-Reformation Archbishop of Canterbury.

Vaughan Williams constructed this work as a *concerto grosso* not for virtuoso interplay, but with three separate ensembles (a string quartet and two string orchestras), with one string orchestra more distant than the other, to "create multiple perspectives in sound." The *Tallis* Fantasia "...looks back to traditional choral works of Purcell, Byrd, and, of course, Tallis. But...also demonstrates an understanding of Debussy and Ravel." The "rapt quietude" of this work (for double string orchestra) gives the first look into the composer's expressive universe.

The Lark Ascending

While Vaughan Williams was far from a virtuoso violinist, he did understand how to write for the instrument. Nowhere is this more clearly on display than in this exquisite austere romance from 1914 for violin and small orchestra with subtle and "delicate coloring", with the violin "conjuring up the song of the lark." The evocation of the flight of the bird is done through the use of cadenzas and lyrical orchestrations, as the listener is caught up in the joyous swoop and soar of aerial flight.

Symphony No.1, 'Sea Symphony'; Symphony No.2, 'London'; Symphony No.4; Symphony No.5

Vaughan Williams' First Symphony was composed between 1903 and 1909. He favored the voice not only in songs but in orchestral works as well. His First Symphony includes two soloists and chorus to sing a text based on a work of Walt Whitman. It is a "gloriously unbridled response to some of (Walt) Whitman's most grandiose poetry."

Vaughan Williams' Second Symphony was composed in 1913. Although the composer insisted he was not trying to compose a musical picture of the city, most people familiar with the work believes it does so very accurately. The best way to put it may be that the composer was attempting to "evoke the essence of London without following a specific program."

In a pattern similar to Sibelius, starting with his Fourth Symphony in 1935, which was knotty and dissonant, most of his subsequent symphonies showed "an ever-increasing harmonic tension." The *Sixth* went so far as to be characterized as 'abstract', but with an 'underlying Englishness.' They are "rugged affairs." The Fourth Symphony is his most dramatic, "a somber, uncompromising work of great impact."

With Symphony No.5 from 1943, dedicated to Sibelius, Vaughan Williams returned to the folk idiom to produce what many consider to be his orchestral masterpiece. "A lush vision of a mythical past...with an *Adagio* for England."

> **Recommended – Vaughan Williams orchestral works**
> Barbirolli/Hallé and Handley/LPO; also, Christopher Warren Green and the ECO give warm, sharp performances of Vaughan Williams' two Fantasies and *The Lark Ascending*, along with Elgar's *Introduction and Allegro for String Quartet and String Orchestra* and *Serenade in E minor*.

Today Vaughan Williams does not enjoy the popularity of Elgar; we still await the rediscovery of Vaughan Williams as happened decades ago.

♪ *Charles Ives (1874-1954)*

Charles Ives was the first American composer to "assert a genuinely American style…to follow his own…instinct", producing in his works vivid fantasy and the boldest imagination. He was the first real 'American' composer. American composers before him (e.g., Edward MacDowell) were mostly trained in Europe and followed European traditions; thus, their music was basically 'European'. MacDowell, in fact, did not want his music considered 'American'. Ives, on the other hand, was one of the first American composers not to think of himself as carrying on the musical heritage of Europe in America. No composer before Ives was able "to find a language that was either singularly American or singularly their own." Unlike other American composers up to that point, Ives did not "straightjacket…native or folk tunes…into a regularized European metrical and tonal framework." Ives combined modern, even radical, compositional techniques with a medley of Americana. He wrote the "most advanced, unorthodox, ear-splitting, grating music composed by anybody anywhere up to that time." Ives looked for musical models other than dead Europeans; as Jan Swafford points out "obsessed by the past, he wrote music of the future."

> *"Our Washington, Lincoln, and Jefferson of music."*
> - Bernstein on Ives

Ives was "imbued with a passion for musical innovation and for instilling into his music a sense of American nationality." While his music was seldom performed during his lifetime Ives can be considered the "father figure of modern American music." With Ives' use of national tunes, ragtime rhythms, hymns, marches and other popular sources, Ives "created the first truly American idiom in music." Perhaps prescient, Ives did not attempt to make his livelihood as a composer; instead, he co-founded Ives and Myrick, before he retired in 1929, the most successful insurance company in the country. In his spare time while building a very successful business, Ives wrote music with dissonances that rivaled Schoenberg's, combined with popular sounds of

Americana. However, unlike Schoenberg, he was clearly ambivalent on tonality: "Why tonality...should be thrown out for good, I can't see," but "why it should always be present, I can't see."

> *"(Music) comes directly out of the heart of experience of life and thinking about life and living life."*
> *- Charles Ives*

> *Ives' "cherished memories of the music of ordinary people became the substance of his art."*
> *- Jan Swafford*

Ives was influenced by Transcendentalism, the philosophy led in America by Emerson and Thoreau; everything around him was "manifestations of God in his infinite variety" and he sought in his music "to unify them by putting them together simultaneously." Transcendentalism holds that "the human mind can go beyond what is seen or experienced," and emphasizes "the spiritual and intuitive over the empirical." He mingles conventional and unconventional elements "with a transcendentalist's faith in the unity behind all diversity." This philosophy "allowed (Ives) to venture beyond the usual limits of musical composition." Ives used what Melvin Berger calls "a sort of musical stream-of-consciousness technique," in which "Ives allows his musical ideas to emerge chainlike in a free association that is loosely linked in one extended outpouring."

Ives used individual scraps of music, which were mostly familiar (hymns, folk tunes) to create a successful, but enormously complex, polyphony. His layering "of seemingly disparate musical materials" would often result "in textures of near-unimaginable complexity." "The collaging of well-known tunes into chaotic textures was but one of Ives' incredible innovations," and a method that would be adopted by several later composers of the 20th century *avant-garde*. Music of chance (indeterminacy) that was later personified by John Cage and characterized by noise and electronic collage derives directly from Ives. His originality "resides...in his heterogeneous combinations of American sounds." Ives' early works were "hyperrealistic reproductions of everyday sonic events." He "wanted his music to arouse the innate grandeur and spirituality of the human community."

Prior to the 1920s Ives toiled in obscurity, any innovations in dissonance not heard by the public. In the 1920s he decided to take matters into his own hands and published a book of his songs and his Second Piano Sonata (he had the means to do this at his own expense). It took until 1927 for an orchestral work by Ives to be heard by the public, well after the bulk of his output had been composed. The fact that he did an imitation of Sibelius, composing almost nothing from 1921 to his death in 1954, worked against his works gaining recognition. Ives attributed giving up composition to, "Nothing sounds right to me anymore." During these thirty-plus years Ives "fiddled much with what he had done in his prime."

As with most *avant-garde* composers Ives despised popular classical music, which he termed 'pretty music'. He is considered a 'forebear' by notable modern American composers Aaron Copland, John Cage, and John Adams. The music of Wagner, Debussy, Ravel, Chopin, Stravinsky, and even Mozart was scorned by him. A notable exception was Beethoven, whom he greatly admired. Taruskin notes that Ives also had an affinity for Brahms, Elgar, Franck and points out that an affinity after World War I for Elgar and Franck would have been considered seriously outmoded. Professor Taruskin takes this further to conclude that, despite all of the dissonance and 'looking-forward' in Ives' music, he was not a 'modernist' but in fact, a 'nostalgist', a social and cultural conservative.

Unfortunately for Ives he "lived in dreadful isolation in an...environment dominated by 19th century German tradition," although Weiss and Taruskin feel that Ives was "unencumbered by the weight of centuries-old tradition" and that Ives agreed with Debussy that "man should try to break the arbitrary limits he himself has imposed through his musical habits on the infinite variety of sound."

The Unanswered Question; Central Park in the Dark

These works comprise the set *Two Contemplations* and were both composed around 1906 and revised in the early 1930s. They are two of Ives' most original well-known works. For an Ives composition *The Unanswered Question* is very approachable. "As with much of Ives' music...(it is) marked by a deep philosophical undercurrent."

The composition is arranged for three groups to engage in a musical argument about man's place in the universe (the 'unanswered question'). The groups, a string orchestra, a solo trumpet, and a quartet of flutes, are not only very different but they are spatially separated as well. The multi-locality of the sets of his *Unanswered Question* was another of his innovators developed in relative isolation to his European counterparts.

In *Central Park in the Dark* the "strings provide a slow, impassive sonic layer. Ives provided the following in his notes to the score, "This piece purports to be a picture-in-sounds of the sounds...men would hear (around 1870) when sitting on a bench in Central Park on a hot summer night." Included in the New York City sound picture are a trolley, a fire engine and a band of street musicians.

Three Places in New England (Orchestral Set No.1)

Possible sketches and fragments existed as early as 1903 and were used to complete the three pieces from 1912-14. Ives had to re-score it for chamber orchestra in 1930 and the work was premiered in New York in 1931. This work, like other Ives pieces from this period, are reminiscent in nature, looking back to the days of his boyhood, creating atmospheres "of recollection by means of misty harmonies…"

The first movement, *The St. Gaudens in Boston Commons,* is based on the monument 'Colonel Shaw and his Colored Regiment' which sits on the corner of Beacon and Park Streets in Boston. The monument honors the 54th Massachusetts, the first all-black Union regiment in the Civil War. The storming of Fort Wagner by this regiment was depicted in the successful movie *Glory*, with an outstanding cast starring Denzel Washington, Morgan Freeman, Matthew Broderick and Andre Braugher. With this piece Ives may actually be looking ahead to black music of the future, e.g., Ellington or Coltrane. However, such resemblances may be nothing more than accidents.

Even though he yearned for a simpler time, his music was the most *avant-garde* of its time. Those statements are certainly true if one accepts the timeline of Ives for his compositions and overlooks possible pre-dating and subsequent revisions, intended to insert 'modern' methods, well after their first completion. Contrary to Ives' claims, some musicologists (e.g., Maynard Solomon) believe much of the work's dissonance was added as Ives arranged *Three Places* for chamber orchestra, and that the original version, completed in 1914 contained far less dissonance and much less of Ives' 'innovations'. This is the subject of much debate, complicated by the fact that little of his music was published during Ives' lifetime, and what he did he published himself. Richard Taruskin has pointed out that Elliott Carter referred to Ives' "jacking up the level of dissonance" in some of his works long after they were ostensibly finished. The controversy continues one hundred year after Ives composed his works "as people hotly debate the ultimate significance of his unique contribution."

Putting aside questions and doubts as to Ives' timelines for completion of particular works in final form and whether he composed "in the most profound isolation compared with other great musical innovators, it can be said Ives "was the first to thoroughly explore the Modernist musical vocabulary," including polytonality, dissonant counterpoint, even atonality and indeterminacy.

Ives' four symphonies span his composing career from the First as his graduation composition from Yale (with composer Horatio Parker) to the Fourth, one of his last and most complex works. He "reminds us that greatness is not merely a matter of polish but of spirit, of substance rather than manner."

Second Symphony

The Second Symphony portrays "the musical feelings of the Connecticut country around here in the 1890s." Not performed in its entirety until 1951 (by the New York Philharmonic), although Ives completed it in 1902, this symphony is a novel blending of "the old Teutonic form" with all kinds of tunes borrowed from all over America, folk tunes, native tunes, marches, and hymns. Ives does not use popular tunes in full but rather blends them in "allusively...put through a sieve of dissonance." In his Second Symphony Ives practically dispenses "with the idea of symphonic themes for a collage of ideas, ranging from Brahms to hymns, college songs, ballads, spirituals, and patriotic anthems."

In addition to the "oddments of Americana" Ives includes tunes that "sound distinctly like Bruckner and Dvořák." In this symphony "romanticism meets the new forces of the 20th century and ultimately succumbs." Under the championing of Bernstein, who called the work "a sort of personal memoir of Ives' own musical experience" and "a sound image of Ives' world at the turn of the century," audiences at the premiere of this work applauded approvingly and the vindication of Ives had begun, fifty years after completion of the work.

Third Symphony, 'Camp Meeting'

Completed in the first decade of the 20th century, this symphony, "a seriously light-hearted work with hymn tunes at its heart" won Ives the Pulitzer Prize in 1948, almost forty years after its completion. Ives, in his typical aloof fashion, ridiculed winning the Prize and gave away the money that came with it. Unlike his other symphonies, the *Third* is lightly-scored with strings and a few winds; it is a "clear and uncluttered reminiscence of 19th-century America...viewed through some of its hymn tunes." The three movements, chocked full of hymn tunes, are themed 'Old Folks Gatherin', 'Children's Day', and 'Communion'.

Fourth Symphony

This grandest of American symphonies was completed in 1916 and is his final large composition. However, as with most of Ives' compositions, parts date from years back; in this case, 1897 up to the acknowledged beginning of the writing process in 1909. With this densely textured work listeners take in all of Ives' innovative techniques as in it Ives "would register the myriad of sounds of home as few people have." The second *Allegretto* movement, according to Jonathan Kramer, "is like a circus, with its nearly constant overlays of...quoted fragments" from so many indigenous tunes of Americana that this movement "seems to be saying that all manner of things...can and do happen, often at once." The third movement is a double fugue, of all things, originating from Ives' student days at Yale under Horatio Parker. The second and fourth movements both contain Ives' most complex structures.

The symphony begins with a short opening Prelude with chorus, which is followed by three substantial movements. The 'aesthetic program' provided by the composer is "that of a searching question of 'What' and 'Why' which the spirit of man asks of life." Although partial premieres of this symphony were given in 1927 (first and second movements) and 1933 (first and third), it had to wait until 1965 to be premiered as a whole. Because it requires three conductors (orchestra, chorus, and extra battery of percussion) Leopold Stokowski was joined by José Serebrier and David Katz at Carnegie Hall.

Stokowski also released a recording of it.

> *"The damndest racket you ever heard."*
> - Jan Swafford on the second movement of Ives' Fourth Symphony

Holidays Symphony (New England Holidays)

This 'symphony' is actually a set of four separate orchestral works written from 1903-13. Although Ives cobbled together a four-movement symphony from them he did state that "they are separate pieces and can be thought of and played as such." The pieces are nostalgic recollections of New England holidays from Ives' childhood. The four, in order, are 'Washington's Birthday', 'Decoration Day' (nowadays celebrated as Memorial Day), 'Fourth of July', and 'Thanksgiving'. Ives, in all four movements, makes appropriate use of the orchestra to perform pyrotechnic feats (#3) and, in 'Thanksgiving', to portray, according to the composer, "the sternness and strength and austerity of the Puritan character."

Recommended – Ives Symphonies
Leonard Bernstein and Michael Tilson Thomas lead the charge in interpretations of Ives' music. Both have studied Ives in detail and bring a scholarly sense to their readings.

Conductor Spotlight – Leonard Bernstein was an American composer, conductor, musician, and first American conductor of a major U.S. orchestra, the NY Philharmonic (1958-1969). He was largely responsible for the resurgence of Mahler's symphonies through his landmark recordings in the 1960s, fulfilling Mahler's prediction that "my time will come."

As conductor Bernstein was known for his personal, if at times self-indulgent, interpretations of the symphonies of Brahms and Sibelius, as well as those of Haydn, Mozart and Beethoven. He had an infectious enthusiasm for Mahler, which produced powerful performances of his symphonies over three decades and roughly two complete cycles. No conductor was more influential than Bernstein in promoting his fellow contemporary American composer Aaron Copland, nor the previously-neglected Charles Ives.

His readings are not viewed positively by all, as he can make "powerful" music seem "mushy" through over-indulgence, in which the performance becomes more about Lenny than about the music. However, no one can deny the talent and impact of this American icon as both composer and conductor.

♪ Edvard Grieg (1843-1907)

Grieg was a Norwegian nationalist who preferred to inject Scandinavian identity into his music instead of the "predominantly German esthetic" prevalent at the time. A Romantic for the first part of his composing career, Grieg turned Norwegian nationalist under countryman and fellow composer Rikard Nordraak. "Together they pored over folk songs and old Norwegian tunes" in an attempt "to create a truly Norwegian musical art."

> *"No chasing after nationalism. I will try to...write from the heart, whether it turns out to be Norwegian or Chinese."*
> *- Grieg*

The sounds of Norwegian folk music permeated the works of Grieg; his music blends "national characteristics with his sensitive feeling for Romantic harmony in a personal, poetic music that has (still) not lost its freshness." As with the music of Sibelius and his native Finland, Grieg's music would come to represent the sound of Norway. Aside from his Piano Concerto, his most famous and best composition, his other popular works are smaller pieces in which "his gift for lyricism" shines through most. "His work...is marked by graciousness of effect, dewy lyricism, and wistful harmonies." These smaller works include both orchestral and works for solo piano. His music is "often bathed in an almost impressionist harmony."

Piano concerto in A minor, Op.16
Both Schumann and Grieg composed one piano concerto, both in the key of A minor. Grieg clearly used Schumann's concerto, which premiered in Leipzig in 1846, as a model for his, composed in 1868 at age twenty-four. From the opening flourish, which "seems the distilled essence of the Romantic concerto," the similarities are established. This has led to the coupling of these two concertos being one of the more popular.

> *Recommended – Grieg Piano Concerto*
> The partnership of Stephen Kovacevich with Colin Davis (1971) has been hailed by critics for its "wholly natural, intimately poetic phrasing." As usual, coupled with the Schumann concerto.

Holberg Suite, Op.40
Grieg wrote several sets of orchestral suites that remain in the active repertory. *Holberg* Suite for string orchestra was originally composed for piano but was expanded to its current version in 1885. Written in the Baroque style, Grieg evokes Bach, Handel, and even Mozart, and makes no attempt to hide the

retro-Baroque intention with movements labeled *Praeludium* (the opening movement), *Sarabande*, *Gavotte*, Air and *Rigaudon*. The work was written to commemorate the 200th birthday of Danish playwright Ludvig Holberg. The suite very effectively shows Grieg's unique combination of Nordic Romanticism with his neo-Classical/Baroque style in the form of a Baroque dance suite.

Symphonic Dances, Op.64

Grieg is beloved in his native Norway to this day, as is Sibelius in Finland. However, "Grieg's reputation has suffered, fairly or not, as a result of his unwillingness to tackle large forms." The four pieces that comprise his Op.64 are as close as he got to a proper symphony. However, there must be more to it than that, as Debussy avoided concertos and symphonies as well and, like Grieg, composed only one string quartet. The difference is that Debussy was a musical trail-blazer, recognized as a great innovator while Grieg utilized existent forms and did not contribute significantly to the evolution of musical forms and styles.

♪ Eastern Europe

Alex Ross in The Rest Is Noise defines three great 'realists' in early 20th century music – Leoš Janáček, Béla Bartók, and Maurice Ravel. Janáček and Bartók were leading nationalistic Czech and Hungarian composers, respectively. Janáček carried forward what had been started by Smetana and Dvořák in forging a national identity for Czech music. The 'realist' label is used for Janáček, Bartók and Ravel because none was born in a city but they went there for their training and livelihood. All three were born in outlying towns and, even years after settling in as urbanites, "never shook the feeling that they had come from somewhere else."

♫ Bedřich Smetana (1824-1884)

The Czech nationalist movement was not "marked from the outset, as was the Russian, by self-conscious efforts to avoid Western influence."

> *"It is to (my homeland) that I shall sacrifice myself."*
> - Smetana

Smetana, the father of Czech nationalist music, had a major influence on Dvořák, Janáček, and Martinů. As with Janáček decades later, Smetana found opera to be a most effective vehicle for expression. Janáček even referred to Smetana as "the sole representation of Czech music," slighting his countryman Dvořák probably because of what Janáček saw as a 'New World' influence as well as Dvořák's coziness with Brahms. The most famous Smetana opera by far is *The Bartered Bride*, while others have remained popular in what is now the Czech Republic and Slovakia. The fact that Smetana grew up speaking German at the virtual exclusion of his native language only strengthened his patriotism and longing to identify himself as a Czech. At age thirty-four Smetana found "to my shame I must confess (my deficiencies) in Czech," but despite this he was "proud to show that my homeland means more to me than anything else."

"In music is the life of the Czechs."
- Smetana

His major instrumental works include his string quartets, one of which, *From My Life*, is the best-known programmatic chamber work, and the six tone poems that comprise his overtly patriotic *Má vlast* ('My Homeland'). The tone poems were composed around icons of Czech nationalism: the river Vltava, the woods and meadows of Bohemia, the mountain Blaník, and the fortress Tabor. *Má vlast* is a captivating narrative "completely dissolved in the history of his nation, in its heroes, mountains, valleys, and streams." In *Má vlast* Smetana invites us to follow the Vltava river that flows through Prague as he takes us to meet defeated Hussite heroes taking refuge in the mountains. Hussites were 15th century Moravians and Bohemians who advocated religious freedom but were ultimately crushed. They became a symbol of freedom for the Czechs. From its first complete performance in November 1882 the collection was and has remained an enduring nationalist demonstration for Czechs.

"He was primarily a tone painter, a descriptive artist." This painting was often autobiographical; as Smetana stated, "My aim was to present to the listener scenes from my life." He was "the foundation of Czech art music" and "holds an especially cherished place in the history of Czech culture." Smetana, as Janáček would later do, tried to avoid traditional German influences in his music as much as possible and to establish an identity for Czech music. He possessed a "steely integrity in serving the national cause." Dvorak, on the other hand, "both venerated and was friendly with Brahms" so Dvořák's music, which has achieved more widespread popularity than the works of his fellow Czechs, was really fusion of traditional German forms with Czech influences.

Ironically, Smetana would fall out of favor with his countrymen for being too influenced by Wagner, despite Smetana's refusal to stage any of the Bayreuth master's music dramas while director of the National Theater repertory. In fact, Smetana dismissed Wagner's works as "foreign in their downright Germanism."

♪ Leoš Janáček (1854-1928)

> *"Moravia alone is enough to give me all necessary inspiration, so rich are her resources."*
> - Leoš Janáček

Together, Dvořák, Smetana, and Janáček make up the triumvirate of great Czech Nationalistic composers. Janáček is the only one whose life and music reached well into the 20th century. As with Smetana, who founded Czech music, and Dvořák, who popularized it, Janáček used many folk-like materials in his works. But unlike fellow Czechs Smetana and Dvořák, Janáček "consciously renounced the styles of Western Europe," and embraced Moravian folk music while rejecting everything German. And as Bartók and Kodály did in Hungary and other parts of Eastern Europe, Janáček in his youth scoured the Moravian countryside for indigenous tunes. His is an "entirely idiosyncratic language based on his folk heritage." He is a composer who straddled the post-Romantic and modern world, as did Schoenberg. His pared-down bare harmonies point forward, while his commitment to tonality looked back.

> *"If I grow at all, it is only out of folk music..."*
> - Janáček

Janáček's style was completely unique and original, created by combining Czech folk-based tunes with melodies influenced by the rhythms and pitch patterns of the Czech language; "very short melodies are his thumbprint." Janáček was determinedly anti-German in his approach to music, no doubt partly responsible for his "half a century of strictly regional (Moravia) fame," marginalized from 'educated German' taste.

One of the great opera composers of the 20th century, early on his music was heavily influenced by his countryman Dvořák. However, he remained virtually unknown until the first decade of the 20th century at age fifty, making him the oldest '20th century' composer. His finest works of his last dozen years were mainly inspired by a frustrated passion for a younger woman. Despite being born in 1854 and in his seventies when 'modern' music began and the world recognized him, Janáček "is customarily treated as a representative '20th century' figure."

After his opera *Jenůfa*, he added a "stark, angular and even rough quality" to his blended melodies and rhythms from Czech and Moravian folk music. Into the 20th century Janáček's music became increasingly rugged and dissonant with harsh harmonies, but it did not become atonal; it remains very accessible. Most of his important works came during WWI or in the 1920s after age sixty in a remarkable burst of inspiration. The success of his opera

Jenůfa in 1915 created a demand for his music. He had "an intensity for nature," his music "full of vitality and color…"

Sinfonietta

As indicated by the title, this is a relatively small-scale work (a 'mini-symphony') and is Janáček's most famous orchestral work. It is "a five-movement work of amazing color and harmonic and orchestral virtuosity." This work was composed in 1925-26, is based on a series of previously composed brass fanfares, and premiered in Prague with the Czech Philharmonic under its legendary conductor Václav Talich. Its youthful vigor belies the fact that Janáček composed the work at age seventy-two.

Nevertheless, *Sinfonietta* is a "youthfully vigorous work, full of life, optimism and originality." The opening fanfare section comes complete with extra military brass, these short and simple fanfares producing "splashes of primary color." The nationalistic spirit took off in Janáček because of the patriotism he felt for his newly-formed Czechoslovakia (created out of World War I). If all of the themes are not actually adopted from folk songs, they sound as if they are.

> *Recommended – Sinfonietta*
> Charles Mackerras/Vienna Philharmonic (Decca) and Simon Rattle/CBSO (EMI). Both are excellent versions.
> *Conductor Spotlight – Charles Mackerras* (1925-2010)
> Raised in upstate New York, he studied in Czechoslovakia with Václav Talich. He is a conductor of an extremely varied repertory, much of it is infused with authenticity through tireless devotion to a scholarship. David Hurwitz has stated that Mackerras, "has not made a bad record." Mackerras is expert and considered an authority on the music of Czech nationalists Dvořák, Smetana, Martinů, but particularly of Janacek.
>
> His performances are marked by tight and polished playing, with ensembles that normally reflect the size of orchestras at the time of the particular music. For his acclaimed recordings of Haydn and Mozart, Mackerras favors the use of smaller 'chamber' ensembles that combine period and modern instruments and a hybrid approach that uses a 'modern' orchestra sized to match period forces. One example of Mackerras' 'scholarly' approach, which is not to everyone's liking, is his observation of all repeats in his Mozart symphonies.

Outside his native land Janáček is probably best-known as one of the more significant 20th century opera composers, with several in the active repertoire, including *Jenůfa*, *The Cunning Little Vixen*, and *From the House of the Dead*. His operas are based on some of the more peculiar subjects in the history of opera and most of them feature women in tragic circumstances. Janáček is also known for his three-movement tone poem *Taras Bulba*; his 'Kreutzer' String Quartet and the Sonata for Violin and Piano remain popular chamber works.

♫ Béla Bartók (1881-1945)

> *"The excesses of the Romantics began to be unbearable to many."*
> - Bela Bartók

Harold Schonberg in his chapter on Bartók ('The Uncompromising Hungarian') in his classic book The Lives of the Great Composers, states at the opening that Bartók "represents the fusion of nationalism and 19th century musical thought into a convulsively powerful means of expression." He looked to take the folk music of his native Hungary, which at the time included parts of Romania, and turn it into 20th century music and "found his personal style in a dissonant, compelling Hungarian nationalism." Bartók "treats the folk music of entirely different cultures (arrangements of Romanian, Hungarian, and Slavic folk songs) very much alike...for the specific purpose of forming a style." He felt that his research into native folk music "freed me from the tyrannical rule of the major and minor keys."

While the Second Viennese School turned to atonality Bartók found "the ideal starting point for a musical renaissance" (Bartók) in the assimilation of 'peasant music'. After Bartók came to America in 1940 he applied his experience researching folk music in his native Eastern Europe to a job at Columbia University with a collection of Serbo-Croatian folk recordings. However, Bartók did not consider himself primarily a 'nationalist' composer. He wanted to be assessed as a composer not as a folklorist.

Bartók was a master of orchestration and with *The Wooden Prince* ballet score (1914-16) "a strongly individual personality emerges" with influences of Strauss and Debussy. The similarities with Stravinsky (when still influenced by Russian folk tunes) include melodies within a narrow range centered around one note and being a "master of percussive dissonance." This placed both of them among "the great rhythmic imaginations of modern times." A difference between Bartók and Stravinsky is that the Russian maintains a homogeneous style within a particular work whereas Bartók "is apt to incorporate diverse elements" within a given composition. His ideal was "to express, in 20th century terms, Bach's texture of contrapuntal fullness, Beethoven's art of thematic development, and Debussy's discovery of the sonorous value of chords." One element Bartók would inject into a work was 'polymodality', the simultaneous combination of different modes (e.g., major and minor), attempting to create a unique chromaticism.

The pantomime *The Miraculous Mandarin* matched the polyphony of *The Rite of Spring* and Bartók included 'stylized noise' (his own words). It was begun in August 1918 in the horrible aftermath of World War I in Europe and contains a cast of thugs, prostitutes, would-be lovers, along with the mysterious title character that creates "a disturbing metaphor for the reigning reality." The full work is a pantomime with libretto by Menyhert Lengyel accompanied by the music of Bartók. Prior to completion Bartók extracted what the orchestral suite from the work.

Bartók produced his masterpieces from 1926-39: the first two piano concertos, string quartets Nos.3-6, the Sonata for Two Pianos and Percussion, the *Music for Strings, Percussion, and Celesta*, and the Second Violin Concerto. As with most 20th century music, but also with other great sets of music such as Beethoven's late string quartets, Bartók's mature works take many hearings to fully absorb. "The dissonances begin to sound pungent instead of fearsome...those savage and eccentric rhythms...all clear up into a direct emotional utterance."

The Piano Concertos

Bartók's three piano concertos are a major contribution to the repertoire. As with Prokofiev and Stravinsky, Bartók saw the piano "as an instrument of percussive rhythm."

> *"One has to go back to Beethoven to find so much fantasy within the rules"*
> - Francis Poulenc on Bartók's piano concertos

The first two piano concertos were composed for Bartók himself, being suitable for an international virtuoso. The First Piano Concerto (composed in 1926; revised in 1929) was premiered in 1927 with Bartók as soloist in Frankfurt with Furtwängler conducting. This muscular concerto dates from a period when Bartók was "exploring relentlessly driving rhythms" and is the best example of how Bartók used dissonance not as harmony but as color "with foreign (i.e., dissonant) notes grafted on (to chords) to add spice...giving it its biting vitality." It presents the German symphonic tradition in a neo-Classical context.

This 'biting vitality', which made his music sound atonal, is on full display in the outer movements, between which Bartók supplies a delicate, but percussive, piece of 'night music.' As did Stravinsky and others, the piano is used as a percussive instrument. In the place of extended melodies Bartók, again like Stravinsky, uses fragments of scales and builds the music "from these small fragments, not from tunes" and "his motives...are in a constant state of regeneration." This concerto, with its relentlessly driving rhythms, was not readily accepted by audiences nor performed by pianists. It is extremely difficult to play and for some time only Bartók played it in concert. Other pianists did not add it to their repertoires.

The lyrical *Third* was written near the end of Bartók's life for his pianist wife and is his last completed work. This concerto, "one of his most unashamedly neo-Romantic in mood," in a clear Mozartian mold, and is much less dissonant than his other mature works. It is lightly orchestrated and contains far less of the conflict between soloist and orchestra found in his first two piano concertos (premiered in 1927 and 1933, respectively). Bartók began the *Third* in poor health in the summer of 1945 and left the last seventeen measures incomplete upon his death. These were completed by his friend, composer Serly. The work premiered in America with fellow Hungarian and Bartók champion Eugene Ormandy conducting his Philadelphians. György Sándor was the soloist.

> *Recommended – Bartók Piano Concertos*
> An original idea that turned out to be very successful was DG having Pierre Boulez lead three different orchestras with a different soloist for each concerto (2005). The soloist/orchestra couplings for *Concertos Nos.1-3*, respectively, are Zimerman/Chicago Symphony, Andsnes/Berlin PO, and Grimaud/London Symphony.
> The other recommendation would be Géza Anda with Ferenc Fricsay leading the Berlin Radio Symphony Orchestra (DG, 1968). For decades this recording by pianist Anda and conductor Fricsay, both Hungarians, has set the standard.

Concerto for Orchestra

This work was commissioned by the Boston Symphony and Serge Koussevitzky. They premiered it in late 1944, less than a year before Bartók's death. The legendary Boston maestro stated that the Concerto for Orchestra was "the best orchestral piece of the last 25 years." Looking back now from 2014, the work may may have been the best orchestral piece of the past eighty or ninety years. The title indicates that the work treats orchestral instruments as soloists, "in a concertante or soloist manner," within a symphonic work, and "every instrument of the orchestra gets a chance to shine." Bartók "treats the instruments in a colorful, soloistic manner, contrasting groups of instruments against the full body of the orchestra." An example is the 'game of pairs' second movement in which pairs of like instruments take turns as soloists. In the fourth movement Bartók famously parodies Shostakovich's Lenigrad symphony, which he had recently heard on radio premiered by Toscanini and the NBC Symphony Orchestra.

Bartók creates a "polyglot diversity" by drawing from folk melodies, North American rhythms, Debussy, Schoenberg, Stravinsky and including for effect "fanfares of all-American brass." The composer characterizes the first movement as stern; the second as 'jesting'; he points out the "lugubrious death song of the third" movement, all a gradual transition to the "life assertion of the last" movement.

This is one of Bartók's more approachable works because it is more expansive and less dissonant than many of his earlier works, although there is no shortage of folk-based melodies and Hungarian dance rhythms. It was his first work to capture the public; unfortunately for Bartók and the public, he practically composed it on his deathbed. He did not live to see much of his other music, such as his concertos but especially his six string quartets, get the attention they deserve.

Music for Strings, Percussion and Celesta

This work, from 1936, is scored for two string orchestras, one on each side of a piano, a celesta, a harp and several other pieces of percussion. The "most remarkable of his orchestral works," is highly original. It is a four-movement concerto grosso in slow-fast-slow-fast format, each with a unique personality, including a fugal first movement. The fast movements contain folk music "cast in a modernistic idiom." The unique scoring and instrumental setup allow Bartók to explore new sonorities. Although Bartók's orchestral works are all harsh and dissonant, they contain plenty of folkish melodies but they stop short of full atonality.

In it a piano, harp, xylophone, timpani and others comprise the 'percussion', and are placed in the middle, with the strings divided on either side. It is Bartók's most dense orchestral works and one of his most difficult to perform. Pierre Boulez characterized the first movement as "a fugue unfolding fanwise to a maximum intensity and then folding back to its initial mystery."

> *Recommended – Bartók Orchestral Works*
> For sheer excitement it is hard to beat Fritz Reiner and his Chicagoans in both of these 20th century orchestral masterpieces.

While Bartók enjoyed a burst of success in 1943-45, his failing health prevented him from fully responding to it. Bartók continued composing up to his death, necessitated by financial straits in the United States. These unfortunate circumstances did result in some of his finest music, including the Viola Concerto, left just short of completion on his deathbed, the Sonata for Solo Violin, and Piano Concerto No.3.

His last work, the Viola Concerto, was commissioned by the noted violist William Primrose. Bartók left this concerto in fragments upon his death in September 1945 but it was fortunately completed by his friend, the composer Tibor Serly, who essentially had to orchestrate the entire work. "It is extremely problematic to orchestrate a viola concerto so that the solo line will not be covered." This is not a problem with the violin and composers had long since learned how to effectively write cello concertos (e.g., Dvořák, Elgar) to give that instrument the prominence enjoyed by violins in violin concertos.

Although Bartók and his works were not fully appreciated during his lifetime; at best his works were met with apathy but sometimes hostility and antagonism. Bartók's music became popular with the public after his death and his works eventually became some of the most often-played of the 20th century repertoire. He is now generally regarded as one of the top five composers of the 20th century, in the company of Stravinsky, Schoenberg, Prokofiev, and Shostakovich. "His greatness lies not so much in his technical and stylistic innovations as in his extraordinary aptitude for creative synthesis." However, his music "exerted very little influence upon the thinking of young composers" as the post-World War II *avant-garde* was drawn to atonality and the composers of the Second Viennese School, particularly Webern.

♪ Zoltán Kodály

Kodály and Bartók met at Budapest's Academy of Music. Kodály collaborated with fellow Hungarian Bartók to scour Eastern Europe for native folk music. As Debussy aimed to break French music from the grip of 19th century Germanic dominance, so Bartók and Kodály incorporated Hungarian folk tunes, "which they hoped would free Hungarian music from the all-pervading German influence." Kodály was determined to use new phonograph recording technology to preserve folk music in its authentic state. He stated, "It is impossible to study folksongs satisfactorily…unless one hears them actually performed…by the peasants themselves (so) that we can be certain as to their correct interpretation."

While Kodály combined the same elements with native folksong as Bartók, Kodály's process "did not produce results of nearly the same artistic quality." The heavy French influence of Debussy Kodály displayed "tempered the strength of the native Hungarian materials." His adventures with Bartók and the indigenous music of Eastern Europe told him what Debussy also knew: "vast possibilities were to be found outside the major-minor system."

Kodály's most popular work by far is the brilliant orchestral showpiece *Háry János* Suite extracted in 1927 from his opera that he composed in 1925-26. The Suite is a six-piece work to portray Háry, a beloved scoundrel from Hungarian folklore who fought in the Napoleanic Wars, as the "typical representative of the whole Hungarian peasantry." The suite includes citations from actual folk material and a prominent part for the zither-like instrument Hungarians call the cimbalon. One of the pieces, titled "The Battle and Defeat of Napoleon," is a caricature of military music and in the opera Kodály absurdly has Háry single-handedly defeat the French army and kill Napoleon himself. Kodály spoke for both himself and Bartók in expressing the thought that "to be a true internationalist, one must first be a nationalist," and the Hungarian spirit is inescapable in Kodály's music. He remains revered in his native Hungary today.

♪ Iberia

♫ Manuel de Falla (1876-1946)

Falla wrote a well-known work that is essentially a piano concerto but titled it to reflect the nationalism and atmosphere of his native land. He developed a diverse Spanish nationalism by collecting and arranging national folk songs. Falla "completely distilled his country's musical voice" and brought Spanish and Andalusian folk and popular music "into a classical context." He also incorporated international influences in his 'Spanish-flavored' music.

Much of the Spaniard Falla's music has been called 'Spanish Impressionism'. Falla developed a new and completely anti-Romantic approach to the piano with his first major work *Cuatro piezas españolas* ('Four Spanish Pieces'). Unlike the French Impressionist masters Debussy and Ravel, who tried to convey a feeling for Spain with *Iberia* and Rapsodie Espagnole, Falla's *Nights in the Gardens of Spain* for piano and orchestra is truly Spanish, albeit with French influences.

Originally seeking a set of nocturnes for solo piano, Falla stated that in composing *Nights* he was inspired not only by festivals and dances but also by melancholy and mystery; that it was written "to evoke places, sensations and sentiments." It has also been claimed (by Spaniards) that some Spanish paintings of gardens inspired Falla; others (Frenchmen) insist the inspiration came from hearing a French poem during his Paris days.

In the style of Debussy the work, begun in 1909 and completed in 1915, is 'Iberian Impressionism' and comprised of three 'nocturnes' connected by a main motive. Falla insisted the music is not descriptive, merely expressive and some of the orchestral coloring is intended to evoke effects peculiar to Andalusian instruments. Also well-known is *El Amor brujo* (1915) with its "vivid evocation of love and witchcraft among the Andalusian gypsies."

His later mature works include *El retablo de maese Pedro* (1919-23) based on an episode from *Don Quixote* and the neo-Baroque Concerto for Harpsichord with Five Solo Instruments (1923-26). As with the nationalist composers of Eastern Europe and Scandinavia, Falla succeeded in making 'serious' music out of the indigenous folk and popular music of his native country. After World War II Falla combined the melodic and rhythmic aspects of Spanish popular music with a neo-Classical approach, resulting in a modern nationalist music. What Bohemia was to Dvořák, Andalusia was to Falla. His colorful rhythms and evocative melodies, drawn from native Spanish tunes, make him a folk hero in Spanish countries today.

♪ Isaac Albéniz (1860-1909)

He spent his childhood as a prodigy being paraded around from age four; at thirteen he was in Cuba, New York and South America. He then returned to Europe and compiled an impressive pedigree, studying piano in Leipzig, Brussels, and Paris with Liszt, d'Indy, and Dukas and inspired future Spanish composers such as Granados (1867-1916) and Falla. "Besides adapting technical features of indigenous Spanish music, he saturated his works with color, the atmosphere of Spain."

Albéniz combined native melodies in a "highly spiced chromatic idiom." His masterpiece is *Iberia*, a set of four books each consisting of three solo piano pieces. Each piece depicts a particular location in Spain and scenes in Spanish life. The work was composed 1906-09 during the difficult last years of his life when he and his wife were ill and his daughter had died. It remains a popular work in the piano repertory today. Based on Andalusian folk tunes, it is full of Spain through and through – exuberant Spanish rhythms and melodies, rich and thick textures, and elaborate ornamentation and "indigenous Spanish dances are everywhere in evidence."

Despite Albéniz's attempts to create a purely Spanish music-world, the influence of Chopin, Liszt, and others is readily apparent in Iberia. The sharp-edged keyboard brilliance is in the spirit of Liszt with an accent of Spanish folk music. In *Iberia* Albéniz collected twelve impressions in four books, suggesting "infinite nuances of atmosphere" and drawing inspiration from Andalusia, the southern-most region of Spain. Some impressions are of a fishing village, a *Corpus Christi* processional and are "at once deliciously evocative and flamboyantly virtuosic." The *El Corpus Christi en Sevilla* is the most famous of the twelve pieces and was orchestrated by Leopold Stokowski.

> *Recommended – Albéniz Iberia*
> The recommendations here are easy: any of the several recordings by Alicia de Larrocha, who has released a recording of these pieces every decade since the 1970s. The Barcelona pianist has a special affinity for this music.

Part 5

Post-Romanticism and the 20th Century

- 21 -

Impressionism
Debussy and Ravel

> "In my own composition I am greatly helped if I have in mind a book, a beautiful picture, or a poem."
> — Sergei Rachmaninoff, who was not an Impressionist composer

The two greatest French masters of the orchestra, Debussy and Ravel, did not compose a symphony. Fauré composed nothing even approaching a symphony or a full-scale concerto. Their elder countrymen Saint-Saëns and Franck both did, as did the disciples of Franck. It has been postulated that it was not a rejection of sonata form by the former group but rather, with Debussy and Ravel, the "feeling for color and light made it inevitable that programme music would exert the stronger appeal."

However, others feel differently noting that while Debussy originally admired Wagner's music and was deeply moved by his music dramas, which he witnessed in Bayreuth in 1888/89, he began to distance himself from the 'Wagner formula' and to seek a 'purer' style. Debussy realized (correctly) that the musical path taken by Wagner, and followed by Mahler and Strauss, both contemporaries of Debussy, was not the road 'modern' music would ultimately follow. Debussy fled once he realized the full implications of Wagner's world, and thenceforth he "shrank from any musical effort that might seem to impose on the listener, let alone overwhelm him."

However, it is also noted that Debussy agreed with Wagner in his assessment that the symphony as a viable form was dead. He summed up his opinion of sonata form as "a legacy of clumsy, falsely interposed traditions…musical mathematics." Debussy's proof was that all composers since had fallen short, if not far short, of Beethoven's powerful works.

> "My God how unbearable these people in skins and helmets become by the fourth night."
> — Debussy at a Wagner *Ring* Cycle

Debussy, as a Frenchman, was sensitive to the heavy influence of German composers on music in his homeland and warned of the "tedious and ponderous Teuton." He added, "To a Frenchman, finesse and nuance are the daughters of intelligence." Debussy's orchestral music "rejected the huge symphonic form of German music (as well as) the traditional classical exposition of Mozart." Instead, his music explored the mysterious relationship between nature and imagination.

> "We ought to have our own music, if possible without sauerkraut."
> — Satie to Debussy

Both Debussy and Ravel were drawn to the Russian masters of orchestral color and atmosphere, but not to the Russian symphonists (the most prominent being Tchaikovsky). They satiated their tastes for a "growing complexity of orchestral textures" with Russian influences, for example, Debussy "inherited the harmonic palette of Mussorgsky." Ravel possessed significant neo-Classical leanings compared to Debussy and he was peerless in his ability to "calculate on paper the effect of a subtle mixture of timbres," leading to his "supreme prowess as an orchestrator."

> *"In Germany, aside from Strauss, we hardly see other than second-rate composers..."*
> \- M. Ravel (letter of 7/7/16)

Impressionism was started in France as a reaction against German Romanticism, although Debussy's music was never fully accepted by the Paris intelligencia, who found his music "a little too murkily mystical." The distinction of Impressionism versus Romanticism is that Impressionist composers "hint at subjects instead of stating them…using lush and somewhat vague harmony and rhythm to evoke… mood, place and natural phenomena" Impressionism "is concerned with something specific but intangible, with something elusive and abstract, with human feelings."

♪ Claude Debussy (1862-1918)

> *"If people insist on wanting to understand what happens in a symphonic poem, we may as well give up writing them."*
> \- Claude Debussy

Impressionism with Debussy should not be confused with the programmatic tone poems of Strauss; in fact, Debussy characterized Strauss's works as 'false grandeur.' We do not find in Debussy's music explicit events or plots. Instead, Debussy's impressionist works were for him a "series of fleeting emotions." His symbolist music was "elusive and shimmering…rather than literal and narrative, like that of Strauss." The works that launched Impressionism began in 1893 with Debussy's String Quartet in G minor, and then the famous *Prelude to the Afternoon of a Faun* the next year with its "voluptuous ambience"…based on the erotic poem by Mallarmé.

Debussy fell under the influence of Wagner in the late 1880s, even attending two Bayreuth festivals, but quickly moved away from the German's massive models in his "honest quest for an unblemished, truthful musical language." This shift led to Debussy's resistance of "the Germanic urge to develop his thematic material: the melody remains static while the accompaniment evolves." But while trying to distance himself from Germanic influences and traditions of form, Debussy did allow Russian influence to shape his approach to music. His use of the whole-tone scale may have been a result of his first trip to Russia in 1881 where he may have been exposed to Glinka's use of it in his works. Debussy was also later influenced by Rimsky-Korsakov and Mussorgsky, two great masters of orchestral color. Debussy's orchestral writing also "displayed the traditional French mastery of the woodwinds."

Debussy wrote in 1907 that "music…is not something that can flow inside a rigorous, traditional form. It consists of colours and rhythmicized time." Debussy had "little affinity for or interest in the symmetry" demanded by working within the boundaries of traditional orchestral forms. As did the Impressionist painters, Debussy wanted to leave some of the 'work' to listeners through suggestion, making an impression. For example, *La Mer* suggests the ocean; the listener is left to blend the sounds to create specific imagery.

La Mer

"The sea held great allure for Debussy" and according to the composer himself, he found himself pulled to the sea throughout most of his life. This tone poem, begun in 1903 and completed in 1905, is considered by some to be a symphony without a first movement. However, Debussy did not intend to write a three-movement symphony, but rather three symphonic sketches as indicated by his subtitle Trois exquisses symphoniques.

La Mer is in three movements, all intended to be very suggestive to listeners. They are: 'From Dawn 'til Noon on the Sea'; 'Play of the Waves'; and 'Dialogue of the Wind and Sea'. The central movement "slips easily from one wave-shaped melodic idea to another." *La Mer* was inspired in part by the world famous wave paintings by the Japanese artist Hokusai. For the first time in his music Nature itself is the subject.

This is not programmatic music as in the sense of the typical Romantic symphonic poems. In *La Mer* the listener does not find the appearance of the sea but rather "an evocation of the magic of the sea." Instead of telling a story Debussy gives an impression. He is a musical painter and wants us to feel the waves in *La Mer*, not see them, through a "series of sense impressions," "to put into music his impressions of visual stimuli;" or as Debussy put it, "trying to achieve…an effect of reality."

Nocturnes

Debussy's Nocturnes are actually a set of three symphonic poems with clear, detailed programs. The first, *Nuages*, is intended to invoke drifting clouds but with a dark, menacing mood. The music of the second, *Fêtes*, symbolizes a celebration, while the third, *Sirenes*, attempts to paint a musical picture of seductive mermaids, and is definitely the most challenging of the three images to conjure up through music. In these 'musical scenes' "an enchanted world seems to rise before us – far-off, antique, misty with distance or bright with the unreal colors of a vision." As with *La Mer* this earlier work (1897-1899) represents the pull of the sea on Debussy.

> *"Music is composed of colors and rhythmic moments of time."*
> *- Debussy*

Images

A set of sonic postcards "trying to achieve something different, an effect of reality," is how the composer explained this orchestral suite. Composed 1906 to 1912, *Images* consists of three pieces containing folk tunes from England ('Gigues'), Spain ('Iberia'), and France (*Rondes de Printemps*, 'Round Dances of Spring'). The very well-known three-movement Iberia is linked by common thematic elements, which Debussy completed in 1908 and premiered in 1910. Iberia is a "brilliantly executed portrait of Spain" with a palette of bold, bright colors. The middle nocturne of *Iberia* is wistful and dream-like while the two outer movements are festive and dance-like, pervaded by Spanish rhythms.

The Spanish composer Manual de Falla felt that Iberia was not an attempt at Spanish music per se "but rather to translate into music the associations that Spain had aroused in him." It is very effective, "particularly its slow and dreamlike section with celesta, oboes and bassoon." *Iberia* is the most popular of the three by far and has become a stand-alone three-part work.

Jeux

Jeux is a startlingly original composition, even for Debussy. It seems to lack continuity and almost completely lacks melody. It "is a mosaic of ideas, many of which seem only half-formed." It concentrates on short wisps of melody, giving the work its fragmentary nature. "Often there is intensity and puzzlement at the same time – a complexity…created by exquisite chords…" This is Debussy's only real ballet score. It was commissioned by Serge Diaghilev for his *Ballets Russes*, and premiered in Paris in May 1915. Two weeks later at the same theatre (*Théâtre des Champs-Élysées*) the same troupe would create an uprising with the premiere of Stravinsky's *The Rite of Spring*. *Jeux* is one of Debussy's most colorful works, despite the composer being less than enthusiastic about the almost plotless story involving three young people playing tennis.

Recommended – Debussy – Orchestral Works
Dutoit, Montreal, 2CD (Decca) and Haitink and the Concertgebouw (Philips), *Prelude to the Afternoon of a Faun, Nocturnes, Images, La Mer*; an exceptional coupling. One cannot go wrong with either the Dutoit or Haitink offerings; masters of color leading the world's most colorful orchestras.

♪ Maurice Ravel (1875-1937)

Ravel's orchestral works and orchestral versions of piano works form a "remarkably varied picture gallery."

Rapsodie Espagnole

Debussy and Ravel each produced a great score intended to evoke images of Spain. Debussy's *Iberia* and Ravel's *Rapsodie Espagnole* were composed a year apart in 1908 and 1907, respectively. "The Ravel orchestration has a springier, lither quality," is a "sultry, virtuoso piece" and his first purely orchestral work.

Ravel's Basque origin (on his mother's side) "held sway over his imagination," and "his mother's memories of a folkish past," sung to Ravel by her as a boy, always influenced his musical tendencies. Much of Ravel's music has a feeling of Spain, and not just the obvious *Rapsodie Espagnole* composed in 1907-08. In this work he puts his "Spanish-Basque heritage proudly on display" creating "transformations of textures and rhythm" and in the finale "a dynamic effect of rhythmic layering." Ravel used Spain as an "inexhaustible source of exotic musical ideas and colorful aural imagery," but, just as Debussy, he also considered Russian influences such as Rimsky-Korsakov's *Capriccio Espagnol*.

Daphnis et Chloe, Suite No.2

Daphnis et Chloe is Ravel's largest work, calling for an enormous orchestra and a wordless chorus. The ballet itself, from 1912, has never been very popular, partly due to the mismatch between Ravel's score, commissioned by Sergei Diaghilev and his Russian dance company, and the other components of it. However, two sets of orchestral suites were extracted from the ballet and the Suite No.2, extracted in 1913, became an extremely popular orchestral work of the 20th century. Igor Stravinsky gushed that *Daphnis et Chloe*, based on a third-century pastoral romance, was "one of the most beautiful products in all of French music."

The second orchestral suite contains three pieces and opens with *Daybreak*, which in the full opera follows a night of terror at the hands of pirates. Using shimmering harps and winds along with low strings, Debussy very effectively conveys the peaceful beginning of a new day, the imagery of a ship setting sail on the ocean, with the wind finally pushing the vessel out to sea. The second piece, *Pantomime*, reunites Daphnis and Chloe, while the third piece is "a sweeping dance that rises to a stunning climax, a Dionysian celebration of physical love." This music would sound a lot more modern if not for its lush harmonies.

La Valse and *Le Tombeau de Couperin*

Both *La Valse* and *Le Tombeau de Couperin* capture Ravel's World War I experiences as an army truck driver who still witnessed the horrible carnage, with *La Valse* starting "in the darkest depths of the orchestra" and ending "catastrophically."

'The Waltz', performed only as an orchestral work, is "both a dazzling incarnation of the 1920s and a dazzling satire of it," with references to the "fury of the war just past." The work is "strikingly contrasted (with) sumptuous harmony and glittering orchestration." Ravel works up a "maelstrom of orchestral sound (that is) elegantly scary." Originally commissioned by Diaghilev as a ballet, the Russian rejected it when Ravel played it for him on the piano, claiming he failed to see how it would work choreographically. Ravel went on to orchestrate the work and perform it anyway. Instead of the merriment of a typical Strauss waltz, *La Valse* has "a sinister atmosphere that becomes frenzied by the end." Ravel himself claims the work describes "flashes of lightning in turbulent clouds reveal a couple waltzing."

Le Tombeau de Couperin is one of several works Ravel originally composed for solo piano and later orchestrated. Ravel's orchestrations of his piano works "soften the edges of the pianistic originals." The six-movement piano version, fittingly written in the form of a baroque dance suite, was finished in 1917 and Ravel orchestrated four movements into a suite less than two years later. *Tombeau*, literally 'tomb', was a term used in the Baroque period, for example, by Francois Couperin, for an elegy piece to a specific person. So Ravel intended to compose an homage to Couperin by composing a suite that contains a series of painful laments, about his friends' deaths in World War I as well as the recent death of his mother.

Tzigane

Ravel's contribution to one-movement virtuoso violin and orchestra showpieces, *Tzigane*, meaning 'gypsy', is marked by its extended, opening cadenza before the entry of the harp. This virtuoso favorite has characteristic gypsy flair. Ravel composed the piece for female Hungarian violin virtuoso Jelly D'Aranyi, who premiered the piano/violin version in 1924. The orchestrated version was completed by Ravel the next year. *Tzigane*, which overflows with virtuoso fireworks, pushed "the violin to its outer limits in a modern idiom rooted in the café gypsy style."

Piano Concertos

> *"The music of a concerto should be light-hearted and brilliant."*
>
> - Ravel

Unlike Debussy, with whom he will be forever linked, Ravel composed some concertos: two for the piano, and both late in his career. Ravel's two piano concertos were both published in 1931 while most of his solo piano and orchestral works were composed before 1920. In the last decade of his life Ravel entered a new phase of consummate mastery with his two piano concertos. The Piano Concerto in G, with its attention-grabbing opening whip crack, was written, according to Ravel, "very much in the same spirit as those of Mozart and Saint-Saëns." The influence of jazz, ragtime and blues is keenly felt in the concerto. It has a quick jazzy feel to it but also reminds the listener of the mood evoked in some of Copland's Americana ballet scores. Sounding more like Gershwin's piano and orchestra works than Mozart, the Concerto in G shows Ravel's "wondrous ability to assimilate different styles of music," including jazz and blues elements. Ravel claimed that this concerto "took two years of work, you know" (1929-31). Scored with a harp and full percussion in addition to a traditional orchestra, the listener can easily hear the influence of jazz, especially Gershwin.

The Concerto in D for Left Hand was commissioned by pianist Paul Wittgenstein. Ravel felt it important to give the solo part as much texture as a concerto for both hands. The thumb is given a prominent melodic role.

♪ *Other Impressionist Composers*

Ottorino Respighi (1879-1936) was unsurpassed as an orchestral colorist; Respighi's orchestral works include "some of the largest and gaudiest blockbusters ever written." He is almost exclusively known for his trilogy of Roman tone poems. The brilliant pictorialism of *Pines of Rome* and *Fountains of Rome*, as well as *Roman Festivals*, make these works the most successful contributions to 20th century orchestral music to come out of Italy.

Given his splashy theatrics and sense for orchestral coloring, it is not surprising that Respighi studied with Rimsky-Korsakov. Both *Pines*, which paints the great pine trees of various places in Rome and *Fountains*, which captures four of the city's famous fountains, combine the harmonic subtleties of Debussy and Ravel with the orchestral splash found in Russian orchestral showpieces (such as those of his teacher, Rimsky-Korsakov). "His finest music drew inspiration from other works of art and nature."

The *Pines* is an excellent example of how Respighi combined influences from the French Impressionists with the brilliant orchestration learned from his teacher. The outer movements, representing the pines of the *Villa*

Borghese and the famous pines of the Appian Way with its "magnificent, spine-tingling crescendo," are brilliant orchestral showpieces. The inner movements clearly show the influence of Debussy. The third movement, *The Pines of the Janiculum*, is famous for the incorporation of actual recorded bird sounds. This is a novelty in impressionist music which previously relied purely on orchestral sounds and timbres to evoke nature.

> **Recommended – Respighi tone poems**
> Sometimes *Pines* and *Fountains* are coupled with the third of Respighi's Roman trilogy, *Roman Festivals*, sometimes with another impressionist work such as Debussy's *La Mer*. Reiner and Chicago are "still unsurpassed for power and excitement," while Toscanini's performance, even in mono, shows "Respighi's inspiration white-hot from the kiln."

Gustav Holst (1874-1934) Although Holst is usually pigeon-holed as a one-hit-wonder with his *The Planets*, he is more accurately a nationalist composer. He wrote mostly songs and hymns and, upon befriending Vaughn Williams, was influenced by English folksong. However, few outside England know this music, but everyone knows *The Planets*, so for this we consider Holst an Impressionist. This famous orchestral suite, despite its huge success and being synonymous with Holst, does not accurately represent Holst's music in general at all.

Holst is much more than *The Planets* but the extraordinary popularity of that gloriously inspired orchestral suite has overwhelmed most serious consideration of his other works and he is often unfortunately seen as the classical music equivalent of a 'one-hit wonder'. He was much better-known in his day than now, and, excepting of course *The Planets*, little of his music remains actively performed.

Each movement represents one of the planets ('Mercury' through 'Neptune'), the known planets from Holst's time as well as the acknowledged planets of today with the recent re-classification of Pluto. Some of the pieces, particularly *Mars* and *Jupiter*, sound like Hollywood soundtracks as Holst's music has definitely influenced composers of film scores.

The fact that clear references to *The Planets* show up in today's music is a tribute to Holst's timeless masterpiece. In fact, it is likely all composers, including the immortals, worked others' material into theirs, consciously or sub-consciously, and some did it for sure. Bach borrowed from Vivaldi's concertos but Bach used any influence from his Italian counterpart as a starting point to create his own unique 'German' music. He certainly did not 'copy' Vivaldi as Bach's works as a whole are far superior to Vivaldi's.

We can only assume other composers took similar approaches, mostly all with limited, if any, success. Of course we will never know as ninety-five percent of past composers and their works have disappeared into oblivion.

> **Recommended – The Planets**
> Dutoit with the Montreal SO is the most widely-acclaimed; either version from Boult, either with the LPO in the late 1970s, or with the Philharmonia in the late 1960s; and the early Karajan recording with the Vienna PO has rightly remained in the catalogue (recently coupled with Monteux's *Enigma* Variations).

Frederick Delius (1862-1934) like Holst an Englishman of German descent, was very opinionated on music, stating, "never believe the saying that one has to hear music many times to understand it." Despite this belief, and his ability to write wonderful melodies, Delius' music does take some time (i.e., at least several if not many listenings) to get used to.

Delius found a champion in conductor Thomas Beecham as early as 1906 and throughout the conductor's career that would last another fifty years. Despite this, most of Delius' music was delayed in being performed and published. In the early 1930s Beecham convinced the gravely ill Delius to visit England (he was living in France). A Delius festival had been arranged by Beecham, who had the means to do this being from the pharmaceutical Beecham family.

> *Beecham on Delius:* "I...regard him as the last great apostle in our time of romance, beauty and emotion in music."
> - Beecham on Delius

In some ways Delius can be considered the "British Fauré" in that it was "highly personal, sometimes delicate, elegant..." and his music "English Impressionism", "an entirely personal music." Like Debussy, Delius completely broke from traditional forms; his music is entirely original. As were the Impressionists, he was a "tone painter" who "wrote beautifully of beautiful things." His miniature tone poems represent "a uniquely poetic, even pantheistic, evocation of nature and the transience of life." His music celebrated the idyllic. Examples include the works *Summer Night on the River* (1911) and *On Hearing the First Cuckoo in Spring* (1912). *Brigg Fair: An English Rhapsody* (1907) is perhaps his greatest and most English-sounding orchestral work.

Delius did not like England and because he came from a wealthy merchant family, he was able to globe trot without concern for money, spending time in Florida, France and Germany.

> **Recommended – Delius**
> Any of the several collections of Delius' music conducted by his champion Thomas Beecham.

- 22 -

Anti-Romanticism
The Second Viennese School

♪ Dissonance and Atonality

Any coverage of the 'Second Viennese School' needs to begin with a discussion of 'dissonance' and 'atonality' and the distinction between the two terms. 'Dissonance' refers to what is heard; 'atonality' refers to the music itself. Dissonance describes the disagreeability of a specific (musical) sound to the listener caused by two or more notes that simultaneously sound to create a harsh, jarring effect. It can be thought of as a "disturbing clash of harmonies." 'Modulation' represents the movement of music from one key to another key, done for effect. It is a means "to provide harmonic variety with a tour through assorted keys." When modulation is done by moving to an adjacent key clockwise on the 'circle-of-fifths' (this is called a 'perfect fifth'), the musical change is very smooth because six of the seven notes of the two adjacent keys are the same and the seventh only differs by a semi-tone (e.g., F to F# in going from key of C major to G major).

> *"Atonality cuts us off from our moorings...(it) forces us more deeply into the ebb and flow of the moment."*
> - Jan Swafford

Atonality is the absence of tonality or key center in a musical work. Most atonal works were written within the last one hundred years and contain plenty of dissonance, but lots of tonal works from the 18th and 19th centuries contain dissonances. The important difference is that tonal works regard dissonances as breaks from stability in the music employed to create tension. Chromatic melody (string of notes separated by half-steps) had been used since the late 16th century "to depict intensities of emotion not easily achieved through the diatonic scale." During the 19th century, composers significantly increased use of all twelve notes of the chromatic scale "to create a turbulent, even devilish atmosphere."

Virtually all music contains some dissonances; however, in tonal music the dissonances are quickly resolved to the satisfaction of the listener. This satisfaction comes from the expectation for tonal music to return to pleasing sounds (i.e., 'consonance', the less frequently used term that is the opposite of dissonance). Dissonance, when it does occur, is expected by the ear to be short-lived. Central to all tonal music is the requirement to make dissonant movement seem graceful "as it arcs away from and back to the home key via an often circuitously long journey." To ensure this, "dissonance must be approached and, above all, resolved in stepwise motion, directly and simply, to the nearest consonance."

The term 'dissonance' should not immediately conjure up an unpleasant sound, "but rather a tense sound that seems to need resolution." If used effectively, dissonance supplies dynamic tension by keeping the listener on edge until the music returns to an agreeable sound (i.e., consonance). Dissonance can additionally be thought of by "its sense of movement" and as "an element of transition…which must be resolved to the ear's satisfaction." For over two hundred years the minor mode has been used as a chromatic device because the minor mode sounds essentially unstable. This is why pieces in the minor tend to have endings in the major, for example, Beethoven's Fifth Symphony finally stabilizes the key of C minor with C major in the finale.

Surprisingly, the first composer to really explore the possibilities of atonal music was probably Liszt, the master Romantic. There are definitely experiments in atonality and unresolved dissonance in his later piano works (1870s and 1880s), especially the *Bagatelle sans tonalite*. These later works of Liszt are much more obscure than his earlier virtuoso piano works, and they seem to not have been composed for public consumption. Perhaps Liszt was aware of their radical and experimental nature.

In non-German-speaking parts of Europe there existed a long-standing resentment toward the Austro-German dominance in the classical repertory. With the outbreak of World War I in 1914, this resentment in France, England, and Russia "blossomed into hate" with composers around non-Germanic Europe calling for rejection of the 'German canon' and what it represented to them at that time and place. By the end of the 19th century Romanticism had become "overblown…decadent, egomaniacal…in short, exhausted." Starting at the beginning of the 20th century many composers abandoned the vast orchestras used by Wagner, Mahler, and Strauss, "tired of the super-saturated sound of the conventional symphony orchestra."

The backlash against Romanticism that began in the first decade of the 20th century really got going during and just after World War I. With the devastating effects of World War I changing forever the fabric of Western Europe, Romanticism was seen as something archaic from a time gone by. Composers associated it "with the pre-war world and thereby with the war itself." Put another way, many thought that the same Europe responsible for the horrors of world war also had created the subjectivity and idealism of Romanticism. "The horror of the First World War…impelled young composers to distance themselves from a blood-soaked Romantic aesthetic." This reactionary movement towards objectivity and away from the extreme emotionalism of late Romanticism can be viewed in hindsight as predictable, if not inevitable.

"Twentieth Century classical composition… sounds like noise to many. It is largely an untamed art…"
- Alex Ross in <u>The Rest Is Noise</u>

With Wagner and his chromaticism, the "feeling of a central key or tonality began to be lost." With the premiere of Tristan und Isolde in 1865 Wagner had already shaken the foundations of the tonal system. Strauss produced a "freer and more sinuous melodic line, of daring leaps and...broader scope." Both Strauss and Mahler "saw music as a medium of conflict, a battlefield of extremes." Then came Debussy, Schoenberg and Stravinsky, who "were the main pathfinders in this uncharted harmonic territory."

"Debussy created his music out of a much more elusive and fragmentary melodic material." Schoenberg took this "harmonic ambiguity" to its "logical conclusions...abandoning...tonality altogether." The result was that "the entire former theory of harmony was thrown overboard." The route to Schoenberg's twelve-tone method and subsequent serialism took him and his two star pupils, Berg and Webern, through an initial period of extreme late Romanticism, demonstrated by their very first works. Then came the 'free atonality' or 'atonal expressionist' period, during which the Second Viennese School composers "were following their intuition rather than rationales and theories." Schoenberg felt this free atonality needed to be put on a leash, and so he developed his twelve-tone method. Jonathan Kramer reminds us not to think of the twelve-tone technique as "a hopeless straitjacket for the composer." However, Kramer also points out that "in the hands of second-rate composers, it can indeed become a substitute for imagination."

> *"There's still plenty of good music to be written in C major."*
> - Arnold Schoenberg

By contrast with tonal music, dissonances in atonal works are rarely resolved. When listening to Schoenberg's atonality "we must listen to melody with a different set of expectations as to what it is going to do." It was this total chromaticism or atonality, this rare resolution of dissonance that made their 'new' music seem like "a revolutionary break with the past." In fact, Schoenberg emphasized that "the history of the development of harmony" is one of dissonance, not consonance, because he felt that it is dissonance that takes music in new directions and continues its evolution and forward progress. In Schoenberg's words it is dissonance that "leads the composer away from well-trodden paths."

Why the decision to leave dissonances unresolved and to formalize its 'emancipation' with his twelve-tone method? Jonathan Kramer points to the time in which Schoenberg lived as well as to the man himself. As a severe man, his severity came through in his music. But it goes beyond that to the "angst of our century." The culture of the late Romantic period died and gave way to tensions that erupted in the First World War. Later in Schoenberg's career World War II broke out, along with the devastation and horrors that characterized "the most intense period in history." Is it any wonder that a very intense person would compose intense music during this period? The composer and musicologist Egon Wellesz stated that the Second Viennese

School was a response to "a climate in which we all sensed the breaking up of civilization as we know it and the collapse of a musical tradition and its language."

Excepting the early tonal works of Schoenberg such as *Verklärte Nacht* and *Pelleas and Mellisande,* all three of the Second Viennese School disliked descriptive titles for their works, especially Webern, and simply called their abstract compositions 'piece', and grouped several pieces together into an opus. Although the use of 'piece' as opposed to traditional titles was meant to demonstrate musical objectivity and possibly anti-Romaniticism, Webern's music (as well as that of Schoenberg and Berg) is hardly objective and impersonal. It is deeply emotional, even the later works that are fully products of the twelve-tone method.

Centered in Paris and Vienna, respectively, both neo-Classicism and atonality (which evolved into serialism with rigorous application of Schoenberg's twelve-tone method) were used to avoid what had been viewed as a period of excess: excess emotion, excessive orchestra sizes (by Mahler and Strauss in particular), excessive lengths of movements within a work (e.g., symphonies of Mahler), and excessive attempts at conveying images and painting musical pictures (i.e., tone poems of Strauss). These excesses led to a perversion of traditional forms. It was time for a change.

Whereas neo-Classicism looked to return to the forms and "constructive principles of the 18th century", serialism established a new form for music in the 20th century, by codifying Schoenberg's twelve-tone method. Serial music was especially attractive to artists in the West during the Cold War "precisely because it was so formalist…it…seemed incapable of being commandeered for purposes of propaganda." Young, post-World War II composers embraced serialism. The view presented by German composer Hans Werner Henze is typical: "dodecaphony and serialism were the only viable new techniques: fresh, and able to generate new musical patterns."

> *"Just as ripe fruit falls from the tree, music has quite simply given up the formal principle of tonality."*
> *- Anton Webern*

♪ The Second Viennese School

The Vienna of 1909-11 saw Mahler compose his Ninth Symphony and Schoenberg his *Five Pieces for Orchestra,* the latter offering an optimistic glimpse of the new century. The two-year period of 1912-13 produced some of the most startlingly original music of all time, made up of unprecedented sounds. Included were Debussy's *Jeux,* Stravinsky's *Rite of Spring,* along with Webern's intense yet intimate *Six Pieces,* Op.6.

Such optimism was short-lived, however, as in just a couple of years the assassination of an archduke would throw Europe into the most brutal three decades of war, depression, and devastation. As Europe spiraled into its first world war, saw the communist takeover of Russia, the impact of the Great Depression, followed by the rise of Nazism and Fascism, Schoenberg, Berg, and Webern moved much further away from the past and abandoned tonality altogether. The twelve-tone method, developed by Schoenberg was adopted enthusiastically by Berg and Webern. Among all the world chaos Schoenberg would impose his twelve-tone system "to impose order on the chaotic chromatic scale." Regardless, these composers did not see themselves as iconoclasts regarding tonality; in fact, Webern pointed out that "it was generations of composers," not the Second Viennese School alone, "who had bent tonality out of shape." While teacher stuck closer to traditional forms, Berg's and Webern's use of traditional forms was freer than Schoenberg's.

Key to the invention and application of the twelve-tone method was the *Tonreihe* ('tone row' or 'series'), a 'row' of notes that consisted of all twelve notes of the chromatic scale in a particular order or 'series'. All twelve notes would be sounded before any of them could be repeated (although this does not strictly hold in many twelve-tone compositions). Schoenberg called his new technique *Reihenkomposition*, or 'composition with rows' but the term *Zwölftontechnik*, "twelve-tone technique" was the one that stuck.

The years between the World Wars saw the rise of tyrants such as Stalin in the Soviet Union, and the rise of the murderous Third Reich of Nazi Germany, led by the personification of evil Adolf Hitler. In addition to the unprecedented death toll of millions of servicemen in World War I, representing a significant percentage of young male Europeans, Paul Griffiths proposes that something abstract, and of relative insignificance to the carnage, had also been a casualty of World War I. That 'something abstract' was the death of confidence in subjectivity – "that consistent voice and consistent temporal flow that gave 19th century music its continuing appeal." Hence, composers moved toward 'absolute' music and objectivity with simultaneous rejection of Romanticism, tonality, and the tried-and-tested, centuries-old forms. "The relatively tranquil and predictable 'old keys' could hardly attain the depth sought by Second Viennese School composers to explore an expressionist emotional world."

That the carnage would be repeated on an even greater scale in the Second World War, and devastate many of the same parts of the world, would only reinforce this objectivity. Sometimes perceived as 'cold' or lacking emotion (i.e., a definition of 'objectivity'), this 'musical objectivity' would prevent any possible rebirth in music with 19th century characteristics. Author and composer Jan Swafford points out that after the horror and chaos of World War I – after all the tragedy set in motion by the dreamy Romantic culture – why wouldn't composers embrace "the serial salvation that Webern promised, something pure and rational and inevitable."

And so the last vestiges of the 19th century are represented by the early music of the 'Second Viennese School' (Haydn, Mozart, and Beethoven comprised the first school). The works of a young Arnold Schoenberg, along with his students Alban Berg, and Anton Webern, would be the 'jumping off point' for '20th century' and 'modern' music. Although Schoenberg's music is highly emotional, his use of the twelve-tone technique led to a rejection of whatever influence the late Romantic period still had on music and a full embrace of dissonance. In particular, in the early works of Schoenberg and Webern "...the emotions expressed are fleeting and irregular...Connections from one musical idea to the next can seem tenuous...Much is turbulent."

Schoenberg, Berg, and Webern (together with their 20th century descendants) felt that tonality was no longer capable of bearing the expressive forces that were being unleashed in the early years of the 20th century. Webern felt it necessary to claim that "the dissolution of tonality wasn't our fault – and we did not create the new law ourselves; it forced itself overwhelmingly upon us." It is curious that Webern felt there was 'blame' to be assigned for the end of tonality despite Schoenberg insisting he was only mapping out the natural evolution of music. One wonders if an art form can naturally evolve to a strict formalism, which points to another curiosity in Webern's quote: "...the new law..." Why should or how is an art form governed by 'laws'. Would not the imposition of laws on art prevent, by definition, the creation of true art?

> *"They are the gentlemen who work with formulas instead of ideas."*
> - Stravinsky on the Second Viennese School

Unfortunately, the mature music of these three composers has never been very popular or often performed, mostly because of the 'difficulty' of listening to twelve-tone compositions with its apparent lack of identifiable melodies. This label has been derogatory in the minds of many music listeners, who marginalize most Post-Romantic music of the last century. While Berg died before the outbreak of World War II and Webern was accidently shot by allied troops at the end of it, Schoenberg fled Nazi Germany for Southern California, joining Stravinsky, Rachmaninoff, and others. Hindemith and Bartók would also follow. Their presence would benefit music in America for decades to come.

♩ Arnold Schoenberg (1874-1951)

> *"You are proposing a new value in place of an earlier one, instead of adding the new one to the old."*
> - Ferruccio Busoni on Schoenberg's atonality

> *"I strive for complete liberation from all forms and symbols of cohesion and logic."*
> -Schoenberg to Busoni

Schoenberg was a contradiction; as critic Harold Schonberg points out, he "was a revolutionary who all his life kept insisting he was a traditionalist," and maintained that all his works had "arisen entirely from the traditions of German music," primarily Bach and Mozart ("My teachers were primarily Bach and Mozart"), but also Beethoven, Brahms, and Wagner. However, he did admit that he had discarded most musical traditions and forms. Although he laid the groundwork for much of music in the 20th century with his atonal twelve-tone method, some of his statements made it sound as if he was an unwilling pioneer, with statements such as, "I am a conservative who was forced to become a radical." This claim of being 'forced' to become a radical contradicts his statements that his 'radical' music was the result of nothing more than the natural progression and evolution of traditional forms. Schoenberg was not deliberately talking out of both sides of his mouth; he was genuinely torn between the past and the changing present, and constantly struggled with them.

> *"It was mainly through J.S. Bach that German music came to decide the way things developed, as it has for two hundred years."*
> - Arnold Schoenberg

Schoenberg, as a German in the second decade of the 20th century, was pro-Germany in World War I and entered the army. "In his zeal for the German cause" he actually drew parallels between Germany's military crushing of France with a denouncement of Bizet, Stravinsky (who was settled in Paris) and Ravel. The following from a letter to Alma Mahler in August of 1914 demonstrates this zeal: "Now we will throw these mediocre kitschmongers into slavery, and teach them to...worship the German God." He later called this his "war psychosis." "Mediocre Kitschmonger?" "Worship the German God?" No wonder he and Stravinsky did not attend each other's barbeques years later when they both had settled and were neighbors in Southern California. But within two decades he was one of the first artists to see Hitler for the monster he was and to fully gauge the extent of growing anti-Semitism.

Verklärte Nacht

The string sextet *Verklärte Nacht* was composed in 1899 and premiered in 1902. It was later rescored by Schoenberg for string orchestra in 1917 with no change to the music itself. Even later Schoenberg refined the work to thin out some of the late Romantic textures. It beautifully combines *Tristan*-like Wagnerian harmony with Brahmsian string sextet. David Dubal calls the work "the last word in *Tristan*-oriented music." It recalls Brahms' two string sextets more than it does the chromaticism of Wagner because it is "much more firmly fixed in specific tonalities." Although tonal, this work definitely "tugs at the limits of tonality" and points listeners in some of the musical "directions Schoenberg was eventually to take."

Verklärte Nacht is "a work of turbulent, superheated late Romanticism...," based on the poem Woman and World by Richard Dehmel. It is a programmatic work in the most traditional ways except in its use of a chamber group. However, the composer did not consider it a tone or symphonic poem despite its clear literary reference. It tells of the passionate meeting of strangers in a bare, cold wood. It is Schoenberg's most approachable work and has remained his most popular and recorded, in both the sextet and orchestral versions.

Pelleas and Melisande, Op.5

Soon after, in 1905 this symphonic poem premiered, based on the same symbolist play of Maurice Maeterlinck that inspired works by Fauré and Ravel. Originally planned by Schoenberg to be an opera as Ravel's, he settled instead on an orchestral work, closer to Fauré's incidental music. As with *Verklärte Nacht*, "here too the orchestra is reinforced to the maximum." It is his only tone poem and is arranged in four main sections, which are cast into smaller sub-units. In the work Schoenberg strains the frontiers of expression by pursuing the prevailing Wagnerian influence to its utmost extreme. Although the work points also to Brahms, Reger, and Strauss, "the world of sound and expressive content were new" and Schoenberg continues exhausting the possibilities of the tonal system. "The chromatic universe was disintegrating."

> *Recommended – Schoenberg post-Romantic works*
> No one beats Karajan and the Berliners in the music of the Second Viennese School. His polish and orchestral refinement seem particularly well-suited to this music. His readings of *Verklärte Nacht* coupled with *Pelleas et Mellisande*, have "an opulence and passion that surpasses all others," making an excellent coupling of two of Schoenberg's early, tonal works.

> *"The great thing that Schoenberg taught us is that there is no real difference between consonance and dissonance."*
> — Otto Klemperer

Schoenberg could not completely deny his music's Romantic origins. He saw the changes in music with time as an evolution and a continuum and saw atonality as the natural progression of this evolution. He hardly saw himself or his novel approaches to his music as radical or revolutionary. Schoenberg's reaction to the uproar and attacks caused by his 'radical' works was to claim they were "the logical, rational outcome of a historical process," which traced back to Beethoven, Mozart and Bach.

Verklärte Nacht carries "Wagnerian chromaticism…to its most extreme form." But it also "marks the beginning of the search for a new musical idiom." This search would take a significant leap forward in 1906 with Schoenberg's first *Chamber* Symphony, Op.9. Although cast in the key of E major, it represents the first step towards the 'suspension of tonality', but not actual 'atonality'. However, the key changes within Op.9, if even identifiable, do not correspond to any traditional harmonic schemes.

At the same time he sought order and structure for this 'new' music, just as there was formal structure to traditional forms. Atonal music, in order to avoid the establishment of key or tonality, used all or most of the twelve notes of the chromatic scale. Schoenberg's twelve-tone method provided a structure for this and serialism would formalize his method further. He saw his twelve-tone method and subsequent serialism as irreversible progress. In what would evolve into full-blown serialism, Schoenberg saw that "a musical work's melodic and harmonic ideas could all spring from a single cell consisting of the twelve notes of the western chromatic scale."

Schoenberg was teacher and mentor to two famous composers who 'apprenticed' under him, Alban Berg and Anton Webern. Webern obtained a Ph.D. in music (in Renaissance composition, specifically the works of Henri Isaac) during which he took private composition lessons with Schoenberg. Shortly after, Alban Berg joined them, forming the 'Second Viennese School'. Schoenberg was paranoid, dictatorial, demanding and authoritarian, and his treatment of these two (Berg in particular) bordered on abusive. Berg, however, took whatever Schoenberg threw at him, as he revered his mentor. The older Schoenberg saw Berg's genius and felt a very demanding approach was necessary to mold the insecure younger Berg.

Contrary to some popular thoughts about Schoenberg rejecting traditional forms, the truth is that he made Berg and Webern compose exercises and works in traditional harmony and counterpoint and all three were "incubated in the golden age of Mahler and Strauss." However, later on in the 1930s/40s all three used the twelve-tone technique developed by Schoenberg. Schoenberg refused to formally teach his students this technique, "insisting instead that they master the traditional counterpoint of Bach and harmony of Brahms." But each of the three took atonal writing in different directions. "Schoenberg explored turbulent expressionism, and Webern wrote remarkable crystalline miniatures, but...Berg...never entirely left Romanticism behind."

Schoenberg's music evolved from *Verklärte Nacht* at the turn of the century to a renunciation of tonality and tonal center altogether. Schoenberg referred to this as the emancipation of the dissonance. By avoiding the establishment of a key there is no modulation (i.e., no changes from one key to another) or any tonality, and dissonances remain mostly unresolved. His First String Quartet in 1907 was thornily contrapuntal but not quite atonal.

"In his early work Schoenberg had stretched Wagnerian chromaticism...he had burst (its) boundaries. By the time of *Pierrot lunaire* (1914), Schoenberg's music was floating free in chromatic space." In 1908-09, with his String Quartet No.2, Op.10 and his first *Chamber* Symphony, Op.9, we see Schoenberg rethinking tonality, moving farther away from it while moving "toward an even more intense expressionism." As with the first String Quartet, both of these works caused a 'ruckus' unprecedented in the performance of music, including "laughter, catcalls...seat-rattling, whistle-blowing (audience members actually brought whistles to the performance) and walkouts," according to Schoenberg student and concert attendee Egon Wellesz.

Five Pieces for Orchestra; Chamber Symphony No.1

The *Five Pieces for Orchestra*, Op.16 were composed in 1909 and premiered in March of 1912. In each of the pieces "the expressionistic atmosphere and the atonal language by which it is expressed are carried to the highest pitch of intensity." The pieces are "brief, self-contained, highly expressive pieces...concerned with individual instrumental color rather than massive orchestral sound" to "express inner emotional states" and summarize anti-Romanticism and the Second Viennese School. Despite the large difference in scale, this work owes a lot to Mahler's music in terms of orchestration and frequent mood changes, although Mahler never abandoned tonality. Its "beguiling array of orchestral timbres" puts it ahead of anything Mahler composed, although its "contrapuntal richness...owes a lot to the older composer." Schoenberg initially gave names to the pieces, at the urging of his publisher, to point listeners in certain directions with titles such as 'Premonitions' for the first piece and 'Chord Colors' for the third.

It should be noted that Schoenberg opposed these names, only relenting at the end, making them either obscure ('The Past') or obscurely technical, not feeling the need "to burden listeners with suggestions of additional significance." Eventually, he would drop the titles for each piece, again to avoid any risk of programmatic or impressionistic interpretations. The 'Colors' (*Farben*) piece could mark the beginning of experimentation in shifting tone colors that would become known as *Klangfarbenmelodie* or 'tone-color melody', "melodic lines made up of changing instrumental colors melting into one another." The *Pieces* show freshness, and are "alive with a confident vitality," giving hints to the "new musical language that would influence most subsequent music."

The First *Chamber* Symphony, Op.9, like the *Five Pieces*, was a transition piece, bridging Wagnerian and Straussian chromaticism with Schoenberg's unique style and logic. It is scored for fifteen solo instruments and remains one of the composer's most frequently performed works.

The Viennese public continued to scoff at Schoenberg's latest works and to vilify the composer. In the first decade of the 20th century the old-fashioned Viennese society, steeped in tradition and guarding the *status quo*, saw Schoenberg's music as a "hostile reminder that their smug, secure world was smoldering with tensions on many levels."

Serialism was what Schoenberg was seeking: "A principle that would secure instrumental forms, as they had been secured by tonal harmony in the past." Schoenberg's first serial works in 1923 had a waltz, a minuet and included an entire Baroque-style suite. Schoenberg was incorporating neo-Classicism in his works of this decade, just as Stravinsky was doing. Debussy died before any of Schoenberg's serial works premiered, so we do not know what the French Impressionist would have thought of the twelve-tone method. We do know that Debussy, in a letter in 1915 to Stravinsky, had characterized the atonal works of Schoenberg that he did hear as "organized ugliness."

Schoenberg formally introduced his twelve-tone method in 1923 with his *Five Piano Pieces*, Op.23. Five years later his Variations for Orchestra, Op.31 premiered with the Berlin Philharmonic under Furtwangler. It was the first twelve-tone work for large orchestra.

Schoenberg was convinced the popularity of his twelve-tone technique would reassert the primacy of Austro-German composition, with its counterpoint and thematic development. He mocked other composers and "vented against the popular styles of the day," such as the 'modern' Stravinsky and "folkloristic composers" (e.g., Bartók), as well as against composers "who mingle dissonance and tonality."

Suite for Piano, Op.25; Suite, Op.29; Variations for Orchestra, Op.31

From 1925-1930 "Schoenberg was at his most inspired in reacting to the hedonistic spirit (of) the Weimar Republic and pre-Nazi Berlin: sardonic, jazzy, living for the moment."

The *Suite for Piano* from 1924 represents Schoenberg's very first work completely written according to his twelve-tone method. The *Variations*, of two years later, was his first orchestral twelve-tone composition. This work "marked a decisive transition from the 'indeterminate abstractness' of atonality to the 'constructive concreteness' of the twelve-tone system." Schoenberg's use of the common Baroque form of the suite "affirmed his kinship with" Bach and Handel. As with the two-hundred-year-old suites of the Baroque, Schoenberg's Op.25 consists of short dance-like forms, which are ideally suited for the experimentation with his new methods.

The *Suite*, Op.29 for the unique ensemble of three clarinets, string trio and piano, contains "bouncy rhythms and disconcerting switches of mood within traditional formal schemes." Within four years of Op.25, his first completely twelve-tone composition, Schoenberg showed an absolute mastery of his serial technique with Op.29. It contains neo-Baroque-styled movements with an opening overture and a gigue for the final movement.

The appearance of the *Variations for Orchestra* in 1928 represented Schoenberg's return to orchestral music after over a decade away from it. The immediate predecessors of Op.25 and Op.31 clearly showed the twelve-tone method applied to selected movements and pieces. This is seen in the *Five Piano Pieces*, Op.23 and the Serenade, Op.24, both from 1923. Op.31 has a main theme, followed by nine variations and concluded with a finale. The theme has a lyrical, melodic character, but one that is vague and mysterious, creating "through the broadened horizons of dodecaphonic counterpoint, a new kind of *Klangfarbenmelodie*."

The *Variations* could have appropriately been called 'Variations for Large Orchestra' because of the forces it calls for including mandolin, harp and celesta. It was Schoenberg's first large-scale twelve-tone work for the public.

Violin Concerto, Op.36; Piano Concerto, Op.42

These two concertos are not easy listening; they are "unrelievedly tense...the intensity never lets up totally," in typical Schoenberg fashion. The Violin Concerto was the first major work Schoenberg composed upon his arrival in the U.S. It was begun in 1934, took two years to complete, and did not premiere until 1940 with Louis Krasner, the soloist who had premiered Berg's Violin Concerto in 1936. Although the concerto has plenty of unresolved dissonance, it has many traditional features, including a finale that is simpler than the preceding movements, hints of sonata form, distinct themes, and long beautiful melodies.

The Piano Concerto, cast in one long movement in four distinct sections, is a product of Schoenberg's days in California teaching music at UCLA and is one of Schoenberg's more approachable twelve-tone compositions. He finished it at the end of 1942 and it was premiered early in 1944 by pianist Edward Steuermann, with Leopold Stokowski conducting the NBC Symphony Orchestra. Stokowski received credit from *avant-garde* composers for performing a new atonal work, which almost certainly would not be well-received by the concert-going public.

♪ Alban Berg (1885-1935)

Alban Berg, who lived his entire life in Vienna, began writing songs in Romantic and Impressionist styles at age fifteen. He had "a mathematical fetish, a love of complexity for complexity's sake." Of Schoenberg and his two famous pupils Berg and Webern, it was Alban Berg who wrote the most passionate music, with a clear connection to the Romantic past. Berg "put a human face on the twelve-tone system..." His music balances "formal rigor and emotional richness...it is tightly constructed and expressive." Despite Berg having no other teacher than Schoenberg, his use of his teacher's twelve-tone technique was different. Berg used Schoenberg's twelve-tone method "as one inventive resource among others, rather than a dominating structural principle" and his approach could not have been what Schoenberg had intended when his student claimed, in a letter to Theodor Adorno, that what attracted him "about Schoenberg's method was its capacity to generate new kinds of tonality." (italics added) Interestingly, the musical philosopher Adorno would be Berg's most famous pupil.

While Schoenberg was clearly an influence on Berg's music, the student took just as much from Debussy and Mahler. Berg had an unquenchable thirst for things dramatic and composer/conductor Pierre Boulez has commented that "there was a lot more to Berg than his immediately accessible romanticisms." This is clear in the Op.6 pieces, which do owe a debt to Schoenberg's *Five Pieces*, Op.16, but whose "music sounds closer to the expressive world of Mahler's Sixth and Third Symphonies and...to the harmonic and orchestral world" of Debussy.

Of the three composers of the Second Viennese School the influence of Mahler is most pronounced on Berg's music with "opulent, upward- and downward-lunging melodies," and Berg, more than his teacher and Webern, was most resistant to abandoning Romanticism; his music never completely stepped out from its shadow. In fact, "Berg can be called the twelve-tone system's most advanced Romantic..." His musical ideas focused "more on harmony than on counterpoint" so that it still related "directly to Romantic tradition." Sections of Berg's music sound tonal; his music has "an emotional directness and openness that can be overwhelming."

"Berg composed communicative, emotional music without compromising his technical sophistication and atonal allegiances." His music has a "greater directness of appeal and overt emotionalism"...than "the more densely-packed scores of Schoenberg" and Berg "...eventually proved to be a formidable challenge to his former teacher."

Although plagued by ill health throughout his life, when he enlisted in the German army during World War I the training almost killed him. He was assigned to ride a desk. This experience in the military, although not as an actual soldier, would provide enough identification with the hapless, tragic, and tormented soldier who would be the lead character in Berg's unrelentingly bleak and macabre *Wozzek*, the first atonal ('free-atonal', not according to twelve-tone methods) opera and still "the closest thing to a popular opera the musical avant-garde ever produced." It is a tribute to Berg's genius, and his ability to create sympathetic figures, that even today his two operas, *Wozzek* and the twelve-tone *Lulu*, remain in the opera repertory.

Three Pieces for Orchestra, Op.6, and Lyric Suite

Berg's Op.6 was composed at the start of World War I in 1913-15, but not performed in its entirety until 1930. The pieces, with their complexity, virtuosity, and firepower represent the maturity of the composer. The three movements are 'Prelude', 'Round Dances', and 'March' and are meant to be symphonic in form; the pieces have a direct link with the sound world of Mahler. The finale, "a huge march in an atmosphere of catastrophe" is clearly influenced by Mahler's *Sixth*. The *Three Pieces* share specific thematic, rhythmic, and harmonic references with Mahler's last symphonies.

Webern conducted the first two movements in 1923 in Berlin. This work is as close as Berg ever came to writing a symphony and "shows him grappling with larger formal issues in response to…Mahler's Ninth." The *Three Pieces* are "Schoenbergian in content but Mahlerian (fully symphonic) in form." Jonathan Kramer points to multiple influences, going back one hundred years, which give *Three Pieces* its extraordinary power and beauty: Schubert's poignant lyricism, Mahler's unique vision, "the free dissonance of Schoenberg and the sensuous colors of Debussy." The third piece, a march, "is a phantasmagoric march for full orchestra."

The *Lyric* Suite, originally cast in six movements for string quartet, was composed over a year from fall of 1925 to 1926. It represents the first work in which Berg strictly employs Schoenberg's twelve-tone method and it clearly "has some of the thorniness one associates with twelve-tone music." The dark, disturbing piece borrows much from Wagner, particularly from Tristan which was regularly referenced by composers in the first two decades of the 20th century. Berg later orchestrated the second through fourth movements, creating one of his most popular works. Decades later it was discovered that Berg had secretly dedicated the work to a married woman with whom he apparently had a secret ten-year affair. Alban's wife Helene got her revenge by living forty-four years after his death; she died in 1979.

> *Recommended – Berg Lyric Suite; Three Pieces for Orchestra*
> Karajan and the BPO (on DG) stand alone in this repertoire as "Karajan effects crystal-clarity in a razor-sharp realization."

Violin Concerto and Chamber Concerto

Berg's Violin Concerto, from the year of his death (1935), was composed to mourn the death of Manon Gropius, the daughter of Alma Mahler and her second husband. Manon died at age eighteen but Berg had known her as a daughter for a long time. It is Berg's single most popular and regularly programmed work, a requiem work that addresses death and transfiguration. Its compelling combination of both tonal and atonal idioms makes it his most accessible score. "Berg's lyric vision finds here its most lofty expression." It is sublimely and exquisitely lyrical, a masterpiece unequalled by any other contemporary composer. It also became his requiem piece as he never lived to see it performed. Ironically, the usually methodical Berg worked quickly on this concerto, completing it only four months before his sudden death at age fifty. Louis Krasner, a virtuoso violinist who was something of a 'modern' concerto specialist, commissioned the work and gave the premiere in Barcelona in early 1936. Krasner argued that Berg could "demonstrate the lyric and expressive potential of twelve-tone music and release it from the stigma of 'all brains, no heart'."

The concerto consists of two movements, each of two parts, giving the work an overall slow-fast, fast-slow format so that the contrast is greatly intensified. There is a recurring theme, fundamental to the work's structure, taken from Bach's chorale *Es ist genug* ("It is enough"), injecting resignation in the face of death (Manon's as well as the composer's imminent demise). Webern was supposed to conduct but was still too upset after a couple of rehearsals and handed the baton over to Hermann Scherchen. It is a twelve-tone masterpiece that appropriately fades out at its conclusion and definitively proves that the "twelve-tone system presents no barrier to music of great beauty." Of the many fine 'modern' violin concertos of the past century, "none is greater or of a finer emotional life than Berg's."

The Chamber Concerto for violin, piano and thirteen winds is "Berg's most rigorous and challenging, and thus his most Schoenbergian, work." Composed in 1923-25, it was among the first of Berg's works to show the influence of his teacher Schoenberg's twelve-tone method, "though the work does not make rigorous consistent use of twelve-tone practices" but rather is freely atonal.

Berg's mature opus output is miniscule for a major composer, only thirteen works. "No other composer has built such a momentous reputation on so few works," although Webern's total oeuvre is of shorter duration, but consists of more works.

♪ Anton Webern (1883-1945)

> *"Webern conveys much by means of the least."*
> - unknown critic

Different from Schoenberg's other student Alban Berg, who looked back from Schoenberg's 'new music', Webern looked forward and turned to the miniature "to get away from the overblown statements of…late romantics."

Schoenberg and Berg can be considered the final offshoots of Romanticism, but not Webern, who "turned his back on tradition and took the plunge into the future." Unlike Berg, who composed little, died early and whose music could not break loose of post-Romanticism, Webern's music was the dominant influence on compositional trends of the 1950s and 1960s. In contrast, Berg's personal style had little influence on later music. Composer and critic Virgil Thomson hailed Webern "as the new god of the young," and his "incredibly tight organization…captured the imagination of composers all over the Western World after World War II."

> *"The incarnation of the most radical side of Schoenberg."*
> - Richard Taruskin

Webern's novel approach to music, in which he treated the tone-row much differently from Schoenberg, has had a tougher time sticking in the repertory than that of his mentor Schoenberg and fellow student Berg. However, Webern's style and works have had the strongest influence on later composers with its extreme economy and concentration. As more and more of the natural world was being explained by science, composers and musicians seemed to "latch on to the ideal of order and clarity in music" and "yearned for strict control backed by scientific principles." Webern's logic and musical purity were perfectly compatible with this movement; he was viewed by many as carrying "the art of music to its logical extreme." Olivier Messiaen and his students Boulez and Stockhausen would take off where Webern had stopped.

> *"When all twelve notes (of the chromatic scale) have gone by, the piece is over."*
> - Anton Webern

With a total output of only thirty-two works (half using Schoenberg's twelve-tone method) Webern created a new style of instrumentation that translates as 'melody of tone-colors', in which he "almost entirely obliterated…the traditional concepts of tutti and melody with accompaniment" and through a "fanatical application of the twelve-tone method" established a "new spareness and economy." This spareness "lets us appreciate how atonality can communicate tenderly, evocatively, movingly…by reducing the notes to the minimum." His works are so compact that, with many movements lasting around one minute, his complete works can fit on roughly three compact discs. Few of his works last more than ten minutes, even if they consist of 'Five Movements' or 'Six Bagatelles'.

> *"By art I mean the capacity for encasing a thought in the clearest, the simplest, that is the most intelligible form."*
> - Anton Webern

His mentor pointed out that it takes restraint to express oneself with the brevity of Webern. Schoenberg summarized Webern's economy of means by observing that "You can stretch every glance into a poem, every sigh into a novel. But to express a novel in a single gesture…" Webern's success in this regard can be traced to his refusal to repeat anything literally and his belief that "once stated the theme expresses all it has to say. It must be followed by something fresh," and "I had the feeling here that when all twelve notes had gone by, the piece was over."

Webern pursued the new musical logic of Schoenberg's twelve-tone method "with the utmost discipline…he turned the technique into a language of almost scientific exactness…and it took Schoenberg's row techniques several degrees further." Whereas Schoenberg's position on serialism ("One has to follow the basic series; but, nevertheless, one composes as freely as before.") left a door open to the post-Romantic, Webern clearly closed that door. When he did look to the past it was before the Romantic, the Classical, and the Baroque; his model for his imitative polyphony was that of the Renaissance.

His early music is "distilled, sounding like Mahler's textures pared to points and outlines." But then Webern clearly "moved ahead of his teacher (Schoenberg) in the expedition to the atonal pole." Melody, in the traditional sense, can be hard to find in Webern's music. He regularly broke up the melody into "small cell-like fragments" which "obliges us to think of individual notes on their own." Listeners sometimes comment that his music "hasn't got a tune." But the "sort of melody (Webern's music) has…obliges us to think of individual notes on their own…the melody may consist largely of huge leaps of well over an octave," played by several different instruments, each playing only two or three consecutive notes of a melody.

Webern's *Passacaglia* for Orchestra, Op.1, is one of his few works in the repertory, and one of the few works that Webern actually casts in a key, D minor. In its rich post-Romantic texture and expansiveness, it is Webern's *Verklärte Nacht*. Its harmonic progressions are Brahmsian but filtered "through a more rigorously Bachian structure." It does not utilize the twelve-tone method but rather is an "intense post-Wagnerian affair," descended from Schoenberg's First *Chamber* Symphony. The *Passacaglia* is Op.1 in designation only; many, many pieces by Webern predate it, with the *Passacaglia* simply signaling the point at which Webern "stopped to say, 'aha – here we have something'."

> "It takes less time to listen to (Webern's music) than to read about it."
> - Jan Swafford

Webern's Concerto, Op.24 is barely six minutes long but is of "truly extraordinary concentration" by eliminating "every decorative element." In the area of chamber music Webern produced his String Quartet, op.28, as well as several sets of pieces for string quartet, including *Five Movements for String Quartet*, Op.5 and Six *Bagatelles* for String Quartet, Op.9. Op.5, from 1909, represents the "distilled essence of expressionism," and Richard Crocker feels the *Five Movements* are "without question the most remarkable pieces of the decade." The harmonic language is rich and pungent, with multiple dissonances. Its twelve minutes "contain more emotional clout than many composers can manage in an hour" and "has a tone of almost unbearable tragedy" in response to the recent death of his mother. It was later scored for full orchestra.

Six Pieces, Op.6 and Five Pieces, Op.10

Webern's *Six Pieces* was composed the same year (1909) as Schoenberg's Op.16 and was Webern's first attempt to apply atonality to a large ensemble. It exudes raw atonality, "arguably the supreme atonal work." Webern, always influenced by Debussy's economy of notes, wrote extremely compressed pieces free of all expressionistic clutter. Each of the pieces "distills the essence of the new musical ideas (of)...Schoenberg." Op.6 plumbs "the depths of Schoenberg's notion of *Klangfarbenmelodie*...(which the latter had) created...with his *Five Pieces for Orchestra*" a few months earlier.

The pieces are not yet twelve-tone or serial in form but they do avoid a tonal center and are too short to support traditional thematic structure yet contain strong emotional undertones. As an example of the reception with which this 'radical' and complex music was received, the *Six Pieces* of Webern were programmed at a Vienna concert in 1913 together with Berg's *Altenberg Lieder*, Op.4. While Webern's pieces elicited only whistling from the audience, Berg's *Lieder* caused a riot and a call to police to restore order. Only two of the *Lieder* caused one of the worst audience riots of the century; imagine if Schoenberg, who directed the program, had presented Berg's entire work. Ironically, a worse shock to Berg came from the strong criticism of his Op.4 songs and censure by none other than Schoenberg himself. A performance in Prague of Berg's twelve-tone opera *Wozzek* in 1926 also caused such a city riot that the mayor fell to a heart attack. These riots and reactions of course occurred when there was no real distinction between 'popular' and 'classical' music, as there is today. Popular music concerts are still capable of generating public misbehavior; however, one has a hard time imagining a classical program, even one comprised solely of atonal works, causing any public release of emotions among concertgoers.

Webern produced his *Five Pieces* during 1911-13 to extend the ideas of the *Six Pieces* "with a particular emphasis on...nuances of soft dynamic levels." Each of the five pieces is less than a minute but "they seem to give off enormous clouds of multicolored sparks" Webern here displays his expert use of the concept of *Klangfarbenmelodie*, a 'melody of tone colors' with each note of a phrase "given to a different instrument, with consequently changing (tone) colors (the *Klangfarben*)" on nearly every note. The pieces are not thematically connected nor do they contain tonal relationships. It is Webern's last orchestral work before his full embrace of the twelve-tone method and Op.10 "is probably the most convincing utilization of *Klangfarbenmelodie* ever." Webern's whittled down twelve-tone music had the "abstract beauty of ice crystals or snowflakes." These "jewel-like pieces" require "microscopic precision" to pull off effectively.

Webern went on to compose serial works including *Symphony*, Op.21 (1927-28), which marked "the beginning of extreme compression…it is widely regarded as a masterpiece in miniature." It is in two movements, one stately and slow, the other "spry, dancing, and jovial: Viennese." His style continued to reflect "his search for an ideal of pure counterpoint carried to the limits of possibility."

Unfortunately, in 1945 he was mistakenly shot and killed by an Allied soldier who was coming to apprehend his son on suspicion of post-war black market dealings. Fortunately, his legacy and a lasting impact from his music had already been firmly established. Although Webern retreated as far as possible from the lush gigantism of late-Romantic music, his economic miniatures seeming to be no more than fleeting wisps of sound sewn together, Mahler and Wagner remained his heroes (as they were to Schoenberg and Berg). Webern even guest-conducted the BBC Orchestra in a triumphant London performance of Mahler's *Eighth* in the 1920s.

While the reaction and reviews to performances of music by Schoenberg, Berg, and Webern are humorous in hindsight, they were merciless at the time. Included were characterizations of the music such as 'sewer smell' and "fragments, rags, sobs, belches." Personal barbs included "fountain-poisoner of German music" (against Berg) and referring to the concert hall in which *Wozzek* was premiered (under the baton of Erich Kleiber) as a public insane asylum. Nevertheless, the music of the Second Viennese School has had the largest influence on music over the past eighty years or so. As pointed out by Aaron Copland, "…all (then) contemporary music owed something…to his (Schoenberg) 'daring'." However, Copland continued that "it was hardly possible to arrive at a conclusive judgment" on the music of Schoenberg, Berg, or Webern "because their works were performed so infrequently."

- 23 -

Stravinsky and Neo-Classicism

"The aim and final reason of all music should be nothing else but the Glory of God and the refreshment of the spirit."
— J.S. Bach

"I consider that music is by its very nature essentially powerless to express anything at all...I evoke neither human joy nor human sadness."
— Igor Stravinsky

Much 20th century music tries to "achieve a taut, vibrant melody from which everything superfluous has been excised...(it) has detached instrumental melody from its vocal origins." This is why one cannot hum along with most 'modern' music (that of either school, Stravinsky or Schoenberg), but the melodies of Classical and Romantic masters can be used for popular songs. 20th century melodies contain "wide leaps and jagged turns of phrase" that are not vocally derived.

In the post-Mahler period there was a de-emphasis of symphonic form in the West. While Prokofiev and Shostakovich would continue to develop the large-scale form and eventually dominate the 20th century symphonic repertoire, the two major schools of influence in the West, the Second Viennese and Stravinsky (i.e., neo-Classicism) either rejected symphonic form (in the case of the former), went back in time to produce more objective neo-Classical works, or revitalized Baroque counterpoint (neo-Baroque). Putting aside the two great Soviet symphonists, the period between the wars left us with very little contribution to the symphonic repertoire in terms of large-scale works. Martinů did not compose his first symphony until the start of World War II and after he arrived in the U.S.

The height of neo-Classicism in the 20th century was between the two world wars as it thrived in Weimar Republic Germany (Hindemith) and Paris (Stravinsky). neo-Classicism "went hand-in-hand with a renewal of interest in contrapuntal procedures." Stravinsky and Hindemith restored the idea of the composer as craftsman. Romantic and Impressionist composers tackled the problem of expression; composers after World War I focused on the problem of formal organization. The audience at a typical symphony concert in the 1920s was more socially diverse than ever and "came out of a simple love of music. But most preferred to hear Brahms." Many composers' works followed a neo-Classical, neo-Baroque aesthetic, with "historical manner expressed in contemporary language." After falling out of fashion (but still occasionally being found useful) in the Classical (e.g., Mozart's finale to his *Jupiter* Symphony) and being relegated to the sidelines by Romantics, archaic repetition in major Baroque forms such as the chaconne and passacaglia would return in the 20th century as "composers pursued ever more arcane musics of the future."

In fact, musicologist Richard Taruskin places the beginning of 20th century music not at the turn of the century but in the 1920s, specifically with Stravinsky's seminal neo-Classical work, the *Octet* in 1923. That ironically places Stravinsky's 'radical' ballets, as well as all Debussy, in the '19th century' together with the post-Romantic works of Strauss and Mahler, an association that Stravinsky and Debussy would have certainly opposed.

Stravinsky revitalized old forms with an ultramodern treatment and modification. He was the most important figure of the neo-Classicist movement but his works might more accurately be described as 'neo-Baroque'. Some neo-Classical works of Respighi actually preceded

Stravinsky's music in the early 1920s, as had Debussy with his late chamber works and Ravel with his neo-Baroque *Le Tombeau de Couperin*, with both French composers writing these works during the First World War.

'Neo-Classicism' is the label used to denote "music that is direct and clear in form, contrapuntal in texture, and restrained in expression." The neo-Classicism of Stravinsky represented "a wholesome return to the formal idea," to build music "out of elements solely derived from the nature of sound." With atonality taking root in the music of Schoenberg and his followers there were only two alternatives: follow the Second Viennese School in their quest to organize the "world of sound by means of a new musical syntax" or, as did most notably Stravinsky and Hindemith, revert to neo-Classical objectivism. Jonathan Kramer sums up Stravinsky's neo-Classical style as, "...not a return to classicism...rather it brings together two eras that have no direct historical contact and thus makes an artificial amalgamation of styles." In fact, James Jolly points out that Stravinsky wrote in "so many styles...(but) is absolutely recognizable in every single piece."

The music of Hindemith and Stravinsky, as well as by Béla Bartók, a nationalist neo-Classical composer, all shared "a profound and emphatic realignment with traditional tonality." Neo-Classicism was 'cool' with a strict rhythm touched by jazz or dance music, but also with "elements of form, gesture and counterpoint from older music." Jazz, with an emphasis on smaller, chamber-like ensembles and with a dominance of melody by winds, was very appealing to composers in the 1920s.

It certainly influenced the chamber works of Stravinsky, Hindemith and Martinů, in which wind instruments are regularly featured. Additionally, the time spent in Paris by Stravinsky and Martinů exposed them to French affinity for winds. In fact, American jazz and blues crossed the Atlantic and infused the neo-Classical works not only of Stravinsky and Ravel (his Piano Concerto in G is a good example) but also of Martinů and Darius Milhaud. On the flip side, European classical influences found their way to the United States as evidenced by pop song writer George Gershwin with his jazz-infused *Rhapsody In Blue* (1924), followed the next year by his first piano concerto. Neo-Classicism provided models of clear form and contrapuntal texture, providing a road map away from Romanticism, which had rejected 18th century models of form.

Many composers abandoned tonality and tradition; Stravinsky held on but even he turned to serialism in the 1950s to get beyond neo-Classicism. Although Stravinsky regularly dismissed Schoenberg's twelve-tone method as "so much Teutonic obscurantism," Stravinsky's acceptance and limited adoption of (at least quasi) twelve-tone techniques corresponded with the death of his rival Schoenberg. For example, while his *Septet* of 1952-53 was twelve-tone to some extent, Stravinsky did not completely go over to dodecaphony, but retained some of his unique characteristic traits.

♪ Igor Stravinsky (1882-1971)

> *"He is a liberator. More than anyone else, he has freed the musical thought of today."*
> - Erik Satie on Stravinsky

Although Igor Stravinsky lived into recent times, his work in the first quarter of the 20th century was the most significant of his career, although he composed for decades more and almost everything he composed seemed influential. Stravinsky was Russian but spent only the early years of his career in Russia. His three great early ballets were written when he was still in Russia; after that he was in Paris, Switzerland, then the U.S. He never lived in the Soviet Union and did not feel the influence of that government on his art or creative process as Prokofiev and Shostakovich did.

He was coldly logical and brilliantly intellectual; the most influential composer of the 20th century. If measured solely in terms of originality, Stravinsky is among the greatest composers of all time. Stravinsky represented a complete rupture with Romanticism. He stated that "…music is…essentially powerless to express anything at all…" "In order to keep his cool, slightly detached image …he denies all expression in his music…but this is a camouflage." To him "music is primarily form and logic…he was interested mostly "in structure, in texture, in balance, in rhythm." He also felt that "it was as essential to see music performed as to hear it." As with Debussy, Stravinsky felt that tonal relationships were "no longer capable of sustaining a lengthy symphonic argument."

Stravinsky avoided traditional forms of development and repetition of themes, preferring straightforward expression in its simplest form. He bluntly stated, "I have no use for 'working out' (i.e., thematic development) in dramatic music." Stravinsky made "rhythm the principal generative element of large-scale composition." To his credit he did not emphasize melody, as he did not have the abilities of others as a melodist (e.g., Prokofiev). In contrast to Schoenberg, who believed that to move music forward order must first be brought to chromatic chaos, Stravinsky, looked to move music forward by looking to the past and believed the "ideal is to be found in the formal balance attained by the great 17th and 18th century composers, the sole repositories of the 'true' sense of tradition."

Stravinsky was not interested in or rejected "any kind of unified field theory" for music, the pursuit of Schoenberg and the Second Viennese School. Stravinsky preferred "to impress his personality on the existing musical world…he was an evolutionary not a revolutionary composer."

> *"His construction sticks out like scaffolding. There's no flow, no natural bridges."* But *"this clarity...must be one of the secrets of Igor Stravinsky's popularity."*
> - Shostakovich in <u>Testimony</u>

Stravinsky was universally recognized as the greatest composer of his time. He came out of the gate very quickly with three of his most popular works, which were very radical for their time, emerging by the time he was thirty. These are the three ballets, *Firebird*, *Petrushka*, and *The Rite of Spring*, which all premiered between 1910 and 1913. Ballet is an offshoot of opera and was extremely popular as the 19th century gave way to the 20th with the famous ballets of Tchaikovsky, Stravinsky, and others.

Stravinsky's first ballet success, *Fireworks* (1908), had strong resonances of Dukas and Rimsky-Korsakov, who were teachers of Stravinsky in St. Petersburg. The music blended French and Russian sounds, which caught the attention of Serge Diaghilev, leader of the *Ballet Russes* troupe in Paris, whose Russian Ballet company had "burst like a gorgeous tropical bird upon the Western World" in 1908. From 1908-1914 Diaghilev and the Russian ballet performed each season in Paris and revolutionized choreography and stage design, dignified by a Pierre Monteux-led orchestra. The reaction of one bourgeois Parisian was that "…something new had been added to the creation of the world on the seventh day." The *Balle Russes* "brought (to Paris) fresh excellence of music by contemporary Russian composers." The visit of a Russian troupe to France was certainly a product of the recent Franco-Russian alliance. Thus Stravinsky began a relationship with Diaghilev that would produce his three famous ballets, *Firebird*, *Petrushka*, and *The Rite of Spring*, all before the outbreak of World War I.

> *"My music is best understood by children and animals"*
> - Stravinsky

♫ The Russian Period – The Ballets

Firebird
Stravinsky's second ballet had its premiere in Paris. The score is a "brilliant exercise in Russian nationalism," a very daring and original work, "extraordinarily skilled synthesis of elements from Rimsky-Korsakov and Glazunov, a masterpiece of orchestral colorism," as well as direct inspiration from Ravel's *Rapsodie Espagnole*. With a "marvelously-wrought evocation of the fairy-tale world…it is full of marvelous inspiration." It is based on the Russian fairy tale of Prince Ivan and the *Firebird* and is set in a wood with a wicked wizard and twelve princesses under a spell. This was the first of

Stravinsky's works to be heard outside of Russia.

Diaghilev took a chance on the young Stravinsky after the former ran out of patience waiting for Anatoly Lyadov (who was much better known at the time than Stravinsky) to fulfill the commission. It was the opportunity Stravinsky needed as "the spectacularly successful premiere in June (1910) instantly made Stravinsky an international star."

Its first performance marked a new age of Russian music to replace the "great age of Russian music" that had died two years earlier with the death of Rimsky-Korsakov, the grand old man of Russian music. Debussy pointed out the "altogether unusual combinations of rhythms." Stravinsky continuously revised the ballet score from 1915-46 with the final version known as the 'Revised 1947 Version'. The result is a thinning out of much of the lush, post-Romanticism in response to post-war neo-Classicism. He later extracted from the complete ballet a suite containing selected music. This *Firebird* Suite has become a very popular work, with its "dazzling orchestral invention and exoticism"

> "The immortal and unhappy puppet, hero of every fair in every country."
> - Stravinsky on *Petrushka*

Petrushka

A year after *Firebird* we see a maturing young composer displaying more confidence and mastery with *Petrushka*, which "exhibits the most perfect melding of music and scene…" Stravinsky took an amazing leap between *Firebird* and *Petrushka*; "Stravinsky found his language…found his identity." In *Petrushka* Stravinsky 'played' with pantonality, two instruments simultaneously playing in different keys. Some themes and motives had dual tonality.

Its polytonality would affect the course of European music and result in "numerous polytonal experiments stemming from *Petrushka*." *Petrushka* is in some ways the most deeply original and characteristic of all Stravinsky ballets; it is "music of power and vitality…with folk tunes…the immortal and unhappy puppet (Petrushka), hero of every fair…" Interestingly, it was originally conceived as a piano concerto or concertino. Stravinsky creates amazingly realistic crowd scenes in the opening and closing, representing an innovation in orchestration.

The Romantic harmony that Stravinsky retained in *The Firebird* was all but abandoned in *Petrushka* (1910-11). In this work his music is lean creating "complex textures by overlaying different streams of music, each with its own rhythm and direction." This work is music of power and vitality with Russian folk tunes to depict the scenes of the ballet: the carnival, the magician, the crowds, the puppet show and the death of Petrushka at the hands of 'the Moor'. With *Petrushka* Stravinsky also showed that folk music could be used without blending the folk tunes into traditional harmony. As a result, the folk music retained more of its freshness and vitality than say Dvořák's folk-tune infused music, which conformed to traditional harmony. Stravinsky demonstrated that folk music did not have to be blended into traditional harmony. It could be used much differently than in Dvořák's symphonies.

Many of the singable melodies derive from Austrian waltzes and Russian folk music. This music was originally received by some audiences as dangerously revolutionary and fearfully dissonant with jagged rhythms and irregular meters. In *Petrushka*, Stravinsky introduced the "Domino technique" of using small modules as building blocks glued together in different ways, thus building larger forms out of the very small units. This technique stayed with his music the rest of his career.

Stravinsky's polyrhythmic, polytonal early ballets pointed to a dissonant future "in their use of a sentiment-free expression and in their air of stark primitivism." In his early ballets "suggestions of polytonality appear side-by-side with overt use of old-fashioned melodic devices." Stravinsky never develops his material in the way the Germans did; he modifies ideas and varies his materials. What we experience superficially as development is really his 'domino technique' of small units being put in different sequences.

The "barbarous quality" of these first two ballets was not lost on listeners, but nothing could have prepared them, or Stravinsky, for the impact of *The Rite of Spring* two years later. The work hit Europe with unprecedented force and "for decades…composers imitated the new rhythms and sonorities" blasting out of this raw ballet. Serge Diaghilev, director of *Ballets Russes*, promised in his press release, "a new thrill that will doubtless inspire heated discussion." The "magnificently calculated chaos" of *The Rite* made it "the Big Bang of modern music." "With its near-total dissonance and breakaway from established canons of harmony and melody" it was a "genuine explosion."

The Rite of Spring

> *"Little melodies arrive from the depths of the centuries."*
> - librettist Jean Cocteau on *The Rite of Spring*

Primordial mutterings at the opening suggest a "strange and ancient landscape;" the "final frenzied moments" with the "percussive orgy of the ritual dance." The bassoon is used in a high register to give color to the beginning of *The Rite*. The "rhythmic world" of the *The Rite* is "dramatically more complex or daring than *Petrushka*." The subject is the "ambiguous triumph and cruelty of spring and the process of natural renewal…" *The Rite* is not only shocking musically; it is also the celebration of primitivism, looking back to pagan ritualism. Stravinsky claimed he got the inspiration for this ballet from a vision in which he imagined "a solemn pagan rite" with elders watching "a young girl dance herself to death" to please the god of spring.

> *"It's rather crude, so much of it calculated for external effect and lacking substance."*
> - Shostakovich on *The Rite of Spring*

Stravinsky's novelties included changing meters with every bar, achieving "jagged and uncouth rhythmic effects." Harsh polychords (combination of two or more traditional chords) are reiterated relentlessly. His use of multiple rhythms, with the number of beats per measure constantly changing, was groundbreaking, and a defiant break from traditional symmetry. "The innovatory force of this remarkable score resides in its rhythmic and metric originality, which is without precedent in…any other European music." In this work Stravinsky used a vast orchestral apparatus, but would never use such outsized forces again. Stravinsky found conventional rhythmic notation unsatisfactory so he changed the time signature almost from bar-to-bar. He "created complex textures by overlapping different streams of music, each with its own rhythm and direction."

In his Expositions and Developments (1962) Stravinsky stated that *The Rite of Spring* and "its highly sophisticated harmonic vocabulary" owe "more to Debussy than to anyone except myself." Indeed, one hears a similarity between the opening bassoon solo of *The Rite* and the opening theme of Debussy's *Prelude to the Afternoon of a Faun*. This bassoon melody is taken from Lithuanian folk tunes. Stravinsky deliberately used the instrument in its highest register to produce an unexpected strained and nasal sounding passage. The composer described the opening section "a sacred terror in the noonday sun." Part One "ends with the sweat-inducing crescendo of *Dance of the Earth*."

In creating the score to *The Rite*, Stravinsky assembled "a fantasy world from scraps of evidence" and "delved into folkloric sources…a book of Lithuanian wedding songs…and…memories of peasant singers" from the region of his birth. He even went so far as to favor folk music from areas that were last to convert to Christianity and had most recently practiced pagan traditions. Richard Taruskin in his book Stravinsky and the Russian Traditions states that the composer drew much more from traditional Russian folk material than had commonly been thought. Taruskin examines in detail the composer's use of folk music in *The Rite of Spring* and calls the work a "great fusion" of national and modern sounds. In the Paris of 1913 the tremendous push of nationalism collided with the 20th century and 'modern' music.

Upon the premiere of several of his works, including *The Rite of Spring* in 1913, Stravinsky stirred up storm after storm, such that the work could have been referred to, as pointed out by Alan Rich, as 'The Riot of Spring'. "Howls of discontent went up from the boxes." But the power and freshness of the music, which was shocking initially, quickly converted the dissenters as boos were replaced with cheers and wild applause in subsequent performances. It is wild music, but at the same time precise and clear.

The raw freshness of *The Rite* was quickly accepted and a new type of composition was born, one in which "melodies would follow the patterns of speech and rhythms would match the energy of dance." The dominance of winds and brass with the relegation of strings to relatively minor participation clearly signaled Stravinsky's increasing anti-Romanticism.

> *Recommended* – **Stravinsky ballets**
> For *Petrushka* and *The Rite of Spring*, Antal Dorati on Mercury; for *The Firebird*, Lorin Maazel, 1957 on DG

♫ The Neo-Classical Period

From Stravinsky's lead in *The Rite of Spring* began a movement across much of Europe for composers to rid themselves of the long-dominant influence of the Austro-German tradition of masters. Composers in non-German Europe, beginning with Debussy, "began to seek a way out of the hulking fortresses of Beethoven's symphonies and Wagner's operas. Teutonism was the common enemy, and devotion to indigenous folk songs escalated with Bartók, Janáček, and Falla.

Contrary to what his most popular ballet scores indicates, Stravinsky was mostly restrained, cool and classical in his music. The "impassioned, exciting, and extroverted" *Rite of Spring* and *Firebird* are more the exception than the rule for this composer. Clearly for many decades the public has preferred the impassioned over the restrained Stravinsky as these ballets dominate his recorded catalogue. Although *The Rite of Spring* quickly became successful outside Russia, within Stravinsky's homeland it was "dismissed...as so much trendy noise."

These colorful early ballets gave way to 'neo-Classicism' by the 1920s, with the revival of counterpoint texture and forms such as fugues and toccatas. Stravinsky sought to demonstrate "how the sounds of old music could be made new." In an apparent contradiction of the return to traditional forms, Stravinsky proclaimed, "The more art is controlled, limited, worked over, the more it is free." But perhaps he helps clarify this paradox by distinguishing 'interpretation' as the flaw of Romanticism, as opposed to 'execution' of exactly what is written as the foundation of modernism, "the tangible result of the postwar triumph of dehumanization."

After using massive orchestral forces for his three great ballets before World War I, Stravinsky turned from "superscores and superorchestras" to works for much smaller ensembles and a "pointed, precise way of writing."

His works during the war use the most economic resources. After the war he continued seeking "an altogether more austere sound world" and he continued to turn "his back on the rich orchestral palette of the pre-war years." "After this his works would be thoroughly western, thoroughly modern."

The work that is generally taken as marking Stravinsky's adoption of neo-Classicism is the ballet *Pulcinella*, which was premiered by Diaghilev and his *Ballets Russes* in 1920. The popular suite from this ballet was extracted by Stravinsky in 1922. Following on the heels of *Pulcinella* were more works composed in the same vein. Included in this period were the *Symphonies of Wind Instruments* (1921) and the *Octet* of 1923 (both works were discussed as chamber works for winds) that also show a return to sonata form. The composer explained that the "discovery of the past was the epiphany through which the whole of my late work became possible."

Stravinsky "took models, usually but not always from the past, and made them his own...He recomposed the music so that it became thoroughly modern and uniquely personal...he tried to show how early compositional devices and idioms can still be used in the 20th century." His neo-Classical works were of a "historical manner expressed in contemporary language", and continued with the Piano Concerto (1924) all the way to 1945 and his Symphony in Three Movements. During his neo-Classical period Stravinsky produced several 'chamber-like' orchestral works for chamber-sized ensembles or orchestras. These often had 'symphony' or 'concerto' in the titles despite not approaching the full-blown versions of those forms. This was common with neo-Classical and neo-Baroque composers; Hindemith's Kammermusik collection is an example that stands out and Martinů composed works with titles such as 'concertino'.

Stravinsky was totally anti-Romantic and his music represented "a complete rupture with Romanticism." Excepting the final period of his career he was committed to "tonality as the chief framework in Western music" and "he breathed new life into...tonality, which invigorated many other composers." He believed music is primarily form and logic, and he was one of music's supreme logicians. From 1911 to the late 1940s Stravinsky was the acknowledged leader of the musical *avant-garde*, and the strongest influence on the contemporary music scene. Harold Schonberg proposes that Stravinsky lived more "for what he did to music rather than for what his music did to the majority of his listeners."

Concerto for Piano and Winds

Stravinsky's adoption of a neo-Classical approach for the 1920s renewed his interest in the piano and highlighted the role of wind instruments in his music from this period. In addition to the Concerto for Piano and Winds the 1920s would also produce his *Octet* and the *Symphonies of Wind Instruments*. The label 'neo-Baroque' is more fitting for this work and others of the period, which follow the general plan of an 18th century *concerto grosso*, but with 20th century Stravinsky touches.

These touches include the composer's usual treatment of the piano as a percussive instrument, "the driving, regular metrics of the Baroque are put through the Stravinskyan rhythm machine." Stravinsky also uses a cyclic procedure with a dotted rhythmic figure appearing at the start and end of the first movement, as well as in the second and third movements. The work premiered in Paris in May 1924 with Stravinsky as soloist.

Stravinsky's Piano Concerto was very influential, most notably on Bartók's First and Second Piano Concertos. Bartók liked Stravinsky's use of Russian folk music in his early ballets, but Stravinsky moved away from this in the 1920s to his objective neo-Classical/neo-Baroque style. Bartók shifted in the same direction towards leaner and more contrapuntal textures.

Capriccio for Piano and Orchestra

Stravinsky acknowledged the influence of Weber and Mendelssohn for his *Capriccio* of 1929, which he intended as a showpiece for piano and orchestra. Although it is "technically demanding for the soloist" it "avoids being an all-out bravura showpiece." The "utterly charming and appealing work" shows dashes of Prokofiev, Saint-Saëns, and even Liszt's 'Hungarianism'. As with the Concerto for Piano and Winds this work is in the traditional three-movement format. Stravinsky divides the orchestra into solo group and full ensemble, as in a Baroque *concerto grosso*, but casting it in his best Hungarian manner.

Symphony of Psalms

This work, a symphony only in the loosest sense, was composed in 1929-30 on commission from the Boston Symphony to mark its fiftieth anniversary. Although Stravinsky used the term 'symphony' for his Symphony of Psalms, Symphony in C, and Symphony in Three Movements, all three works are unlike anything we would normally associate with the term or with the Germanic symphonic tradition. They are symphonies in name only.

The Symphony of Psalms is in three movements with Latin texts for choir and orchestra. It is a neo-Classical work. Stravinsky said that "sacred art...must abide by...ancient principles..." It is even proposed that Stravinsky, who claimed to have written the work "in a state of religious and musical ebullience," had found religion at a "time of danger."

However, Stravinsky avoids religious self-expression and cultivates "an impersonal, objective liturgical persona." His inscription on the score read, "Composed to the greater glory of God" and it is true that he returned to the Russian Orthodox Church around this time. This is more than a little curious given Stravinsky's claim that music should express nothing. It is based on Psalms 39, 40, and 150 and the contrapuntal writing for chorus and orchestra looks back to the cantata of the Baroque.

Violin Concerto

When it was suggested that he compose a violin concerto Stravinsky, a pianist, replied, "But I am not a violinist!" However, Paul Hindemith, an accomplished violist, convinced him that he could use that apparent deficiency as an advantage because Stravinsky would "avoid routine technique" and would bring "ideas which would not be suggested by the familiar movement of the fingers."

The concerto premiered in Berlin in 1931 with Stravinsky leading the Berlin Radio Symphony Orchestra. Samuel Dushkin, the violinist who commissioned the work, was the soloist. Stravinsky gave it wind instrument heavy orchestration, resulting in an effective contrast of the relative coolness of woodwind and brass with the warmth of the solo instrument. Stravinsky, in program notes he provided, wanted this concerto to be more chamber music in nature than orchestral, and he stated that he "did not care about exploiting the violin virtuosity." Towards this end there is frequent pairing of the soloist with another instrument.

The concerto has four movements instead of the standard 19th century three and they have titles of *Aria*, *Capriccio* and *Toccata*. Stravinsky made no secret that he had no use for the great violin concertos of the repertory such as those by Beethoven and Brahms; "to my mind, the only masterpiece…is Schoenberg's," which (conveniently) was composed after Stravinsky's. In effect, Stravinsky is saying that he took no cues for his concerto from any of the existent ones.

> *Recommended – Stravinsky Orchestral Works*
> There is the massive set of Stravinsky's Ballets and Orchestral Works by Ernest Ansermet and the *L'Orchestre de la Suisse Romande*.
> Good individual CD's are available on Naxos with Robert Craft conducting the Philharmonia or London Symphony.
> *Violin Concerto* – Perlman, Boston SO, Ozawa

Symphony in Three Movements

This symphony is utterly different from the Symphony in C, which represented an intensification of Stravinsky's neo-Classicism. This work pictures a world at war, with some of its various ideas suggested by wartime newsreels. Stravinsky stated that, "the symphony was written under the impression of world events (1942-45)…they excited my musical imagination." He intended each episode of the symphony to represent a specific impression of the war. However, Stravinsky insisted that, in spite of his indications to the contrary, "the symphony is not programmatic."

It was "his most potent music for orchestra since *The Rite*." Although Stravinsky at first insisted that this work "has no program," he later admitted that "the whole feeling of the work was bound up with his emotional reactions to World War II." It is a work of contrasts, "the most obvious is that of harp and piano, the principal instrumental protagonists." It was composed from 1942-45 and premiered in the first month of 1946 by the New York Philharmonic led by Stravinsky himself. The work, which characteristically uses the piano as a rhythm instrument, is "one of the most gripping and effectively executed scores of the 20th century."

> *"Whatever else serial music may be, it is certainly pure music."*
> *- Stravinsky in 1952*

To Stravinsky, "atonality implied anarchy, a state of lawlessness against which Stravinsky wanted to dictate the Bachian reaction." Although Stravinsky "did not (for the most part) go the atonal route of some dissonance-driven 20th century composers," he did finally succumb to serial form for some of his post-World War II compositions, including the *Movements* for Piano and Orchestra (1959). By 1959 Stravinsky had completed the transition to serialist, with the heaviest influence coming from Anton Webern, not Berg and Schoenberg (the latter being his neighbor at the time in southern California). This despite Debussy's prediction that "When he (Stravinsky) is old he will be unbearable…he will admit no other music." Movements resembles chamber music in which Stravinsky constantly changes the ensemble and uses the piano not as a soloist but as the principal role. Stravinsky, "staunch in his elaborate tonalism, would…finally become refreshed through Schoenberg's innovations."

♪ Paul Hindemith (1895-1963)

> *"One can still learn much from Papa Haydn."*
> *- Paul Hindemith*

Paul Hindemith began playing stringed instruments at age seven, left home at eleven to play in beer gardens and night clubs, and by the time he was in his twenties could play just about every instrument of the orchestra at least adequately. From this humble start Hindemith would end up as a professor of music at Yale University.

Hindemith was anti-Romantic and influenced by the German Baroque and Classical tradition, producing works of uncomplicated grace. He "showed a deep feeling for…the stately forms of the Renaissance and the Baroque;" the counterpoint of Bach, the polyphony of the Renaissance, and the balance, clarity and sturdiness of construction of the Classical period. Of the composers of the early 20th century he met 18th century specifications most closely. He was one of the few composers since the Baroque to revise the genre of the solo string sonata with his solo viola sonatas.

His music is "a model of workmanship in the mainstream of Baroque and Classic German music," evolving as "a most unusual harmonic and melodic language." Hindemith, one of the best practitioners of modern polyphonic texture of the 20th century, created a "new sound palette through Bachian counterpoint" using regular, carefully-balanced rhythms. He acknowledged that he wrote a lot of music but thought eighty percent of it was bad. Hindemith defended writing the bad eighty percent because without it he would not have composed the other twenty percent.

Between World Wars I and II he was considered, with Stravinsky and Schoenberg, one of the three leading 'radical' composers. However, Hindemith "pursued a consistently tonal path throughout his career." Although his music did strike listeners in the 1920s as highly dissonant, it always remained key-centered. His particular type of neo-Classicism was termed 'new objectivity' for its "great emphasis on the rules that govern the arts." His counterpoint was termed 'linear counterpoint'; it was dissonant, freed from all harmonic restrictions.

So while he started out 'radical' he ended up conservative, along the way composing music that was "modern in style yet thoroughly approachable." He "showed an exceptional command of the orchestra" and used elaborately contrapuntal forms such as the passacaglia and fugue. He was "enormously prolific" and an accomplished violist who toured with the Amar Quartet and premiered Walton's Viola Concerto in 1929 as soloist. Although "Hindemith's music has exerted no significant influence on composers of later generations…(it remains) a fitting monument to the neo-Classical ideals of the 20th century."

He composed in almost every musical genre, was the consummate craftsman who, in addition to being a virtuoso violist, could effectively play every major orchestral instrument. Hindemith possessed "an intimate knowledge of the performative, mechanical, and idiomatic possibilities and properties of each instrument." Not surprisingly, he wrote music for a wide variety of instruments, including at least one sonata for each in the orchestra. Some of his horn sonatas have even been adapted for the saxophone, in Hindemith's time a popular jazz instrument, but not a traditional instrument of the orchestra. The incorporation of saxophone into Hindemith's neo-Classical works is a good example of the cross over between jazz and classical music that was going on between the two world wars.

> *"The days of composing for the sake of composing are perhaps gone forever."*
> -Paul Hindemith

His music is intense with a rough and rowdy edge, and as with his Russian contemporaries, Hindemith saw the piano as a 'percussion instrument', telling musicians to "look on the piano as an interesting kind of percussion instrument and act accordingly." He believed strongly "that music should be useful and practical, and should not be a vehicle for self-expression." Hindemith drew attention for his 'utilitarian' music, in German *Gebrauchsmusik*, translated 'workaday music' or 'music for use', as opposed to 'music for music's sake'. It was anti-Romantic and "vehemently anti esthetic art...anti-transcendent, anti-idealist ideal...this was sheer subversion...(to the) heroic romantic tradition."

Hindemith stressed the mastery of musical craft. Under the liberal Weimar Republic of 1920s Germany, conditions were very favorable for *Gebrauchsmusik*. Other composers of this utilitarian music were Krenek, Weill, and Eisler. The term 'workaday music' is used to characterize his many assorted works for one to two amateur players. His sonatas, playable by 'amateurs', are not aimed at the overspecialized virtuoso of the Romantic Era but rather the versatile craftsman of the Classical period. Hindemith's dedication to the composition of works for amateurs was indicative of his teaching nature, as evidenced by the several professorships he held in Europe, Turkey, and the United States. His *Gebrauchsmusik* compositions may seem to lack a final polish but this was deliberate as Hindemith decried the modern orchestras that had "degenerated into mere distributors of superrefined sounds." Hindemith believed strongly in the ethical imperatives of music and the moral obligations of the musician.

As with most composers of the 20th century (as well as the Baroque) Hindemith's music is an acquired taste that requires repeated listening to fully reap the rewards of its "logic, organization and integrity." As a German and a 'modern traditionalist' (or neo-Classicist) he was devoted to counterpoint. In a way he was an early 20th century version of Brahms, looking back as far as Baroque forms and even to the origin of counterpoint in the Renaissance. Hindemith believed that sounds and forms of classical music must be used "to turn our soul towards everything noble, superhuman, and ideal." As such, he opposed Schoenberg's techniques and "steadfastly adhered to...tonality."

Mathis der Maler
'Matthew the painter' was commissioned by Wilhelm Furtwangler (1933-34) and was Hindemith's first symphonic essay. It was originally intended as an opera, from which he extracted, before completion, a three-movement symphonic suite. The work is based on artist Matthias Grünewald (c.1460-1528) who joins in a peasant revolt. There are three movements, each based on one of Grünewald's paintings: *Angelic Concert*, which was to be the prelude to Hindemith's opera; *Entombment*, an orchestral interlude from the final act; and *The Temptation of St. Anthony*, the opera's dream sequence. "The symphony ends in a blazing affirmation of faith, in God, and in the power of art." Although often referred to as a symphony, it lacks the wholeness required of a 'symphony'.

It is "a dramatic allegory about the artist's dilemma in a turbulent society." *Mathis der Maler* is more post-Romantic than neo-Classical; in fact, in some of the louder full orchestral sections *Der Maler* sounds like Herr Mahler. Although Furtwangler staunchly defended Hindemith and this work, the Nazis had already begun their campaign against the composer, branding his music as 'culturally Bolshevist' and Hindemith as an 'atonal noisemaker', despite the fact that Hindemith's works were tonal compared to much of the 'modern' music composed in Europe after World War I. The *Mathis der Maler* symphonic extract had to have its premiere during World War II in neutral Switzerland.

> "Paul Hindemith has burst like fireworks over New York, scattering performances everywhere."
> - Elliott Carter in 1939

In 1938 his music was officially banned in Germany and all subsequent premieres of his works took place in other countries. Hindemith finally had enough of Hitler and his propaganda minister Goebbels, and went to the United States in 1939, becoming a professor at Yale until 1953.

Konzertmusik; Symphony in E-Flat

Hindemith used the vague title *Konzertmusik* for three consecutive Opus numbers, Op.48 for viola and chamber orchestra; Op.49 for piano, two harps and brass; and Op.50 for brass and strings. The Op.50 was commissioned by the Boston Symphony for its 50th anniversary in 1931.

The Symphony in E-Flat is one of Hindemith's first works composed in the U.S. (1940). Commissioned by Koussevitzky and premiered by the Minneapolis Symphony under Mitropoulos, it is chock full of glorious brass fanfares.

Symphonische Metamorphosen

The *Symphonic Metamorphoses after Themes of Carl Maria von Weber* is a four-movement orchestral showpiece composed in 1943. As Hindemith had finally gotten out of Nazi Germany, the work premiered in January 1944 with NY Philharmonic under Artur Rodzinski. It is an immediately attractive work, "full of colorful writing enhancing striking themes" from Weber's incidental music.

Hindemith adapts some of Weber's themes in this orchestral suite. It contains a powerful march-finale and a long scherzo that is virtuosic in the extreme. This work and *Mathis der Maler* are Hindemith's most popular orchestral scores.

> **Recommended** – *Mathis der Maler* (orchestral suite) – Wolfgang Sawallish/Philadelphia Orchestra-EMI (19xx), on a CD that also includes strong performances of the *Symphonic Metamorphosis* and *Nobilissima Visione* his next two most popular works for full orchestra.

♪ *Kammermusik*

Kammermusik is a collection of seven concertos for various instruments (piano, violin, cello, viola, and even one for organ) and chamber orchestras of various combinations of mostly winds with a few strings. Although Hindemith called these 'chamber' works they are better characterized as 'mini-concertos' because of the ensemble size and the use of an identified soloist in each. Although composed for moderately-sized orchestra, the "instrumental demands are certainly 'chamber sized'." The series defined an influential neo-Classical impulse of German music in the 1920s. The numbering is confusing: Nos.1-7 correspond to Op.24:1, 36:1-4, and 46:1-2; therefore, to minimize confusion these are usually designated as Nos. 1-7 without inclusion of the opus numbers.

The first is actually a *concerto grosso* for twelve instruments with the remaining concertos for cello, piano, violin, viola, viola *d'amore*, and organ, respectively. The prominence of the winds in the various concertos of *Kammermusik* clearly shows the composer's association with jazz and popular music. With Nos. 2-7, composed 1924-27, Hindemith wrote for ensembles that "renounce the harmonically oriented balance of 19th century chamber music and take their stimulus from Bach's *Brandenburg* Concertos, focusing on…wind and brass…" In a way, these mini concertos are the *Brandenburgs* of the 20th century and Hindemith's "instincts had always been towards the 'objective' musical values of strong polyphonic interest." The *Kammermusik* set represents for listeners today a return to a lost era.

Kammermusik No.1 is a suite for twelve players and is a short, cheerful, four-movement work of fifteen minutes. With it Hindemith "abruptly aligned himself with Stravinsky and Milhaud…" No.2 followed three years later and is a piano concerto. As with the first piece of the series the orchestral ensemble is twelve players. This work is in ways a neo-Baroque concerto, a *concerto grosso*, but with 20th century piano writing.

The next four mini-concertos (Nos. 3-6) are for single string soloist; in order, cello, violin, viola, and the all-but-forgotten Baroque *viola d'amore*. These all look back to Baroque suites and concertos as all are in four or five movements instead of the standard three movements of concertos of the previous 150 years. The work for cello soloist (1925) is a cello concerto ingeniously scored for an ensemble of ten solo instruments. Including the one among the *Kammermusik* works, Hindemith wrote three piano concertos. The other two are his Piano Concerto and the *Concert Music*, Op.49. His neo-

Classical concertos are closer in form to "baroque ideals" than to "the practices of the Viennese classics."

The one work in three movements, No.7 features the organ as solo instrument with eleven winds and a few strings. It is "the grandest and most festive of all..." An interesting feature of the *Kammermusik* series is the noticeable scarcity of accompanying violins and violas, and the dominance by winds. Hindemith shares this affinity for winds with fellow neo-Classicist Stravinsky. There are no violins at all in No.4 (for solo violin) and No.5 has neither violins nor violas.

> **Recommended** - For a complete set of the *Kammermusik*, Abbado and players from the Berlin Philharmonic (and pianist Lars Vogt) are recommended (EMI). Chailly and Concertgebouw members also distinguish themselves (Double Decca). Abbado includes Hindemith's Viola Concerto *Der Schwanendreher*, while Chailly does not.

♪♩ Music for Strings and Orchestra

Although Hindemith could play practically any instrument and play it well, he was most proficient as a violist. Therefore, some of his best concerto writing is for viola and orchestra.

The *Trauermusik*, ('Mourning music') is a miniature four-movement 'requiem concerto' for viola or violin or cello and string orchestra. It begins right away with the theme of death in a funeral march. There is even an adaptation as a sonata for violin and piano. Its most common form though is for viola and small orchestra. The *Trauermusik* is *Gebrauchsmusik* with emotion. The dark and strained tone of the viola is well suited.

Der Schwanendreher ('The Swan Turner') from 1935 is in the standard three movements, is Hindemith's only full-scale viola concerto, and is one of three viola concertos by Hindemith. The earlier two, discussed above, are from the *Kammermusik* series: No.5 for viola and No.6 for viola *d'amore*, the latter being "more hard-edged and elaborately contrapuntal." 'The Swan Turner', a reference to medieval times, is the title of the song used in the finale, *Aren't You the Swan-Turner?*

Perhaps the conditions brewing in 1935 Germany stirred up in Hindemith a longing for "a lost era of harmony and humanity." This longing, if actually the case, would have been naïve, as life for just about all in the Middle Ages, excepting the upper classes and clergy, was miserable. Nonetheless, in *Der Schwanendreher* the composer vividly conjures up "a medieval minstrel embellishing a variety of folk songs," as Hindemith does incorporate original folk tunes into the musical fabric. The music has a clearer tonality and less dense polyphony than his works of the previous decade and is the most famous of the dozen or so works that the composer wrote for himself to perform as soloist.

The cello concertos are two of Hindemith's most powerful orchestral works. One is part of the *Kammermusik* set of concertos (No.2) for soloist(s) with small orchestra, while the second, from 1940 for full orchestra, is among his greatest works. The composer stated that he wanted to write a "piece for the cello like the Violin Concerto."

Hindemith wrote two violin concertos, one being *Kammermusik* No.4, dominated by wind instruments, and his 1935 Violin Concerto for full orchestra, a more lyrical work than the earlier mini-concerto. This work "builds on the tradition of the genre in the 19th century while not forsaking the concertante approach of the 18th." In Hindemith's later concertos and symphonies, starting with his departure from Germany, "one can detect a vision of a music that might synthesize the inheritance of tonal music from the Middle Ages to the 20th century…"

Although his early works were viewed as clearly 'modern' and Hindemith was seen as such, after World War II he was seen as a conservative in light of the emergence of the avant-garde. Simply put, "Hindemith could not follow the process of tonal 'break-down'…his musical instinct bound him…to the fugal spirit of Bach." Because of this, Hindemith has mistakenly gotten the unfortunate label of 'uninspired technician' by some, but he was certainly inspired by German tradition, particularly Baroque counterpoint and J.S. Bach.

♪ Bohuslav Martinů (1890-1959)

Martinů was a contemporary of Hindemith; a Moravian who spent parts of his career in Paris and America. As with Hindemith, a contemporary and fellow neo-Classicist, Martinů remains an obscure figure to most casual classical music listeners, primarily due to the lack of a 'masterpiece' or an instantly-recognizable work. This is a shame because both Hindemith and Martinů composed prolifically in many forms, including a large variety of chamber works for seemingly endless ensembles. Where Hindemith favored strings, particularly the viola, Martinů had a special affinity for the flute. Their music remains for most an undiscovered treasure chest of great music that bridges Baroque and Classical forms with 20th century 'modernism'.

Martinů's music is set apart from Stravinsky's and Hindemith's by its larger scale, as evidenced by his six major symphonies and five piano concertos, and the fact that it is less harsh and remained romantic at its core. Many feel its shimmering textures and half-realized melodies make Martinů's music unique and instantly recognizable. His "scores don't amble or glide; they skip, dance, caper and frolic." His orchestration, with its "block chords and massed sonorities, results in a 'wall of sound'." Martinů's music is "usually quite angular" but possesses "innate lyricism."

Some critics feel this makes Martinů's longer pieces tend toward sameness. The atmospheric, easy-listen style at times reminds some of the American composer Howard Hanson. Martinů's harmonies are "partly naturally Czech...but have an added Vaughan Williams-like modality and an air of Ravelian impressionistic magic." David Ewen goes even further and points to the impressionism of Debussy as a dominant influence on Martinů.

Before leaving Bohemia in 1923 for Paris, Martinů was a violinist in the Czech Philharmonic. Arriving in Paris he was "well-armed with late Impressionism and folkloristic tendencies" as well as "for thinking on quite a grand scale." He was a neo-Classicist Czech nationalist who honed his craft in Paris falling under the influence of Stravinsky, Debussy and *Les Six* composers, as well as American jazz, which had become popular with Parisians. He wrote a great deal of music in all possible genres, including six substantial symphonies and a large number of concertos. His style began as romantic and even impressionist, then evolved into a jazzy neo-Baroque, as evidenced by his *Concerto Grosso* of 1937. He even claimed Corelli as his favorite composer.

His music has been described as "quasi-neo-Baroque," although it was "never associated with any particular school, finding his own voice in the synthesis of the most diverse influences." The works of Martinů are characterized by "distinctive, unorthodox chord progressions that defy traditional tonal logic." "He succeeded in amalgamating Czech musical traditions with contemporary Western trends." With time, Martinů's music became infused with "the romantic strain that was at the core of his nature."

Continuous changes in meter and extended tonality, with occasional harsh dissonances that also incorporates elements of jazz characterize Martinů's music. According to conductor and musicologist Christopher Hogwood, "waywardness of meter" and "perpetual syncopation" characterizes Martinů's compositional style. Some of his orchestral works are of a purely orchestral nature while others are *concertante* works for chamber orchestra with titles such as serenade, *sinfonietta*, and partita. After World War II, he settled in the U.S. and became lushly romantic. He held posts as professor of music at several institutions including Princeton. Martinů was a master technician, a perfect craftsman, "longing for an earlier formality." Through it all Czech/Moravian folk music was always his point of reference. "Czech folk music...shaped his melodic and rhythmic invention in general."

♫ Symphonies

Martinů contributed valuable works to nearly every area of the repertory. Although some of his over 300 compositions are not of the highest quality, his six symphonies are widely held as among his best works. As was the case with Brahms, Martinů waited until he was well established in his fifties to present his First Symphony to the world in 1942 on commission from the

Boston Symphony Orchestra. Together with Sibelius, Vaughn Williams, and Shostakovich, he is counted with the greatest symphonists of the 20th century, all six of which he composed from 1942-53 after settling in the U.S. Martinů never liked or adjusted to America or the American way of life; "...what he saw as the slick American way of life sickened him."

> *"The artist is always searching for the meaning of life,*
> *his own and that of mankind, searching for truth."*
> *- Martinů*

Martinů's period of symphonies upon his arrival in the United States followed a decade of neo-Baroque forms (e.g., *concerto grosso*). The six symphonies are all different and do not seem to be influenced much by preceding symphonies. As someone who relied strictly on traditional forms, none of the six symphonies "breaks new ground formally, yet they each establish a world that is radiant and vital...The melodic inspiration is strong." "He chooses thematic germs that will lead to a lot of development."

Martinů created a music identifiable by its "nervous, gliding, motoric rhythms" combined with folk-like melodies. He rarely used an actual folk song but instead created pseudo-Bohemian and pseudo-Moravian melodies combined with "exotic sonorities...Eastern percussive effects...always a piano somewhere...working on a rhythmic basis." The seemingly ever-present piano in so many of Martinů's works "is partly soloistic but frequently reverts to a sort of *basso continuo* role." The use of piano as bass accompaniment also shows the influence of jazz.

Martinů's symphonies are 'Mahler-lite', utilizing large orchestras with lush textures contrasted with powerful rhythms and folk music, but not weighted down by the extreme orchestral bombast and emotional excesses of Mahler's huge works. Conductor and pianist Vladimir Ashkenazy feels Martinů's symphonies "show the very harmonious development of a dedicated composer." The symphonies are all around thirty minutes without post-Romantic excess or pretension, making them instantly accessible but thoroughly modern. However, none of the six are staples of the symphonic repertoire.

Martinů's sixth and final symphony (1953), the three-movement *Fantasies Symphoniques*, is the best-known, although the *First*, *Fourth*, and *Fifth* are popular as well. Of the *First*, conductor Serge Koussevitzky, who commissioned the work, recommended to Martinů, "you cannot change a single note...it is a classical symphony." In it, Martinů uses "several unifying devices to make a cohesive whole of the four movements." The Fifth Symphony contains a "lovely slow movement flute solo and a rich vein of lyrical ideas." It also possesses "an indefinable Czech character that suggested a latter day Dvořák."

> "Martinů never composed anything he'd need to be ashamed of."
> - pianist Rudolf Firkusny

It took the usually fast-working Martinů a surprising two years to complete his *Fantasies Symphoniques* after receiving the commission from the Boston Symphony and Charles Munch in 1951. His final symphony uses a slow-fast-slow three-movement structure built on a three-note motif that begs comparison to similarly-structured French orchestral works. The symphony alternates mystery with great lyrical warmth and, as its subtitle suggests, it explores deep veins of fantasy. In it Martinů also decided against the use of piano as a percussive instrument, although he had in fact originally planned to use three pianos in the *Sixth*!

Virgil Thomson, upon hearing the First Symphony, commented, "the shining sounds of it sing as well as shine." As Stravinsky used his Symphony in Three Movements in response to the horrors of World War II, so Martinů captured in his Third Symphony the sorrow he felt in response to the atrocities, which included the Nazis overrunning his native land.

> **_Recommended_ – _Martinů Complete symphonies_**
> Belohlavek and the Czech Philharmonic (Chandos or Supraphon) or Thomson and the Royal Scottish NO (Chandos, 2005). An exciting coupling of the *Fifth* and *Sixth Symphonies* is by the Czech PO and Ančerl (Supraphon, 1960s), who championed the exile composer in his native Czechoslovakia.

Apart from his symphonies, Martinů's orchestral masterpiece is the three-movement, quasi-Impressionist work *Frescoes of Piero della Francesca*. Each of the movements was inspired by church-wall paintings that the composer saw during his tour of Italy late in his career (1954-55). Among the depictions that inspired Martinů are the Queen of Sheba and the Emperor Constantine. The work premiered at the 1956 Salzburg Festival with Rafeal Kubelik, its dedicatee, conducting.

♪ *Concertos*

The influence of the late Baroque *concerto grosso* is seen in the "sometimes over-busy contrapuntal textures of Martinů's chamber works." His chamber output contains some fifty works. A sense of exile can be felt in much of his music. He spent much of his life in exile outside his native Bohemia.

> "My melody, rhythm and sonority stem directly from my Czech nature and they are linked with Smetana and Dvorak."

His most famous concerto is the *Double* Concerto scored for two string orchestras serving as bookends to the piano and timpani. It is a neo-Classical concerto grosso with two orchestras pitted against each other. It is known for its intense slow movement, capturing Martinů's feelings "after the betrayal of his country at Munich" in 1938 and subsequent Nazi occupation. It was written under the imposing doom for his Czech homeland brought on by the Munich Agreement. It is "one of the strongest and most-compelling of Martinů's many works...the basic emotion is not despair but rather," according to the composer, "revolt, courage and unshakable faith in the future."

From start to finish the work "bristles with nervous energy, horror, and sorrow." In true neo-Classical/Baroque style, the piano receives a "genuinely *concertante* role,...sometimes part of the ensemble and sometimes spotlit as a soloist." This work does have its detractors; Christopher Hogwood finds it "too unrelentingly and gratingly dissonant throughout."

Martinů was also prolific in the piano concerto form, composing five 'piano concertos' and a *Concertino* for Piano and Orchestra. The best-known is Piano Concerto No.4, *Incantations*, a two-movement work that has remained in the concerto repertoire. In it Martinů "ventures into modernist angularity á la Hindemith." Piano Concerto No.4 "covers a great deal of emotional distance and psychological distance...like so much of Martinů's music is emotionally volatile...goes from zero to sixty very quickly...you're on a pretty vigorous emotional roller coaster." By casting the concerto in two movements Martinů claimed "I am trying to escape the traditional form of the piano concerto which is geometrical...leaving little opportunity for free development..." His Third Piano Concerto was written for Rudolf Firkusny, Martinů's friend and long-time champion of his music.

Another nod to the Baroque is Martinů's Harpsichord Concerto, composed in a modern Bachian style. He also contributed, among others, two cello concertos and an oboe concerto. The Oboe Concerto includes a harpsichord part and is scored for chamber orchestra. His concertos, while certainly not staples of the repertoire, do occasionally appear on programs. For example, his later Piano Concerto No.4 from 1956 was programmed by the New York Philharmonic, with Garrick Ohlsson as soloist, in November 2009 while the First Cello Concerto remains one of Martinů's most popular orchestral works.

> *Recommended – Martinů Concertos*
> For the *Double* Concerto the nod goes to Belohlavek and the Czechs on Chandos for state-of-the-art recordings. For vintage performance, the composer described Kubelik's 1950 performance with the Philharmonia as "powerful and awe-inspiring as a storm at sea."
> Complete Martinů *Piano Concertos* – Emil Leichner as soloist with the Czech Philharmonic under Belohlavek. There is a

> brand new recording of the *Second* and the *Fourth* by pianist Robert Kolinsky with Ashkenazy and the Sinfonieorchester Basel (Ondine, 2009). *Cello Concerto* – if you can find the Fournier/Fricsay recording; otherwise, Wallfisch with Belohlávek/Czech PO (Chandos, 2009).

Despite his large and varied output Martinů remains a relatively obscure composer. Possible reasons are that he not only leaned on traditional forms but also broke no new ground, while most of his well-known contemporaries either broke new ground musically or did so with traditional forms. He was also probably born too late, although this was not as much of a problem for his contemporary Hindemith. While Martinů's oeuvre does not boast a work instantly identified with him (e.g., Stravinsky's *The Rite*), this again is also the case with Hindemith. Another possibility is his classification as neo-Baroque and neo-Classical instead of as a Czech nationalist. As a result, he is excluded from discussions of the great Czech composers Dvořák, Smetana, and Janáček. Unlike the great Czech triumvirate, Martinů spent the bulk of his career outside his native Moravia in Paris and the U.S.

Critics and musicologists cannot seem to make up their minds on Martinů's place in musical history. Most all agree that after Janacek, Martinů is the second greatest Czech composer of the 20th century. But David Dubal opines that many of Martinů's works "fizzle out for lack of sustained inspiration." Curiously, several survey books make no mention of him (Schonberg, J. Kramer, P. Goulding) while others give him a fair amount of coverage (R. Hemming).

It is likely that his output is uneven because he composed rapidly and rarely revised his work. Martinů "didn't like revising very much, which may have been one of his weaknesses, but his strengths are so abundant that that doesn't matter."

The late 1930s and 1940s for music was the period of the rapid rise of the 'Darmstadt *avant-garde*' which unfairly condemned all neo-Classical music as the artistic counterpart to political totalitarianism. This was in reaction to the totalitarian regime in Russia, the rise and fall of Nazi Germany, but also to the Soviet-style communism taking root in post-war Eastern Europe. Artists saw so much of Europe and so many of their fellow musicians come under government control and oppression. As a result, not just the music of Martinů, but also that of his important contemporaries such as Albert Roussel, Arthur Honegger, Francis Poulenc, Darius Milhaud and others virtually vanished from concert podiums and have returned only since the end of the 20th century. The music of Martinů received an additional lift in 2009 from the 50th anniversary of his death, with an increase of concerts and recordings focused on his music.

- 24 -

Two Russian Giants
Prokofiev and Shostakovich

Two great Soviet composers of the 20th century, known mostly for their orchestral music, deserve detailed discussion. Both Shostakovich and Prokofiev were Russians who lived and composed under the Soviet Union. Shostakovich is the greatest modern-day symphonist while Prokofiev composed an incredible variety of works that remain popular, including symphonies, concertos, sonatas, and orchestral suites from film scores. However, both are prime examples of how world events early in the last century forever changed the musical landscape.

Music composed after World War I needs to be considered separately and in context. The music of these two great Soviet composers was heavily influenced by their government and their creative talents were greatly suppressed by Soviet communism. Alex Ross in The Rest Is Noise appropriately titles his chapter on music in Stalin's Russia, "The Art of Fear", evoking the multiple layers of "one of the great nightmares of 20th century cultural history," that would cause Prokofiev and Shostakovich to both "endure a long string of humiliation." Coupled to these great nightmares was "the onset of the most warped and tragic phase in 20th century music: the total politicizing of the art by totalitarian means," not only in the Soviet Union but in the totalitarian regimes so common in Europe during the second quarter of the last century, in Germany, Italy, Spain and Hungary.

The Soviet Union in the 1930s banned all music that had any hint of abstractionism; art was turned into a vehicle for Soviet propaganda with music "evaluated not on its own merits but on its doctrinal purity." The state that had arisen out of revolution now "began to turn out art of a…uniformity of expression that (was) the antithesis of revolution." Any music that did not glorify the proletariat was dismissed; any music that was judged 'modern' or dissonant was condemned as decadent and was not allowed to be heard by Soviet citizens, who under state-central control could not be allowed to judge music for themselves.

While there certainly is plenty of dissonance in the work of both these composers, they could only adopt 20th century 'modernist' tendencies in limited doses and avoided producing atonal works. In fact, Prokofiev's music was a "tug-of-war between motoric modernism and Romantic lyricism." Their music was, in some ways, neo-Classical (sometimes blatantly so with Prokofiev) and often neo-Baroque. Shostakovich effectively used "the recurring bass lines of the passacaglia (a Baroque form) to suggest the inescapable tensions of modern existence."

In 1948 the Politburo, led by communist party leader Andrei Zhdanov, issued a 'Resolution' accusing Prokofiev, Shostakovich and most other leading Soviet composers of composing music that was unbecoming a Soviet. The Central Committee cited a need for their composers to restore "high-quality works worthy of the Soviet people." (read: meeting the criteria of the Politburo's cultural ideology office and usefulness for state propaganda.) Soviet composers "must reject as useless and harmful garbage all the relics of bourgeois formalism in musical art" ranted fellow composer Tikhon Khrennikov. Khrennikov threw his colleagues 'under the bus' in exchange for a powerful position in the musical bureaucracy.

'Formalism' was essentially "any style that smacked too strongly of Western modernism." Soviet music must be used "to portray the eternal battle between good Soviets and their class enemies"…and to show "the struggle of conflicting tendencies." Artists "were obliged to curtail experiment (in music) in support of official doctrine." This was the foundation for the concept of 'Socialist Realism' in the Soviet arts with "demands for 'songfulness' in Soviet music by the party leadership." Central to the concept of Social Realism was conservatism and traditionalism, following the manner of The Mighty Five and Tchaikovsky. Impressionism and Serialism were to be shunned. The Resolution of 1948 essentially initiated a "musicological inquisition", which effectively quashed "any lingering ideas of individuality" among composers living within the Soviet system.

Restrictions did ease up starting around 1950 with Khrushchev coming to power. He acknowledged the crimes of Stalin and took steps to exonerate the celebrated composers who had been vilified by the 1948 Resolution. In 1958 Khrushchev announced that Stalin had been 'subjective' in his approach to works of art and the new leader removed the 'formalist' label from Shostakovich's music. A further relaxation was allowed by Brezhnev in the mid-1960s.

In 1979, a few years after Shostakovich's death, an English translation was published of <u>Testimony</u>, the supposed memoirs of the composer. In this work Shostakovich reveals his true feelings on the Soviet system but more interestingly, the fact that he disguised these feelings in several key works which were, in a way, a subtle form of protest music. The First Violin Concerto is one of the major examples of such a work, written in the middle of Zhdanov's purge of 1948 and held back from publication by Shostakovich until after Stalin's death.

To the great credit of Prokofiev and more so of Shostakovich (who lived twenty years longer under the Soviet system) both learned to compose successfully under strict parameters. It was not at all easy for either of them. Prokofiev still produced music denounced by the central committee, which pointed out that the composer "has even now not yet outgrown the childish dogma of innovation for the sake of innovation…"

But one has to wonder what Shostakovich and Prokofiev, as well as scores of other Russian composers forced to work their craft under Soviet rule, would have produced had their creative talents been allowed to flow unchecked. While Prokofiev did not possess his countryman's skills for orchestration, Shostakovich did not have Prokofiev's gift of melody and lyricism.

As with Shostakovich, Prokofiev's best works "clearly transcend any political context." "The majority of my symphonies are tombstones," said Shostakovich, alluding to honoring by his compositions Russians who were killed but whose families were unable to bury. Adding emphasis, "I dedicate my music to them all."

> *"Prokofiev always made more of a splash and seemed more interesting."*
> - Dmitri Shostakovich in <u>Testimony</u>

♪ Serge Prokofiev (1891-1953)

Prokofiev's fellow Russian Stravinsky never matched the early popular successes of his ballet scores and so embraced neo-Classicism. Then, towards the end of his career, incorporated atonality and serialism, after rejecting the 'Schoenberg school' for years. However, Prokofiev never looked back and made no secret about his rejection of influences from the past, and "ran the gamut of styles without ever losing his own." But as it turned out, he was heavily influenced by what had preceded him.

Prokofiev remains one of the most played and recorded composers of the 20th century. He created lasting symphonies (his First and Fifth), piano and violin concertos, several piano sonatas, orchestral suites of film scores and the ever-popular *Peter and the Wolf*. Prokofiev can be considered a 20th century Mendelssohn or Tchaikovsky; a tunesmith with an endless well of melodies whose gift surpassed rivals such as Stravinsky and Shostakovich. This gift for melody, combined with his progressiveness, has been described by Lawrence Kramer as "a tug-of-war between motoric modernism and Romantic lyricism."

> *"I want nothing better, more flexible or more complete than the sonata form, which contains everything necessary for my structural purposes."*
> - Serge Prokofiev

With the Russian revolution in 1917 Prokofiev headed to America. It was a very productive year, resulting in his Visions fugitives, the Violin Concerto in D, and his First Symphony, *Classical*. However, Prokofiev was not accepted in New York in the early 1920s; his icy, irritating disposition certainly did not help matters. Audiences responded well to his virtuosic piano playing but listeners generally did not take to his music and so he fled America for Paris. In 1936 he returned to the Soviet Union to settle in Moscow, naively believing that the Soviet bureaucracy would not bother a composer of his stature.

When Prokofiev returned to the Soviet Union he had by coincidence just committed himself to what he called a new simplicity, a conservative modernism rooted in Classical and Romantic tradition. This view just happened to agree with the socialist-realist ideology that was being promulgated at the time in the Soviet Union. Thus, upon returning to his homeland his music enjoyed official 'acceptance'. Although Prokofiev "towed the company line" and personally was treated relatively well by the Soviet machine, friends of his spoke of a "mask of optimism" behind which lurked "the feeling of profound and terrible insecurity."

Prokofiev was extremely active in the 1930s and 1940s, producing in a variety of genres works that would become international favorites. From this period are Violin Concerto No.2 (1935), the symphonic fairy tale for children *Peter and the Wolf* (1936), ballet music for *Romeo and Juliet* (1935) and the film scores for *Lt. Kije* (1934) and *Alexander Nevsky* (1939), extracting concert suites from both of these scores. In the 1940s he continued with Piano Sonata No.7, the Second String Quartet, and Symphony No.5.

While all these works continued to be rhythmically, melodically and harmonically Prokofiev, the 'age-of-steel' modernity of his earlier works was not as pronounced. The middle-aged Prokofiev had become a gentler, slightly watered-down version of his younger self.

> "It seemed to me that if Haydn had lived in this century, he would have retained his own style while absorbing certain things from newer music."
> - Prokofiev

Symphony No.1, 'Classical'

Prokofiev attempted to write a 20th century Haydn symphony, which has remained one of his more popular works. Both Shostakovich and Prokofiev had neo-Classical tendencies but more so Prokofiev with the blatant Classical Symphony and his greater talent for melody. Prokofiev believed in what he called 'light-serious' or 'serious-light' music. Such music according to the composer "should be primarily melodious" with clear and simple melodies but not repetitive or trivial. This happens to describe Prokofiev's music very effectively because he was a very gifted melodist (arguable the greatest of the 20th century) and many of his contemporaries emphasized rhythm over melody (e.g., Stravinsky, who also resided in Paris while Prokofiev lived there).

The *Classical* Symphony shows no signs of the war tearing Europe apart in 1916-17. It links Classical period form and style with the "harmonic and rhythmic gestures of the early 20th century." The third movement is a clear break from Classical form and instead represents neo-Baroque, using a gavotte (a dance movement typical of Baroque suites) in place of the usual minuet and trio of Haydn and Mozart.

Symphony No.5

Prokofiev's Fifth Symphony was also hailed as an "inspirational 'war symphony';" however, unlike Shostakovich's *Leningrad* Symphony (No.7) it lacked any program to connect it directly to battle, although Prokofiev clearly followed Shostakovich's Fifth Symphony as a model. Prokofiev characterized his most famous symphony as "the culmination of a long period of my creative life" and "a symphony of the greatness of the human spirit, a song of praise of free and happy mankind." The grim presence of World War II can be felt in this "work of epic scope and noble character." Prokofiev conducted the premiere in Moscow in January 1945.

This symphony is a clear commitment to socialist-realism, composed in the popular fashion of four traditional movements. As with Shostakovich's popularly-fashioned symphonies, brass and percussion are effectively utilized to evoke military associations. The final rondo lets the symphony end with a positive mood, thus bringing a sign of hope through the *Fifth* in the "middle of a political ice age."

The First and Fifth Symphonies are by far the most popular of Prokofiev's seven symphonies. The other five contain much enjoyable music in typical Prokofiev style, particularly the *Sixth*.

Piano Concertos

The five piano concertos were all composed by the time Prokofiev was forty-two, so they are mostly representative of early Prokofiev. Piano Concerto No.1, Op.10 was composed 1911-12 and premiered in 1912 in Moscow with the composer as soloist. It is a clear anti-Romantic work composed while he was still a student at the Romantically-oriented St. Petersburg Conservatory. As a soloist and composer for piano, Prokofiev saw the piano as a percussion instrument and had no use for the tradition that came down from Chopin and Liszt.

> *"They say you cannot give a recital without Chopin?*
> *I'll prove that we can do very well without Chopin."*
> - Prokofiev

The Second Piano Concerto, Op.16, was composed right after the first in 1912-13 and revised in 1923 with Prokofiev again the soloist for the premiere of the revised version, this time in Paris under Serge Koussevitzky. Parisians did not receive the revised work much better than the original version had been received in St. Petersburg. This work too was written while he was at the Conservatory, the work of a young man in his early twenties.

Piano Concerto No.3, Op.26, his most well-known and performed, had a more indirect route to completion than its predecessors. In it Prokofiev used materials dating back to as early as the First Piano Concerto, but did not finish it until 1921. This time the composer went across the Atlantic to premiere the concerto later that year in Chicago. It too is brilliant but less taxing than the Second.

His Fifth Piano Concerto is a "pithy, technically difficult work in five short movements."

String Concertos

Prokofiev's First Violin Concerto was begun in 1913 and completed in 1917. It premiered in 1923 on a programme that also included Stravinsky's *Octet*. The concerto is highly original; it breaks from the traditional fast-slow-fast structure of concertos and instead ends slowly and softly. The first movement is not in sonata form but is rather "a rhapsody-like chain of freely-evolving ideas." This violin concerto was used by William Walton as the model for his Viola Concerto, although Walton remained closer to sonata form in his first movement.

The premiere of Violin Concerto No.2 in G minor, Op.63 was given in 1935 by Robert Soetens as soloist in Madrid. A recording with Soetens and the BBC SO under Henry Wood made a year later recently surfaced and was released in the December 2009 issue of *BBC Music Magazine*. Prokofiev wrote that he wanted to make his Second Violin Concerto "different from No.1 in terms of both music and style."

The 'Symphony-Concerto' (or *Sinfonia Concertante*) is actually a cello concerto "on a heroic scale, geared to exploit the technical mastery of (cellist) Rostropovich." This concerto had an interesting origin, beginning in 1938 with the disastrous premiere of Prokofiev's 'Cello Concerto', the composer revised the work a decade later, calling it 'No.2'. The Symphony-Concerto is actually the second major re-working (completed in 1951-52) of his cello concerto, which he officially named *Sinfonia Concertante* (in E minor, Op.125). It premiered posthumously in 1954 with Rostropovich as soloist with the Danish Radio Orchestra in Copenhagen. "The virtuoso demands on the soloist in the Prokofiev, especially in the central movement, make this one of the most challenging scores in the cello repertoire."

> *Recommended – Prokofiev Concertos*
> *Piano Sonata No.8* and *Piano Concerto No.5* by Richter and the Warsaw NPO under Rowicki is an excellent coupling. A good version of his most popular piano concerto, *No.3*, is by Argerich with Montreal under Dutoit. Among complete sets of the piano concertos, the 1974 set by Beroff and the Gewandhaus, Leipzig under Masur is recommended (EMI) as is the recent acclaimed set by Bavouzet with Noseda and the BBC Philharmonic (Chandos, 2014).
> *Symphony-Concerto* – Han-Na Chang, LSO/Pappano or Capuçon with Mariinsky Theatre Orchestra/Gergiev (Virgin, 2010); *Violin Concertos* – Shaham with Previn and the LSO

While he was alive and actively composing Prokofiev was labeled the 'age of steel' composer for his strong anti-Romanticism, particularly prior to the 1940s. His music disturbed many in his day but also "acutely resonated with the needs and aspirations of a public traumatized by autocracy and war." The current view of him, however, with the benefit of at least a half century of hindsight, is much different. As with others of his time, Prokofiev's music while highly dissonant, was tonal, composed within traditional frameworks and according to 19th century forms. The music of Prokofiev is not profound; it is "lean, clear, pointed", exuding "confidence and an enormous athleticism." Personally, Prokofiev did not fare as well as Shostakovich did in their country; the Soviet machine ground him down, culminating in the 1948 resolution. This gradually sapped his creative energies as well as his health.

♪ Dmitri Shostakovich (1906-1975)

Shostakovich's ancestors were actually from Poland. His great-grandfather was exiled to the Russian wilderness after the Polish uprising of 1830. Shostakovich is primarily known as the composer of fifteen 20th century symphonies, the most important set of any composer born in the 20th century. However he composed lasting works in many genres, including fifteen string quartets. Shostakovich revived the dying genre of the symphony in the early 20th century. But he composed well in several forms, and together with Bartók, contributed one of the two key sets of string quartets in the 20th century (covered in Chapter 11). Shostakovich had a "career-long preoccupation with finding an appropriate balance between musical form and emotional content." His personality had "a split focus: concern for tradition against challenge of it."

    He was a virtuoso pianist whose early works were extraordinarily advanced, often sharp and satirical, full of youthful nervous energy. Shostakovich placed great importance on orchestration. Unlike many composers he did not compose his orchestral works as piano reductions first but wrote down the complete score from the start. As a young composer "Shostakovich seemed to be a faithful adherent of the…Rimsky-Korsakov school of composition." His composition teacher at the Petrograd Conservatory was the son-in-law of the Russian master of orchestral color. "On a musical plane, Shostakovich had seen himself as Mussorgsky's successor…"

    "His most familiar tones are savage irony and tragedy," because of Stalin's Russia. But to stay in the dictator's favor and to ensure survival of his music (and possibly his life), Shostakovich was forced to become a 'safe' composer starting in the 1930s. Gone were the "dash, sparkle, and modernity he had shown in the First Symphony…and the Piano Concerto." Officially, Shostakovich saw the "narrow-minded dogmatism" of serialism as "an obstacle for any imagination and individuality." However, it is not clear if these were only the opinions he expressed publicly as in private circles he expressed admiration for works by Boulez and Stockhausen. But Shostakovich endured and was able to "preserve his musical self under potentially annihilating pressure."

> *"I don't think that Prokofiev ever treated me seriously as a composer; he considered only Stravinsky a rival..."*
> – D. Shostakovich

♪ The Symphonies

Shostakovich's symphonies, taken together, "paint a comprehensive autobiography" of the composer. And as with Mahler's symphonies, Shostakovich's have provoked musical commentators "to read into them complex psychological interpretations." The works reach outward while his solo piano music probes increasingly inward with dissonant and sparse linear textures. Of his fifteen symphonies, some are forgettable and far from his best efforts (e.g., No.2 and No.3), although it is hard to know his motivation given his situation in the Soviet Union. Some stretch the definition of 'symphony', with No.13 'Babi Yar' actually a choral setting of a poem and No.14 a series of tragic songs for voice and small orchestra and could be considered lightly orchestrated *Lieder*. However, his symphonic masterpieces are those in which he stays closest to the traditional form: the First, Fifth, Seventh, and Tenth, with the Fourth and Eighth also recognized as significant.

Symphony No.1

His First Symphony was composed at age nineteen while still at the Conservatory. It is a "symphony on a grand scale...with juicy melodic content and rich-sounding orchestration." It is heavily post-Romantic, fusing elements of Mahler and Tchaikovsky symphonies, but with the added feature of a pronounced role for the piano in the second and fourth movements. The third movement especially is very Mahler-like. Shostakovich would move away from the extended themes and turn-of-the-century lyricism in his later large symphonies. The best-known, beginning with Symphony No.4, are on a massive scale, with individual movements in several symphonies approaching a half-hour.

Shostakovich took influences from contemporary Soviet artists and combined them with the "'objectivist' tone of Hindemith, Weill, Bartók and...Stravinsky." The symphony premiered in Leningrad in May 1926, then it was taken to Berlin where it was premiered by Bruno Walter. Walter also led performances of it in Munich and Vienna. Two years later Stokowski introduced it to America, and so the *First* was established as one of the modern staples of the symphonic repertory.

The work successfully captures the spirit of youth and has an unfading freshness despite its rhythmic stops and starts and dissonances, which make it clearly a work of the 20th century. In it "youthful assurance blazed forth" with an "unusually gripping narrative drive."

Symphony No.4

This represented his most ambitious work to-date; the dark, ominous score requires a mammoth orchestra of up to 130 players. It "is Shostakovich's encounter with Mahler, a flawed masterpiece yet pivotal in his evolution." It was clearly influenced by Mahler's idea of symphony as 'psychological theatre'; it most resembles Mahler's *Sixth* "in the drawn-out anguish of its close." This work was composed at the time of Stalin's criticism of *Lady MacBeth of Mtsenk* and the subsequent ramp up of artistic and creative suppression by the state. During this time Shostakovich came under severe criticism for not "listening to the desires and expectations of the Soviet public." "Instead of repenting I composed my Fourth Symphony", the composer explained, going further to characterize his *Fourth* as 'a very imperfect, long-winded work that suffers from grandiosomania." It was begun in 1935 but disappeared in 1936, withdrawn by Shostakovich under pressure from government officials interested only in music that could be used as communist propaganda.

Not surprisingly the *Fourth* was rejected by the cultural police as being of "diabolical complexity," with Shostakovich being accused of rejecting criticism. And so the *Fourth* was not allowed to be performed. It was thus hidden by the composer and did not premiere until 1961 with the Moscow Philharmonic and Kiril Kondrashin.

> *"I left a concert thinking about others instead of myself...this is the main strength of Shostakovich's music for me."*
> - Solomon Volkov

Symphony No.5

Shostakovich was officially censured on account of Stalin's reaction in 1936 to his opera *Lady MacBeth*, characterized as "chaos instead of music" by *Pravda*. Whether or not he had a change of heart and was truly contrite after the reaction from the State to his Fourth Symphony is doubtful. But with his *Fifth* (Op.47) he certainly was successful in giving that impression. The composer responded to this "just criticism" by producing arguably his finest symphony, the *Fifth*, enthusiastically accepted by the Soviet leaders. Shostakovich even included the subtitle, "A Soviet artist's answer to justified criticism."

After his *Fourth*, the *Fifth* represents a major compromise by Shostakovich and accommodation of the Soviet cultural police. But it had the desired effect as it was just what the authorities were looking for and "Shostakovich was instantly rehabilitated." This "forced compromise" looked back to Tchaikovsky and Borodin without any "leftist distortion" and provided, again according to *Pravda*, "what the Soviet audience expects and looks for in music." Of course in the Soviet Union the 'audience' was not consulted.

The symphony was what Stalin and his music hacks were looking for: a grand four-movement symphony in the style of Beethoven, starting in minor key but resolving in an exultant major. It is accessible, conventionally-styled and structured in the symphonic tradition of a tragic start in a minor key leading to a triumphant, heroic conclusion in the major, *à la* Beethoven's *Fifth*. Maxim, the composer's son and accomplished musician, indicated that the *Fifth* is his father's 'heroic' symphony, to portray the struggle to overcome obstacles to gain victory.

> "This is not music; this is high-voltage, nervous electricity."
> - anonymous listener to the Fifth Symphony

This symphony was premiered in November 1937 by the legendary Yevgeny Mravinsky and the Leningrad (formerly and presently the St. Petersburg) Philharmonic. The symphony was belittled by some Western critics as a 'concession' to political pressure. Save for the finale, Shostakovich made few concessions, and, mostly avoiding the terms of social realism, returned to a traditional four-movement format and a 'normal-sized' orchestra. In it Shostakovich shows his hallmark of brilliant orchestration, and each instrument is given its own evocative character.

Symphony No.7, *Leningrad*

This symphony, designated by the composer as 'Dedicated to the city of Leningrad' was twisted into a propaganda tool as the Soviet leadership interpreted it to honor Soviet defenders against the Nazis in the Battle of Leningrad. However, Shostakovich claimed he had the idea for such a symphony before the war and that he "was thinking of other enemies of humanity when (he) composed the theme." "Shostakovich played cat and mouse with the Soviet authorities for his entire career."

This did not prevent this symphony from being dismissed for years as wartime propaganda. In it Shostakovich tried to capture the emotions of battle, to celebrate the citizens of Leningrad who suffered through the 900 day siege of their city by the Germans.

> "The Nazi barbarians seek to destroy the whole of Slavic culture."
> - Shostakovich in response to the siege of Leningrad

Shostakovich attached a program to the symphony with the first movement being particularly descriptive. According to the composer, "the exposition tells of the happy, peaceful life of people..." There is then an attention-getting "invasion episode" in the development section depicting war bursting into "the peaceful life of these people."

The premiere in Leningrad was during the long siege; the citizens had already endured th suffering for some time. It was performed by surviving members of the Leningrad Radio Orchestra along with musicians recalled from the war front. Soviet leadership played this up as a major propaganda event.

Although this symphony was used to rally the citizens of Leningrad besieged by the Nazis, Shostakovich stated that he was not limiting the meaning of the music only to his countrymen; rather, he claimed to have in mind victims of "all forms of terror, slavery, the bondage of the spirit." This is then followed by an extended repetition of "one rather simple-minded idea" with the continuous rhythm of a snare-drum rapping underneath.

Arturo Toscanini conducted the American premiere of the *Leningrad* in July 1942 and NBC radio broadcast the performance. It was "the most spectacular new-music event of the radio era." However, "the Seventh has not worn too well past its function as an Allied icon."

Symphony No.8
The Seventh Symphony was a description of war, a programmatic work with each movement evoking an aspect of war. The *Eighth* is instead a contemplation of war. Shostakovich dedicated this second war-era symphony, composed at the height of the war in 1943, to conductor Evgeny Mravinsky. It is a monumental work, unquestionably grim. The work, with the massive opening movement typical of this composer's great symphonies, is "inescapably pessimistic" and "lacked the propaganda possibilities" of its predecessor. However, it was accepted by the socialist realism police because it was a "truthful reflection of the horrors and losses of war." The opening theme in the deep strings recalls the opening cello theme and atmosphere of his Fifth Symphony. It powerfully evokes "the eerie detachment that war induces in its survivors." To muster that effect Shostakovich does not bring the enormous energies of the work to any type of resolution, but instead leaves the work "hanging, almost as if...ended with a question mark."

Symphony No.9
After the two massive, wartime symphonies, the siege-of-Leningrad inspired Seventh Symphony, and the chilling Eighth, the Ninth Symphony is a welcomed contrast. At less than thirty minutes it is half the length of its two predecessors and much lighter in spirit. It is "a merry, exuberant, light-hearted work...to celebrate the victorious end of the war." The "seemingly light neoclassical" work brings a new level of irony to Shostakovich's symphonies.

Stalin was angry with Shostakovich because the composer refused to use his Ninth Symphony as a majestic triumphant work that "would have hailed the genius and wisdom of the leader." Instead, the *Ninth* is full of sarcasm and bitterness, a "slight and whimsical opus in the spirit, the composer suggested, of Haydn."

Symphony No.10

The Tenth Symphony was written right after Stalin's death in 1953 and is but one of the few "indisputable masterpieces penned in the second half of the 20th century." As a musical portrait of Stalin shortly after his death, "it offers a glimpse into the darkest…corners of the composer's soul." The symphony begins, as is typical with Shostakovich, with an extended first movement, which is almost as long as the three subsequent movements. In Testimony Shostakovich reveals (assuming the work is authentic) that the "furiously sinister" second movement represents a "portrait of Stalin himself."

Shostakovich's late-period music was a "desolate psychological terrain." Alex Ross refers to "the ironic, self-flagellating, death-obsessed Shostakovich;" the Soviet system had worn him out. Finally, in the Thirteenth Symphony Shostakovich lashes out and bases the symphony on anti-Stalinist poems, yielding his boldest political statement of the period. The work "reveals the composer in a stark and bitter mood, using dark and brooding orchestral colors."

The first movement, based on the poem *Babi Yar*, mourns not only the victims of the Holocaust but the victims of Stalin's terror as well, including the massacre of Jews in Kiev during World War II. However, because it is so heavily propagandist it remains seldom performed, despite the attention *Babi Yar* draws to one of the long list of World War II horrors.

Recommended – Shostakovich Symphonies

Symphony Nos.1 & 7 'Leningrad' – Bernstein and the Chicago SO (DG, 1989), in a grammy-winning performance, deliver powerful performances that take advantage of the Chicago brass section in the *Leningrad*. Bernstein stretches it to over eighty-five minutes but effectively holds things together.

Symphony No.4 – Recorded in 1994 but surprisingly not released until almost a decade later, the performance by Myung-W Chung and the Philadelphians (DG) has received much acclaim. Chung turns out to be an excellent interpreter and has an orchestra linked with this music for decades through the commitments of both Stokowski and Ormandy to bring the music of Shostakovich to American audiences.

Symphony No.5 – a performance by the combination that premiered this symphony, Mravinsky, who knew the

> composer, and the Leningrad Philharmonic, is available. Some online critics complain of audience coughing but the performance by Mravinsky and the orchestra he led for fifty years, more than makes up for the sore throats. Also recommended is the offering of both the *Fifth* and *Ninth* symphonies by A. Rahbari and the Belgian R&TV Orchestra (Naxos). "Rahbari's reading (of *No.5*) is most convincing, with dramatic tensions finely controlled..."
> *Symphony No.8* – made toward the end of his career and life, the version by Rostropovich, the great cellist and friend of Shostakovich, with the LSO (LSO Live, 2002) effectively captures the essence of this powerful war-era symphony.
> *Symphony No.10* – either recording by Karajan and the BPO, the late 1960s or the later digital set. Both show that this conductor had the measure of this work, "superbly moulded with genuine tragic feeling and authenticity...with a fierce brilliance to project the score's climaxes pungently."

♪ The Concertos

Shostakovich wrote two concertos each for cello, violin and piano. The First Piano Concerto is an early work, the First Violin Concerto was composed just after World War II, but the remaining four concertos are later, post-Stalin Soviet works.

Cello Concertos, No.1 in E-flat, Op.107; No.2, Op.126

Shostakovich's two cello concertos were both written for the great Russian cellist Mstislav Rostropovich, who premiered the works. The premiere of No.1 was given in 1959 with the Leningrad Philharmonic under the legendary conductor Yevgeny Mravinsky. Shortly after this, it was given its American premiere by Rostropovich with the Philadelphia Orchestra during a trip by Soviet musicians, including the composer. The work "feeds on grim memories" and the four-note recurring first theme "is questioning and nervous."

Violin Concertos, No.1 in A minor, Op.77; No.2 in C-sharp minor, Op.129

Similar to the cello concertos, both violin concertos were written for, dedicated to, and premiered by the great Russian violinist David Oistrakh (with Mravinsky and the Leningrad Philharmonic). Also, as was the case with the cello concertos, the works were both begun after the age of forty. No.1 was originally designated Op.99 to be consistent with its appearance in 1955, Shostakovich would insist that it be known as Op.77 to indicate that it was written years earlier, during the Zdanov purge and the 1948 'Resolution'. The Second Violin Concerto is not as flashy as the *First* and is more introspective.

The First Violin Concerto is striking in style and structure and at roughly forty minutes it is a very long concerto. Its dedicatee Oistrakh commented that it "does not fall easily into one's hands." Instead of the usual three concerto movements there are four distinctly varied movements plus a huge five-minute cadenza between the *passacaglia* third and burlesque final movements.

> *Recommended – Shostakovich Violin Concertos*
> Hilary Hahn with the Oslo Philharmonic under Marek Janowski (Sony, 2002). For vintage recordings Oistrakh with Mravinsky is the clear choice.

Piano Concertos, No.1 in C minor, Op.35; No.2 in F, Op.102

The two piano concertos are much different from each other; No.1 is young and daring, even with a trumpet sharing soloist duties. It was completed in 1933 and had its American premiere the following year in Philadelphia under Leopold Stokowski with Eugene List as soloist. "Its prankish humor can be explained as a challenge to the traditional Russian concerto style."

In No.2 the very opening of the *Allegro* first movement almost sounds like something lifted from Tchaikovsky's *Nutcracker*, but the piano quickly enters and away we go on a dizzying ride. There is a beautiful slow movement that shows the composer at his most lyrical, and contrasts effectively with the light-hearted dual of soloist and orchestra in the finale and the whirlwind opening movement. The Second Piano Concerto was a graduation gift from Shostakovich to his son Maxim in 1957.

Shostakovich's popularity in the West took off in the 1980s as cycles of his symphonies were recorded. Listeners began to identify with the plight of a genius composer ground down by an ideological steamroller, who still managed to express himself and create, despite the considerable forces against him, music of power, dignity, but also infinite sadness.

Boris Schwarz, in the New Grove Composer Biography Series, sums up Shostakovich as an "eclectic progressive, rooted in tradition and tonality, yet using dissonance and occasional atonality as expressive means." Ted Libbey captures Shostakovich's legacy very well in stating that it is "his music, not (Stravinsky's and Schoenberg's), which – above all (in) its grasp of suffering and sadness – revealed the essential truth of the time."

Shostakovich's death in 1975 left a temporary void in Soviet (Russian) music that was filled quickly by Alfred Schnittke, Sofia Gubaidulina, and the Estonian Arvo Pärt. The unique style of Pärt is covered later under Minimalism, although he cannot be singularly classified.

> *"I set down a beautiful chord on paper*
> *– and suddenly it rusts."*
> - Alfred Schnittke

Neither can Schnittke be placed under a single school; he could more appropriately be placed in almost every school. Instead, he created a name for his style, 'polystylistics' that Adam Ross describes as the "gathering up in a troubled stream of consciousness the detritus of a millennium of music." Schnittke wanders deeply into the labyrinth of the past with music ranging from medieval chant and Renaissance mass to twelve-tone writing and touches of modern pop.

- 25 -

Populism and Traditionalism
Copland, Britten and Barber

Two phenomena occurred in 20th century music that were unprecedented. First, music was deconstructed away from rigid Western forms (e.g., sonata form). The second phenomenon was the way music was generated, from a fascination with individual tones leading to atonality, and the "concept of the sound environment" to the use of electronic means.

After the devastation and tragedy of World War II, there was a movement among critics and younger composers to totally embrace atonality and serialism, and to attack and "distance themselves from totalitarian aesthetics." Neo-Classicism was included among totalitarian aesthetics. Both Stravinsky and Hindemith, whose music continued to be tonal after 1945, were attacked by musical philosophers such as Theodor Adorno, who felt that "preserving tonality in the modern era…" was "tantamount to Nazi kitsch." Others, such as René Leibowitz, proposed that atonality displayed "uncompromising moral strength."

However, serialism was not the panacea originally thought for 'modern' composers. Populists such as Aaron Copland (who was a serialist early in his career), Walter Piston, and Benjamin Britten achieved widespread popularity not approached by Schoenberg or his disciples. However, both the American avant-garde, represented by John Cage, Milton Babbitt, Elliott Carter, and the European led by teacher Olivier Messiaen and students Pierre Boulez and Karlheinz Stockhausen, held mostly to their guns in their devotion to serialism. Stockhausen would migrate to Cage's indeterminacy and Messiaen rejected serialism to develop his unique musical sound world.

By the 1960s composers were appearing who felt that none of the above approaches led anywhere. Populism was stale and serialism was a dead end. Thus, minimalism was born as a reaction to 'modern' music up to that point.

> *"Music is meaningless noise unless it touches a receiving mind."*
> - Paul Hindemith

As the 20th century progressed, classical music "lost part of its emotional transparency." It was no longer "utterly available" but became harder to hear, even alienating many by being perceived as "a disciplined procedure that required training by experts (to be fully enjoyed)." The melodies of Mozart, Schubert, Chopin and Tchaikovsky "were shaped to the curve of the human voice" while 20th century composers "detached melody from its vocal origins." However, it is clear that techniques of orchestration continue to evolve. Contemporary composers have learned from the experience of predecessors in their brilliant and clever handling of the orchestra.

> *"The leaders of the modern movement wished only...to make their music express their own time."*
> *- Joseph Machlis*

Sibelius lived until 1957 but had not produced any music of substance in three decades. Berg and Webern died in 1935 and 1945, respectively; the former at a young age, the latter the victim of a gunshot from an over-zealous Allied soldier at the end of World War II. Bartók died in 1945 and Prokofiev in 1953. However, both Stravinsky and Shostakovich lived into the 1970s and were able to record stereo performances of their works with themselves as conductor and/or soloist.

The rise of serialism in the first half of the 20th century was followed by its application to all elements of a composition; that is, to harmony and rhythm in addition to melody (i.e., 'total serialism'). This distinction leads to two phases of 'modern' music in the 20th century. The first was just before World War I with the seminal works of Debussy, Stravinsky, and Schoenberg. The second phase started just after World War II with the *avant-garde* school of Boulez and Stockhausen in Europe and Cage and Babbitt in America.

After World War II the Cold War era 'modern' composers, and the critics supportive of them, obsessed "on the moral corruption of tonality and the righteousness of the twelve-tone method." These artists realized that atonal polyphony was less popular but held that it only mattered that it was aesthetically more honest. Schoenberg was still the "patron saint of new music after 1945" as he "quickly emerged as the shining beacon for young German (and French) composers." But it was his student Webern and his incredibly tight organization that swept along the international *avant-garde*. In fact, it was widely held by the younger generation of post-World War II composers (e.g., led in Europe by Pierre Boulez) that it was Webern and not Schoenberg who had carried the art of music to its logical extreme.

Post-World War II composers adopted what Alex Ross calls "catastrophic style"; the recent tragedies of the first half of "the century of death" justifying "their instinctive attraction to the dreadful and the dire." According to Adrian Leverkuehn, Thomas Mann's Faustian composer, the approach of the 20th century modernist composer is summed up as "only by striking the dark note can he achieve true seriousness and originality." With the certainty of science providing an explanation for so much of the world around us, composers were drawn to certainty in composition as well, seeking strict control and precision instrument construction. By the 1960s 'modern' music was totally dissonant with melody and harmony abolished. It was total polyphony.

♪ Aaron Copland (1900-1990)

The 'dean of American composers', Copland began as a major composer of the avant-garde, but it is his populist works evoking Americana for which he is remembered. Copland was awarded the 1945 Pulitzer Prize for the ballet Appalachian Spring, reflecting the surge of populism and neo-Classicism taking place in American music with composers, in addition to Copland, such as Samuel Barber, Roy Harris, William Schuman, Howard Hanson and the young Leonard Bernstein.

The full ballet, commissioned by Martha Graham for the Elizabeth Sprague Coolidge Foundation, was composed in 1943-44. Set in the hills of Pennsylvania it tells the story of the celebration in spring by newlyweds for their newly-built farmhouse, a sort of Pennsylvania *Rite of Spring*. The suite version of *Appalachian Spring* for full orchestra, a scaled-down, full-orchestra version of the ballet, "may be...the most-loved orchestral work ever written in America," with its variations on the Shaker song 'Simple Gifts' instantly recognizable. However, this is the only use of actual folk tunes; instead, "like Bartók and Falla, Copland has distilled the character of folk music and imbued the entire fabric with its essence."

> *"Music that is born complex is not inherently better or worse than music that is born simple..."*
> *- Aaron Copland*

Early on he was influenced by Stravinsky and the result in the 1920s was polyrhythmic music (e.g., the Piano Concerto of 1926), which absorbed elements of jazz and tone colors of ragtime and the blues. Later in the decade Copland adopted a stringent dissonant style that he described as "more spare in sonority, more lean in texture" compared to his works earlier in the decade. But at the same time Copland became increasingly dissatisfied "with the relationship between the living composer and the listening public."

While most of his contemporaries moved further away from the public, Copland described the course he was choosing in his 1941 work Our New Music. His new direction was "to see if I couldn't say what I had to say in the simplest possible terms." Therefore, in the late 1930s, dissatisfied with the public's indifference to his abstract 'modern' works (and one of the few composers who cared), he changed his style and produced the music most people know, the "tuneful and atmospheric scores." "Copland's use of transparent, widely-spaced sonorities...creates a distinctive sound that...has become the quintessential musical emblem of America."

Copland provides the following account of this third shift in style: "I began to feel an increasing dissatisfaction with the relations of the music-loving public and the living composer." This is a soft-pedaled way of acknowledging that his music, and most of his contemporaries, was not very popular. He also stated about his fellow composers, "It seemed to me that we composers were in danger of working in a vacuum."

Copland's move away from abstract music to Americana ballet scores led to his music being loved instead of merely respected, and secured his place with the music-loving public. Incorporating folklore, gospel hymns, cowboy songs, the ballets *Billy the Kid*, *Rodeo*, and *Appalachian Spring* from 1938, 1942, and 1944, respectively, remain his most popular works. Also in similar style but with a Latin flavor are the orchestral pieces *El Salón México* and *Danzón Cubano*, the former a flamboyant, exotic orchestral work, full of Mexican tunes and rhythms. The 'danzón' is the Latin version of the waltz. Both of these pieces were originally composed for two pianos and shortly after were fully scored by Copland. However, these popular works represent only one segment of his output.

His Third Symphony was written between the American landing on Normandy in the summer of 1944 (D-Day) and the summer of 1946; it is "the Great American Symphony to end all American symphonies." It possesses a triumphant mood at the victory of war, "an effective memento of its euphoric time." However, once the euphoria wore off some critics complained that the symphony's finale was pomp and overblown.

> *Recommended – Copland Orchestral Music*
> A classic recording is by Antal Dorati and the London Symphony (Mercury, 1961, compilation 1991), which contains *Appalachian Spring* and *Billy the Kid* as well as the shorter pieces *Danzón Cubano* and *El Salón México* (with the Minneapolis Symphony).

Copland had to tolerate concerted efforts by the press and by his own government, in the era of McCarthyism and red hysteria of the late 1940s and 1950s to denounce his works as communist propaganda. The term used back then for left-leaning artists was 'fellow traveler' and Copland's works were censored and removed or prohibited from many programs and performances. Ironically, the red hysteria led many in the United States to act in the same totalitarian manner toward artists as the Soviet Union did toward Shostakovich and Prokofiev.

Even populist works such as *A Lincoln Portrait* and *The Tender Land* were painted as somehow subversive and anti-American. Copland characterized this atmosphere, one that certainly helped bring about the progressive social movements of the 1960s, as one of suspicion, ill-will and dread; an atmosphere in which an artist, forced to live in it, "will end up creating nothing." One can almost hear Shostakovich, "Aaron, I know how you feel."

In the 1950s Copland shifted styles a fourth and final time, adopting Schoenberg's twelve-tone method into works such as his Piano Quartet.

Copland felt comfortable moving away from explicitly 'American' music and themes, "having achieved the unity he sought between musical technique and national identity,"

♪ Benjamin Britten (1913-1976)

> "(Music) demands as much effort on the listener's part as the other two corners of the triangle, this holy triangle of composer, performer, and listener."
> - Benjamin Britten

Britten was the most important English composer in the Post-World War II era. He was a lyrical master craftsman, a classicist devoted to the Baroque forms of canon, fugue, and *passacaglia* who never substantially changed his style, one that can be described as "eclectically conservative" as it is strongly tonal but makes use of 'modern' techniques. Britten opposed the self-imposed regimentation of the *avant-garde* composers of the Cold War era and favored tonality. He was also a musical dramatist, creating some of the best operas of the 20th century such as *Peter Grimes* (1945), *Billy Budd* (1952), *Death in Venice* (his final work for stage in 1973), among others.

> "I try to write as Stravinsky has written and Picasso has painted."
> - Benjamin Britten

The success of *Peter Grimes* quickly gained Britten international acclaim and secured his reputation. He became "England's most celebrated living composer…a patriotic icon,…a focus of British pride," as well as the first English composer to have his operas become repertoire staples. Living well into the stereo recording age and possessing multiple musical talents of pianist and conductor in addition to composer, Britten has left us not only recordings of his own compositions, but of other composers' works as both conductor and performer.

> "I want my music to be of use to people, to please them…I do not write for posterity."
> - Britten

The *Simple* Symphony, Op.4 was composed in 1934 at the age of twenty-one. It is cast in the traditional four movements for string orchestra, including a boisterous *bourreé* and a sentimental *sarabande*, and consists of tunes and melodies from Britten's childhood.

While at London's Royal College of Music in the 1930s he studied with composer Frank Bridge and would compose his masterpiece for string orchestra in 1937, *Variations on a Theme of Frank Bridge*, Op.10. As in the *Simple* Symphony Britten references the Baroque in this eleven-part work, but also Classical period terms for movements, including a 'funeral march', a fugue and finale, an *aria Italiana*, and a *Wiener* Waltz. This tribute to his teacher would establish an international reputation for Britten.

The well-known *Young Person's Guide to the Orchestra*, Op.34 (1946) is intended to be instructive (if narrated) through its variations and fugue on a Purcell theme (from *Abdelazer*). Although originally written for a documentary on the instruments of the orchestra, it is very enjoyable for the music itself and the music-only version remains more popular. In this 'guide' each section of the orchestra is highlighted in one of the thirteen variations. All are brought together in the superbly crafted concluding double-counterpoint fugue.

According to Yehudi Menuhin, Britten had a "wonderful sensitivity for children...a creative genius who never grew up." The Aldeburgh Festival, which still takes place each summer, was started by Britten in 1948 at his home.

Although Britten will remain better known for his operas and choral works, many of his instrumental works have held a place in classical music. In addition to his most popular works described above Britten composed such works as the three neo-Baroque suites for solo cello, as well as three string quartets, and one concerto each for violin, piano, and cello (the last titled a 'symphony').

> ***Recommended – Britten Orchestral and Chamber Music***
> As pianist: Schubert's *Arpeggione Sonata*, Schumann's *Fünf Stücke*, and Debussy's Cello Sonata with Rostropovich; as conductor: Mozart Piano Concertos, with pianist Clifford Curzon (1960s Decca). As composer/conductor: *Young Person's Guide* (without narration); *Simple* Symphony; *Bridge* Variations, English Chamber/LSO (Decca, early 1960s).

♪ Samuel Barber (1910-1981)

Samuel Barber "was a traditionalist who never abandoned tonality. He...maintained a healthy interest in all kinds of music" and could not have cared less if his music was scorned by the *avant-garde*. "Barber's style is essentially diatonic, in spite of a few chromatic touches...the basic element is lyricism...emotional, dramatic, and expressive passages...provide a strong link with the past." His early training as a singer gave all his music a lyrical melodic bent.

> *"My personal style is born of what I feel...I am not a self-conscious composer."*
> - Samuel Barber

As Britten did in England, Barber developed an individual style without departing radically from the past and "remained stubbornly resistant to influences foreign to his own aesthetic." Contemporary American composer John Corigliano describes Barber's style as "...an alternation between post-Straussian chromaticism and often diatonic typical American simplicity." "His music conveys a distinctively expressive warmth and humanity that ensures its durability." Barber was a melancholic who suffered from depression; "his sorrow is a profound lyrical force."

His first major success was his Overture to the *School for Scandal*, Op.5 which he wrote at age twenty-one while still a student in Philadelphia at the Curtis Institute of Music.

Although some in the *avant-garde* viewed Barber's compositions as reactionary, he was not influenced by that 'peer pressure'; instead "a great quantity of his work contains a striking nostalgia, a longing for an evergreen past." He was not "given to change our world of music or our perception of it." Barber was the consummate traditionalist; a post-Romantic after post-Romanticism was no longer. But, make no mistake, his works clearly belong to the 20th century; for example, his Piano Sonata (1949) uses twelve-tone rows but in a tonal framework.

Adagio for Strings

This single-movement work, the string quartet version of which is the slow movement of Barber's First String Quartet, is one of the most popular and most performed works of the 20th century. It is a prime example of Barber's neo-Romanticism, "a slow, minor-key lament, which evokes deep sadness in those who hear it...an icon of American grief." It was composed in 1936 and the version for string orchestra that has become so well-known premiered in 1938 with the New York Philharmonic under Toscanini.

Its long lines and rich harmonies have made it popular for use in films; its most famous use in Oliver Stone's antiwar film *Platoon* "gave voice to the insanity of war." Over the decades it has become "America's secular hymn for grieving our dead" used at presidential funerals as well as the funerals of Einstein and Grace Kelly.

> *Recommended – Barber Adagio for Strings*
> Schippers and the NYPO (Sony, 1960-63, compilation 1997) include the *Adagio for Strings*, *Overture to the School for Scandal*, the *Second Essay for Orchestra*, Op.17, and some instrumental interludes from operas by Menotti, Berg, and Indy. Performances by a promising conductor who died too young.

Capricorn Concerto, Op.21; Violin Concerto, Op.14; Cello Concerto, Op.22; Piano Concerto, Op.38

Barber's Violin Concerto (1939) is second in popularity only to his *Adagio for Strings* and is the most romantic of Barber's works. In his Cello Concerto from 1945 Barber "sought to combine the songlike poetry of his Violin Concerto with the spiciness of Capricorn."

The *Capricorn* Concerto from 1941 is unique with its scoring for flute, oboe, trumpet, and strings, which suggests a kinship with the Baroque concerto grosso. It is different from Barber's other orchestral music in its lack of big melodies. Instead, it is "an amalgam of motivic ideas expertly traded off among soloists and strings."

Barber's music was neo-Romantic, lyrical and, as displayed by a work such as his *Capricorn* Concerto, he could also produce a light-hearted 20th century *concerto grosso*. Similar to Stravinsky's *Dumbarton Oaks* concerto, a less overt tribute to Bach's *Brandenburg* Concerto No.3, the *Capricorn* Concerto is a tribute to Bach's *Brandenburg* Concerto No.5.

Barber's Piano Concerto, a later composition from 1962 and his final masterpiece, won the composer the Pulitzer Prize. Although it contains a beautiful second movement it hasn't sustained the popularity it seemingly deserves. Barber intended the concerto to be premiered by his favorite pianist, John Browning, with the Boston Symphony under Leinsdorf.

> *Recommended – Barber's Concertos*
> The Piano, Cello, and Violin Concertos are available together in one excellent recording with Leonard Slatkin conducting (RCA/BMG, 2005). The soloists are John Browning, Steven Isserlis, and Kyoko Takezawa for the Piano, Cello, and Violin Concertos, respectively. For the *Capricorn*, it is again Slatkin and the St. Louis SO, with soloists Berg, Bowman, and Slaughter (RCA/BMG, 1990)

Cello Sonata

Barber's Cello Sonata is among the more traditional chamber works of the mid-20th century. It is a product of his student days when he was still "very much under the spell of Brahms, whose autumnal darkness pervades much of this work." The work shows that at age twenty-two Barber was already capable of handling the intricacies of sonata form. Cellist Gregor Piatagorsky championed this work and helped establish it as a key addition to American works for the cello.

- 26 -

The Avant-Garde and Minimalism

"The key to the understanding of contemporary music lies in repeated hearing; one must hear it till it sounds familiar..."
— Roger Sessions

There have been many different approaches to music in the past sixty years. Schoenberg's twelve-tone method was developed formally into serialism, which led to 'total serialism'. One can add to this 'indeterminacy', 'experimentation', 'mikropolyphonie', and, finally, 'minimalism' and still be missing some labels.

Of composers of the first half of the 20th century, the post-World War II *avant-garde* was indebted most to Webern. This avant-garde rapidly assimilated Webern's concepts, leading to the "totally organized music of Messiaen, Babbitt, and Boulez." *Avant-garde* is the term used for artists who disregarded normal aesthetic values in their works. The difference between the atonality of the Second Viennese School and that of Boulez and Stockhausen (the Darmstadt School) is that Schoenberg and his disciples used the twelve-tone system "in the service of traditional aesthetic norms."

Some composers dug in their heels and remained committed to a style or school (e.g., Boulez with strict serialism). Carter, Boulez, and Babbitt held onto serialism and continued composing knotty, dissonant scores. "Serialism of one kind or another remained the dominant aesthetic of the 1950s and 1960s." Other composers began the move back towards tonality and their styles evolved and diverged in the Post-World War II years. Aaron Copland and Olivier Messiaen are two prominent examples of this 'evolving 20th century composer'. Others, such as John Cage, can only be classified as deliberate experimentalists. According to musical philosopher Theodor Adorno, composers could not avoid dealing in their music with society's tensions. The effect on the staunchly modern young avant-garde was consistent with Adorno's belief that as societies became more divided and complex, so should music to reflect that reality; 'art imitates life'. Boulez and Adorno were in agreement that serialism, being the most complex and intellectual form of music, was therefore the most advanced.

♪ The Avant-Garde

Harold Schonberg has concluded all three editions of his <u>The Lives of the Great Composers</u> (extending twenty-seven years from 1970-1997) with the same observation: that Western music in the decades since World War II "saw a hiatus in the mighty line of powerful, individualistic composers…from Monteverdi through Stravinsky and Schoenberg." At the end of the third edition Schonberg emphasizes that the observation he first made in 1970 still holds in 1997.

♪ Milton Babbitt (1916-2011)

Milton Babbitt was a mathematician who taught at Princeton for almost fifty years, essentially throughout the Post-World War II *avant-garde*. However, his formal degrees were in music, not math. Babbitt can be summed up as a "technologically oriented, mathematically inclined, twelve-tone, academic composer." Babbitt "treated serialism as a branch of mathematics." According to John Rockwell, author of All American Music, Babbitt is "perhaps the most complex composer ever," although he has stiff competition from Elliott Carter. Babbitt has been a steadfast advocate of 'total serialism', often in combination with electronic music and effects. Some feel that "Babbitt's music is full of wit and sparkle...rhythm at every level is one of the most forceful elements of (his) music."

Although his chief influences were Schoenberg and Webern, "compression of music takes on new meaning in his work." Considered the "leader of the American school of Serialism," Babbitt was a pioneer of the 'total serialism' movement, whereby each element of a composition (tempo, timbre, etc., not simply only pitch) is generated according to a formal system; that is, a total organization of all aspects of music within a composition. His extreme pieces are composed by controlling each aspect with a series, his 'total serialist' works have twelve rhythmic values, twelve levels of volume, etc. However, the significance of 'twelve' in aspects other than pitch or melody appears to be arbitrary.

In its strictest form (and the form used by Babbitt) total serialism controls all aspects of composition – pitch, rhythm, and dynamics. It involves composing with patterns of musical intervals rather than with themes or motives. The distinction may at first appear subtle but can have very significant results on the music heard. Composition by musical intervals gives little or no regard to what sound(s) are produced, it is the interval that rules; on the other hand, themes or motives are constructed purely for the way they sound and the effect they will have. *Three Compositions for Piano* and *Composition for Four Instruments*, both composed at Princeton in 1948, were the first works to apply total serialism. Babbitt has been heavily involved with the Columbia-Princeton Electronic Music Center.

> *"The public likes it and we must always agree with the public."*
> - Massenet

Babbitt and Carter (as well as others) rejected "Copland-style populism." In a 1958 article in *High Fidelity* magazine titled "Who Cares if You Listen?" Babbitt called for composers to withdraw from public and eliminate society from musical compositions. While this may at first seem an outrageous position, we must put ourselves in his shoes. Ever since Beethoven was accorded demigod status things had been steadily going downhill for living composers in general. By the second half of the 20th century composers figured that if no one was going to be interested in their music they might as well write for themselves. By the 1960s he was working only with electronic synthesizers and could not only compose but perform his works by himself in a studio.

> *"It has been the lonely modernist's chief consolation (that) prestige attaches itself more readily to the esoteric than to the popular."*
> — Richard Taruskin

♫ Elliott Carter (1908-2012)

Possibly the most admired of modern composers by his colleagues for setting a very high bar for 'serious' composition, Carter counts Ives, Scriabin, Stravinsky, and jazz as his influences. He studied with Walter Piston and Gustav Holst. His music is "thorny, dense, and formidably intellectual" and creates a "counterpoint of sharply differentiated lines." The most conspicuous features of his music are "the extreme fluidity of both rhythm and tempo…(and) the enormous variety of detail." "The outstanding characteristics of Carter's music are rhythmic complexity and concentrated texture (which) goes far beyond that of earlier composers." "While not necessarily serial, Carter habitually moved through the twelve-tone field in such a mercurial fashion as to seem keyless to older ears." Although known for works of awesome complexity that can be described as "polyrhythmic dissonance," his early works, up to around age thirty, leaned in a neo-Classicist direction. Worshipped in professional circles, some critics have accused him of "difficulty for the sake of difficulty."

The public does not share in the admiration and Carter's extreme complexity has led to works that are practically inaccessible to the listening public. He does not seem to care and thinks it was a mistake that at one time (but no longer) he had a "professional and social responsibility to write interesting, direct, easily understood music." Carter stated his atonal First String Quartet was written only to be "very interesting to myself and so say to hell with the public and with performers." Unfortunately, this elitist attitude could only further thwart any chance of acceptance by the public of 'difficult' and 'modern' music.

The titles of his more significant works are traditional; for example, a piano sonata from the 1940s, *Variations for Orchestra* (1955), the Piano Concerto (1965), and the Concerto for Orchestra (1969). The Concerto for Orchestra "consists of four separate ensembles using four distinct styles of music," employing string quartet tactics in a "much larger and…diverse ensemble."

Carter's description of his music as "mosaics of fragments and short, overlapping episodes," could describe much of modern music. In his *Double*

Concerto for Harpsichord and Piano with Two Chamber Orchestras from 1961 Carter has created a confrontation between two groups of players to form a 20th century *concerto grosso*, and a work declared a masterpiece by Stravinsky. According to the composer, "the concerto, although continuous, falls into seven large, interconnected sections." At times during the seven-movement work Carter has one orchestra going in one direction at one tempo while the second goes in another direction at a different tempo. Both the harpsichord and piano are surrounded by their own nineteen-piece orchestra. Its seven movements hinge on the central *Adagio*, with a harpsichord cadenza (second movement) and piano cadenzas (sixth movement) included in a work that "follows an overall principle of perpetual variation." The musicologist Charles Rosen was the pianist for the work's premiere at New York's Metropolitan Museum of Art.

His five string quartets, composed over a forty-four year period (1951-1995) are acknowledged as modern marvels of the idiom, with No.5 completed when the composer was in his late eighties. In his quartets Carter "aspires toward a conversational flexibility...bestowing an individual character upon each member of the ensemble." The composer aims for "a form that is simultaneously organic and fragmented." Two of the quartets won him Pulitzer Prizes (No.2 from 1959 and No.3 from 1971) and they are the likely works to take hold in the repertory, if any do. He celebrated his 100th birthday in 2008.

> *Recommended – String Quartets*
> In recognition of his centennial, the Pacifica Quartet has released two CDs (Naxos) containing the five string quartets. And the Juilliard String Quartet has always endorsed Carter's music with its recordings. If you enjoy string quartets it might be worth a listen to see how far the idiom has come since Haydn.

Elliott Carter wrote much chamber music in addition to his string quartets, ranging from Neo-Baroque to the incredibly complex *avant-garde*. The earlier works are relatively approachable for 20th century works and less complex than his later orchestral works. In them he gives each instrument a distinct role in a dramatic work. His *Pastoral* for Clarinet and Piano is an early clarinet sonata consisting of a single, substantial movement of just less than ten minutes. The Woodwind Quintet is a short, serenade-type work in two movements from 1948, totaling around eight minutes. Carter also produced a significant, jazz-influenced Cello Sonata (in four movements) that represented the start of a distinguishing feature of his music, the innovative 'metric modulation' in which he transitions from one tempo and meter to another through "an intermediary stage that shares aspects of both."

Perhaps the closest comparative 20th century well-known chamber work to Carter's *Sonata for Flute, Oboe, Cello and Harpsichord* is Debussy's *Sonata for Flute, Viola and Harp*, which is really a 'trio sonata'. This fifteen-minute work by Carter from 1952 gives the harpsichord a "neo-Classic treatment...as a texture separate from the other instruments."

An interesting set is Carter's *Eight Etudes and a Fantasy*. These pieces have their origin from Carter's teaching days in the early 1950s when he asked his students to compose some short pieces to show the unique features of each woodwind instrument. Unfortunately for the students Carter was not happy with the results and ended up sketching some brief pieces of his own, which he later expanded to the full *Eight Etudes and a Fantasy* for flute, oboe, clarinet, and bassoon. Each of the pieces displays, as Carter intended, a "distinct musical or instrumental effect" and it is "a piece of great charm and wit that has become a concert favorite." The work premiered in 1952.

A much later chamber work is the Quintet for Brass. As with the earlier Etudes above, this quintet is designed to display the particular character of the specific ensemble instruments. Composed during the summer of 1974, it is divided into nineteen short sections with every third section being for the entire ensemble. In between are duos and trios for various combinations of French horn, two trumpets, and two trombones.

Even more recent are the Quintet for Piano and Winds (1991) and the Quintet with Strings (1997). Oboist Heinz Holliger encouraged Carter to compose a wind quintet for the same combination as Mozart's and Beethoven's. In the work Carter creates three instrumental characters: piano, horn, and reed trio, each with "its own type of expressivity and character derived from its instrumental capabilities." The Quintet with Strings is a piano quintet consisting of one big movement of over twenty minutes divided into several sections.

"Many of the most gifted composers and performers of the 20th century, from Stravinsky onwards, have professed admiration of, but also bafflement by, Carter's forms and choices." Carter's music is much more frequently performed outside of the United States; by his own admission Carter makes "thirteen times as much in royalties from European performances as from American ones."

♪ Olivier Messiaen (1908-1992)

He began as a devout serialist but discarded it in favor of his devout Catholicism, in addition to influences from paganism, pantheism and ornithology, the last influence resulting in his trademark bird calls as part of his compositions. Influenced by Satie and Debussy, as well as by "Hindu chant, medieval plainsong (and) Aztec and Inca pipe music," Messiaen applied these to the methods of the Second Viennese School. He "broke through...with a new dreamlike style" and became a major influence on, as well as teacher of, avant-gardists Stockhausen, Boulez and Xenakis with his "spirited innovations and embracing of new instruments and cultures." Messiaen "presided over the transfiguration of tonality," pursuing a "deep investigation into sound itself." Many terms can and have been used in an attempt to classify the music of Messiaen, including "like glinting stars on a clear night," but none has been adequate to capture the aesthetic of this unique composer, who "sought to embody in music a stance of ecstatic contemplation."

A church organist in Paris at the same parish for sixty years until his death in 1992, Messiaen's music had a unique appeal, "sweet water in the desert of postwar musical systems and –isms." Virgil Thomson summed up Messiaen's style as "a technique of great complexity and considerable originality." Messiaen has stated that, "My music depends on uneven beats, as in nature." His music is notable especially for its rhythm and Boulez points out that his former mentor's biggest contributions were to rhythm.

His religion-tinted works actually defy classification, perhaps why several have actually entered the repertory, including the gargantuan *Turangalila* Symphony, which was commissioned by Koussevitzky and the Boston Symphony, with no limit on length or orchestral forces. Bernstein would conduct the 1949 premiere. Messiaen derived the title from two Sanskrit words, *turanga* meaning 'measurement of time by movement', and *lila*, meaning the 'the intervention of divine will on the cosmos.' The "continuous piano line…and sparkling use of vibraphone, glockenspiel, and *Ondes Martenot* (an early electronic instrument) made it sound quite unique."

The Bostonians did not get short-changed by Messiaen. With ten movements consuming over seventy-five minutes this massive work, requiring an orchestra of more than one hundred players, does not seem a likely candidate for commercial recordings. However, several recordings have remained in the catalogue, been re-issued, and recent new recordings have been made by prominent composers (Salonen and Rattle). The *Turangalila* represents "Messiaen's musical cosmology maximalized to the very limit."

Messiaen's relative popularity was also buoyed from being the first major avant-gardist to return to a tonal-based music. The very real impact of this is seen in the seismic shift in the 1970s and a worldwide flight from serialism. The serialists had drifted too far from Schoenberg's founding concepts, becoming too academic, engaging in complexity for its own sake. Schoenberg foresaw the potential danger of reducing his twelve-tone method to rigid analyses, but post-World War II serialists, the so-called 'post-Webernists', had too often neglected "the importance of impulse, intuition, spontaneity." While Webern certainly taught the *avant-garde* composers he inspired the value of making every note count, many of Webern's followers "seem merely to be playing mah-jongg with notes." For Schoenberg the composition itself always trumps the method of composition; the means was not more important than the end.

Messiaen's most famous work, and one of the most courageous compositions of the 20th century, is his 'Quartet for the End of Time' (*Quatour Pour la Fin Du Temps*). The apocalyptic title is completely understandable; Messiaen's deep Catholicism led him to draw from the *Book of Revelation* given the circumstances. It was composed while he was imprisoned in a Nazi prison camp in 1941. The circumstances surrounding this work make it unique and very special; its composition is a tribute to the human spirit, a "statement of faith and resilience."

Messiaen scored the work for the players and instruments he had available to him in the prison, the cellist Etienne Pasquier, violinist Jean LeBoulaire, and clarinetist Henri Akoka. These musicians either happened to have their instruments with them in the prison or were somehow able to procure one, as Messiaen found a playable piano. The clarinet playing style of the Algerian Akoka would influence "Messiaen's future musical preferences."

The instruments are piano, clarinet, violin and cello, by coincidence the same ensemble as Hindemith's quartet. The work is unconventional, almost fifty minutes, and in eight movements, with "fluttering clarinet and ethereal, open-ended piano tones," the work was heavily influenced by Asian Indian music. It was first performed in the Stalag 8A prison camp in Silesia in 1941 to an audience of 400 inmates. This figure is sometimes grossly exaggerated to as many as 5,000 but the building in which it was performed only had capacity for a few hundred. Unlike traditional chamber music, the players do perform as extended soloists in the movements, with the long third movement, 'Abyss of the Birds', being for unaccompanied clarinet and written for Akoka. The fourth movement is essentially a one-movement clarinet trio.

Although some of Messiaen's works are among the most popular and most recorded of the post-World War II period, "some find his music interminably long-winded and totally undigestible." Musicologist Richard Taruskin claims an influence on Messiaen by Scriabin, going so far as to combine the two composers in the same chapter in volume four of his *magnum opus* The Oxford History of Western Music under Taruskin's discussion of Maximalism and Transcendentalism. Scriabin did produce some of the greatest post-Romantic piano music. Although Messiaen shares Scriabin's blend of the sensuous and the mystic, Scriabin was a nut with a radical view of religion that put him at its center as a god-like Wagnerian figure, a messiah. Messiaen, on the other hand, was a church organist with a spirituality rooted in the Catholic faith. Scriabin's egocentrism increased exponentially in his orchestral works which are the epitome of self-indulgence, and would have culminated in Scriabin's insane plan for the thankfully unrealized *Mysterium*. Unlike the *Gesamtkunstwerke* of Wagner, which were stage works with actors and props, Scriabin's vision for *Mysterium* literally would have occurred. This vision had as its climax the gathering of mankind to the Himalayas with the outcome the creation of a new race.

♪ Pierre Boulez (1925-2016)

"I think that music should be collective magic and hysteria."
- Pierre Boulez

Shostakovich called Boulez "the arch-apostle of modernism." As a young artist Boulez railed against any music not radical enough for him. From his days as a student in Nazi-occupied Paris he approached music and his musical cause with "the intensity of a resistance patriot." Specifically, he saw the neo-Classicism of the inter-war years as a 'distraction'. In the immediate wake of World War II he began attacks against composers who did not fully embrace complete atonality and serialism, including an unforgivable condescension toward Stravinsky. Boulez was an extreme iconoclast, using the "polemical articles he wrote during his twenties" to furiously take to task...Schoenberg, Berg, Bartok, and Stravinsky, and even his mentor Messiaen. Messiaen's reaction to his rebel student was simply to state that "Boulez was in revolt against everything."

Boulez showed an almost Stalinist contempt for all new music that did not meet his criteria of hard-core serialism with no hints of neo-Classicism. His own words sum up his outlook in the early 1950s, "...any musician who has not experienced...the necessity of the dodecaphonic language is USELESS." (The capitals are Boulez's) Favoring Webern over even Schoenberg and denouncing the latter for holding onto the emotional past and not cutting it loose completely, Boulez published the manifesto *Schoenberg est mort* ('Schoenberg is dead') only seven months after Schoenberg's death.

Although Boulez always put Stravinsky's music among the broad range of first half 20th century compositions he rejected, a look at the catalogue today shows beyond any doubt whose music people are interested in (Stravinsky's) and whose music remains esoteric and unknown to most. Boulez's own apparent insistence on radicalism for its own sake would indicate that he probably considers his music's lack of broad appeal as a positive.

Boulez picked up where Anton Webern left off, taking serialism beyond simply pitch to apply serial methods to other musical elements, striving for 'total serialism.' His "glittering, violent, and emotional music" advanced the development of serialism. An example is his Piano Sonata No.2 (1947-48), "a work of Beethovian range and power" which is "a four-movement torrent in which all music's easy consolations are obviated or disrupted." Boulez's "writing demands the utmost virtuosity from the performer." His Second Piano Sonata "is a staggering display of pianistic virtuosity." His work for two pianos Structures (1957) represents the first work of total serialism.

> *Recommended – Piano Sonata No.2* – Maurizio Pollini (DG)

One of the more prominent composers of the 20th century, Boulez has also had a distinguished career as a conductor, including a stint as conductor of the New York Philharmonic in the 1970s, succeeding Leonard Bernstein. For decades he has been as devoted to conducting as to composing. Not surprisingly, as a conductor he specializes in 20th century music, but includes some of Mahler's symphonies in his discography. Boulez is as good a conductor of modern music as he is a composer and proponent of it. Despite his enormous influence on modern music, within France and outside, his own compositions, while praised, have still not taken hold in the active repertory. In 1976 he formed the *Ensemble InterContemporain*, one of the best European ensembles for the performance of contemporary music. It includes noted pianist Pierre-Laurent Aimard.

♫ *György Ligeti (1923-2006)*

Ligeti's best-known works are among the most popular and performed of any composer of the second half of the 20th century. Despite losing much of his family in concentration camps, then enduring his native Hungary succumbing to communism, he still "nonetheless found it in him to write music of luminosity and wit." His early works clearly show the influence of his countryman Bartók. As with most composers of the period his musical influences are varied and eclectic, including the influence of African music in his dance rhythms, the repetitive sounds of Minimalism, the avant-garde of the Darmstadt School, and the Impressionism and neo-Impressionism of Debussy and Messiaen, respectively. He also counts as influences older composers of keyboard miniatures such as Chopin and Schumann and back to Domenico Scarlatti.

Ligeti's early set of piano pieces *Musica ricercata* (1951-53), named after the polyphonic Baroque form, were influenced by Bartók's *Mikrokosmos* as well as Stravinsky. The first piece contains two tones, the second three, and so on so that the eleventh piece uses all twelve pitches and "hovers between academic orthodoxy and deep reflection." The set, although utilizing various Renaissance and Baroque tricks, represents Ligeti's dabble into twelve-tone writing, although with a unique approach through the eleven pieces that produces a rich diversity of material, including some that is folk-based. With much of Ligeti's music atonality becomes mystical and otherworldly.

His three books of piano études, while difficult are accessible and are among the most popular of late 20th century piano pieces. They display the same influences of Debussy's set. There are, so far, three books of études starting in 1985 with Ligeti continuing to add to the total, which he sees as an ongoing series.

> "The only musical instrument in my childhood home was the gramophone."
>
> - György Ligeti

Ligeti, looking back in 1993, summed up the *avant-garde* he had been a part of: "Tonality was definitely out. To write...even non-tonal melodies was absolute taboo. (This music) worked when it was new, but it became stale." Ligeti went on to explain that he felt as if "in a prison: one wall is the *avant-garde*, the other wall is the past" (i.e., tonality). He rejected 'systems' and artificial methods (i.e., serialism) that were all the rage with the *avant-garde* and he distanced himself from it. Composer George Benjamin points out that Ligeti's music, as opposed to much *avant-garde* music "was smooth and seamless like a huge wave."

Ligeti's 'solution' was to move away from serialism and towards what he termed *mikropolyphonie*, a polyphony based on minute details, a method of "composition with blocks of sound," referred to as 'tone clusters', "out of which he could draw swathes of different textures." The result, according to Adam Ross, is music "in which melody and harmony seem to vanish into an enveloping fog of cluster chords." It is a "style forged from chromatic cluster chords that are devoid of conventional melody, pitch and rhythm..." As part of this, Ligeti looked to extend the use of *Klangfarbenmelodie* ('tone-color-melody') developed by the Second Viennese School. However, Ligeti's *Klangfarbenmelodie* uses blocks of sound instead of single notes, manipulating them to produce the "effect of colors emerging, altering, disappearing..." He elevated "texture and color to the status of primary compositional elements along with melody, harmony, and rhythm."

One of his better-known orchestral works, *Atmospheres* (1961) is for large orchestra without percussion and focuses almost exclusively on sound texture (timbre) or 'sound mass'. *Atmospheres* "projects a series of sound 'clouds' of changing density and color." It is a study in orchestral timbre in which "the listener hears an all but motionless series of sound evolutions unfolding at various moments." In Ligeti's music "shapes come out of the shadows, dark cedes to light."

A similar work for large orchestra from the same time period (1960) is *Apparitions*, which is "maximalization of the most radical aspects of Bartók's music...an adaptation (of it) to the reigning ideologies and methodologies of Darmstadt...in a context completely devoid of folklore." Ligeti uses instruments "with dazzling effect...(his) use of micro-intervals, amorphous textures, and delicate wind-tones is especially effective," in addition to Cagean effects such as bassoonists playing without reeds and smashing a bottle in a metal-plated crate as a percussive device. Ligeti referred to his final style, which was a kind of harmonic kaleidoscope, as 'non-atonality'.

In chamber music he has highlighted winds with his Trio for Violin, Horn and Piano (1982) and *Ten Pieces for Wind Quintet* (1968). The *Trio* bears the subtitle "homage to Brahms" but, while the form may be traditional, beginning with a distorted variation of the 'farewell' motif from Beethoven's Op.81a sonata, the music is purely 20th century.

Ligeti also composed one concerto each for piano, violin, and cello, all in his unique micropolyphonic *Klangfarbenmelodie*, with an "emphasis on diverse layerings and superimpositions, with many novel effects of timbre and tuning." His Cello Concerto (1967) was earlier than his Violin Concerto and Piano Concerto. The Violin Concerto, from the 1980s, is one of the finest concertos for string soloist of its time.

> **Recommended – Ligeti**
> Pierre-Laurent Aimard, a friend of the composer, has recorded much of Ligeti's solo piano music including the sets of *Études*. A good recording is the CD with three Ligeti concertos, for piano, for violin, and for cello, by the *Ensemble InterContemporain* led by Pierre Boulez (DG, 1994). Aimard is the pianist of this ensemble.

♪ Indeterminacy: Cage and Stockhausen

♫ John Cage (1912-1992)

The *avant-garde* around 1970 was divided into two camps: the first was that of Boulez and the fussy, control-freakish serialists; the second was led by John Cage, the shaggy-dog, do-you-own-thing school.

In opposition to the strict parameters of serialism, John Cage's style established 'indeterminacy', allowing the performers the freedom to determine certain aspects of the score, as a leading musical style for the second half of the 20th century. Based in California he created a disorganized 'music of chance', which valued individual, randomly chosen sounds and was "aimed at freeing the performer from the literal execution of a fixed sequence of notes."

"The most drastic thing Cage did…was to throw out conventional musical rhetoric as it had existed for hundreds of years." His methods "created opportunities for experiencing sounds as themselves, not as vehicles for the composer's intentions." "Cage puts responsibility on his musicians to make decisions that can…affect every parameter of the music…an idea of musical democracy. Some musicians aren't ready to accept that; they'd rather play the notes on the page…"

> *"With Cage, music is like an art object to be viewed."*
> – Alex Ross

Indeterminacy goes well beyond differences simply in interpretation so that no two performances of a work are musically exactly alike. Cage took music, which had always been 'organized sound', and made it completely disorganized with works such as *Music of Changes* and *Imaginary Landscape No.3* (1942), and he repeatedly challenged the core concepts of music itself.

Cage's father was a successful inventor and this spirit of innovation was a huge influence on the son's innovative approach to music, seeking to create something no one else had before created; fashioning Cage as a 'musical inventor'. This led him to create music with 'instruments' that were not considered musical; at the extreme, household items such as tin cans, utensils, and kitchen containers. He invented the 'prepared' piano in 1938 to emphasize the percussive qualities of the instrument, sensing that 20th century composers such as Stravinsky and Prokofiev had exhausted those qualities and modification to the instrument was needed for his purposes.

> *"I don't have an ear for music...I can't remember a melody."*
> – John Cage

Cage studied at UCLA with Schoenberg, although his later devotion to indeterminacy as a reaction to the formalism of serialism would make him the anti-Schoenberg. One of his 'innovative' gimmicks was the 'prepared' instrument. An example is the placing of common objects inside a piano "causing it to sound like a multihued percussion instrument." Because this process cannot be reproduced identically, the prepared piano contributes to the indeterminate character of the music. He then moved on to embrace chaos rather than try to order it, introducing randomness or 'indeterminacy' to his compositions. Some aspects of a score or composition were left to chance, sometimes literally to a flip of a coin, as in Music of Changes from 1951.

His most notorious work, *4'33"*, was actually nothing musical, just a 'player' sitting in silence at a piano for four and a half minutes. In it "Cage finally dared to offer complete emptiness." To add to the experience, Cage actually had the 'pianist' break up the work into three movements, indicated by lowering and raising the piano cover. His idea was to have the audience focus on the random ambient 'music', the pianist simply an enabler.

4'33" remains Cage's most misunderstood piece. It is not about silence but "the sound of the environment – knocking down the doors of the auditorium to let the world in." "Cage considers silence a very integral part of a piece of music, given equal importance with the sounded notes." However, Cage's 'silence' is not absolute silence; "whenever there are people…there is some kind of sound…caused by nature or traffic." 'Traffic' referring here to any human activity. Cage had this to say on his work of 'silence': "What they thought was silence…was full of accidental sounds." (wind, raindrops, talking, etc.)

However, Cage could compose according to traditional forms; his Concerto for Prepared Piano and Orchestra (1950-1) follows the traditional three-movements. According to Cage, the work, like many concertos from the 19th and 20th century, is a drama between the romantically expressive piano and the orchestra. When motivated, Cage produced lyrical, accessible music, as demonstrated by his *magnum opus* for the prepared piano, the relatively traditional *Twenty Sonatas and Interludes* composed 1946-48. These pieces are "Eastern-inspired piano pieces of exquisite calm." Maro Ajemian, an important new-music advocate of the time, performed the premiere in 1949, which gave Cage's profile a huge international boost. The score includes meticulous instructions on how to prepare the piano. Bolts, screws, rubber, and plastic are inserted to alter the strings. Cage conceived of the whole work as "a bringing together of…eight emotions, with their tendency toward tranquility." Cage described the 'white emotions' as being the "heroic, the erotic, the mirthful, and the wondrous; the 'black emotions' being fear, anger, disgust, and sorrow."

Some critics, starting in the 1970s with the rise of minimalism, have labeled Cage's musical experimentations as "nihilistic musical deconstructions" that ultimately led nowhere. But fans of Cage's indeterminacy and of *4'33"* see it as "a kind of artistic prayer…that opened ears and allowed one to hear the world anew." Other leading composers who can be classified under indeterminacy are Lukas Foss (1922-2009) and Karlheinz Stockhausen.

♪ Karlheinz Stockhausen (1928-2007)

The term indeterminacy can be applied to the works of the German Stockhausen, but it would certainly only partly cover his range. Stockhausen is one of the best-known leaders of the European *avant-garde*, a counterpart to American John Cage. Both infused randomness (or 'indeterminacy') in their works and to an increasing amount as they matured. They looked to take music on new pathways. Stockhausen and Pierre Boulez shared Webern's principles of compression and rigour as the foundation for their techniques. Both continued the evolution of music where Anton Webern had left it; namely, to continue the "attempt to achieve minute control over all the elements of composition," leading to 'total serialism.' Boulez and Stockhausen, together with Luigi Nono, led a summer music school in Darmstadt, the German city that had served as the ideological headquarters of the new *avant-garde* movement since the end of World War II.

> *"In a world bombarded by images, the function of music is to awaken the inner man."*
> - Karl Heinz Stockhausen

Most of Stockhausen's landmark, totally serial works were composed between 1952-1964, including his seminal work of electronic music *Gesang der Jünglinge* ('Song of the Youths', 1955-56). He was a student of Messiaen who became a jazz pianist and took an interest in physics and acoustics. His *Electronic Studies* (1953-54) was the first published 'electronic music.' Stockhausen was a "stylistic chameleon" flip-flopping from total serialism to indeterminacy and often incorporating electronic effects and extra-instrumental effects. His work for solo percussion, *Zyklus*, is an extreme example of indeterminacy that can start anywhere in the score and proceed in virtually any direction.

Stockhausen was something of a pop culture figure, appearing in the crowd of heroes on the cover of the Beatles' *Sergeant Pepper's* album. The Beatles claimed to have been influenced by his transformations of sound through electronic means. Stockhausen stated that my music has "no recapitulation, no variation, no development." To this could be added "no listeners." Deutsche Grammophone withdrew Stockhausen's entire catalogue in the 1990s while, through the end of the first decade of the 21st century, re-issues and, more importantly, brand new performances of works by Messiaen, Stravinsky, Shostakovich, and Bartók continue to be released.

Some consider Stockhausen's work to be "characterized more by industry and facility than musical imagination." The *avant-garde* strongly disagrees but the public has spoken. Some critics have pointed out the irony that serial music, which is by definition the most organized music, often sounds chaotic and disorganized to most listeners. This all begs the question that Harold Schonberg poses about serialism never taking hold with the public or in the repertory: "Could it be that…the fault lay not with the public but with the composer?"

Total serialism, which was what the avant-garde espoused religiously, represents strict control over all aspects of the music but ironically, tends to make music sound totally random, and totally uninteresting as anything more than an academic exercise. In the end, serialism held much more interest for composers than it did for the public. "Serialism failed to live up to its promise as the new international language of music." It is the best example of how the creators of art, no matter how talented and well intentioned, cannot force the public to embrace their work; popularity can only come from the people.

♪ Post-Modernism: Minimalism

> *"Once musicians obtained every-thing they had imagined in their most daring dreams, they started again from scratch."*
> - Kurt Weill

The decline of serialism was followed by the rise of minimalism in the 1960s and 1970s. The century that began with Impressionism ended with Minimalism, which "appeared as just another strand in the rich fabric of contemporary music." Minimalism was the answer for many composers "looking for a way forward from Schoenberg and Serialism," as well as away from the post-war avant-garde. Philip Glass characterized the *avant-garde* around this time as "dominated by maniacs...who were trying to make everyone write this crazy creepy music."

Put another way, Minimalism is "viewed as a response to the largely academic, elitist climate of 'new' music in the 1950's and 60's." The reaction to the 'Darmstadt school' of the avant-garde in Europe was that "many resented on social grounds the idea of a music that disclosed so little to an ordinary listener." Minimalism was "the first style of literate music making originating in America to have the same transformative impact on European musicians that earlier European innovations previously had on Americans."

> *"Atonality, rather than being the Promised Land so confidently predicted by Schoenberg, Boulez and Babbitt, proved to be nothing of the kind (and)...was unable to reproduce its initial harvest."*
> - John Adams in <u>Hallelujah Junction</u>

Minimalism generally uses "concentrated sound units" stated over and over with only gradual changes in tonality, texture, etc. In its obsessive repetition it is a revolt against serialism, its complexities and lack of repetition. A minimalist composer must come up with good musical ideas in order to "present patterns that will hold the listener's interest through all that repetition," as the tonal harmonies change very slowly. With Minimalism in particular it helps the listener to have some idea of what Minimalism is all about; otherwise, one can find the music monotonous. A fan of Classical or Romantic period works might wonder, "Where is the exposition? Where is the development?"

> *"Believe it or not, I have no real interest in music from Haydn to Wagner."*
> - Steve Reich

Minimalism counts as its founders La Monte Young and Terry Riley, who started the movement in the 1960s. Terry Riley's *In C* blazed the path for the movement by showing the appeal of sharing simple repeated motifs between players. Young explained Minimalism as "that which is created with a minimum of means." However, it really gained traction with the works of the better-known Minimalists Steve Reich, Philip Glass, and John Adams. However, these three do not feel that the Minimalist classification accurately or completely describes their work over their careers. This is especially true of Adams, whose wide interests and styles certainly extend well beyond literal Minimalism.

The relative popularity of minimalism as 'modern' music is due to its immediate approachability and the little effort required by the listener. It also has a "strong pulse, paralleling popular music's beat." Even people who thought they did not like classical music found themselves drawn to "this flow of sequential patterns. Unlike serialism and the subsequent experimental methods of both the European and American *avant-garde*, minimalism actually achieved some measure of acceptance by the listening public and established some works in the repertory. However, these works are primarily the minimalist operas of Philip Glass and John Adams.

Minimalism borrowed from bebop and jazz and its extreme reaction against serialism showed that American composers who were children during World War II could not relate to the angst of serialists such as Stockhausen and Boulez who "were portraying...what it was like to pick up the pieces of a bombed-out continent after World War II." Unlike the *avant-garde*, Minimalist composers "sought social connection, not alienation."

♫ Erik Satie (1866-1925)

It is necessary to begin coverage of Minimalist composers with Erik Satie, the 'father of Minimalism,' despite being dead for decades by the 1960s. His simpler, repetitive music "seemed...more fitting to a new age." The "symmetrical repetition" of Satie's music "is the essence of Minimalism," making him a pioneer of the 20th century *avant-garde*, as his music even inspired the 1980s 'New Age' movement in music. Maurice Ravel considered Satie's genius to be completely ahead of its time and Minimalism was not only foreshadowed by the piano pieces of Satie but also by Ravel's *Bolero* (1928) and its infectious repetition.

> "Satie was...starting European musical history all over again."
> - Reinbert De Leeuw

"The apostle of simplicity," the 'anti-Impressionist' who pre-saged Minimalism, Erik Satie "served as a catalyst for many young Moderns...(he) was a breath of fresh air in an age dominated by Mahler and Strauss." Although the musical style of Satie strongly influenced Ravel, Milhaud, Busoni, and even Copland, his works "never won a firm place in the repertory." Much of his music parodied Impressionism, which he did not see as a future path for music but more as a short-lived fad. He "reacted against...the luscious complex harmonies cultivated by Debussy and fellow Impressionist composers," but at the same time wanted no part of the German tradition that so dominated 19th century music. He was "anti-Teutonic in every fiber of his being."

Satie developed the template for the "kind of impersonal music that" composers sought after World War I: "music stripped of nonessentials down to its 'bare bones'." Satie called this "music without sauce." He is best known for his short piano pieces ('miniatures'). Satie offers "cool refreshment" in his piano pieces, which initially "may seem to lack substance" but on repeated hearings "the childlike lyricism emerges." With the "clear melodic phrases, exquisite lightness, and fresh texture" Satie's three sets of miniatures, *Trois Sarabandes*, *Trois Gymnopedies*, and the six *Gnossiennes*, from 1887, 1888 and 1890, respectively, "literally blew away the pomp and rhetoric of the old order."

These sets, written before the age of twenty-five, contain "symmetrical phrases repeated over and over" and a persistent rhythmic pattern that look decades ahead to Minimalism. "Instead of offering variety...his piano pieces are all ostentatiously plain and unemotional." His use of "modal and unresolved chords opened new possibilities for Debussy and Ravel." With his three *Gymnopedies* of 1888 Satie discarded virtuosity and complexity for simplicity and "anticipated the unresolved chords and quasi-modal harmonies of Impressionism." The pieces have little, if any development, and no transitions, only a prolonged instant, a "miraculous economy of texture." The *Trois Gymnopedies* would be quickly orchestrated by Debussy in 1896. A habit of Satie's, perhaps thankfully not taken up by other and future composers under his influence, was his use of crazy titles for many of his pieces; e.g., one translates as 'Four Veritable Flabby Pieces for a Dog', and seemingly loses nothing in translation.

Satie's music is "one side of the *avant-garde* which wittily upends conventional ideas." The Second Viennese School would be another side which upended conventional forms with a very serious and formal approach (i.e., the twelve-tone method) and considered itself in the natural progression of great composers and the natural evolution of Western music. Satie could not even begin to take himself this seriously.

> **Recommended – Satie piano works**
> Most pianists fall into the trap of playing Satie's miniatures too fast but Satie intended them to be 'exquisitely slow.' Only Reinbert De Leeuw (Philips, mid-1970s) follows the composer's instructions, but many listeners will find the pace too dull. Good alternative collections are available by French pianists Pascal Rogé and Jean-Ives Thibaudet.

♪ LaMonte Young and Terry Riley

The two American pioneers of Minimalism would be eclipsed by Glass and Reich within a decade of its 'birth'. While lacking commercial success, LaMonte Young and Terry Riley are the recognized founders of the musical movement that would become as popular as Copland's orchestral Americana portraits, while far eclipsing any serial works. Together they created Minimalism with "elements of Debussy, Satie, Webern, Ives, Messiaen, Grainger, but above all Cage and Stockhausen." The music of these composers combined with influences from the music and writings of John Cage and post be-bop jazz such as John Coltrane and early Miles Davis. Both were also influenced by Indian Raga while Young counted chant and Indonesian gamelan music as additional influences.

> "...I am not interested in good; I am interested in new..."
> - LaMonte Young

Minimalism can be traced LaMonte Young's groundbreaking 1958 work Trio for Strings, which follows "a carefully plotted serial procedure" but takes "Webernian focus to an extreme." Another major work was *The Well-Tuned Piano*, five hours of music with an obvious Baroque reference, conceived in 1964 but not recorded until 1981. Young's "compositions are predicated on the idea of infinite extension in time, achieved with the aid of electronic drones...a principle of 'sustenance', or long-sustained sounds."

Terry Riley simply saw serial music as neurotic. He met LaMonte Young while studying composition at Berkeley around 1960. Riley replaced Young's sustenance of sound with 'looping', a landmark change in the development of Minimalism that allowed the new music to be performed live in real time. According to Riley, this music could be *avant-garde* and attract an audience too, correctly predicting the future popularity of Minimalist works.

His work *In C* is the seminal Minimalist work, pushing the movement into the commercial limelight in 1964, becoming "a platform upon which the Minimalist movement was built." *In C* consists of fifty-three 'modules' (i.e., measures) and can last anywhere from 30 to 180 minutes. The large variation in time comes from the freedom given performers to repeat any of the modules any number of times before moving to the next. This practice was termed 'looping.' The modules can be played by any number of any kind of instruments, including human voice.

♪♩ Steve Reich (1936-)

> *"I don't want people to find my music 'interesting'; I want them to be deeply moved by it."*
> - Steve Reich

Reich's "lively, pulse-oriented music of great color" is "rooted in the syncopations of jazz." Reich trained musically as a percussionist, including the study of African drumming. According to Reich his influences come from his love of jazz, Bach, and Stravinsky. In the 1970s he composed landmark Minimalist works such as *Drumming* (1971) and Reich moved to a more diverse harmonic style with *Music for Eighteen Musicians* (1976), *Music for a Large Ensemble* (1978), and his *Octet* (1979). Professor Richard Taruskin feels that Reich gave "classical music back first its youth and finally its soul in the waning years of the 20th century."

Reich emphasized the importance of hearing the compositional processes used by the composer in the music. According to Reich, these processes should have an "audible connection," and he has stated that he does not know "any secrets of structure that you can't hear." Reich uses 'progressive canons' to introduce "a form of Western contrapuntal complexity into the texture" of his works. His early technique of 'phasing' features two tracks (the two tracks can be two tapes, instrument/tape, etc.) set out at slightly different speeds to slowly shift 'out of phase,' leading to new harmonies. Reich has a strict, tonal melodic style. But with his works of the mid-70's, starting with *Music for Eighteen Musicians*, Reich adopted a different Minimalist aesthetic of 'pulse' or 'pulsing', which has no relation to melody. "The ecstatic, driving pulse, launched in the very first bar, never lets down." A work such as *Eighteen Musicians* has been summed up as "created to never really end, or begin, it is a giant, beautiful circle of sound that is to be approached from any angle."

With his *Variations for Winds, Strings and Keyboard* (1980) Reich moved to an orchestra scale as opposed to previous chamber ensembles. The repetitions are effective at producing a "hypnotic, but soothing, kind of poetry." Reich's pulsing technique results in music "sounding like a night drive through a neon city with bright sounds appearing on the horizon, coming closer, then disappearing behind."

> **Recommended – Steve Reich Variations**
> San Francisco Symphony with Edo De Waart conducting (Philips) are excellent in the minimalist repertoire and Reich wrote *Variations* for this orchestra.

Reich's chamber work *Different Trains* won a Grammy Award in 1989. It is a three-movement work, of approximately thirty minute duration, for string quartet and tape. It is Reich's "somber evocation of his childhood with its quiet, disturbing references to the Holocaust." The three movements are *America – Before the War*, *Europe – During the War*, and *After the War*. Recorded on tape to be played on top of the music are interviews with people about their experiences before, during, and after World War II (hence the three movements), including the horrors experienced by concentration camp survivors. The second movement's collage of speech melodies is drawn from archival tapes of Holocaust survivors recalling their trip to Auschwitz. Reich "created a powerful work with a deeply emotional edge rare in new music," using "fragments of speech in a darkening reminiscence of rail travel in the 1940s," and "based the melodic content...on the contour and rhythm of ordinary human speech."

Another Reich work using sampled sound effects, along with chamber ensemble, is *City Life*, which gives a "turgidly bleak portrait of New York City," Reich's hometown.

> *Recommended – Reich Different Trains*
> The Kronos Quartet specialize in 20th century chamber music and their recording sets the standard, coupled with Pat Metheny performing *Reich's Electric Counterpoint* (Nonesuch, 1990).

♫ Philip Glass (1937-)

> *"I spent years subtracting things from my music. Now I'm deciding what to put back in."*
> - Philip Glass

The above quote sums up the dilemma faced by so many post-World War II composers: how far to push Minimalism before the pendulum must be brought back toward center? Glass shared Reich's views on Serialism, summing it up as a "one-way-ticket-to-nowhere." Reich had not been as harsh when stating that the "work of Schoenberg and Boulez had no rhythm nor melodic organization." Despite the strong feelings of both composers toward Serialism, it is possible for a listener to find both minimalist and serial works appealing provided (as is the case with all music) they are of high quality and have something to say musically.

Philip Glass has long been a cultural icon and "has given a dose of much-needed glamour to the status of the classical composer in contemporary life." His compositions are characterized by the application of non-Western techniques, including the "elaborate rhythmic structure of Indian music."

"The building blocks of Glass's music are cells which rarely change radically nor develop beyond strictly limited confines." His music helped popularize Minimalism by playing simple, short melodic patterns (not even full melodies) over and over, expanding and contracting rhythmically, but taking time to produce any significant change.

After initially sharing an ensemble to perform their music, both Reich and Glass formed their own ensembles. The Philip Glass Ensemble was formed to perform his works. One of Glass's early seminal Minimalist works, *Music in Twelve Parts*, was written over a three year period (1971-74) and contains over six hours of music that represents "a summation of past techniques and a look forward to the future." Initially Reich and Glass were mutually supportive of each other's efforts, even performing together. However, Glass and Reich separated ways as the former was drawn to the theater and had a greater affinity for the rock scene. Interestingly, Glass's operas "had a strong and openly acknowledged influence on the art-rock of the 1970s and 1980s."

By the late 1980s "Glass had reached some sort of truce with the ideas of melody and conventional musical structure." His *Glassworks* from 1981 is "a concoction of smooth horns, strings and lovingly coaxed electronics." With "an amiably soft-edged minimalist sound," it represents one of his most successful releases. Scored for two flutes (or two saxophones) and strings it takes the form of a *chaconne* with the strings playing a single harmonic sequence over and over again as the wind soloists play melodic variations with Glass' characteristic arpeggiated figures blended in. Propulsive *arpeggio* figuration is a recurring feature of Glass's works. In addition to versions with the two standard wind scorings there is at least one recording in which additional strings take the parts of the usual duo wind soloists.

Through 2012 Glass had composed ten symphonies, more than most composers. His *Low* Symphony from 1992 was derived from the David Bowie/Brian Eno album *Low*. Although Glass borrows themes from Bowie and Eno, he does not quote them directly but rather builds his own themes and variations on some of the main themes of the rock album.

Recently, Glass was commissioned to compose a piano concerto by several Nebraska organizations for the Bicentennial celebration of the journey of Lewis and Clark. This concerto is programmatic, with each of the three movements representing highlights of the explorers' adventures. The middle movement, for example, is simply titled, *Sacajawea.*

His Violin Concerto from 1987 was his first major work for conventional orchestra and his first mature essay for a concert hall setting. The slow movement, with a *passacaglia* bass line, gives the work a neo-Baroque touch. Continuing in the neo-Baroque vein are his *Concerto Grosso* and Harpsichord Concerto. Glass has composed several Minimalist concertos that are quite lyrical (for Minimalist works), including a cello concerto, his Piano Concerto No.2, and the interestingly innovative Saxophone Quartet Concerto and *Concert Fantasy for Two Timpanists.*

As is the case with fellow minimalist John Adams, Glass is best known for his operas. The most famous is *Einstein on the Beach*, which was very successful in the mid-1970s. His diverse compositions include the first-ever soundtrack for the 1931 horror movie *Dracula*, a string quartet performed by the Kronos Quartet. But perhaps Glass' most accessible music is that for solo piano, including his collection of *Études*. While solidly minimalist in their repetition they also possess sufficient harmonic variation and occasional tunefulness to appeal to broad audiences.

> **Recommended** – *Philip Glass, Live from SoHo*, Orange Mountain Music, 2010.

♪ Arvo Pärt (1935-)

The early works of Estonian Arvo Pärt are characterized as neo-Classicical/Baroque. He then entered a period of serial composition, followed by an attempt to blend serialism with his earlier style. This blend did not satisfy his musical needs either, so in the 1970s he created a unique style that was "greatly simplified, austere and essentially tonal." Having reached this point Pärt characterized it as, "I work with very few elements (and) build with the most primitive materials." Pärt is among late 20th century composers who "combined a radical simplification of material and procedures with a return to diatonic music."

Pärt is devoted to Eastern Orthodox Christianity and most of his later works are infused with "an intense spiritual pleading," leading some to refer to his style as 'holy minimalism.' His deeply religious nature and the influences of chant and its mystical connotations come through in his music, which "always points to an unchanging, transcendent refuge for the world-weary." Pärt's music is "introspective, mystical…(it) can cast a spell on listeners," and it "pursues an austerely beautiful simplicity that suggests spiritual illumination." It has also been characterized as "Medieval music seen through a contemporary sensibility."

Pärt coined the term 'tintinnabulation' (literally 'the ringing of bells') to describe some of his works that contain two voices; one voice stepping around a central note to create the melody, while the second voice "rings out the notes of the tonic triad around it," like bells ringing. This effect was first used in the short piano piece *Für Alina* in 1976.

His works are well-represented on recordings with his most popular being *Tabula Rasa* (1977), composed for fellow Latvian, violinist Gidon Kremer. The 'blank slate' is Pärt going from strict process to free expression, starting from scratch with his final style, the novel holy minimalism, after moving on from serialism. This *concerto grosso* is a double concerto scored for two violins with string orchestra and a 'prepared' piano. The prepared piano produces an "alienated tone color effect."

The work is in two movements totaling around thiry minutes. The first movement, *Ludus*, "consists of progressively lengthening and loudening bouts of fiddling activity" and *Silentium* or 'silence'. *Silentium*, "infused with a...single omnipresent harmony (is) a startlingly successful evocation of stillness." The first movement grows "until it bursts into a climactic cadenza" for the violins, while the second movement ends quietly "as the music subsides into the depths." The music "keeps disappearing into silence, and then returning." *Tabula Rasa* shows a "clear sense of the...sprirtual underpinnings of" tintinnabulation method, which results in "a continuously shifting surface of consonances and dissonances..."

Other of his better-know works include *Fratres*, "a sort of wordless chorale in irregular meter (that) exists in numerous arrangements..." and his *Cantus in Memory of Benjamin Britten* for string orchestra and bell, which is strikingly minimalist with similarities to Steve Reich's phase-shifting music. The various versions of *Fratres* include one for eight cellos, for wind octet and percussion, for strings and percussion, for cello and piano, and for string quartet.

Of his three early symphonies, Nos.1 and 2, from 1964 and 1966 respectively, are twelve-tone works while the *Third* (1971), considered a transition piece between Pärt's neo-Classical/atonal and austere periods, is "serene and tonal in contrast to the angst of the first two." In parts it has a neo-Classical, Martinů-like feel (with bells instead of piano) to it but the slow sections are more uniquely in Pärt's austere style. Forty years after his Third Symphony,

Pärt returned in 2010 with Symphony No.4. Over those forty years "he has developed a vocabulary of singular intensity and cohesion." His works have been "linked ever more clearly with his Orthodox faith but employing an ever-expanding range of musical and linguistic color."

> *Recommended* – **Arvo Pärt** *Tabula Rasa*
> Not surprising, the 1984 recording by Kremer remains the standard, with the Lithuanian Chamber Orchestra conducted by Saulius Sondeckis, violinist T. Grindenko, and Russian composer Alfred Schnittke handling the prepared piano (ECM, 1984). Also includes *Fratres*, Pärt's work for multiple cellos.

♪♪ John Adams (1947-)

Adams embraced the Minimalism of Reich and Glass but does not consider himself strictly a minimalist, which he defines as "building large, expressive structures by the repetition of small elements." Adams and Arvo Pärt can be considered 'post-Minimalists'. Over time Adams "has relied less on minimalist techniques and more on traditional harmonic and contrapuntal means." In fact, "the folkloric, vernacular elements (of some of his works) suggest that he is a successor of Copland rather than a rival to Carter."

The New England-born, Harvard-educated, San Francisco-based composer was the composer-in-residence (1979-85) of the San Francisco Symphony and head of the new music program at the San Francisco Conservatory from 1972-82. Adams, as a New Englander, has been compared to another New Englander, the Yale-educated Charles Ives; both "never coy about using vernacular and banal elements."

Adams' work is much broader than Minimalism itself and it has been difficult to assign his works to one particular school or movement. His minimalism is not as repetitive (some would say 'monotonous') and strict to the form as Reich and Glass; in fact, it is really post-Minimalism. His many operatic and symphonic works stand out among contemporary classical compositions for their depth of expression, their sonic brilliance, and the profoundly humanist nature of their themes.

Adams is best-known for the Minimalist operas *Nixon In China*, *The Death of Klinghoffer*, and *Captain Atomic*, the last about Manhattan Project leader and nuclear physicist Robert Oppenheimer. Adams' operatic topics are often controversial and based on current or recent events. In this century he was commissioned by the New York Philharmonic to compose a memorial to the victims of the 9/11 terrorist attacks. The result was the chorale work, *On the Transmigration of Souls* (recorded by the New York Philharmonic under Lorin Maazel).

> *"A creative mind whose entire life ran unfailingly against the grain of society."*
> — John Adams on Schoenberg

Many Minimalist composers have moved away from strict adherence to the form and in later works utilize larger forces and incorporate longer melodic lines and lusher harmonies in their compositions. This school is usually termed 'post-Minimalist'. This is especially true for John Adams; his forty-minute symphony *Harmonielehre* (composed 1984-85) is "a statement of belief in the power of tonality...a wedding of *fin-de-siecle* chromatic harmony with the rhythmic and formal procedures of Minimalism (not) too rigorously bound to the practices of either tradition... shades of Mahler, Sibelius, Debussy and the young Schoenberg are everywhere in this strange piece," and Adams cites as turn-of-the-century influences such works as *Parsifal*, Mahler's *Tenth*, Sibelius' *Fourth*, and Schoenberg's *Gurreleider*. The work is named for the 1911 treatise on harmony by Schoenberg and is borderline Mahlerian. However, Adams has his issues with Schoenberg's twelve-tone method, calling it "an over-ripening of 19th century individualism." According to the composer, *Harmonielehre* marries Minimalism with "the harmonic and expressive world of...late Romanticism..."

His popularity took off in 1986 with his lively composition *Short Ride in a Fast Machine*, a five-minute ride that is as catchy as a minimalist work can be. It is also as minimally Minimalist as a Minimalist work can be. *Short Ride* is the second piece of Adams' *Two Fanfares*; the first being *Tromba Lontana*. Adams sometimes uses traditional titles for works, e.g., his Chamber Symphony and Violin Concerto; at other times he creates a unique title such as *Gnarly Buttons* and *Century Rolls* for a clarinet concerto and piano concerto, respectively.

Shaker Loops from 1978 contains four movements for string septet (Adams would offer a version for string orchestra in 1983). Adams regards *Shaker Loops* as one of his first truly characteristic works and also one of the first in which he applied Minimalism, but in a manner termed 'post-Minimalism' by the composer. Adams sought to "transform minimalism into something richer and less rigid," with greater dynamic contrasts. He realized "the limitations of a technique that placed so much emphasis upon repetition."

The 'Loops' are melodic patterns of different lengths shaped by the seven strings. This work, as well as others such as *Harmonium*, owes much "to the perpetual motion ostinatos of Sibelius (and) expands the Adams palette of Sibelian ostinatos and floating ambiences." Shaker refers to the New England religious community Adams was familiar with who are known for their 'shaking' dances of worship. In the work Adams draws a comparison between their shaking and the quick movement of bow across string used to effect in this work.

> *Recommended – John Adams Orchestral Works*
> Because of Adams' close relationship over the years with the SFSO and Edo de Waart, recordings by that team are generally highly endorsed. However, the composer, an excellent conductor of his own works, has released recordings of many of his works leading the SFSO, the St. Luke's CO, and the London Sinfonietta. Other notable conductors who stand out in the works of Adams include Simon Rattle, Esa Pekka Salonen, and Kent Nagano.

Bibliography and Further Reading

"Writing about music is like dancing about architecture."
- Anonymous

The following bibliography groups the books together into several arbitrary categories. This survey is not meant to indicate superior works at the exclusion of lesser works. These are simply the works that I used in the course of putting this book together. There are, of course, scores of excellent biographies on individual composers or on a very small set of composers.

Some of the books detail the movements of works, e.g., what form a movement is in, key modulations, development of themes, etc. I have noted some of these below but a very good source for this information are the liner notes that accompany CDs. This may not be a solution for those who download but some on-line offerings do come with 'digital liner notes' that are downloadable as a .pdf file.

General Interest and Encyclopedic Works

The New Grove Dictionary of Music and Musicians, 2nd ed, Stanley Sadie, ed. Oxford University Press, 2004.
This is really a library of classical music in 29 volumes. Certainly much more information for mostly all individuals as well as a price tag to go with it. However, we are lucky that many libraries consider it an essential volume, so it remains within reach of everyone.

The Oxford Companion to Music, Latham, Alison (ed.), Oxford University Press, 2002.
An update of a volume that dates back to 1938. A wealth of information is packed into its almost 1500 pages that goes beyond 'classical' music to include discussions on jazz, pop and dance.

The Musical Companion, A.L. Bacharach, J.R. Pearce, eds. Harvest/HBJ, 1984.
A timeless classic with contributions from eminent musicologists.

The Cambridge Companion to the Concerto, S. Keefe, ed. Cambridge University Press, 2005.

Copland, Aaron, **What to Listen for in Music**. New York: Signet Classic, 1939, renewed 1985.
"...a brilliant range of common sense non-technical discussion." – J.H. Jacobson

Libbey, Ted, **The NPR Listener's Encyclopedia of Classical Music**, New York, NY: Workman Publishing, 2006.

Hinson, M. Guide to the Pianist's Repertoire, 3rd edition. Indiana University Press, 2001. *An A to Z encyclopedia on the keyboard and its artists*

Csampai, A., Holland, D. Der Konzert Führer. Hamburg: Rohwolt Verlag GmbH, 2005 (in German).
An encyclopedic 1350 pages covering the orchestral music of almost 300 individual composers, many of whom are overlooked by others, from 1700 to the turn of the 20th century.

Compendia of Recommended Recordings

These works center on the particular works of composers and provide criticism of available performances of the works, but not of the compositions themselves (All Music Guide... excepted). There is also limited information on the lives of the composers and works are rarely put into any context. But these volumes are the best publications for determining the best (and not so good) performances of a particular work and for building a classical collection of definitive recordings beyond the staples of the repertory. Because these books almost all exceed 1,000 pages, it is no surprise that they contain 'a lot of information about a lot' of composers, performers, works, etc.

Penguin Guide to Compact Discs and Cassettes, I. March, E. Greenfield, R. Layton, eds. London, Penguin Group, multiple editions released over the years.
I primarily used the 'New Edition' of 1992.

The Grammophone Classical Music Guide, J. Jolly, ed. Grammophone Publications.
Analogous to the Penguin Guides, usually a new edition released for each year.

All Music Guide to Classical Music, C. Woodstra, G. Brennan, A. Schrott, eds. San Francisco, CA: Backbeat Books, 2005.
An excellent source for short anecdotes about several pieces in each genre by many composers, together with recommended recordings. This volume is also a listener's guide and contains detailed information on the individual movements within given works.

Classical Music, A. Morin, ed. San Francisco, CA: Backbeat Books, 2002.

1001 Classical Recordings You Must Hear Before You Die, Matthew Rye, ed. Quintessence, 2007.

How to Build a Classical Collection

Unlike the 'compendia' books above, these works are designed for someone with a much smaller collection of classical music, and focus on a handful of recordings for the works discussed. Also, these works usually limit themselves to well-known composers.

Bookspan, Martin, <u>101 Masterpieces of Music and Their Composers</u>. New York: Doubleday, 1973.
Although the recommendations are by now all historic recordings, Bookspan's strong opinions and musical analysis remain timeless and entertaining. This book doubles as a listener's guide and contains detailed information on the individual movements within given works.

Dubal, David, <u>The Canon of Classical Music</u>. New York: North Pointe Press, 2001.
Covers from the Baroque to the 21st century, details the masters and hundreds of minor composers. A very readable, occasionally humorous, always enjoyable book by the program director for two decades of the now-defunct legendary New York Classical music station WNCN.

Goulding, Phil G., <u>Classical Music: The 50 Greatest Composers and Their 1,000 Greatest Works</u>. New York: Fawcett Books, 1992.
A late-comer to classical music helps neophytes find their way in the maze of composers, works, and recordings, using rankings and lists to help matters.

Hemming, Roy, <u>Discovering Great Music</u>. New York: Newmarket Press, 1988.
Hemming covers a lot of ground in this book, but nothing in much detail. This is one of the few books to consider Martinů a major composer. Much of the book is taken up with recommended recordings by different formats, a topic which is now outdated.

Jacobson, J.H., <u>The Classical Music Experience</u>. Naperville, IL: Sourcebooks, 2003.

Kramer, Jonathan, <u>Listen to the Music</u>. New York: Schirmer Books, 1988.
A collection of the author's program and concert notes, covering over 50 composers and a couple of hundred of their works. This book contains detailed information on the individual movements within given works.

Swafford, Jan, <u>The Vintage Guide to Classical Music</u>. Vintage, 1992.
One of the best all-around works covering 100 composers, 500 years of music and including a glossary of terms and a guide to building a classical collection. If you wanted to give a friend with a growing interest in classical music only one book on the topic, this would be the one.

Historical Surveys

Abraham, Gerald, <u>The Concise Oxford History of Music</u>. London: Oxford University Press, 1979.

Burkholder, J.P., Grout, D.J., Palisca, C., <u>A History of Western Music</u>, 8th edition. New York: W.W. Norton, 2009.
One of the classic texts covering music from its beginnings. Actually, any edition you can get your hands on going back to the first edition from 1960 is worth looking into.

Einstein, Alfred, <u>A Short History of Music</u>, 3rd ed. Hippocrene Books, 1987.
By one of the all-time leading musicologists, the original edition was published in 1917.

Einstein, Alfred, <u>Music in the Romantic Era</u>, New York: W.W. Norton, 1947.

Ewen, David, <u>David Ewen Introduces Modern Music</u>, 2nd ed. Philadelphia: Chilton, 1969.

Griffiths, Paul, <u>A Concise History of Western Music</u>. Cambridge University Press, 2006.
Packing two millennia of music history into a couple of hundred pages unavoidably omits centuries and many topics, but what Griffiths does cover is, as usual, well written, opinionated and enjoyable.

Heartz, Daniel, <u>Mozart, Haydn and Early Beethoven: 1781-1802</u>. New York: W.W. Norton, 2008.
Daniel Heartz's sequel to his 2003 book Music in European Capitals: The Galant Style, 1720-80. As a review states, "A vivid portrait of Mozart and Haydn's greatest achievements and young Beethoven's works under their influences.

Katz, Ruth, <u>A Language of its Own: Sense and Meaning in the Making of Western Art Music</u>. University of Chicago Press, 2010.

Lang, Paul Henry, <u>Music in Western Civilization</u>. New York: W.W. Norton, 1941 (republished 1997).
Another great book and one of the best-written works available. The book was never revised (evidence of its timelessness) and the 1100 pages remain as they were in 1941 – classic.

Machlis, J., <u>Introduction to Contemporary Music</u>, 2nd edition. New York: W.W. Norton, 1979.
A textbook style book that covers not only 20th-century music in detail but the Post-Romantic music leading up to it.

Rosen, Charles, The Classical Style: Haydn, Mozart, Beethoven, expanded edition. New York: W.W. Norton, 1997.
A very detailed and scholarly dissection by the noted pianist-author of the musical developments that led to the compositions of the great three composers and how they perfected the forms. Chock-full-of musical score excerpts to add flavor for the established musician. Mr. Rosen's writing style will draw you in.

Rosen, Charles, The Romantic Generation. Cambridge, MA: Harvard University Press, 1995.
The same plentitude of musical score excerpts appears in this work as well, and again, amateurs like myself need not be afraid.

Steen, Michael, The Lives and Times of the Great Composers. Oxford University Press, 2004.

Swafford, Jan, The Vintage Guide to Classical Music. Vintage, 1992.
This is such a good book and provides so much that I had to list it twice.

Taruskin, Richard, On Russian Music. Berkeley, CA: University of California Press, 2009.
If the title interests you; if not, probably too much detail

Taruskin, Richard, Oxford History of Western Music (5-volume set). Oxford University Press, 2009. Vol.1, "The Earliest Notations to the Sixteenth Century"; Vol.2, "The Seventeenth and Eighteenth Centuries"; Vol.3, "The Nineteenth Century"; Vol.4, "The Early Twentieth Century"; Vol.5, "The Late Twentieth Century".
Never dry and often opinionated, this massive exploration of music by the eminent musicologist from 'first notations' through the present, occupies five volumes and almost 4,000 pages. It can be had in paperback for under $150, or one can purchase any of the five volumes separately. Two of the five volumes cover the 20th-century, so it is exceptional in its coverage of 'modern' music.

Weiss, Piero; Taruskin, Richard, Music in the Western World: A History in Documents, 2nd ed. Belmont, CA: Schirmer Cengage Learning, 2008.
An excellent collection of primary sources from Ovid to Corigliano, with illuminating annotation by Professors Weiss and Taruskin.

Musicology and Music within a Social/Historical Context

Most of the works in this category are very detailed and often academic. They look at the history, business, and/or social forces behind music; at music beyond music. For the most part they provide 'a lot about a little', meaning they really drill down into specific times, composers, historical events, etc, or are presenting and supporting a thesis. Some can really bring composers to life by providing historical context and building a narrative around it.

Adorno, Theodor, <u>Essays on Music</u>. R. Leppart, ed., S. Gillespie, transl., UC Press, 2002.

Blanning, Tim, <u>The Triumph of Music</u>. Cambridge, MA: Belknap Harvard, 2008.
A well-known historian traces music's path and prominence through history, from court and church servants to today's rock stars.

Crocker, R.L., <u>A History of Musical Style</u>. New York: Dover Publications, 2011.

Kramer, Lawrence, <u>Why Classical Music Still Matters</u>. Berkeley, CA: University of California Press, 2007.
A very readable book that attempts to address its title. The reader must determine if Kramer is successful or not.

McCarthy Draper, Maureen, <u>The Nature of Music, Beauty, Sound, and Healing</u>. New York, NY: Riverhead Books (Penguin), 2001.

Lebrecht, Norman, <u>The Life and Death of Classical Music</u>. Anchor Books, 2008.
An at-times hilarious journey through the business behind Classical Music by a man who has focused his writings in this area.

Prendergast, M., <u>The Ambient Century</u>. New York: Bloomsbury, 2000.

Ross, Alex, <u>The Rest is Noise</u>. New York: Picador, 2007.
Contains excellent and well-written treatments of the Second Viennese School, Richard Strauss, Prokofiev, and Shostakovich, as well as the second half of the last century.

Ross, Alex, <u>Listen to This</u>. New York: Farrar, Strauss and Giroux, 2010.

Hamilton, Andy, <u>Aesthetics & Music</u>. London: Continuum Publishers, 2007.

Sachs, Harvey, <u>The Ninth: Beethoven and the World in 1824</u>. New York: Random House, 2010.

Composer Biographical

These works are arranged by composer, and usually cover their works while describing composers' lives. They provide 'a lot about a lot'. Of course there are dozens of excellent works dedicated to specific composers, but such a list is beyond the scope here.

Grove, George, <u>Beethoven and His Nine Symphonies</u>, 3rd ed. (1898). Dover Publications, 2012.
A timeless classic from the founding editor of the <u>Grove Dictionary of Music and Musicians</u>. It provides expert analysis interspersed with composer quotes and extracts from Beethoven's correspondence. One gets a full sense of Beethoven's thought process and circumstances surrounding each symphony.

Kramer, Jonathan, <u>Listen to the Music</u>. New York: Schirmer Books, 1988.
A collection of the author's program and concert notes, covering over 50 composers and a couple of hundred of their works. This book contains detailed information on the individual movements within given works.

Lampert, V., Somfai, L., Noble, J., White, E.W., Kemp, I., <u>The New Grove Modern Masters</u>. NY: WW Norton, 1984.
Concise biographies of Bartok, Stravinsky, and Hindemith detailing their important works and legacies

Morris, Edmund, <u>Beethoven: The Universal Composer</u>. New York: Harper Collins, 2005.

Robbins Landon, H.C., The Symphonies of Joseph Haydn (1955); Haydn: A Documentary Study (1981); Haydn: Chronicle and Works, 5 vols. (1976-80).
Three key works from the late and greatest Haydn scholar who was responsible more than anyone for the re-discovery of Haydn and established the chronology of the symphonies with his 1955 work.

Schonberg, Harold, <u>The Lives of the Great Composers</u>, 3rd edition. W.W. Norton, 1997.
A classic, updated to include Minimalism. One of the best and most comprehensive works covering the major composers from the Renaissance to 20th century. A 'must-have' providing a narrative of the select composers' lives, with notable works sprinkled in.

Solomon, Maynard, <u>Beethoven</u>. NY: Schirmer Trade Books, 2001

Tibbetts, John, <u>Schumann - A Chorus of Voices</u>. New York: Amadeus Press, 2010.

Volkov, Solomon, <u>Testamony: The Memoirs of Dmitri Shostakovich</u>. Transl. A.W. Bouis. New York: Harper and Row, 1979.

Works about Classical Music Forms and Genres

Hefling, Stephen, <u>19th Century Chamber Music</u>, 2nd edition. Routledge, 2003.

Berger, Melvin, <u>Guide to Chamber Music</u>. New York: Dodd, Mead & Co., 1985.

Berger, Melvin, <u>Classical Sonatas: Music for One or Two Instruments</u>. Anchor Books, 1990.

Keller, Hans, <u>The Great Haydn Quartets</u>. London: Oxford University Press, 1986.

Keller, James, <u>Chamber Music: A Listener's Guide</u>. London: Oxford University Press, 2010.
A comprehensive survey of chamber music that does not neglect the 20th-century, covering even Ruth Crawford Seeger. It includes obscure composers Joan Tower, Silvestre Revueltas, and Osvaldo Golijov, and even Fanny Mendelssohn and Clara Schumann. It considers chamber music of three or more performers so duo sonatas are not covered.

McCalla, James, <u>Twentieth Century Chamber Music</u>. Routledge, 2003.

Rognoni, Luigi, The Second Vienna School: <u>The Rise of Expressionism in the Music of Arnold Schoenberg, Alban Berg, and Anton von Webern</u>, transl. R. Mann. London: John Calder, 1977.
This is the most detailed study of the major works of Schoenberg, Berg, and Webern to appear in one volume. For those who are curious about twelve-tone music this work will provide greater understanding and possibly enjoyment of the "most significant music of the twentieth century."

Charles Rosen, <u>Sonata Forms</u>. NY, NY: WW Norton & Co, 1988.

Steinberg, Michael, <u>The Concerto</u>. London: Oxford University Press, 1998.

Steinberg, Michael, <u>The Symphony</u>. London: Oxford University Press, 1995.

Ulrich, Homer, <u>Chamber Music</u>, 2nd ed. New York: Columbia University Press, 1966.

Notes – Part 1

Preface
[1] see P.Goulding or T.Libbey, <u>NPR Guide to Building a Classical Music Library</u>; "makes little effort...happened as they did." R.Taruskin, vol.5, p.x; "program-note writing"   H.Schonberg, <u>The Lives of the Great Composers</u>, 3rd edition. NY: W.W. Norton, 1997, p.16.

Chapter 1
What is Classical Music?
R. Hemming, <u>Discovering Great Music</u> pp.3-4; For an excellent history of the evolution over at least the last five thousand years, see Chapter 1 (R. North) of <u>The Musical Companion</u> or <u>A Concise History of Western Music</u> by Paul Griffiths or <u>A Short History of Music</u> by Alfred Einstein

Music Before 1717 – the Renaissance
"the period when the values...", B. Tuchman, <u>The March of Folly</u>, p.52; "prevailing texture...", Burkholder, Grout, Palisca, p.300; "assumed unquestioned leadership...", P.H. Lang, p.176; ibid, p.193; "rippling passage work...", ibid, p.363; "desire to avoid mere repetition...", ibid, p.246; "The spirit of the Renaissance...", ibid, p.435; "the many colored richness...", Draper, p.96; "became the creator...", P.H. Lang, p.234; "are among music's...", D. Dubal, p.13; "incense-diffusing softness", P.H. Lang, p.234-36; "the culmination of...", ibid, pp.226, 230; "combination of Germanic earnestness...", ibid, p.230; "He cherished the great traditions...", ibid, p.231; "abstruse polyphonic designs", A. Ross, <u>Listen to This</u>, p.30; "they wanted a simple line...", H. Schonberg, p.26; "by providing a sense of...", P. Griffiths, pp. 45-47; "secular strains infiltrated...", A. Ross, <u>Listen to This</u>, p.28; "the knotty interweaving...", ibid; "clarity and balance...", P. Goulding, p.45; "In this time dissonances...", Weiss, Taruskin, p.95; "the first artist to revive...", P.H. Lang, p.339; "strict rules and ever-murmuring...", H. Schonberg, p.23; "highly sophisticated part-song...", Weiss, Taruskin, p.120; "natural prosody of the words.", A. Copland, p.37; "with their variety of mood...", H. Schonberg, p.31; "a repertoire of textures...", ibid, p.32; "but Monteverdi's huge contribution...", Morin, p.595; "Monteverdi's famous opera *Orfeo*...", H. Schonberg, p.26.

The Baroque
"Music prior to this arbitrary...", Taruskin, v.2, p.216; "outstanding late practitioners...", ibid, p.218); In counterpoint there is often..., see detailed discussion in Chapter 3; A critical development that began..., P. Griffiths, pp.92-3; "The system of major-minor harmony,...", ibid, p.111; "At a time when many composers...", Taruskin, v.2, p.225; "it seems likely that...", Copland, p.66; "backup music designed to give...", P. Goulding, p.443; however, less than ten years later..., P. Griffiths, p.123; In the last decade of his life..., Weiss, Taruskin, p.217; "was notoriously criticized...", *ibid*.

Classical Period
"like the same number of windows...", T. Smith, NPR, p.2; "well contained within the form.", J. Machlis, p.10; "proceeding from assertive thematic ideas...", A.

Ross, Listen to This, p.46; "unified representation of a...", C. Rosen, The Romantic Generation, p.132; Classical composers did not care for..., H. Schonberg, p.81; "otherwise intangible emotions...", quote by E.Dusinberre of the Takacs String Quartet; "remnants of Barbarism and bad taste.", M. Solomon, p.386. For a good discussion of tonality and equal temperament in the transition from High Baroque to Classical period, see C. Rosen, The Classical Style, pp.23-29; "essentially accessible to anyone...", T. Smith, NPR, p.2; "from the scintillating gracefulness...", P.H. Lang, p.719; "Solomon feels the period...", M. Solomon, p.386; "deification of man's mental life...", P.H. Lang, p.731; "The gradual reconquest...", C. Rosen, The Classical Style, p.135; "The greatest contribution...", ibid, p.44; But it took Haydn and Mozart..., ibid, p.45; At its worst, the style *gallant*..., H. Sachs, The Ninth, p.48; "created a style in which...", C. Rosen, The Classical Style, p.44.

Romantic Period
"Its chief characteristics...", T. Blanning, p.98; "The sacralization of music...", *ibid*, p.104; Whereas, with the Classical period composer...indifferent to public acclaim. Weiss, Taruskin, p.287; "could express their...into artistic expression.", H. Sachs, p.77; "The essence of Romanticism is...", H. Schonberg, p.142; "the incessant absorption of new material...", A. Einstein, A Short History of Music, p.188; Composers were drawn to..., H. Schonberg, p.142; Composers of the Classical period...and rebels against tradition., J. Machlis, p.6; "the broad middle class public...", Weiss, Taruskin, p.296; "reactions against French culture's...", H.Sachs, p.71; "the first of the true Romantics.", H. Schonberg, p.147; The layout of his piano music...more glitter than substance., *ibid*, p.149; "introduced a harmonic vocabulary...", *ibid*, p.145; "the entire harmonic vocabulary...", *ibid*, p.142; "unusual tonal combinations...", *ibid*, p.142; Mendelssohn, on the other hand,...first time in 1829. P. Griffiths, p.183; "more interested in what...", Musical Companion, p.47; "were celebrities idolized...", J. Kramer, p.632; The symphonies of Mahler...first half of the 20th century. *ibid*, p.363.

20th Century
Harsh, percussive tonal effects..., Copland, p.69; Whereas Bach and Mozart...rarely without it. Draper, p.49; The early Modernist period...as a mark of vitality. R. Taruskin, v.4, p.1; "remains the heart of...", L. Kramer, pp.69-70; "that the major and minor key...", D. Dubal, p.503; The revolutionary Impressionist sounds...in the 20th century. H. Schonberg, pp. 454-55; "dared to make his ear...", Copland, p.59; "orchestration shimmers with...", J. Machlis, pp.91,95; "the last stylistic synthesis of the century" and "the clear articulation...or rustling of leaves.", P.H. Lang, p.1018; "The seemingly apocalyptic...of security and norms." McCalla, p.xv; Indeed, the writing of...of the Romantic composers. H. Schonberg, p.589; "a principal hostility to..." L. Kramer, p.69; "its abstraction and refinement of thought", J. Machlis, p.37; "compositional problems rather than...personal feelings." *ibid*, p.39; "desire...for condensation of style...and transparency of texture." *ibid*; "composers turned away from...Wagnerian histrionics." *ibid*, p.153; "for the human resources...", S. Finkelstein, liner notes for Shostakovich *Symphonies No. 1&5*, Koussevitzky, Omega Classics, 2000; "greater contrapuntal complexity..." MC, p.340; "great structure assembled..." H. Schonberg, p.465; "a revolutionary break...", J. Kramer, p.112; "a direct outgrowth of...", McCalla, p.xv; "more rigorously athematic...", A. Copland, p.61; "the reestablishment of traditionalism...", McCalla, p.xv; "mind-bending harmonies...", A. Ross, The Rest is Noise, p.386; "an art of the dead...", A. Ross, Listen to This, p.XVI; "...the serious artist should stop...", *ibid*, p.42; "the modernist strain in...", A. Ross, Listen to This, p.67;

Sentiment is "the essential...of romantic music.", A. Einstein, <u>A Short History of Music</u>, p.249; "Beethovenian urge to speak to all...", P. Griffiths, p.260; "music was becoming simpler...", *ibid*, p.265; "to fit intellectual concepts." Draper, p.49; Boulez felt that musical progress..."who had carried forward...progress...before (World War II)." P. Griffiths, p.270; Indeed, the post-World War II..."logic and musical purity." H. Schonberg, p.595; "confidence in subjectivity", P. Griffiths, p.247; "something in the *Zeitgeist*...scientific principles", H. Schonberg, p.594; "in the 1930s/40s...", A. Ross, <u>Listen to This</u>, p.386; "music's inclination to settle...", P. Griffiths, p.271; "By the middle of...sounding at once.", J. Swafford, p.30; "dissonance, density,...", A. Ross, <u>Listen to This</u>, p.387.

Chapter 2

"these composers have something to say...", R. Hemming, p.3 ; "Classical music asks its listeners...", L. Kramer, p.87; "How much does the (composer) impose...", MC, p.715; "The gulf which we have built...", N. Reich in <u>Robert Schumann</u>, p.179; "distances us from the distracting immediacy of everyday life.", L. Kramer, pp.13-14; although not all musicologists agree that classical does relax us, L. Kramer, p.34; "All music trains the ear to hear it properly, but classical music...wants to be explored, not just heard.", L. Kramer, p.11; "with the music's capacity to absorb us." *ibid,* p.11; "by subtracting what is irrelevant...of sound that reaches our ears." *ibid*; "The ear should be the final arbiter in all musical compositions.", letter to editor, *Classic FM*, August 10, 2010; "...classical music demands a bit more...worth the bother." L. Kramer, p.32; "by subtracting what is irrelevant...reaches our ears", *ibid*, p.11; "The now in which we hear it...when the piece was composed." P. Griffiths, p.7; "A composition is...an organism...seen in a different light by various interpreters." Copland, p.215; "as refracted by the personality...", *ibid*, p.215; "Classical performances...story without rewriting it", L. Kramer, p.41; "With orchestral or chamber music,...suffused by the sound", *ibid*, p.141; "Something distinctive and particular...music to make it live", *ibid*, p.25; "listener hears only unrepeated...musical events", Burkholder, *et al.*, p.920.

The Accessibility of Music

"And the listener had to flip sides..., A. Rich in A. Copland, p.xii; "every piece of music...", *ibid*, p.xv; "Harmony is...brought...", L. Kramer, p.44; "generally has more immediate appeal...", A. Copland, p.89; "the contrasts in Beethoven's music...", Draper, p.91; "moves by reason of separate..." A. Copland, p.86; "to pander to audiences who liked...", T. Blanning, p.60; "you pick up new clues...", Draper, p.67; "

Absolute, Impressionist, and Programmatic Music

'Absolute' music can be defined..., <u>The Musical Companion</u>, p.235; "speaks solely a tongue...", *ibid*, p.246; "depend not one whit...extra-musical implications." M. Bookspan, p.73; However, programmatic music...attempting to portray. <u>The Musical Companion</u>, p.109; "express only mood...purely musical terms." H. Schonberg, p.158; "the image of the desired ideal", A. Einstein, <u>Essays on Music</u>, Faber and Faber, 1958, p.3; "that art must always be...", *ibid*.

Availability of Recordings

Norman Lebrecht postulates..., N. Lebrecht, <u>The Life and Death of Classical Music</u>. NY, NY: Anchor Books, 2007.

Introduction to Part 1
"the instrument par excellence...", L. Kramer, Why Classical Music Still Matters. Berkeley, CA: University of CA press, 2007, p.135; "virtuosity in itself...", The Musical Companion, p.715; "and you are playing romantically,", Taruskin, v.4, p.475.

Chapter 3
"embodied calm, assured,...human clarity", P.H. Lang, p.321; "discovered the great possibilities...of musical instruments", ibid, p.324; "A Baroque composition reveals...shape of its melody", C. Rosen, The Classical Style, p.76.

Polyphony, Counterpoint and Fugue
"The best homophony still...in each part", J. Swafford, p.93; "The purpose of Baroque counterpoint...", C. Rosen, The Romantic Generation, p.5; Counterpoint "exalts...values of music.", J. Machlis, p.37; "...challenges the creative imagination", ibid; "Bach's fugue is the...", A. Einstein, A Short History of Music, p.137; "Every instrument that was capable...", ibid; "is a brilliant summation...", M. Hoffman, The NPR Classical Music Companion. NY: Houghton Mifflin, 1997; "fugues differ from other...", H. Ulrich, p.170; "one voice and now...", C. Rosen, The Romantic Generation, p.355; "a series of episodes...", A. Copland, p.137; "crystallization of imitative polyphony...", The Musical Companion, p.106; "Fugue is...geometrical in the...", D. Barenboim, Music Quickens Time. London: Verso Books, 2008, p.25; "In fugal writing...(Bach's) works...", H. Ulrich, p.101.

Johann Sebastian Bach
"not only attained an unsurpassed...", T. Dickey in All Music Guide, p.1540; "a brilliant work containing...", T. Smith, p.3; "spoke frankly of having to...", J.R. Gaines, An Evening In the Palace of Reason, p.167; "Bach perceived possibilities...", A. Morin, p.30; "unparalleled mastery of craft...", McCarthy Draper, p.80; "it is as though the 17th century...", italics added by the author, A. Einstein, A Short History of Music, p.136; "thought of himself as a...", A. Morin, p.21; "mastered with mathematical precision...", Rough Guide, p.18; As has been pointed out, A. Morin, p.33; "require the singing and sensitive...", E. Wen, liner notes for A. Schiff The Well-tempered Clavier, Book 2, Decca; "Bach's genius to evoke timeless...any specific instrumental environment." M. Perahia, liner notes for M. Perahia Bach Goldberg Variations, Sony, 2000; Hans von Bülow pointed out that..., Martin Meyer, liner notes for Beethoven Cello Sonatas, Schiff/Perenyi, ECM, 2004; Bach transends..."to attain the zenith of his art.", A. Morin, p.36; "a journey of extraordinary transformations...", Rough Guide, p.18; Each is an...imagination and power. S. Ledbetter, liner notes for Bach English Suites, Perahia, Sony, 1999; "a collection of stylized dances...virtuosity of the performer...", ibid; "possesses characteristics consistent...national identity", 1001 Classical Recordings You Must Hear Hear Before You Die, M. Rye, ed., Universe, 2008, p.110; "each is an extraordinary example...", Crocker, p.330; "the supreme specimens of their kind...", A. Einstein, Essays, p.42; "one encounters a breadth of imagination...", H. Ulrich, p.102; "with due respect...that after...", E. Wen, liner notes for A. Schiff The Well-tempered Clavier, Book 2, Decca; "sounds much more effective...", A. Morin, p.35; "wonderfully serene harmonic progressions." P. Griffiths, p.116; "in different tempi and...the material is more appropriate." E. Wen, liner notes; "contain the most lyrical effusion...smallest space", Crocker, p.332; "underlying, almost pervasive spirit...prevailing joy", J. Siepmann; "incredibly complicated networks of parts...", Draper, p.38; "Certainly the contrapuntal technique...short of virtuosic", E. Wen,

liner notes; "with their ultimate *raison d'etre*...", 1001 Classical Recordings..., p.97; "all the harmony...up to four voices...", L. Kramer, p.207; Pablo Casals..., N. Lebrecht, "The Life and death of classical music", NewYork: Anchor Books, 2007, p. 172; "trying to recreate the evocative melodies...", N. Clein in *Grammophone*, Aug 2010; "spacious arpeggios (and) runs...", L. Kramer, p.26; "These are the most intricate...", A. Morin, p.29; "finest single movement...", T. Potter, liner notes to *Bach Sonatas & Partitas*, Itzhak Perlman, EMI, 2005; "a quarter-hour-long soliloquy...", A. Ross, Listen to This, p.30; "a kind of death dance...", Draper, p.82;"harmonic richness and contrapuntal intimacy...", Z. Minderovic, All Music Guide, p.1542; "outstanding for their complexity,..." 1001 Classical Recordings..., p.98; "humble, unglamorous, workaday. He remained for life in the musical environment to which he had been born." Taruskin, Oxford History..., v.2, p.218.

Domenico Scarlatti
"the first composer with a fine ear...", C. Rosen, The Classical Style, p.79; "an attempt to make a real...", *ibid*, p.43; "reveal a consistent step...", H. Ulrich, p.118.

George Friedrich Handel
"Much of the expressive force of...", C. Rosen, The Romantic Generation, p.27; "The nobility of Corelli's ideals...", H. Ulrich, p.94. "was the quintessential musical polyglot." Taruskin, Oxford History..., v.2, p.222; "Handel's stays in Hamburg,... grow continuously in breadth and freedom." A. Einstein, A Short History of Music, p.138; "how a musician could become rich...", T. Blanning, The Triumph of Music. Cambridge, MA: Belknap Press/Harvard, 2008, p.24; "might serve as a...", (Einstein, Essays,p44); "demanded a singing style...", H. Schonberg, The Great Pianists, Simon & Schuster, 1987, p19; "His music, characteristic of the French Baroque... emphasizing melody with accompaniment." Morin,p242.

Couperin and Rameau
"in which the heroic dimensions...", Weiss, Taruskin, p.200; "Rameau was the supreme composer... looking forward to Romanticism and Impressionism." Dubal, p.63.

Chapter 4
Mozart, Haydn, and Beethoven
"no radical movement away from...", Rosen, The Classical Style, p.380; "By the late 1780s there was...", *ibid*, p.xv; "were considered a coherent group...", *ibid*, p.xvi; "is a reflection of a mind...", Ulrich, p.201-2; "When Beethoven left Bonn... the great master who was past sixty." C. Rosen, The Classical Style, p.19; "was increasingly seen as the...", R. Wigmore, "The Poor Man's Mozart?", *Grammophone*, June 2009; "Haydn scholar Richard Wigmore... all composers of instrumental music.", *ibid*; "Maybe part of the relative neglect... with his gift for the theatrical.", C. Hogwood, interview in *Grammophone*, May 2009; "he brought to perfection those already in existence.", J. Nicholas, The Great Composers. London: Quercus, 2007, p.40; "Mozart "moved beyond Haydn...deep into the spirit realm.", Wigmore, *Grammophone*, June 2009; "Haydn's music manipulates and thwarts... to the full expressive range of his music.", *ibid*; "Haydn allows his music... complete melodies of Mozart", Rosen, The Classical Style, p.394; "The insistent repetition of smaller units...", *ibid*, p.250, parentheses are Rosen's; "Haydn is interested in the directional power...", *ibid*, p.129; "The opening of a work by Mozart... movement away from the

tonic.", *ibid*, p.186; "mastery of subtle and complex...", Wigmore, *Grammophone*, June 2009; "Haydn was the most playful... that no other composer enjoyed." Rosen, The Classical Style, p.129; "have relatively little of...", Wigmore, *Grammophone*, June 2009; "art...leads through opera" and opera "became...", Lang, p.646; "No composer has been more innovative...", Rosen, The Classical Style, p.508; "each major work ventures into...", Draper, pp.76-77; "by infusing them with new force...", Berger, p.22; "Beethoven was in a position to select...", Crocker, p.415; "Beethoven never relinquished his reliance... boundaries and maximizing their coherence." Solomon, p.385; "The mature Beethoven underwent the influence...", A. Copland, p.213; "The whole immense wealth of (the 18th) century...", Lang, p.752; "established the model of the composer as the angry, unhappy, original, uncompromising genius...", Blanning, p.99; "he has for years resided in Vienna in open hostility...", Weiss, Taruskin, p.280; While Beethoven's *Fourth* and *Fifth* concertos... provides the most listening pleasure. Goulding, p.125; "Mozart lacked the temperament...", D. Heartz, Mozart, Haydn and Early Beethoven, p.4; "still worked within the... the greatest goal of a musician." Sachs, p.31; "and as such superior in his own mind... to become a legend in his own time." Blanning, p.34; "we've come to expect (an) artist...", Draper, p.88; His predecessors, including Haydn... rather, they supplied a commodity. Schonberg, p.111; "certainly more stable than the mercurial,...", Wigmore, *Grammophone*, June 2009.

The Classical Style and Sonata Form
"evolved through the combined experience...", Copland, p.92; "the symmetrical resolution of opposing...", Rosen, The Classical Style, p.83; "immeasurably increased the power of dissonance,...", ibid, p.120; "marked music's shift from church to... did not want to think." H. Schonberg, The Great Pianists, p.19; "The whole tendency of the classical style... ornamentation of the Rococo" Rosen, The Classical Style, p.101; "the rising aspirations of the commercial class...", Rosen, The Classical Style, p.333.

Sonatas and Sonata Form
"applied in a loose manner to individual...", Libbey, p.794; "a sonata was any organized series...", Rosen, The Classical Style, p.53; "'Sonata form' is not a definite form...", Rosen, The Classical Style, p.30; "ability to present and develop...", T. Blanning, The Pursuit of Glory, p.483; "The classical style appears inevitable...", C. Rosen, The Classical Style, p.57; "The most common Baroque form is...", *ibid*, p.61; "the emotional force of the classical style...", *ibid*, The Classical Style, p.74; "The dramatic character of...", *ibid*, p.70; "brought instrumental music to full maturity...", Swafford, p.169; "depends upon the unification...", Short History of Music, p.150; "a sophisticated large-scale structure...", Swafford, p.168; "in such a way as to create...", Machlis, p.617; The "opposed affects" made possible... of longing and anger, of pleasure and pain." M. M. Solomon, Mozart: A Life. Harper Perennial, 2005; "The use of repeats is transformed...", Rosen, The Classical Style, p.395; "a special division reserved for the extension...", Copland, p.151; "The quality of the development is the test...", H. Schonberg, p.93; The contrast "sets off and...", Machlis, p.14; "the principle of thematic development... harmonic surprises for the development." Rosen, The Classical Style, p.124; "deconstructed and combined...", J. Martineau, The Elements of Music, NY: Walker & Co., 2008; "a recapitulation that begins in...", Rosen, The Romantic Generation, p.341; "The tone is often courtly,... made his "jokey and/or folksy." Swafford, p.171; Beethoven did not simply replace... B-varied scherzo', Musical Companion, p.86-7.

Other Forms
"the middle section represents a step...", L. Kramer, p.56; "the most 'open' of musical procedures...", Lang, p.396; "the game is to get maximum...", Swafford, p.171; "Anchored in...the theme,...", Draper, p.42; "plain and uncompromising theme...", Swafford, p.171; "...like a series of short excursions...", Draper, p.40; Cyclical form was very attractive... give it more personal urgency." Rosen, <u>The Romantic Generation</u>, p.89.

Chapter 5
"Even more so than the string quartet,...", C. Rosen, <u>Beethoven Piano Sonatas: A Short Companion</u>. Yale University Press, 2001, p.4; "showed still less consideration...", *ibid*, p.5; "Beethoven's music...demands more...", *ibid*, p.xii; "the way for the professional concert pianist...", *ibid*, p.4.

Mozart
"This most spontaneous of melodists...," <u>Short History of Music</u>, p.165; "they strongly prefigure Beethoven's famous 'C minor mood'." W. Kinderman, liner notes for M. Uchida, "Mozart Complete Piano Sonatas, Philips, 1990; "strength and grace...in the most polished and ingenious manner...", <u>Short History of Music</u>, p.176; "propelled the pianist to the front rank of instrumentalists." Blanning, p.177.

Haydn
"sanest and most spontaneous of...", Short History of Music, p.158; "he was thrown upon his own resources (to) develop...", Ulrich, p.158; "was the synthesis of all this into...", Lang, p.632; "strength and serious purpose (but with)...melodic style." <u>Short History of Music</u>, p.158-59; "ideal balance of homophony...than rhythmic and motivic." Lang, p.625; He "seldom repeated himself...characteristic musical ideas." Ulrich, p.161; "new world of art...to its supreme flowering." Lang, p.625; "a most personal expression...wit, humor, joy, and sorrow." *ibid*; "a miracle of wit, lyricism and beautiful playing," Morin, p.434.

Beethoven
"upon himself as...an artist." Schonberg, p.111; "he was a creator,...ideas and originality." *ibid*, p.112; Beethoven's "is the most powerful...by one composer." *ibid*, p.123; "always turned toward...of the (piano) itself." Crocker, p.447; "the piano went from gently...modern instrument." H. Goodall, *Classic FM*, Aug, 2010; "consciously made (his piano sonatas) so...mastered Haydn and Mozart." Einstein, <u>The Romantic Generation</u>, p.38; "Beethoven planted bombs under their seats." Schonberg, p.113; "a fiction for the purposes of analysis;" Rosen, <u>The Classical Style</u>, p.389; "limited themselves to...levels of experience." Solomon, <u>Beethoven</u>, p.251; "Beethoven's turn to compositions of...currents of contemporary history." *ibid*, p.252-53; "they served him only as...more acute approach." Martin Meyer (transl. R. Evidon), "A Dialogue through all the Tones, Beethoven as Chamber Musician", liner notes to *Beethoven, Complete Music for Piano and Violincello*, Schiff and Perenyi, ECM, 2004; "the simplest, most...at the very opening." Rosen, <u>The Classical Style</u>, p.405; "extended Haydn's technique to...language without violating its spirit." *ibid*, pp.407&400; "The extent to which Beethoven manipulated...revive many musical procedures" *ibid*, pp.449&458; "Probably only Mozart and Schubert...all over the world." Sachs, p.46; "the profundity and largeness of...to music." Ulrich, p.249; "struggle is sublimated

into ecstasy...after and discovered;" Solomon, p.385; "a new vehicle for...thoughts." *ibid*, p.395; "late style into its sources...the history of music." Solomon, p.387; The Beethoven of the late period...the contemporary musical language." Rosen, The Classical Style, p.449; "were increasingly instilled with...with infinite inventiveness." Solomon, p.254; "a new synthesis of Classicism...new century." Lang, p.752; "earlier piano sonatas were...expression and structural cogency." Plantinga, p.92; "this eerie, obsessive/compulsive...", P. Clark, "Breaking the Mold," *Classical FM*, Aug 2010; "a huge march in an atmosphere of catastrophe." Berger, Classical Sonatas, p.38; "represent a growth in artistic...", Rosen, The Classical Style, p.399; "twin peaks in the middle-period range...exults in the major key...pursues its minor-key drama to the bitter end." D. Matthews, liner notes for *Beethoven: Sonaten*, Gilels, DG, 1972/73/74; "potentialities of both instrument...", Solomon, p.255; "finally arrived at a conception...formulated as one." Rosen, The Classical Style, p.399; "slow movements are organically connected with the finales." Solomon, p.256; "begins in ominous mystery" J. Henken, LAPhil.org; "the tragic passion is rushing...in a nihilistic frenzy." Morris, p.144; "The first movement of the *Waldstein*...other work of Beethoven." Rosen, The Classical Style, p.396; "often marked by a reflective lyricism,...", P. Petazzi, transl. K. Chalmers, R. Osborne, liner notes for *Beethoven: Die spaeten Klaviersonaten*, Pollini, DG, 1977; "bursts with youthful,...of desolate longing," Morris, p.137; "childlike purity of this melody,..." W. Kempff, liner notes *Beethoven: The Late Piano Sonatas*, Kempff, DG, 1965; "an unreserved lyricism...the tender refrain." Petazzi; "probes deep inside the world...", H. Fladt (transl. S. Spencer), liner notes for *Beethoven: Piano Sonata Nos.27-31*, Gilels, DG, 1972/75/86; "the gates leading to the world...", W. Kempff, liner notes for W. Kempff, "Beethoven, The Late Piano Sonatas, DG, 1965; "The basic chromaticism of the minor...diatonic major." Rosen, Beethoven's Piano Sonatas, p.11; "adherence to and a rebellious...Classical style," Solomon, p.418; "highly concentrated exploration of...textures." *ibid*, p.386; "Variation form joins fugue...", *ibid*, p.395; "produced a synthesis of fugue...", Rosen, The Classical Style, p.502; "form one of the pillars...last years." Solomon, p.391; "The *Hammerklavier* is not typical...of his last period." Rosen, The Classical Style, p.434; "a new and original work of uncompromising greatness." *ibid;* "a magnification of scale and an intensification of contrast." Solomon, p.418; "full-blooded, quasi-orchestral...finest modern instruments." W. Kempff, liner notes for W. Kempff, "Beethoven, The Late Piano Sonatas, DG, 1965; "passages of such contrapuntal density...the late years of Liszt." Morris, p.196; "a demonstration of power..." it marked the "emancipation of piano music...", Rosen, The Classical Style, p.404; "The *Hammerklavier* is less the...act of Titanic rage." R. Osborne, liner notes, 1977; "a new vehicle for his most imaginative musical thoughts." Solomon, p.395; "giving new vitality to old contrapuntal forms" Rosen, The Classical Style, p.502; "the integration of unity and variety,...", L. Kramer, p.112; "is unequalled in the entire...Chopin, Brahms." W. Kempff, liner notes, 1965; "massive fugue created in wrath..." *ibid;* "arena for confrontation,...unrelenting conflict." H. Fladt (transl. M. Whittall), liner notes for Beethoven *Hammerklavier Sonate*, Gilels, DG, 1983; "with a variety of rigorous...improvisatory tone." Solomon, p.395; "the recurrence of alternating...of motivic forms." Rosen, The Classical Style, p.498; "The vision is particularly elusive...particularly sublime." G. Larner, liner notes for *Stephen Hough in Recital* Hyperion, 2009; "arena in which a life and struggle is to take place,...from the gloom...from this world to the next." W. Kempff, liner notes, 1965; "public taste was for shorter, less-demanding fare." M.Donat, "A Fragment, a Fantasy and Some Riddles", in liner notes for *Schubert Piano Sonatas D.840/894*, Uchida, Philips, 1997; "nothing more than ideas...lyrical moments." Einstein, The Romantic Generation, p.70; "often deliberately superficial...variations" Solomon, p.130; "developing the implications of the...four-movement cycles." *ibid*, p.129; "real crown of his contribution...voices, registers, and rhythms." M. Meyer, Schiff/Perenyi liner notes, 2004; "at once a stupendous practical joke"...while "...and mastery of form." A. Morin, p.122; "above all a discovery...musical elements." Rosen, The Classical Style, p.445.

Schubert
"rested his case for Schubert's...sonatas." L. Kramer, p.111; "to the fact that Schubert...figures of music..." Schonberg, p.125; "in part the most significant...post-classical composer." Rosen, The Classical Style, p.516; "moves with great ease...held it together." *ibid*, p.520; "Schubert is extremely direct...it's very immediate." P. Boulez, interview to B. Finane, *Listen*, Summer 2010, p.40; "is amazing how consistently Schubert... contemporary (Beethoven)." Schonberg, p.131-2; "basic ideas are either...rarely germinal motives." Abraham, p.625; "a marvelous flow of melody" plus... "handling of tonality, full...force of sustained lyricism." Ulrich, p.281; "stand on the same exalted...sonatas of Beethoven." Libbey, p.745; "Each movement is based somewhat...set of variations." Rosen, The Romantic Generation, p.580; "less difficult but brilliant pieces in a lighter style." M. Donat, "Free From Beethoven's Shadow", liner notes for *Schubert Piano Sonatas D.958/959*, Philips, 1997; "bleak and austere work...limitations of the piano," M. Donat, liner notes for *Schubert Piano Sonatas D.850/784*, Uchida, Philips, 2000; "show an almost total disregard for...are absent." B. Johnston in All Music Guide, p.1201; "is the most brilliant and extrovert...extremely energetic." *ibid*; "preoccupation with dark self-knowledge" L. Kramer, p.60; "By 1800 music for piano was public..." Rosen, The Romantic Generation, p.363;

Chapter 6
The Birth of Romanticism
"a symbol of greatness, heroism and genius for generations to come." Sachs, p.167; "sets in motion the lever of fear,...", *ibid*; "overflows from the boiling cauldron...", Lang, p.752; "one of the turning points...to the end of High Classicism", Morris, p.181; "The Romanticists emphasized the individual...", *ibid*, p.1023; "gradual unfolding and illumination of reality." Rosen, The Romantic Generation, p.194; "represents sentiment only ambiguously...", *ibid*, p.132; "looked to Beethoven as they formed...", *ibid*; "he dared to breach the classical rules...", Steen, p.305; "as the highest expression of subjective innerness." Rognoni, p.xv; "their first thoughts tended to be their best ones...", Crocker, p.427; "All that is most interesting in the next generation...", Rosen, The Classical Style, p.379; "watershed between the century of musical craftsmanship...", Rognoni, p.xv; "Romantic style did not come from Beethoven...", Rosen, The Classical Style, p.385; Charles Rosen sums up this widespread...., Rosen, The Romantic Generation, p.352; "the audible experience of fugue...", *ibid*, p.354; "Perhaps nothing characterizes a style better...", *ibid*, p.457; "the delight in sound...", *ibid*, p.40; Revolution and other subsequent ideological movements..., Katz, p.1; "boundless idealism and exaltation...", Swafford, pp.344-45; "taste for imagining oneself in strange lands...", Steen, p.305; "surrendered him to the Philistines...", Einstein, The Romantic Generation, p.46; "demanded something else of music; they demanded...", *ibid*, p.44; "highly colored historical novels...", Dubal, p.148; "the old aesthetic of the hierarchy of genres," and "had already shaken it to its foundations." Rosen, The Romantic Generation, p.699; "understood its capricious imagination...", *ibid*, p.706; "The fundamental task and achievement...", *ibid*, p.699; "tone color was (only) applied...", *ibid*, p.39;

"explore new types of color...", Dubal, p.148; "the first composer with an eye...", Einstein, The Romantic Generation, p.56; "breathed a mysterious, supernatural,...", Dubal, p.148; "towards extreme intimacy and absorption,...", Einstein, The Romantic Generation, p.50; "The sonata was as archaic...", Rosen, The Classical Style, p.32; "offered themselves as real,...", L. Kramer, p.145; "to spread out the unlimited possibilities...", ibid, p.146; "the lyrical expression of Nature...", Rosen, The Romantic Generation, p.124-25; "condemned to be a missing link...", Morin, p.459; "more impressive than profound...", ibid.

The Early Romantics
Robert Schumann
"the origin of all that is poetic for his music." J. Demus in J. Tibbetts, p.161; "to yoke together musical ideas...", Rosen, The Romantic Generation, p.673; "He constantly swayed between elation...", The Gift of Music: Great Composers and their Influence. J.S. Smith and B. Carlson, p.106; "give a clue to the mood,...", Schonberg, p.179; "Arguably, none investigated the Romantic's obsession...", gramophone.net, June 2010; Schumann "achieved the most powerful...", Rosen, The Romantic Generation, p.648; "striking, dramatic and powerful works,..." from which springs an "inspired flow of melody...", The Musical Companion, p.612; Schumann's piano music is autobiographical... C. Floros (transl. R. Evidon), liner notes for Schumann: Davidsbündlertänze/ Concert sans orchestra, Pollini, DG, 2001; "between profound seriousness and pointed...", Short History of Music, p.200; "The great art of the Romantic generation...", Rosen, The Romantic Generation, p.298; "The moods and forms they encompass are myriad,...", gramophone.net, 6/2010; "loosely knit structures...many small cameos...welding them all together...", ibid; "the technique of creating a cycle of 'fragments'." Rosen, The Romantic Generation, p.58; "his ability to make a unity...", ibid, p.673; "As if there were nothing higher...service of poetical expression." Einstein, The Romantic Generation, p.52; "in his music technique is the servant...", Short History of Music, p.200; "his melodic genius lay in...", Rosen, The Romantic Generation, p.703; "uses a lot of baroquish motor rhythms...", J. Tibbetts, p.168; "it is more through the fear of being...", A. Schiff in ibid, p.165; "To wander is the Romantic tradition; one yields to it...seamless and cohesive whole." 1001 Classical Recordings, p.243; "was freighted from the beginning...", Taruskin, v.3, p.309; "neither starts from a point of stability...", Rosen, The Classical Style, p.514; "with a sweep and energy...", Rosen, The Romantic Generation, p.100; "are often nothing more than a...musical seed." ibid, p.71; "spiritual diaries as well as music." Schonberg, p.169; Although Schumann seems to compose...but especially Bach. S. Isserlis in Grammophone, 9/2010; "established an entire aesthetic..." Schonberg, p.169; "apprentice work, his graduation piece,...", Rosen, in J. Tibbetts, p.163; "The succession of short pieces corresponds...", L. Gerber, liner notes for Schumann: Symphonic Etudes / Papillons, Perahia, CBS, 1977; "the suggestion of airiness and flight is clearly borne out by the music." B. Johnson at allmusic.com; "is the subtlest, most mysterious,...", Rosen, The Classical Style, p.223; "unimaginative bourgeois...and pretentiousness in music." Schonberg, p.177; "the fashionable mass producers of...", Weiss and Taruskin, p.305; "absolute nonsense. It's not interesting...of music." V. Feltsman in J. Tibbetts, p.193; "very dangerous to play in public; I think...artists." J. Tibbetts, supplemental CD; "juxtaposition of rhythms that are not...", ibid; "was the extrovert, violent...", Rosen, The Romantic Generation, p.98; "steeped himself in the tales of E.T.A. Hoffmann,...", A. Ross, Listen to This, p.297; "a whiff of brimstone hovering...", J. Tibbetts, supplementatl CD; "all week at the piano...all at once." R. Brautigam in J. Tibbetts, p.204; "As a whole, the Novelletten are extremely busy,...", ibid, p.203; "These are not woodland depictions without

complications." C. Eschenbach in *ibid*, p.213; "harmless urban fictions of country life." Rosen, The Romantic Generation, p.221; "is a very advanced, *avant-garde*...", C. Eschenbach in J. Tibbetts, p.213; "had the most trouble with this piece...", P. Frankl in *ibid*, p.358; "fragile music...best...to play it alone without an audience...", R. Brautigam in *ibid*, p.359; "to endow the music with...", Rosen, The Romantic Generation, p.677.

Chopin

"combination of melodic and harmonic...", H. Schonberg, p.194; "link poetically expressive melody...", J. Reel in All Music Guide, p.281; "Chopin's music is largely derived from...", Rosen, The Romantic Generation, p.285; "two voices playing the same melody...", *ibid*, p.349; "the supremacy of the Italian-style melody...", *ibid*, p.350; "unique among instrumental composers...", *ibid*, p.328; "Chopin has transferred Italian operatic...out of one." *ibid*, p.354; "Mendelssohn complained that you couldn't tell...", Swafford, p.28; "music was more influenced by Classical...", Jessica Duchen, *BBC Magazine*, Feb 2010; "Beethoven's thunder appealed to Chopin far less...", J. Distler, *Listen*, Summer 2010, p.50; "the expression at once of the soul...", Short History of Music, p.241; "most original in his use of...He was both the "most conservative..." Rosen, The Romantic Generation, p.471; No other music of his time...with such complex art." *ibid*, p.341; "magnified aura of brilliance,...", *ibid*, p.335; "was devoted to the service of the most...", Short History of Music, p.241; If the time 'stolen' is not quickly...for good." The Musical Companion, pp.59-60; "The true musician...takes something from time...", *ibid*, p.715; "scatter like pinpoints of flame." Schoenberg, p.193; "pure virtuosity with an aristocratic and poetic kind", *ibid*, p.194; "made possible the kind of experimentation....", Rosen, The Romantic Generation, p.399; "within his self-imposed limitation he was perfection itself," Schonberg, p.196; "An aura of mystery and magic surrounded...cast a spell on his listeners." Weiss/Taruskin, p.313; "The fusion of narrative and lyric in the Ballades...", Rosen, The Romantic Generation, p.322; although Charles Rosen finds this highly doubtful. *ibid*, p.322; On the other hand, the *Scherzos*..., I. Kolodin, liner notes for *The Chopin Ballades & Scherzos*, A. Rubinstein, RCA, 1960; "Throughout his life Chopin's outmoded sense..." Rosen, The Romantic Generation, p.87; "retains a feeling for a continuous, uninterrupted..." *ibid*, p.323; "a kaleidoscope of images that reveal..." I. Kolodin, liner notes, 1960; "gathers momentum slowly, like a story..." Rosen, The Romantic Generation, p.322; "so urgent a part of its total effect," I. Kolodin, liner notes, 1960; "extraordinary...in the varied colors of its...", T. Parry, liner notes for *Chopin Favorite Piano Works*, Ashkenazy, Decca; "where substance and high-octane virtuosity staggeringly mesh!" J. Distler, p.50; "a clear incapacity for attaining...", Rosen, The Romantic Generation, p.284; "a form in which musical substance..." *ibid*, p.363; "a short piece in which the musical interest..." *ibid*; "string of arpeggios with an almost..." *ibid*, p.362; "For Chopin and many others, *The Well-Tempered Clavier*..." *ibid*, p.555; "lyrical pieces with long dreamy...accompaniments." J. Distler, p.50; "cultivated it as both an idea and a genre." C. MacDonald, *BBC Music Mag*, Feb 2010; "At a time when most concert...for intimate expression", *ibid*; "use of *arpeggio* figures wrapped...sustaining pedal." *ibid*; "enriching the harmonic content...more speculative and elaborate." Libbey, p.552; "progressively more and more encrusted with chromatic ornament." The Musical Companion, p.66; "wonderfully polished jewels of reflective lyricism and expressive nostalgia." T. Parry, liner notes; "subtle mood studies intended..." Morin, p.228; "...the idea of creating...what he was about." pianist Peter Donohue; "There's a sort of contrapuntal...study of Bach." Martin Roscoe; When Chopin arrived in

Vienna...spinning furiously in three-quarter time". Bookspan, pp.126-7; "rather limited genre" and Chopin's waltzes..."genius and powers of invention." T. Parry, liner notes; "most impressive example of a set of tiny Fragments," Rosen, The Romantic Generation , p.83; "In the *Preludes* there is...character and sentiment" *ibid*, p.86; "are more concentrated...separate individual, and complete in itself." *ibid*, p.87; "Chopin expended great subtlety...from one prelude to the next." *ibid*, p.86; "evoke images of the high drama of Poland's history." Morin, p.229; "a stately processional dance...never previously associated with it." J. Siepmann, *BBC Music Magazine*, Feb 2010; "an image of heroism...volatile keyboard epics." J. Distler, p.51; "a straightforward reflection of...as well as the future." D. Nice, *BBC Music Mag* Collection liner notes, Feb 2010; "with a repertoire of motifs...traditions of European music." Rosen, The Romantic Generation, p.413; "It was in Chopin's playing...have been most remarkable." *ibid*; "They constantly veer between...charming and audacious." J. Distler, p.51; "From the mazurka...Wagner, Debussy, and Schoenberg." J. Siepmann, *BBC Music Magazine*, Feb 2010; "They have an almost supernatural difficulty." pianist Nikolai Demidenko; "perhaps nowhere else do we feel...craftsmanship and passionate intensity." Rosen, The Romantic Generation, p.452; "The Romantic grotesque...as in the mazurkas." *ibid*, p.427; "transform the mazurka...into something more ambitious." *ibid*, p.425; "we find the first of Chopin's...opening theme,"..."most spectacularly in the Fourth Ballade." *ibid*, p.432; "feverish galloping of the opening movement" J. Duchen, *BBC Music Mag*, Feb 2010; "all the previous ingredients...into a compelling whole." D.Nice, *BBC Music Magazine* Collection, Vol.18, No.6; "Chopin's mastery of tone color...unsurpassed before Debussy." Rosen, The Romantic Generation, p.471; "something repulsive about it," *ibid*, p.283; "traditional elements and the conservative craftsmanship" *ibid*, p.284; "'poem of death' for...it contains a funeral march." H. Grimaud to M. Church, liner notes for Grimaud: *Chopin/Rachmaninov Piano Sonatas*, DG, 2005; "a minute and a half...moving at breakneck pace;" L. Kramer, p.164; "bizarre-sounding scherzo of Prokofiev's Third Symphony." A. Walker, *BBC Music Magazine*, Feb 2010; "compromised neither his sense of style nor the energy of the form." Rosen, The Romantic Generation, p.466; "a bewildering variety of surface change." *ibid*; "he communicated his feeling with almost hypnotic intensity" Bookspan, p.129; "fresh and musically instinctive approach...performances must be judged." E. Levi, *BBC Music Magazine*, Feb 2010; "bristle with imagination, vitality and insight" Bookspan, p.129

Franz Liszt
"a theatrical prophet who...a poetic-romantic vision." G. Larner, liner notes, 2009; "right-thinking music lovers looked on with horror" Rosen, The Romantic Generation, p507; 510; "colossal technique, an unprecedented sonority" Schonberg, p.197; "the transition of musician from servant to master." Blanning, The Triumph of Music, p.57; "heroic virtuosity...make the keys bleed." L. Kramer, p.142; "fresh infusion of Eastern European...among the earliest nationalists." Morin, p.220; "represents the Romantic era at its most public." Musical Companion, p.612; "tried to modify...a more poetic style," "the piano could be...a virtuoso instrument" "virtuosity could have a musical meaning." Schonberg, pp.191,199; "to create heroic self-portraits and vast panoramas." The Rough Guide to Classical Music , 4th ed., Rough Guides publishing, 2005, p.37; "a heroic and even explosive scale;" Schonberg, p.204; "of almost fiendish difficulty." Morin, p.519; "tremendous operatic paraphrases for solo piano." Schonberg, pp.199-204; "a vast amount of great...an almost limitless public." Musical Companion, p.715; It is these vulgar yet great works...- *to sum up the opinions of many serious critics and musicologists - RG*; "he had little feel for the quality of

his musical material" C. Rosen, The Romantic Generation, p.540; "organic unity becomes established." At the Piano with Liszt, M. Hanson, ed., Van Nuys, CA: Alfred, 1986, p.7; "greatest achievement was...musician from servant to master." T. Blanning, The Triumph of Music, p.57; "freedom of form, not formlessness." Short History of Music, p.219; "thematic metamorphosis as a means of organic unification." Musical Companion, p.337; "its own kind of unity without falling back on old forms," Schonberg, p.204; "crisscrossed Europe dozens of times...virtuoso of the piano." Bookspan, p.216; "made a vast amount of great... an almost limitless public." Musical Companion, p.716; "Everywhere he went he was received with rapture," T. Blanning, The Triumph of Music, p.55; "headquarters of the progressive musical movement" H. Schonberg, p.202; "Liszt's last piano works...compromise to public taste." P. Kennedy, liner notes for *Liszt Piano Recital*, Andsnes, EMI 2001; "texture and intensity of sound...in the development of new forms." Rosen, The Romantic Generation, p.541; "In his concentration on tone color musician...was turned upside down by Liszt." *ibid*, p.507; "us realize how misleading...when dealing with the 19th century." *ibid*; "with the etude and the characteristic...greatest revolutions of keyboard style." C. Rosen, The Romantic Generation, p.491; "skirt the edge of the impossible in piano technique" *ibid*, p.493; "pruned of their Romantic excesses." *ibid*; "developed new effects of realization" *ibid*, p.507; "The etude is the most striking product of the 19th-century Baroque revival." *ibid*, p.365; "In fact, nothing was ever...material for Liszt's compositions." *ibid*, p.540; "cheap, urban popular music." *ibid*; "as a set of character variations on the crusader's 'song'." G. Larner, 2009; "similarly explores subtle methods...a range of evocative moods." *ibid*; "built on a technique of character...more flamboyant pyrotechnics." *ibid*; "often vaguely hymn like...with healing potential." L. Kramer, p.171; "tone poems that sum up...places he visited." G. Stewart, amazon.com review of Brendel/Kocsis, *Années de pélerinage, Books 1-3*, Philips, 1999, posted 11/10/07; "the tempos are mostly...meditative or mournful." www.classicalarchives.com.

Johannes Brahms
"like a grumpy Santa Claus...an overbearing professor." A. Ross, Listen to This, p.296; "the renovation of music as an abstract art and the resuscitation of its traditional forms" "chiefly concerned with achieving structural integrity." "nowadays it seems obvious that Brahms...greatly renewed it," C. MacDonald, "Johannes Brahms, The Great Romantic" *Grammophone*, Dec 2010; "had made a huge impact on the evolution of music in the 20th century." *ibid*; "combines rigorous argument with...nuanced, and emotionally probing." Libbey, pp.84-5; "hides within it...tenderest kind of private feelings." R. Osborne, liner notes for *Brahms: The Piano Concertos*, Gilels/Jochum, DG, 1972; "The sense of the irrecoverable...that he was born too late." C. Rosen, The Romantic Generation, p.522; "Beethoven's piano was as different...from Bach's harpsichord." Blanning, The Triumph of Music, p.186; "even in his youth he was a master of the twilight tone." A. Ross, Listen to This, p.305; "pensive tone hangs over so much of the late Brahms." *ibid*, p.308; "the entire range of music...repeatedly in 20th century composers." Burkholder, Grout, Palisca, p.726; "infused new life into forms which the romantics had weakened" Short History of Music, p.238; "technical perfection in the classical sense...his ideals lay in the past." *ibid*, p.236; "the spirit of Beethoven and Schumann" and "creating a series of abstract sounds" H. Schonberg, p.302; "offers large structures without the pitfalls of the sonata." Lang, p.921; "the archaic effect of stanza and refrain is more literally indicated." C. Rosen, The Romantic Generation, p.323; "He was extraordinarily imaginative...ideas into innovative textures." Burkholder, J.P., Grout, D.J., Palisca p.723; "set out his variations as a string...harmonic plan of the theme." *ibid*;

"playing of such unmannered beauty...Brahms face-to-face." A. Ross, Listen to This, p.345; "The sense of modernity...often deeply melancholy." L. Kramer, p.63; "more security, confidence...sophisticated harmonically and rhythmically." Schonberg, p.300; "tried to recapture variation...and to develop the thematic material organically..." Short History of Music, pp.237-38; "wrote a very tender...unique in the music of his time." "vehicles for his most intimate thoughts", "a perfect expression of subtle feeling". Musical Companion, p.614; "a musical novella in seven chapters." R. Osborne, liner notes, 1972; "hides within it, whole...kind of private feelings." *ibid*; "they tilt toward dark keys...elusive to be considered occasional pieces." A. Ross, Listen to This, p.307; "combines technique with a mellow, golden glow." "a musical novella in seven chapters." R. Osborne liner notes; "Schumann's lovely sketches one step further." H. Schonberg, p.300.

Gabriel Faure
"ranges from the gently reflective to the profoundly searching." Penguin Guide, p.385; "is a lyricist...continuous from first to last bar." S. Johnson, liner notes for *Faure Piano Quartets*, Domus, Hyperion, 1986; "one of the most supple, elegant and refined of all composers" H. Schonberg, p.407; "a world of ultra sensitivity girded with searing passion." Morin, p.313; "contain some of Fauré's most haunting inspiration." Penguin Guide, p.386; "the eminently French qualities of taste, clarity, and a sense of proportion." Machlis, p.56.

Edvard Grieg; Sergei Rachmaninoff
Grieg felt that only in...he clearly imitated a folk melody. E. Grieg to H.T. Finck, 17-July-00; "the most effective anti-modernist standard bearer." R. Taruskin, Oxford History..., v.4, p.553; "powerful, sensitive, willful piano playing" A. Loesser and C. van Ausdall, liner notes for Byron Janis, Rachmaninoff Piano Concertos Nos.2 and 3, Minneapolis SO/LSO, Dorati (Mercury, 1960/61); "essentially the same kind of music throughout his life" H. Schonberg, p.510; "without indulging in Lisztian pyrotechnics." *ibid*, p.512; "is couched in the melancholy...pervades much of his music." G. Norris, Russian Masters 2, p.92; "must surmount...challenges to create a vivid musical impression." C. MacDonald, *BBC Music Magazine*, May 2010; "fuse technical and musical challenges with evocative poetic vision." T. Parry in 1001 Classical Recordings..., p.593; "history may eventually come...the triumphant return to tonality." J. Kramer, p.538.

Chapter 7

Impressionism
"piano music...actually anticipate Debussy." J. Fisk, ed. Composers On Music, Eight Centuries of Writings, 2nd ed., Northeastern Univ. Press, 1997; "principal extramusical influences...not the visual arts." McCalla, p.xii; "small musical units...into a great system of architecture." Lang, p.1020; "had some nasty things to say about Ravel." Schonberg, p.468.

Claude Debussy
"music reflects...the complicated soul of the turn-of-the-century." Lang, p.1021; "imitated the dreamy qualities...Impressionist paintings." Draper, p.14; "connect sensory, emotional and imaginative experiences to one another." Libbey, p.171; "Debussy's music does...strive to convey...music that came before." Berger, p.145; "attempted to create...literature permeated with ambiguity." Lang,

p.1023; "depict personal responses to the...They wanted to suggest rather than state..." Berger, p.146; "...spiritually akin to Impressionism and Symbolism...and Oriental melody." *ibid*; "used short melodic fragments...pieces of stained glass." Goulding, p.332; "infallible instinct for the...make his piano music unique," Schonberg, p.462; "fragmentary motives and little flashes..." to create "...light and shadow." Draper, p.14; "developed new theories of light and color in music" Schonberg, p.453; "brought to music...unique surface beauties." Dubal, p.444; "no one since Chopin...as did Debussy." Libbey, p.172; "deeply mistrustful of tradition...the creation of music." Weiss, Taruskin, p.355; "abhorred the egocentric hero worship...of (Wagner)." Lang, p.1021; "the 'Wagnerian revolution'...the door on the past." Weiss, Taruskin, p.355; "destroyed 19th century rhetoric." Schonberg, p.452; "to all the musical possibilities explored in the 20th century." Libbey, p.170; "Debussy's whole-tone scale...relationship." The Musical Companion, p.351; "elusive melodies and harmonies favored by Impressionism." Machlis, p.91; "used chord changes...not to heighten feeling" Crocker, p.479; "reflections in water,... quietude of moonlight." Prendergast, p.10;
"principles of texture, sonority and tone color." M. Donat, liner notes for M. Uchida: *Debussy Etudes*, Philips, 1990; "ultravirtuosic (and possess) "a certain icy fury." A. Ross, The Rest Is Noise, p.105; "is a loving reflection of Debussy at his most human and humorous." L. Shulman, NJSO concert notes, 2010.

Maurice Ravel
"a piece of melodic genius...20th century modernism." Prendergast, p.12; "innovative inelastic movement...revolution of the 1960s." *ibid*, p.14; "achieved a kind of clockwork...without sacrificing panache." Libbey pp.665-7; "His love of all things...intricate logic of his writing." J. Haylock, *Classic FM*, Apr 2010; "needed not one jot of correction." Prendergast, p.14; "dash of Spanish influence and just a bit of American jazz." Morin, p.738; "nocturnal stillness and translucent...piano creations." Prendergast, p.12; "expressed itself in the transformation...most viscerally exciting of musical gestures." Libbey, pp.665-7; "already had the sophisticated precision of his mature style" H. Schonberg, p.468; "strikes out into uncharted territory...in his harmonic development." S. Wright, liner notes for *Ravel Piano Music*, Collard, EMI, 2004; "The world of piano music was turned upside-down by *Gaspard de la Nuit*," J. Haylock, *Classic FM*, Apr 2010; "alluring nightmare of a work" Morin, p.742; "his neo-classical delight in rethinking popular idioms of the 17th century." *ibid*.

Alexander Scriabin
"divine tonal colorist," "full of mysterious vibrations." Dubal, p.513; "represents the darker and...the Russian artistic psyche." "the voluptuous haziness of post-Wagnerian harmony." Swafford, p.343; "breathtaking in their melodic prodigality...infused with mercurial sensations, breathless palpitations..." Dubal, p.513; "represent an intensive flowering of a more individual manner." Hugh MacDonald in New Grove Russian 2, p.55; "speaks its own language...'Russian-ness' or nationalistic traces in it." Y. Sudbin in *BBC Music Mag*, Oct 2010; "ever more incandescent, intoxicated, trancelike, and fevered." Dubal, p.514; "dissonances take on radiant auras of stability" Griffiths, p.236; "the world's first twelve-tone composition" R. Cummings in All Music Guide, p.1245; "that tone alone no longer suffices." Lang, p.1025; "rely less on thematic structure...harmonic and textural intensity." MacDonald, p.63; "the Chopinesque model steeped...dissolution and tonal indeterminism." Rognoni, p.xxv; "achieved a maximum compression of form...astonishingly varied within their terse format." Musical Companion, p.623; "series of incarnations to ever-

higher spiritual spheres," F.E. Kirby, <u>Music for Piano, A Short History</u>. Singapore: Amadeus Press, 1995, p.319; "in the coming regeneration of the world through a cataclysmic event." H. MacDonald, p.58; "a mystical devil-worshipping avant-gardist." Y. Sudbin in *BBC Music Mag*, Oct 2010; "elaborate program, ending with…cosmic dance of the atoms." H. Schonberg, p.517; "for the first time…between light-color and sound." Rognoni, p.xxv; "a supernatural dream, and whose mind…speculations, hallucinations, and dementia." Lang, p.1025; "the last extravagant faith…and in art as humanity's salvation." Dubal, p.512.

20th Century
Béla Bartók
"a decisive, almost ideological…the 'natural phenomenon' of folk music." Lampert, Somfai, Noble, *et al.*, p.37; "remained quite apart from the neo-Classical endeavors." *ibid*; "20th century re-examination of Bach's approach to this genre." <u>Musical Companion</u>, p.664; "chosen to challenge Bach on his own ground" *ibid*.

Serge Prokofiev
"reflects the nervous anticipation…", B. Berman, <u>Prokofiev's Piano Sonatas: A Guide for the Listener and the Performer</u>. New Haven, CT: Yale University Press, 2008, p.151; "projects the anguish and the…", *ibid*; "looks back to those terrible…", *ibid*; "contrast between simple lyricism and horrifying violence." D. Hurwitz, amazon.com review; "ponderous." Taruskin, v.5, p.9; "sound like moments of authentic inspiration, caught on the wing." M. Harrison, liner notes for *Prokofiev Piano Concertos*, Beroff, EMI, 1988.

Notes – Part 2

Introduction to Part 2
"does not depend for its effects…", H. Ulrich, <u>Chamber Music</u>, p.2; "not a medium for storytelling …", Ulrich, p.5; "to make it yield all its…", MC, p.719; "the listener…is often so lost…", Ulrich, p.5; "the listener…is often so lost…", MC, p.507; "The highly developed Viennese musical life…", Lang, p.642;

Chapter 8
"characteristically English vein of melancholy." Grammophone, Sept 1971; "disregarding the inroads of the concerted manner of composition," Lang, p.369; "the harmonic background…indications given by a figured bass (*i.e.*, the continuo)." D. Tovey, <u>The Forms of Music</u>, p.6; "It is not enough to hear…will allow us to boast of its conquest." E. Blom in <u>Musical Companion</u>, p.719; "consistently leaves nothing undetermined…or in permanent subordination." *ibid*; "began to weave the pretty…into more serious, substantial musical fabrics" Berger, p.186; "idiom midway between orchestral music and true chamber music." P. Holman, liner notes for *Beethoven: Septet/Sextet*, Gaudier Ensemble, Hyperion, 1992; "stimulated by the extensive Austrian tradition of divertimento writing." D.W. Jones, "The Origins of the Quartet," in <u>The Cambridge Companion to the String Quartet</u>, R. Stowall, ed. Cambridge University Press, 2003, p.182; "Even at the end of the turbulent…the traditional criteria still hold." McCalla, <u>20th</u>

Cent. Chamber Music, p.vii; "had earlier been an overwhelmingly 'absolute' or 'pure music' genre," *ibid*, p.viii;

Chapter 9
"to regard himself as playing...", Musical Companion, pp.516-7; "were expected to be simple enough...", Rosen, p.46; "adorned by an optional 'accompaniment'...", B. Jacobson, liner notes for *Schubert: Complete Trios*, Beaux Arts Trio, Philips, 1995; "genre almost invariably proves troublesome" M. Jameson, AMG, p.912; "a distillation of Mozart's technique and...", Rosen, p.281; "stands alone, far above all...", *ibid*; "from the viewpoint of depth...", Berg, p.311; Alfred Beaujean sees a look ahead to Schubert..., A. Beaujean (transl. R. Jordan), liner notes for *Mozart: Complete String Quintets*, Grumiaux Trio, A. Gérecz, M. Lesueur, Philips, 1967/74; "speaks of the poet's most subjective dreams and desires...", Lang, p.644; "rarely has a piece for such small forces...", Morin, p.625; "the greatest little-known treasure...", Morin, p.427; "Beethoven faced the challenge of blending...", L. Lockwood, M. Kroll (eds.) The Beethoven Violin Sonatas, Univ. of Illinois Press, 2004, p.2; "heartfelt, exquisite communicativeness...", Solomon, p.253; "atmosphere of experimentation and complex references..." M. Meyer (transl. R. Evidon), liner notes for A. Schiff/M. Perényi, "Beethoven: Complete Music for Piano and Violincello", ECM, 2004; "still belong to the category of...", *ibid*; "melodies not infrequently rough,...", *ibid*; First paragraph material supported by: Plantinga, p.91; Short History of Music, p.180; "never achieved a true trio style...", G. Abraham, p.617; "The opening movement has the noble sweep...", Draper, p.93; "the most magnificent of all piano trios...", Morris, p.146; "the age of heroes and nobles was drawing...", Berger, p.59; "always...the inexhaustible melodist"..."the lighter tones...". Short History of Music, p.191; "noble melodies, piquant rhythms...", Ulrich, p.278; "gentle tempi...introspection and poignancy." G. Johnson, liner notes for *Schubert Arpeggione Sonata, etc.*, Britten/Rostropovich, Decca, 2007.

Schumann and Mendelssohn
"elfin, scurrying scherzos." Short History of Music, p.196; "all three...have charm, vitality and musicianship." Penguin Guide, p.621; "a brilliantly structured piece...", H. Wallace, *BBC Music Mag*, 4/10; The three pieces "were conceived..."urgent resolve of the third." J. Chissell, liner notes for *Schumann Chamber Music*, M. Argerich, et al., EMI, 1995; "more personal (than *Op.80*),..." J. Warrack, liner notes for *Schumann Piano Trios, etc.*, Beaux Arts Trio, Philips, 1997; "a well-proportioned work,...", P. Lamb, liner notes for Dartington Piano Trio, "Fanny Mendelssohn and Clara Schumann Piano Trios" Helios, 1989.

Brahms
"cultivated an esoteric style founded..." Taruskin, v.3, p.731; "the intense fascination Brahms' chamber music..." *ibid*, p.732; "formal display of erudition...full-blooded romanticism." M.Furman, liner notes for *Brahms Cello Sonatas*, Ma/Ax, RCA, 1985; "an authentic Romantic flamboyance..." C. MacDonald, *Grammophone*, Dec 2010.

Dvořák, Grieg, Tchaikovsky and Rachmaninoff
"retreated from an uncompromising Wagnerian...". J. Clapham, liner notes for *Dvořák Piano Quintets*, S. Richter/Borodin String Quartet, DG, 1984; "how this nationalistic strain...", Berger, p.155; "has a characteristic freshness..." *Grammophone*, review, 10/94; "represent his dedication to the nationalist impulse...", Ulrich, p.330; "the charming theme in a number...chords and flashing

arpeggios." Ulrich,p327-28; "has the gloomy charm of youthful morbidity..." J. Leonard in All Music Guide, p.1063; "the sincerity of his grief..." G. Norris, p.80; "are imbued with lyrical fervor..." Penguin Guide, p.820.

French Sonatas and Trios

"its neatness, finish, clear outlines...tradition come shining through." Schonberg, p.343; "late flowering of Classical elements...composers a century before his time." Ulrich, p.324; "a paucity of profound feeling," and "a lack of real inspiration in melodic writing." Ulrich, p.324; "his unique harmonic style, characterized by rich modulations and chromatic wandering." ibid, p.320; "speaks the loudest of all his compositions...turmoil and argumentative-type writing." Nicola Benedetti in BBC Music Magazine, Mar 2010; "His music is characterized...formal innovation, and religious idealism." Ulrich, p.319; Some detect an atmosphere of ...Romanticism by a return to counterpoint. Griffiths, p.251; "musical development in which...within an entire composition." Schonberg, p.404; "only a few primal themes...metamorphosed as the work progresses." J. Martineau, The Elements of Music. NY: Walker and Co., 2008; "sought to blend rigorous formal training with soaring lyricism." Libbey, p.241; "superb synthesis of Franck's own...and the Viennese Classical tradition." B. Johnston in All Music Guide, p.465; "reaches out and involves...strength and beauty of its lyricism." Bookspan, p.166; "on a note of calm repose." ibid, p.167; "restless, churning section with vivid accents and strong syncopation." ibid; "preoccupation with German polyphony." Lang, p.926; "tossed from one instrument and echoed by the other." ibid; "a mighty affirmation of victory." ibid; "their particular flavour being unlike that of any other chamber music." The Musical Companion, p.553; "achieve a graceful union of classical form and romantic content." Machlis, p.56; "is to French chamber music what Schumann and Brahms are to German." Morin, p.312; "the soaring, songlike lines...very much Fauré's personal language." J. Duchen in 1001 Classical Recordings You Must Hear Hear Before You Die, M. Rye, ed., Universe, 2008, p.396; "succeeds in unifying string and keyboard texture" F. Pott; "is mostly a meditation on two themes." R. Nichols, liner notes for *Debussy, Ravel, Fauré: Piano Trios*, Florestan Trio, Hyperion, 1999; "continuation of recent French classicism...hothouse of individualistic emotions." McCalla, p.xiii; "a synthesis between the new directions of...Couperin and Rameau." Berger, p.147; "slyly sneak glances at Rameau and Couperin." Griffiths, p.241; "perfumed with the palmy air of the French Baroque." A. Ross, The Rest Is Noise, p.105; "as free-flowing and harmonically...the most passionate and violent of the three." Morin, p.256; "harsh, discontinuous, largely without a sense of key." Crocker, p.479; "manages to fuse elements...wholehearted affinity for gypsy violin playing." B. Johnston in All Music Guide, p.357; Instead, it shows the young...melodies with the surrounding material. R. Nichols, liner notes; "tuneful gumdrop of a piece" Morin, p.255; Malay verse form...extraordinarily intricate structure. R. Nichols, liner notes; "eleven statements of an eight-bar...and then receding again," ibid; "his most potent jazz stylizations." Taruskin, v.4, p.606.

20th Century

"disclose a Classical clarity of form." Ulrich, p.364; "from dry humor to fierce abandon, from suave lyricism to intense drama." ibid, p.363; "a distillation of wartime feelings" Morin, p.714; "exceedingly profound work...rewards for patient listeners." R. Cummings in All Music Guide, p.1036; "lyrical warmth with his playful mischief." ibid; "true Classical sonata-allegro form...virtuosic fire that will always say 'Prokofiev' to us." B. Johnston in All Music Guide, p.1035; "hammered into a brutal march," Morin, p.865; "in the more comforting key of

E major." P. Morita in All Music Guide, p.1265; "rife with cynicism, despair, and mockery." G. Olson in All Music Guide, p.1265; "coarse, repetitive sawing from the cello" *ibid*; "rude, comically sinister finale," *ibid*; "the morbid and gloomy...most of the late quartets." R. Cummings in All Music Guide, p.1270; "a masterly exploration of baroque techniques in modern terms." The Musical Companion, p.662; "he was thought of as...a hick." Taruskin, v.4, p.423; "virtually a life's work crammed...unprecedented rejuvenated creative vitality." Taruskin, v.4, p.424; "...the natural rhythmic patterns of the Czech language...lines, or large blocks of sound." Z. Minderovic in All Music Guide, p.651; "ability to adopt his music...characteristics of the Czech language." *ibid*; "brisk, effective storytelling." J. Stevenson in All Music Guide, p.657; "reveal a creative mind of fertility and invention." J. Haylock, Classic FM, Feb 2010; "a seriously rewarding work...marvelous dramatic thrust." S. Ritter, Fanfare, Mar/Apr 2010, p.241; "motoric rhythms (of Roussel that) would...for the rest of (his) life." All Music Guide, p.804; "one of his darkest and most dramatic duo works." *ibid*.

Chapter 10

"The string quartet...clearest non-vocal state." Rosen, The Classical Style, p.137; "the most elevated, expressive, and...combination in all music...", Solomon, p.133; "Its very timbre creates a sense..." Copland, p.78; "demands scrupulous musicianship", for anything less is "mercilessly exposed in a string quartet." The Musical Companion, p.516; "abundance of melodic force...endless resource." Einstein, Short History of Music, p.177;

Haydn and the Birth of the String Quartet

"Haydn both broke...durable models." All Music Guide, p.567; "Haydn brought all the...on his chamber music." Rosen, The Classical Style, p.45; "endowed it with the power...without flying apart." *ibid*, p.287; "developed a style in which...curbed or tamed his irregularities." *ibid*, p.112; "into a style of convincing logic and permanent validity." Lang, p.632; "toward the point where it...forms of composition." R. Cummings in All Music Guide, p.915; "entirely from its pre-eminence...death of Schubert." Rosen, The Classical Style, p.137; "the form and instrumental...we know it today." Berger, p.187; "It was from Haydn...to compose quartets." L. Kemp, liner notes for Quatour Ysaÿe: *Mozart: Haydn String Quartets*, Ysaÿe Records, 2003; "his themes often recur... fashion." Ulrich, p.202; "the expected thing takes place,...interesting ways." *ibid*; "The trios became more boisterous as Haydn grew older." Rosen, The Classical Style, p.340; "now he begins to dazzle even his colleagues." Ulrich, p.166; "Haydn shows a new...possibilities of the cello," *ibid*, p.167; "The individual character...Haydn's principal concern at this time." Crocker, p.379; "hyper-emotive aesthetic movement" Keller, p.215; "quite a new and special way." "Haydn's technique of...almost any material, and absorb it." Rosen, The Classical Style, p.341; "ripened (Haydn's) ideas and the...style *galant* disappeared." Lang, p.630; "the powerful influence emanating...spiritual disciple and friend, Mozart." Lang, p.630; "in an entirely new manner...and a more elaborate rhythmic scheme." Ulrich, p.171; "essential to the method of thematic development," C. Rosen, The Classical Style, p.xiii; "builds the melodies up out of...from several microcosmic musical gestures," Berger, p.197-98; "standard accompaniment fragments...used them in both melody and accompaniment." E. Weimer, ref at bottom of Rosen, The Classical Style, p.xiv; "single innovation (was) the touchstone of classical counterpoint." Rosen, The Classical Style, p.xiv; "that he was well on his way...of all musical forms, the string quartet." Berger, p.197; "the independent solo writing entails... and complex contrapuntal display." Rosen,

The Classical Style, p.139; "partial return to the rich and more 'learned' technique of the High Baroque" *ibid*; "The mature power and variety...were never surpassed by Haydn." Rosen, *ibid*, p.140; "a cue for any chattering to cease." R. Wigmore, "The Poor Man's Mozart?", *Grammophone*, June 2009; "more experimental and innovative than earlier compositions" Berger, p.213; "...flamboyant contrasts of texture, register, and dynamics." R. Wigmore, liner notes for *Haydn String Quartets*, Op.74, Lindsay String Quartet, ASV, 2004; "are marked by a profusion of arresting textures." R. Stowell, Cambridge Companion..., p.206; "The dawn of Romanticism is noticeable in the string quartets of Op.74." Berger, p.213; "The texture...a perfect blend of homophonic and contrapuntal writing" Berger, p.226; "in these quartets the highest point of Haydn's creative activity is reached." Ulrich, p.183; "he only had the strength to finish the middle movements of his last quartet." Rosen, The Classical Style, p.136; "The development of his genius is laid down for all to see." Ulrich, p.205; "are, to be truthful, the fruit of long and laborious efforts." Mozart quote; "For variety of thematic matter, concentration of musical thought...among the most perfect chamber works ever composed." Musical Companion, p.522; "as the finest example of Mozart's genius." Ulrich, p.199; "exhibit a perfect amalgam of the Rococo and Classical spirits." Berger, p.287; "quickly gives notice...a new phase of his musical development." I. Kemp in Lampert, Somfai, Noble, *et al.*; "buoyant, transparent melody;" "brims with rhythmic and contrapuntal invention." C. Vigeland, The Mostly Mozart Guide to Mozart, p.79; "what was then an almost alarming display of dissonant chromaticism." Dubal, p.103; "chromatic meanderings" "unresolved harmonies over a throbbing cello line" J. Reel in All Music Guide, p.916.

Beethoven
"ability to embrace the whole range of human emotion, from dread of death to love of life..." Morris, p.3; "chose to stretch the string quartet toward symphonic dimensions." Libbey, p.122; "The risk-taking and compositional challenges...the quartets are staggering and inspirational." M. Donat, liner notes for *Beethoven: Razumovsky Quartets, Harp Quartet*, Takacs Quartet, Decca, 2002; "direct and passionate expression of emotion...introverted in his late piano sonatas and string quartets." Draper, p.87; "the artist as a unique, dignified prophet of society." A.Morin, p.87; "most ambitious single project...composed in 1798-1800 and published in 1801. Solomon, p.133; "dipping a toe into string quartet waters." M. Donat, liner notes for *Beethoven: The Early String Quartets*, Takacs Quartet, Decca, 2004; "increasingly uncomfortable with the elegant confines..." "hard-edged accents and intensified dramatic contrasts." *ibid*; "essentially remain traditional and even conservative...the most prestigious genre of the Classical style." Solomon, p.134; "an interesting beginning to an extraordinary journey" E. Dusinberre, liner notes for *Beethoven: The Early String Quartets*, Takacs Quartet, Decca, 2004; "fine slow movement...tragic utterances among his earlier music." M. Donat, liner notes for *Beethoven: The Early String Quartets*; "widely admired as its companions...elsewhere in Beethoven's string quartets." *ibid*; "the music crackles with vitality, wit, and daring ingenuity," E. Dusinberre, liner notes for *Beethoven: The Early String Quartets*, Takacs Quartet, Decca, 2004; "often speaks with a gruff Beethovian accent," *ibid*; "material of diametrically opposed character." M. Donat, liner notes for *Beethoven: The Early String Quartets*; "with its seemingly mystical...dynamic, thrusting scherzo." *ibid*; "a good deal better-behaved." *ibid*.

The Middle Period
"his style had changed almost beyond recognition" M. Donat, liner notes for

Beethoven: Razumovsky Quartets, Harp Quartet, Takacs Quartet, Decca, 2002; "uncompromising in their severity and intellectual rigor," Morris, p.120; "a continental divide in the history of the quartet." *ibid*; "by 1806 Beethoven was…in any species of polyphony." *ibid*, p.121; "concentrated power and energy that tap into…his greatest orchestral works." J. Duchen, "A Pure Vision," *Classic FM*, Aug 2010; "challenged the traditional notion of chamber music as a vehicle for domestic music making." M. Donat, liner notes for *Beethoven: The Middle String Quartets*; "pervasive atmosphere of grief." *ibid*; "but for a later age." Berger, pp.45-46; "only gradually gropes its way towards the home key." M. Donat, liner notes for *Beethoven: Razumovsky Quartets, Harp Quartet*; "one may legitimately speak of these quartets as 'symphonic quartets'." Solomon, p.260; "a trio of sharply characterized, consciously differentiated individuals." *ibid*; "altogether well-behaved," "bold individuality of its slow opening page" "unnecessary jumble of harsh dissonances," M. Donat, liner notes for *Beethoven: Razumovsky Quartets, Harp Quartet*; "diabolical scherzo, full of hammering figures." Ulrich, p.253; "formed his main creative…final three years of his life." M. Donat, liner notes for *Beethoven: The Late String Quartets*, Takacs Quartet, Decca, 2004; "Its abrupt transitions, changes of mood…to Beethoven's late masterpieces in the form." E. Dusinberre, liner notes for *Beethoven: The Late String Quartets*, Takacs Quartet, Decca, 2004; "stands at the gateway to the third." Ulrich, p.253.

The Late Period

"crystallized avant-garde currents among Viennese intellectuals." Solomon, p.415; "As his hearing faded…he longed to touch the infinite…to embrace all humanity." Draper, p.94; "exceptionally strong unity that binds (them) together." M. Donat, liner notes for *Beethoven: The Late String Quartets*; "expressive heart of the work as a whole," *ibid*; "variation form joins fugue as one of the leading features." Solomon, p.395; "sublime soliloquies of a lonely soul" "represent…the supremist height to which music has attained." Short History of Music, p.186-87; "show a new-found interest in the discipline of the fugue." M. Donat, liner notes for *Beethoven: The Late String Quartets*; "with our sense of the passage of time" S. Johnson, liner notes; "incomprehensible, like Chinese…" Solomon, p.417; "withstand the shock of the new." *ibid*; "are generally agreed to represent the summit of instrumental music in the West." Morris, p.213; "Does there still remain alive in…Beethoven's own *Op.18* had exemplified?" Einstein, The Romantic Generation, p.38; "there is no poignancy or sentiment…the most divinely inspired music in the literature." Ulrich, p.254; "a natural outgrowth of the last piano sonatas," Solomon, p.419; "perhaps to reestablish Beethoven's control of the medium." *ibid*, p.418; "contains only the ruins of…his genius, often buried under arid rubble." Blanning, Triumph of Music, p.101; "experimental works that create a variety of new formal structures." Solomon, p.418; "carry music to a height that actually seems to transcend music." Schonberg, p.122; "song of gratitude to God after recovering from a serious (abdominal) illness." Draper, p.94; "music here appears to become an implicit agency of healing, a talisman against death." Solomon, p.420; "rudely interrupted by a parody of a march" E. Dusinbarre, liner notes for *Beethoven: The Late String Quartets*; "is as different as could be imagined…fugal writing." M. Donat, liner notes for *Beethoven: The Late String Quartets*; "Like the fugal finale of the *Hammerklavier Sonata*…writing at its most intractable," *ibid*; and "can alienate with its sheer furosity and scale." Dusinbarre, liner notes for for *Beethoven: The Late String Quartets*; "Its subject is marked…veers toward brash dissonance." J. Keller, p.73; "may appear to be a nostalgic reminiscence of Mozart and Haydn," Rosen, The Classical Style, p.511; "Beethoven came home at last...expressiveness of the earlier (four late) quartets." Solomon, p.424.

Chapter 11
Franz Schubert
"on lyric moments and rich harmonies at the expense of figuration and tonal plans." Crocker, p.429; "Schubert works within the late and loosely organized post-classical style." Rosen, The Classical Style, p.517; "The 'great' Schubert shows himself first in the C minor string quartet of 1820." Abraham, p.625; "are still based on intimate, economical chamber music techniques." Ulrich, p.274; "the inner joy and vivacity that filled the earlier works is gone," *ibid*, p.273; "Beethoven's titanic figure loomed large over Schubert's life." Peter Clive, Schubert and His World, cited in H. Sachs, p.171; "What Schubert could only suggest in his *Lieder* here finds exhaustive expression." quote by Alfred Einstein, unattributed; "offers perhaps the most...from the lines of true Classicism." Ulrich, p.277; "Schubert returns to classical principles...if not as complete, as Beethoven." Rosen, The Classical Style, p.521;

Romantic Period Quartets
"Mendelssohn had a genuine understanding of what Beethoven was up to in his last years." Rosen, Romantic Generation, p.578; "so flagrant as to constitute a public homage to Beethoven." *ibid*, p.574; "could not think of work...barrenness in the mind and heart." "perhaps the most intensely tragic work" "characterized by extreme, often unresolved tension." M. Struck-Schloen (transl. J. Scheffel), liner notes for Mandelring Quartet, "Mendelssohn Complete Chamber Music for Strings, Vol.II, Audite, 2012; "music generally seeks to avoid...implied by the string quartet." Rosen, The Classical Style, p.137; "proof of mastery, and a nostalgic recall of the great classicists," *ibid*; David Soyer, cellist of the Guarneri String Quartet, unattributed; "in the glorious slow movement...the happiness of his first love." Penguin Guide, p.980; "his most experimental work" but "many of his most beautiful inspirations." Morin, p.287; "folksy, concise, and easy to follow." Morin, p.288; "and his confident mastery of the quartet medium." Berger, p.166; "suffer from their complexity;" "worked over nature." Morin, p.176; "immediately identifiable language...and melting lyricism." J. Keller, p.108; "more room for more expansive lyricism." *ibid*, p.109; "deeply serious and uncompromising pieces" "been known to find both pieces somewhat forbidding." *ibid*; "too delightful for words, with its delightful, mocking conclusion." Quote attributed to Clara Schumann.

French Romantic String Quartets
"be taken as a symbolic renunciation of Wagner." Crocker, p.477; "so vigorous, so thoughtful in its passion." "fuses Debussy's harmonic and...cyclic treatment of themes." Grout, p.602; "Its varied tonal effects...an excellent musical counterpart" Berger, p.147; "written at a time when poetry...influences upon his music" "no poetic or visual allusion." C. Dingle, BBC Music Mag, Feb 2010; "In the name of the gods of music...do not touch a single note." "makes the violin sound like an entirely different instrument." Draper, p.37; "enigmatic and otherworldly...last (musical) utterance." Penguin Guide, p.384; "a rarefied distillation of the whole miniature musical culture," P. Griffiths, The String Quartet. New York: Thames and Hudson, 1983, p.210; "remarkable example of contrapuntal mastery." Morin, p.313.

Borodin, Grieg, and Tchaikovsky

"by far the single most popular piece of chamber music" "it is beautifully composed...sweet, gentle..." Schonberg, p.362; "pouring out long, exquisitely...and glorious themes." "as an expression of love for his wife." S.Johnson in <u>1001 Classical Recordings...</u>; "one can (still) detect...against musical conservatism." Berger, p.82; "teutonically academic 'pure' music" D. Brown, p.65; "aims at breadth, vigor, flight of...tone for the instruments.", "all have the rhythmic verve...of folk dances." Berger, p.183; "has been arranged for every conceivable instrumental combination." Berger, p.439.

20th Century

"tax the players to the utmost...rather than scare off, prospective performers." <u>The Musical Companion</u>, p.574; "deep insights into the character...immensely resourceful, composer." *ibid*, p.575; "not only his personal creative...of half a century as well." Thomas May, amazon.com editorial review; "very elaborate works and all very different from one another." Taruskin, v.4, p.400; "found in the string quartet...cogently expressive yet fully discursive." Crocker, p.494; "The grave opening fugue" "owes much to the example of Beethoven's *Op.131*" <u>The Musical Companion</u>, p.572; "the essence of his national folk...highest forms of Western art music." Grout, p.617; "has a great deal of the strange... harmonies as well as in its rhythms." Grout, p.614; "created a series of works...one disclosed new musical possibilities." Ulrich, p.355; "a new brand of folk-based musical realism" A. Ross, <u>The Rest Is Noise</u>, p.88; "destructive urban influence," "the contaminating influence of cosmopolitan culture." *ibid*, p.89; "heed mainly to people on the social margins" *ibid*; "he has completely absorbed...tradition into his own musical thinking." Berger, p.13; "but Bartók's ardor for...going over the brink" A. Ross, <u>The Rest Is Noise</u>, p.90; "has a sense of a note...sometimes called 'chromatic tonality'." Swafford, p.277; "finding his basic material in music...and a more generalized expression." Griffiths, p.266; "personal creative evolution" "hothouse romanticism" "the deeply tragic zeitgeist of half a century as well." T. May, Amazon.com 'Best of 1998' review; "almost every melodic fragment appearing in various guises," Berger, p.11; "to synthesize the influences of peasant song and art music." Lampert, Somfai, Noble, *et al.*, p.12; "begins with music of exacerbated personal feeling" "in an exuberant medley of village dances." Griffiths, p.242; "are in a new, wild, cataclysmic world...the rebound of the string against the fret board." Schonberg, p.576; "Bartók came closest to the extreme...clouded over or completely eliminated." Crocker, p.498; "audacious in concept and brilliant in execution" Berger, p.15; "a unique central movement...by neighbors of similar character..." Taruskin, v.4, p.402; "is an almost motionless 'night music'," *ibid*; "advanced shapes and textures are now concentrated in the inner movements." Crocker, p.500; "sonata-like balance between movements of scherzo and nocturne type." Lampert, Somfai, Noble, *et al.*, p.61; "it is not difficult to hear...tottered on the brink of destruction." Berger, p.19; "ensemble of virtuosi, as they tax the players to the utmost." The Musical Companion, p.574; "In their breadth of vision...legitimate progeny of Beethoven's." Machlis, p.188; "are a drama of volatile, fluctuating emotion..." A. Corleonis in <u>All Music Guide</u>, p.657; "predominately serious, deeply felt work." Berger, p.339; "Prokofiev only allows the occasional...in the first two movements." D. Nice, *BBC Music Magazine*, April 2010; "long emotional Andante (is) the quartet's crowning...sense of inner strength and fortitude." Berger, p.340; "one of the most immediately attractive quartets in the repertoire." David Gutman, Grammophone, Mar 2010; "music's primitive power and...naïveté with menacing belligerence" Berger, p.341; "a series unparalleled in the 20th century for its all-inclusive breadth", M. Struck-Schloen (transl. D. Babcock), liner notes for Mandelring Quartet, "Shostakovich Complete String Quartets", Audite, 2011; "long, flowing contrapuntal movements, wandering and almost improvisatory in nature." The Musical Companion, p.574; "became his favorite medium...narratives full of blankly winding fugues." A. Ross, The Rest Is Noise, p.280-81; "increasingly served to make an indictment...individual in the inhuman system." M. Struck-Schloen (transl. D. Babcock), liner notes for Mandelring Quartet, "Shostakovich Complete String Quartets", Audite, 2011; "six movements of unrelenting gloom." Dubal, p.626; "rigorous struggles of the Fifth;" A. George, liner notes for *Shostakovich String Quartets*, Fitzwilliam String Quartet, Decca, 1979; "the hallowed genre with deliberately shallow material." B. Schwarz, L. Fay, in The New Grove Russian Masters 2, G. Abraham, H. MacDonald, B. Schwarz, R. McAllister, G. Norris, eds. W.W. Norton, 1986, p.187; "so full of spring-like innocence." M. Struck-Schloen (transl. D. Babcock), liner notes for Mandelring Quartet, "Shostakovich Complete String Quartets", Audite, 2011; "enthusiasm for difficult forms of instrumental music without text." *ibid*; "one of the most extraordinary autobiographical pieces in musical history."A.Ross, The Rest Is Noise, p.475; "intensely poignant and personal in the slow movements...its use of homophonic and polyphonic textures." B. Schwarz, L. Fay, p.194; "The fury of some sections could outpunch heavy rock music." R. Ainsley, BBC Music Magazine, May 2009; "sounds that are as bleak...his music would not have aspired to such tragic heights." Draper, p.52; "entirely abstract, gentle and optimistic in tone." Berger, p.415; "one of Shostakovich's most serene and untroubled compositions," A. George, liner notes; "Few works...life in a more personal, poignant, and anguished way..." Berger, p.416; "hold the listener's attention, providing an extremely moving musical experience." Berger, p.417; "Increasingly bleak and despondent, his fifteen quartets represent a diary of his ever more desperate, tormented existence." E. Eisler, amazon.com review.

Chapter 12

"Placing the minuet second...throws the expressive weight...towards the latter half" Rosen, The Classical Style, p.280; "with occasional prominent solos and dialogues for two of them." Deryk Cooke, liner notes for *Mozart: The String Quintets*, Grumiaux Trio, A. Gérecz, M. Lesueur, DG, 1967/74; "Mozart's first viola in no way...Luigi's (first cello)." *ibid*; "is the most complex contrapuntal...many years to come." Rosen, The Classical Style, p.265; "grander in scope than anything...even for the orchestra." *ibid*, p.266; "the brilliance of the individual instruments...with passages of exceptional virtuosity." *ibid*, p.281; "Playing on this level is...pantheon of great Mozart recordings." Morin, p.641; "suffused with the warmth and intimacy of Hausmusik." Berger, p.381; "is largely an independent...foundation for the piano (and) strings." Ulrich, p.273; "vastly expanded range of sonorities" Berger, p.387; "manages a careful balance...music and true romantic poetry." M. Struck-Schloen (transl. D. Babcock), liner notes for Mandelring Quartet, "Shostakovich Complete String Quartets", Audite, 2011; "based on catchy opening...times in several different settings." R. Kapilow, All You Need to Do Is Listen, Wiley, 2008; "treat the piano as a soloist constantly in the spotlight." J. Warrack, liner notes, 1997; "so buoyant and so full of life. It's really infectious music" Paul Katz in Robert Schumann, p.285; "one of the most inspired things ever written by anybody." E.Ax in Robert Schumann, p.286; "continuous use of short...sequential patterns...forward without varying the pattern." Rosen, The Romantic Generation, p.705; "he did not expand the means of his art." The Musical Companion, p.542; "daunting legacy bequeathed" "there is a deeper generic structure...that signifies its ancestry." Richard Kramer, liner notes for *Brahms Piano Quartets*, Ax, Stern, Laredo, Ma, Sony, 1988; "among them there is not...be said that 'Homer nodded'." The Musical Companion, p.541; "makings of tragedy" "profound disturbances" "is all grace and romance" R. Kramer, liner notes; "variations and permutations". R. Kramer, liner notes; "precisely evokes the exuberance of a Gypsy wedding band." A.Ross, Listen To This, p.302; "potent combination of driving passion (and) lyrical grace…" Morin, p.177; "continuously building on germinal ideas…series of variants of its opening measure." Burkholder, Grout, Palisca, p.722; "sunny and pleasant in outlook…the music of Mozart and Beethoven." Berger, p.89; "quieter and more reflective than the first sextet," J. Palmer in All Music Guide, p.195.

19th Century France
"inhabit a more private world," Penguin Guide, p384; "contain some of the darkest…moments in (his) chamber music." Morin, p.313; "intellectual, contrapuntal writing" "ever-gutsy sensuality." J. Duchen, review in *BBC Music Magazine*, July 2009; "puts you completely under its spell." *ibid*; "evolve into one another." "language of seamless flow, almost never of dramatic interruption." "as unobtrusive equal in the dialogue" "pervasive web of harmonic richness." F. Pott, liner notes for *Fauré String Quintets*, Domus, Hyperion, 1995; "an outpouring of powerful and vigorous chamber music." *ibid*.

Eastern Europe
"Dvořák wrote melodies that grew…Germanic craftsmanship learned from Brahms and Beethoven." B. Adolphe, liner notes for *The Juilliard String Quartet Turns Fifty*, 1996; "far more assured…capacity for rich, massive sonorities" Richard Wigmore, liner notes for *Dvořák Piano Quartets*, Domus, Hyperion, 1988; "built on the grand scale of Brahms' Piano Quartets" online review by 'Santa Fe listener', Amazon.com Mar 15, 2009; "a beautifully played Dvořák program with charm and warmth." *ibid*; He took much longer to move…piano as well as the strings. Wigmore liner notes; "understated, lyrical opening…business of the first movement." J. Smaczny, liner notes for *Dvořák: Violin Concerto, Piano Quintet*, Chang, Andsnes, et al., EMI, 2003; The popularity of this work is undoubtedly…brooding nature of so much of his music. J. Keller, NYPhil.org program notes; "a work of a neo-Classical stance…juxtaposed in an effective manner," B. Schwarz, L. Fay, p.187.

Chapter 13
"he (had written) only one flute…at least one flute quartet." E. Bromberger, LAPhil.org; "Brief and straightforward…instrument in the process." *ibid*; "to write all-wind music at the top of his form." Swafford, p.172; "that the idealism of Mozartean music manifests itself most palpably." Lang, p.641; "powerful, penetrating piece that…Mozart explored in his great operas." Morin, p.628; "spectacular, hauntingly beautiful set of variations" *ibid*; "allows the clarinetist to display great virtuosity." B. Robins in All Music Guide, p.912; "an elaborate, refined piece…bit as demanding as a string quartet." M. Hasel, liner notes for *Mozart/Beethoven: Quintets for Piano and Winds*, Berlin Philh. Wind Quintet/S. Hough, BIS, 2007; "full of gentle, amiable music", E. Bromberger, LAPhil.org concert notes; "The viola has a range…the bright upper register of the violin." *ibid*; "exploited wittily and skillfully." A. Beaujean (transl. J. Poole), liner notes for *Mozart: Clarinet Quintet, Horn Quintet, Oboe Quartet*, ASMF Chamber Ensemble, Philips, 1980; "one of the jewels of the repertory…infectious high spirits." Morin, p.639; "denounced it for lacking seriousness" Berger, p.42; "a few moments in the spotlight." S. McGinnis, liner notes for *Schubert Octet*, Hausmusik, EMI, 1991; "found at last a perfect medium for the expression of his own humanity." Short History of Music, p.238; "by endeavoring to restore the balance and clarity of the

past." Ulrich, p.340; "the paradigm of his autumnal style." Morin, p.177; "gleams forth over murmuring strings...the mood is perfectly blissful." L. Kramer, Why Classical Music Still Matters, Berkeley, CA: UC Press, 2007, p.35; "old and creatively exhausted." L. Kramer, p.36; "the sound of a romantic longing very familiar to members of Brahms' generation." *ibid*, p.46; "in many ways looks back nostalgically to his youth." S. Coburn in All Music Guide, p.196; "a great deal less harmonically adventuresome." B. Johnston in All Music Guide, p.357; its "mess of 18th century mannerisms." "the latent objectivity of modern music to full consciousness." Taruskin, v.4, p.447; "lamenting cries (and) meandering chants", A.Ross, The Rest Is Noise, p.104; "only a system of sounds, which...according to purely musical affinities." Taruskin, v.4, p.469; "kind of disjointed, collage-like form." C. Anderson-Bazzoli, LAPhil.org concert notes; "While invoking the outdoor wind divertimentos...and emotional indulgences." O. Howard, LAPhil.org concert notes; "contain almost none of the post-Romantic...German modernist music in the 1920s." A. Carpenter in All Music Guide, p.609; "an undercurrent of bitterness and irony...political unrest in Germany at the time." Berger, p.234; "bubbles forth with great enthusiasm and fresh ideas" (F. Stover in All Music Guide, p.657; "whispered nocturnal flutterings and...along mountain streams." Berger, p.19.

NOTES – Part 3

Chapter 14

Mendelssohn "never wrote a more perfect work" and this Overture "has remained eternally fresh." Schonberg, p.214; The loose structure of tone poems..."seemingly fragmentary nature" of his piano works. Libbey, p.430; "the descriptive impulse from...the overture as a genre." Griffiths, p192; "Beethoven had done all there was...", Schonberg, p.430.

Suites, Divertimenti, and Variations
"not a stepping-stone to quartet...spiritual and technical maturity with", Lang, p.647; "because of the opportunities it affords for...pictorial orchestration." The Musical Companion, p.332.

Evolution of Orchestral Music – Symphony & Concerto
"extreme and hostile...High Renaissance polyphony." Weiss & Taruskin, p.139; "in the direction of the 'musical speech'...to a simple accompaniment." *ibid*, p.139; "The first man to think instinctively...drawing "a spectacular variety of ear-tweaking combinations." J. Haylock, *Classical FM*, 4/2010; Thus, sonata form and three- and four-movement...a climax and dénouement. Rosen, The Classical Style, p.155; "Between the instructional works of the late Baroque...and spread of the public concert." Rosen, The Romantic Generation, p.362-63; "new stylistic principle of graduated transition dynamics." Lang, p.711; "was the creation of abstract patterns of pitch and rhythm...generally expected from performers." Rosen, The Romantic Generation, p.28; "now wishing to exercise...the handling of inner parts", Crocker, p.356; "The orchestral music of...still a 'chamber art'." Lang, p.714; "It wasn't until as recently as...something like its modern form...", J. Haylock, Classic FM, April 2010; "The institution of public concerts had been...most notably the Classical symphony." Weiss, Taruskin, p.248; "It was the gradual spread...its dependence on court and church." Rosen, The Romantic

Generation, p.71; "rise of trivial 'salon music' that attended the rise of the bourgeoisie." Weiss, Taruskin, p.273; "applied timbres to an orchestral...master painter's brushstrokes." Lang, p.954.

Evolution of the Symphony
"...indeed, the whole German symphony...of the old opera sinfonia." Crocker, p.438; "the creation of an original expressive language." Crocker, p.359; "frequent, unpredictable placement of..."in a rapid alternation of light and dark." *ibid*; "the form in which...grips with big emotions." Copland, p.159; With this great symphony...and even metaphysical statements. Libbey, p.836; "drove orchestral virtuosity to previously...consummate master of his instrument." Lang, Chap 19.

Development of the Concerto
"flashy and full of 'inspired' effects...Liszt and Paganini." Weiss & Taruskin, p.134; "became the essence and symbol of baroque chamber music." Lang, p.367; "is the dialogue between...soloist(s) and orchestra." The Musical Companion, p.103; "The Baroque concerto is...ripieno and solo sections." Rosen, p.197; "give the soloist-protagonist a dramatic life...that of these two protagonists." The Musical Companion, p.111; "offers a parade of the main ideas of the movement." Plantinga, p.13; "seeks to deepen and ...wealth of pianistic textures." L.Kramer, p.102; "with the development of...shorter pieces for piano and orchestra." The Musical Companion, p.640-41; "the piano encounters an 'objective'...proceeds to make it 'subjective'." L.Kramer, p.100.

Orchestral Music of the Baroque
"The guiding theme of music...constant decline in polyphony," Lang, p.377; "united all the threads developed...sonority and polyphonic construction." Lang, p.368; "was preoccupied with...new concepts of melodic beauty." Ulrich, p.52; "delicately stylized dances...and broadly flowing largos." Lang, p.369; "clearly manifest the sense...found before only in vocal music." Crocker, p.303; "in a mixed homophonic and imitative style...expressively melodious bass lines." Ulrich, p.78; "bringing about corresponding harmonic mismatches." Griffiths p.103; "enlarged the solo passages in the concerto grosso...passionate fresco of dramatic contrasts." Lang, p.484; "advanced the concerto more than any other composer...or 'programmatic' writing." A. Mellor, Classic FM, 2/2011; "the particular atmosphere, flavor, and spirit of each season." Minderovic, p.1541; "Vivaldi experimented with a range... driving rain to bird song." *ibid*; "a flight from counterpoint...progress towards the Classical style"... M. Talbot, *Classic FM*, 2/2011; "Vivaldi developed tremendous rhythmic drive...pathos or poignancy in the slow." Ulrich, p.93; "join winds to the strings for rousing and delectable music." Morin, p.380; "performances of eloquence and...that add a feeling of zestful chance-taking." *ibid*; "the old plush Handel, but dramatic and swaggering." *ibid*, p.381; "a citizen of the world who finally settled down in Britain." Lang, p.526; Bach "seemed unaware of the existence...an unlimited creative capacity." *ibid*, p.527;

Johann Sebastian Bach
"work exhibits a remarkable unity...the genres in which he composed." J. Lester, p.vii; "Bach was less attracted to trio sonatas, more to virtuoso solos." Crocker, p.330; "Perhaps the most brilliantly diverse instrumental anthology ever assembled." All Music Guide, p.1542; "microcosm of Baroque music..the era's emotional universe." Libbey, p.87; "Baroque jam session, the way different instruments take the spotlight." Draper, p.82; "kaleidoscope of counterpoint is

endlessly varied and fascinating." J. Kramer, p.7; "there is nothing about its character to deter the casual listener." J. Keillor, All Music Guide, p.66; "a mathematical delight in the...variations on the same theme." Grammophone Classical Music Guide, 2009, p.XXVI; "those select few who truly understood his art." Quote from Bach scholar Randolph Currie; "same unfathomable and mysterious musical world...the last string quartets of Beethoven." Ulrich, p.106; "the independence and opposition of voices through tone color and phrasing." Rosen, The Romantic Generation, p.6; "demonstrates the full arsenal of the Baroque composer of fugues..." J. Keillor, All Music Guide, p.66; "More than almost any other work...may be understood and its purpose revered." Ulrich, p.107; "with his own more vigorous breath...to the utmost completeness and grandeur." Einstein, p.132; "stand or fall by the treatment of the...*Largo*." 1001 Classical Recordings You Must Hear Hear Before You Die, M. Rye, ed., Universe, 2008, p.96; As pianist Helene Grimaud noted...by choice but of necessity. H. Grimaud, radio interview with E. Forrest, WQXR, 25-Feb-09.

Chapter 15
"Haydn and Mozart...the expressive and the elegant could join hands." Rosen, The Classical Style, p.44; "a partner or a rival...impulse to significant change." L. Kramer, p.49; "that mysterious unity...like different aspects..." Short History of Music, p.161; "convinces us that each finale is the inevitable outcome" *ibid*.

Joseph Haydn
"The consistency of Haydn's output is almost greater than any other composer." D. Boyd, 'Haydn Seek', Grammophone, 7/09; According to pianist Howard Shelley...energy, and contrast. Grammophone,7/09; "lusty, peasant-like minuets," Schonberg, p.94; "Haydn's impressive series of 100-odd symphonies...and after." Crocker, p.372; "For Haydn, the overall form...to form a complete musical experience." *ibid*, p.425; "developing a pregnant idea through all imaginable metamorphoses." Lang, p.632; "music to be listened to for its own expressive value." Crocker, p.378; "as if to say to people...but look how effective it can be'." Shelley, Grammophone, 7/09; "new expressive freedom, a freedom from convention." Rosen, The Romantic Generation, p.135; "dramatic, passionate, and at times demonic tone" Lang, p.630; "took on a new emotional intensity (and) dramatic sense of urgency and energy." Berger, p.186; "tempestuous fast movements and dramatic changes of tempo and dynamic." BBC Music Magazine, 7/09; "curiously relentless character which eventually distorts the traditional style." Crocker, p.373; "harshly dramatic and fiercely emotional without a trace of sentimentality." Rosen, The Classical Style, p.146; "dramatic, highly personal and mannered...rationalism and classicism of the older generation." T. Blanning, The Pursuit of Glory: Europe 1648-1815. Viking Penguin, 2007, p518; "subjectivism, emotional excess, spontaneity, violence, even a kind of anarchism." Blanning, The Triumph of Music, p.94; "became broader than it had ever been, deeper, more expressive." Schonberg, p.89; "deep inner balance" and..."character with a minimum of means." Crocker, pp.404-05; "an approachable, popular style...inventive mastery of form." L. Kemp, liner notes for Haydn *Paris Symphonies*, Philh. Hung., Dorati, Decca, 1971; "it is only in the 1780s...elements of folk style at will." Rosen, The Classical Style, p.330; "which has the most holy religious character," A. Fischer, 'Haydn Seek' Grammophone, 7/09; "Not a measure (of the *Paris* symphonies)...is not marked by Haydn's wit." Rosen, The Classical Style p.159; "Haydn's most massive expansion of sonata form until then." *ibid*, p.160; "finely developed sonata-rondos...quality of the initial movements." Lang, p.631; "The slow movements of many of...of his chamber music." Rosen, The Classical Style, p.45; "reveal new

relationships between the introductions and the following allegros." *ibid*, p.269; "For beauty, power and range,...created in so short a time." Morin, p.430; "the different orchestral colors...a new kind of mass sonority." Rosen, The Classical Style, p.143; "rarely displays the extraordinary passion of the finest works of the 1770s." *ibid*, p.xv; "more powerful than (his) finest works...are certainly more efficient." *ibid*; "sophisticated control to relate...the music with great energy." *ibid*; "lack of a precise definition...(a) nebulous quality" *ibid*, p.347; "until the listener no longer knows when to expect it." *ibid*, p.337; "heedless of rules, who traded in the inspired-unexpected...better than the gloomiest artists." Wigmore, "The Poor Man's Mozart?" *Grammophone*, June2009; "adored from St. Petersburg to Seville...while remaining...a servant." Morris, p.46.

Mozart
Mozart "perfected as he created the form of the classical concerto." Rosen, p.263; "Mozart's music is at once...its depth, its subtlety, its passion." Schonberg, p.103; "to a certain part of the 19th century...so 'godlike' a perfection..." Short History of Music, p.3; "the piano's exposition is...the orchestral ritornello." Rosen, The Classical Style, p.206; "bound himself only...reformulated anew for each work." *ibid*, p.210; "the entrance of the soloist...on the stage of a drama." *ibid*, p.197;
"In terms of Mozart's style, dramatization means development...and modulation." *ibid*, p.203; "independent creations based...contrast between solo and orchestra..." *ibid*, p.210; "none is without a matchless contribution from his pen," Short History of Music, p.165; "The miracle of Mozart's style was...departure in the history of music." Rosen, The Classical Style, p.218; "an exalted level" infusing them "with an otherworldly purity and spirituality." Morin, p.629; "to be expanded and intensified by...the great Romantics who followed." *ibid*; "integrate elements...rich...polyphonic textures." Steinberg, p.280; "the keyboard concerto was a personal vehicle...presenting himself to the public." Plantinga, p.286; "had not broken, except in small details...style of his contemporaries." Rosen, The Classical Style, p.214; "Where listeners would have expected...rejoinder from the soloist." J. Magnum, LAPhil.org; "has a depth of feeling...that have made the concerto endure." J. Kramer, pp.428-9; "as an expression of grief and despair...is the same tragic power recaptured." Rosen, p.211; "This concerto is the last of the miraculous harvest of 1784," Steinberg, p.301; "The first two movements of...contrapuntal imitation." Rosen, The Classical Style, p.226; "the greatest of all Mozart's concerto finales...and opera buffa style." *ibid*; "This concerto is Mozart's first true essay in orchestral grandeur." Rosen, The Classical Style, p.236; "over a troubled accompaniment we hear one of the world's astounding melodies..." Steinberg, p.307; "both grand and gentle, it offers...and audaciously personal." Steinberg, p.308; "little ambition by way of...lyric and softly moonlit." Steinberg, p.310; "no worries in it...the worries come in the second movement." Andsnes, interview, available on YouTube; "in which the piano and orchestra cavort...seemingly most perfect masterpieces." N. Zaslow, ed. The Complete Mozart, WW Norton, 1990, p.133; "The soft but tumultuous strains...unease, portending tragedy." D. Heartz, Mozart, Haydn and Early Beethoven. Norton, 2008, p.108; "began with a melody...pleasant anticipation of its return." *ibid*; "brooding chromaticism and stormy outbursts" N. Zaslaw, ed. The Complete Mozart. NY: WW Norton, 1990, p.131; "a clear instance of an 18th century happy ending." *ibid*; "darkened mood, chromatic instabilities, and stormy patches" *ibid*, p.133; "With all its dramatic power...detail of the string quartet." Rosen, The Classical Style, p.250; "more intimate (and) it evades the theatricality of (K.466)." *ibid*, p.245; "almost neutral character of the material" *ibid*, p.251; "meant more to please...and stir the

emotions." Steinberg, p.280; "ability to draw the utmost poignance of expression from the simplest means." Rosen, The Classical Style, p.243; "the most 'progressive' of all Mozart's works...as the greatest of early Romantic concertos." Rosen, The Classical Style, p.258; "depend more upon the delicate...interplay of concerto style." *ibid*, p.260; "provides the ideal mix of purity and profundity." Morin, p.629; "sonority inspired by the...himself to play, is unique." Rosen, The Classical Style, p.214; "sparkles with the wit that is typical of Mozart at his happiest," J.Kramer, p.454; "hardly the trifling showpiece...of other clarinet concertos." J. Kramer, p.421-22.

Symphonies
"he leaves the hearer out of breath," quote of violinist K.D. von Dittersdorf; "far too many notes," quote of Emperor Joseph II; "of much greater depth, confidence, brilliance, and power" Schonberg, p.103; It is in these three symphonies...voice as a symphonist. J. Kramer, p.464; "bathing in a refined...projects gentleness and high hopes." Morin, p.620; "perhaps the richest...before Beethoven's Seventh Symphony." Rosen, The Classical Style, p.347; "provided Mozart with the...was ever to know," J. Kramer, p.475; "This gave Mozart the opportunity...plan more exciting and expressive." Crocker, p.407; "excite wonder even for...output is a creative miracle." Bookspan, p.278; "between grace and melancholy...on a dark background." Short History of Music, p.177-78; "the characteristically liquid sound...throughout the work..." Bookspan, p.279; "wonderful clarinet writing and Haydnesque ingenuity." BBC Music Magazine, May 2009; "behind the gentle yet intense song of the violins." Bookspan, p.282; Sir Charles also points out...almost jolly symphony. BBC Music Magazine, May 2009; "magnificent coda where all...one of music's greatest triumphs." L. Shulman, NJSO program notes, 2009; "introduce all kinds of contrapuntal devices...overwhelming passages..." Schonberg, p.105; "makes a direct appeal even on the casual listener." R. Wigmore, liner notes for Mozart *Symphonies 35-41*, Böhm, DG, 1976.

Beethoven
"not just to create music...highest artistic worth." Sachs, p.14; "big-caliber artillery pointed at the future." *ibid*, p.13; "Beethoven the virtuoso felt free...by Beethoven the composer." L. Plantinga, Beethoven's Concertos. NY: W.W. Norton, 1999; "youthful preoccupation intimately bound up...for the composer-virtuoso's performances" *ibid*, p.4; "shows Beethoven struggling toward...achieved by Haydn and Mozart." *ibid*, p.92; "are fairly unadventurous...in the nature of the piano writing," Solomon, p.136; "has a Promethean strength of purpose...something altogether more epic." The Musical Companion, pp.636; "model of Classic-Romantic concerto form for the 19th century." Solomon, p.136; "a new note of passion enters...Mozart's *C minor Concerto* (No.24) The Musical Companion, p.637; "full of Mozartean reminiscences." Rosen, The Classical Style, p.389; "entrance of the piano in the first measure...*Piano Concerto No.9*." *ibid*, p.391; "a vividly etched dialogue between piano and strings." Plantinga, p.185; "And yet out of this...bold and life-affirming *Fifth Piano Concerto*." E. Baker, Classical FM, Mar 2010; "storming solo cadenzas, has a royal majesty;" The Musical Companion, p.637; "so far ahead of its time that...grow into the music." NJSO, Program Notes, 2008-09; "bombast of scales, arpeggios, trills, thunderous chords, and the like." *ibid*; "serene bliss" of the second movement "follows...in the first movement..." Draper, p.37; "heroic struggle of the first movement...rest in the second movement." *ibid*, p.58; "irrepressible joyride" and one of Beethoven's "most delightful and positive conclusions." NJSO, Program Notes, 2008-09; "stylistic range that can only be

called Protean." Morris, p.119; "The opening theme quietly...in concerted woodwinds." Plantinga, p.217; "summons up the imagined simplicity...in the countryside." Plantinga, p.218; "seems to have differed appreciably from the version we know." Plantinga, p.235.

The Symphonies
"one major work with another...all geothermal heat;" Morris, p.136; "begat the decidedly unheroic Fourth...transluscent delicacy...exuberant display of power" *ibid;* Beethoven's *Third, Fifth* and *Ninth* Symphonies...marvelous economy. Martin Meyer, liner notes for *Beethoven Cello Sonatas*, Schiff/Perenyi, ECM, 2004; "to get beyond this...own style and career." Kramer, p.75; "a caricature of Haydn pushed to absurdity." Kramer, p.75; "a gross monster, a hideously writhing wounded dragon." Sachs, p.15; "the first of Beethoven's immense expansions of classical form." Rosen, p.392; "limited themselves...to a purification of feelings." Einstein, Music in the Romantic Era, W.W. Norton, 1947, p.42; "is fundamentally a show...flexes his muscles." Sachs, p.141; "to the heroic, to the religious, to the moral." *ibid;* "too much that is glaring and bizarre." Morris, p.116; "strange modulations and violent transitions...where one would derive no pleasure from it..." Weiss, Taruskin, p.279; "the musical public of Beethoven's time was ...was indeed a remarkable proof of musical intelligence." Lang, p.1026; "inspired by a modern hero...no less evident a role." Einstein, Music in the Romantic Era, p.45; "willful break with tradition." Weiss, Taruskin, p.279; "rapped out with neither ceremony nor apology." L. Kramer, p78; The "purity of form and depth...the very ethos of heroism." Short History of Music, p.182; "miraculously balances the tension...and humor can exist side-by-side." Draper, p.37; "to give a bit of emotional respite." Sachs, p.14; "From the Eroica Symphony onward...of a genius in full control." Morris, p.121; "exceptional example of how...can get out of a few notes..." T. Smith, The NPR Curious Listener's Guide to Classical Music, Perige Trade, 2002, p.3; "four-note rhythmic figure...all movements in various guises" J. Kramer, p.648; "one of the most violent, conflict-ridden pieces ever composed." L. Kramer, p.174; "an effort to get from turmoil...evolves from dark to bright." L.Kramer, p.176; "coda that serves also...striking turn toward bright C major." Crocker, p.420; E.T.A. Hoffmann described the link...giving way to "radiant blinding sunlight," Morris, p.144; "The triumphant effect of the eruption...long stretch of harmonic ambiguity." Swafford, p.273-74; "represents a retreat from the militancy of the Fifth," L. Kramer, p.184; "all painting in instrumental music...discover the situations themselves." Kramer, p.91; "is evidently done for effect – if splendidly." Griffiths, p.180; "is the fulcrum of the Pastoral Symphony...narrative direction to the whole." L. Kramer, p.178; "bathed in a benign luminous energy," L. Kramer, p.174; "massive, muscular, louder than...explosion of superhuman energy." Morris, p.148; "short on themes but long on rhythmic drive," Crocker, p.421; "short and deliciously witty" Morris, p.148; "full of sly humor." Griffiths, p.158; "it seems to be the most infectiously joyous thing man has ever made." *BBC Magazine*, Jan 2010; "the music se ems to descend...again more ecstatically than before." *ibid*; "to mind the lightness and clarity of the 18th century Viennese style." Rosen, The Classical Style, p.510; "civilized gaiety" that marked the classical style "makes its last...the last string quartets." *ibid*, p.98; "swamped by sentiment." *ibid*; "the most profound message of brotherhood and hope." A. Mellor, *Classic FM*, Aug 2010; "turning once again to the...with its grand-manner Empire style." Solomon, p.406; "The Ninth consolidated and elaborated...and transcended them." Sachs, p.3; Author Harvey Sachs feels...aftermath of revolution and Napoleon. see *ibid*, p.95; "begins quietly but not calmly...seems to be moving towards us." *ibid*, p.136; "Beethoven compresses human life into a

quarter of an hour." *ibid*, p.135; "to analyze such a composition...long hesitated to undertake." *ibid*, p.130; "freely rearranged...in accordance with his own poetic vision." Solomon, p.408; "the simplest harmonies are presented...imbued with unutterable significance," Crocker, p.423; "in simpler progressions but in curious rhythms;" *ibid*, p.421; "swirls continuously upwards...it is in a dynamic A-B-C-D form." Sachs, p.86; "The opening is...full of rich invention...of the colossal theme." Weiss, Taruskin, p.284; "conceived partly as a parody of the first movement." Rosen, The Classical Style, p.280; "emerges from the orchestral narrative...with audacious brilliance." S. Johnson, BBC *Magazine*, Feb 2010; "The contrast between the marvelously...the fourth never fails to jar." Sachs, p.150, for an in-depth historical as well as expert musical analysis of Beethoven's Ninth, the reader is referred to Sachs' entire work. "the variation set is completely transformed...work in miniature." Rosen, The Classical Style, p.440; "the variation finale of Beethoven's Ninth was a model for both Schumann and Liszt." Rosen, The Romantic Generation, p.480; "Beethoven managed without intellectual condescension...anthem-like tune of the finale." Morris, p.211; "represents struggle...so monumentally anguished a cry." Schonberg, p.123; "not as a master of the universe...thoughts and emotions." *Classic FM*, Aug 2010.

Schubert
"there are poignant passages in...beauty and pain seem inseparable," Draper, p.26; "forms and textures of Mozart...own without ever turning back." Schonberg, p.132; "to wander and become diffuse," Schonberg, p.134; "a consolidation of techniques" G. Crankshaw, liner notes for *Schubert Complete Symphonies*, VPO/Kertesz, Decca, 1991; "a glorious outpouring of melody." 1001 Classical Recordings..., p.230; "the darkest, grimmest, most 'pathetic' mood." Taruskin, Oxford History of Western Music, v.3, p.108; "is valued for the lyricism of its themes, not for its overall form." Crocker, p.429; "declares Schubert to be Beethoven's peer." Short History of Music, p.191; "had an enormous influence on composers...from Bruckner to Dvořák," Taruskin, Oxford History of Western Music, v.3, p.87.

NOTES – Part 4

Chapter 16

"Berlioz, Schumann, Liszt and Wagner...the musical life of Europe." Weiss, Taruskin, p.296; "discouraged the composition of new...during the next half century." A. Peter Brown, The Symphonic Repertoire, vol.4, The Second Golden Age of the Viennese Symphony, Indiana Univ. Press, 2004, p.1; "and then reconciling them into some synthetic whole." A. Boime, in Tibbetts, p103; "symphonic space for evocative...a ceremony in Cologne Cathedral" Griffiths, p.186; Interestingly, composer Lukas Foss...with Schubert's and Mendelssohn's L. Foss in Tibbetts, p.278; "you never have big melodies, like a Tchaikovsky symphony." W. Sawallisch in Tibbetts, p.275; "absolute music in the Beethovenian mould." R. Wigmore, liner notes for *Schumann Complete Symphonies*, Staatskapelle Dresden, Sawallisch, EMI, 2002; "represents Schumann's most radical...together all four movements." *ibid*; On the other side, Lukas Foss...we should trust him. L. Foss in Tibbetts, p.278; "very lugubrious kind of...opening of the Second Symphony" P. Ostwald in Tibbetts, p.266; "all those short entrances...like an echo coming back." W. Sawallisch in Tibbetts, p.276;

"Schumann did not completely succeed in his symphonies, partly because he never learned to think in terms of orchestral sound." see Crocker, p.443; "has a Mendelssohnian grace and lightness of touch" R. Wigmore, liner notes for Schumann Complete Symphonies; "charming and so Mendelssohnian...counterpoint in the last movement." M. Alsop in Tibbetts, p.275; "a continuously developing lyricism...the first two movements." Rosen, The Romantic Generation, p.689; "magnificent work with both Handelian...found in any concerto." S. Isserlis in Tibbetts, p.366; "lesser-known works, which still deserve to be heard." "Local locals: Eric Wyrick", interview by J.A. Wolkoff, 8/13/09, online at Maplewood.blogs.nytimes.com.

Felix Mendelssohn
"by far the most restrained...in the 1830s and 1840s." Schonberg, p.218; "his devotion to clarity and balance look back to the Classical era." Morin, p.573; "for lyrical melodic lines and delicate, transparent textures," Rosen, The Romantic Generation, p.569; "versatile, craftsmanlike composer whose...poles of classicism and romanticism." R. Larry Todd, Mendelssohn, A Life in Music. NY: Oxford Univ. Press, 2003, p.xix; "has clear lines and...avoids the sweeping Romantic gesture." Schonberg, p.218; "masterpieces of refinement, lightness, clarity, and control," Short History of Music, p.196; "tender, wistful, whimsical, or spritely." Crocker, p.438; "sweet, pure, perfectly proportioned master." Schonberg, p.221; "there is indeed something elfin about it." Schonberg, p.214; "was absolutely perfect and was always...delving deeper into things." E. Leinsdorf in Tibbetts, p.266; "ever developed beyond the supreme fluency and grace of his early masterpieces." Morin, p.573; "he never lived up to his initial creative promise." Schonberg, p.211; "that threatened the established order of things." *ibid*, p.212; "the Romantics did not speak the same language." *ibid*, p.219; "real conflict was lacking in his life as in his art." Short History of Music, p.196; "along with inexorable vivacity." The Musical Companion, p.641; "most successful synthesis...with the Romantic virtuoso form," Rosen, The Romantic Generation, p.586; "produced the quintessential Romantic concerto," Morin, p.576; "most sublime and original...compositions." H. Hahn, liner notes for *Mendelssohn/Shostakovich Violin Concertos*, Sony, 2002; "revealed a forcefulness...amiable whimsy or tenderness." Crocker, p.438; "masterful integration of virtuosity and...effortlessly from the violin..." Kramer, p.407; "transformed his personal travelling experiences into poetic sound images." M. Struck-Schloen (transl. J. Scheffel), liner notes for *Mendelssohn: Complete Chamber Music for Strings, Vol.2*, Mandelring String Quartet, Audite, 2012; "elfin spirit leaps out...conception of orchestral writing." D. Dubal, p.216; "garlands of flute tone woven around the strings." Morin, p.573; "especially engaging...one of Mendelssohn's inspired ideas – simple and beautiful." Kramer, p.409; "deplored music with explicit extra musical references." *ibid*, p.414; "in the whole first movement...of a Scottish highland mist." *ibid*;

Frederic Chopin
"Chopin solved many of the problems confronting Schumann by avoiding them," Crocker, p.444.

Franz Liszt
"sections merging freely and lacking the customary development." L. Shulman, NJSO program notes, 2010; "show a profound understanding of the integration between soloist and orchestra." *ibid*; "forceful opening gesture...octaves and clangorous chords," Steinberg, The Concerto, p.242; "a sweetly harmonious, sensitive...woodwinds and muted strings." *ibid*; "extroverted to the point of

exhibitionism…flame-throwing pianist…" Bookspan, p.217; "the first perfect realization…treated on variation principles…undergoes constant transformations and disguises,…purpose of unity within variety." Kramer, p.347; "The seven-note recurring…the outset by the clarinets" H. Glass, LAPO program notes, online; "in the work in different guises…together with thematic logic." L. Shulman, NJSO program notes, 2010; "to focus on the individual timbres of instruments." *ibid*; "reveal an experimental approach… matching of soloist and orchestra." J. Williamson, liner notes for *Liszt Piano Concertos Nos.1&2, Totentanz*, K. Zimerman, BSO, Ozawa, DG; "by transforming the thematic material…portray a programmatic subject." Burkholder, Grout, Palisca, p.728; "the very essence of gypsy soul and wild abandon." Morin, p.517.

Richard Wagner
"made up for his deficiencies by instinct and a profound musicality." Schonberg, p.269; "hours…poring over scores of Beethoven symphonies." *ibid*, p.270; "a high degree of…restless, searching tonal instability," AMG, p.1473; "his melodies and harmonies…Wagner often used dissonant chords." Swafford, p.275; "took chromaticism as far as it could go within the key system" The Musical Companion, p.66; "the tonal harmonic system to near bursting point." J. Haylock, Classic FM, July 2009; "His aesthetic was perhaps…music has ever known" AMG, p.1473; "the most subjective of all artists." A.Einstein, Music in the Romantic Era, NY: WW Norton, 1947, p.40; "Wagner's achievements…the artist is the incarnation of his age." Short History of Music, p.214; "was his positioning of music…it has never been dislodged." T. Blanning, The Triumph of Music, p.59; "rapturous musical creativeness" produced…, see Short History of Music, p.227; "the text merely floated on top of the rich orchestral sonorities." Crocker, p.457; "a chaos of unconnected sensual elements…the perfect blend of poetry and music." Sachs, p184-85; "Practically every 19th century composer…spiritual as well as musical preceptor." Weiss, Taruskin, p.322; "caused the orchestra to burst…message for all mankind," Crocker, p.457; "sounded the death knell of…a viable independent genre." Weiss, Taruskin, p.322; "that the mantle of Beethoven had fallen on their shoulders" *ibid*, p.324; "that music was to be valued for its emotional or symbolic content." *ibid*, p.343; "an independent existence and…drama and the other arts." *ibid*, p.326; "only the total work of art…could redeem humankind from the abyss." Blanning, The Triumph of Music, p.106; "capable of one-upping Mozart or Beethoven;" Sachs, p.185; "a degree of megalomania that approached…that is unpleasant in human character." Schonberg, p.268; "must endure. His work…cannot be ignored." Sachs, p.189; "Through much of the latter half…the European artistic avant-garde." *ibid*, p.186; "An imagination so powerful…succeeding generations…is conceivable without him." Taruskin, Oxford History…, v.3, p.479; "rule by the best…seduced the imagination of Europe" Tuchman, p.299; "all great art must be based on mythology." Schonberg, p.272; "unbroken drama expressed in unbroken music." Schonberg, p.273; "illustrates Wagner's unrelenting effort to make music overwhelmingly convincing." Crocker, p.460; "gods, goddesses, earth-mothers…through love wins out." Schonberg, p.285; "had acquired an oppressive atmosphere of obligatory reverence." Tuchman, p.293; "the faithful absorbed the master's works 'as if they were receiving Holy Communion'." *ibid*; "The opening chords of Tristan were…a breakaway, a new concept." Schonberg, p.277; "for Wagner a stable key is …by remote modulations." Crocker, p.462; However, Richard Taruskin does not see…"the historicist tendency to write history backward…goal-oriented evolution through history. Thomas May, amazon.com review; "a reactionary with a social vision…caused by modernization." Taruskin, Oxford History…, v.4, p.3;

Chapter 17
Hector Berlioz
"Only a genius could have overcome...the paths he took." Schonberg, p.152-54; "sincerely believed that anybody becoming...on the road to hell," Schonberg, p.156; "the forms he used were different...tried to shape his materials." *ibid*, p.153; "was the foundation of all composition." Rosen, The Romantic Generation, p.555; "super-heated imagination", *ibid*; "the first composer consistently...the nature of the instruments." Quote from Richard Strauss; "With Berlioz you have a wide range...just one given character." K. Kolb in Tibbetts, p.264; "the more colossal the means...the better he felt." Einstein, The Romantic Generation, p.39; "preoccupied...with extreme and gigantic aims." Short History of Music, p.215; "To his inflamed imagination...generalized and ambiguous in meaning." *ibid*; "Mendelssohn was sanitized to perfection...excessive enthusiasm or exaggeration." M. Steen, p.337; "the projection of the ego...the artist as inspired lunatic." Rosen, The Romantic Generation, p.543; "exploited a satanic public image...taste for the macabre." *ibid*, p.472; "sharp satire and wit, mingled with considerable bitterness." Weiss, Taruskin, p.298; "produced an unceasing inventiveness in...orchestral color." Griffiths, p.180; "all other musical means...of orchestral color." Short History of Music, p.216; "first to express himself autobiographically...into a 'drama with voices'." Lang, p.859; "there nevertheless was a great deal of tradition in his music," Schonberg, p.160; "uncontrollable instincts of youth (with) restraint, clarity, and proportion." *ibid*; "ignored most of Mozart." *ibid*; "Berlioz was the only man...Beethoven come alive again." *ibid*, p.162; "Of all who dared rival Beethoven...than young Hector Berlioz." Crocker, p.434; "Beethoven (to Berlioz) stood for all...against all that was trivial in music." Weiss, Taruskin, p.299; "continuing the symphonic ideal...a poetic idea in music." Lang, p.859; "the symphony responds to the abstract-musical only." *ibid*, p.860; "Our Hero experiences in the course of his drugged dreaming," Bookspan, p.77; "a kind of five-act drama of nightmares and hallucinations." Weiss, Taruskin, p.301; "first major figure in European music...Beethoven's last creative phase." Sachs, p.176; "concepts of color and sonority...estimates of orchestral sound." Schonberg, p.157; "the unity of his symphonic whole" Short History of Music, p.217; "saw in every Frenchman an agent of the revolution." J. Kramer, p.115; "is wonderfully alive, marvelously sonorous – because of its orchestration." *ibid*, p.122; "rather, it is a work...were unlike those of any other composer." *ibid*, p.123; "was left on the periphery of the musical establishment" M. Steen, p.304.

Cesar Franck
"to go to the edge of tonality...a feeling of transcendence," Libbey, p.242; "odd combination of Wagnerian...and Bachian rigor." Morin, p.323; "recapitulation...but here it is in an alien key...recalls all the themes..." *ibid*; "haunts the work no less pervasively than it had haunted Bruckner's Third Symphony." Taruskin, Oxford History..., v.3, p.776; "returned in its original form in the coda to the finale." *ibid*, p.777; "only a few primal themes...metamorphosed as the work progresses." Copland, pp.156-57; "deft dovetailing of piano and orchestra." A. Corleonis, All Music Guide, p.466; "one of the glitterati of the French musical scene." *ibid*, p.465; "a set of six free-flowing variations enclosed by an introduction and finale." O. Howard, LAPhil.org concert notes; "is built mainly on the piano's...from the variation melody." *ibid*.

Camille Saint-Saëns
"probably the most awesome child prodigy in the history of music." Schonberg, p.341; "worked prolifically in all forms...of purity, clarity, refinement, and

Classicism." *ibid;* And he despised Debussy's music. Schonberg, p.342; "did not make much headway." *ibid;* "elegant but superficial…the French Mendelssohn", *ibid;* "bad music that was well written." *ibid;* "being unwilling to sully his facility with depth or originality." Swafford, p.342-43; "heaviest of lightweights…full of wit, color, melody and imagination." Morin, p.782; "a luscious depth." Dubal, p.340; "triumphant chords…majestic full voice", Libbey, p.585; "blazing heart-on-sleeve melodies…capacity to sing and growl." H. Wallace in <u>1001 Classical Recordings You Must Hear Hear Before You Die</u>, M. Rye, ed., Universe, 2008, p.382.

Chapter 18

Wagner considered the symphony "redundant" by the 1840s. Griffiths, p.203; "upholding the primacy of sonata form" Swafford, p.169; "represented Russian melancholy expressed in German forms." Schonberg, p.512.

Johannes Brahms
"the renovation of music as…resuscitation of its traditional forms," Libbey, p.85; "without which serial music of the 20th century would be unthinkable." Csampai and Holland, p.504 (transl. R.G.); "combines rigorous argument with…and emotionally probing." *ibid;* "stooped to no trickery…music beautiful for its own sake." <u>The Musical Companion</u>, p.278; "immense power…full of inspired individual touches." *ibid;* "metamorphose from the comparatively unbridled…second half of the 19th century." (S. Isserlis in Grammophone, Sept 2010; "a mannequin with a somewhat narrow heart." Goulding, p.170; "The new symphony…is a possession…pleasure and fruitful study." *ibid*, pp.170-73; "he had before him the fearsome specter of the Beethoven Ninth" Schonberg, p.296; "the creation of true music…acquired by years of study." <u>The Musical Companion</u>, p.277; "Beethovenian spiritual journey of (its) outer movements" B. Johnston, in All Music Guide, p.189; "like Beethoven's Ninth (Brahms' First)…to attain a final victory." Ross, <u>Listen to This</u>, p.300; Also, the intensely dramatic…Schumann's *Fourth Symphony*. MacDonald, Grammophone, Dec 2010; "succeeded in establishing a motivic continuity…continued throughout the four movements." T. Sick, transl. J.S. Rushworth, liner notes for *Brahms Symphonies*, István Kertész, Decca, 1996; The two serenades were viewed…"emotional density" of the symphonies. A. Morin, p.172; "begins with a dipping-and-rising…kernel of the entire piece." Ross, <u>Listen to This</u>, p.294; "an odd mix of overt heroism and dense formal logic" B. Johnston, in <u>All Music Guide</u>, p.189; "the *Third* leads neither to victory nor to tragedy, but ends in resignation and hard-won calm." M. Steinberg, <u>The Symphony</u>, p.80; "the strict musical architecture…passion of the Romantic era." M. MacDonald in <u>1001 Classical Recordings…</u>, p.428; "epic tragedy and melodic lyricism find their most powerful expression." *ibid;* "combination of tragic feelings and heart-rending melancholy" Dubal, p.325; "a vision 'seen through a glass darkly…the grandeur of its conception." <u>The Musical Companion</u>, p.281; "The finale of Brahms' Fourth is…musical history stripped to the bone." A. Ross, <u>Listen to This</u>, p.311; "perhaps the most extraordinary…post-Beethoven and pre-Mahler era." *ibid;* "On a melody (St. Anthony Chorale)…both in terms of design and content. <u>The Musical Companion</u>, p.333; "a single tune, examines it from every…angle, and puts it back together." T.Smith, <u>The NPR Curious Listener's Guide to Classical Music</u>. Perige Trade, 2002, p.4; "richness of expression and unerring taste…dry, artificial, and (even) grotesque." <u>Composers on Music</u>, 2nd ed., J. Fisk, ed., Northeastern, 1997, p.132; "roughly equal footing, as one troubled mind commiserating with another." Ross, <u>Listen to This</u>, p.296; His music has a 'sunset' quality about it, L. Foss in Tibbett, p.277; "the tone of late-night

consolation...chief gift to the human race." Ross, Listen to This, p.300; "touched the profoundest depths of inspiration...orchestral trickery." The Musical Companion, p.278; "vehicle for virtuoso display with orchestral accompaniment." A. Morin, p.173; "creating a more equal partnership between soloist and orchestra." ibid; Harold Schonberg characterized..."keeper of the flame" Schonberg, p.290; "music combined a sensitivity...unmatched by other romantics." Morin, p.170; "Sturm und Drang turbulence," MacDonald, Grammophone, Dec 2010; "concerto is not a war; it is a creative debate rooted in conflict." R. Osborne, liner notes for Brahms Piano Concertos, Gilels/Jochum, 1996; "classically-grounded...very much from Beethoven tradition...heavy in orchestration." Interview with Leif Ove Andsnes, YouTube; "functions as a palate cleanser in between substantial courses." H. Smith in 1001 Classical Recordings..., p.420; "sunny, idyllic works abounding in melodic...rhythmic robustness and warm flow of harmony" Bookspan, p.97; "Brahms had written one against the violin." ibid, p.98; "one of his least memorable creations, suffering from unimaginative piano writing." The Musical Companion, p.693; "Throughout the concerto both soloists...orchestra in a bid for supremacy." T. Williams, BBC Magazine, Dec 2009; "magnificent piece...it has a powerful sense of suppressed energy." The Musical Companion, p.694.

Antonin Dvořák
"sums up the emotional experience...Romantic feeling in every bar." C. MacDonald, Grammophone, Dec 2010; "Dvořák was singularly endowed with...the 'classical' and the 'futurist'." Taruskin, "Nationalism: Colonialism in Disguise?", in New York Times, 8/22/93; "tight control of formal structure...can go anywhere at any time." Morin, p.279; "to an obscurity which is out...true worth." R. Minshull, liner notes for Dvořák: Complete Symphonies, LSO, István Kertész, Decca, 1991; "marks the beginning of his true maturity as a symphonic composer." ibid; "cheerful assurance" and "gives no hint...at his lack of recognition." ibid; "can easily stand beside his better known, later symphonies." J.Kramer, p.248; "witnessed a sea change in his approach to composition." Jan Smaczny, BBC Magazine, Mar 2010; "consciously molded in the traditions of Viennese Classicism" ibid; "ideas linked by rhythmic rather than melodic features." ibid; "is the majestic culmination of Dvořák's evolving symphonic style." R. Cowan, BBC Music Magazine, July 2009; "did it imply that...was in some sense inherently American?" Taruskin, v.3, p.755; "marked the birth of modern Czech music," K. Schumann (transl. J. Coombs), liner notes for Dvořák: Orchestral Music, BRSO, Kubelik, DG, 1975-77; "symbol of nature as the basis of all life." ibid; "central European folk tales...not always have a happy ending." L. Shulman, NJSO concert notes, 2010; "orchestrated in bright primary colors...traditional Czech folk dances." J.E. Bedell, www.bsomusic.org, 2008; "more sophisticated concert dances...removed from their folk origins." ibid; "poignant Siegfried Idyll-style harmonies." D. Joffé, BBC Music Magazine, July 2009; "astonishingly inventive use of texture," J. Smaczny, liner notes for Dvořák: Serenades, VPO, Myung-Whun Chung, 2003; "It is not often played...difficult and not 'pianistic' at all." Martin Helmchen, Classic FM, February 2010.

Piotr Tchaikovsky
"affords multiple insights into..."a form for developing reasoned musical discussion." N. Goodwin, liner notes for Sibelius Complete Symphonies, Oslo PO/Jansons, Chandos, 1988; "had much more sympathy with the life...of all the Russian composers." Steen, p.659; "gulf between people's taste and the expert's opinion." ibid, p.661; "a means to express his most inward thoughts and feelings." N. Goodwin; "no 19th century composer was...personal disclosure

through music." Weiss, Taruskin, p.338; "less a form for developing...his most inward thoughts and feelings." N. Goodwin; "melodic themes borrowed from Ukrainian folksong" *ibid*; "the music reflects a wholly unmorbid side of the composer's personality." *ibid*; "offering tremendous drama and outpouring of indelible melody." T. Smith, The NPR Curious Listener's Guide to Classical Music. NY, NY: Penguin Putnam, 2002, p.208; "great eruptions of fiery passion as well as the expression of profound defeatism." K. Franke (transl. J. Coombs), liner notes for Tchaikovsky Symphonies 4-6, Leningrad Philharmonic, Mravinsky, 1978-9; "If Beethoven's Fifth is Fate...trying to get out." N. Goodwin; "though by its close the symphony has done away with the difference." L. Kramer, p.51; "is a large self-contained whole...encloses another." *ibid*; "shatters the stillness. Sheer turmoil follows", *ibid*; "the long dying-away...sole substance of the finale," L. Kramer, p.51; "ending what Tchaikovsky had virtually composed as his own epitaph." N. Goodwin; "peculiar alternation of melancholy...of grief and joy." Libbey, p.214; "reflected a conscious premonition of death on (his) part." N. Goodwin; "begins at a peak of magnificence...in search of a new theme." L. Kramer, p.63; "its grandiose, Listzian pages... Rubinstein's refined and intimate style." J. Haylock, *BBC Music Magazine* collection, v.18, no.10;

"with greater finesse or panache, not even Rachmaninov." R. Dettmer in The All Music Guide, p.1390; "tormented and overwrought soul...submission with emotional extremes." M. Morrison in *ibid*; Tchaikovsky completely approved...events recount it that way. see P. Kerotsky's narrative of events at musicweb- International.com.

Rachmaninoff
"could...do nothing right by most contemporary critics and composers...an inspired tunesmith...aspire and then decline in nostalgia." C. MacDonald, BBC Music Mag, May 2010; "his music's surface brilliance masks...in the image of the romantic melodist." *ibid*; "has none of No.2's more indulgent or excessive qualities." *ibid*; "almost everything grows from the first movement's initial bars." *ibid*; "at a time when audiences...19th century 'classics' into the 20th century." Taruskin, Oxford History..., v.4, p.553; "stripped-down, sinewy, athletic...in its expressive gestures." *ibid*; "embodies his late style...world's irresistible melodies," Steinberg, The Concerto, p.367; "the demonic Paganini in its use of the Gregorian *Dies Irae* chant." Morin, p.728; "are more firmly entrenched...than those of any other 20th century figure," Libbey, p.657; "Rachmaninoff may have contributed nothing...highly personal, as Tchaikovsky did." Schonberg, p.521; "display...a greater confidence in the handling of large-scale structures." The New Grove Russian Masters 2, G. Abraham, H. MacDonald, B. Schwarz, R. McAllister, G. Norris, eds. W.W. Norton, 1986, p.92; "mild metric shifts, jagged rhythms, and chromatic harmonies," J. Kramer, p.537.

Chapter 19
Anton Bruckner
"embraces the naïveté of the folk music of Upper Austria," The Musical Companion, p.269; "Basic to Mahler's melodic inspiration...vital and most genuine essence." Rognoni, p.xxiii; "almost always an impetuous...first movement of vast proportions." Rognoni,p.xxi; "The Mahler symphonies represent...romanticism to the point of saturation." *ibid*; "offered a different answer...at the turn of the 20th century." Morin, p.534; "the symphonic tradition of Beethoven filtered through the Wagnerian experience." Rognoni, p.xix; "The Bruckner symphony brims and blazes with an inner spiritual fire." *ibid*; "once more attained the monumental stature of true symphony." Short History of Music, p.239; "somewhat incoherent outer movements." *ibid*; "but when it

comes to musical expression...how he uses musical form." W. Sinkovicz, liner notes for *Bruckner Symphony No.5*, LPO, Welser-Möst, 1994; "There are aspects of Bruckner's...in a more modern way." *ibid*; "direct descendent of the old Austrian instrumental church-music composers" Short History of Music, p.221; "expression of transcendent emotion and a confession of personal faith." Libbey, p.92; "humble church organist" whose...Church permeated his music. *ibid*, p.93; "love of nature, piety...and mysticism." Short History of Music, p.239; "preclassical structural devices" and they bear "unmistakable traces of organ improvisation." Taruskin, Oxford History..., v.3, p.746; "with its luxuriant orchestra...its complex motivic textures." *ibid*; "romantic of the first order...basis of his symphonies." Short History of Music, p.239; "is much more revolutionary than people usually perceive." W. Sinkovicz, liner notes for *Bruckner Symphony No.5*, LPO, Welser-Möst, 1994; Rumor had it that Hanslick...prevent performances of his works. R. Bogar and L. Biancolli, The Concert Companion, 1947; "his success as an improviser...work in stone for all time." The Rough Guide to Classical Music, 5th ed., J. Staines, ed., Rough Guides Ltd., 2010, p.114; "based on a more literal reading of (Bruckner's) hand-written scores." *ibid*; "awe-inspiring grandeur, innocence, and sense of space" The Musical Companion, p.270; "makes his nine symphonies into densely woven polyphonic designs." Swafford, p.341; "a vague agitation in the strings...then builds up in a crescendo." Burkholder, Grout, Palisca, p.731; "...the highly charged intensity of his style was attributed to neuroticism." Berger, p.119; "in beating his own symphonic path Bruckner...musical language is immediately recognizable." W. Sinkovicz, liner notes for *Bruckner Symphony No.5*, LPO, Welser-Möst, 1994; "but underneath...were clearly organized...mortar to hold them together." T.Smith, p.2; "visionary expression with a broad yet cogent development of...material." Libbey, p.93; "slow, inexorable, solemn procession of harmonies." Schonberg, p.441; "a world of spirits in the bass...steps of the bass...had cosmic importance." *ibid*; "staggeringly complex yet always logical." T. Williams, *BBC Magazine*, Feb 2010; "emerge from darkness into light." W. Sinkovicz, liner notes for *Bruckner Symphony No.5*, LPO, Welser-Möst, 1994; "incredibly modern and so totally weird...throws everything upside down," *ibid*; "most generously melodic of the symphonies...and one of warm serenity." S. Johnson in 1001 Classical Recordings..., M. Rye, p.424; "unfolds in visions of religious ecstasy" W.G. Reisig, All Music Guide, p.225; "unleashes the brass as if a dozen cavalries were coming." Swafford, p.342; "somewhat pruned and with many dramatic new features." *ibid*; "wide interval leaps and grinding dissonance." *ibid*; "...the violence alternating with near-serenity...personality and giving them form." M. Tanner, *BBC Music Magazine*, Feb 2010.

Gustav Mahler
Conflict-ridden, Mahler saw himself...rule of conventional formal language. M. Meyer (transl. R. Evidon), liner notes for A. Schiff/M. Perenyi: *Beethoven Complete Music for Piano and Violincello*, ECM, 2004; "futile struggle to make sense out of life." Schonberg, p.443; a term coined by German music historian Rudolf Stephan. Taruskin, v.4, p.6; "so great that the whole world is actually reflected therein..." *ibid*; "In (Mahler's) music there is everything... own fears, doubts and suffering." M. Jansons, *Grammophone*, Mar 2010; "recast them into one immense musical edifice." Rognoni, p.6; "Just as Wagner had introduced...Mahler restored opera to the symphony." Rognoni, p.xxi; "My music is, everywhere and always, only a sound of Nature." Schonberg, p.447; "in search for his God." J. Kramer, p.364; "steeped in the mysticism of natural beauty...life, death and renewed life." *ibid*; "each of Mahler's symphonies...questions eternally plaguing him." Schonberg, p.438; "the breakup of Classical models...as

a bold personal statement." Burkholder, Grout, Palisca, p.773; "unconscious attempts to rewrite the adagio of (Beethoven's) Ninth." Schonberg, p.449; "There are sections in most... conquers Mahler the Deep Thinker." *ibid*; "but they are strongly linked...material as of narrative." Griffiths, p.216; "already enjoys immortality here on earth." Mahler to a critic, 1906; "convinces me that Mahler was right in ultimately dropping this movement." Bookspan, p.228; "with an elemental hum...all registers of the strings," A. Ross, The Rest Is Noise, p.21; "deliberately left unassimilated...style in which they are embedded." Rosen, pp.332-33; "and absolutely nothing dramatic...the very end (of the opening movement)." D. Hurwitz, The Mahler Symphonies: An Owner's Manual. Amadeus Press, 2004, p.3; Mahler faced some trouble...considered it too modern. J. Kramer, p.360; "mock funeral march and the turbulent...audience with problems." *ibid*; Mahler claimed the connection between...symbolizing the burying of the 'hero' of his First. Mahler to critic Max Marschalk, March 26, 1896; "essentially optimistic...from a song of death to a song of hope." J. Kramer, p.364; "there is no judgment...there is no punishment...we know and are." D. Murray, liner notes for *Mahler Symphony No.2*, CBSO, Rattle, 1987; "always the hope of the new mingled with the death of the old." J. Kramer, p.364; "to supply added variety and invoke...of Beethoven's Ninth." Griffiths, p.216; "begins with a furious orchestral assault and progresses to a huge choral and orchestral climax." T. Willams, *BBC magazine*, Feb 2010, p.56; "a chamber or neo-classical symphony." I. Fischer, BBC Music Magazine, Mar 2010; "could probably get a perfect...universe of Gustav Mahler" BBC Music Magazine, Mar 2010; "proceeds from death to resurrection...moves from death to life." J. Kramer, p.377; "a compound of airy lightness and ornate melancholia," Prendergast, p.5; "It's kind of timeless, almost defying gravity in the way it flows." M. Stenz, BBC Magazine, Mar 2010; "his darkest emotions...composing at those times. J. Kramer, p.379; "This strange, dark, massive work confused listeners." J. Kramer, p;380; "the tragic aspects of the symphony become most clear," J. Kramer, p.382; "the ending...shattering in the whole repertoire." M. Tilson Thomas, BBC Music Magazine, Mar 2010; "unremittingly in the minor"..."transformation into a glorious ending or peaceful resignation." S. Coburn in All Music Guide, p.788; "unmistakably a dance of death." S. Johnson, *BBC Music Magazine* Collection, v.18, no.13; "breathe an inner serenity and resignation." Machlis, p.65; "synthesis of the sharp-edged style...with the rarefied, contrapuntal technique" *ibid*; "music that is more closely allied...than with Mahler's earlier romanticism." *ibid*; "the inner tensions of the first two movements." J. Kramer, p.394; "broadly sweeping Adagio...into a purely spiritual realm." *ibid*, p.395; "a magnificent conclusion to his symphonic struggles." Dubal, p.433; "heaven-storming hero of mythical proportions." D. Dubal, The Essential Canon of Classical Music. NY,NY: North Star Press, 2001, p.148; "attacks death head-on with music of profound violence and irony." S. Coburn in All Music Guide, p.789; "that punishment awaited those who challenged certain forces." Schonberg, p.439; "This all but fizzled out in Austria and Germany with the death of Mahler." D. Fanning in The Cambridge Companion to the Symphony, J. Horton, ed. Cambridge University Press, 2013; "Through a loosened key structure...full of intense yearning." Prendergast, p.5; "express anything, and that his..."arouse passions" in the audience. from Stravinsky's 1935 autobiography; "the most serious and accomplished musicians...existential and musical conundrums he created." Michael McManus, "A Mahlerian Odyssey," *Grammophone*, March 2010.

Richard Strauss
"The anguished idealism of Mahler...Strauss towards music and the world." Weiss, Taruskin, p.353; "the concept of music as expression...with a literary or

philosophical outline." Bookspan, p.382; "in favor of a freewheeling, moment-to-moment, poetically-inflamed narrative." Ross, The Rest Is Noise, p.16; "what the concerto grosso had been to the Baroque." Schonberg, p.430; "Liszt's natural successor." *ibid*; "carried the symphonic poem to more daring feats of description" Tuchman, p.298; "man in struggle and search... battle, love and death," *ibid*, p.308; "generated a constant atmosphere of excitement and electricity." Schonberg, p.427; "retained for Germany...had culminated in Wagner." Tuchman, p.291; "thrust into soloistic prominence," Machlis, p.72; "aggrandized and enlarged choreographically...highest degree of acrobatic virtuosity." Rognoni, p.xvi; "dissonance speaks of personal feeling...Austro-German Romantic tradition." "most all-embracing harmonic logic, that dissonance was most powerfully felt" Griffiths, p.234-5; "the anguished idealism of Mahler...towards music and the world." Weiss, Taruskin, p.353; "exercised little or no influence...vulgar, over orchestrated." Schonberg, p.436; "to take the huffings and puffings" "flawed by the desire to put effect over substance." *ibid*, p.435-6; Strauss sought to make "music...describe characters, emotions, and events. Tuchman, p.296; "the program was mainly a stimulus...could stand on its own." J. Kramer, p.710; "those who really understand how...don't need it (a program) at all." R. Strauss, unattributed; "the mood of a scene, or a general feeling." Hemming, p.16; Strauss used the hero from a poem...but a more complicated figure. Bookspan, p.385; "irrepressible adventurer" and, according to Tovey...wheresoever it might be found." "a heroic proclamation from the four horns in unison." *ibid*, p.386; "detested everything that was not Brahms or Schumann." Tuchman, p.297; "represent the death of a person...highest artistic goals" "perfected in the most glorious...not fulfill here on earth." R. Drakeford, liner notes for *R. Strauss: Five Great Tone Poems*, Concertg. Orch., Haitink/Jochum, 1994; "every kind of instrumental device (to portray Till's) adventures..." Tuchman, p.298; "most programmatic piece by music's most programmatic composer." J. Kramer, p.710; "who shook off the chains of tradition...burden of the past," Tuchman, p.299; "varying in tempo and tone...same supply of thematic material." Griffiths, p.216; "he never put up much of a fight against the horrors of the Nazi regime." Schonberg, p.435; "wanted to have the best...his music and make money." *ibid*; "rotten character...completely lacking in...impulses of shame and decency." A. Ross, The Rest Is Noise, p.384.

Jean Sibelius
"found fresh new means...working within accepted traditions." D. Hurwitz, Sibelius Orchestral Works: An Owner's Manual. Amadeus Press, 2007, p.5; "with darker shades of the musical...atmosphere of his beloved native land." NYPhil.org concert notes; "whatever elements he borrowed...degree of character found nowhere else." D. Hurwitz, Sibelius Orchestral Works: An Owner's Manual, p.6; "severity of form, and profound...between all the motifs." Liner notes for *Sibelius: The Symphonies*, Philh. Orch., Ashkenazy, Decca, 1977; "favored pithy, compact motifs, rather than extended melodies." Berger, p.420; "succeeded in stamping his own...antiquated symphonic forms." A. Ross, The Rest Is Noise, p.174; "the largest, most serious, and most complex of all musical genres." D. Hurwitz, Sibelius, Orchestral Works: An Owner's Manual, p.4; "haunting lyrical passages of yearning, melancholy, and nostalgia." NYPhil.org concert notes; "typical orchestral dramas...down themes into murmuring textures." A. Ross, The Rest Is Noise, p.177; "There is a subtle coherence...counters its seemingly shapeless quality." B. Wise in The All Music Guide, p.1278; "decked out in all the lush raiment of late 19th century orchestration." Machlis, p;79; "terse, elusive work...a sustained deconstruction of symphonic form." A. Ross, The Rest Is Noise, p.178; "new formal methods

based on fragmentation and recombination." B. Wise in The All Music Guide, p.1278; "the sensuous radicalism of Debussy…new possibilities in…orchestral color," A. Ross, The Rest Is Noise, p.179; "moved away from the lush orchestral…urge to lighten the orchestral texture." Machlis, p.79; "is the quintessence of Sibelius…intensity, and thematic unity;" "emotion is tautly controlled within…clean-lined, orchestral texture." Grout, p.594; "material is handled with the utmost economy." Machlis, p.79; "Sibelius' 4th symphony experimented with passages of indeterminate tonality." The Musical Companion, p.351; "haunted, with textures of an almost Webern-like spareness." C. Morrison in The All Music Guide, p.1279; "bleakest expression" to-date…disenchantment with the world." D.Gutman in 1001 Classical Recordings…, p.592; "music as forbidding as anything…claustrophobic grimness…gravitational force on the music…same unresolved conflicts." A. Ross, The Rest Is Noise, p.179; "protest against the music of today." Liner notes for *Sibelius: The Symphonies*, Philh. Orch., Ashkenazy, Decca, 1977; "the organic evolution of material during the course of a work." Libbey, p.837; "ends not with a bang…but with a leaden thud." A. Ross, The Rest Is Noise, p.180; "many composers chose to concentrate on more economical forms," Griffiths, p.239; "an unconventional and staggeringly original work." A. Ross, The Rest Is Noise, p.180; "as if the composer were trying to flee into a mythic past." *ibid*, p.183; "the purest, most inward…ever revealing all of its secrets." R. Dettmer in The All Music Guide, p.1279; "most outrageous expressionist experiments…iconoclasm of Les Six in France." L. Shulman, NJSO Program Notes, 2009; "has a seemingly inexhaustible capacity…same basic germinal ideas." R. Layton, liner notes for *Sibelius Symphonies 2, 5, 7, etc.*, Koussevitzky, Pearl; "into one continuous structure…anchored on a grand theme for solo trombone." A. Ross, The Rest Is Noise, p.184; "the acme of formal unity" "rustling of strings under fragments of solo woodwind melody." Burkholder, Grout, Palisca, p.595; "by tugging at both ends…the gaps that opened in the middle." The Musical Companion, p.48; "his visionary, myth-based musical style…" Libbey, p.833; "shape to what a wanderer feels as he walks alone." A. Ross, The Rest Is Noise, p.449; "compresses centuries of Finnish folklore… into eight minutes of music." L. Shulman, NJSO program notes, 2009; "raw emotionalism dominates…Finlandia grabs both heart and gut." *ibid*; "the connection to traditional tonality grows ever more tenuous." A. Ross, The Rest Is Noise, p.184; "especially remarkable concentration…dazzling sonic imagination." Libbey, p.833; "arrived at a final synthesis in a style of Classical tranquility." Burkholder, Grout, Palisca, p.594; "This time the reviews were merely indifferent." Lebrecht, p.170; "unblinking conviction" *ibid*, p.171; "lionized as a new Beethoven in England and America" but "dismissed as a kitsch composer in" Austria-Germany. A. Ross, The Rest Is Noise, p.171; "the last of the heroes…music from cerebral modernism." *ibid*, p.187; "his expansive symphonies and evocative…intellectual market value" A. Ross, The Rest is Noise, p.188; "boring Nordic dreariness" the critic Heinrich Strobel; "the work of Sibelius…fundamentally lacks any good qualities." from an analysis Theodor Adorno prepared for the Princeton Radio Research Project (*whatever that was – RG*); "an honorable place among the minor composers." Schonberg, p.399; "who found fresh new means…working within accepted traditions." Hurwitz, Sibelius, An Owner's Manual, p.5; "personal style that stands outside the status quo of perpetual progress." A. Ross, The Rest Is Noise, p.192; "reaction to the post-Civil War repressive society," "age, burn-out and painful self-criticism" M.S. Rohan, *BBC Magazine*, Jan 2010.

Chapter 20

"only when needed within an already formed style." Rosen, The Classical Style, p.332; "one of the weapons by which...from the domination of foreign music." Grout, p.584; "systematically incorporated the folk...their countries into their music." Goulding, p.525; "impulse to get below surface politeness to the roots of things." Short History of Music, p.240; "the characteristics and the emotions...ear of the listener." M. Steen, p.693; "for a pretechnological past...for a lost world...elegies for the golden age." A. Ross, The Rest Is Noise, p.174; "the most inventive and spontaneously musical of all national composers." Short History of Music, p.243; "remained loyal to...that hidden empire of peasant music." A. Ross, The Rest Is Noise, p.121; "love of country began to fill the empty spaces in the heart." Tuchman, p.250.

Russia, Glinka, and The Mighty Five
"the attempt to build a national Russian school on a foundation of folklore," Taruskin, v.3, p.464; "sank deep into Glinka's mind...shapes into his own melodic invention." D. Brown, The New Grove Russian Masters 1. W.W. Norton, 1997, p.2; "what Weber had done for Germany...sophistication of the classical traditional to create" T. Blanning, The Triumph of Music p.296; "has a recognizably Russian exuberance...distinct from conventional Western practices." D. Brown, p.30; "more readily in terms of full melodic statements and subsequent variation," *ibid*; "of a musical fabric woven...upon an evolving tonal scheme." *ibid*; "the overbearing leader...who encouraged its Russian nationalism." J. Kramer, p.484; "to discover their own ways...materials nearest at hand, folk songs." Grout, p.584; "His music seems to penetrate the Russian soul." Steen, p.647; "a unique figure who invents a world of stunning novelty." D. Brown, The New Grove Russian Masters 1. W.W. Norton, 1997, p.ix; "witches music, in the form of a tone poem." "something new and is bound...impression on a thoughtful musician." Griffiths, p.200; "determination of the Russian nationalists...composers in absolute music." Grout, p.585; "scenes of Russian heroic antiquity" and oriental voluptuousness." Taruskin, v.3, p.789; "as a picture of old Russia." J. Kramer, p.136; "tried consciously to make...and the rhythms have a decidedly Russian feeling." J. Kramer, p.135; "inspired mix of imagination and orchestral skill." Morin, p.759; "knew every instrument's capabilities...new tone colors for them." Dubal, p.382; "helped turn Rimsky's mind towards exotic themes." G. Norris, *Grammophone*, Sept 2010; "eventually embraced the more disciplined...from his Western European contemporaries." J. Kramer, p.484; "kaleidoscope of fairy-tale images and...painted a more luxuriant canvas," Dubal, p.383; "unfolds as a lush and exotic musical representation of the 1001 Nights." Swafford, p.343; "the Spanish themes of dance character...orchestral effects." "one of the all-time tours de force of instrumental imagination," Swafford, p.343; "single-handedly kept the nationalist flag...symphonies, concertos, ballets, and quartets." J. Haylock, Classic FM, Mar 2010; "the Romantic style that he clung to was already in terminal decline." *ibid*; "against the prevailing tide...Romanticism alive until the 1930s." *ibid*.

Great Britain
"lifted British music from its post-Handel and post-Mendelssohn doldrums." Schonberg, p.501; "proved to be a concept brimful with motivating force" T. Blanning, The Triumph of Music, p.236; "wove all the elements...the fabric of English music." Dubal, p.59; "that at times anticipated the chromaticism of the Romantics," Schonberg, p.492; "land without music." A. Ross, The Rest Is Noise, p.173; "a flood of pent-up musical energy" Morin, p.294; "representative of English music on the international scene." Machlis, p.291; "did not rock the

boat." "writing very proper and not very original music." Schonberg, p.493; "sometimes viewed as the artistic exponent of the virtues of the empire." A. Mellor, *Classic FM*, Sept 2010; "the Wagnerian apparatus of leitmotifs...of the British Empire at its height." A. Ross, The Rest Is Noise, p.13; "plush, expressive-but-not-excessively-so orchestral style." Swafford, p.344; "mixture of idealism and imperialism...found perfect expression in (Elgar's) music." Machlis, p.56; "an emotional kaleidoscope" Morin, p.294; "the guns of August blasted away the context of his music." Steinberg, The Concerto, p.186; "He believed that it was a...the quaint sounds of the past." Schonberg, p.495; "but his music is not in the least touched by English folk song." Grout, p.595; "both virtuosically orchestrated...diverse range of moods." Taruskin, v.3, p.806; "arguably the most difficult," The Musical Companion, p.670; "with a deeply personal impulse...as has ever been written." *ibid*, p.671; "infinitely subtle, reflective slow movement." *ibid*; "resigned, melancholy, moody, introspective, even tormented." Steinberg, The Concerto, p.186; "one can sink as into a comfy chair." Swafford, p.344; "filled with sadness and disillusionment" "end of a civilization." Dubal, p.404; "victorious swagger" "rhapsodic virtuosity" "a musical conversation of shyness...of daring and attack." (A. Mellor, *Classic FM*, Sept. 2010; "remarkably original masterpiece...moments of sudden lyrical sweetness." D. Jaffe, *BBC Music Magazine*, July 2009.

Ralph Vaughn Williams
"saturated himself in folk song...free himself from foreign influences." Schonberg, p.506; "Better a limited but honest music than imitation." *ibid*; "an orchestral stew of several existing (English) folk airs." Goulding, p.495; "a massive, broad, bare choral style" Machlis, p.294; "create multiple perspectives in sound." M. Hayes, "Tallis Fantasia" *Grammophone*, Dec 2010; "...looks back to traditional choral works...an understanding of Debussy and Ravel." Nigel Gayler, *Classic FM*, Feb 2010; The "rapt quietude" of this work...the composer's expressive universe. Libbey, p.907; "delicate coloring" "conjuring up the song of the lark." The Musical Companion, p.673; "gloriously unbridled response...Whitman's most grandiose poetry." Libbey, p.907; "evoke the essence of London without following a specific program." S. Whalley, 1001 Classical Recordings..., p.608; "an ever-increasing harmonic tension." Schonberg, p.508; "a somber, uncompromising work of great impact." Machlis, p.295; "A lush vision of a mythical past...with an Adagio for England." R. Ainsley, *BBC Music Magazine*, May 2009, p.57; "to find a language...American or singularly their own." "straightjacket...native or folk tunes...European metrical and tonal framework." McCalla, p.xiv; "most advanced, unorthodox...anybody anywhere up to that time." Schonberg, p.556; "obsessed by the past, he wrote music of the future." J. Swafford, Charles Ives: A Life with Music. New York: W.W. Norton, 1998; "imbued with a passion for...music a sense of American nationality." A. Rich in A. Copland, What to Listen for in Music, p.IX; "father figure of modern American music." *ibid*; "created the first truly American idiom in music." Swafford, p.374; "to unify them by putting them together simultaneously." "the human mind can go beyond what is seen or experienced," Berger, p.238; "the spiritual and intuitive over the empirical." *ibid*; "with a transcendentalist's faith in the unity behind all diversity." Grout, p.592; "allowed (Ives) to venture...limits of musical composition." Berger, p.238; "Ives allows his musical ideas...loosely linked in one extended outpouring." *ibid*; "of seemingly disparate musical materials" "in textures of near-unimaginable complexity." All Music Guide, p.644; "The collaging of well-known tunes...but one of Ives' incredible innovations." J. Kramer, p.328; "resides...in his heterogeneous combinations of American sounds." "hyperrealistic reproductions of everyday sonic events." A.

Ross, The Rest Is Noise, p.143; "wanted his music to arouse...of the human community." Swafford, p.434; "Nothing sounds right to me anymore." "fiddled much with what he had done in his prime." Taruskin, The Danger of Music and Other Anti-Utopian Essays. UC Press, 2010, p.52; He is considered a 'forebear'...and John Adams. Taruskin, "Underneath the Dissonance Beat a Brahmsian Heart" in the New York Times, 5/16/04; "lived in dreadful isolation...19th century German tradition," Dubal, p.504; "unencumbered by the weight of centuries-old tradition" "man should try to break...on the infinite variety of sound." Weiss, Taruskin, p.360; "As with much of Ives' music...deep philosophical undercurrent." All Music Guide, p.644; "strings provide a slow, impassive sonic layer." J. Grimshaw, All Music Guide, p.643; "of recollection by means of misty harmonies..." Griffiths, p.256; "jacking up the level of dissonance" Taruskin, "Underneath the Dissonance Beat a Brahmsian Heart" in the New York Times, 5/16/04; "as people hotly debate the ultimate significance of his unique contribution." J. Kramer, p.327; "was the first to thoroughly explore the Modernist musical vocabulary," Swafford, p.378; "reminds us that greatness...of substance rather than manner." J. Swafford, Charles Ives: A Life with Music. W.W. Norton, 1998, p.434; "the musical feelings of the Connecticut country around here in the 1890s." from Ives' notes to the work; "allusively...put through a sieve of dissonance." Schonberg, p.560; "with the idea of symphonic themes...spirituals, and patriotic anthems." S. Schwartz, at Classical.net; "oddments of Americana" J. Kramer, p.325; "sound distinctly like Bruckner and Dvořák." ibid, p.326; "romanticism meets the new... century and ultimately succumbs." Morin, p.467; "a seriously light-hearted work with hymn tunes at its heart" ibid; "clear and uncluttered reminiscence...through some of its hymn tunes." D. Lewis in All Music Guide, p.642; "would register the myriad of sounds of home as few people have." J. Swafford, Charles Ives..., p.1; "is like a circus, with...quoted fragments" J. Kramer, p.332; "seems to be saying that...can and do happen, often at once." ibid.

Edvard Grieg
"Together they pored over...a truly Norwegian musical art." Dubal, p.375; "national characteristics with his sensitive...has (still) not lost its freshness." Grout, p.591; "his gift for lyricism" Morin, p.368; "His work...dewy lyricism, and wistful harmonies." Swafford, p.343; "often bathed in an almost impressionist harmony." Dubal, p.377; "seems the distilled essence of the Romantic concerto," Swafford, p.343; The suite very effectively shows...form of a Baroque dance suite. Dubal, p.378; "Grieg's reputation has suffered...unwillingness to tackle large forms." D. Hurwitz, Sibelius Orchestral Works: An Owner's Manual, p.4.

Eastern Europe
"never shook the feeling that they had come from somewhere else." A. Ross, The Rest Is Noise, p.86; "marked from the outset...to avoid Western (European) influence." Grout, p.589; "to my shame I must confess...means more to me than anything else." T. Blanning, The Triumph of Music, p.285; "completely dissolved in the history...mountains, valleys, and streams." Lang, p.657; "He was primarily a tone painter, a descriptive artist." Dubal, p.299; "My aim was to present to the listener scenes from my life." "the foundation of Czech art music" and "holds an especially cherished place in the history of Czech culture." ibid; "steely integrity in serving the national cause." T. Blanning, The Triumph of Music, p.288; "both venerated and was friendly with Brahms" ibid, p.291; "consciously renounced the styles of Western Europe," Grout, p.589; "entirely idiosyncratic language based on his folk heritage." Dubal, p.397; "very short melodies are his thumbprint." J. Stevenson, All Music Guide, p.657; "half a century of strictly

regional (Moravia) fame," Taruskin, v.4, p.422; "is customarily treated as a representative '20th century' figure." *ibid*; "stark, angular and even rough quality" Schonberg, p.387; "an intensity for nature," "full of vitality and color..." The Musical Companion, p.348; "a five-movement work of amazing color and harmonic and orchestral virtuosity." Morin, p.470; "youthfully vigorous work, full of life, optimism and originality." J. Kramer, p.336; "splashes of primary color." L. Kramer, p.67.

Béla Bartók
"represents the fusion of nationalism...powerful means of expression." Schonberg, p.567; "found his personal style in a dissonant, compelling Hungarian nationalism." Dubal, p.505; "treats the folk music of entirely...for the specific purpose of forming a style." Rosen, p.332; "a strongly individual personality emerges" "master of percussive dissonance" Machlis, p.187; "the great rhythmic imaginations of modern times." *ibid*; "is apt to incorporate diverse elements" *ibid*; "to express, in 20th century terms...discovery of the sonorous value of chords." Grout, p.614; "a disturbing metaphor for the reigning reality." S. Lacoste, LAPhil.org concert notes; "The dissonances begin to sound...a direct emotional utterance." Schonberg, p.576; "as an instrument of percussive rhythm." Machlis, p.188; "exploring relentlessly driving rhythms" J. Kramer, p.29; "with foreign (*i.e.*, dissonant) notes...giving it its biting vitality." *ibid*, p.31; "from these small fragments, not from tunes" J. Kramer, p.30; "his motives...are in a constant state of regeneration." Schonberg, p.573; "one of his most unashamedly Neo-Romantic in mood," Hemming, p.40; "in a concertante or soloist manner," Bartók quote; "every instrument of the orchestra gets a chance to shine" Lebrecht, p.191; "treats the instruments in a colorful...against the full body of the orchestra." Hemming, p.39; "polyglot diversity" "fanfares of all-American brass." A. Ross, The Rest Is Noise, p.328; "most remarkable of his orchestral works," The Musical Companion, p.347; "cast in a modernistic idiom." Taruskin, v.4, p.394; "It is extremely problematic...solo line will not be covered." J. Kramer, p.41; "His greatness lies not so much...extraordinary aptitude for creative synthesis." Lampert, Somfai, Noble, *et al.*, p.78; "exerted very little influence...thinking of young composers" Schonberg, p.572; "which they hoped would...the all-pervading German influence." Dubal, p.656; "did not produce results of nearly the same artistic quality." F.E. Kirby, Music for Piano, A Short History. Singapore: Amadeus Press, 1995, p.316; "tempered the strength of the native Hungarian materials." *ibid*; "vast possibilities were to be found outside the major-minor system." Griffiths, p. 223; "typical representative of the whole Hungarian peasantry." J. Kramer, p.343.

Iberia
"completely distilled his country's musical voice" "into a classical context." Morin, pp.308-9; "vivid evocation of love and witchcraft among the Andalusian gypsies." Morin, p.309; "Besides adapting technical features...with color, the atmosphere of Spain." D. Ewen, Ewen's Musical Masterworks, 2nd ed. NY: Bonanza Books, 1967, p.2; "highly spiced chromatic idiom." Schonberg, p.392; "indigenous Spanish dances are everywhere in evidence." Kirby, p.331; "infinite nuances of atmosphere" Ewen, p.2; "at once deliciously evocative and flamboyantly virtuosic." Libbey, p.349.

NOTES – Part 5

Chapter 21

"feeling for color and light...would exert the stronger appeal." The Musical Companion, p.339; he began to distance himself from...to seek a 'purer' style. Schonberg, p.454-55; "shrank from any musical effort...let alone overwhelm him." Crocker, p.476; "rejected the huge symphonic form...classical exposition of Mozart." Prendergast, p.9; "inherited the harmonic palette of Mussorgsky." The Musical Companion, p.339; "calculate on paper the effect...supreme prowess as an orchestrator." *ibid*, p.173; "a little too murkily mystical." A. Ross, The Rest Is Noise, p.97; "hint at subjects instead of...using lush and somewhat vague... place and natural phenomena" L. Van de Sande, amazon.com, 6/23/05; "is concerned with something...and abstract, with human feelings." J. Kramer, p.268.

Claude Debussy
"series of fleeting emotions." J. Kramer, p.231; "elusive and shimmering...and narrative, like that of Strauss." B. Tuchman, The Proud Tower, MacMillan, 1966, p.314; "voluptuous ambience"...based on the erotic poem by Mallarmé. Prendergast, p.8; "honest quest for an unblemished, truthful musical language." A. Ross, The Rest Is Noise, p.44; "the Germanic urge to develop...static while the accompaniment evolves." *ibid*, p.47; "displayed the traditional French mastery of the woodwinds." Machlis, p.100; "little affinity for or interest in the symmetry" Goulding, p.332; "slips easily from one wave-shaped melodic idea to another." Griffiths, p.222; *La Mer* was inspired in part...by the Japanese artist Hokusai. Prendergast, p.10; "an evocation of the magic of the sea." J. Kramer, p.231; "series of sense impressions," Schonberg, p.463; "to put into music his impressions of visual stimuli." J. Kramer, p.223; "an enchanted world seems to rise...unreal colors of a vision." Grout, p.603; "brilliantly executed portrait of Spain" Libbey, p.349; The middle nocturne of *Iberia*...dance-like, pervaded by Spanish rhythms. J. Kramer, p.225; "but rather to translate...Spain had aroused in him." "particularly its slow and dreamlike... celesta, oboes and bassoon." Prendergast, p.11; "is a mosaic of ideas, many of which seem only half-formed." J. Kramer, p.226; "Often there is intensity and puzzlement...created by exquisite chords..." Griffiths, p.240.

Maurice Ravel
"remarkably varied picture gallery." Morin, p.738; "The Ravel orchestration has a springier, lither quality," Schonberg, p.473; "sultry, virtuoso piece" Morin, p.739; "held sway over his imagination," "his mother's memories of a folkish past," A. Ross, The Rest Is Noise, p.92; "Spanish-Basque heritage proudly on display" "transformations of textures and rhythm" "inexhaustible source of exotic...colorful aural imagery," Libbey p.665-7; "a sweeping dance that rises... celebration of physical love." J. Kramer, p.561; "in the darkest depths of the orchestra" "catastrophically." G. Lamer, "Maurice Ravel" in *BBC Music Magazine*, May 2009; "both a dazzling incarnation...dazzling satire of it," A. Ross, The Rest Is Noise, p.120; "fury of the war just past." A. Ross, The Rest Is Noise, p.121; "strikingly contrasted (with) sumptuous harmony and glittering orchestration." "maelstrom of orchestral sound (that is) elegantly scary." Morin, p.740; "a sinister atmosphere that becomes frenzied by the end." "flashes of lightning in turbulent clouds reveal a couple waltzing." J. Kramer, p.569; "soften the edges of the pianistic originals." L. Kramer, p.159; "the violin to its outer

limits...in the café gypsy style." J. Haylock, *Classic FM*, April 2010; "wondrous ability to assimilate different styles of music," Dubal, p.553.

Other Impressionist Composers
"some of the largest and gaudiest blockbusters ever written." Libbey, p.673; "His finest music drew...works of art and nature." L. Shulman, NJSO program notes, 2010; "magnificent, spine-tingling crescendo," L. Shulman; "Respighi's inspiration white-hot from the kiln." Morin, p.751; "British Faure" "highly personal, sometimes delicate, elegant..." "English Impressionism", "an entirely personal music." Schonberg, p.501; "tone painter" "wrote beautifully of beautiful things" "a uniquely poetic, even pantheistic, evocation of nature and the transience of life." Morin, p.260.

Chapter 22
Dissonance and Atonality
"disturbing clash of harmonies." Copland, p.61; "to provide harmonic variety with a tour through assorted keys." Swafford, p.273; "to depict intensities of emotion not easily achieved through the diatonic scale." Ulrich, p.200; "to create a turbulent, even devilish atmosphere." A. Ross, p.212; "as it arcs away from and back...often circuitously long journey." L. Kramer, p.44; "dissonance must be approached...to the nearest consonance." Rosen, The Romantic Generation, p.553; "but rather a tense sound that seems to need resolution." J. Kramer, p.597; "its sense of movement" quote from Walter Piston, unattributed; "an element of transition...resolved to the ear's satisfaction." Quote from Igor Stravinsky; There are definitely experiments...especially the Bagatelle sans tonalite.; "blossomed into hate" A. Ross, The Rest Is Noise, p.101; "overblown...decadent, egomaniacal...in short, exhausted." Swafford, p.345; "tired of the super-saturated sound of the conventional symphony orchestra." The Musical Companion, p.568; "with the pre-war world and thereby with the war itself." Griffiths, p.253; "The horror of the First World War...blood-soaked Romantic aesthetic." A. Ross, Listen to This, p.48; "feeling of a central key or tonality began to be lost." Copland, p.58; "freer and more sinuous melodic line...broader scope." Copland, pp.45-6; "saw music as a medium of conflict, a battlefield of extremes." A. Ross, p.5; "were the main pathfinders in this uncharted harmonic territory." Copland, p.58; "Debussy created his music out of a much more elusive and fragmentary melodic material." *ibid*, p.46; "logical conclusions...abandoning...tonality altogether." "the entire former theory of harmony was thrown overboard." *ibid*, p.57; "were following their intuition rather than rationales and theories." Swafford, p.392; "a hopeless straitjacket for the composer." "in the hands of second-rate composers...substitute for imagination." J. Kramer, p.592; "we must listen to melody...as to what it is going to do." The Musical Companion, p.66; "a revolutionary break with the past." *ibid*, p.112; "the history of the development of harmony" Machlis, p.20; "Angst of our century." J. Kramer, p.597; "a climate in which we all sensed...of a musical tradition and its language." The Musical Companion, p.342; "constructive principles of the 18th century", "precisely because it was so formalist...commandeered for purposes of propaganda." Taruskin, v.5, p.17.

The Second Viennese School
"to impose order on the chaotic chromatic scale." Swafford, p.442; "it was generations of composers," "who had bent tonality out of shape." *ibid*, p.276; "that consistent voice and consistent...music its continuing appeal." "The relatively tranquil and predictable... explore an expressionist emotional world." *ibid*; "the serial salvation that Webern promised, something pure and rational

and inevitable." *ibid*, p.447; "...the emotions expressed are fleeting...Much is turbulent." McCalla, p.xii.

Arnold Schoenberg
"was a revolutionary who...insisting he was a traditionalist," "arisen entirely from the traditions of German music," Schonberg, p.578; "In his zeal for the German cause" A. Ross, The Rest Is Noise, p.72; "the last word in Tristan-oriented music." Dubal, p.538; "much more firmly fixed in specific tonalities." McCalla, p.3; "tugs at the limits of tonality" "directions Schoenberg was eventually to take." J. Kramer, p.606; "a work of turbulent, superheated late Romanticism...," Libbey, p.739; "here too the orchestra is reinforced to the maximum." Rognoni, p.8; "the world of sound and expressive content were new" *ibid*, p.10; "The chromatic universe was disintegrating." *ibid*, p.15; "an opulence and passion that surpasses all others," M. MacDonald in 1001 Classical Recordings You Must Hear Hear Before You Die, M. Rye, ed., Universe, 2008, p.536; "the logical, rational outcome of a historical process," A. Ross, The Rest Is Noise, p.62; "Wagnerian chromaticism...to its most extreme form" Rognoni, p.4; "marks the beginning of the search for a new musical idiom." *ibid*, p.5; "a musical work's melodic and harmonic...notes of the western chromatic scale." M. Hayes, *BBC Music Magazine*, Jan 2010, p.56; dictatorial, demanding and authoritarian...threw at him, as he revered his mentor. J. Kramer, p.110; "incubated in the golden age of Mahler and Strauss." A. Ross, The Rest Is Noise, p.70; "insisting instead that they master the traditional counterpoint of Bach and harmony of Brahms." J. Kramer, p.592; "Schoenberg explored turbulent expressionism...entirely left Romanticism behind." C. Culver, Amazon.com customer rev, 7/18/08; "In his early work Schoenberg...was floating free in chromatic space." Swafford, p.275; "toward an even more intense expressionism." Libbey, p.739; "the expressionistic atmosphere and the atonal...carried to the highest pitch of intensity." Rognoni, p.20; "brief, self-contained, highly expressive pieces...massive orchestral sound" to "express inner emotional states" Hemming, p.159; "beguiling array of orchestral timbres" A. Ross, The Rest Is Noise, pp.57-8; "contrapuntal richness...owes a lot to the older composer." J. Kramer, p.598; "to burden listeners with suggestions of additional significance." J. Kramer, p.600; "melodic lines made up...colors melting into one another." Swafford, p.446; "alive with a confident vitality," "new musical language that would influence most subsequent music." J. Kramer, p.599; "hostile reminder that their smug...with tensions on many levels." Dubal, p.535; "A principle that would secure instrumental...by tonal harmony in the past." Griffiths, p.254; "vented against the popular styles of the day," "folkloristic composers" "who mingle dissonance and tonality." A. Ross, The Rest Is Noise, p.216; "Schoenberg was at his most inspired...jazzy, living for the moment." A. Whittall, Grammophone, June 2010; "marked a decisive transition from...concreteness' of the twelve-tone system." Rognoni, p.67; "affirmed his kinship with" Bach and Handel. Machlis, p.251; "bouncy rhythms and disconcerting...within traditional formal schemes." A. Whittall, Grammophone, June 2010; "through the broadened horizons... a new kind of Klangfarbenmelodie." Rognoni, p.95; "unrelievedly tense...the intensity never lets up totally," J. Kramer, p.593.

Alban Berg
"a mathematical fetish, a love of complexity for complexity's sake." A. Ross, The Rest Is Noise, p.71; "put a human face on the twelve-tone system...formal rigor and emotional richness...it is tightly constructed and expressive." Libbey, pp.56-7; "as one inventive resource...than a dominating structural principle" M. Hayes; "about Schoenberg's method was...generate new kinds of tonality." A. Ross, The

Rest Is Noise, p.226; "there was a lot more to Berg than his immediately accessible romanticisms." A. Morin, p.131; "music sounds closer to the expressive...to the harmonic and orchestral world" J. Kramer, p.112-13; "opulent, upward- and downward-lunging melodies," A. Ross, The Rest Is Noise, p.70; "Berg can be called the twelve-tone system's most advanced Romantic..." Dubal, p.505; "more on harmony than on counterpoint" "directly to Romantic tradition." M. Hayes; "an emotional directness and openness that can be overwhelming." McCalla, p.xvi; "Berg composed communicative, emotional music...sophistication and atonal allegiances." D. Davis, Amazon.com editorial review; "greater directness of appeal...densely-packed scores of Schoenberg" The Musical Companion, p.342; "...eventually proved to be a formidable challenge to his former teacher." M. Hayes; "the closest thing to a popular opera the musical avant-garde ever produced." Swafford, p.438; "a huge march in an atmosphere of catastrophe" Griffiths, p.241; "shows him grappling with larger...Mahler's Ninth." Libbey, p.56-7; "the free dissonance of Schoenberg and the sensuous colors of Debussy." J. Kramer, p.113; "is a phantasmagoric march for full orchestra." A. Ross, The Rest Is Noise, p.71; "has some of the thorniness one associates with twelve-tone music." Swafford, p.442; "Karajan effects crystal-clarity in a razor-sharp realization." (amazon.com online review, 1/30/05; It is Berg's single most popular...makes it his most accessible score. S. Coburn in All Music Guide, p.140; "Berg's lyric vision finds here its most lofty expression." Rognoni, p.124; "demonstrate the lyric and expressive...from the stigma of 'all brains, no heart'." Steinberg, p.97; "twelve-tone system presents no barrier to music of great beauty." Swafford, p.440; "none is greater or of a finer emotional life than Berg's." Dubal, p.580; "Berg's most rigorous and challenging, and thus his most Schoenbergian, work." "though the work does not make rigorous consistent use of 12-tone practices" All Music Guide, p.138; "No other composer has built such a momentous reputation on so few works," Swafford, p.440.

Anton Webern
"to get away from the overblown statements of...late romantics." J. Kramer, p.794; "turned his back on tradition and took the plunge into the future." Rognoni, p.315; "as the new god of the young," A. Ross, The Rest Is Noise, p.417; "incredibly tight organization...Western World after World War II." Schonberg, p.595; "latch on to the ideal of order and clarity in music" and "yearned for strict control backed by scientific principles." *ibid*; "the art of music to its logical extreme." *ibid*, p.597; "almost entirely obliterated...the traditional concepts...new spareness and economy." The Musical Companion, p.174; "lets us appreciate how atonality...by reducing the notes to the minimum." Penguin Guide, p.1193; "with the utmost discipline...row techniques several degrees further." Swafford, p.445; "distilled, sounding like Mahler's...teacher (Schoenberg) in the expedition to the atonal pole." A. Ross, The Rest Is Noise, p.125; "small cell-like fragments...of individual notes on their own." The Musical Companion, p.66; "sort of melody (Webern's music) has...huge leaps of well over an octave," *ibid*; "through a more rigorously Bachian structure." Rognoni, p.317; "intense post-Wagnerian affair," Dubal, p.657; "stopped to say, 'aha – here we have something'." B. Johnston in All Music Guide, p.1497; "distilled essence of expressionism," Swafford, p.447; "without question the most remarkable pieces of the decade." Crocker, p.507; "contain more emotional clout...can manage in an hour" and "has a tone of almost unbearable tragedy" *ibid*; "truly extraordinary concentration...every decorative element." Schonberg, p.598; "arguably the supreme atonal work." Ross, The Rest Is Noise, p.68; "distills the essence of the new musical ideas (of)...Schoenberg." Hemming, p.210; "the depths of Schoenberg's notion of Klangfarbenmelodie...his Five Pieces for

Orchestra" J. Keillor in <u>All Music Guide</u>, p.1497; "with a particular emphasis on…nuances of soft dynamic levels." Hemming, p.211; "they seem to give off enormous clouds of multicolored sparks" A. Rich in Copland, p.225; "given to a different instrument…changing (tone) colors (the Klangfarben)" Schonberg, p.588; "is probably the most convincing utilization of Klangfarbenmelodie ever." J. Keillor in <u>All Music Guide</u>, p.1497; "abstract beauty of ice crystals or snowflakes." A. Ross, <u>Th e Rest Is Noise</u>, p.214; "jewel-like pieces" require "microscopic precision" A. Rich, p.226; "the beginning of extreme compression…a masterpiece in miniature." A. Carpenter in <u>All Music Guide</u>, p.1496; "spry, dancing, and jovial: Viennese." Swafford, p.448; "his search for an ideal…carried to the limits of possibility." Rognoni, p.17; "…all (then) contemporary music …to his (Schoenberg) 'daring'." "it was hardly possible to arrive at a conclusive judgment" "because their works were performed so infrequently." P. Goulding, p.23.

Chapter 23

"achieve a taut, vibrant melody…melody from its vocal origins." Machlis, p.14; "wide leaps and jagged turns of phrase" *ibid*; "went hand-in-hand with a renewal of interest in contrapuntal procedures." Libbey, p.542; "came out of a simple love of music. But most preferred to hear Brahms." A. Ross, <u>The Rest Is Noise</u>, p.120; "historical manner expressed in contemporary language." Schonberg, p.484; "composers pursued ever more arcane musics of the future." A. Ross, <u>Listen to This</u>, p.48; "music that is direct and clear in form, contrapuntal in texture, and restrained in expression." Taruskin, v.2, p.114; "out of elements solely derived from the nature of sound." Machlis, p.161; "world of sound by means of a new musical syntax" Rognoni, p.62; "…not a return to classicism…an artificial amalgamation of styles." J. Kramer, p.732; "a profound and emphatic realignment with traditional tonality." <u>The Musical Companion</u>, p.629; "elements of form, gesture and counterpoint from older music." Griffiths, p.250.

Igor Stravinsky

"In order to keep his cool, slightly detached image …but this is a camouflage." Esa-Pekka Salonen, *Grammophone* "The Real Great Composers No.35", June 2010; "music is primarily form and logic…"in structure, in texture, in balance, in rhythm." Schonberg, p.486; "it was as essential to see music performed as to hear it." Morin, p.198; "no longer capable of sustaining a lengthy symphonic argument." White and Noble, p.141; "I have no use for 'working out'…in dramatic music." B. Tuchman, <u>The Proud Tower</u>, p.339; "rhythm the principal generative element of large-scale composition." Libbey, p.818; "ideal is to be found in…the sole repositories of the 'true' sense of tradition." Rognoni, p.x; "to impress his personality on the…evolutionary not a revolutionary composer." Lampert, Somfai, Noble, et al., p.187; "burst like a gorgeous tropical bird upon the Western World" B. Tuchman, <u>The Proud Tower</u>, p.336; "brought (to Paris) fresh excellence of music by contemporary Russian composers." *ibid*.

The Russian Ballets

"brilliant exercise in Russian nationalism," "extraordinarily skilled synthesis of elements…masterpiece of orchestral colorism," Libbey, p.818; "marvelously-wrought evocation of the fairy-tale world…it is full of marvelous inspiration." <u>The Musical Companion</u>, p.344; "the spectacularly successful premiere…Stravinsky an international star." Malcolm Hayes, *BBC Music Magazine*, May 2010; Its first performance marked a new age…the grand old man of Russian music. Schonberg, p.365; "dazzling orchestral invention and exoticism" C. Dingle in <u>1001 Classical Recordings…</u>, p.588; "exhibits the most perfect melding of music and scene..." Libbey, p.819; "Stravinsky found his language...found his identity." Esa-Pekka Salonen and James Jolly in *Grammophone* "The Real Great Composers No.35", June 2010; "numerous polytonal experiments stemming from Petrushka." Schonberg, p.480; "music of power and vitality...unhappy puppet (Petrushka), hero of every fair..." Tuchman, The Proud Tower, p.339; "complex textures by overlaying...each with its own rhythm and direction." Griffiths, p.237; "in their use of a sentiment-free expression and in their air of stark primitivism." Ulrich, p.341; "suggestions of polytonality appear...overt use of old-fashioned melodic devices." *ibid*, p.367; "for decades...composers imitated the new rhythms and sonorities" Schonberg, p.481; "a new thrill that will doubtless inspire heated discussion." "magnificently calculated chaos" "the Big Bang of modern music." Libbey, p.819; "With its near-total dissonance and breakaway from established canons of harmony and melody...genuine explosion." *ibid;* "strange and ancient landscape;...final frenzied moments...percussive orgy of the ritual dance." T. Smith, The NPR Curious Listener's Guide to Classical Music. Perige Trade, 2002, p.170; "dramatically more complex or daring than Petrushka." Esa-Pekka Salonen and James Jolly in *Grammophone*, "The Real Great Composers," No.35, June 2010; "ambiguous triumph and cruelty of spring and the process of natural renewal..." Lampert, Somfai, Noble, *et al.*, p.128; "jagged and uncouth rhythmic effects." A. Copland, p.32; "The innovatory force of this remarkable score...any other European music." The Musical Companion, p.345; "created complex textures by...each with its own rhythm and direction." Griffiths, p. 237; "its highly sophisticated harmonic vocabulary" "more to Debussy than to anyone except myself." The Musical Companion, p.345; "ends with the sweat-inducing crescendo of *Dance of the Earth*." A. Ross, The Rest Is Noise, p.99; "a fantasy world from scraps of evidence" *ibid,* p.113; "delved into folkloric sources...a book of Lithuanian wedding songs...memories of peasant singers" *ibid*, p.97; "Howls of discontent went up from the boxes." *ibid*, p.81; "melodies would follow...would match the energy of dance." *ibid*, p.83; "impassioned, exciting, and extroverted...rule for this composer. J. Kramer, p.727; "dismissed...as so much trendy noise." A. Ross, The Rest Is Noise, p.103; "how the sounds of old music could be made new." *ibid;* "the tangible result of the postwar triumph of dehumanization." Taruskin, v.4, p.476; "superscores and superorchestras" "pointed, precise way of writing." Schonberg, p.483; "his back on the rich orchestral palette of the pre-war years." The Musical Companion, p.345; "After this his works would be thoroughly western, thoroughly modern." Griffiths, p.249; "took models, usually but not always from the past,...idioms can still be used in the 20th century." J. Kramer, p.755; "historical manner expressed in contemporary language" Schonberg, p.483-84; "a complete rupture with Romanticism." "tonality as the chief framework in Western music" "he breathed new life into...tonality, which invigorated many other composers." Dubal, p.566-67; "for what he did to music rather than for what his music did to the majority of his listeners." Schonberg, p.486-90; "the driving, regular metrics...through the Stravinskyan rhythm machine." O. Howard, LAPhil.org concert notes; "technically demanding for the soloist" "avoids being an all-out bravura showpiece." *ibid*; "in a state of religious and musical ebullience," Libbey, p.837; had found religion...at a "time of danger." Griffiths, p.260; "an impersonal, objective liturgical persona." Lampert, Somfai, Noble, *et al.*, p.156; "his most potent music for orchestra since The Rite." A. Ross, The Rest Is Noise, p.418; "the whole feeling of the work...reactions to World War II." Libbey, p.837; "the most obvious is that of harp and piano, the principal instrumental protagonists." J. Kramer, p.753; "one of the most gripping and effectively executed scores of the 20th century." *ibid*; "atonality implied anarchy...dictate the Bachian reaction." Taruskin, v.4, p.678; "did not (for the most part) go...dissonance-driven 20th century composers," Goulding, p.260; "staunch in his elaborate tonalism, would...through Schoenberg's innovations." Dubal, p.537.

Paul Hindemith
"showed a deep feeling for...the Renaissance and the Baroque;" A. Ross, The Rest Is Noise, p.198; "a model of workmanship...of Baroque and Classic German music," "a most unusual harmonic and melodic language." Schonberg, p.545; "new sound palette through Bachian counterpoint." online @ NYPhil.org; "pursued a consistently tonal path throughout his career." The Musical Companion, p.345; "great emphasis on the rules that govern the arts." M. Berger, Chamber Music, p.231; "modern in style yet thoroughly approachable." Libbey, p.332; "showed an exceptional command of the orchestra" *ibid*; "Hindemith's music has exerted no...neo-Classical ideals of the 20th century." Ian Kemp in Lampert, Somfai, Noble, *et al.*, p.258; "an intimate knowledge of the performative...and properties of each instrument." J. Grimshaw in All Music Guide, p.611; "look on the piano as an...instrument and act accordingly." A. Ross, The Rest Is Noise, p.199; "that music should be useful...be a vehicle for self-expression." Lampert, Somfai, Noble, *et al.*, p.255; "vehemently anti esthetic art...this was sheer subversion...heroic romantic tradition." Taruskin, "In Search of the 'Good' Hindemith Legacy," *New York Times*, 1/8/95; "degenerated into mere distributors of superrefined sounds." quote of P. Hindemith, unattributed; "logic, organization and integrity." Schonberg, p.546; "to turn our soul towards everything noble, superhuman, and ideal." quote of P. Hindemith, unattributed; "steadfastly adhered to...tonality." Machlis, p.197; "The symphony ends in...and in the power of art." Herbert Glass, LAPhil.org concert notes; "a dramatic allegory about the artist's dilemma in a turbulent society." Lampert, Somfai, Noble, *et al.*, p.258; "full of colorful writing enhancing striking themes" E. Greenfield in *Grammophone*, June 2010; "renounce the harmonically oriented balance of 19th century...focusing on...wind and brass..." Lampert, Somfai, Noble, *et al.*, p.248; "instincts had always been... values of strong polyphonic interest." M. MacDonald, liner notes for Hindemith *Kammermusik 1-7; Der Schwanendreher*, EMI, 2007; "abruptly aligned himself with Stravinsky and Milhaud..." Lampert, Somfai, Noble, *et al.*, p.243; His neoclassic concertos are closer..."the practices of the Viennese classics." Musical Companion, p.346; "the grandest and most festive of all..." MacDonald, liner notes; "more hard-edged and elaborately contrapuntal." Musical Companion, p.675; "a lost era of harmony and humanity." MacDonald, liner notes; "a medieval minstrel embellishing a variety of folk songs," Musical Companion, p.675; "builds on the tradition of the genre...the *concertante* approach of the 18th." Lampert, Somfai, Noble, *et al.*, p.265; "one can detect a vision of a music...Middle Ages to the 20th century..." *ibid*; "Hindemith could not follow the process...to the fugal spirit of Bach." Rognoni, p.51.

Bohuslav Martinů
"scores don't amble or glide; they skip, dance, caper and frolic." A. Mellor in *Classic FM*, Feb 2010; "block chords and massed sonorities, results in a 'wall of sound'." "usually quite angular" "innate lyricism." G. Richards in *Grammophone*, Jan 2010; "partly naturally Czech...an air of Ravelian impressionistic magic." A. Mellor; David Ewen goes even further...as a predominant influence on Martinů. Ewen, p.374; "well-armed with late Impressionism...for thinking on quite a grand scale." 'Christopher Hogwood on Martinů,' *Grammphone* Collector's Edition, July 2009; "quasi-neo-Baroque." Morin, p.561; "never associated with any...synthesis of the most diverse influences." Barbara Moroncini, LAPhil.org program notes; "distinctive, unorthodox chord progressions that defy traditional tonal logic." Libbey, p.468; "He succeeded in amalgamating Czech musical traditions with

contemporary Western trends." Machlis, p.445; "the romantic strain that was at the core of his nature." *ibid*; "longing for an earlier formality." 'Christopher Hogwood on Martinů'; "Czech folk music...and rhythmic invention in general." The New Grove Dictionary of Music and Musicians, S. Sadie, ed. 6th ed. London: MacMillan, 1980, v.11, p.733; "...what he saw as the slick American way of life sickened him." The New Grove Dictionary of Music and Musicians, v.11. Grove, 1995, p.733; "breaks new ground formally...The melodic inspiration is strong." Musical Companion, p.261; "He chooses thematic germs that will lead to a lot of development." 'Christopher Hogwood...; "nervous, gliding, motoric rhythms" Hemming, p.111; "exotic sonorities...working on a rhythmic basis." 'Christopher Hogwood...'; "is partly soloistic but frequently reverts to a sort of basso continuo role." Morin, p.561; "several unifying devices to make a cohesive whole of the four movements." F. Stover in All Music Guide, p.802; "lovely slow movement flute solo and a rich vein of lyrical ideas." *Classic FM*, April 2010; "an indefinable Czech character that suggested a latter day Dvořák." P. Lambert, The Grammophone Collection: Bohuslav Martinů, *Grammophone*, Dec 1990, pp.1167-71; "sometimes over-busy contrapuntal textures of Martinů's chamber works." Musical Companion, p.548; "after the betrayal of his country at Munich" Machlis, p.445; "one of the strongest and...basic emotion is not despair but rather," "revolt, courage and unshakable faith in the future." Hemming, p.111; "bristles with nervous energy, horror, and sorrow." B. Hodges, Amazon.com, 2/5/02; "genuinely concertante role,...ensemble and sometimes spotlit as a soloist." The Musical Companion, p.694; "too unrelentingly and gratingly dissonant throughout." 'Christopher Hogwood on Martinů,' *Grammphone* Collector's Edition, July 2009; "ventures into modernist angularity á la Hindemith." Santa Fe Listener; "covers a great deal of emotional distance...you're on a pretty vigorous emotional roller coaster." G. Ohlsson, YouTube interview; "I am trying to escape the traditional form...leaving little opportunity for free development..." P. Lambert "The Grammophone Collection: Bohuslav Martinů" *Grammophone*, Dec 1990, pp.1167-71; "fizzle out for lack of sustained inspiration." Dubal, p.663; "didn't like revising very much...strengths are so abundant that that doesn't matter." G. Ohlsson, YouTube interview; For elaboration on the information of the final paragraph, see A. Brezina, "Martinů Revisited: the rediscovery of a many-sided Czech composer of the 20th century" in *Czech Music*, July 2008.

Chapter 24

"one of the great nightmares of 20th century cultural history," A. Ross, The Rest Is Noise p.236; "endure a long string of humiliation." *ibid*, p.237; "the onset of the most warped...of the art by totalitarian means," *ibid*; "evaluated not on its own merits but on its doctrinal purity." *ibid*; "began to turn out art of a...the antithesis of revolution." *ibid*; "tug-of-war between motoric modernism and Romantic lyricism." L. Kramer, p.159; "the recurring bass lines of the...inescapable tensions of modern existence." A. Ross, The Rest Is Noise, p.477; "to portray the eternal battle...and their class enemies" "the struggle of conflicting tendencies." "were obliged to curtail...in support of official doctrine." S. Morrison, The People's Artist Oxford Univ. Press, 2009, p.2; "demands for 'songfulness' in Soviet music by the party leadership." A. Ross, The Rest Is Noise, p.245; "musicological inquisition", "any lingering ideas of individuality" *ibid*, p.279; "clearly transcend any political context." Libbey, p.647; "a tug-of-war between motoric modernism and Romantic lyricism." L. Kramer, p.160.

Serge Prokofiev

"ran the gamut of styles without ever losing his own." Morin, p.707; "mask of optimism..."the feeling of profound and terrible insecurity." A. Ross, The Rest Is Noise, p.266; "harmonic and rhythmic gestures of the early 20th century." M. Henke, transl. G. Standwell, liner notes for Prokofiev *Symphony Nos. 1&5*, Phila. Orch., Ormandy, Sony, 1993; "inspirational 'war symphony';" A. Ross, The Rest Is Noise, p.272; "work of epic scope and noble character." Libbey, p.646; "middle of a political ice age." M. Henke; "pithy, technically difficult work in five short movements." David Hurwitz, amazon.com; "a rhapsody-like chain of freely-evolving ideas." S. Keefe, p.148; "on a heroic scale, geared to...mastery of (cellist) Rostropovich." T. Williams, *BBC Music Magazine*, Dec 2009; "The virtuoso demands on the soloist...scores in the cello repertoire." M. Cookson, MusicWeb International, online review at ArkivMusic.com; "acutely resonated with the...public traumatized by autocracy and war." J. Horowitz, "A Moral Beacon Amid the Darkness of a Tragic Era." *NY Times*, 2/6/00; "lean, clear, pointed"..."confidence and an enormous athleticism." Schonberg, p.528.

Dmitri Shostakovich

"career-long preoccupation with finding...musical form and emotional content." Libbey, p.774; "a split focus: concern for tradition against challenge of it." B. Schwarz, L. Fay, in The New Grove Russian Masters 2, G. Abraham, H. MacDonald, B. Schwarz, R. McAllister, G. Norris, eds. W.W. Norton, 1986, p.183; "Shostakovich seemed to be a...Rimsky-Korsakov school of composition." Volkov, p.xxiii; "On a musical plane, Shostakovich had seen himself as Mussorgsky's successor..." *ibid*, p.xxvi; "His most familiar tones are savage irony and tragedy," Swafford, p.472; "dash, sparkle, and modernity...and the Piano Concerto." Schonberg, p.532; "narrow-minded dogmatism" "an obstacle for any imagination and individuality." M. Struck-Schloen (transl. D. Babcock), liner notes for Mandelring Quartet, Shostakovich *Complete String Quartets*, Audite, 2011; "preserve his musical self under potentially annihilating pressure." A. Ross, The Rest Is Noise, p.248; "paint a comprehensive autobiography" Dubal, p.624; "to read into them complex psychological interpretations." Hemming, p.16; "symphony on a grand scale...with juicy melodic content and rich-sounding orchestration." Schonberg, p.528; "'objectivist' tone of Hindemith, Weill, Bartók and...Stravinsky." A. Ross, The Rest Is Noise, p.244; "youthful assurance blazed forth" with an "unusually gripping narrative drive." *ibid*, p.243; "is Shostakovich's encounter with...yet pivotal in his evolution." B. Schwarz, L. Fay, p.184; "in the drawn-out anguish of its close." A. Ross, The Rest Is Noise, p.253; "Shostakovich was instantly rehabilitated." Libbey, p.775; "was thinking of other enemies...composed the theme." Schonberg, p.536; "Shostakovich played cat and mouse...authorities for his entire career." Swafford, p.472; "invasion episode" "the peaceful life of these people." Ross, The Rest Is Noise, p.269; "all forms of terror, slavery, the bondage of the spirit." *ibid*; "the most spectacular new-music event of the radio era." *ibid*, p.327; "the Seventh has not worn too well past its function as an Allied icon." Swafford, p.476; "truthful reflection of the horrors and losses of war." Taruskin, v.5, pp.8-9; "hanging, almost as if...ended with a question mark." Libbey, p.775; "a merry, exuberant, light-hearted work...to celebrate the victorious end of the war." B. Schwarz, L. Fay, p.189; "seemingly light neoclassical" work...to Shostakovich's symphonies. iTunes review; "would have hailed the genius and wisdom of the leader." Volkov, p.xxxvi; "slight and whimsical opus in the spirit, the composer suggested, of Haydn." Taruskin, v.5, p.13; "indisputable masterpieces penned in the second half of the 20th century." Libbey, p.775; "it offers a glimpse into the darkest...corners of the composer's soul." *ibid*; "desolate psychological terrain."

A. Ross, The Rest Is Noise, p.476; "the ironic, self-flagellating, death-obsessed Shostakovich." *ibid*, p.484; "reveals the composer in a stark and bitter mood, using dark and brooding orchestral colors." B. Schwarz, L. Fay, p.195; "Rahbari's reading (of *No.5*) is most convincing, with dramatic tensions finely controlled..." Penguin Guide, p.951; "superbly moulded with genuine tragic...to project the score's climaxes pungently." Penguin Guide, p.955; "feeds on grim memories" "is questioning and nervous." Steinberg, p.435; "Its prankish humor can be explained...the traditional Russian concerto style." B. Schwarz, L. Fay, p.184; "eclectic progressive, rooted in tradition...occasional atonality as expressive means." *ibid*, p.202; "gathering up in a troubled stream...detritus of a millennium of music." A. Ross, The Rest Is Noise, p.576.

Chapter 25

"concept of the sound environment" Prendergast, p.2; "distance themselves from totalitarian aesthetics;" A. Ross, The Rest Is Noise, p.389; Adorno expounds upon this in his book Philosophy of New Music; "preserving tonality in the modern era..." "tantamount to Nazi kitsch." A. Ross, The Rest Is Noise, p.388; "lost part of its emotional transparency." Machlis, p.14; "a disciplined procedure that required training by experts (to be fully enjoyed)." *ibid*; "were shaped to the curve of the human voice" "detached melody from its vocal origins." *ibid*; The second phase started...and Cage and Babbitt in America. J. Kerman, Contemplating Music. Harvard Univ. Press, 1986, p.14; "patron saint of new music after 1945" "quickly emerged as the...young German (and French) composers." A. Ross, The Rest Is Noise, p.381.

Aaron Copland

"may be...the most-loved orchestral work ever written in America," Swafford, p.471; "like Bartók and Falla...and imbued the entire fabric with its essence." Liner notes for Copland *Appalachian Trail, etc.*, Dorati, Mercury, 1991; "with the relationship between the living composer and the listening public." H. Stevens, E. Bruck, liner notes for Copland, *Appalachian Spring, et al.*, LSO/Minn.SO, Dorati, Mercury, 1957/61; "tuneful and atmospheric scores." Schonberg, p.565; "Copland's use of transparent, widely-spaced sonorities...has become the quintessential musical emblem of America." Burkholder, Grout, Palisca, p.888; "the Great American Symphony to end all American symphonies." Taruskin, v.5, p.3; "an effective memento of its euphoric time." *ibid*, p.6; "will end up creating nothing." A. Ross, The Rest Is Noise, p.417; "having achieved the unity...musical technique and national identity," Berger, p.132.

Benjamin Britten

"England's most celebrated living composer...a focus of British pride," A. Ross, The Rest Is Noise, pp.449, 468; All are brought together...concluding double-counterpoint fugue. Dubal, p.634; "wonderful sensitivity for children...a creative genius who never grew up." Dubal, p.631.

Samuel Barber

"was a traditionalist who never...interest in all kinds of music" J. Kramer, p.24; "Barber's style is essentially diatonic...provide a strong link with the past." Ulrich, p.371; "remained stubbornly resistant to influences foreign to his own aesthetic." *ibid*; "...an alternation between post-Straussian chromaticism...and humanity that ensures its durability." Hemming, p.36; "his sorrow is a profound lyrical force." T. Larson, The Saddest Music Ever Written: The Story of Samuel Barber's Adagio for Strings. New York: Pegasus Press, 2010, p.ix; "a great quantity of his work contains a striking nostalgia, a longing for an evergreen past." Dubal, p.680; "given to change our world of music or our perception of it." M. Steinberg, The Concerto, p.21; "a slow, minor-key lament, which evokes...an icon of American grief." T. Larson, p.vii; "gave voice to the insanity of war." *ibid*, p.viii; "America's secular hymn for grieving our dead" *ibid*; "sought to combine the songlike...with the spiciness of Capricorn." Morin, p.76; "an amalgam of motivic ideas expertly traded off among soloists and strings." *ibid*, p.75; "very much under the spell...darkness pervades much of this work." Morin, p.77;

Chapter 26

"totally organized music of Messiaen, Babbitt, and Boulez." Schonberg, p.591; "in the service of traditional aesthetic norms." All Music Guide, p.1550; "Serialism of one kind or another remained the dominant aesthetic of the 1950s and 1960s." Rough Guide to Classical Music, 5th ed. Rough Guides, 2010, p.384; "saw a hiatus in the mighty line...from Monteverdi through Stravinsky and Schoenberg." Schonberg, p.619; "technologically oriented, mathematically inclined, twelve-tone, academic composer." W. Duckworth, Talking Music. NY: Schirmer Books, 1995, p.52; "treated serialism as a branch of mathematics." J. Swafford, p.397; "Babbitt's music is full of wit and sparkle...rhythm at every level is one of the most forceful elements of (his) music." McCalla, p.xxi; "compression of music takes on new meaning in his work." Dubal, p.684; "leader of the American school of Serialism," Schonberg, p.598; "Copland-style populism." A. Ross, The Rest Is Noise, p.438.

Elliott Carter

"thorny, dense, and formidably intellectual" Dubal, p.678; "counterpoint of sharply differentiated lines." Burkholder, Grout, Palisca, p.921; "the extreme fluidity of both rhythm and tempo...the enormous variety of detail." Taruskin, v.5, p.262; "The outstanding characteristics of Carter's music...that of earlier composers." Ulrich, p.375; "While not necessarily serial...as to seem keyless to older ears." Crocker, p.520; "polyrhythmic dissonance," Schonberg, p.611; "difficulty for the sake of difficulty." *ibid*, p.612; "professional and social responsibility to write interesting, direct, easily understood music." Elliott Carter quote, unattributed; "very interesting to myself...the public and with performers." A. Ross, The Rest Is Noise, p.440; "consists of four separate ensembles using four distinct styles of music," "much larger and...diverse ensemble." A. Cassidy, Classical.net; "follows an overall principle of perpetual variation." Machlis, p.511; "aspires toward a conversational flexibility...character upon each member of the ensemble." P. Quantrill in 1001 Classical Recordings..., p.889; "a form that is simultaneously organic and fragmented." E. Carter quote, unattributed; "neo-classic treatment...separate from the other instruments." Grammophone, Sept 1971; "distinct musical or instrumental effect" "a piece of great charm and wit that has become a concert favorite." Berger, p.124-25; "its own type of expressivity and character derived from its instrumental capabilities." E. Carter quote, unattributed; "Many of the most gifted composers and performers...bafflement by, Carter's forms and choices." A. Tsioulcas, "Who Gets Carter?" *Grammophone*, Feb 2008; "Thirteen times as much in royalties from European performances as from American ones." *ibid*.

Olivier Messiaen

"Hindu chant, medieval plainsong...Aztec and Inca pipe music," Prendergast, p.38; "broke through...with a new dreamlike style" *ibid*; "spirited innovations and embracing of new instruments and cultures." *ibid*, p.40; "presided over the transfiguration of tonality," "deep investigation into sound itself." A. Ross, The

Rest Is Noise, p.495-96; "like glinting stars on a clear night," Prendergast, p.40; "sought to embody in music a stance of ecstatic contemplation." Burkholder, Grout, Palisca, p.911; "sweet water in the desert of postwar musical systems and –isms." Morin, p.585; "continuous piano line...and sparkling use...made it sound quite unique." Prendergast, p.39; "Messiaen's musical cosmology maximalized to the very limit." Taruskin, v.4, p.240; "the importance of impulse, intuition, spontaneity." Machlis, p.251; "seem merely to be playing mah-jongg with notes." Swafford, p.443; "statement of faith and resilience." Morin, p.586; "Messiaen's future musical preferences." R. Rischin, For the End of Time: The Story of the Messiaen Quartet. Cornell Univ. Press, updated 2006, p.13; "fluttering clarinet and ethereal, open-ended piano tones," Prendergast, p.39; This figure is sometimes grossly...had capacity for a few hundred. R. Rischin; "some find his music interminably long-winded and totally undigestible." Dubal, p.679; Scriabin did produce some of the greatest post-Romantic piano music, "Chopin filtered through Grieg and Tchaikovsky" Julian Haylock, BBC Music Magazine, Mar 2010.

Pierre Boulez
"the intensity of a resistance patriot." Griffiths, p.270; "polemical articles he wrote during his twenties"...even his mentor Messiaen. P. Griffiths, Modern Music and After: Directions Since 1945, Oxford University Press, 2011, p.5; "Boulez was in revolt against everything." ibid; "glittering, violent, and emotional music"..."a work of Beethovian range and power"..."a four-movement torrent...consolations are obviated or disrupted." Griffiths, p.271; "is a staggering display of pianistic virtuosity." The Musical Companion, p.628.

Gyorgy Ligeti
"nonetheless found it in him to write music of luminosity and wit." A. Ross, The Rest Is Noise, p.485; *"hovers between academic orthodoxy and deep reflection."* G. Ligeti (transl. D. Feurzeig, A. McVoy), liner notes for Ligeti: Works for Piano, Aimard, Sony, 1996; "Tonality was definitely out. To write...but it became stale." ibid, p.506; "in a prison...the other wall is the past" ibid; "was smooth and seamless like a huge wave." BBC Music Magazine, Jan 2010; "composition with blocks of sound...out of which he could draw swathes of different textures." Griffiths, p.288; "in which melody and harmony...an enveloping fog of cluster chords." A. Ross, Listen To This, p.48; "style forged from chromatic cluster...conventional melody, pitch and rhythm..." R. Cummings in All Music Guide, p.744; "effect of colors emerging, altering, disappearing..." Griffiths, p.288; "texture and color to the status...along with melody, harmony, and rhythm." Steinberg, p.225; "projects a series of sound 'clouds' of changing density and color." ibid; "the listener hears an all but...unfolding at various moments." E. Eriksson in All Music Guide, p.746; "shapes come out of the shadows, dark cedes to light." A. Ross, The Rest Is Noise, p.509; "maximalization of the most radical...ideologies and methodologies... completely devoid of folklore." Taruskin, v.5, pp.50-51; "with dazzling effect...wind-tones is especially effective," Dubal, p.687; "emphasis on diverse layerings and...effects of timbre and tuning." The Cambridge Companion to the Concerto, S. Keefe, ed., p.168.

Indeterminacy: Cage and Stockhausen
"aimed at freeing the performer...of a fixed sequence of notes." Libbey, p.441; "The most drastic thing Cage did...as it had existed for hundreds of years." A. Ross, Grammophone, March 2010; "created opportunities for experiencing...for the composer's intentions." Burkholder, Grout, Palisca, p.932; "Cage puts responsibility on his musicians to make decisions that can...rather play the notes

on the page..." P. Clark and B. Brandt, Grammophone, Mar 2010; "causing it to sound like a multihued percussion instrument." Libbey, p.101; "Cage finally dared to offer complete emptiness." Griffiths, p.303; "the sound of the environment...auditorium to let the world in." A. Ross, *Grammophone*, Mar 2010; "Cage considers silence...given equal importance with the sounded notes." Kyle Gann, No Such Thing as Silence, John Cage's 4'33". New Haven, CT: Yale University Press, 2010, p.ix; "whenever there are people...caused by nature or traffic." *ibid*; "Eastern-inspired piano pieces of exquisite calm." Prendergast, p.1; "a bringing together of...their tendency toward tranquility." T. May, LAPhil.org concert notes; "nihilistic musical deconstructions" Schonberg, p.612; "a kind of artistic prayer...allowed one to hear the world anew." K. Gann, p.11; "stylistic chameleon" Libbey, p.809; "characterized more by industry and facility than musical imagination." Crocker, p.523; Some critics have pointed out...chaotic and disorganized to most listeners. Schoenberg, p.600; "Could it be that...with the public but with the composer?" *ibid*, p.603; "Serialism failed to live up...international language of music." Swafford, p.447.

Post-Modernism: Minimalism

"appeared as just another strand in the rich fabric of contemporary music." Griffiths, p.293; "looking for a way forward from Schoenberg and Serialism," Prendergast, p.92; "dominated by maniacs...everyone write this crazy creepy music." A. Ross, The Rest Is Noise, p.548; "viewed as a response to the largely...music in the 1950's and 60's." A. Cassidy, Classical.net; "many resented on social grounds...so little to an ordinary listener." Taruskin, v.5, p.37; "the first style of literate music...innovations previously had on Americans." *ibid*, p.X; "present patterns that will hold the listener's interest through all that repetition," Morin, p.748; "strong pulse, paralleling popular music's beat." Griffiths, p.292; "were portraying...what it was like...continent after World War II." A. Ross, The Rest Is Noise, p.517; "sought social connection, not alienation." Taruskin, "A sturdy bridge to the 21st Century." New York Times,8/24/97.

Erik Satie

"seemed...more fitting to a new age." Prendergast, p.6; "symmetrical repetition" "is the essence of Minimalism," *ibid*. p.8; "The apostle of simplicity," Machlis, p.122; "served as a catalyst for...dominated by Mahler and Strauss." Dubal, p.504; "never won a firm place in the repertory." Machlis, p.122; "reacted against...by Debussy and fellow Impressionist composers," Machlis, p.119; "anti-Teutonic in every fiber of his being." Dubal, p.441; "music stripped of nonessentials down to its 'bare bones'." Machlis, p.122; "may seem to lack substance" "the childlike lyricism emerges." Dubal, p.637; "clear melodic phrases, exquisite lightness, and fresh texture" "literally blew away the pomp and rhetoric of the old order." Prendergast, p.6; "symmetrical phrases repeated over and over" Machlis, p.122; "Instead of offering variety...all ostentatiously plain and unemotional." Burkholder, Grout, Palisca, p.796; "modal and unresolved chords opened new possibilities for Debussy and Ravel." *ibid*; "anticipated the unresolved chords and quasi-modal harmonies of Impressionism." Grout, p.606; "miraculous economy of texture." Grout, p.607; "one side of the avant-garde which wittily upends conventional ideas." Burkholder, Grout, Palisca, p.796.

LaMonte Young and Terry Riley

"elements of Debussy... but above all Cage and Stockhausen." Prendergast, p.95; "a carefully plotted serial procedure" "Webernian focus to an extreme." J. Grimshaw in All Music Guide, p.1527; "compositions are predicated on the idea...'sustenance', or long-sustained sounds." Taruskin, v.5, p.360; "a platform upon which the Minimalist movement was built." K. Grimshaw in All Music Guide, p.1099.

Steve Reich

"lively, pulse-oriented music...rooted in the syncopations of jazz." Morin, p.748; "classical music back first its youth...years of the 20th century." Taruskin, "A Sturdy Bridge to the 21st Century" in *The New York Times*, 8/24/97; "a form of Western contrapuntal complexity into the texture" Taruskin, v.5, p.390; "The ecstatic, driving pulse...never lets down." J. Adams, Hallelujah Junction, Picador, 2009, p.95; "created to never really end, or begin...to be approached from any angle." Matt-SPV, iTunes customer review, 3/20/07; "hypnotic, but soothing, kind of poetry." Penguin Guide, p.844; "sounding like a night drive through...then disappearing behind." iTunes Album Review; "somber evocation of his childhood...references to the Holocaust." J. Adams, Hallelujah Junction, p.95; "created a powerful work with a deeply emotional edge rare in new music," Morin, p.748; "fragments of speech in a darkening reminiscence of rail travel in the 1940s," Griffiths, p.313; "based the melodic content...on the contour and rhythm of ordinary human speech." Taruskin, "A Sturdy Musical Bridge to the 21st Century" in *The New York Times*, 8/24/97; "turgidly bleak portrait of New York City," Morin, p.748.

Philip Glass

"has given a dose of...classical composer in contemporary life." J. Adams, Hallelujah Junction, p.94; "elaborate rhythmic structure of Indian music." Libbey, p.271; "The building blocks of Glass's music...develop beyond strictly limited confines." *Grammophone*, June 1990; "a summation of past techniques and a look forward to the future." Prendergast, p.136; "had a strong and openly...art-rock of the 1970s and 1980s." Taruskin, v.5, p.391; "Glass had reached some sort of truce...conventional musical structure." R. Thomas in 1001 Classical Recordings..., p.921; "a concoction of smooth horns, strings and lovingly coaxed electronics." Prendergast, p.137; "an amiably soft-edged minimalist sound" J. Grimshaw in All Music Guide, p.498.

Arvo Pärt

"greatly simplified, austere and essentially tonal." Libbey, p.599; "combined a radical simplification...with a return to diatonic music." Burkholder, p.957; "an intense spiritual pleading," Libbey, p.599; "always points to an unchanging, transcendent refuge for the world-weary." Morin, p.693; "introspective, mystical...(it) can cast a spell on listeners," Draper, p.60; "pursues an austerely beautiful simplicity that suggests spiritual illumination." T. May, Amazon.com review; "Medieval music seen through a contemporary sensibility." P. Hiller, *BBC Music Magazine*, 12/09, p.122; "rings out the notes of the tonic triad around it," Libbey, p.599; "alienated tone color effect." John Henken, LAPhil.org; "consists of progressively lengthening and loudening bouts of fiddling activity" Taruskin, v.5, p.404; "infused with a...startlingly successful evocation of stillness." *ibid*, p.406; "clear sense of the...spriritual underpinnings of" All Music Guide, p.982; "a continuously shifting surface of consonances and dissonances..." *ibid*; "until it bursts into a climactic cadenza" "as the music subsides into the depths." Henken, LAPhil.org; "keeps disappearing into silence, and then returning." P. Hiller; "a sort of wordless chorale...exists in numerous arrangements..." Taruskin, v.5, p.404; "serene and tonal in contrast to the angst of the first two." Morin, p.692; "he has developed a vocabulary of singular intensity and cohesion." I. Moody, *Grammophone*, Awards issue, 2010; "linked ever more clearly with...range of musical and linguistic color." *ibid*.

John Adams
"building large, expressive structures by the repetition of small elements." J. Adams, <u>Hallelujah Junction</u>, p.93; "the folkloric, vernacular elements...rather than a rival to Carter." A. Whittall in <u>The Cambridge Companion to the Concerto</u>, Simon P. Keefe, ed. Cambridge University Press, 2005; "has relied less on minimalist...harmonic and contrapuntal means." Burkholder, p.956; "never coy about using vernacular and banal elements." <u>The Rough Guide to Classical Music</u>, 4th ed., Rough Guides, 2005, p.1; "a statement of belief in the power of tonality...a wedding of...are everywhere in this strange piece," J. Adams, <u>Hallelujah Junction</u>, p.130; "transform minimalism into something richer and less rigid," <u>Rough Guide</u>, 4th ed, p.2; "the limitations of a technique that placed so much emphasis upon repetition." *ibid*, p.1; "to the perpetual motion ostinatos of...Sibelian ostinatos and floating ambiences." Morin, p.1-2.

Adams, John
Chapter 26

Albeniz, Issac
Chapter 20

Arensky, Anton
Piano Trio - Chapter 9

Babbitt, Milton
Chapter 26

Bach, Johann Sebastian
Goldberg Variations, Keyboard Suites and Partitas – Chapter 3
Well-Tempered Klavier – 3
Unaccompanied Cello Suites - 3
Unaccompanied Violin Sonatas and Partitas - 3
Brandenburg Concertos – 14
Harpsichord, Violin Concertos -14
Orchestral Suites, *The Art of the Fugue, A Musical Offering* -14

Barber, Samuel
Chapter 25

Bartók, Béla
String Quartets - Chap 10
Concertos, Orchestral works - 20

Beethoven, Ludwig van
Piano Sonatas - Chapter 5
Violin Sonatas, Cello Sonatas - 8
String Quartets - 9
Piano Concertos, Symphonies – 15
Overtures - 15

Berlioz, Hector
Chapter 17

Borodin, Alexander
String Quartets - Chapter 10
Orchestral works - 20

Boulez, Pierre
Chapter 26

Brahms, Johannes
Solo Piano Music – Chapter 6
Piano Trios - 9
String Quartets - 10
Piano Quartets, Piano Quintet – 11
String Quintets, String Sextets - 12
Wind Chamber Music – 13
Concertos, Serenades, Symphonies – 18

Britten, Benjamin
Chapter 25

Bruckner, Anton
Chapter 19

Cage, John
Chapter 26

Carter, Elliott
Chapter 26

Chopin, Frederic
Ballades; Scherzos; Etudes; Nocturnes; Waltzes; Preludes; Polonaises; Mazurkas; Piano Sonatas – Chapter 6
Piano Concertos - Chapter 16

Copland, Aaron
Chapter 25

Corelli, Arcangelo
Concerto Grossi - Chapter 14

Couperin, Francois
Music for Harpsichord - Chapter 3

Debussy, Claude
Solo piano music – Chapter 7
String Quartet - 10
Orchestral Music - 21

Delius, Frederick
Chapter 21

Dvořák, Antonin
Piano Trios - Chapter 8
String Quartets - 10
Piano Quartets, Piano Quintets - 11
Concertos, Symphonic Poems, Symphonies - 18

Edward Elgar
Concertos, *Enigma Variations*, Symphonies – Chapter 20

Franck, Cesar
Violin Sonata – Chapter 8
String Quartet - 10
Piano Quintet – 11
Symphony in D - 17

Fauré, Gabriel
Music for solo piano - Chapter 6
String Quartet - 10
Piano Quartets and Quintets - 11

Glass, Philip
Chapter 26

Glinka, Mikail
Chapter 20

Grieg, Edvard
Lyric Pieces - Chapter 6
Violin Sonatas, Cello Sonata - 8
String Quartet - 10
Piano Concerto - 20

Handel, George Friedrich
Chamber Sonatas, Harpsichord Suites – Chapter 3
Concerti Grossi - 14
Water Music - 14

Haydn, Joseph
Piano Sonatas - Chapter 5
Piano Trios - 8
String Quartets - 9
Symphonies, Concertos - 15

Hindemith, Paul
Chapter 23

Holst, Gustav
Chapter 21

Ives, Charles
Chapter 20

Janáček, Leos
String Quartets – Chapter 10
Sinfonietta - 20

Kodály, Zoltan
Chapter 20

Ligeti, Gyorgi
Chapter 26

Liszt, Franz
Piano Sonata, Transcendental Etudes, *Paganini Etudes*, Hungarian Rhapsodies – Chapter 6
Piano Concertos, Tone Poems - 16

Lully, Jean-Baptiste
Chapter 14

Mahler, Gustav
Chapter 19

Martinů, Bohuslav
Sonatas, Trios – 9
Chamber music for Winds - 13
Symphonies, Concertos - 23

Mendelssohn, Felix
String Quartets - Chapter 10
Octet, op.20; Quintet - 11
Concertos, Symphonies, Overtures - 16

Monteverdi, Claudio
Chapter 1

Mozart, Wolfgang Amadeus
Piano Sonatas – Chapter 5
String Quartets - 9
String Quintets - 11
Piano Concertos, Concertos for Strings - 15
Wind Concertos, Symphonies, Serenades and *Divertimenti* - 15

Pärt, Arvo
Chapter 26

Prokofiev, Serge
Violin Sonatas, Cello Sonatas – Chapter 9
String Quartets - 10
Piano Concertos, Violin Concertos, Symphonies - 24

Purcell, Henry
Sonatas of Three Parts - Chapter 14

Rachmaninoff, Sergei
Solo Piano Music – 6
Piano Concertos – 20
Piano Trios and Cello Sonata - 9

Rameau, Jean-Phillippe
Chapter 3

Ravel, Maurice
Solo Piano Music - Chapter 7
String Quartet - 10
Piano Concertos - 21

Reich, Steve
Chapter 26

Scarlatti, Domenico
Keyboard Sonatas - Chapter 3

Schubert, Franz
Solo Piano Music – Chapter 5
Piano Trios - 9
String Quartets - 10
Trout Quintet; Quintet in C - 11
Symphonies - 15

Schumann, Robert
Solo Piano Music – Chapter 6
Trios – Chapter 9
String Quartets – 10
Piano Quartet; Piano Quintet - 11
Piano Concerto, Violin Concerto, Symphonies - 16

Shostakovich, Dmitri
Solo Piano Music – Chapter 7
Cello Sonata, Piano Trio - 9
String Quartets - 10
Piano Quintet - 11
Symphonies - 24

Sibelius, Jean
Symphonies, Tone Poems, Violin Concerto – Chapter 19

Smetana, Bedrich
String Quartets - Chapter 10

Stockhausen, Karlheinz
Chapter 26

Strauss, Richard
Chapter 19

Stravinsky, Igor
Chapter 23

Tchaikovsky, Piotr Ilych
Piano Trio - Chapter xx
String Quartets - 10
Piano Concertos, Violin Concerto, Symphonies - 18

Vaughn Williams, Ralph
Chapter 20

Vivaldi, Antonio
The Four Seasons – Chapter 14

Wagner, Richard
Chapter 16

A

Abbado, Claudio.....*285, 303*
Abel, C.F.....*61*
absolute music......*24,29, 444*
Academy of Ancient Music.....*264-5,270*
Academy of St. Martin in the Fields Chamber Ensemble.....*236*
Adams, John.....*ii,312,410*
Adorno, Theodor.....*1,395,450, 500,502*
Africa....*139*
African music.....*510,519*
Aimard, Pierre Laurent..... *510,512*
Ajemian, Maro.....*514*
Akoko, Henri.....*508*
Alban Berg Quartet.....*209*
Aldeburgh Festival.....*505*
Aldol Reaction.....*401*
Alps.....*356*
Alsop, Marin.....*311*
Amar Quartet.....*156,471*
Amazon.com.....*vi*
America.....*185-6,207,338, 348-50, 395,444,486,491, 493,495-6,501-2*
Americana......*25,409,412,435,501-2*
American Revolution.....*98*
Amsterdam.....*256*
Ancient Greece.....*250*
Anda, Géza.....*284,421*
Andalusia.....*424-5*
Andalusian folk music..... *424-5*
Anderson, Hans Christian *121*
Andsnes, Leif Ove.....*77, 127,132, 134, 182,229, 361,421*
Angelich, Nicolas....*130*
Annunzio, Gabriele d'....*52*
anti-Romanticism.....*404, 448*
anti-semitism.....*380,389, 445*
Arabia.....*139*
Aranyi, Jelly d'.....*435*
Archbishop of Canterbury.....*407*

Archbishop of Salzburg..... *62*
Argerich, Martha....*124, 143,169-70,220,226,359*
Arrau, Claudio.....*83*
Ashkenazy, Vladimir.... *134,165, 167,361, 393, 395,478,480*
atonality.....*16,18,20,411,419,422,439-42,444,446, 449,453,455*
Auer, Leopold.....*358*
Auschwitz.....*520*
Austria.....*255,257,381*
Austrian folk tunes.....*366,376*
Austrian-Hungarian Empire..... *398*
avant-garde....*16,25,99, 110,134, 248,366,391, 410-11, 422,468, 475,480, 500-1,504-6,502-3,505, 508,510-12,514-19*
Ax, Emmanuel....*157,226*
Aztec and Inca pipe music.....*507*

B

Bach, Carl Philipp Emanuel..... *12,13,43,43, 64,254,279-81*
Bach *Gesellschaft*......*44*
Bach, Johann Christian *10, 43, 75,153, 220,280*
Bach-*Werke-Verzeichnis* *45*
Balakirev, Mily.....*400*
Ballets Russes.....*433,463*
Barbirolli, John.....*297,408*
Barcelona......*425,452*
Barenboim, Daniel.....*22,161, 165,283,334, 352*
Baroque.....*ii,iii,38,39,40-4,47-8,52-5, 80, 84,97-8,100,104,112-3,125,129, 131, 142-43, 147,154-5, 160,166,180,182,184-5,188, 190-1,202,13,246, 248-54,257-9,261-70, 272,281,284,294, 403, 415,448-9,454,504,510, 519*
Baroque suites.....*10*
barroco.....40

609

Barschay, Rudolf.....216
Bartók *pizzicato*.....209, 213
baryton.....60
Basque.....434
basso continuo...9
Battle of Leningrad.....493
Bavaria.....117,314
Bavarian Radio Symphony Orchestra.... 308,351
Bayreuth.....13,298,300,417,430-31
Bayreuth Festival....323-4
Bax, Arnold.....239
Beatles.....515
Beaujean, Alfred.....162
Beaux Arts Trio.....157,164, 174, 176,224,226,229
be-bop jazz.....518
Beecham, Thomas.....277,303, 343,437-38
Beethoven, Karl van..... 80,198
Beethoven, Kaspar van..... 198
Beethoven String Quartet..... 183,217
bel canto..........60,117,122
Belgian Radio & TV Orchestra 495
Bell, Joshua.......24
Benedetti Michelangeli, Arturo...361
Benjamin, George..... 297, 511
benzene derivatives..... 401
Berg, Helene.....452
Berg, Jacob.....507
Berger, Melvin.....409
Berio, Luciano....
Berkeley.....519
Berlin.....165,171,238,298,347,356,395,446,449,451-2,469,491
Berlin Philharmonic....*222,255-7, 285,289-90,292, 300,302,334, 338, 345,349,352,357, 373, 380,421,474,495*
Berlin Radio Symphony Orchestra.....421, 469
Berlin Wall.....298
Bernstein, Leonard.....v, 256,292, 309,311, 375, 380,409,412-13, 494-5, 501,507,510
Béroff, Michel.....149
Bertrand, Aloysius.....142
Bettelheim, Dolf.....224
binary form.....64,69
Birtwhistle, H.....20
Bizet, Georges.....249
Blaník.....416
Blom, Eric.....25,26,152, 289
blues.....137,435,502
Boccherini, Luigi....221-3,311
Bohemia.....174,184,228,347-51, 424,476, 479
Bohemian dance.....350
Böhm, Karl.....222,285, 289-90, 300,303
Bonaparte, Napoleon.....292,295, 298,380, 423
Bonn.....124,291,299
Book of Revelation.....507
Bookspan, Martin.....178, 300
Borodin, Alexander.....138, 209-10,217, 338,391
Borodin Quartet....157,210, 217, 230
Borodin Trio.....176
Boston.....357-8,411
Boston Commons.....411
Boston Symphony.....255, 330, 338,395,421,468-9,473,477-8, 507
Boulez, Pierre.....156,331,421-2, 450,453,490
bouree.....248
Boult, Adrian.....332,406, 437
Bowie, David.....522
Bowman, Peter.....507
Brain, Dennis.....285
Braugher, Andre.....411
Brautigam, Ronald.....110
Brazilian folk tunes.....v
Brendel, Alfred....77,87,89,91,93, 124,292
Brezhnev, Leonid....485
BBC Music Magazine.....vii

BBC Symphony Orchestra.....297,456
Bridge, Frank.....504
British Empire.....404
Britten, Benjamin.....169, 283
Brno.....184,351
Broderick, Matthew..... 411
Brodsky, A......358
Brown, David.....400
Browning, John......109, 507
Bruch, Max.....312,352
Bruckner Society.....368, 371
Brussels.....424
Brymer, Jack.....236
Budapest Academy of Music..... 423
Buchberger Quartet..... 193
Buckley, William F.....78
Bülow, Hans von.....45, 48, 128, 132,345, 358,384-5
Burgundy.....3
Burleigh, Harry.....349
Busoni, Ferruccio.....270, 444,517
Byrd, William.....407
Byron, Lord........99

C

Caccini, Guilio.....7,113
cadenza.....259-61,266
Cage, John.....410
Cairo.....334
California.....444-5,450, 512
Calvinism.....43
Cannabich, Christian..... 253
cantabile style.....75,82-3
canzone.....5,257
Capuçon brothers.....170
Carnegie Hall.....93,361, 413
Carter, Elliott.....9,411
Casals, Pablo.....49
cassation.....249,260
Catholicism.....374,379,381,507-9
Caucasus Mountains..... 215

Celibidache, Sergiu.....352
Centennial Exposition Universelle.....139
Central Committee....484-5
Central Park.....410-11
Cervantes, Miguel de..... 387
chaconne.....248,270
Chailly, Riccardo.....373
Chang, Sarah.....178,182, 229
chanson.....257
Chausson, Ernest 177,331
Chen, Wendy.....182
Chicago.....488
Chicago Symphony Orchestra....255-6,292,332,334,338,345,359, 380,394,421,436,494
Chinese.....200
Christianity.....379
chromaticism.....1,399,403,419,440-1,445-8
chromatic scale..... 439, 443,446-7,453
Chung, Myung-Whun..... 495
City by the Sea....117
City of Birmingham SO.....335,418
Civil War.....411
Classical period.....iii,40,42,47, 54, 73, 77, 79,81, 154-5,162, 171,189,196, 234-5,242,246, 249,251, 253-4,257-9,262,272, 281, 284,289,293-4,339,345
Classical Style.....75,83,96, 98, 106,174, 188,190,197,201,229
Classicism......96,205
Clement, Franz.....293
Clementi, Muzio.....74,79,117
Cleveland Orchestra..... 255-6, 277,292,303,345,349,351,423
Cliburn, Van.....359
Cold War.....20,442,501, 504
Coltrane, John.....411,518

Columbia Princeton Electronic Music Center....503
Columbia Symphony Orchestra 297,373
Columbia University..... 419
Communist Manifesto 30
Comte d'Ogny.....274
concertante style.....221, 246, 249,258,261, 332
Concertgebouw Orchestra (Amsterdam) 255,330, 357, 373,402,433
concerto grosso.....246, 258,261-3,265-6,269,271-2,290,506
Connecticut.....412
consonance.....439,441,456
continuo.....250,252-3, 257,266-7
Cooke, Deryk.....367,379
Cooper, Barry.....290
Copenhagen.....489
Copland, Aaron.....ii,1,21,23-28, 227,240, 326,332, 360,435,456
Corelli, Archangelo.....9,10,52-4, 251,258,261-62,264,269,476
Corigliano, John.....505
Coriolanus.....301
Cöthen.....ii,2,43,46-8,50,249,266
Council of Trent...6
Count Giovanni de Bardi.....250
Count Keyserlingk.....10,45
Count Lamoral van Egmont..... 301
Count Razumovsky.....198
Count Thun-Hohenstein 287
counterpoint.....6,7,9,11,17,18,40-4, 48,52,54,97-8,111,116,119-20,128-9,447,449,451,456
country and western music.....22
Couperin, François.....137,142, 154,180,435
Cowboy songs.....502
Croatia.....212
Crocker, Richard.....79,265
Crossley, Paul....132
Crusades....126
Cuba.....424
Cui, Cesar.....362,400
Curtis Institute of Music 506
Curzon, Clifford.....281,332,345, 505
cyclic form.....71,177-8,258,272, 274,332
Czech folk music....347,350-51,476-7
Czecholslovakia.....398-9,418
Czech Philharmonic.....351, 418, 476,478, 480
Czech Republic.....352,416
Czerny, Carl.....82,198, 292-3
Cziffra, Georges....125-6

D

Dante String Quartet..... 209
Dallas Symphony.....361
Danzi, Franz.....234
Darmstadt.....480,514
Darmstadt School.....502, 510-11,516
Dartington Trio.....171
Das Kunstwerk der Zukunft 321
David, Ferdinand....314
Davidsbund society.... 106,108
Davis, Colin....229,277, 308,330, 345,414
Davis, Miles.....518
Dearling, Robert.....369
Dehmel, Richard.....230, *445*
De Jean, Ferdinand.....234
Delius, Frederick.....403, 437-38
De Niro, Robert....117
Derry, Michael.....23
Desprez, Josquin....4-6
Dettmer, Roger.....392
Deutsche Grammophone 31
development.....61,64-70
Diabelli, Anton.....84-5,87-8,92
Diaghilev, Serge.....433-4
diaphony.....2
diatonic scale.....439
Diémer, Louis.....332

Dies Irae....318,361-62
d'Indy, Vincent...131,177,331-2, 424
dissonance.....409-12,419-20, 439-41,443,446-7,451, 455
de Larrocha, Alicia.....425
divertimento.....248-9, 254,258-8,273,289
Domino technique...464-5
Domus.....157,228-9
Donat, Misha.....91
Doráti, Antal.....256,277, 357, 361,401,423. 503
Downes, Olin.....395
Draculu.....522
Dresden....101,169,216,309-11,322
Dresden Staatskapelle.....373
Dryden, John.....403
Dubal, David.....445,480
Dukas, Paul.....424,463
Dumay, Augustin....161, 175
Dumka.....174,231
Dunstable, John.....403
Du Pré, Jacqueline.....334, 352
Durchführung.....67
Dushkin, Samuel.....469
Düsseldorf......102,127,169,309-11
Dutoit, Charles.....433,437

E

Early Baroque.....40
Eastern Orthodox Christianity 522
eBay......vi
Ecole Niedermayer.....131
Edwardian Era.....404
Ehnes, James.....182
Einstein, Albert.....185,506
Einstein, Alfred.....2,14,30,44, 193,200,279-80,287,303,313, 367,370
Eisenstadt.....63,278
Eisler, Hanns.....472

Elizabeth Sprague Coolidge Foundation.....501
Ellington, Duke.....v,21, 411
Emerson, Ralph Waldo..... 409
Emerson String Quartet.....157, 193,203,205,209-10,214,217, 229
Emperor Constantine..... 479
Emperor Friedrich Wilhelm..... 194
Emperor Joseph II.....283
Enlightenment...12,80,96
English Chamber Orchestra..... 269,408,505
English folksong.....436
English Hymnal.....407
Eno, Brian.....522
Ensemble Inter Contemporain 510,512
Erben, Karel Jaromír......350
Erlenmeyer, Emil.....401
Eschenbach, C....110
Essays on Music......30
Eszterháza.....76,99,253
Esterházy family....76,274, 276, 278
Exposition.....64-7,70
Eusebius.....102,106-8
Ewen, David.....476

F

Falla, Manuel de.....466
Farrenc, Louise....107
Fascism.....392,442
Fate.....354-56
Faust.....342
Feltsman, Vladimir......106
Field, John.....117
54th Massachusetts.....411
Finland.....132,366,398,414-15
Finnish folklore.....389,393
Firkusny, Rudolf.....478-9
Fischer, Iván.....277,377
Fitzhagen, William.....358
Fitzwilliam Quartet.....217

Flegeljahre…..103,105,107
Fleisher, Leon…..157,292, 345
Florence…9,53
Florentine Camerata…..7,113, 250-1,261
Florestan……102,106-8
Florestan Trio…..157,182
Florida…..438
folk music…..ii
Formalism…..484
Fort Wagner…..411
Foss, Lukas…..105,309-10,514
Fournier, Pierre…..352
Frankfurt…..420
Frankl, Peter……110
Frederick the Great…..268
Freed, Richard…..301
Freeman, Morgan…..411
Freemasons…..320
French Impressionism….. 406, 424
French Revolution….. 13,98
Friedrich Wilhelm II …..165,222
Fricken, Ernestine von …..107-9
Fricsay, Ferenc…..421
Frisch, Walter…..342
Fugue…..40-2,46-50
Furtwängler, Wilhelm….. *300, 343,420,472*

G

Gaffigan, William…..312
Galileo, Vincenzo…..250
Galitzin, Prince Nikolas …..200, 202
gamelan…..139
gaudeamus igitur…..338,342
gavotte…..248
Gebrauchsmusik….184,241,472, 475
Genoa…..330
Gérecz, Árpád…..222
Gergiev, Valery…..402
German Chamber Philharmonic Bremen …..297
German Expressionism….. 180

Gershwin, George….v,19, 435, 461
Gesamtkunstwerk…..146,321, 509
Gewandhaus…..206
Gewandhaus Orchestra…..252, 273,313-14,316
gigue…..246,248
Gilbert, Kenneth…..47
Gilels, Emil…..75,83,86, 132,345
Glazunov, Alexander…..312,362, 402-3
Glikman, Isaak…..216
Glinka, Mikail…..399-400,431
Glory…..411
Goebbels, Joseph….473
Goethe, Johann Wolfgang von….. 47,79, 99,155, 268, 274,301,342
Goldberg, J.G.…..10,45
Goldberg, Szymon…..161
Goodman, Benny…..242
gospel hymns…..502
gothic…..369
Gould, Glenn…..45,267
Gounod, Charles…..331, 334
Graf, Max…..370
Graham, Martha…..501
Grainger, Percy…..518
Gramophone……v,vii
Grammy Award…..520
Granados, Enrique…..424
Grand Duke Paul of Russia…..190
Graun, C.H….13
Great Depression…..392,449
Great Dome of Köln…..311
Gregorian Chant…..2,201
Griffiths, Paul…..23,155,180, 296,443
Grimaud, Hélène…..270,421
Gropius, Manon…..452
Grout, Donald…..30
Grumiaux Trio…..163,222
Grünewald, Matthias….472
Gubaidulina, Sofia…..497
Guiness Book of World Records …..141

gypsy.....228,231,435

H

Haas, Robert.....368,372
Hahn, Hilary.....345
Haitink, Bernard....361,433
Hallé, Charles.....121
Hallé Orchestra.....408
Hamburg......53,127
Hamelin, Marc-Andre.....77,121
Handley, Vernon.....408
Hanson, Howard.....501
Hannover.....52-3
Hanslick, Eduard......128,173, 251,339-40,347,358,368-9, 384,386-7
Harasiewicz, Adam.....130
Harmonicon, The.....299
Harmonie.....235,240
Harmoniemusik.....155,234
harmony......27-28
Harnoncourt, Nikolas.....266,284
Harrell, Lynn.....167
Harris, Roy.....501
Harvard University....524
Haslinger, Tobias.....92
Hasse, Adolf.....13
Hausmusik (ensemble).....225
Hausmusik.....152,222
Haylock, Julian....144
Hebbel, C.F.....110
Hebrides....315-16
Heidelberg, University of.....401
Heifetz, Jascha.....51,345,359,394
Heine, Heinrich.....124
Helsinki.....390
Hemming, R.....2,22
Hesse, J.A....13
Henze, Hans Werner.....442
Hewitt, Angela.....49
Heymann Quartet.....209
High Baroque...8-10,12,52,58,65, 69,258
High Fidelity.....504
High Renaissance...6,7,40,250
Hiller, Ferdinand.....326
Hindu Chant.....507
Hitler, Adolf.....389,436,442,473
Hoboken, Anthony van.....77
Hoffmann, E.T.A.....96,98,107, 109,296
Hogwood, Christopher.....265, 270,477,479
Hokusai, Katsushika.....432
Holberg, Ludvig.....415
Holliger, Heinz....506
Holocaust.....183,520
Holst, Gustav.....436-7,504
homophony.....6-9,27,29,40,63, 66
Honegger, Arthur.....20,480
Horowitz, Vladimir.....52,109,361
Hough, Stephen......*115,124,127, 335,361*
Hummel, Johann Nepomuk *14,100,120*
Hungarian folk music.....211-12,423
Hungarian folklore.....423
Hungarian Gypsy folk tunes 125
Hungarian Quartet.....214
Hungary.....212,398,417,419,423
Hurwitz, David....141,254,376, 390,418
Hussites.....416

I

idée fixe.....*71,329-30*
Imai, Nobuko.....*330*
imitative polyphony....42
Immerseel, Jos van.....*298*
Impressionism......*16,29,30,55,13 5,137-40, 147,209,239,385*
Indeterminacy.....*502,512-15*
Internet.......*31*
Ireland, Patrick.....*236*

Irish Folksong.....*117*

Isaac, Henri.....*447*
Isserlis, S....*101,312,507*
Italian opera.....*52-3,111-2,253-4*
Italian style.....*46,53*
Ives, Charles.....*524*
Ives and Myrick.....*409*

J
Jacobson, J.H.....*28*
Jaeger, Augustus.....*405*
Jandó, Jenó.....*49,77*
Janis, Byron.....*361,401*
Janowski, Marek....*496*
Jansons, Mariss.....*215,357,402*
Järvi, Neeme.....*402*
Järvi, Paavo.....*297*
jazz.....*19,22,137,142,181,435,461,471,474,476-7,502,504-5,514,517-19*
Jean Paul.....*103,105,107*
Joachim, Joseph.....*223,312,344-45,352*
Jochum, Eugene.....*345,373*
Johnson, Julian.......*23*
Juilliard String Quartet.....*157,214,224,230*

K
Kabardian folk music.....*215*
Kalevala.....*394*
Kammermusik.....*152*
Kamu, Okko.....*359*
Karajan, Herbert von.....*256-7,285,300-2, 343,352,357,359, 373,393,437,446,452,495*
Karlsruhe.....*371*
Karl Theodor.....*234,253*
Katz, David.....*413*
Katz, R....*4,398*
Kelly, Grace.....*506*
Kempff, Wilhelm.....*85-6,292*

Kennedy, Nigel.....*345,359*
Kertész, István.....*283,341,343, 347,349*
Khrennikov, Tikhon.....*484*
Kindertotenlieder.....*378*
King Arthur.....*403*
King of Bavaria.....*314*
King George I.....*265*
King, Stephen.....*350*
Kirov Orchestra.....*402*
Kissin, Evgeny.....*93,107,134*
Klangfarbenmelodie.....*448-9, 455-6,511-12*
Kleiber, Carlos.....*31,297,303,343*
Kleiber, Erich.....*456*
Klemperer, Otto.....*345,373,380, 446*
Klinger, Maximillian.....*274*
Klopstock, Friedrich Gottlieb..... *376*
Knecht, Heinrich.....*296*
Köchel, Ludwig von......*74*
Kocsis, Zoltán *147*
Kodály Quartet.....*193*
Kodály, Zoltan....*49,212,398, 417,423*
Köln.....*378,387*
Kondrashin, Kiril.....*318,359,402, 492*
Königsberg.....*321*
Koussevitzky, Serge....*146,241, 395,400, 421,473,478,488,507*
Kovacevich, Steven......*87,130, 236,345,414*
Kramer, Jonathan......*iv,378,412, 441,451, 461,480*
Kramer, Lawrence.....*2,17,23,26, 126,238, 486*
Krasner, Louis.....*450,452*
Kremer, Gidon.....*284,523-4*
Kreisler.....*109*
Krenek, Ernst.....*472*
Kronos Quartet.....*520,522*
Krushchev, Nikita....*485*
Kubelik, Rafael.....*349,351,479-80*
Kubrick, Stanley.....*387*
Kundera, Milan.....*396*

L

Lahti Symphony Orchestra.....*394*
Lake Lucerne.....*361*
Lalo, Edouard.....*131,176,312, 344*
Lamartine, Alphonse de.....*319*
Ländler......*22,366,372,376*
Landowksa, Wanda....*47,54*
Lang, P.H.....*5,8,17,81,96,163, 190,249, 268,273,328*
Laredo, Jaime.....*157,163,184, 226*
Lasso, Orlando di.....*6*
Latham, Peter.....*128*
Layton, Robert.....*390*
LeBoulaire, Jean.....*508*
Le Guay, Claire-Marie.....*224*
Leibowitz, René.....*395,500*
Leinsdorf, Erich.....*313,507*
Leipzig.....*7,46,48,51,63,200,313- 14,316,344,368,414,424*
Leipzig Conservatory.....*168-9*
Leitmotif.....*319,322*
Leitner, Ferdinand.....*292*
Lenau, Nikolaus.....*385*
Lengyel, Menyhert.....*420*
Leningrad.....*491,493-4*
Leningrad Philharmonic....*256, 357,495-6*
Les Six.....*392*
Lesueur, Max.....*222*
Leutgeb, Ignaz.....*236,285*
Leverkuehn, Adrian.....*501*
Levi, Hermann.....*340,372*
Levine, James.....*93,284,292,334*
Levy, David Benjamin.....*298*
Lewis and Clark.....*522*
Libbey, Ted....*496*
Lieder.......*v,13,29,88-9,91,100, 375*
Ligeti, Gyorgy.....*142*
Lindsays, The.....*193,203*
Linz.....*287,367*
Lipatti, Dinu.....*118,121*
Liszt-Wagner, Cosima.....*320,322*
Litton, Andrew.....*361*
Lobkovitz, Prince.....*192*
London.....*52-3,241,276,315,348, 356,456*
London Philharmonic.....*255,332, 359, 408, 437*
London Symphony Orchestra..... *255,303,318,345,349,357,361, 421,503,505*
Longfellow, Henry Wadsworth *349*
Lord Byron.....*355-56,385*
Los Angeles Philharmonic.....*255*
Louis XIV....*54,261,403*
Löwe, Ferdinand.....*368-9,372*
Lugano Festival.....*170,226*
Luisi, Fabio.....*373*
Lully, Jean-Baptiste.....*54,261- 2,267*
Lupu, Radu.....*91,93,110,130,161*
Luther, Martin......*5*
Lyadov, Anatoly.....*463*
Lydian mode.....*201*

M

Ma, Yo-Yo.....*49,156-7,163,226, 278*
Maazel, Lorin.....*335,359,524*
MacBeth.....*167*
MacDowell, Edward.....*408*
Machlis, Joseph.....*500*
Mackerras, Charles.....*265,277, 288-9,349, 351,418*
Madame Blavatsky.....*145*
Madrid....*488*
madrigal...*5,6,8*
Maeterlinck, M.....*446*
Magdeburg.....*321*
Mahler, Alma.....*378,445,452*
Mallarmé, Stéphane.....*431*
Mandelring Quartet.....*217,224*

Manhattan Project.....*524*

Mann, Klaus.....*388*
Mann, Thomas.....*388,501*
Mannheim.....*153-4,220,234-5*
Mannheim Court Orchestra.....*253-4*
Mannheim School.....*153*
Mannheim Steamroller.....*253*
Manze, Andrew....*264,270*
Marsalis, Wynton.....*278*
Marwood, Anthony.....*228*
Marx, Karl......*30*
mathematics.....*430*
Maximalism.....*508*
McCarthy-Draper, Maureen.....*16,42*
McCarthyism.....*503*
McCreesh, P.....*263*
Meiningen.....*341,382,384-5*
Mendelssohn, Fanny...*170-1,205-6*
Menotti, Gian Carlo.....*506*
Menuhin, Yehudi.....*147,312,505*
Messiaen, Olivier.....*27,453*
Mexican tunes.....*502*
Meyer, Martin....*45*
Michelangelo......*127*
Mickiewicz, Adam.....*112,114*
micropolyphonie.....*502,511*
Middle Ages.....*2,475*
Mighty Five, the....*210,385,399-402,485*
Milhaud, Darius.....*239,461,474,480,517*
Milstein, Nathan....*50*
minimalism.....*ii,iii,142,497,500*
Minnesota (Minneapolis) Symphony..... *256,361,393,423,473,503*
minuet and trio.....*68,70-1*
Mitropoulos, Dmitri....*473*
modulation.....*439,447*
Molina, Tirso de.....*385*

monophony...2
Montagu, J.....*128*
Monteux, Pierre.....*332,343,437, 463*
Monteverdi, Claudio.....*8,22,250,252*
Montreal Symphony Orchestra *433,437*
Moravia.....*184,398,417*
Morin, A......*vi,264*
Mørk, Truls.....*175*
Moscow.....*215,486-8*
Moscow Philharmonic.....*256, 492*
motet...5,6,8
Mount Everest.....*195*
Mozart, Leopold.....*193*
Mravinsky, Yvgeny.....*357,492-3,495-6*
Mühlfeld, Richard.....*238*
Munch, Charles....*330,478*
Munich.....*154,314,491*
Munich Agreement.....*479*
Musicus Consentius Wien.....*266*
Mussorgsky, Modest......*30,138,142,399-401,430-1*
Muti, Riccardo.....*256,357,402*
mysticism.....*366-7,373-4,379*

N

Napoleon.....*13,14,292,295,298,380,423*
Napoleonic Wars.....*118,199,423*
National Society of Music.....*131*
Nationalistic Impressionism..... 147
NBC Radio.....*493*
NBC Symphony Orchestra.....*421, 450*
Native American music.....*207*
Nature.....*367,370,373-4,384, 390,394 ,430, 432,436,438*
Naxos.....*32*
Nazism.....*20,213,321,392,396,442*
Nebraska.....*522*
neo-Baroque.....*84,147,149,190, 232,284, 407,415,424,505,522*

neo-Classicism.....*iii,v,17,18,20,
25,42,240-2, 255, 372,392-3,
404,415,420, 424,430, 442,449,
500-1,504,509,522-3*
neo-Romanticism.....*420,506*
Netherlands.....*301*
Netherlands Schools...*4,6,8*
Neue Freie Presse.....*339*
Neue Zeitschrift für Musik.....
101,303
New England.....*524-5*
New Grove Dictionary of Music
.....*264*
New Jersey Symphony Orchestra
....*311-12*
New World.....*207*
New York....*213,360,411,424,
486,520*
New York Herald Tribune.....*395*
New York Philharmonic.....*255-
6,349,361, 375,380,395,412-
13,470,480,506,510,524*
New York Times.....*395*
Nice, Italy.....*330*
Nice, D.......*120*
Nichols, J....*123*
Nietzsche, Friedrich.....*321,387, 398*
Nono, Luigi....*514*
Nordraak, Rikard.....*414*
Normandy.....*144,502*
Norrington, Roger....*20,275*
North Africa.....*212*
Norway.....*398,414-15*
Nowak, Leopold.....*368,372*

O

objectivity.....*440,442*
occult.....*145*
Ode to Joy.....*298-9*
Ogdan, John.....*134*
Ohlssohn, Garrick.......*103,480*
Oistrakh, David.....*183-4,345,496*

Opera.....*247,250-1,253-4,258-9*
Oppenheimer, Robert.....*524*
Oramo, Sakari.....*335*
oratorio.....*5,7,9,10*
Orchestra of St. Luke's.....*265, 277*
Orchestra National de France..... *335*
Orfeo.....*8*
organic halogens.....*401*
Ormandy, Eugene.....*256,360-
62,394, 421,495*
Orthodox Church.....*399*
Oslo Philharmonic.....*357,496*
Ostwald, Peter.....*310*
Ottaway, Hugh......*282*
Our New Music.....*502*
Oxford University.....*275*

P

Paganini, Nicolo......*108,112,121,
123,125, 129-30,133-4,251,257,
312,328-9,361*
Palestrina, Giovanni Pierluigi
da.....*4,6*
Pappano, Antonio.....*361*
Paris.....*20,113,118,122,177,185,
209,274-5,280,317,395,424,431,
433,442, 445,486-8,507,509*
Paris Conservatory.....*107,131,
139,143,228,252*
Paris Exposition.....*138*
Parker, Horatio.....*412-13*
Pärt, Arvo.....*497*
Pasquier, Etienne.....*508*
passacaglia.....*248*
Paul, Jean.....*107*
Paungartner, Sylvester.....*222*
Pavel Haas Quartet.....*215*
peasant music.....*398,419*
Pennsylvania.....*502*
Perahia, Murray.....*45,47,91,93,
107,116, 126,134,267,269,283*
Perényi, Miklós.....*166*

Perlman, Itzhak….50,161,165, 167,170,284
Peter the Great….399
Petrograd Conservatory…..490
Philadelphia…..506
Philadelphia Orchestra….256, 309,360,394, 402,495
Philadelphia Sound…..256
Philharmonia Hungarica…..277
Philharmonia Orchestra…..285, 301,303, 373,380,393,395,437
Philharmonic Society of London …..348
Philistines…….99,106,108
pianoforte…..279
Piatogorsky, Gregor…..507
Pierguigi, Giovanni…..6
Pihad, Emmanual….285
Pinnock, Trevor…..266-7,270,277
Pires, Maria João…..161,175
Piston, Walter…..500,504
Pittsburgh Symphony Orchestra …..359
Plantinga, Leon…..293
Platoon…..506
Pletnev, Mikail…..52,134
Pleyel, Ignaz…..342
Pogorelich, Ivo….52,143
Poland…..113,116,118-9,317,490
Polish dances…..111
Polish Uprising of 1830…..490
Politburo…..484
polka…..207
Pollini, Maurizio…..86,104,107, 116-7,119, 121,124,149
polymodality…..419
polyphony…..4,6-9,12,17,28,40-2,63,66,70, 76,84-5,97,101,111-12,120,128,250-1,261, 501
polystylistics…..497
populism…..500-1
Pörtschach…..172
Poulenc, Francis…..420,480
post-Minimalism…..524-5

post-Romanticism……*ii,v*,135, 139,146, 230,238,241, 366, 369, 379,384-5,388, 390,392,397,366, 385,391,444,453-4,506
post-Straussian chromaticism …..505
Potsdam…..268
Prague…..173,207,287,347-48, 351, 356, 416,418,455
Prague Chamber Orchestra….. 289
Pravda…..492
Pressler, Menahem…..157,229
Previn, Andre…..361
Primrose, William…..422
Prince Christian Ludwig…..266
Prince Esterhazy….33,63
Prince Leopold…..ii,43
Princeton University…..185,477, 503
programmatic music…….27,29,30
Proud Tower, The…..398
Psalter…..407
Puccini, Giacomo…..iv
Pulitzer Prize…..412,501,505,507
Purcell, Henry…..154,261-63, 403-4,417,504

Q

Quartetto Italiano…..193,205
Queen of Sheba….479

R

ragtime…..502
Rahbari, A…..495
Rameau, Jean-Philippe….10,137, 142, 154, 180
Ramm, Friedrich…..236
Raphael…..127
Ratatouille…..339
Rattle, Simon…..418,507,525
RCA…..32
recapitulation…….64-7
Reger, Max…..446
Reihenkomposition…..443
Reiner, Fritz…..256,345,359, 422,436

Rellstab, Ludwig.....*200-1*

Renaissance.....*ii,2,40,43,98,101, 131,250, 257,263,269-70,403, 447,454*
Resolution of 1848.....*485*
Respighi, Ottorino.....*385,436*
Rhine River....*102,344*
Rhodes, Samuel.....*224*
ricercar.....*5,257,268*
Rich, Alan....*26,466*
Richter, Hans.....*341,372*
Richter, Karl.....*269*
Richter, Johann Paul Friedrich.....*107*
Richter, Sviatoslav.....*vi,75,89,91, 93,107, 111,124,134,149,157, 166,183-4,220, 229,308,318,401*
Riga.....*322*
Ring Cycle.....*216,247,430*
ripieno.....*258,266*
ritornello.....*259*
Ritter, Alexander.....*382-3,386*
River Thames.....*265*
Robbins Landon, H.C.....*164,192, 275,278*
rock 'n' roll......*22*
Rockwell, John.....*503*
rococo.....*12,13,40,54,59,63-4,98,155,189, 191,194,237,252, 258,280,283*
Rodzinski, Artur.....*473*
Rogé, Pascal.....*178*
Rognoni, L.....*145*
Rolland, Romain.....*74,387*
Romania.....*212*
Romantic period.....*ii,24,27,29, 40,42, 82, 160, 177, 196,220, 225,246,248-9, 251, 255, 259-60, 269-70,339,343,349,352*
Romantic Style.....*61,63,89*
Romanticism....*1,2,96-101,110, 122,133, 142,172,174,177, 179, 398,403,407,412,415, 431,440-1,443,445,447,450,453*
Rome.....*52-3,124,264,314-15,330*
Rondo form...*68,70,246,249, 259,284,290*
Roscoe, Martin.....*79*
Rosen, Charles.....*2,12,41,61,64-5,79, 85, 87,96-8,100,110-11, 114-16,121, 125, 137, 251,257, 281,283,299,505*
Ross, Alex.....*16,19,24, 128,171, 240, 343,389,396,415,440, 484, 494,497,501*
Rossini, Gioachino.....*247*
Rostropovich, Mtislav.....*49,164 ,166,169, 182-3,352,359,488-9, 495,505*
Rousseau, J.J....*12*
Roussel, Albert.....*186,480*
Rowicki, Witold.....*308*
Royal College of Music.....*504*
Royal Philharmonic......*277,303*
Royal Scottish National Orchestra.....*373, 478*
rubato.......*113*
Rubinstein, Anton.....*120,175*
Rubinstein, Arthur.....*83,112, 115-6,118,120-1*
Rubinstein, Nicolai...*175,357-58*
Rückert, Friedrich.....*378*
Russia.....*ii,133,139,215,338,361, 385, 396,431,440,442*
Russian folk music.....*210,240, 400,419*
Russian Nationalism.....*210*
Russian Orthodox Church.....*469*
Russian Revolution.....*486*

S

Sachs, Harvey.....*30,96,290,295, 298*

St. Anthony Chorale.....*342*
St. Louis Symphony Orchestra.....*507*
St. Petersburg.....*256,277,362, 399,463,488*
St. Petersburg Conservatory..... *488*
Salomon, Johann Peter.....*253, 276,288*
Salonen, Esa-Pekka.....*507,525*
Salzburg.....*13,279-80,284,286, 290*
Salzburg Festival....*479*
Salzburg Mozarteum.....*284*
Sanderling, Kurt.....*85*
Sándor, György.....*147,421*
Santa Claus....*127*
San Francisco Conservatory..... *524*
San Francisco Symphony Orchestra.....*520,524*
sarabande.....*248*
Satie, Erik.....*iii,430*
Sawallisch, Wolfgang.....*256,309-11*
Saxony.....*10,52*
Scandinavia.....*424*
Scarlatti, A......*9,53,510*
Scarlatti, D....*10,48,51-4,69,149*
Schalk, Franz.....*368-9*
Scherchen, Hermann.....*452*
Schiff, András......*31,32,44-5,47, 49,52,77,166,270,286*
Schiller, Friedrich.....*98,298-9*
Schindler, Anton.....*379*
Schippers, Thomas.....*506*
Schmeider, Wolfgang....*45*
Schnabel, Artur.....*93*
Schnittke, Alfred.....*497*
Schonberg, Harold........*iv,52,122, 201,248, 313,323,326,328,343, 370,373-4, 382, 384, 396,404, 407,419,444,468,480,503,513*
Schubart, Christian Daniel.....*253*
Schubert, Ferdinand.....*304*
Schuman, William.....*21,501*
Schumann, Clara...*102,106-8,110,127, 170, 223-4,308, 311,340*

Schwarz, Boris.....*496*
Scotland.....*315-16*
Scott, Walter......*99,109*
Scottish Chamber Orchestra..... *289*
Scottish Folksongs.....*117*
Second Viennese School.....*18, 25,260,324, 372,374,419,422, 438-9,441-4,446-8, 450, 456, 460-2,502,507,511,518*
Sechter, Simon.....*367*
Seidl, Anton.....*349*
Serbo-Croatian folk music.....*419*
Serebrier, José.....*413*
Sergeant Pepper's......*515*
serenade.....*246,249-50,254,258-60*
serialism.....*366,382,434-5,439-41,454,500-1,502-3,507,509-17, 521-3*
Serkin, Rudolf.....*345*
Serly, Tibor.....*421-22*
Seville.....*277*
Shaker.....*502,525*
Shakespeare, William.....*167,248, 301,315, 319,327-8,330,383*
Shaw, George Bernard.....*97*
Shelley, Howard.....*270*
Shostakovich, Maxim.....*492,496*
Simrock, Friedrich August.....*226, 346-47, 351*
Sinatra, Frank.....*360*
sinfonia concertante.....*272,284*
Sinopoli, Giuseppe.....*303*
Slatkin, Leonard.....*507*
Slaughter, Susan.....*507*
Slavonic folk tunes.....*229,419*
Slovakia.....*416*
Smithson, Harriet.....*329*
Soetens, Robert.....*488*
Solomon, Maynard.....*12,96,188, 411*
Solti, Georg.....*380*
sonata-allegro form.....*246*
sonata da camera.....*258*
sonata da chiesa.....*258*
Sonata form.....*63-70,275,280,*

292,302
Song of Hiawatha…..*349*
South America…..*424*
Souza, John Philip…..*31*
Soviet Union…..*20,145,182-3, 382,396,443,462,484,486,491-2,503*
Spain…..*402,424-5,433-4*
Spanish folk music…..*425*
Spanish Impressionism…..*424*
Spanish Nationalism…..*423*
Spillville, Iowa…..*349*
Spitz, Jonathan…..*311*
Spohr, Louis…..*224*
spirituals…..*207*
Staatskapelle Dresden…..*303, 309-11,330*
Stadler, Anton…..*235*
Stalin, Joseph…..*145,216,443, 484-5,490-2,494-5*
Stalin Prize…..*232*
Stamitz, Johann…..*61,153,253-4*
Steinberg, Michael…..*283*
Stenz, Markus…..*378*
Stephan, Rudolf…..*373*
Stern, Isaac…..*157,163,226*
Steuermann, E…..*450*
Stockhausen, Karl Heinz…..*453, 490*
Stokowski, Leopold…..*270,402, 413,425,450,491,495-6*
Stone, Oliver…..*506*
Stösslova, Kamila…..*214*
Stott, Kathryn….*132*
Stradivari…..*261*
Strasburg…..*274*
Strauss, Johann……*118*
Sturm und Drang…..*190,253,273-4,276-7,286*
Swafford, Jan…..*40,216,409,413, 439,443,455*
style *galant*…..*12,13,63-4,189-91,220,237,274,279,283*
Sudbin, Yevgeny…..*145*

Suppé, Franz von…..*247*
Sutre, Guillaume…..*178*
Swedish Radio Symphony Orchestra….*352*
Swiss Alps…..*172*
Switzerland…..*172,356*
symbolism…..*209*
symbolist…..*137-8*
Szell, George…..*256,292,303, 309,343, 345,349,351-52,357, 423*
Szigeti, Joseph…..*242*

T

Tabor…..*416*
Tafelmusik…..*153,155*
Takacs Quartet…..*201,203,205, 214*
Takezawa, Kyoko…..*507*
Talich, Václav…..*418*
Tallis Thomas…..*403*
Tapio…..*393*
Tarantella…..*197*
Taruskin, Richard…..*iii,147,324, 349,410-11,453,460,466,504, 508,519*
Taverner, John…..*403*
Tchaikovsky, Modest…..*356*
Telemann, Georg Philipp…..*153*
Temirkanov, Yuri…..*353*
Tetzlaff, Christian…..*182*
Teutonic Legends…..*247*
The Rest Is Noise…..*415*
thematic transformation…..61, 67,71,310, 317-9,332,224
theme and variations…..*69-70*
Third Reich…..*388,443*
Thomson, Bryden…..*478*
Thomson, Virgil….*185,395,453, 478,507*
Thoreau, Henry David…..*409*
1001 Arabian Nights…..*402*
three-part form…..64,66,68-9

Thun.....172-3
Thurber, Jeannette.....*349*
Tilson Thomas, Michael.....*2,413*
Tintinnabulation.....*523*
Tintner, George.....*373*
toccata.....5
Tokyo String Quartet.....*214*
Tolstoy, Leo.....165,214
Tomes, Susan.....*157*
tonality.....*439-40,442-50*
tone row.....*443*
Tonreihe.....*443*
Toscanini, Arturo.....*32,295,299, 343,421, 436,493,506*
Totenfeier.....*377*
Tovey, Donald.....*82,128,192, 224,277,287-8,386,394*
Transcendentalism.....*409,508*
Transylvania.....*124,212*
<u>Treatise on Modern Instrumentation and Orchestration</u> (Berlioz).....*327*
Trio sonata.....*249,252,256-7, 262,264-5,268*
Tuchman, Barbara.....*384,398*
Turkey....*212,472*
Twelve-tone method.....*18,25, 441-56,501,503*
2001: A Space Odyssey.....*387*

U

Übermensch.....*321*
Uchida, Mitsuko.....*75,89,93*
UCLA.....*450,513*
Ukrainian folk song.....*174,215, 354*
Ulrich, Homer.....*152,204*
United Nations.....*298*
United States.....*ii,461,472-3,477*

V

Vänskä, Osmo.....*393-4*
Varèse, Edgard.....*v*
Verdi, Guiseppe.....*v,6*

Victorian Era.....*404*
Vienna.....58,61-3,75-6,83,88-9,118,128, 154,162,164,173,195-6,228,236-7,253, 257,270,276, 279-88,286-7,291-92, 294,298, 338-39,351,358,*368-9,371, 374, 379, 384,442,450,455,491*
Vienna Opera.....*374-5,377*
Vienna Philharmonic.....*255,284-5, 290, 297,300,341,343,373,418, 437*
Viennese style.....58,250
Villa-Lobos, Heitor.....v
Viñes, Ricardo.....*137,140*
viola d'amore.....*475-6*
viola da gamba.....*266*
Vivaldi, Antonio.....*40,52,256,259,261, 263-5,267,269,370,437*
Vltava River.....*416*
Voigt, Lars.....*182-3*
Volkov, Solomon.....*492*

W

Wagner, Cosima.....*384*
Walt and Vult....*107*
Walter, Bruno.....*297,373-4*
Walton, William....*471*
Warren-Green, Christopher.....*408*
Warsaw National Philharmonic *308*
Washington, Denzel.....*411*
Weber, Carl Maria von.....*14,99-100,398-9*
Weill, Kurt.....*i,472,491*
Weimar.............*46,51,124,269,31 8,384*
Weimar Republic.....*449,460,472*
Weiss, Piero.....*410*
Weissenberg, Alexis.....*21*
Wellesz, Egon.....*441,447*
Welse-Möst, Franz.....*371*
Western forms.....*500*

Westminster Abbey.....*403*
Weltanschauungsmusik.....*373*
Weltschmerz.....*102*
What to Listen for in Music (Copland) *332*
Whitman, Walt.....*408*
Wieniawski, Henryk....*312*
Wigmore, Richard.....*59,278*
Wind Chamber Music Society of Frankfurt.....*241*
Wings.....*92*
Wittgenstein, Paul.....*435*
Wolff, Hugo.....*v*
Wood, Henry.....*488*
World War I.....*15,17,20,25,142-3,146, 179-81,184,213,255,277, 360, 392,398,404-5,410.418,420, 434-5,440-3,445, 451,460-1,463, 467,471-2,501,517*
World War II.....*15,20,27,143, 147,164,182,185,300,331,362, 368,388,396,422,424,441-4,453, 460,470-1,473,475,477-8,487, 494-5,500-1,503,509,514,517, 520*
Wörther Lake.....*172*
Wurtz, Charles-Adolphe.....*401*
Wyrick, Eric.....*312*

Zilberstein, Lilya.....*226*
Zimerman, Krystian.....*421*
Zuckerman, Pinchas....*165*

X
Xenakis, Iannis.....*507*

Y
Yale University.....*412-13,470, 473,524*
Ysaÿe, E.....*177*
Ysaÿe Quartet.....*178*

Z
Zaslaw, Neil.....*64*
Zeitgeist.....*20,30,274*
Zhdanov, Andrei.....*484*

www.ingramcontent.com/pod-product-compliance
Lightning Source LLC
Chambersburg PA
CBHW031423160426
43195CB00010BB/599